MAJOR PRINCIPLES OF MEDIA LAW

Second Edition

Wayne Overbeck, Ph.D., J.D.

Member of the California Bar
California State University, Fullerton

and

Rick D. Pullen, Ph.D.

California State University, Fullerton

HOLT, RINEHART AND WINSTON

NEW YORK   CHICAGO   SAN FRANCISCO   PHILADELPHIA   MONTREAL
TORONTO   LONDON   SYDNEY   TOKYO   MEXICO CITY
RIO DE JANEIRO   MADRID

Library of Congress Cataloging in Publication Data

Overbeck, Wayne.
    Major principles of media law.

    Includes index.
    1. Mass media—Law and legislation—United States.
2. Freedom of information—United States.   I. Pullen,
Rick D.   II. Title.
KF2750.09   1985   343.73′099   84-19240
                                    347.30399

ISBN 0-03-001514-6

Address correspondence to:
383 Madison Avenue
New York, N.Y. 10017
All rights reserved
Printed in the United States of America
Published simultaneously in Canada
5 6 7 8 9   016   9 8 7 6 5 4 3 2 1

CBS COLLEGE PUBLISHING
Holt, Rinehart and Winston
The Dryden Press
Saunders College Publishing

PREFACE

This book is intended to be, above all, a clear and concise summary of the major principles of media law—at a time when communications law is growing more complicated by the day.

In the preface to the first edition of this book, we pointed out that thousands of appellate court decisions on media law had been published in the last half century. We suggested that it was unrealistic to ask undergraduate students to learn all of them. Thus, our goal was to write a textbook that would focus on the main points, citing the most important court decisions and statutory enactments in each area of communications law. In selecting from the vast amount of available material, we concentrated on concepts and cases that we felt would still be important by the time today's students are working professionals. To that end, we said we were omitting some of the older court decisions and emphasizing general principles wherever possible.

That's what we said in 1981. Three more years have passed, and the nation's appellate courts have given us another 750 new decisions on communications law, give or take a few. The United States Supreme Court released no fewer than eleven media law decisions during the first half of 1984 alone, and Congress has acted on numerous media-related issues, as have the regulatory agencies. While this book was in page proof form late in 1984, Congress abruptly broke a long stalemate and passed a comprehensive cable television bill. As our editors at Holt, Rinehart and Winston have discovered, keeping a manuscript current in this field requires repeated editorial revisions—right up to the time the presses roll.

Given the pace with which communications law is growing and changing, the need for a major-principles approach to the subject seems greater than ever. In discussing the dramatic new developments of the past three years, we have tried to summarize the major trends and issues wherever possible. In fact, many of the trends that we noted in our first edition have continued and become dominant features in the regulatory landscape.

Three years ago, we said the American mass media were on the brink of a new technological revolution, a revolution so profound that it might render the print and electronic media almost indistinguishable. We predicted that the law would have to either treat all media alike or tolerate an absurd double standard: Material that would be Constitutionally protected if placed on the home television screen by a cable system or a newspaper would be illegal if put there by a broadcaster. The old rules—under which the print media enjoy greater First Amendment rights than the broadcast media—were being called into question, another trend that has continued through the early 1980s.

The preface to our first edition predicted fundamental changes in the regulatory environment for the mass media. We pointed out that FCC seemed to be launching a major reevaluation of the regulatory philosophy it had followed since the New Deal era in the 1930s. We said the FCC was looking less and less to content controls such as the Fairness Doctrine as tools to foster good public service by broadcasters. Instead, the commission was starting to look to the marketplace to provide better public service. To that end, the FCC seemed ready to open up the radio spectrum to more broadcast voices and to encourage the development of new electronic media.

By late 1984, much of this had happened. Both radio and television have been deregulated in many ways, and radio deregulation has been largely affirmed by the courts. In fact, in its amazing *League of Women Voters v. FCC* decision, the Supreme Court for the first time overturned a Congressional restriction on broadcast content on First Amendment grounds. Moreover, the court seemingly invited the FCC or Congress to abolish the Fairness Doctrine itself. And the FCC has indeed launched a proceeding to eliminate the Fairness Doctrine, a controversial proposal that is supported by many people but that has also drawn fire from critics in Congress and elsewhere. Meanwhile, the FCC has opened the way for so many new electronic communications systems that we have added a separate chapter about the new communications technologies.

In view of these new developments, our chapter on broadcasting and cable has a non-traditional emphasis. While it covers the traditional material about the Fairness Doctrine, the Equal Time provision and the licensing process, it emphasizes the FCC's new philosophy of creative spectrum management and deregulation. The chapter also includes a discussion of the spectrum itself to clarify the problems involved in the FCC's efforts to put more stations on the air. In some print-oriented media law courses that do not serve broadcasting students, this material may not be assigned, but we felt it should be included because so many programs today offer broadcasting, advertising, and public relations as well as the traditional print journalism major.

In other areas, too, we call attention to new trends that have become apparent in recent years. In the all-important chapter on libel, we emphasize and re-emphasize the major principles that one must understand to avoid lawsuits. But we also address such alarming new developments as the tendency for juries to award multimillion-dollar judgments in libel cases and the propensity of libel plaintiffs to use pretrial discovery procedures more aggressively than ever before. And, of course, we discuss the implications of *Calder v. Jones* and *Keeton v. Hustler*, the Supreme Court's rulings on long-arm jurisdiction and the mass media. We also point out that not all of the new developments in libel law have been bad for the media, as the *Bose v. Consumer's Union* decision illustrates.

Nor have the media fared badly in lawsuits involving the problems of newsgathering. Indeed, the Supreme Court has repeatedly affirmed the right of the press and public to attend court proceedings. The recent *Globe Newspaper, Press-Enterprise*, and *Waller v. Georgia* decisions all reinforced the media's right to cover the courts. The fair trial-free press chapter emphasizes these developments, while summarizing other aspects of this troublesome field as well. Chapters Eight and Nine discuss other aspects of the law of newsgathering: reporter's privilege, shield laws, and freedom of information under statutory laws and the First Amendment.

Elsewhere in the book, we have endeavored to present a mixture of major principles and new developments. The chapter on copyright law includes a summary of the main provisions of the 1976 Copyright Act and a discussion of the copyright implications of the new technologies. Yes, there is a summary of the Supreme Court's long-awaited *Sony v. Universal Studios* decision, but the chapter also discusses important but less-noticed new developments in such diverse fields as music copyrights, computer software copyrights, and cable copyrights. And the copyright chapter includes a section on trademark law that should be particularly helpful to advertising and public relations students.

The antitrust chapter deals with the monopoly and cross-ownership problems created by the new technologies as well as a review of media monopoly and cross-ownership issues. The regulatory groundrules and policy implications of the new electronic media—direct broadcast satellites, multi-point distribution service, teletext, videotex(t) and the like—are discussed in Chapter Fifteen, the new chapter that focuses on the communications revolution and the law.

Like the broadcasting chapter, the advertising chapter focuses on the trend toward deregulation. Perhaps nowhere is this philosophy more evident than at the Federal Trade Commission, which was stripped of key regulatory powers in 1980 and then voluntarily abandoned many of its other regulatory policies of the 1970s under a new chairman appointed by Ronald Reagan.

The advertising chapter also notes the Supreme Court's ongoing efforts to protect both commercial speech and non-commercial corporate speech, a trend that began in the mid-1970s and has continued with new decisions in the 1980s. Advertising students should also be particularly interested in the expanded "right of publicity" section in the chapter on privacy law.

However, not every chapter in this book looks to the future. One must know where we've been as well as where we're going to understand media law. Chapter Two traces the long and sometimes bitter struggle for freedom of expression from its English roots to the twentieth century. Then Chapter Three looks at modern-day prior censorship in its various forms, including restraints via discriminatory taxation, judicial restraints based on national security concerns, pretrial discovery under the *Seattle Times v. Rhinehart* rule, literature distribution problems, and ordinances banning newsracks.

Before we discuss any of this, however, we start by explaining how the legal system works. This book was written for journalism and communications students and professionals, not for lawyers. Nothing that we say about media law would make much sense without an explanation of the legal process in America. To illustrate how the system works, we trace one famous lawsuit (the *New York Times v. Sullivan* libel case) from the initial filing to the Supreme Court.

Because of its special relevance to both students and faculty, there is also a separate chapter on freedom of the student press, a chapter that summarizes the major cases on both the college and high school level and offers practical suggestions for student editors facing censorship-minded administrators.

In studying mass media law, it is easy to overlook the major legal and ethical issues amidst the details. Therefore, after devoting 15 chapters to the specifics of the law, we conclude with an Epilogue in which we step back and look at the ongoing issues in the field—the problems that may well defy solution in the 1980s and beyond.

On some of these controversial issues, there are deep conflicts between journalists and the legal community. In addressing these issues, we offer a lawyer's perspective as well as a journalist's. We try to explain why each side takes the position it does. However, our own sympathies are usually with the media, and we have not tried to conceal that fact. On occasion, we express opinions, particularly in discussing the jailing of reporters in Chapter Eight.

Throughout this book, we have tried to make the presentation comprehensible and interesting without sacrificing accuracy or precision. Thus, we include boxed chapter summaries to highlight some of the main points. Also, we have omitted footnotes. Every case we mention carries a legal citation—in the text where it would be placed in a court opinion—and our quotations from other published materials are attributed and cited. But we feel, as do several other authors of law texts written mainly for undergraduates, that extensive footnoting is neither necessary nor conducive to clarity.

However, the lack of footnotes in no way implies that we do not believe in sending students to original sources. Indeed, we think finding and reading at least a few of the most important court decisions in their original unedited versions is an important part of the learning process. Many instructors ask their students to look up the key cases or otherwise research some aspects of media law for themselves, using the legal research methods described in Chapter One.

Nevertheless, we doubt that undergraduates—or even law students—are likely to read and absorb every important case during a one-semester course. Law students, for instance, spend three years learning law by the casebook method—but before they take the bar exam most of them attend a bar review course where the major principles of each subject are summarized clearly and concisely. We were mindful of the success of these bar reviews when we chose our style and approach for this text.

We received valuable assistance from many people as we wrote this book and then revised it for the second edition. Our colleagues at California State University, Fullerton, helped us in many ways. Marc Nurre of the *San Bernardino* (California) *Sun* wrote the section describing CompuServe in Chapter 15, and did it on a moment's notice. His thesis—that the main appeal of videotext is interpersonal communication and not mass communications—is an insight we would otherwise have missed.

We also appreciate the suggestions made by those who reviewed our manuscript for the first and second editions: James Fields, University of Wisconsin; Gary Kebbel, Northern Illinois University; William Hall, Ohio State University; Mike Kautsch, University of Kansas; Robert Hughs, Virginia Commonwealth University; Steven Helle, University of Illinois; Daniel W. Pfaff, Pennsylvania State University; Conrad Smith, Idaho State University, and Jay G. Sykes of the *Green Bay (Wis.) News-Chronicle*.

We especially wish to pay tribute to Clifton O. Lawhorne, a professor at the University of Arkansas, Little Rock, whose career was cut short by his untimely death in 1983. Cliff was a fine teacher and a legal scholar, but most important, he was a friend. Many of the ideas expressed in this book were Cliff's before they were ours. His encouragement and counsel were very valuable to us.

Finally, we want to thank our families for their support while we were so preoccupied with this project. To Donna and Lara, and to Jill, Mindy, Reid, and Erica go our heartfelt words of appreciation.

Wayne Overbeck
Rick D. Pullen
October, 1984

CONTENTS

14 FREEDOM OF THE STUDENT PRESS

15 NEW TECHNOLOGIES AND MEDIA LAW

TABLE OF CASES

LAW, LAWMAKERS, AND LAWSUITS

America is a nation of laws, but it is also a nation of lawyers and lawsuits. Both the number of lawsuits being filed and the number of people employed as lawyers have doubled in the last two decades. For good or ill, more and more people with grievances are looking to the legal system for redress.

The mass media have not escaped this flood of litigation. The nation's television networks, major newspapers, newsmagazines, wire services, and advertising agencies are constantly fighting legal battles. Just a few decades ago, media executives only rarely needed legal advice to perform their duties properly. But today, few major communications businesses operate without lawyers on their staffs, or at least on retainer.

Moreover, legal problems are not just headaches for top executives. Working journalists run afoul of the law almost daily. So many reporters have faced jail sentences for standing by their journalistic principles that the imprisonment of a journalist is no longer front-page news, except perhaps in the locality where it happens.

Million–dollar lawsuits are no longer unusual in the mass communications field, and the big national media are by no means the only targets. For example, a medium-size newspaper in Idaho was recently ordered to pay $1.9 million in a libel case—not because the newspaper published some horribly libelous falsehood but merely because the paper refused to say who told a reporter where to find public records about wrongdoing by an insurance company. A higher court set aside that ruling, but it cost the paper thousands of dollars in legal fees to defend the case.

More than ever before, a knowledge of mass media law is vital for a successful career in mass communications. This textbook was written for students planning such careers and for professionals seeking an overview of media law. Since most readers will be neither lawyers nor law students, the first step is to explain how the American legal system works. This chapter does that, describing the various kinds of law and tracing a typical case through the courts.

THE KEY ROLE OF THE COURTS

Mass media law is largely the result of court decisions. Even when a law is based on an act of Congress or a provision of the U.S. Constitution, the courts play a decisive role in shaping the law. Courts have the power to establish "legal precedent," handing down rules to be followed by lower courts. In so doing, appellate courts have the power to modify or even overrule the enactments of state legislatures and Congress.

However, not all court decisions establish legal precedents, and not all legal precedents are equally important as guidelines for later decisions. The United States Supreme Court is the highest court in the country: its rulings are binding on all lower courts. On matters of state law, next most influential are the highest courts of the 50 states (called state supreme courts in most states). On federal matters the U.S. Courts of Appeals rank just below the U.S. Supreme Court in precedent-setting authority. All of these courts are "appellate" courts; cases are appealed to them from the trial courts.

There is an important difference between trial and appellate courts. The major function of the appellate courts is to hand down precedent-setting decisions that interpret the meaning of law. The trial courts, on the other hand, are responsible for deciding factual issues (such as the guilt or innocence of a criminal defendant). And this fact-finding process does not normally establish legal precedents. The way a judge or jury decides a given murder trial, for instance, sets no precedent at all for the next murder trial. The fact that one alleged murderer may be guilty doesn't prove the guilt of the next murder suspect.

In civil (i.e., noncriminal) legal proceedings, this is also true. A trial court may have to decide whether a newspaper libeled the local mayor in reporting a scandal involving him. Even if the paper did—and if the mayor wins his lawsuit against the paper—that doesn't prove the next newspaper story about a mayoral scandal is also libelous. Each mayor—or murder suspect—is entitled to his or her own day in court.

The trial courts have the final say about these questions of fact. An appellate court may rule that a trial court misapplied the law to a given factual situation, but the appellate court doesn't ordinarily reevaluate the facts on its own. Instead, it sends the case back to the trial court with instructions to reassess the facts under new legal rules written by the appellate court. For instance, an appellate court might decide that a certain piece of evidence was illegally obtained and cannot be used in a murder trial. It will order the trial court to reevaluate the factual issue of guilt or innocence, this time completely disregarding the illegally obtained evidence. Such a ruling may well affect the outcome of the case, but it's the job of the trial court to decide that question, just as it is the job of the appellate court to set down rules on such legal issues as the admissibility of evidence.

This is not to say trial courts never make legal (as opposed to fact-finding) decisions. They do so every time the law must be applied to a new factual situation, but when a trial court issues an opinion on a legal issue, that opinion carries little weight as legal precedent.

Sometimes there is high drama in the trial courtroom, and that may result in extensive media coverage. One trial verdict may even inspire (or discourage) more lawsuits of the same kind. However, the outcome of a trial rarely has long-range legal significance. Meanwhile, a little-noticed appellate court decision can fundamentally alter the way we live. That's why a textbook such as this must focus on appellate court decisions, and especially rulings of the U.S. Supreme Court.

TYPES OF LAW

The Constitution

When we use the term "law," we are actually referring to many different kinds of rules and regulations, ranging from the bureaucratic edicts of administrative agencies to the unwritten principles we call the "common law." The most important law in America is the U.S. Constitution itself. No other law that conflicts with the Constitution is valid. The U.S. Constitution is the basis for our legal system: it sets up the structure of the federal government and defines federal-state relationships. It divides authority among the three branches of the federal government and limits their powers, reserving a great many powers for the states and their subdivisions (such as cities and counties).

Of particular interest to the mass media is the First Amendment to the Constitution, which in a mere 45 words sets forth the principles of freedom of the press, freedom of speech, and freedom of religion in America. The First Amendment says, "Congress shall make no law. . . abridging the freedom of speech, or of the press. . . ."

What do those words mean? The job of interpreting what they mean has fallen to the appellate courts, which have written thousands of words in attempting to explain those 45 words. For instance, the First Amendment sounds absolute when it says "Congress shall make no law. . . ." However, the courts have repeatedly ruled that those words are not absolute, and that freedom of expression must be balanced against other rights. In practice, the First Amendment should really be read more like this: "Congress shall make almost no laws. . ." or "Congress shall make as few laws as possible. . .

abridging freedom of speech, or of the press. . . ." The chapters to follow will discuss the many other rights that the courts have had to balance against the First Amendment.

Another point about the First Amendment is that it originally applied only to Congress and to no one else. It was written that way because its authors trusted their state governments not to deny basic civil liberties much more than they did the new federal government. However, it became clear over the years that state and local governments also at times violated the basic rights of their citizens. Hence, the Supreme Court eventually responded by ruling that the First Amendment's safeguards protected citizens from abuses by state and local governments as well.

Chapter Two describes the evolution of freedom of expression in America. It is sufficient here to remember that the U.S. Constitution plays the central role in American law. No law may be enacted or enforced if it violates the Constitution. The courts—particularly the U.S. Supreme Court—play the central role in interpreting what the Constitution means, often in practical situations that the Founding Fathers never dreamed of when they wrote the document 200 years ago.

In addition to the federal Constitution, each state has its own constitution, and that document is the basic legal charter for that state. No state law that conflicts with either the state's own constitution or the federal Constitution may be enacted or enforced. Each state's courts must interpret the state constitution, invalidating laws that conflict with it.

Likewise, many cities and counties have "home rule" charters that establish the fundamental structure and powers of local government. Like the state and federal constitutions (which local governments must also obey), local charters are basic sources of legal authority. On the other hand, many local governments operate under the general laws enacted by state legislatures rather than their own local charters.

In all of these circumstances, the courts must decide when a government action—be it an act of Congress or the behavior of the local police department—violates one of these basic government documents. When this happens, it is the job of the courts to halt the violation.

The Common Law

Another very important—and sometimes misunderstood—kind of law in America is the common law. The common law is an outgrowth of an English judicial tradition that was brought to America by the early colonists. It is a huge body of law based on many years of accumulated judicial precedents— judge-made rules that govern a variety of legal questions without being written down in any one place.

When the American government took its present form with the ratification of the Constitution in 1789, the entire English common law as it then existed became the basis for the American common law. Since then, thousands of additional decisions of American courts have expanded and modified the common law in each state.

It should be emphasized that the common law is mainly state law and not federal law; an important U.S. Supreme Court decision so ruled years ago. Each state's courts have developed their own judicial traditions, and those traditions form the basis for that state's common law, which may vary from the common law of other states.

Like federal Constitutional law, the common law can grow and change without any formal act of a legislative body precisely because it is judge-made law (often called "case law"). When a new situation arises, the appellate courts may establish new legal rights, acting on their own authority. A good example of the way the common law develops a little at a time through court decisions is the emergence of the right of privacy. As Chapter Five explains, there was no such legal right until the twentieth century. But as the mass media became more powerful and pervasive, the need for such a right became apparent. The courts in a number of states responded by allowing those whose privacy had been invaded to sue the invader, establishing precedents for other courts to follow.

In addition to privacy law, several other major areas of mass media law had their beginnings in the common law tradition, among them libel, slander, and the earliest forms of copyright protection.

If this all happens through judicial precedent, with the courts obligated to follow the example set by earlier decisions, how can the common law correct earlier errors?

The common law system has survived for nearly a thousand years precisely because there are mechanisms to allow the law to change as the times change. Courts don't always follow legal precedent; they have other options.

When a court does adhere to a previous decision, it is said to be observing the rule of *stare decisis*. That Latin term, roughly translated, means "Let the precedent stand." However, courts need not always adhere to the rule of *stare decisis*. Instead, a court faced with a new factual situation may decide that an old rule of the common law should not apply to the new facts. They may be sufficiently different from those in previous cases to justify a different result. This is called "distinguishing" a case, and when an appellate court does it, the common law grows and keeps up with changing times.

Another option, of course, is for a court to decline to follow precedent, even though the factual circumstances and issues of law are virtually identical. When an appellate court does that, it is called "reversing" or "overruling" a precedent, and it is considered appropriate when changing times or changing conditions have made it clear that the precedent is unfair or unworkable.

A good example of this process is the 1954 ruling of the U.S. Supreme Court in the famous school desegregation case, *Brown v. Board of Education* (347 U.S. 483). There was a precedent, an 1896 Supreme Court decision called *Plessy v. Ferguson* (163 U.S. 537). In that earlier case, racial segregation had been ruled Constitutionally permissible as long as the facilities for different races were "separate but equal." But in 1954 the Supreme Court pointed out that more than half a century's experience under the *Plessy v. Ferguson* rule proved it didn't work. The Supreme Court noted that separate facilities were almost always unequal, thus ruling that the public schools of America had to be desegregated.

As a result of that new decision, the precedent from the 1896 case was no longer binding and a new precedent replaced it. Although this decision was based on an interpretation of the U.S. Constitution and is an example of Constitutional law rather than common law, it nicely illustrates just how law develops over the years, as the courts adapt their judicial tradition to meet new conditions. In the development of the common law as in Constitutional law, the appellate courts have a central place in the lawmaking process.

Statutory Law

The third major type of law in America is the one most people think of when they hear the word "law." It is statutory law, a sweeping term that encompasses acts of Congress, laws enacted by state legislatures, and even ordinances passed by cities and counties.

If Constitutional and common law are largely unwritten, or at least uncodified, forms of law because they are the result of accumulated court decisions, statutory law is just the opposite. It is law that is written down in a systematic way. Statutory laws are often organized into "codes." A "code" is a collection of laws on similar subjects, indexed and arranged by subject matter. Much federal law is found in the "United States Code." On the state level, much statutory law is similarly organized, although not all states refer to their compilations of statutory laws as codes.

Although statutory law is created by legislative bodies, the courts have an important place in statutory lawmaking just as they do in other areas of law. That is true because the courts have the power to interpret the meaning of statutory laws and apply them to practical situations. For this reason, law books containing statutory laws are often "annotated." This means each section of the statutory law is followed by brief summaries of the appellate court decisions interpreting it. Thus, one can quickly learn whether a given statutory law has been upheld or if it has been partially or totally invalidated by the courts. Annotated codes also contain cross-references to other relevant analyses of the statutory law, such as attorney general's opinions or articles in law reviews.

Why would a court invalidate a statutory law? It can happen for several reasons. First, of course, if the statute conflicts with any provision of the appropriate state or federal constitution, it is invalid. In addition, it is not unusual for there to be conflicts between two statutory laws enacted by the same state legislature or by Congress. When that happens, the differences must be reconciled, and that may mean reinterpreting or even invalidating one of the laws. In addition, courts may void laws that conflict with well-established (but unwritten) common law principles. For instance, journalists' "shield laws" (discussed in Chapter Eight) have sometimes been overruled by courts that felt these laws infringed on their prerogatives under the common law.

There is considerable interplay between the courts and legislative bodies in the development of statutory law. As already indicated, often a new legal concept is recognized first by the courts, whose decisions will make it a part of the common law. At some point, a legislature may take note of what the courts have been doing and formally codify the law on that subject by enacting a statute. The courts may then reinterpret the statute, but the legislature may respond by passing another statute intended to override the court decision. We will see precisely this sort of interplay between a legislative body and the courts in several areas of mass media law, particularly in such areas as copyright, reporter's privilege, and broadcasting.

One point to emphasize here is that this interplay can occur only where a court has based its decision to invalidate or modify a statutory law on something other than a Constitutional principle. When a court says such a principle is involved—and no higher court disagrees—the only way to reverse the court decision is by a Constitutional amendment. Of course, as times change the judiciary may come to interpret the Constitution differently, as happened in the landmark school desegregation decision mentioned earlier.

Administrative Law

Another important kind of law in America is administrative law. Within the vast bureaucracies operated by the federal government and many states, there are numerous agencies with the power to adopt and enforce administrative regulations, and these regulations have the force of law.

Such agencies often have authority that would seemingly violate the traditional concept of separation of powers. They may write the rules, enforce them, and try alleged violators, handing out criminal penalties to those convicted. One important check on these agencies is that their decisions can be appealed to the courts. This means that the appellate courts have an important role even in this kind of lawmaking.

However, many of these agencies were created by legislation, and in recent years Congress and the various state legislatures have proven that they can take back some of the authority they handed out, either directly by rewriting the enabling legislation or indirectly by budget cuts. A notable example of this is the new limitations imposed on the Federal Trade Commission by Congress in 1980 (see Chapter 12).

Among the thousands of government agencies with administrative rule-making powers, probably the most important for mass communicators are the Federal Trade Commission (which regulates advertising) and the Federal Communications Commission (which regulates broadcasting and cable).

Many agencies at the state level also have administrative lawmaking authority. For instance, most states have administrative agencies that regulate public utilities and transportation within their boundaries.

Actions in Equity

One final kind of "law" that should be mentioned here is not really a form of law at all but an alternative to the law.

Hundreds of years ago in England, it became obvious that courts sometimes caused injustices while acting in the name of justice. There are some circumstances in which faithfully applying the law simply does not result in a fair decision. For example, the common law has always held that "damages" (money) would right a wrong, and that the courts should not act until an injury actually occurred—and even then they could do nothing except to order a payment of money to compensate the injured party. Obviously there are times when letting a court sit back and wait for an injury to occur just isn't satisfactory. The harm that could result might be so severe that no amount of money would make matters right. A good example of an occasion when an action in equity would be appropriate is when highway builders are about to excavate and thus destroy an important archeological site. Those seeking to preserve the site cannot wait until after an injury occurs and sue for damages. The artifacts that would be destroyed might be priceless.

The concept of equity is an old one: it developed in medieval times. Early in the development of the English common law, people facing irreparable injuries began to appeal to the king, since he was above the law and could mete out justice when the courts could not—or would not. As the volume of requests for this sort of special consideration increased, kings began to appoint special officers to hear appeals from those who could not get justice in the courts of law. Such officers came to be known as "chancellors" and their court became known as the "court of the chancery." As time went on, this brand of justice based on the dictates of someone's conscience came to be known as "equity."

The concept of equity works in much the same way today, but in America the same courts that apply the law usually entertain actions in equity, too.

Unlike the law, which has elaborate and detailed rules, equity is still a system that seeks to offer fairness based on the dictates of the judge's conscience. Equity is only available in situations where there is no adequate remedy under the law, and only then if the person seeking "equitable relief" is himself being fair to the other parties in a dispute.

ORGANIZATION OF THE AMERICAN COURT SYSTEM

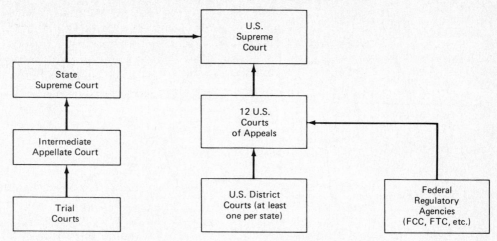

Fig. 1-1 The American Legal System. This simplified chart shows the portions of the regulatory and judicial system of most interest in the study of mass media law. The state court system diagrammed at left is typical of those in large states; smaller states usually do not have intermediate courts and appeals are routed directly from trial-level courts to the state's highest court. Decisions of a state's highest court, and decisions of lower courts that can be appealed no further, may be appealed to the U.S. Supreme Court if a federal question is involved. Decisions of federal regulatory agencies such as the Federal Communications Commission may be appealed to the U.S. circuit Courts of Appeals, and from there to the Supreme Court.

There are certain kinds of legal actions that are based on equity rather than law. Probably the most important for our purposes are injunctions, which are court orders requiring people to do something they are supposed to do (or to refrain from doing something that would cause irreparable harm). Chapter Three discusses several attempts by the federal government to prevent the publication of information that government officials felt would cause irreparable harm to national security. When a court orders an editor not to publish something, that is ordinarily an example of an action in equity.

THE COURT SYSTEM

Now that we have summarized the various sources of law, the next step is to describe the state and federal court systems in the United States.

Figure 1-1 shows how the state and federal courts are organized. In the federal system, there is a nationwide network of trial courts at the bottom of the structure. Next higher are twelve intermediate appellate courts serving various regions of the country, with the Supreme Court at the top of the system.

Fig. 1-2 Service Areas of the U.S. Courts of Appeals. This map shows which portion of the nation is served by each federal appellate court. The new eleventh circuit, serving Alabama, Florida, and Georgia plus the Canal Zone, was established in 1981 as a separate unit. The twelfth circuit is Washington, D.C., and its circuit court hears appeals of many federal agency decisions. Thus its decisions are often very important in mass media law.

District Courts

In the federal system there is at least one trial court called the "U.S. District Court" in each of the 50 states and the District of Columbia, with some of the more populous states having several such courts.

As trial courts, the U.S. District Courts have limited precedent-setting authority. Nevertheless, there are occasions when a U.S. District Court opinion is recognized as a precedent. The primary duty of these courts, however, is to serve as trial courts of *general jurisdiction* in the federal system; that is, they handle a variety of federal civil and criminal matters.

Circuit Courts of Appeals

The next level up in the federal court system is the U.S. Courts of Appeals, often called the "circuit courts" because the nation is divided into "circuits." Each circuit court serves a specific geographic area, and there were ten regional circuits for many years. In 1981, an eleventh circuit was created by dividing the enormous circuit that served the rapidly growing southern states into two separate units. A twelfth circuit court sits in Washington, D.C. Figure 1-2 shows which states fall into each federal circuit.

Just a year after the eleventh circuit was created, still another federal circuit court was established. In 1982, the Federal Courts Improvements Act established the Court of Appeals for the Federal Circuit. Unlike the other circuit courts, this one serves no single geographic area. Instead, it has general jurisdiction over certain special kinds of cases, including patent and customs appeals and some claims against the federal government. This court is the product of a merger of the old Court of Claims and the Court of Customs and Patent Appeals.

As this book went to press, Congress was considering legislation to create still another federal circuit court, this time by dividing the enormous ninth circuit, which had served a far-flung area including the island of Guam in the western Pacific Ocean, Alaska, Hawaii, and the entire West Coast. For one federal circuit to serve all of that territory was asking just a bit much, proponents of another judicial split argued. The proposed division would leave California, Nevada, and Arizona in the ninth circuit and create a new circuit court to serve the Pacific Northwest, Alaska, Hawaii, and U.S. possessions in the Pacific.

The losing party in most U.S. District Court proceedings has a right to appeal the decision to the circuit court serving that region of the country.

The decisions of the circuit courts produce many important legal precedents; on federal questions the rulings of these courts are second in importance only to U.S. Supreme Court decisions. Each circuit court has a large number of judges, but most cases are heard by only three of them. Two of the three constitute a majority and may issue the "majority opinion," which sets forth the court's legal reasoning that led to the decision. Sometimes a case is considered so important that all justices serving on a given circuit court will decide the case. When that happens, it is called hearing a case "en banc."

Since these appellate courts decide only matters of law, there are no juries in these courts. Juries only hear trial court cases, and even then their role is limited to deciding factual issues (such as the guilt or innocence of a criminal defendant) and not legal issues. Appellate cases are always decided by judges alone, unassisted by a jury—both in the federal and state court systems.

One point should be explained about the significance of the legal precedents established by the federal circuit courts. As long as the decision does not conflict with any U.S. Supreme Court ruling, each circuit court is free to arrive at its own conclusions on issues of law. A circuit court is not required to follow precedents established by other circuit courts around the country, although precedents from other circuits usually carry considerable weight and are often followed.

Nevertheless, there are occasions when two different circuit courts will rule differently on the same legal issue. When that happens, the trial courts in each region have no choice but to follow the local circuit court's ruling. Trial courts located in other circuits may choose to follow either of the two conflicting precedents, or they may follow neither. Since this kind of uncertainty about the law is obviously bad for everyone, the U.S. Supreme Court often intervenes, establishing a uniform rule of law that is binding all over the country.

Circuit courts of appeals have jurisdiction to hear cases from a variety of sources. As already indicated, appeals from the federal trial courts go to the circuit courts. But in addition, appeals of the decisions of many special-purpose courts and federal administrative agencies are routed to the circuit courts. For instance, decisions of both the Federal Trade Commission and the Federal Communications Commission may be appealed to these courts. The U.S. Court of Appeals serving the District of Columbia is highly influential on federal regulatory matters: because of its location it hears hundreds of appeals of federal agency rulings each year.

The U.S. Supreme Court

The U.S. Supreme Court is, of course, the highest court in the country. Its nine justices are the highest-ranking judges in the nation, and its decisions represent the most influential legal precedents, binding on all lower courts.

Because of this court's vast authority, it is common for people involved in a lawsuit to threaten to "fight all the way to the Supreme Court." However, very few cases have any real chance to make it that far up through the system. The U.S. Supreme Court is, after all, only one court, and it can only decide a limited number of cases each year. The Supreme Court accepts only a few hundred cases annually for a full hearing—out of at least 5,000 petitions for a hearing. Obviously, some screening is required.

In doing the screening, the Supreme Court tries to hear those cases that raise the most significant legal issues, those where the lower courts have flagrantly erred, and those where conflicting lower court decisions must be reconciled. However, the fact that the Supreme Court declines to hear a given case does not mean the high court agrees with the decision of a lower court. To the contrary, the Supreme Court may disagree with it, but it may choose to leave the decision undisturbed because it has a heavy caseload of more important matters. The fact that the Supreme Court declines to review a lower court decision establishes no precedent: for the Supreme Court to refuse to hear a case is not the same as the Supreme Court hearing the case and then affirming the lower court's ruling. When the Supreme Court declines to take a case, the lower court ruling on that case remains in force—but it is still just the decision of a lower court.

The nine justices conduct a vote to decide which cases they'll hear of the many appealed to them. Under the Supreme Court's rules of procedure, it takes four votes to get a case on the high court's calendar.

Cases reach the U.S. Supreme Court by several routes. For one, the Supreme Court has "original jurisdiction" over certain cases (that is, it is the first court to hear that kind of case). Disputes between two states are an example of this kind of case. Then there are a limited number of cases in which the losing party in the lower courts has a right to appeal to the Supreme Court.

Finally, and most important, there are a vast number of cases that the Supreme Court is not required to hear; the losing party in a lower court asks the highest court to hear the case voluntarily. This is called petitioning the Supreme Court for a "writ of certiorari." Technically, certiorari is an order from the Supreme Court to a lower court to send up the records of the case. "Certiorari granted" means the Supreme Court has agreed to hear an appeal, while "certiorari denied" means the Supreme Court has decided not to hear the case.

This certiorari procedure is by far the most common way cases reach the Supreme Court, although many more petitions for certiorari are denied than granted, as already suggested. Cases may reach the Supreme Court in such appeals from both lower federal courts and from state courts. The U.S. Supreme Court often hears cases that originated in a state court, but only when an important federal question, such as the First Amendment guarantee of freedom of the press, is involved. Most of the Supreme Court decisions on libel and invasion of privacy that will be discussed later reached the high court in this way.

The U.S. Supreme Court will consider an appeal of a state case only when the case has gone as far as possible in the state court system. That normally means the state's highest court must have either ruled on the case or refused to hear it.

The State Courts

Each of the 50 states has its own court system, as already indicated. Larger states such as California, New York, Ohio, Pennsylvania, Texas, Illinois, and Michigan have two levels of state appellate courts plus various trial courts, duplicating the federal structure.

In these states, the intermediate appellate courts (usually called simply "courts of appeal") handle a variety of cases that the state supreme court has no time to consider. The state supreme court then reviews only the most important cases. Worth special note is the New York system, which is structurally similar to the systems in other populous states, but with opposite nomenclature. In New York, the "supreme court" is a trial court that also has intermediate appellate jurisdiction; there are many such courts in the state. New York's highest court is the Court of Appeals.

In smaller states, the trial courts send cases directly to the state supreme court, which may have from three to nine or more justices to hear all appeals in the state. As both the population and the volume of lawsuits increase, more and more states are adding intermediate appellate courts.

The states tend to have a much greater variety of trial courts than does the federal government, since the state courts must handle many minor legal matters that are of no concern to the federal courts. A typical state court system includes some kind of local court that handles minor traffic and civil matters and perhaps minor crimes. Such courts are often called municipal courts, county or city courts, justice courts, or the like.

In some states the highest trial courts not only hear the most important trials but also perform some appellate functions, reviewing the verdicts of the lower trial courts.

State and Federal Jurisdiction

It may seem inefficient to have two complete judicial systems operating side by side. Wouldn't it be simpler and less expensive to consolidate the state and federal courts that operate in each state? Perhaps it would, but one of our strongest traditions is power sharing between the federal government and the states. We'll have separate state and federal laws—and separate court systems to interpret them—throughout the foreseeable future.

How then is authority divided between the federal and state courts? State and federal authority sometimes overlaps, but basically the state courts are courts of "residual" jurisdiction; that is, they have authority over all legal matters that are not specifically placed under federal control. Anything that isn't a "federal question" falls within the jurisdiction of the state courts. However, state courts may also rule on issues that *are* federal questions, such as First Amendment rights.

What makes an issue a federal question? The Constitution declares that certain areas of law are inherently federal questions. For instance, the Constitution specifically authorizes Congress to make copyright law a federal question. And Congress, acting under the authority of the Constitution, has declared copyrights and many other matters to be federal questions. Congress has used its Constitutional power to regulate interstate commerce as a basis for federal regulation of broadcasting, for instance.

Thus, certain legal disputes are federal questions because of their subject matter. In addition, federal courts may step into almost any area of law if a state court ruling conflicts with the U.S. Constitution. Much of mass communications law is a study of this kind of conflict. In almost every area discussed in this textbook the U.S. Supreme Court has intervened at one time or another, interposing federal Constitutional requirements on the states. Most often, of course, the Constitutional issue is freedom of expression as protected by the First Amendment; the Supreme Court has often overruled state laws and court decisions that violated it.

In addition to these federal questions, there is another reason the federal courts will sometimes agree to hear a case: diversity of citizenship. This principle applies only when a citizen of one state sues a citizen of another state: if you're a New Yorker and you are involved in a serious auto accident with a Pennsylvanian, you may avoid a lawsuit in the Pennsylvania state courts under the diversity principle.

The framers of the Constitution felt it would be unfair to force anyone to fight a lawsuit on someone else's "home turf," so they ordered the federal courts to provide a neutral forum to hear these disputes involving citizens of two different states. The theory is that a state court might be biased in favor of its own citizens and against outsiders. When a federal court hears a case that would be a state matter if it involved two citizens of the same state, it is said to be a federal case because of *diversity jurisdiction* rather than *federal question jurisdiction*. In diversity lawsuits, the trial may still occur in the home state of one of the litigants, but in a federal rather than a state court.

There are limits on diversity jurisdiction. If there were not, the federal courts might be overwhelmed by minor cases. To avoid that problem, federal courts accept diversity-of-citizenship cases only when the dispute involves more than $10,000. And there has to be *complete* diversity. That is, all of the parties on one side of a lawsuit must come from a different state than anyone on the other side. That means, for instance, that a lawsuit by a New Yorker against an individual from New Jersey and a company in New York would not qualify as a diversity case.

Sometimes there is considerable legal maneuvering when a case does qualify for federal jurisdiction, either because a federal question is involved or because there is diversity of citizenship. One side may want the case kept in state court, while the other prefers a federal court. Such a case may be filed in a state court, removed to federal court, and eventually sent back to a state court.

One more point about federal-state relationships bears explaining. As we have already said, certain legal matters are exclusively federal concerns, either under the Constitution or an act of Congress. In those areas, the federal government is said to have "preempted the field." That is, no state law in this area is valid; the federal government has exclusive jurisdiction. Copyright law is one such area.

In certain other areas of law, Congress has enacted some federal laws without preempting the field. The states may also enact laws in these areas, providing that the state laws do not conflict with any federal laws. These are called areas of "concurrent jurisdiction." Examples of this in media law include the regulation of advertising, antitrust law, and trademark regulation. A typical dividing line in such an area of law is the one that exists in trademark regulation, where the federal Lanham Act protects trademarks of businesses engaged in interstate commerce, while many states have laws to protect the trademarks of local businesses.

In addition to the areas of law preempted by the federal government and areas of concurrent jurisdiction, of course, a large number of legal matters are left to the states—unless a state should violate some federal principle in the exercise of its authority. Libel and invasion of privacy are two areas of media law that are essentially state matters.

Criminal and Civil Cases

Another distinction we need to explain is the difference between civil and criminal lawsuits. In a criminal case, someone is accused of committing an act that is considered to be an offense against society as a whole—a crime. Therefore, society as a whole ("the people" if you will) brings charges against this individual, with the taxpayers paying the bill for the people's side of the case. If the person accused of the crime ("the defendant") is impoverished, the taxpayers will also pay for his or her defense by providing a lawyer from the local (or federal) public defender's office. Defendants who are more financially secure will hire their own defense lawyers, but the basic point to remember is that the legal dispute is between the defendant and "the people"—society as a whole. Moreover, because the defendant's life or liberty may be at stake, the prosecution must prove guilt "beyond a reasonable doubt." This is a difficult standard of proof.

In a civil case, it's a different matter. Here, one party claims another party injured him or her individually, without necessarily doing something so bad it is considered a crime against society as a whole. It's just a dispute between two individuals (or two corporations, or two government agencies, etc.). The courts simply provide a neutral forum to hear this private dispute. The burden of proof is correspondingly lower in civil cases: to win, a litigant must usually prove his or her case by "the preponderance of the evidence," but not necessarily "beyond a reasonable doubt," as in criminal cases.

Don't assume that all legal matters are either criminal or civil matters—some are both. The same series of events may lead to both civil and criminal litigation. For instance, someone who has an auto accident while intoxicated may face criminal prosecution for drunk driving as well as civil lawsuits from the victims for personal injuries and property damage, among other things.

THE PROFILE OF A LAW SUIT

Perhaps the best way to illustrate how the legal system works is to follow a lawsuit through the courts, step by step. We'll trace a civil case called *New York Times v. Sullivan* (376 U.S. 254), a libel suit that is usually remembered for the very important legal precedent it established. Its effect on libel law is discussed in Chapter Four. However, *New York Times v. Sullivan* is also an excellent case to illustrate court procedures, since the case was carried through almost every step that occurs in civil law suits.

When someone thinks a newspaper story has injured his reputation, he has a right to sue the newspaper for damages (i.e., money) to compensate for his losses. This case involved such a lawsuit between an individual named L. B. Sullivan and the corporation that produces the *New York Times*.

The case began after the *New York Times* published an advertisement from a group of black civil rights leaders that described instances of alleged police brutality in the South. Some of the incidents occurred in Montgomery,

Alabama. The ad was essentially accurate for the most part, but it did contain several errors of fact. The ad didn't name any individual as responsible for the alleged police misconduct.

Nevertheless, Sullivan, who was one of three elected commissioners in Montgomery and the man in charge of police and fire services there, contended that his reputation had been damaged by the ad, so he hired a lawyer and sued the *New York Times* for libel. He contended that to criticize the police was to criticize the city commissioner who oversees the police department. The result was a lawsuit that went all the way to the U.S. Supreme Court after a variety of intermediate steps.

When Sullivan's lawyer filed the papers required to initiate the lawsuit (a document called the "complaint"), the clerk of the trial court assigned the case a number for record-keeping purposes, and the case became known as *Sullivan v. New York Times*. In our legal system, court cases are identified by the names of the parties to the dispute, with a little "v." (for versus) between the two names. When there are multiple parties on either side, the case is popularly identified by the name of the first person listed on each side. The name of the party bringing the lawsuit (the "plaintiff") appears first, followed by the name of the party defending (the "defendant"). When a case is appealed, the two names are sometimes reversed. Hence, this case later became known as *New York Times v. Sullivan*.

As the plaintiff, Sullivan was seeking an award of monetary damages. The *New York Times*, of course, wanted to convince the court it had done nothing to injure Sullivan and that damages should therefore not be awarded.

Sullivan could have chosen to sue the *New York Times* in the New York state courts, but at that point in history many southerners bitterly resented northern efforts to promote the civil rights of blacks in the South. To many in Alabama, the *New York Times* symbolized all that they disliked. Thus, Sullivan's lawyer knew his client would have a much more sympathetic jury in Alabama than in New York. Besides, it would certainly be more convenient for them (but not for the *Times*) to try the case there.

Having filed the complaint in the proper Alabama trial court, the next step was to "serve" the *New York Times*. That is, a "process server" had to deliver a copy of the papers announcing the lawsuit to an appropriate representative of the newspaper. Some states permit the plaintiff to simply mail a copy to the defendant, depending on the nature of the case.

Serving the *New York Times* was a bit of a problem for Sullivan, since the paper didn't have any offices or regular employees in Alabama. Shortly after Sullivan initiated his law suit, a *Times* reporter visited the state to cover a civil rights demonstration, but *Times* lawyers in New York advised the reporter to leave the state before Sullivan's process servers could catch up with him, and he did so.

Sullivan ultimately served the papers on an Alabama resident who was a "stringer" (a part time correspondent) for the *New York Times*. The *Times* immediately filed a motion in the Alabama courts to "quash" (invalidate) the service of process. Anxious to gain jurisdiction over the *Times*, the Alabama court denied the motion—and then found a technicality in the *Times'* legal petition that enabled the Alabama courts to hear the case.

Given the sentiments of many Alabama residents toward the *New York Times*, this would seem to have been an ideal case to be tried in federal court on a diversity of citizenship basis. However, the Alabama courts ruled that the *Times* had voluntarily consented to Alabama jurisdiction by the manner in which the motion to quash the process service was worded.

Although it had a daily circulation of only 390 in the entire state and about 35 in the Montgomery area, the *New York Times* would be forced to submit to the jurisdiction of the Alabama state courts due to a legal technicality.

Once the Alabama court established jurisdiction, the paper was forced to respond to the lawsuit. The newspaper filed a reply (called the "answer"), denying Sullivan's claims.

If no answer had been filed, the *New York Times* would have "defaulted." That means the court would have been free to award Sullivan whatever he asked for, without the paper having any say in the matter. But the *Times* did file an answer, denying any "liability" (responsibility for the alleged wrong).

Pretrial Motions

The *Times* also initiated a series of legal motions designed to get the case thrown out of court before trial by saying, in effect, "Look, this is nothing but a harassment lawsuit, and we shouldn't be put to the expense of a full trial."

Two kinds of pretrial motions can lead to a dismissal of the case before trial. One is called a "demurrer" (or simply a "motion to dismiss") and it contends that there is no legal basis for a lawsuit, even if every fact the plaintiff alleges is true. The other kind is a motion for "summary judgment," and it usually is based on the contention that there is no factual basis for a lawsuit even if all the facts that the plaintiff alleges are completely true. A summary judgment motion may also be made when one side contends that there is no real disagreement between the parties about the facts, and that the judge should decide the case without further proceedings.

The *Times* filed a series of demurrers, arguing that, among other things, the ad in no way referred to Sullivan and thus there was no legal basis for Sullivan to sue. (You have to be identified before you can sue for libel, as Chapter Four explains.)

Demurrers and motions for summary judgment are particularly important for the mass media, because the media are often sued by people who may be embittered over unfriendly news coverage but who have no valid basis for a lawsuit. In such cases, the media may be entitled to a dismissal without the expense of a full trial. However, pretrial dismissals deny plaintiffs their day in court. Thus, a court reviewing such a request must give the plaintiff the benefit of every doubt. A pretrial dismissal is improper if there is any reasonable possibility the plaintiff could win at a trial.

This point is important because a number of the Supreme Court decisions adverse to the media have come on appeals of motions to dismiss a case before trial.

When a newspaper or television station, for instance, is denied a pretrial dismissal and the U.S. Supreme Court affirms the denial, that does not mean the Supreme Court thinks the plaintiff will eventually win the lawsuit. Rather, it merely says that the plaintiff might have some slight chance to win and, in our system of justice, has a right to try. If you keep that point about court procedures in mind, some of the seemingly anti-media decisions we discuss later may not appear quite so harsh.

Returning to the Sullivan case, the Alabama court denied all of the *Times'* motions to dismiss the case before trial, and a trial was eventually scheduled.

Discovery

After the legal maneuvering over motions for summary judgment and demurrers, there is another very important pretrial procedure: the process of *discovery*. It is a process that allows each side to find out a great deal about the strengths and weaknesses of the other side's case. Each "litigant" (i.e., party to the lawsuit) is permitted to ask a variety of oral and written questions of the opposition and may even get to meet and question hostile witnesses. As a result, a defendant can find out how substantial the plaintiff's losses really were, for instance. And each litigant can size up the other's witnesses to see whether they will be credible in court. Much important information is revealed during discovery.

Why do courts allow discovery? Experience has shown that allowing discovery encourages many out-of-court settlements of lawsuits that would otherwise clog up the courts. If you find out that your opponent really does have a good case against you, you'll be much more likely to make a generous settlement offer. Actually taking a case to trial costs time and money, so it's in everybody's interest to see cases settled out of court whenever possible. The more each side knows about the other's case, the more likely they are to reach an agreement on their own.

However, in our sample case Sullivan and the *New York Times* were hopelessly far apart; no settlement was possible. Sullivan was suing for half a million dollars, and the *Times* was contending that this was ridiculous. With a circulation of only 35 in Sullivan's county, and with him never mentioned either by name or title, the *Times* felt there was simply no way the ad could have done half a million dollars worth of damage to the man's reputation.

The Trial

Sullivan and the *New York Times* squared off in a courtroom for trial. The first step in the trial was the selection of a jury, a process that raises another interesting point about civil cases.

Jury rights in civil cases differ somewhat from those in criminal cases. A defendant's right to a trial by a jury is one of the cornerstones of our criminal justice system, but no such stringent Constitutional safeguards are involved in civil cases. There is a growing trend toward reducing the size of civil juries from the traditional panel of 12 to as few as six persons, and to allow verdicts to be rendered by nonunanimous civil juries.

In fact, many civil cases are tried without any jury because the losing side could be stuck with a bill for the jury, a risk neither side wishes to take. (By contrast, the defendant never has to pay for asserting his Constitutional right to a jury trial in a criminal case.) Moreover, as a matter of strategy some civil litigants avoid jury trials. But on the other hand, there are instances where a civil plaintiff may insist on a jury trial in the hope that the jurors will become emotional and award a big judgment. That happened in the Sullivan case.

Sullivan's lawyers were not unaware of the hostility many white southerners felt toward both the civil rights movement and the *New York Times* in the early 1960s when this case was tried (blacks were still rare on Alabama juries at that point). The lawyers felt—correctly—that their client would do well before a jury.

Thus, the trial began. Sullivan, as the plaintiff, presented his evidence first, and then the *New York Times* responded. The plaintiff always goes first, the defendant last. A variety of witnesses testified for each side, with Sullivan's witnesses saying that they indeed associated him with the actions of the Montgomery police, and that they would think less of him if they believed the charges in the *New York Times* advertisement. Other witnesses testified to what they claimed were inaccuracies in the ad.

In its response, the *Times* contended that publishing the ad was protected by the First Amendment and that the ad in no way referred to Sullivan.

The significance of these arguments will become more clear in Chapter Four, which discusses what one must prove to win a libel suit and what a newspaper must prove to defend itself in such a suit.

Finally, all of the evidence was in, and the judge instructed the jury on the law. He told the jurors the material was legally libelous. Thus, their job was to decide only whether the *Times* was responsible for the publication and whether, in fact, the ad referred to Sullivan. The judge ruled that Sullivan did not need to prove any actual monetary losses because of the ad, since damages could be presumed from any libelous statement under Alabama law.

Finally, the jury adjourned to a private room and arrived at a verdict: a judgment of half a million dollars (the full amount requested) for Sullivan. They would see to it the *Times* would pay for its decision to publish an ad alleging police brutality in Montgomery, Alabama.

After that verdict was rendered, the *New York Times* took two important procedural steps. The first was to file a motion for a new trial, citing what it claimed were errors and irregularities in the original trial. That motion was promptly denied in this case, but that doesn't always happen.

If a trial court judge feels the jury improperly weighed the evidence or was not impartial, or if improper evidence was presented at the trial, or if various other procedural errors occurred during the trial, the losing side may be entitled to a new trial. In this case, the motion for a new trial was denied. Then the *Times* exercised its other option, appealing the verdict to the Alabama Supreme Court.

The Appeal

When a case is appealed, the nomenclature changes a little. The party that appeals the case becomes the "appellant," while the other side becomes the "respondent." When the losing side at the trial level appeals, the names get reversed, as we already suggested would happen in this case. Hence, the *New York Times* became the appellant and Sullivan the respondent: the case became known as *New York Times v. Sullivan*.

The Alabama Supreme Court agreed to hear the *New York Times v. Sullivan* case. When an appellate court grants an appeal such as this one, several things occur. First, each side submits a "brief" which is an elaborate argument of the legal issues involved in the case: a "brief" is not always brief. The appellant's brief must argue that the trial court erred in applying the law to the facts at hand, while the respondent must defend the trial court's decision.

After the briefs are filed and read by the appellate justices, oral arguments are usually scheduled. At oral arguments the lawyers for each side are given a short period of time to highlight their main points. The justices may ask them questions, sometimes on obscure points, forcing the lawyers to use up their time allotment without ever getting to their most important arguments.

After the oral arguments, the justices informally vote on the case to see how they will rule. Once the positions of the various justices are clear, one justice will be assigned to write the "majority opinion"—the opinion that will prevail and become a legal precedent. If other justices disagree with this opinion, they may write "dissenting opinions," opinions in which they argue that the majority is in error. Or a justice may agree with the result reached by the majority but disagree with some of the reasoning. When that happens, the result is a "concurring opinion." A justice may also concur with another's concurring or dissenting opinion.

Dissenting and concurring opinions are important, because as times change it is not unusual for a new majority to coalesce around what was once a minority viewpoint. A dissenting opinion may become the foundation for a later majority opinion.

When the appellate opinion is then published—that is, printed in a law book that provides a verbatim record of all published decisions of the particular court—that decision officially becomes a legal precedent, adding a little more to the accumulated weight of case law.

Not all appellate opinions are published: many courts publish only their most important opinions. The unpublished ones have little weight as legal precedents because they are not readily available to judges or to lawyers arguing later cases. In some states—California, for instance—only a small percentage of all appellate court rulings are published, and the unpublished ones are not considered to be legal precedents at all. In fact, the California Supreme Court sometimes eliminates lower court rulings that it dislikes by simply ordering them "decertified for publication." The decertified lower court decision may still appear in law books, but it doesn't officially exist.

There are other occasions when an appellate court decision will lose its significance as a legal precedent. For instance, this also occurs when a higher court decides to review the decision and issue its own ruling on the issue.

In the *New York Times v. Sullivan* case, the Alabama Supreme Court affirmed the judgment of the trial court in full, upholding the half-million-dollar libel award to Sullivan. In an elaborate legal opinion, the Alabama Supreme Court defended the trial court's finding that it had jurisdiction over the *New York Times*. Then the court upheld the trial judge's controversial jury instructions, in which he told the jurors Sullivan didn't need to prove any actual losses to win his case. Finally, the state supreme court affirmed all other aspects of the decision, including the large award of damages.

After this setback, the *New York Times* had one hope left: the chance that the U.S. Supreme Court might agree to hear the case in spite of the fact that civil libel had traditionally been purely a matter of state law. The *Times* petitioned for a "writ of certiorari," contending that this kind of a libel judgment violated the First Amendment because it would inhibit public discussion of controversial issues.

To the amazement of some legal experts, the U.S. Supreme Court agreed to hear the case.

The U.S. Supreme Court Ruling

When the *New York Times v. Sullivan* case reached the U.S. Supreme Court, all of the steps just described happened again. Elaborate briefs were filed by both sides, and oral arguments were heard by the nine Supreme Court justices. Then the justices conferred privately and Justice William J. Brennan was selected to write a majority opinion in what was destined to become the most famous court decision of all time on libel law.

Chapter Four describes the legal reasoning of the Supreme Court in this landmark decision. At this point, we'll simply say the *New York Times* won. The decisions of the Alabama courts were "reversed and remanded." That means the Supreme Court invalidated the lower court decisions and ordered the Alabama trial court to reconsider the facts of the case under new legal rules set down by the Supreme Court.

As a practical matter, sometimes a decision like this one terminates the case, because the plaintiff knows he cannot hope to win a trial conducted under the new legal ground rules. When the U.S. Supreme Court "reversed and remanded" the Alabama court's decision, this case was terminated—in fact if not in legal theory.

Other Options

In addition to reversing and/or remanding a lower court ruling, there are several other options open to an appellate court. The decision can be upheld ("affirmed") or it can be affirmed in part and reversed in part. But whatever the ultimate outcome of the case at trial, often the most important aspect is the precedent-setting ruling of an appellate court. In the study of mass media law, you will encounter cases where the discussion centers on a major legal issue—and the final disposition of the lawsuit isn't discussed. After a landmark appellate ruling, it may take many more years to complete all of the various legal maneuvers at the trial court level and conclude a lawsuit—or the matter may be terminated as soon as a high appellate court rules.

Certainly a valid criticism of the American legal system is the length of time it takes to get a case to trial, up through the appellate courts and then back to trial again if necessary. If "justice delayed is justice denied," as critics of the system have suggested, the route through the American court system often includes enough detours to deny justice to many.

Another ethical issue raised by all of this, of course, is the prohibitive cost of justice. By the time a case reaches the U.S. Supreme Court, each side may have spent several hundred thousand dollars in legal fees, court costs, and even printing bills. The Supreme Court doesn't expect to see typewritten briefs: briefs are supposed to be neatly (and expensively) printed, even though the press run is relatively short.

OTHER CONCEPTS: TORTS AND DAMAGES

Two other legal concepts that need to be explained in this introductory chapter are the concepts of "torts" and "damages."

To explain what a tort is, we can simply say that most civil lawsuits not based on a breach of contract are tort actions. A tort is any civil wrong that creates a right for the victim to sue the perpetrator. Almost any time one party injures another, the resulting lawsuit is a tort action.

If you are walking across the street and you're struck by a car driven by a careless driver, you have a right to sue for your personal injuries in a tort action for "negligence." Should the doctor at the hospital forget to remove a sponge from your body after an emergency surgery, you could sue him for the tort of "medical malpractice."

On the other hand, if you could prove that the car struck you not because the driver was careless but because a manufacturing defect caused the steering to fail, you could sue the manufacturer for the tort of "products liability."

Finally, if the local paper said you were fleeing the scene of a crime you committed when the car struck you, you could sue the paper for the tort of libel—unless, of course, you really were escaping after committing a crime.

All of these legal actions, and dozens of others, fall into the broad category called torts. The person who commits the wrong is called the "tortfeasor"; he becomes the defendant in the lawsuit and his victim is the plaintiff.

Several of the important legal actions affecting the mass media are tort actions. Examples include libel and slander, invasion of privacy, and unfair competition.

To win a tort lawsuit the plaintiff generally has to show that there was some sort of wrongful act on the part of the tortfeasor, often either negligence or a malicious intent. The plaintiff also has to show that he suffered some kind of "damages," although courts are sometimes permitted to presume damages where certain kinds of wrongful acts have occurred.

This brings us to the definition of damages, which is a central point in this introduction to mass media law. There are three basic kinds of damages: general damages, special damages, and punitive damages.

General damages are a form of monetary compensation for losses incurred under circumstances in which the injured party cannot place a specific dollar amount on his loss. In an auto accident where you suffer personal injuries, for instance, you may win general damages to compensate you for your pain and suffering, which is obviously an intangible. In a libel suit, the plaintiff seeks general damages to repay him for embarrassment and loss of prestige in the community, another intangible.

Special damages are a bit different. Here, the plaintiff must prove his out-of-pocket monetary losses to win compensation. In the auto accident we've been using as an example, perhaps you can show that your doctor and hospital bills came to a certain amount of money. Maybe you can also show that you were unable to work for several months or years, or maybe you needed at-home nursing care or rehabilitation. These are all things for which courts can establsh specific dollar values. Special damages are intended to compensate you for these kinds of provable losses.

On the other hand, punitive damages are not based on any tangible or intangible loss. Instead, they are intended as a punishment for the person who commits a maliciously wrongful act. For the victim, they constitute a windfall profit—and the Internal Revenue Service taxes them as such. For the wrongdoer, they're a form of noncriminal punishment, imposed by the court to deter such wrongful actions. Punitive damages are only awarded in those tort actions where the victim can prove there was malice on the part of the tortfeasor. As we'll see in Chapter Four, the term "malice" has more than one meaning in law. For the purpose of winning punitive damages in most tort actions, it means ill will or evil intentions toward the victim. In libel cases, it has a different meaning, but either way, it's difficult to show malice—unless the tortfeasor actually set out to injure someone deliberately.

As we'll see later, keeping track of these three kinds of damages is important in several areas of mass media law. Sometimes one type of damages is available but not another. It is not unusual for a plaintiff in a libel suit, for example, to be denied a right to sue for anything but special damages because a newspaper has printed a retraction. This concept will be discussed in Chapter Four.

Sometimes other terms are used to describe the various types of damages. "Actual damages" means provable losses, including out-of-pocket losses (special damages) and, in some instances, some intangible but none-theless real losses (i.e., general damages). "Presumed damages" are damages that a court assumes occurred without any proof. For many years, libel plaintiffs were awarded presumed damages without having to prove the defamation actually caused any injury.

HOW TO FIND THE LAW

Once you understand the various kinds of law—and how the American legal system fits together—it isn't difficult to teach yourself the law on any given subject. Legal research (the process of finding out what the law is on a subject) involves nothing more than knowing how to use some basic reference books that every well-stocked law library keeps on its shelves. Most county court-houses either have a law library or are located near one since judges who must make legal decisions daily need ready access to the laws on which to base their decisions. Also, every accredited law school has an extensive law library. Most of these law libraries are open to the public. You can go in and look up the law for yourself, and this section tells how to do so.

Court Decisions

Precedent-setting appellate court decisions are not difficult to look up, because there's a "citation" system that will tell you where to find each case. Throughout each chapter in this book you'll find citations to important court decisions in that area of media law. After the names of the two parties in the case, you'll see the case citation (a series of numbers and letters). We've already discussed the landmark libel decision, *New York Times v. Sullivan.* When you look up that case in this or any other law-oriented book, you'll see this legal citation after the name of the case: 376 U.S. 254. The letters and numbers tell you exactly where to find the full text of the Supreme Court's ruling.

The "U.S." in the middle tells you which court ruled on the case because it stands for "United States Reports," a series of books carrying the official text of Supreme Court decisions. Thus, to find the decision, you'd ask the law librarian where the "U.S. Supreme Court Reports" are kept. When you find this large collection of identical-looking volumes, the rest is simple. The first number in the citation (376) refers to the volume number of the law book in which the *New York Times v. Sullivan* case appears. You would look down the row, find the volume labeled "376" on the binding, and pull it out.

Now you're there. The number after the "U.S." is the page number where the text of the case begins. Turn to page 254 in volume 376 of the United States Reports, and there's *New York Times v. Sullivan*. Before the actual text, there are some introductory notes explaining the decision, designed to facilitate a quick review of the highlights of the case.

Some citations conclude with the year of the decision in parentheses.

You can look up any other published appellate court decision in exactly the same way. Chapter Six mentions a well-known copyright decision, *Rosemont Enterprises v. Random House*, and its legal citation is "366 F.2d 303." That case was decided by a federal circuit court of appeals, not the U.S. Supreme Court, and the letters in the middle tell you that. "F.2d" means "Federal Reporter, second series," a set of law books containing decisions of the various U.S. Courts of Appeals. Why "second series"? The publisher of these books began producing them many years ago, and after a time the original editorial treatment and even the style of the binding seemed old-fashioned. Thus, the publisher modernized the book and started a second series, beginning again with volume number one in the new series.

To find the *Rosemont* case, then, you would first locate the Federal Reporter, second series, in the law library. Then you'd look for volume 366 and turn to page 303.

In this textbook you'll see a variety of other legal citations to court decisions, and in each instance the letters in the middle tell you which court decided the case. Those decisions of the federal district courts that are published as legal precedents (many are not) appear in the "Federal Supplement" (abbreviated "F.Supp." in citations).

The same principle applies to citations in the state courts. In Chapter Five there's a reference to a privacy case called *Briscoe v. Reader's Digest*, 4 Cal.3d 529. That's a decision of the California Supreme Court, and the case appears in the "California Supreme Court Reports, third series." To find the case, you would find volume 4 of that series and turn to page 529. Chapter Eight cites a case on reporter's privilege named *Zelenka v. Wisconsin*, 266 N.W.2d 279. It's a decision of the Wisconsin Supreme Court, but the citation refers to the "Northwestern Reporter, second series." That series carries important court decisions from a number of midwestern states. It is a part of the "National Reporter System," one publishing house's collection of regional reports together covering all 50 states.

By the way, don't assume that your local law library only has reports of your own state's precedent-setting court decisions. Any large law library will have the National Reporter system and perhaps other sets of volumes reporting the major cases of the state appellate courts around the country. Whether you're in New York, Florida, or Alaska, you'll probably find the text of state supreme court decisions in the other states.

In many instances, you will discover that your law library has more than one set of law books reporting the most important court decisions. This is true in part because there are competing legal publishing houses, each seeking to offer a full set of reports of the major appellate cases. To illustrate by returning once again to *New York Times v. Sullivan*, here's a more complete set of citations to that case: 376 U.S. 254, 84 S.Ct. 710, 11 L.Ed.2d 686 (1964). Don't be intimidated by all those numbers: let's take it a step at a time. You already know what "376 U.S. 254" means, and that's all you need to know to find the case in the official United States Reports. But suppose somebody else is using the crucial volume of that set when you visit the law library. No problem. Just go to the next citation. "S.Ct." means "Supreme Court Reporter," and if you pull down volume 84 and look on page 710, there's your case. Or you could go to "L.Ed.2d," which means "Lawyer's Edition, U.S. Supreme Court Reports, second series," and pull down volume 11 and look on page 686. In each of these law books, the text of the Supreme Court decisions is exactly the same, but the introductory matter and editorial treatment vary slightly. Many law libraries keep all three of these sets of Supreme Court rulings in their collections.

In the mass communications field, another convenient way to look up court decisions is to check *Media Law Reporter*. One volume is published each year, and it carries the full text of most precedent-setting court decisions on media law, including Supreme Court decisions, lower federal court rulings, and state cases. You will find a number of citations to *Media Law Reporter* in this book.

Legal Encyclopedias

We have just described the method of looking up the text of any major appellate court decision, but what happens if you don't have any names of court decisions and you want to learn something about the law on a particular topic?

In that case, the first place you check is a legal encyclopedia. Legal encyclopedias are just like the regular encyclopedias you've used for years— except that they discuss only legal subjects. There are two leading legal encyclopedias in America, again produced by different publishing houses: "American Jurisprudence," or "AmJur" for short, and "Corpus Juris Secundum," or "CJS." The publisher of the "CJS" (Latin for "body of the law, second edition") is now producing a set called "Corpus Juris Tertium," or "body of the law, third edition."

Despite their intimidating names, these sets of legal encyclopedias are not difficult to use. The many legal topics they treat are listed in alphabetical order, with brief summaries of the major legal principles in each area. The only trick is knowing where to look for a particular subject, and for that there's a comprehensive index at the end of each set. If you want to know more about libel law, for instance, you would look up the word "libel," and you would be told where to go for more information. It's not always that straightforward, because the name you have in mind may not be the key word under which that subject is indexed; you may have to think of some synonyms. Once you hit the right word in the index, it will lead you directly to a summary of the law you want, whether it's bankruptcy or crimes, unfair competition or medical malpractice.

As well as these national legal encyclopedias—which try to summarize the general rules of law around the country—there are legal encyclopedias that specifically summarize the laws of one state. Most of the populous states have such encyclopedias, bearing names such as "Florida Jurisprudence," "California Jurisprudence," "Texas Jurisprudence," or "New York Juris-pru-dence."

One thing you need to be aware of when you consult a legal encyclope-dia is the existence of "pocket parts." The law changes every year, often dramatically. Thus, what a legal encyclopedia says in its main text is supplemented by annual updates that are tucked into a pocket at the back of each volume. Make it a habit to check the pocket part first, lest you waste time learning something that is no longer valid law.

Annotated Codes

Once you have read a survey of your subject in a legal encyclopedia, you might want to learn more about the subject by actually reading some of the court decisions and statutory laws summarized in the encyclopedia. We've already described the method of finding court decisions, working from the case citations found in any law book. Looking up the text of a statutory law is often even easier.

Many of the important state and federal laws are organized by subject matter. To look up a statutory law, you locate the appropriate book of state or federal statutes: a legal encyclopedia will refer you to statutory laws as well as court decisions that pertain to your subject. If you wanted to read the federal Copyright Act, for instance, you would use its legal citation, which is "17 U.S.C.A. 100 et seq." That means Title 17 of the United States Code Annotated, section 100 and following sections. To find the text of the Copyright Act, you would ask the law librarian where the U.S. Code volumes are kept, and then look up section 100 in Title 17. The number before the name of a state or federal code is always the title, book, or volume number, and the number after the name will lead you to the correct chapter and section. The nomenclature varies somewhat from state to state, but the principles are the same.

There are two things to remember in looking up statutory laws in this fashion. One is that the most complete sets are annotated. That is, they contain brief summaries of court decisions interpreting the statutory laws as well as the text of the laws themselves. It's important to look through these annotations to make sure the law you're learning has not been overruled by a court decision.

Another thing you must do to make sure your law is still in effect is to once again check the pocket part. Almost any code book that isn't completely revised every year (or more frequently) will contain a pocket part, just as a legal encyclopedia does. That pocket part will tell you of amendments to the law, if any, and of any new court decisions interpreting it.

Like encyclopedias, the annotated collections of statutory laws are extensively indexed. If you want to learn what the law of libel is in West Virginia, for instance, you can simply look up libel in the index to the "West Virginia Code" and then turn to the appropriate sections to find both statutes and summaries of cases mentioned in the annotations. In some chapters of this book, we'll conclude with suggestions for simple legal research you can do to learn exactly what the laws are on the particular topic in your state. No comprehensive national survey textbook can hope to summarize the law in each state in great detail, but you can fill in those details for your own state in this fashion.

Administrative Regulations

Administrative law is such a vast and amorphous thing that we will not devote much space to the problems of researching it here. However, students with a special interest in broadcasting, for instance, should be aware that the regulations of the Federal Communications Commission are organized to facilitate research.

Title 47 of a legal work called "The Code of Federal Regulations," or "CFR" for short, contains the FCC's rules and regulations. Working from the table of contents, you can quickly look up the FCC's rules on a particular point of broadcast regulation in CFR.

CFR is updated frequently, since the administrative agencies whose regulations appear in it are constantly changing their rules.

Further Information

In summarizing the methods of legal research, we have attempted to do in a few pages what an entire course does in law school. There is no way we could tell you about all of the details of this kind of specialized research. But on the other hand, you probably won't be using this know-how to prepare a detailed brief for the U.S. Supreme Court at this point. All you need now is a general overview of the law.

However, there are a couple of additional things you should remember if you undertake a serious legal research project. One is that the courts are constantly interpreting and reinterpreting their previous decisions. Thus, before you cite any court decision, you need to make sure it has not been reversed by a higher court or a later decision. The way you do that is to consult a cross-reference index called "Shepard's Citator." If you're involved in serious legal research that involves cases, ask someone at the law library to explain how to use "Shepard's" so you won't make the mistake of writing ten pages about a court decision that has been reversed.

Finally, you should feel free to ask questions when you visit a law library. The people at the desk are paid to help you, and a law library is often visited by people who know far less about the law than you do if you've read this far. Don't refrain from asking a question out of fear you'll sound ignorant. If you don't know where something is—or don't quite know what you're looking for—ASK.

2

THE TRADITION OF FREEDOM

Americans are sometimes accused of taking freedom for granted. It is easy to talk about the First Amendment almost as if it were a universal law of nature, a principle that always existed and always will.

That, of course, is not the case. The civil liberties that exist today in the United States and a few other western-style democracies are unique in world history. These freedoms were won through centuries of bitter struggle, and they could easily be lost. Only a small percentage of the world's population enjoys these basic freedoms even today.

In much of the modern world, government leaders consider such things as "national security" (or their own personal security in office) more important than their peoples' freedoms. Many leaders see the mass media only as tools of propaganda or national development, weapons to be used against their rivals, both foreign and domestic. It was not too many years ago that the leaders of what are today's democracies viewed mass communications in much the same way.

The story of how earlier generations won the freedoms we enjoy today is an important chapter in the study of mass communications law, perhaps the most important chapter of all.

CENSORSHIP IN ENGLAND

This summary of the evolution of freedom of expression could begin with the ancient Greeks, were this a survey of the philosophical underpinnings of western civilization. But for our purposes, the story begins in England several centuries ago.

In the 1600s, England was caught up in a battle that mixed politics and religion. The monarchy and the Church of England were determined to silence dissenters, many of them Puritans. Moreover, the religious and political struggle was closely linked with an economic battle between the aristocracy and the rising middle class.

Leaders on both sides of this ideological battle understood the importance of the printing press and sometimes resorted to heavy-handed efforts to censor ideas they considered dangerous. More than one Englishman was jailed, tortured, and eventually executed for expressing ideas unacceptable to those in power.

Official censorship was enforced through a licensing system for printers that had been introduced as early as 1530. The licensing denied access to printing presses to people with unacceptable ideas, but it also enabled government representatives to preview and pre-censor materials before publication. Moreover, by making the possession of a license to print a coveted privilege, it was possible to control underground printing. The licensed printers themselves would help ferret out bootleg presses to protect their own self-interests.

By the early 1600s this censorship was being used to suppress all sorts of ideas that threatened the established order. This inspired some of the leading political philosophers of the day to write eloquent appeals for freedom of expression as a vital adjunct to the broader freedom from religious and political oppression they sought. An early apostle of freedom of expression was John Milton, who in 1644 wrote his famous argument against government censorship, *Areopagitica*. Milton's appeal to the Long Parliament for freedom contained this statement:

> Though all the winds of doctrine were let loose to play upon the earth, so Truth be in the field, we do injuriously by licensing and prohibiting to misdoubt her strength. Let her and Falsehood grapple; who ever knew Truth put to the worse in a free and open encounter?

Out of this passage several modern ideas emerged, including the concept that a "self-righting process" would occur through open debate of controversial issues. In effect, Milton said censorship was unnecessary because true ideas would prevail over false ones anyway. Milton advocated something of a "marketplace of ideas." But ironically, Milton and many of his fellow Puritans had no intention to offer the sort of freedom they sought for themselves to those whose ideas they considered false or subversive. Milton's appeal for freedom specifically excluded "popery (support for the Roman Catholic Church) and open superstition" and ideas that were "impious or evil."

In fact, after the Puritan movement led by Oliver Cromwell gained control of England and executed King Charles I in 1649, Milton accepted a government appointment as an official censor. By 1651—only seven years after he appealed to the government to allow true and false ideas to struggle for popular acceptance—Milton was issuing licenses and thus engaging in the prior censorship of ideas. Moreover, Cromwell's government imposed strict Puritan moral standards on England, showing little tolerance for the beliefs of other religious groups. Nevertheless, Milton's *Areopagitica* was an eloquent appeal for freedom of expression and an important influence on later English political thought.

In fairness to Cromwell's followers, we should also point out that some went much further than Milton did in advocating freedom of expression. For instance Roger Williams, a onetime Puritan minister in the Massachusetts Bay colony who was exiled to Rhode Island for his controversial religious ideas, later returned to England and wrote *Bloudy Tenent of Persecution for Cause of Conscience* in the same year as Milton's *Areopagitica*. Williams urged freedom of expression even for Catholics, Jews and Moslems—people Milton would not have given any place in his marketplace of ideas.

Perhaps even more emphatic in their arguments for freedom from censorship in the 1640s were the Levellers, a radical Puritan group. Their tracts consistently contained passages condemning censorship and the licensing system. In their view, free expression was essential to the religious freedom and limited government authority they so fervently sought. Among the leaders of the Leveller movement were William Walywyn, Richard Overton, and John Lilburne.

In a 1648 petition to the Parliament, the Levellers appealed for a free press. When "truth was suppressed" and the people kept ignorant, this ignorance "fitted only to serve the unjust ends of tyrants and oppressors." For a government to be just "in its constitution" and "equal in its distributions" it must "hear all voices and judgments, which they can never do, but by giving freedom to the press."

Despite the rhetoric of the Puritans, England restored the monarchy in 1660 and the licensing of printers continued (although Parliament by then had a much larger say in the process). Although the post-1660 Restoration period was marked by unprecedented freedom—and even bawdiness—in English literature, it was also a time of religious repression. A 1662 act of Parliament, for instance, limited the number of printing presses and prohibited the printing of books contrary to the Christian faith as well as seditious or anti-government works.

As the struggle between the monarchy and Parliament became more intense in the late 1600s, new philosophers of free expression emerged. Perhaps chief among them was John Locke. His ideas were not necessarily original, but he presented them so eloquently that he is remembered as one of the most important political theorists of his time. Locke's famous "social contract" theory said that governments were the servants of the people, not the other way around. Locke believed men were endowed with certain natural rights, among them the right to life, liberty and property ownership. In effect, Locke said that men strike a deal with a government, giving it the authority to govern in return for the government's promise to safeguard these natural rights.

Central to these natural rights, Locke felt, was freedom of expression. Thus, when the English licensing system came up for review in 1694, Locke listed 18 reasons why the act should be terminated. The act was allowed to expire, primarily because of "the practical reason arising from the difficulties of administration and the restraints on trade." For a fuller description of the struggle for freedom of expression in England, see Fred Siebert's classic work, *Freedom of the Press in England, 1476-1776* (Urbana: University of Illinois Press, 1952).

Other forces in English society were also providing impetus for freedom of expression. For one, Parliament gained a major victory over the monarchy in the Glorious Revolution of 1688. James II, an avowedly Catholic king so offensive that several warring factions united against him, fled the country that year. Then in 1689 Parliament enacted a Bill of Rights and invited William of Orange and his consort Mary, James' Protestant daughter, to assume the throne with strictly limited powers. In the Declaration of Rights, William and Mary accepted these conditions, ending England's century-long struggle between Parliament and the monarchy.

In addition, a two-party system was emerging in England; the times were ready for open, robust political debate. The two parties, the Whigs and Tories, both relied extensively on the printing press in taking their views to the people.

Nevertheless, if prior restraint was a thing of the past as England moved into the 1700s, the crime of seditious libel remained a viable deterrent to those who might publish defamatory tracts.

A good illustration of this problem was the 1704 case of John Tutchin, who was tried for "writing, composing and publishing a certain false, malicious, seditious and scandalous libel, entitled, *The Observator* (see *Rex v. Tutchin*, 14 Howell's State Trials 1095).

Tutchin was convicted of the crime, and in the process the presiding judge defined the common law on seditious libel:

> To say that corrupt officers are appointed to administer affairs, is certainly a reflection on the government. If people would not be called to account for possessing the people with an ill opinion of the government, no government can subsist. For it is very necessary for all governments that the people should have a good opinion of it. And nothing can be worse to any government, than to endeavor to procure animosities, as to the management of it; this has been always looked upon as a crime, and no government can be safe without it be punished.

This common law rule did not go unchallenged for long. Free press advocates, perhaps strengthened by their victory in abolishing licensing, opened the eighteenth century with a flurry of articles advocating greater freedom. Nevertheless, criticism of the government remained a crime throughout the century, with the truthfulness of the criticism not a defense against the charge. The prevailing legal maxim was, "the greater the truth, the greater the libel."

How could this be? The assumption underlying this philosophy was reminiscent of Milton: if a printer publishes a false attack on the government, it will be disregarded by the people; if, on the other hand, a truthful attack is published, the people are likely to lend it credence and perhaps revolt, causing disorder and anarchy.

Parliament itself recognized the abuses possible under the common law of seditious libel, and in 1792 the Fox Libel Act was passed. That act permitted juries, rather than judges, to decide whether a statement was libelous. Prior to that time, the law allowed the jury to determine only whether the defendant was guilty of printing the libelous publication. The judge ruled on the legal question of whether the material was actually libelous.

This legal reform did not eliminate seditious libel prosecutions, but it did make it more difficult for a government to punish its critics because a jury, whose members might well sympathize with the defendant's allegedly libelous statements, could decide if the statement was libelous.

An additional reform came in 1843, further strengthening the rights of those who would criticize the government in England. In that year, Parliament passed Lord Campbell's Act, establishing truth as a defense in all seditious libel cases. Thus, the old maxim, "the greater the truth, the greater the libel," was at last abolished.

While the struggle for freedom of expression was being fought in England, a parallel battle was under way in the American colonies.

FREEDOM IN A NEW NATION

Although many of the early colonists in North America left England or the European continent to escape religious or political oppression, they found (or created) an atmosphere of less than total freedom in some of the colonies here. As the Puritans gained control in New England, they established close church-state ties, and persons with unpopular religious or political ideas were little more welcome here than they had been in England.

In fact, the first laws that restricted freedom of the press in North America preceded the first newspaper here by some 30 years. Even without any specific authority, colonial rulers often simply assumed they had the right to censor dissenting publications because the authorities had that right in England. Even after licensing was abolished in England, colonial leaders continued to act as if they had licensing powers, and several colonial newspapers carried the phrase "published by authority" in their mastheads years after the right to publish without government permission was won in England.

Moreover, in North America as in England, seditious libel prosecutions were used as a means of controlling the press, as were laws that placed special tax burdens on newspapers. The Stamp Act of 1765, for instance, taxed newspapers by forcing publishers to purchase stamps and attach one to each copy. The result was such blatant defiance of British authority that it helped inspire the eventual revolution against the mother country.

Early in the colonial publishing experience there was a seditious libel case that became a cause celebre on both sides of the Atlantic: the trial of John Peter Zenger in 1735 (*Attorney General v. John Peter Zenger*, 17 Howell's State Trials 675).

Zenger, a German immigrant, was the publisher and printer of the *New York Weekly Journal*. His paper became a leading voice for the opposition to a particularly unpopular royal governor, William Cosby. After some legal maneuvering, the governor was able to have Zenger jailed and charged with "printing and publishing a false, scandalous and seditious libel, in which. . . the governor. . . is greatly and unjustly scandalized, as a person that has no regard to law nor justice."

Zenger was fortunate enough to have Andrew Hamilton of Philadelphia, one of the most respected lawyers in the colonies, make the trip to New York for his defense. And Hamilton, ignoring the orders of Cosby's hand-picked judge, appealed directly to the jury. He urged the jurors to ignore the maxim of "the greater the truth, the greater the libel" and to decide for themselves whether the statements in question were actually true, finding them libelous only if they were false.

"Nature and the laws of our country have given us a right—and the liberty—both of exposing and opposing arbitrary power. . . by speaking and writing truth," Hamilton said.

In urging the jury to ignore the judge's instructions and decide whether the publication was actually libelous, Hamilton was clearly overstepping the bounds of the law. A less prestigious lawyer might have been punished for an action so clearly in contempt of the court's authority. However, Hamilton wasn't cited, and his eloquent appeal to the jury worked: the jury returned a not-guilty verdict.

It would be difficult to overstate the importance of the Zenger trial in terms of its psychological impact on royal governors in America. Still, its direct effect on the common law was minimal. Even in those days, a criminal trial verdict established no binding legal precedent. English courts continued to punish truthful publications that were critical of government authority. For instance, the trial of John Wilkes for publishing a "wicked and seditious libel," a 1763 English case, made it clear that the common law had not been changed by the Zenger trial.

Nevertheless, the argument was made again and again that mere words critical of the government—and especially truthful words—should not be a crime. In 1773 the Rev. Philip Furneaux wrote that only overt acts against a government should be punished:

> The tendency of principles, tho' it be unfavourable, is not prejudicial to society, till it issues in some overt acts against the public peace and order; and when it does, then the magistrate's authority to punish commences; that is, he may punish the overt acts, but not the tendency which is not actually harmful; and therefore his penal laws should be directed against overt acts only.

THE FIRST AMENDMENT

When a series of incidents strained relations between England and the colonies past the breaking point, the colonists declared their independence in 1776. Yet even in breaking with England, the Americans borrowed heavily from the mother country. Thomas Jefferson's ideas and even some of his language in the Declaration of Independence were borrowed from English political philosophers, notably John Locke. Locke's natural rights and social contract ideas appear repeatedly in the declaration.

After independence was won on the battlefield, the new nation briefly experimented with a weak central government under the Articles of Confederation and then became a unified nation under the Constitution, which was ratified by the states in 1789. Despite its ratification, many Americans feared the new federal government, particularly because the Constitution had no guarantees that basic civil liberties would be respected. Although the defenders of the Constitution argued that these civil liberties were firmly entrenched in the common law we had inherited from England, many were wary. Some states ratified the Constitution only after they received assurances that it would be amended quickly to add a Bill of Rights.

That promise was kept. In the first session of Congress, the Bill of Rights was drawn up and submitted to the states to ratify. It was declared in force late in 1791. Of paramount concern to the mass media, of course, is the First Amendment, which reads:

> Congress shall make no law respecting an establishment of religion, or prohibiting the free exercise thereof; or abridging the freedom of speech, or of the press; or the right of the people peaceably to assemble, and to petition the Government for a redress of grievances.

Taken literally, the First Amendment is everything that any free press advocate could hope for, but those words have not often been taken literally. In fact, the exact meaning of those words has been vigorously debated for nearly 200 years now.

The record of the Congressional debates surrounding the drafting of the Bill of Rights is so sketchy that it is impossible to be certain what Congress had in mind. Constitutional scholars have advanced various theories, but most doubt that the majority of the framers of the Constitution intended the First Amendment to be an absolute prohibition on all government actions that might in any way curtail freedom of the press.

If the First Amendment is not absolute, then, it must really mean something like this: "Congress shall make *almost* no laws. . . abridging freedom. . . of the press. . ."

The crucial question, then, and the one that is the focus of the rest of this chapter, is this: which restrictions on freedom are Constitutionally permissible and which ones are not? Many scholarly works have been published attempting to answer this question; several historians have dedicated much of their lives to examining records, debates and documents of the period in an attempt to find the answers. Some of their conclusions will be presented shortly.

Whatever the first Congress intended in drafting those words, it was only a few years later that Congress passed a law that seemed to be a flagrant violation of the First Amendment. In 1798 Congress hurriedly approved the Alien and Sedition Acts, two laws designed to silence political dissent in preparation for a war with France, a war that was never declared. The Sedition Act made it a federal crime to speak or publish seditious ideas. The law had one important safeguard: truth was recognized as a defense. Nevertheless, a fine of up to $2,000 or two years' imprisonment was prescribed for any person who dared to:

> . . .write, print, utter or publish, or . . .knowingly and willingly assist or aid in writing, printing, uttering or publishing any false, scandalous and malicious writing or writings against the government of the United States, or either house of the Congress of the United States, or the President of the United States, with intent to defame the said government, or either house of said Congress, or the said President, or to bring them, or either of them, into contempt or disrepute; or to excite against them, or either or any of them, the hatred of the good people of the United States, or to stir up sedition within the United States.

There were about 25 arrests and 15 indictments under the act. All were aimed at opponents of President John Adams and the Federalist Party, which then controlled Congress and had enacted the law over non-Federalist opposition. Even though the Federalist press was often guilty of vicious attacks on Thomas Jefferson and other non-Federalist government officials, no Federalist was ever prosecuted under the Sedition Act.

One historic trial resulting from the Sedition Act was that of Dr. Thomas Cooper, who was charged with publishing a list of mistakes he thought Adams had made as president (*U.S. v. Cooper*, 25 F. 631, 1800).

Cooper, who later became president of Columbia College, made statements at his trial that were widely circulated, condemning the restrictions placed on the press by the Sedition Act. Cooper pointed out that "in the present state of affairs, the press is open to those who will praise, while the threats of the law hang over those who blame the conduct of the men in power."

Furthermore, he said that if freedom of discussion is stifled, then the avenues of information are closed. The electorate cannot wisely select political leaders then, since those in power have thrown "a veil over the grossest misconduct of our periodical rulers," Cooper said.

In reply, Samuel Chase, the Federalist judge who presided over Cooper's trial at a federal court in Pennsylvania, told the jury:

> All governments which I have ever read or heard of punish libels against themselves. If a man attempts to destroy the confidence of the people in their officers, their supreme magistrate, and their legislature, he effectually saps the foundation of the government.

The jury convicted Dr. Cooper. Elsewhere in the United States, about seven others were similarly convicted, and several of them became folk heroes among a populace that was increasingly dissatisfied with the Federalist leadership.

The emerging opposition political party—Jefferson's anti-Federalist movement—capitalized on this unrest and gained a wide base of popular support in part because of the heavy-handedness of the Federalists.

Jefferson, then the vice president, strenuously opposed the Alien and Sedition Acts. The Kentucky and Virginia legislatures passed resolutions, encouraged by Jefferson, that purported to "nullify" these laws, thus raising questions about states' rights that would not be resolved until the Civil War.

James Madison, later to be Jefferson's vice president and the nation's fourth president, made it clear in drafting the Virginia Resolution that he felt the Sedition Act was a violation of the First Amendment. Madison believed the First Amendment was supposed to be an absolute prohibition on all actions of the federal government that restricted freedom of the press.

Jefferson probably agreed. In one letter to a friend, he wrote: "I am. . . for freedom of the press and against all violations of the Constitution to silence by force and not by reason the complaints or criticisms, just or unjust, of our citizens against the conduct of their agents."

When Jefferson ran for president in 1800, he made the Alien and Sedition Acts a major issue; public discontent over these laws was certainly an important factor in his victory. Immediately after his inauguration, Jefferson ordered the pardon of those who had been convicted under the Sedition Act.

However, Jefferson's record as a champion of a free press was not entirely unblemished. During his presidency he was subjected to harsh personal attacks by some opposition newspapers. Although he usually defended the right of his foes to express their views, he eventually became so annoyed that he encouraged his backers to prosecute some of his critics in state courts.

FIRST AMENDMENT SCHOLARS' VIEWS

The Sedition Act expired in 1801, and it was more than 100 years before Congress again attempted to make criticism of the government a federal crime.

However, this does not prove the First Amendment was intended to eliminate seditious libel as a crime, and the debate over that issue has continued into this century. Historian Leonard Levy, a leading Constitutional scholar, has written:

> What is clear is that there exists no evidence to suggest an understanding that a Constitutional guarantee of free speech or press meant the impossibility of future prosecutions of seditious utterances. ... The security of the state against libelous advocacy or attack was always regarded as outweighing any social interest in open expression, at least through the period of the adoption of the First Amendment.

Levy argues that most likely the framers of the First Amendment weren't certain what its full implications were, but that most of the framers believed future prosecutions for seditious utterances were possible.

On the other hand, Harvard Professor Zechariah Chafee wrote that the First Amendment was indeed intended to eliminate the common law crime of seditious libel "and make further prosecutions for criticism of the government, without any incitement to law-breaking, forever impossible in the United States."

Chafee, in his 1941 work, argued that freedom of expression is essential to the emergence of truth and advancement of knowledge. The quest for truth "is possible only through absolutely unlimited discussion," Chafee said. Yet, he noted that there are other purposes of government, such as order, the training of the young, and protection against external aggression. Those purposes, he said, must be protected too, but when open discussion interferes with those purposes, there must be a balancing against freedom of speech, "but freedom of speech ought to weigh heavily on that scale."

Chafee argued against prior restraint of expression unless it was very clear that such expression imperiled the nation. He wrote:

> The true boundary line of the First Amendment can be fixed only when Congress and the courts realize that the principle on which speech is classified as lawful or unlawful involves the balancing against each other of two very important social interests, in public safety and in the search for truth. Every reasonable attempt should be made to maintain both interests unimpaired, and the great interest in free speech should be sacrificed only when the interest in public safety is really imperiled, and not, as most men believe, when it is barely conceivable that it may be slightly affected. In war time, therefore, speech should be unrestricted by the censorship or by punishment, unless it is clearly liable to cause direct and dangerous interference with the conduct of war.

Chafee's boundary line, then, is that point where words will incite unlawful acts. As we'll see later, that is precisely the point at which the Supreme Court has drawn the line in recent decisions on the meaning of the First Amendment.

A third noted Constitutional scholar, Alexander Meiklejohn, agreed for the most part with Chafee's interpretation of the First Amendment. He said that only expression that incites unlawful acts should be punishable. Further, he said, incitement does not occur unless an illegal act is actually performed and the prior words can be directly connected to the act. Then, and only then, can words be punished in spite of the First Amendment.

Meiklejohn said that the First Amednment was written during a time when large sections of the population were hostile to the form of government then being adopted. Thus, the framers knew full well that a program of political freedom was a dangerous thing. Yet, Meiklejohn said, the framers chose to write the First Amendment as it is and not the way the courts have rewritten it during the twentieth century. He said that if the framers had wanted the federal government to control expression, the First Amendment could have read:

> Only when, in the judgment of the legislature, the interests of order and security render such action advisable shall Congress abridge the freedom of speech.

Both Chafee and Meiklejohn felt that the voters must be well informed to make wise decisions. Both endorsed Milton's "marketplace of ideas" concept, and Meiklejohn supported Milton's view that truth will prevail in this clash of ideas:

> No one can deny that the winning of the truth is important for the purposes of self-government. But that is not our deepest need. Far more essential, if men are to be their own rulers, is the demand that whatever truth may become available shall be placed at the disposal of all the citizens of the community. The First Amendment. . . is a device for the sharing of whatever truth has been won.

Much of what we have just discussed is quite theoretical, but the views of scholars such as Chafee, Meiklejohn, and Levy have often influenced the U.S. Supreme Court when it was forced to make difficult decisions about the scope and meaning of the First Amendment in the real world.

Whatever the framers of the Constitution and Bill of Rights intended, the question received little attention in the 1800s.

NINETEENTH-CENTURY PRESS FREEDOM

The nineteenth century was a time when Americans were preoccupied with such overriding issues as national expansion and slavery. There was surprisingly little attention given to the meaning of the First Amendment, except during the Civil War.

In 1812 the U.S. Supreme Court ruled that the federal courts had no authority to entertain actions involving common law crimes such as criminal libel. In *U.S. v. Hudson and Goodwin* (7 Cranch 32), the high court said this area of law fell within the exclusive domain of the states, a philosophy that has remained largely unchanged ever since.

If the federal government stayed out of mass media law during much of the nineteenth century, the states filled the void. Throughout the century, the states were expanding their statutory and common law in such areas as libel and slander.

One of the best known state cases was the 1804 libel trial of Harry Croswell in New York (*People v. Croswell*, 3 Johnson's Cases 336). Croswell attacked President Jefferson in print and was prosecuted for criminal libel. He was convicted, but he appealed to a higher state court. His defense attorney, Federalist leader Alexander Hamilton, argued that truth plus "good motives for justifiable ends" should be a defense in such cases.

Although Croswell lost when the appellate panel of four judges deadlocked 2-2, the concept that truth should be a libel defense was sometimes called the "Hamilton doctrine" and was adopted in a number of states in that era. For instance, the New York legislature recognized the truth defense by statute in 1805—and added a provision empowering the jury to determine whether the statement in question was actually libelous. Some states had recognized truth as a libel defense even before that time and, of course, the 1798 Sedition Act had recognized it on the federal level. Nevertheless, what the distinguished Philadelphia lawyer, Andrew Hamilton, had argued for in the Zenger trial 70 years earlier gained general acceptance in American law only after another distinguished lawyer named Hamilton made it his cause as well.

Aside from the gradual evolution of libel law, probably the most significant conflict over American freedom of the press in the 1800s resulted from the War Between the States. A vigorous antiwar movement emerged in the North during the Civil War, and antiwar editors came to be known as Copperheads. Many of them tested freedom of the press in wartime to the limit, openly advocating a southern victory.

The Copperheads' rhetoric often hindered recruiting for the Union Army. On several occasions, military commanders in the North acted against Copperheads, creating a difficult dilemma for President Lincoln, who was deeply committed to the First Amendment but also wanted to end the war quickly. He is generally credited with exercising great restraint in the face of vicious criticism from the Copperhead editors. On one occasion he actually countermanded a general's decision to occupy the offices of the *Chicago Times* to halt the paper's attacks on the war effort.

However, in 1864 Lincoln reached his breaking point when two New York newspapers published a false story claiming there was to be a massive new draft call—an announcement sure to stir violent antidraft riots. The president allowed the editors to be arrested and their papers occupied by the military until it was learned the papers got the story from a forged Associated

Press dispatch that they had every reason to believe was authentic. As it turned out, the story was fabricated by an unscrupulous journalist who hoped to make a stock market killing in the panic he expected the story to produce.

In the pre-war South, a number of states enacted "gag laws" that prohibited the circulation of newspapers and other materials advocating the abolition of slavery. Although these laws were clearly acts of prior censorship and violated the spirit of the First Amendment, the First Amendment had not yet been made applicable to the states, and these laws were never tested for their constitutionality.

Even some northern states attempted to curb abolitionist literature through various laws; these laws too escaped Constitutional scrutiny because the Bill of Rights didn't apply to the states.

However, in the aftermath of the Civil War, the Fourteenth Amendment was approved, requiring the states to afford their residents basic civil liberties. The appropriate part of the Fourteenth Amendment reads thus:

> No state shall make or enforce any law which shall abridge the privileges or immunities of citizens of the United States; nor shall any State deprive any person of life, liberty or property, without due process of law; nor deny to any person within its jurisdiction the equal protection of the laws.

Like the First Amendment, this amendment had far-reaching consequences that were not fully understood when it was adopted. Its immediate impetus came from the desire to protect the former slaves from oppressive legislation in southern states. But in more recent times the "liberty" clause of the Fourteenth Amendment has been relied upon repeatedly to make the various federal rights guaranteed in the Bill of Rights applicable to the states. More will be said later of this trend.

JOHN STUART MILL'S PHILOSOPHY

As we conclude our discussion of freedom of expression in the nineteenth century, one additional point deserves special mention—the writings of the nineteenth century English political philosopher, John Stuart Mill.

Mill's *On Liberty*, first published in 1859, defined the limits of freedom and authority in the modern state. He recognized that by the mid-1800s the important role of the press as one of "the securities against corrupt or tyrannical government" was well recognized—at least in such countries as England and the United States. He stressed that any attempt to silence expression, even that of a one-person minority, deprives mankind of something important. He said that "if the opinion is right, they (mankind) are deprived of the opportunity of exchanging error for truth; if wrong, they lose what is almost as great a benefit, the clearer perception and livelier impression of truth, produced by its collision with error."

Although Mill discussed liberty generally, he presented four basic propositions in defense of freedom of expression. First, he said an opinion may contain truth, and if one silences the opinion, the truth may be lost. Second, there may be a particle of truth within a wrong opinion, and if one silences the wrong opinion, he is likely to lose that particle of truth. Third, even if an accepted opinion is the truth, the public tends to hold it not on rational grounds but as a prejudice unless forced to defend it. And fourth, a commonly held opinion loses its vitality and its effect on conduct and character if it is not contested from time to time.

In these terms, Mill expanded upon Milton's "marketplace of ideas" concept. The impact of these ideas on the evolution of freedom of expression became evident in the twentieth century.

SEDITION IN THE TWENTIETH CENTURY

Wars and the threat of wars tend to make lawmakers worry more about national security and less about such abstractions as freedom of speech. The Alien and Sedition Acts of 1798 were passed at a time when war with France seemed imminent, and the Civil War created pressures for censorship of those who opposed that war effort.

Early in the twentieth century, this nation became involved in what many Americans thought would be the war to end all wars: World War I. In preparing the country for this all-out war, Congress again decided that domestic freedom would have to be curtailed. The result was the Espionage Act in 1917, which was expanded by the Sedition Act in 1918.

In passing these laws, Congress was not merely expressing its own collective desire to suppress unpopular views. In fact, there was a growing worldwide movement for fundamental social change, a movement many Americans found threatening. Already, Marxist revolutionaries were on the move in Russia, and socialists, anarchists, and Marxists were highly visible in this country. Moreover, we were about to undertake a war against Germany, and yet there were millions of persons of German descent living in America. In addition, labor unions such as the International Workers of the World (the "Wobblies") were gaining wide support and calling for basic changes in the capitalist system.

The Espionage Act was passed shortly after the United States entered World War I. It prohibited seditious expression that might hurt the war effort. This federal law was particularly aimed at those who might hamper armed forces recruiting, and it was written so broadly that it could be applied against grandmothers who wrote letters urging their grandsons not to join the army.

Unlike the 1798 Sedition Act, which resulted in only a handful of prosecutions, the 1918 law was vigorously enforced. About 2,000 persons were arrested for violating the Espionage and Sedition acts and nearly 1,000 were convicted. Several of the convictions were appealed to the U.S. Supreme Court, which upheld every conviction it reviewed.

The first case to reach the Supreme Court was *Schenck v. U.S.* (249 U.S. 47) in 1919. Charles T. Schenck, general secretary of the Socialist Party, and another socialist were convicted under the Espionage Act and state anarchy and sedition laws for circulating about 15,000 leaflets to military recruits and draftees. The tracts denounced the draft as an unconstitutional form of involuntary servitude, banned by the Thirteenth Amendment. They urged the draftees not to serve and called the war a cold-blooded venture for the profit of big business.

When their conviction was reviewed by the Supreme Court, the socialists argued that their speech and leaflets were protected by the First Amendment. The court rejected that argument. In a famous opinion written by Justice Oliver Wendell Holmes Jr., the court said:

> We admit that in many places and in ordinary times the defendants in saying all that was said in the circular would have been within their Constitutional rights. But the character of every act depends upon the circumstances in which it is done. The question in every case is whether the words used are used in such circumstances and are of such a nature *as to create a clear and present danger* that they will bring about the substantive evils that Congress has a right to prevent. (emphasis added)

In short, the Supreme Court said the First Amendment is not absolute. Congress may abridge freedom of speech whenever that speech presents a "clear and present danger" to some other more important national interest than freedom of speech.

In reaching this conclusion, Holmes made his famous analogy: "free speech would not protect a man in falsely shouting fire in a theatre and causing a panic." Thus, he wrote, free speech can never be considered absolute. Instead, each abridgment of freedom must be weighed against its purpose to decide if it is an appropriate or inappropriate one.

Although the clear and present danger test has proved to be vague and difficult to administer, it replaced a common law test for allegedly dangerous speech that was even more difficult to administer without unduly inhibiting freedom. The old common law test, known as the "reasonable tendency" or "bad tendency" test, was established in England in the 1700s and adopted as American common law along with the rest of the English common law. This test could be used to forbid any speech that might tend to create a low opinion of public officials, institutions, or laws. It gave prosecutors wide latitude to prosecute anyone charged with the crime of seditious libel.

Whatever its limitations, the "clear and present danger" test was more precise and offered more protection for unpopular speech than the old "reasonable tendency" test.

Following the *Schenck* decision, the Supreme Court quickly upheld the convictions of two other persons charged with violating the Espionage Act: Jacob Frohwerk, a German language newspaper editor, and Eugene V. Debs, the famous leader of the American Socialist Party who later received nearly a million votes for president of the United States while in jail.

Eight months after the *Schenck*, *Frohwerk* (249 U.S. 204) and *Debs* (249 U.S. 211) decisions, the Supreme Court ruled on another Espionage Act case, *Abrams v. U.S.* (250 U.S. 616). The convictions of Jacob Abrams and four others who had published antiwar leaflets were upheld, but this time the court had a new dissenter: Justice Holmes had rethought his position and wrote an eloquent defense of freedom of expression that was joined by Justice Louis Brandeis.

In the majority opinion that affirmed the convictions, Justice John Clarke said:

> The plain purpose of their propaganda was to excite, at the supreme crisis of the war, disaffection, sedition, riots, and, as they hoped revolution, in this country for the purpose of embarrassing and if possible defeating the military plans of the Government in Europe.

The primary goal of Abrams and his co-defendants, Clarke said, was to aid the enemy. That constituted a clear and present danger to national interests.

But on the other hand, Holmes and Brandeis replied:

> It is only the present danger of immediate evil or an intent to bring it about that warrants Congress in setting a limit to the expression of opinion where private rights are not concerned. Congress certainly cannot forbid all effort to change the mind of the country. Now nobody can suppose that the surreptitious publishing of a silly leaflet by an unknown man, without more, would present any immediate danger that its opinions would hinder the success of the government arms or have any appreciable tendency to do so.

Elsewhere in the dissenting opinion, Justice Holmes added this appeal for a free exchange of ideas:

> . . .When men have realized that time has upset many fighting faiths, they may come to believe even more than they believe the very foundations of their own conduct that the ultimate good desired is better reached by free trade in ideas—that the best test of truth is the power of the thought to get itself accepted in the competition of the market, and that truth is the only ground upon which their wishes safely can be carried out.

This opinion was very influential in later years, but at the time it was a minority view. Neither the country nor the Supreme Court was in a mood to be tolerant toward political radicals.

In the last Espionage Act case it reviewed, the Supreme Court affirmed a lower court ruling that denied second-class mailing privileges to the *Milwaukee Leader,* the best known Socialist paper in the country. The high court found that articles in the *Leader* "sought to convince readers. . . that soldiers could not be legally sent outside the country," and thus the sanctions were appropriate (*U.S. ex rel. Milwaukee Social Democratic Publishing Co. v. Burleson*, 255 U.S. 407, 1921).

By today's standards, these Supreme Court decisions seem very repressive. The expression of views that would have been considered well within the protection of the First Amendment in more recent times led to criminal prosecutions during World War I. Obviously, First Amendment law was in its infancy at that point. The courts felt little obligation to observe the niceties of Constitutional law at a time when leftists seemed threatening to many Americans.

STATE SEDITION LAWS

During the first part of the twentieth century, at least 20 states enacted their own laws against various kinds of political radicalism. The common element in these laws was a fear of groups that sought to change the American political and social system and advocated force as a means of accomplishing their goals. The constitutionality of these laws was soon challenged by those convicted under them, and it wasn't long before some of these cases reached the U.S. Supreme Court.

Probably the most important of these state sedition cases was *Gitlow v. New York* (268 U.S. 652), which reached the Supreme Court in 1925. Benjamin Gitlow, a New York socialist, and three others were convicted of violating a state criminal anarchy law by writing a document called the "Left Wing Manifesto." They were also convicted of distributing a paper called *The Revolutionary Age*.

Gitlow argued that the New York law violated his freedom of expression, as guaranteed under the First Amendment. In so doing, he was asking the high court to reverse an 1833 decision that said the Bill of Rights only applied to the federal government (*Barron v. Baltimore*, 7 Peters 243). Gitlow contended that the Fourteenth Amendment's requirement that the states safeguard the "liberty" of their residents meant the civil liberties guaranteed in the Bill of Rights could no longer be violated by the states.

By making this argument, Gitlow won a tremendous long-term victory for freedom of expression, but he lost his own appeal. In an amazingly brief passage, the Supreme Court completely rewrote the rules on Constitutional law, holding that the Fourteenth Amendment had indeed made the First Amendment applicable to the states. But then the court said the First Amendment did not protect Gitlow's activities, thus upholding the New York conviction.

The court said, "a state in the exercise of its police power may punish those who abuse this freedom by utterances inimical to the public welfare, tending to corrupt public morals, incite to crime, or disturb the public peace."

Two years later, the Supreme Court affirmed another state conviction in a case that produced a famous opinion defending freedom of expression. In that case (*Whitney v. California*, 274 U.S. 357), Charlotte Anita Whitney was prosecuted for violating a California criminal syndicalism law, a law that made it a felony to belong to a group that advocated forcible change. Whitney was a member of the Communist Labor Party, but she had argued against its militant policies at a meeting just before her prosecution.

Despite these mitigating circumstances, the Supreme Court affirmed her conviction. For technical reasons, Justice Brandeis concurred in the court's decision rather than dissenting, but his concurring opinion (which Justice Holmes joined) was an eloquent appeal for freedom:

> Those who won our independence by revolution were not cowards. They did not fear political change. They did not exalt order at the cost of liberty. To courageous self-reliant men, with confidence in the power of free and fearless reasoning applied through the processes of popular government, no danger flowing from speech can be deemed clear and present, unless the incidence of the evil apprehended is so imminent that it may befall before there is opportunity for full discussion. If there be time to expose through discussion the falsehood and fallacies, to avert the evil by the processes of education, the remedy to be applied is more speech, not enforced silence.

Brandeis said he believed that free speech should be suppressed only in times of emergency and that it was always "open to Americans to challenge a law abridging free speech and assembly by showing that there was no emergency justifying it."

The Supreme Court finally reversed a conviction for expressing radical ideas for the first time in another 1927 case, *Fiske v. Kansas* (274 U.S. 380). In that case, a defendant was prosecuted merely for belonging to the International Workers of the World, and the primary evidence against him was the preamble to the "Wobblies'" constitution. There was no evidence that he had advocated or engaged in any violent or otherwise unlawful acts. The court said the preamble simply didn't present sufficient evidence of unlawful goals to justify the conviction.

THE SMITH ACT

The 1918 Sedition Act, like its 1798 predecessor, was only in force a short time: it was repealed in 1921. Some parts of the 1917 Espionage Act were not repealed, but that law was specifically written so that it only applied in wartime. Thus, for nearly two decades after 1921, there was no federal law prohibiting seditious speech. But as World War II approached, those who felt the need to curtail freedom in the interest of national security again gained support. Finally, a sedition law was attached to the Alien Registration Act of 1940, popularly known as the Smith Act because one of its sponsors was Congressman Howard Smith of Virginia.

Not only were the new sedition provisions attached to an essentially unrelated bill, but the whole thing happened so quietly that many free speech advocates didn't realize what had happened until months later.

Among other things, the new sedition law made it a crime to advocate the violent overthrow of the government or even to belong to a group that advocated overthrowing the government by force. In addition, there were provisions making it a crime to proselytize for groups with such goals. The law did not require proof that the group might actually carry out any of these goals before its members could be prosecuted; mere advocacy was sufficient.

The 1940 law was rarely used at first. In fact, compared to other wars, World War II elicited little domestic opposition, perhaps because of the manner in which the United States became involved in that war as well as the widely publicized atrocities of the Nazis. However, during the tense "cold war" era that followed World War II, the Smith Act was used to prosecute numerous members of the American Communist Party.

The Smith Act's constitutionality was first tested before the U.S. Supreme Court in a 1951 case involving 12 alleged Communists, *Dennis v. U.S.* (341 U.S. 494). Eugene Dennis and the others were tried on charges of willfully and knowingly conspiring to overthrow the U.S. government by force. After a controversial nine-month trial, they were convicted and the Supreme Court eventually upheld the convictions.

Chief Justice Fred Vinson's opinion, in which three other justices joined, didn't specifically apply the "clear and present danger test" to the activities of the defendants. Instead, the court adopted a test that had been formulated by Learned Hand, a famous appellate court justice who heard the case before it reached the Supreme Court. Justice Hand's test is this:

> In each case (courts) must ask whether the gravity of the "evil," discounted by its improbability, justifies such invasion of free speech as is necessary to avoid the danger.

By using Justice Hand's modified version of the "clear and present danger" test, it was possible for the Supreme Court to sustain the convictions without any evidence that there was a real danger that the Communists could achieve their stated goals. Justice Vinson ruled that the American Communist movement, tiny though it was, constituted a sufficient "evil" to justify the limitations on freedom of speech inherent in the Smith Act. For the moment, it would be unlawful even to belong to an organization that advocated the violent overthrow of the government. Chief Justice Vinson wrote:

> Certainly an attempt to overthrow the Government by force, even though doomed from the outset because of inadequate numbers or power of the revolutionists, is sufficient evil for Congress to prevent.

Justice Vinson continued:

Overthrow of the Government by force and violence is certainly a substantial enough interest for the Government to limit speech. Indeed, this is the ultimate value of any society. . . .

After winning the *Dennis* case, the U.S. Justice Department began a new series of prosecutions under the Smith Act. During the early 1950s at least 121 persons were prosecuted under the act's conspiracy provisions, and many others were prosecuted under the provisions outlawing mere membership in organizations advocating the violent overthrow of the government.

This may seem to be an alarming violation of the American tradition of free speech, but it was in keeping with the mood of the times. The early 1950s were the heyday of McCarthyism, a time when prominent Americans were accused of pro-Communist sympathies, often with little or no proof. For example, a number of well-known writers and motion picture celebrities were blacklisted in the entertainment industry after undocumented charges were made against them. In Congress, the House Committee on Un-American Activities conducted investigations that its critics felt were little more than witch-hunts designed to harass those with unpopular ideas.

However, the times were changing, and so was the makeup of the U.S. Supreme Court. Senator Joseph McCarthy of Wisconsin, the man whose name is synonymous with the red scare, was censured by his Congressional colleagues, and public disapproval of his tactics increased notably by the time of his death in 1957. Meanwhile, the Supreme Court had gained several new members, most notably Chief Justice Earl Warren, who led the court into an unprecedented period of judicial liberalism. Warren was appointed in 1953 after the death of Chief Justice Vinson.

In 1957 the Supreme Court responded to these changes by modifying the *Dennis* rule in another case involving the prosecution of alleged Communists under the Smith Act, *Yates v. U.S.* (354 U.S. 298). In this case, the Supreme Court reversed convictions or ordered new trials for a total of 14 persons charged with Communist activities. In so ruling, the high court focused on the distinction between teaching the desirability of violently overthrowing the government as an abstract theory and actually advocating violent action. The court said the convictions had to be invalidated because the jury instructions did not require a finding that there was any tendency of the advocacy to produce forcible action.

The court said the Smith Act could only be used against "the advocacy and teaching of concrete action for the forcible overthrow of the Government, and not of principles divorced from action." The Supreme Court did not return to the "clear and present danger" test as such, and the court insisted it was not abandoning the *Dennis* rule. But the new requirement of proof that the defendant was calling for action rather than teaching an abstract doctrine made it very difficult to convict anyone under the Smith Act. As a result, this controversial law was almost never used against political dissidents after that time.

Perhaps this was fortuitous timing, because in the 1960s there was a period of political dissent unprecedented in twentieth-century America. Thousands—and eventually millions—of Americans came to disagree with their government's handling of the Vietnam War, and countless numbers of them vocally demanded changes in the political system that led to this unpopular war. Had this happened at a time when the government was prepared to vigorously enforce the Smith Act (and when the courts were willing to brush aside the First Amendment and let it happen) far more people than were jailed under the World War I Sedition Act might have been imprisoned for opposing the government during the Vietnam War.

The First Amendment protection for those accused of seditious speech was again expanded in a controversial 1969 Supreme Court decision involving a Ku Klux Klansman. In that case, *Brandenburg v. Ohio* (395 U.S. 444), a man convicted of violating an Ohio criminal syndicalism law contended that his conduct was protected under the First Amendment. Brandenburg spoke at a Klan rally that was filmed. Part of the film was later televised nationally. Much of what was said was incomprehensible, but the meaning of other remarks was quite clear. Brandenburg urged sending "niggers" back to Africa and Jews to Israel, and also talked of the need for "revengeance."

Was this a call for action that could be prosecuted under the *Yates* rule, or was it merely the teaching of abstract doctrine? In resolving that question, the Supreme Court went beyond the Constitutional protection it had afforded speech in the *Yates* decision. In *Brandenburg,* the court said the First Amendment even protects speech that is a call for action, as long as the speech is not likely to produce *imminent* lawless action. Thus, the point at which the First Amendment ceases to protect seditious speech is not when there is a call for action, but when that call for action is persuasive and effective enough that it is likely to produce imminent results.

The court said:

> . . .(T)he Constitutional guarantees of free speech do not permit (state regulation). . . except where the speech is directed to inciting or producing imminent lawless action, and is likely to incite or produce such action.

Brandenburg's criminal conviction was reversed, and the Supreme Court invalidated the Ohio criminal syndicalism law itself. In so doing, the Supreme Court reversed the 1927 *Whitney v. California* decision, in which a state law very similar to Ohio's had been upheld. This provides an interesting illustration of the way a dissenting or concurring opinion of one generation can inspire a majority opinion in another. Justice Brandeis' concurring opinion in *Whitney* argued for an imminent danger requirement: Brandeis said the First Amendment should not permit sanctions for political speech unless it threatens to provoke imminent lawless action. More than 40 years later, the entire Supreme Court adopted that view in the *Brandenburg* decision, repudiating the majority opinion in *Whitney.*

Does this new imminence requirement mean that the First Amendment never allows speech to be made a crime unless there is a call for action that may actually lead to unlawful acts? When the speech is political, the answer to that question would be yes. However, the Supreme Court has also dealt with various other circumstances in which speech may be punished.

For example, the high court has often upheld obscenity laws, ruling that the First Amendment does not protect speech or writings that are legally obscene. The problem in that area, of course, is deciding whether a particular work is obscene, a task that has sometimes fallen to the Supreme Court. Chapter 10 discusses the problems of obscenity and the First Amendment.

Another kind of speech that the Supreme Court has said may be prohibited in spite of the First Amendment is what have been called "fighting words." A famous 1942 Supreme Court decision (*Chaplinsky v. New Hampshire*, 315 U.S. 568) upheld the criminal conviction of a man who used words likely to produce an immediate violent response—a breach of the peace. Thus, speech likely to cause a fight, such as calling someone a "damned fascist" in the heyday of Hitlerism (as happened in *Chaplinsky*), may be prohibited.

In addition, the Supreme Court has allowed a variety of other limits to be placed on speech. Many of these limits are prior restraints—laws that prohibit the speech from occurring in the first place as opposed to punishing the speaker afterward. The next chapter discusses the problems of prior restraint and the First Amendment.

GUIDELINES FOR INTERPRETING THE CONSTITUTION

In tracing the development of First Amendment freedoms, we have noted several philosophies and "tests" that have been proposed to aid in interpreting what the First Amendment means. Because interpreting the First Amendment (and the rest of the Constitution) is so central to the study of mass media law, we will summarize some basic principles of Constitutional interpretation at this point.

Almost every dispute about Constitutional rights involves some kind of a *balancing test*. The courts must weigh conflicting rights and decide which is the most important. That means sometimes one Constitutional principle must give way to another: there are few absolutes in Constitutional law.

That fact, of course, is unfortunate for the mass media. Were the First Amendment an absolute, many of the legal problems the media face would not exist. Given an absolute First Amendment, there would be no such thing as sedition or prior restraint, and it is doubtful the media could even be held accountable for libel and slander, invasions of privacy, or copyright infringements. Certainly there would be no obscenity law and no limits on media coverage of the criminal justice system. But if that were the case, many of society's other interests would be forced to yield to freedom of speech and freedom of the press.

Fortunately or unfortunately, depending on your point of view, the *absolute theory* of the First Amendment has never been the majority view on the U.S. Supreme Court. Some of the founding fathers, such as James Madison, may have considered the First Amendment something of an absolute safeguard for free speech, and two well-known Supreme Court justices who served in the Warren years (Hugo Black and William O. Douglas) took an absolutist position.

However, the majority view has always been that the First Amendment must be weighed in the balances against other rights and social needs. Thus, the task for the courts over the years has been to develop appropriate guidelines to assist in this balancing process.

One of the best-known of these guidelines for balancing the First Amendment against other interests has been the *clear and present danger* test. As already noted, it was first cited by Justice Oliver Wendell Holmes in the 1919 *Schenck* decision. In the years since, it has sometimes been applied to political speech cases, although in recent years the Supreme Court has not mentioned it in the leading decisions on free speech. As Chapter Eight explains, the Supreme Court has also applied the "clear and present danger" test in resolving conflicts between the media and the courts. In many of those cases, the Supreme Court has been forced to weigh the First Amendment guarantee of a free press against judges' rights to exercise their contempt of court powers, and the concept of "clear and present danger" has been used in this balancing process.

Some Constitutional scholars argue for a *preferred position* test as an alternative to balancing the First Amendment against other rights and social interests. In their view, the First Amendment should occupy a preeminent place in Constitutional law and should rarely give way to other interests. They suggest the Warren Court leaned toward that view of the First Amendment. Indeed, many of the decisions most favorable to the media were handed down by the Warren Court.

In a more general way, the Supreme Court always uses a kind of "preferred position" test in weighing constitutionally protected interests against other values. In *U.S. v. C.I.O.* (335 U.S. 106), a 1948 case, Justice Wiley Rutledge articulated this view. He noted that the normal rule of judicial interpretation requires the courts to adopt a presumption in favor of the validity of legislative acts. However, he said, when a legislative act restricts First Amendment rights, the presumption must be reversed so that there is a presumption against the validity of the law rather than in favor of its validity. Thus, he advocated a "reverse presumption of constitutionality" when a statutory law is challenged on Constitutional grounds.

The concept that the rights protected by the Bill of Rights occupy a preferred position compared to other interests has been mentioned in a number of other Supreme Court decisions. However, on a practical level that bias in favor of Constitutional rights does not necessarily translate into tangible results. What the court still does is balance the competing interests—albeit with the scales tipped slightly toward Constitutional rights.

The Supreme Court has also developed a series of more specific guidelines to use in evaluating claims that a given statutory law or government action violates a Constitutional right.

When a statute (or a state's application of the common law) is challenged, the court normally looks for nothing more than a *rational relationship* between the law and a legitimate government goal. When a state law is challenged, for instance, the state may attempt to defend it by showing that the law bears a rational relationship to its police power or its duty to promote the health and welfare of its citizens.

However, when the claim is that the statute violates a fundamental right protected by the Constitution, the state must show a *compelling state interest* to justify the statute. The state must, in effect, convince the court that its objective in enacting this statute is of such overriding importance that a fundamental right (such as freedom of expression) must give way. A good example of this is described in Chapter 12, where the Supreme Court's landmark decisions on the First Amendment and commercial speech are discussed. In those cases, the high court has repeatedly forced the states to show a *compelling state interest* to justify restrictions on the right to advertise (see, for instance, *Bigelow v. Virginia*, 421 U.S. 809, 1975).

Another way the courts, and particularly the U.S. Supreme Court, evaluate challenged state and federal statutes is to decide whether they are *vague* or *overly broad*. If a law that limits Constitutionally protected rights is so broad that it inhibits freedom more than is necessary for a legitimate government purpose, or if it is so vague it is difficult to know exactly what speech or conduct is prohibited, it may be invalidated for vagueness or overbreadth.

If a court is going to invalidate a statutory law, it has two options: (1) to find that the law is unconstitutional and thus void under all circumstances; or (2) to find that it is unconstitutional only as it has been as applied to the person suing. Moreover, given an ambiguous law, the courts have an obligation to resolve the ambiguity in such a way as to avoid a Constitutional conflict if possible. The U.S. Supreme Court has the final say in construing the language in federal statutes, but the state courts have the final say in interpreting state laws. The U.S. Supreme Court can only decide whether a state law is unconstitutional as interpreted by the state courts; it cannot reinterpret the statute.

This means the U.S. Supreme Court sometimes has to send a case back to a state court to find out what a state law means. Once the state court spells out the meaning, the nation's highest court can then decide whether the law—as interpreted by the state court—actually violates the U.S. Constitution. If it does, it is invalid, of course. But if the state court can interpret the law in such a way as to avoid a conflict with the U.S. Constitution, the law is valid.

Obviously, determining whether a given statute or government action violates the Constitution is a difficult and subjective job. The Supreme Court has a variety of guidelines that it may choose to follow (or choose to ignore) in any given situation. Critics of the process suspect that whatever test is or isn't applied in a particular case, the ultimate outcome of the case depends more on the values and priorities of the nine justices than on how the facts measure up against one or another set of guidelines. In short, whatever other test may be applied, cases are decided on the basis of a balancing process in which various competing interests and social objectives are weighed.

THE FUTURE OF FREEDOM

In this chapter, we have traced 300 years of struggles for freedom of expression. Of the total history of humanity, that is but a tiny portion. Where, then, is freedom going in the next 300 years?

Obviously, no one can really answer that sort of question. The status of freedom in the coming centuries depends on who runs the country (and, more important, which societies are dominant on the world scene). But in the shorter run, it depends on who is appointed to the U.S. Supreme Court, the federal appellate courts, and the appellate courts of the 50 states. It is these people who will shape the law.

Another factor that will determine how much freedom there is in future centuries is the degree to which societies such as ours feel secure. Whenever a society feels threatened by subversive forces within and powerful enemies abroad, freedom suffers. All one need do to see that is to look at the abridgments the First Amendment has suffered over the past 200 years when war seemed imminent.

In addition, the extent to which there is freedom in the future will depend on the conduct of the mass media. Yellow journalism, monopolistic business practices, and denials of public access invite punitive responses by governments. If they are to preserve their freedom, the media must stand firm against abuses by governments at all levels, but they must also be responsible in exercising that freedom.

3

PRIOR RESTRAINT IN MODERN AMERICA

Legal controls on the mass media generally fall into two categories: prior restraint and subsequent punishment. A prior restraint is an act by a government agency to prevent facts or ideas considered unacceptable from ever being published. Under a subsequent punishment system, on the other hand, the publisher or broadcaster is free to disseminate the questionable material, but must be prepared to face the consequences afterward.

Prior restraints are usually a far greater threat to freedom than subsequent punishments. If the media are free to publish controversial facts and opinions without government interference beyond the threat of punishment afterward, at least a few courageous publishers and broadcasters will take the risk and make the questionable material public. If the material turns out to be of social importance, the publisher may still be punished, but at least the people will have the information and a public dialogue can begin. However, if a government can prevent the publication from ever occurring, the public may never know about important facts or ideas, and the democratic process may be thwarted. A democratic society cannot long survive without a press free of prior censorship by government.

Fortunately, most of the legal controls on the press in modern America are subsequent punishments, not prior restraints. Much of the struggle for freedom of the seventeenth and eighteenth centuries was a battle against prior restraints, and that battle was largely won by the time the First Amendment was ratified. Nevertheless, prior censorship occasionally occurs in America today, the First Amendment notwithstanding. These instances of prior restraint typically involve conflicts between the right to publish and other important societal needs. Often the conflict is between freedom of expression and the government's claim that a certain story, if published, will do irreparable harm to national security.

Half a century ago, the U.S. Supreme Court made it clear that prior restraints are generally improper in America. That ruling came in a landmark 1931 decision, *Near v. Minnesota* (283 U.S. 697). The case resulted from a Minnesota statute that allowed government officials to treat a "malicious, scandalous and defamatory newspaper" as a public nuisance and bar its publication. Under this law, a county attorney brought suit to stop publication of *The Saturday Press*, a small weekly newspaper produced by Howard Guilford and J. M. Near.

Guilford and Near had published several articles critical of certain public officials over a period of two months. In their attacks, they charged that a Jewish gangster controlled gambling, bootlegging and racketeering in Minneapolis. They claimed law enforcement agencies did little to stop this corruption. In particular, they accused the police chief of gross neglect of duty, illicit relations with gangsters, and participating in graft.

A trial court ruled the paper a public nuisance under the Minnesota law and banned its further publication. The Minnesota Supreme Court affirmed the ruling, and Near appealed to the U.S. Supreme Court, contending that his First and Fourteenth Amendment rights had been violated.

In a decision that made Constitutional history, the Supreme Court overturned the lower courts and allowed Near to continue publishing. In a narrow 5-4 decision, the high court traced the history of prior restraints and concluded that a newspaper may not be censored before publication except under very exceptional circumstances. Chief Justice Charles Evans Hughes wrote:

> The fact that for approximately one hundred and fifty years there has been almost an entire absence of attempts to impose previous restraints upon publications relating to the malfeasance of public officers is significant of the deep-seated conviction that such restraints would violate Constitutional rights. The general principle that the Constitutional guaranty of the liberty of the press gives immunity from previous restraints has been approved in many decisions under the provisions of state constitutions.

In reaching this conclusion, the court cited James Madison's interpretation of the First Amendment as well as the views of William Blackstone, a highly respected British jurist of the eighteenth century. The court noted Blackstone's argument against prior restraints but in favor of punishments afterward for those whose publications turn out to be unlawful.

The Supreme Court also pointed to the *Schenck v. U.S.* case (discussed in Chapter Two) as an example of an exceptional circumstance in which prior restraint might be proper. Chief Justice Hughes said that, in addition to prior censorship in the interest of national security, prior restraints might be proper to control obscenity and incitements to acts of violence. The court said, "the Constitutional guaranty of free speech does not protect a man from an injunction against uttering words that may have all the effect of force."

In the half-century since the landmark *Near v. Minnesota* decision, the closeness of the vote against prior restraints has often been overlooked. The dissenters in *Near*, who needed just one more Supreme Court justice on their side to prevail, would have allowed prior restraints under many more circumstances. In fact, their reading of history led them to believe that the only form of prior restraint the First Amendment was actually intended to prohibit was licensing of the press by the executive branch of government.

Despite the closeness of the decision, the *Near* case established a pattern that the Supreme Court has consistently followed in the decades since. The court has repeatedly invalidated prior restraints on the media, declaring that prior censorship would be possible under the right conditions but failing to find those conditions. One of the few exceptions to this rule arises when the news media obtain confidential information through the pretrial discovery process in a civil lawsuit. In such cases, the Supreme Court has allowed prior restraints, a point discussed later in this chapter.

In 1971 the Supreme Court was confronted with the question of allowing a prior restraint in the case of *Organization for a Better Austin v. Keefe* (402 U.S. 415). Jerome Keefe was a real estate broker who allegedly engaged in "blockbusting" tactics in the community of Austin, near Chicago, Ill. He was accused of attempting to panic white residents into selling at low prices to escape an influx of blacks that he claimed were moving into their neighborhoods. The Organization for a Better Austin (OBA), trying to halt this white flight, began circulating fliers attacking the "panic peddling" methods of Keefe. Keefe got an injunction that prohibited the OBA from distributing its fliers or picketing. The order was affirmed by an Illinois appellate court, and OBA appealed to the U.S. Supreme Court.

The Supreme Court invalidated the injunction, noting that peaceful pamphleteering is protected by the First Amendment, and its prohibition is a prior restraint. The court said:

> Any prior restraint on expression comes to this court with a "heavy presumption" against its Constitutional validity. Respondent thus carries a heavy burden of showing justification for the imposition of such a restraint. He has not met that burden.

THE "PENTAGON PAPERS" CASE

One month after the Keefe decision, another prior restraint issue surfaced—this one pitting then-President Richard Nixon's administration against two of the nation's leading newspapers, the *New York Times* and the *Washington*

Post. The case came to be known as the "Pentagon Papers" case, although its official name is *New York Times v. U.S.* (403 U.S. 713).

A secret Defense Department study of American policy in Vietnam was surreptitiously photocopied and portions of it were given to several newspapers. It revealed questionable policy decisions by several presidents that led the country into the Vietnam War.

When the first installment of a planned series based on the secret study appeared in each newspaper, the Nixon administration demanded that the *Times* and *Post* halt all further stories on the subject. When they refused, the Justice Department secured a temporary order from a federal district judge forbidding the *Times* to publish any more articles on the "Pentagon Papers." The judge then changed his mind and vacated the order, but a federal appellate court reinstated it. The case was immediately appealed to the U.S. Supreme Court. Meanwhile, another federal appellate court refused to stop the *Post* from publishing more stories about the "Pentagon Papers."

In view of the flagrant prior censorship the order against the *Times* involved, the U.S. Supreme Court justices decided the case only two weeks after the controversy arose, working during what would otherwise have been their summer recess. The Nixon administration argued that publication of the "Pentagon Papers" would endanger national security and damage U.S. foreign relations.

The newspapers replied that this was a clear-cut First Amendment issue involving information of great importance to the American people. Further, the newspapers contended that the entire classification system under which these documents were declared secret should be revised.

The Supreme Court voted 6-3 to set aside the prior restraint and allow the publication of articles based on the "Pentagon Papers." Journalists proclaimed the victory as if it were the outcome of the Super Bowl. *Newsweek*, for instance, put "Victory for the Press" in bold yellow type on its cover. Inside, the magazine said this: "Few clearer gauges of the sanctity of the First Amendment freedoms, few plainer demonstrations of the openness of American society, could be imagined than the High Court's ruling in favor of the press."

Unfortunately, it wasn't that clear cut.

In a brief opinion, the court had simply said the government had failed to prove that the articles would endanger national security sufficiently to justify prior restraint of the nation's press. In the majority were Justices Black, Brennan, Douglas, Marshall, Stewart, and White. The minority consisted of Justices Harlan and Blackmun and Chief Justice Burger.

In addition to the brief opinion by the court, each of the nine justices wrote his own separate opinion explaining his views. When legal scholars began analyzing those nine separate opinions, they realized the decision was no decisive victory for the press.

Only two of the justices (Black and Douglas) took the absolutist position that prior restraints such as the government sought would never be Constitutionally permissible. Justice Marshall said the courts should not do by injunction what Congress had refused to do by statutory law (i.e., authorize prior censorship). Justice Brennan said the government simply hadn't satisfied the very heavy burden of proof necessary to justify prior censorship in this particular case.

However, the other five made it clear they either favored censorship in this case or would support criminal sanctions against the nation's leading newspapers after publication of the documents. At least two justices (Harlan and Blackmun) favored prior restraint in this case, while Chief Justice Burger voted to forbid publication at least until the lower courts had more time to consider the matter, although he didn't really address the substantive issue of prior restraint. Justices White and Stewart said the government had not justified prior censorship but they made it clear (as did Burger) that they favored criminal prosecution of the editors after publication for revealing the secret documents.

Thus, the "Pentagon Papers" case was not a clear-cut victory for freedom of expression, but at least the nation's press was allowed to publish stories based on the documents. No journalist was ever prosecuted in connection with the "Pentagon Papers," although the government unsuccessfully prosecuted Dr. Daniel Ellsberg, the social scientist who copied the documents in the first place.

The question of prior restraint in the interest of national security arose again in a 1979 case, *U.S. v. The Progressive* (467 F. Supp. 990). This case was never given full consideration by a court of appeals, let alone the Supreme Court, so it has little value as a legal precedent. Nevertheless, it did dramatize the conflict between freedom of the press and national security.

The Progressive, a liberal magazine, was planning to publish an article entitled, "The H-bomb Secret: How We Got It, Why We're Telling It." The author, Howard Morland, had assembled an apparently accurate description of a hydrogen bomb through library research. The magazine sent the article to the federal government prior to publication with a letter requesting that its technical accuracy be verified. The U.S. Department of Energy responded by declaring that publication of the article would violate the secrecy provisions of the 1954 Atomic Energy Act. The U.S. Justice Department sought a court order prohibiting publication.

Federal Judge Robert Warren issued an order forbidding the magazine to publish the article. He said the article could "accelerate the membership of a candidate nation in the thermonuclear club." He distinguished this case from the "Pentagon Papers" case in that he said the H-bomb article posed a current threat to national security. Also, he ruled, a specific statute prohibited publication of this article, whereas there was no statutory authorization to pre-censor the "Pentagon Papers." Ultimately, though, he offered a very pragmatic argument:

Faced with a stark choice between upholding the right to continued life and the right to freedom of the press, most jurists would have no difficulty in opting for the chance to continue to breathe and function as they work to achieve perfect freedom of expression.

Doubting that the issue was quite that black and white, *The Progressive* appealed Warren's ruling. However, before a federal appellate court could decide the case, articles describing an H-bomb in similar detail appeared in other publications, rendering the case moot. Once the information was published elsewhere, the government dropped its attempt to pre-censor the magazine article.

Therefore, the *Progressive* case left many important issues unresolved. One of the most troubling is that the information for the article was gleaned from non-classified sources, yet when it was put into an article questioning the classification system, the U.S. government tried to censor it. Also, Judge Warren's abandonment of the First Amendment invited appellate review. In reviewing Warren's order, a higher court might have clarified the extent to which the national security classification system overrides the First Amendment.

CIA CONTRACTS AND THE RIGHT TO PUBLISH

Another challenge to the classification system has come from two former employees of the Central Intelligence Agency, both of whom published books on their CIA experiences. In both instances, the agency attempted to pre-censor the ex-employees' writings under a provision of their employment contracts that prohibited them from publishing information they gained as CIA agents without the agency's prior approval. Both employees contended these contract provisions violated their First Amendment rights.

The first case, *U.S. v. Marchetti* (466 F.2d 1309, 4th cir. 1972) arose after Victor L. Marchetti left the CIA and published both a book and a magazine article critical of CIA activities. When the agency learned he was about to publish still another book, it got a court order temporarily halting the project. After a secret trial (much of the testimony was classified), the court ordered Marchetti to submit everything he might write about the CIA to the agency for approval. Marchetti appealed that decision, but it was largely affirmed by the U.S. Court of Appeals.

However, the appellate court said the CIA could only pre-censor classified information, and after further legal maneuvering a district court allowed the agency to censor only 27 of 166 passages in the new book that the agency wanted to suppress.

Although the U.S. Supreme Court refused to review the *Marchetti* case, in 1980 the court did rule on a similar case, *Snepp v. U.S.* (444 U.S. 507). Frank Snepp resigned from the CIA in 1976 and wrote a book alleging CIA ineptness in Vietnam. He did not submit it for prior CIA approval, as required by his employment contract. After its publication, the U.S. government filed a breach of contract suit against Snepp. Snepp contended the contract violated his First and Fifth Amendment rights.

A trial court ordered Snepp to turn over all his profits from the book to the government and submit any future manuscripts about the CIA to the agency for prior approval. An appellate court reversed that ruling in part, prompting the Supreme Court to hear the case.

The Supreme Court reinstated the trial court's order against Snepp without even hearing full arguments from both sides: the court never let Snepp present his case. But the high court upheld the validity of the contract, ignoring the prior censorship implications of such contracts. The court said: "He (Snepp) deliberately and surreptitiously violated his obligation to submit all material for prepublication review. Thus, he exposed the classified information with which he had been entrusted to the risk of disclosure."

The *Snepp* decision, then, was decided as it was because of the provisions of Snepp's CIA employment contract and would not be applicable to persons who had not signed such contracts. However, this led many journalists to wonder what would happen if the government decided to impose similar contracts on other government employees. They didn't have to wonder for long.

In 1983, Ronald Reagan issued a presidential directive requiring that more than 100,000 government employees sign agreements consenting to "prepublication review" of their writings by government censors—for the rest of their lives. The order applied to high-level employees of the Defense, State, and Justice Departments, among others. The directive produced immediate protests from civil libertarians, the mass media, and members of Congress.

Critics warned that the plan would eliminate any semblance of informed public debate about the government's handling of many foreign policy—and even domestic—issues. If this is a government of the people, they asked, shouldn't the people have a right to know when their leaders make deals with foreign governments? Isn't it in the public interest for government employees with troubled consciences to be able to speak out when they believe a government agency is abusing its powers?

As the outcry against this lifetime censorship plan grew, Congress intervened. Congress attached language that would delay implementation of the plan to a bill the president wanted, and he reluctantly signed the bill in late 1983. Then in early 1984 Reagan agreed to temporarily shelve his proposal and work for a new "bipartisan" plan to censor the writings of government employees.

At this writing, it was not clear what this new "bipartisan" censorship plan would include. What was clear is that the Reagan administration wanted to defuse the controversy—and keep things quiet until after the 1984 election. But those who opposed the whole idea of government censorship wondered why, after all of these years, the writings and speeches of thousands of government employees should be subject to any new censorship policy.

Moreover, some critics of the plan to censor present and former government employees were troubled by another, less publicized aspect of the program: a second "nondisclosure agreement" that some four million persons

(including about 1.5 million civilian employees of companies having government contracts) were being asked to sign. That form does not authorize direct
prior censorship, but it does authorize the government to secure court orders
to censor those who might otherwise speak or write about things the
government says they shouldn't discuss for "national security" reasons. In the
long run, this second agreement—which was not withdrawn along with the
more publicized one—could do even more to restrict national debate about
military and foreign policy issues, critics warned.

RESTRAINT VIA DISCRIMINATORY TAXATION

One of the oldest forms of government control over the mass media is
discriminatory taxation. Authorities in seventeenth- and eighteenth-century
England used taxes as a means of controlling the press. One of the major
grievances of the colonists before the revolutionary war was the Stamp Act,
which taxed newspapers. After independence, attempts to single out newspapers for special taxes were rare in America, but a classic example of such a
tax cropped up in the 1930s.

In 1936, just five years after its landmark *Near v. Minnesota* decision, the
Supreme Court decided *Grosjean v. American Press* (297 U.S. 233). This case
arose because the state of Louisiana, dominated by Governor Huey "King-
fish" Long's political machine, had imposed a special tax on the gross receipts
of the 13 largest papers in the state, 12 of which opposed Long. The tax
applied to total advertising receipts of all papers and magazines with a
circulation over 20,000 copies per week.

The newspapers challenged the tax in court and a federal district court
issued an order barring the tax as a violation of the First Amendment. The
Supreme Court heard the case on appeal and unanimously affirmed the lower
court.

In an opinion by Justice George Sutherland, the court traced the history
of taxes on knowledge in England and America. Sutherland said the First
Amendment was intended to prevent prior restraints in the form of discriminatory taxes. He noted that the license tax acted as a prior restraint in two
ways. First, it would curtail advertising revenue, and second, it was designed
to restrict circulation. The Louisiana tax, Sutherland said, was "not an
ordinary form of tax, but one single in kind, with a long history of hostile
misuse against the freedom of the press."

This Supreme Court decision, however, did not free the media from
their normal tax obligations as businesses. That principle was illustrated in a
1953 California case, *City of Corona v. Corona Daily Independent* (115
Cal.App.2d 382). The *Daily Independent* refused to pay a $32 city business
license fee, claiming the fee was a violation of the First Amendment. The
appellate court ruled:

There is ample authority to the effect that newspapers and the business
of newspaper publication are not made exempt from the ordinary forms

of taxes for the support of local government by the provisions of the First and Fourteenth Amendments.

The U.S. Supreme Court refused to review that decision. Taxation as a means of controlling or punishing the media is clearly prohibited by the First Amendment; routine taxation of all businesses (including media businesses) is not.

However, *Corona* and *Grosjean* are not the only cases involving the question of discriminatory taxes against the media. In 1983, the Supreme Court faced the issue again in a case involving a Minnesota tax on some—but not all—newspapers.

Minnesota created a "use" tax on the ink and newsprint used by newspapers in 1971. But after some of the smaller papers complained of the economic hardship the tax caused, the legislature rewrote the law to exempt the first $100,000 in newsprint and ink each newspaper purchased annually. Thus, the law in effect exempted small newspapers or, to put it another way, singled out the large newspapers for a special tax. In 1974, one newspaper company—the *Minneapolis Star and Tribune*—paid about two-thirds of the total amount the state collected from all Minnesota newspapers through this tax. Citing the *Grosjean* precedent, the *Star and Tribune* company challenged the constitutionality of the tax.

In *Minneapolis Star and Tribune v. Minnesota Commissioner of Revenue* (103 S.Ct. 1365, 1983), the Supreme Court voted 8-1 to overturn Minnesota's tax on ink and newsprint. Justice Sandra Day O'Connor, writing for the court, warned that because such a tax "targets a small group of newspapers," it "presents such a potential for abuse that no interest suggested by Minnesota can justify the scheme." Justice William Rehnquist dissented, arguing that the use tax in question was less of a burden than the normal sales tax paid by other businesses. (Minnesota exempted newspapers from the state sales tax, a practice that is common in other states as well.) Rehnquist said the state was actually conferring a benefit on the press, something the states may do without violating the First Amendment.

However, the majority's view was that the Minnesota tax was a problem precisely because it singled out certain newspapers for a tax not paid by others. Had Minnesota merely imposed a uniform sales or use tax on all businesses, there would have been no First Amendment issue.

Also, Justice O'Connor emphasized that this case was not comparable to *Grosjean* in that there was no evidence that Minnesota's discriminatory tax was created to punish large newspapers for their editorial views. But the potential for such abuses was enough to render the tax unconstitutional.

CONTROLS ON DISTRIBUTION

The United States has never had any formal licensing system for the print media, perhaps because of the abuses of licensing in seventeenth century England (discussed in Chapter Two). The nearest thing to licensing in

America has been attempts by governments and private entities to control the distribution of printed materials. Usually these controls involve requiring someone's "permission" before any material may be distributed, with the permission available only to certain favored publications. Such controls are often attempted, despite the First Amendment. In fact, the U.S. Supreme Court has often been asked to rule on the validity of this kind of prior restraint.

The constitutionality of such restraints was first tested in connection with the proselytizing activities of the Jehovah's Witness movement. Since this religious group engages in door-to-door and street corner soliciting for a cause unpopular with many Americans, its efforts led to restrictive ordinances in a number of cities by the late 1930s. The Witnesses challenged these limits on their First Amendment rights in a series of law suits, several of which reached the U.S. Supreme Court by the early 1940s.

The first of these Jehovah's Witness cases was *Lovell v. City of Griffin* (303 U.S. 444), decided in 1938. Alma Lovell, a Witness, circulated pamphlets in Griffin, Ga., without the city manager's permission, something a local law required. She was fined $50, but she took her case all the way to the Supreme Court and won.

The Supreme Court found the ordinance invalid, saying it "strikes at the very foundation of the freedom of the press by subjecting it to license and censorship." The city claimed the First Amendment applied only to newspapers and magazines, and not to Ms. Lovell's pamphlets. The Supreme Court disagreed: "the liberty of the press is not confined to newspapers and periodicals. It necessarily embraces pamphlets and leaflets. These indeed have been historic weapons in the defense of liberty."

Moreover, the court went to some length to make it clear the First Amendment protects the right to distribute literature as well as the right to publish it.

Elsewhere, a number of communities attempted to curb Jehovah's Witnesses by using anti-littering ordinances against them. Several of these laws were considered by the Supreme Court in a 1939 case, *Schneider v. State of New Jersey* (308 U.S. 147).

The court said a city indeed has the right to prevent littering, but it must do so by punishing the person who actually does the littering, not by punishing someone who hands literature to willing recipients. The person handing out a pamphlet cannot be punished even if the recipient later throws it away, the high court said.

In *Schneider*, the Supreme Court also invalidated a city ordinance that required anyone seeking to distribute literature door to door to get police permission first.

The court said giving the police discretion to decide which ideas may and may not be advanced by neighborhood canvassing is a violation of the First Amendment. The court said a city may limit the hours of door-to-door soliciting, but requiring a permit in advance is unconstitutional when the permit system gives the police discretion to approve permits for causes they like and deny permits to unpopular causes.

In 1942, the Supreme Court first approved and then invalidated another city ordinance that had been used against a Jehovah's Witness, this one simply requiring a $10 "book agent" license for all solicitors. In this case (*Jones v. Opelika*, 316 U.S. 584), the high court initially upheld the license requirement. But some 11 months later, the court vacated its decision and adopted what had been a dissenting opinion as the majority view. The court's final decision was based on the fact that the ordinance gave city officials discretion to grant or revoke these licenses without explaining why the action was taken.

As a result of these Jehovah's Witness cases, it is now a settled principle of Constitutional law that local authorities may not arbitrarily grant solicitation permits to popular ideas while denying them to unpopular ones. A permit system that merely controls the time, place, and manner of solicitation by all groups is valid, as long as it is not so restrictive that it has the effect of preventing the dissemination of ideas.

However, these cases all involved the acts of government agencies that attempted to control the dissemination of ideas in public places or by door-to-door canvassing. Is the rule different if the soliciting is to occur in a private place, such as a company-owned town or a shopping center?

The Supreme Court first addressed that issue in a 1946 case, *Marsh v. Alabama* (326 U.S. 501). The case arose in Chickasaw, Alabama, a company town owned by Gulf Shipbuilding. The distribution of literature without permission of the town's authorities was forbidden.

The case arose when a Jehovah's Witness tried to pass out tracts there. She was told that permission was required before solicitation was allowed, and that she would not be given permission. She was ordered to leave, and when she refused she was prosecuted for trespassing.

Even though the entire town was privately owned, the high court stood by its earlier decisions in the *Marsh* case. Noting that for all practical purposes this company town was a city, the court applied the same rules to it as had been applied to other cities. The court pointed out that the town was in fact open to the public and was immediately adjacent to a four-lane public highway. Even though the streets were privately owned, the public used them as if they were public streets. The court said:

> Ownership does not always mean absolute dominion. The more an owner, for his advantage, opens up his property for use by the public in general, the more do his rights become circumscribed by the statutory and Constitutional rights of those who use it.

More than 20 years later, the Supreme Court applied the same kind of logic to a private shopping center in *Amalgamated Food Employees Local 590 v. Logan Valley Plaza* (391 U.S. 308, 1968). This case involved union picketing, which had been forbidden on shopping center premises. The union challenged this rule and won.

The Supreme Court compared the private shopping center to the private town in *Marsh*, and said the same right to distribute literature existed here.

However, the court said a factor in its decision was that the case involved a labor dispute to which a merchant in the shopping center was a party. The court did not say whether the First Amendment would have applied if there had not been a close relationship between the picketing and a merchant in the shopping center.

However, in 1972 the Supreme Court decided *Lloyd Corp. v. Tanner* (407 U.S. 551), a case involving a shopping center where there was no relationship between the material being distributed and the business of the shopping center. This decision allowed a very large shopping center in Portland, Oregon, to ban anti-Vietman War protesters who wanted to pass out literature.

In the years between the *Logan Valley* decision and this one, four Nixon appointees had replaced key members of the liberal Warren court, and these four justices helped create a new majority that backed away from the court's previous rulings about literature distribution on private property. The court said there was no Constitutional right to distribute literature in this case, particularly because there was no relationship between the literature and the business being conducted at the shopping center. However, the majority opinion did not specifically say it was overruling the *Logan Valley* decision.

In 1976 the Supreme Court came full cycle, specifically stating it had reversed the *Logan Valley* decision as it decided another shopping center case, *Hudgens v. NLRB* (424 U.S. 507). This case involved warehouse employees of the Butler Shoe Company who were on strike. When they picketed a Butler store in an Atlanta shopping center, the center's management ordered them out of the mall. The National Labor Relations Board held this to be an unfair labor practice, and the shopping center owner appealed.

The *Hudgens* majority made it clear that there was no longer any Constitutional right to distribute literature at a private shopping center, even if the literature specifically involved a labor dispute with a merchant doing business there. The court said that, if First and Fourteenth Amendment rights are involved, the content of the material should be irrelevant; it shouldn't matter whether the literature has anything to do with the business being conducted at the shopping center or not. Whatever the subject matter of the literature, there is no Constitutional right to distribute it at a private shopping center, the *Hudgens* majority ruled. This would not preclude the NLRB from ordering an employer to allow picketing on another legal basis, but the court ruled out any such right under the federal Constitution.

There were those who thought *Hudgens* settled the matter of literature distribution at private shopping centers, but they were wrong. In 1980, the Supreme Court made another sharp turn in its circuitous route through this area of law in the case of *Pruneyard Shopping Center v. Robins* (447 U.S. 74).

This case presented the conservative majority on the Supreme Court with a classic confrontation between private property rights and states' rights, two causes that have sometimes been rallying cries of conservatives. At a shopping center near San Jose, California, a group of high school students tried to distribute literature opposing a United Nations resolution against

"Zionism." They were refused permission, and they sued in California's state courts. The state Supreme Court said that the California Constitution provides a broader guarantee of free expression than the federal Constitution. The California court said there is a right to distribute literature in private shopping centers in California, even if no such right is required by the federal Constitution.

The center's owners appealed to the U.S. Supreme Court, contending that this California Supreme Court ruling denied them their property rights and due process rights under the federal Constitution. The respondents replied, of course, in states' rights terms, asserting the right of a state to afford its citizens more free speech rights than the federal Constitution mandates.

In a 7-1 opinion, Justice William Rehnquist chose states' rights over property rights, ruling that the California Supreme Court decision violated no federal right of the shopping center owners that was as important as a state's right to define freedom for its citizens. Rehnquist said the U.S. Supreme Court's earlier rulings on access to shopping centers were not intended to "limit the authority of the state to exercise its police power or its sovereign right to adopt in its own Constitution individual liberties more expansive than those conferred by the Federal Constitution."

In short, the Supreme Court affirmed California's right to create broader rights than the federal Constitution requires. The effect of the *Pruneyard* decision is to leave it up to other state legislatures and courts to decide whether to grant literature distribution rights in private places similar to those now in effect in California.

If the federal Constitution does not guarantee a right to distribute literature at private shopping centers, what about other public and quasi-public places? Are the Jehovah's Witness decisions still valid? The U.S. Supreme Court addressed that question in an important 1981 decision, *Heffron v. International Society for Krishna Consciousness* (452 U.S. 640).

Like members of the Jehovah's Witness movement, Krishna adherents believe their faith requires them to distribute literature to the public. In recent years, Krishna members have attempted to promote their faith and solicit funds in many places where people gather, often citing the earlier Jehovah's Witness cases to support their right to do so. The *Heffron* case arose when Krishna members were refused permission to distribute literature and solicit funds freely at the Minnesota State Fair. They were told they could only do so at a single booth. Under the fair's rules, booths were available to all groups on a non-discriminatory first-come, first-served basis.

The Krishna movement challenged the rules as a violation of the First Amendment, and the case eventually reached the U.S. Supreme Court. Krishna followers argued that distributing literature and soliciting funds are actually part of the movement's religious ritual, required of all members. To limit these activities is a violation of the First Amendment as interpreted in the *Schneider* and *Lovell* cases (discussed earlier), they contended. Minnesota fair officials conceded that Krishna followers, like Jehovah's Witnesses or anyone else, have a Constitutional right to propagate their views at the state fair. However, they said it was necessary to restrict all such groups to booths to keep the fair orderly.

The Supreme Court majority agreed. The court said it is not a violation of the First Amendment to require Krishna followers to practice their religion at a booth rather than at large throughout the state fair. The majority opinion pointed out that Krishna members remained free to mingle with the crowd and orally present their views, but it upheld the rule limiting solicitations and literature distribution to individual booths at the fair. The court pointed out that if the Krishnas were allowed to proselytize throughout the fairgrounds, all other groups would have to be given the same privilege.

In short, the First Amendment requires officials to allow all groups reasonable access to government-controlled public events and places, but still permits reasonable restrictions on the time, place, and manner of literature distribution. Private facilities such as shopping centers, however, are a different matter. If a state wishes to require public access to such places for literature distribution, it may do so, but the federal Constitution does not guarantee any such right.

NEWSRACK ORDINANCES

If California has taken the lead in guaranteeing freedom of expression at shopping centers, it has also taken the lead in denying freedom of expression via street corner vending machines.

The city of Glendale, Calif., adopted an ordinance that set a limit of eight newsracks at each place in town where newsracks were permitted. The ordinance established an order of preference for awarding access to the newsracks, with first priority to daily newspapers and second priority to general circulation weekly papers.

As a result, some newspapers were denied newsrack space altogether, including *The Weekly People*, the paper of the Socialist Workers Party. The party sued the city, charging a violation of the First and Fourteenth Amendments. A trial court ruled the ordinance unconstitutional, but the California Court of Appeals reversed the ruling. The appellate court said that sometimes a means of expression must be limited to avoid interference with the rights of others to go about their business. It said the constitution does not require a community to put up with an unlimited number of newsracks along the right of way.

Further, the appellate court said the ordinance did not discriminate on the basis of the content of the publications. The court said: "they (the ordinance's provisions) are mechanical, they do not leave anything to the discretion of the public works director. . . ."

Both the California and U.S. Supreme Courts refused to review the appellate court decision (*Socialist Labor Party v. Glendale*, 82 Cal.App.3d 722, 1978).

However, if local authorities arbitrarily decide which newspapers can be sold via newsracks based on their content, or if newsracks are banned altogether, there are First Amendment problems. Lower courts in both Pennsylvania and New York have overruled arbitrary controls and outright bans on newsracks (for instance, see *Philadelphia News, Inc. v. Borough C. Etc., Swarthmore*, 381 F.Supp. 228; and *Westchester Rockland Newspapers v. Yonkers*, 5 Med.L.Rptr. 1779). Even in California, a city may not ban all newsracks outright. Nor may it arbitrarily remove newsracks without providing the publisher with an opportunity to challenge the action at a hearing. To do either would violate the First Amendment, the state Supreme Court said in 1977 (*Kash Enterprises v. City of Los Angeles*, 19 Cal.3d 294).

PRIOR RESTRAINTS AND CONFIDENTIAL INFORMATION

Another kind of prior restraint the media have encountered in recent years is the result of state efforts to keep certain kinds of information about crime confidential. The fair trial-free press problem is discussed more fully in Chapter Seven, but at this point we should note several U.S. Supreme Court decisions overturning court orders and state laws forbidding the media to publish confidential information.

These cases typically involve the publication of the names of juvenile suspects and rape victims. This issue also has privacy implications, which are discussed in Chapter Five. However, when a court orders or a statute forbids the publication of such information, that constitutes a prior restraint and raises Constitutional questions apart from the privacy and fair trial-free press implications.

Some would say that these are really subsequent punishment cases rather than prior restraint cases, since they generally involve laws that prescribe criminal sanctions for publishing the forbidden information. However, they represent an arm of the government specifically telling the media what may and may not be lawfully published. In that respect, they constitute prior restraints, although perhaps not of the same magnitude as a law that forbids a publisher to sell his newspapers on the city streets.

In any event, there is often only a fine line between prior restraint and subsequent punishment. The "Pentagon Papers" case is unquestionably a prior restraint case, but even there no government official actually seized control of the *New York Times* pressroom to censor the paper. Instead, a court order was issued—an order the editors could have ignored if they had been willing to face a subsequent punishment (a contempt of court citation involving a fine or a short jail sentence).

In most totalitarian societies, there is a very clear distinction between prior restraints and subsequent punishments. Prior restraints in those societies often take a very tangible form: a visit from government censors accompanied by troops, or worse. The authorities may well use physical force to restrain the publication of forbidden material.

In most democracies, on the other hand, the distinctions between prior restraints and subsequent punishments tend to be much more subtle. The prior restraints are rarely if ever accompanied by the kind of physical force that would be needed to actually prevent publication. Rather, the prior restraints are almost always merely court orders or laws that editors are free to disobey—provided they are prepared to face still more subsequent punishments.

Nevertheless, the law makes a distinction between prior restraints and subsequent punishments, and says that prior restraints are usually much more Constitutionally suspect than subsequent punishments. The cases involving confidential information illustrate this point.

The Supreme Court first dealt with a state prohibition on publishing the names of rape victims in 1975, overturning a Georgia law that made it a crime to publish the names. In that case (*Cox Broadcasting v. Cohn*, 420 U.S. 469), a television reporter had obtained the name of a rape victim from a court record, and the station later faced a civil invasion of privacy suit for broadcasting the name. The U.S. Supreme Court said the First and Fourteenth Amendments do not permit criminal sanctions or civil invasion of privacy lawsuits for the publication of truthful information lawfully obtained from official court records.

Two years later the U.S. Supreme Court stepped in to overturn an Oklahoma court order that banned publication of the name of an 11-year-old boy allegedly involved in a fatal shooting. The case was *Oklahoma Publishing v. District Court* (430 U.S. 377, 1977).

Reporters were present at the boy's initial detention hearing and learned his name. Local newspapers and broadcasters carried the name in their coverage of the story. A judge ordered the media not to publish the boy's name or picture again, and the Oklahoma Publishing Company appealed the order to the state Supreme Court, which upheld it. The U.S. Supreme Court then reversed, finding the order amounted to prior censorship in violation of the First and Fourteenth Amendments. The high court relied on *Cox Broadcasting* as a precedent, and said there was no evidence that the press acquired the information unlawfully or even without the state's permission.

In 1979, the Supreme Court intervened once more to halt a Constitutional violation in this kind of situation. In this case (*Smith v. Daily Mail*, 443 U.S. 97), the high court voided a West Virginia law that imposed criminal sanctions for newspapers that published the names of juvenile offenders. One youth allegedly killed another at a junior high school. Reporters got his name by monitoring police radio broadcasts and by talking to eyewitnesses. They published the name.

The Supreme Court again ruled that a truthful account of lawfully obtained information was being punished. Thus, the West Virginia law was invalidated on Constitutional grounds. One aspect of the law that particularly amazed Justice Rehnquist, who wrote a concurring opinion, was that it forbade newspaper publication of juvenile names while not outlawing a broadcast of the names.

The publication of another kind of confidential information produced a 1978 U.S. Supreme Court decision, *Landmark Communications v. Virginia* (435 U.S. 829). The case involved the *Virginian Pilot*'s coverage of the proceedings of a state commission reviewing a judge's performance in office. The paper published the name of the judge, among other information. Virginia had a law making these proceedings confidential. The paper was criminally prosecuted and fined for publishing this information, and the state Supreme Court affirmed the judgment.

The U.S. Supreme Court ruled that the Virginia law violated the First Amendment. The court said judges have no greater immunity from criticism than other persons or institutions. When a newspaper lawfully obtains information about a proceeding such as the one in question, the paper may not be criminally punished for publishing what it learns. The Supreme Court said:

> If the Constitutional protection of a free press means anything, it means that government cannot take it upon itself to decide what a newspaper may and may not publish. Though government may deny access to information and punish its theft, government may not prohibit or punish the publication of that information once it falls into the hands of the press, unless the need for secrecy is manifestly overwhelming.

Thus, a pattern has clearly emerged from these Supreme Court decisions. A state need not release information about juveniles, rape victims, or judges, but if the mass media somehow lawfully obtain this kind of information, they cannot be punished for publishing or broadcasting it. Nor may courts or legislatures engage in prior restraint by forbidding the publication of such information once the media have it.

PRIOR RESTRAINTS AND PRETRIAL DISCOVERY

The mass media's freedom from prior restraints is not as clear when the media obtain confidential information during the pretrial discovery process in a lawsuit (explained in Chapter One). In a 1984 decision that troubled many journalists, the U.S. Supreme Court ruled that the *Seattle Times* and the *Walla Walla (Wash.) Bulletin-Union* could not publish information they obtained while defending a libel suit against a religious group (*Seattle Times v. Rhinehart*, 104 S.Ct. 2199).

The case arose after the two papers carried articles about the allegedly bizarre behavior of the Rev. Keith Milton Rhinehart, leader of a religious group called the Aquarian Foundation. Rhinehart and several followers sued the two papers; during the discovery process the papers obtained the group's membership and donor lists, tax returns, and other financial information. A trial court ordered the newspapers not to publish this information—an order that amounted to a prior restraint.

However, the Supreme Court drew a distinction between the traditional kinds of prior restraint and court orders involving discovery. The high court pointed out that the papers would be free to publish the information in question if they obtained it independently from other sources. However, when a party to a lawsuit is under court orders to give confidential information to the other side, there should be some assurances that the information will remain confidential, the Supreme Court said.

This was not the first time the media had lost a case involving prior restraints in this sort of situation. A year before the *Seattle Times* decision, the Supreme Court refused to overturn a similar prior restraint in a case involving actress Shirley Jones and her husband, Marty Ingels. In that case, the *National Enquirer* was under a court order forbidding it to publish information it might obtain about Jones and Ingels during the discovery process in a libel suit they filed against the paper. The lawsuit stemmed from an *Enquirer* article saying Ingels had cheated stars and terrorized his staff, and that Jones was "driven to drink by his bizarre behavior." A Los Angeles Superior Court judge allowed the *Enquirer* to ask questions about Jones' and Ingels' personal lives during the discovery process—but ordered the paper not to publish anything it might learn.

The California Supreme Court refused to overturn this order, and the U.S. Supreme Court declined to accept the case for review. (The Supreme Court did rule on another aspect of the *Jones-Enquirer* libel case, as explained in the next chapter).

In short, prior restraints appear to be permissible when they involve information obtained during the pretrial discovery process. It may seem ironic, but judges tend to be more willing to let the news media publish material that might affect national security than they are to let the media publish stories based on information they learn while defending civil lawsuits.

A Summary of
Modern Prior Restraints

WHAT IS A PRIOR RESTRAINT?

A prior restraint is a government act to prevent facts or ideas considered unacceptable from ever being published. It is a far greater abridgment of freedom of expression than a subsequent punishment system, which allows publication but punishes the publisher afterward for any harm that may result.

ARE PRIOR RESTRAINTS PERMITTED IN AMERICA?

Under the First Amendment, prior restraints are permitted only under extremely compelling circumstances, with the agency of government that seeks to impose such censorship required to carry a very heavy burden of proof to justify it.

WHEN WOULD A PRIOR RESTRAINT BE CONSTITUTIONAL?

In the "Pentagon Papers" case, the Supreme Court ruled that prior censorship would be permissible if the government could prove that irreparable harm to national security would otherwise result. However, the government was unable to prove national security was sufficiently endangered to justify prior restraint in that case.

ARE CONTROLS ON DISTRIBUTION PRIOR RESTRAINTS?

Laws forbidding the distribution of newspapers or other literature constitute prior restraints, and such laws have often been invalidated by the courts. Under this rationale, laws against pamphleteering on public property are particularly suspect. For a time, the Supreme Court even said the First Amendment required businesses to allow literature distribution in quasi-public places such as shopping centers, but the court has abandoned that rule. However, if a state wishes to create such literature distribution rights under its own laws, it is free to do so.

HOW DO THESE PRINCIPLES AFFECT THE MASS MEDIA?

Several courts have said it is unconstitutional for a community to outlaw all street-corner newsstands. Also, laws forbidding the media to publish information they have in their possession are usually unconstitutional, even if the information concerns confidential legal matters such as juvenile court proceedings. The media may not have a right to gather this kind of news, but the courts cannot ordinarily prevent its publication once the media have it.

4

LIBEL AND SLANDER

Ever since American journalists won their basic First Amendment freedoms, their most serious ongoing legal problem has been the danger of being sued for libel or slander. Other threats to journalistic freedom arise from time to time, but over the past two centuries libel has been a continuing legal problem, with thousands of judgments rendered and thousands more cases settled out of court. Even the fear of libel suits often leads journalists to suppress stories they would otherwise publish, thus engaging in a form of self-censorship that may not always be in the public interest.

Libel judgments today are bigger than ever. Hostile juries sometimes hand out punitive damage awards against newspapers, magazines, and broadcasters without worrying much about the validity of the libel claim itself.

A single libel suit can be financially devastating even to a powerful media corporation. The Libel Defense Resource Center, a New York-based organization that monitors libel cases nationally, reported in 1984 that there had been no fewer than 22 different million-dollar libel judgments against the mass media in the early 1980s.

Although most of the large libel judgments are eventually overturned by appellate courts, the cost of defending such a lawsuit runs into thousands or even millions of dollars. For a small-market broadcaster or newspaper publisher, the cost of a libel suit—even one that is eventually won in court—can put the company on the brink of bankruptcy.

For example, in 1981 the Alton (Ill.) *Telegraph* filed for bankruptcy court protection after losing a $9.2 million libel judgment for a story that was never published in the paper. The case was eventually settled for $1.4 million; the paper managed to borrow enough money to stay in business, but just barely. The case arose because the paper investigated what it felt were questionable business dealings by a local developer. Two reporters sent a memorandum summarizing their findings to federal law enforcement officials (at the federal officials' request), but they decided not to publish the story in the paper because they did not consider their documentation adequate. Still, the developer sued, alleging that he suffered serious business reverses because he was libeled in the memo, and the paper was almost put out of business by the incident (*Green v. Alton Telegraph*, 438 N.E.2d 203, 8 Med.L.Rptr. 1345, 1982).

Well-known national media often find that they are even bigger targets for angry jurors. A jury recently awarded a former "Miss Wyoming" beauty contest winner $26.5 million for a fictitious article in *Penthouse* magazine that never mentioned her name. The judge thought the verdict was excessive, so he reduced it to a mere $14 million! An appellate court eventually set aside the verdict altogether, but by then *Penthouse* had spent roughly a million dollars on legal fees (*Pring v. Penthouse*, 695 F.2d 438, 1983).

But the cost of defending the Miss Wyoming libel case was small compared to the legal bill *Penthouse* ran up in another celebrated libel case. The magazine published an article alleging that Rancho La Costa (a Southern California resort) was built with laundered organized crime money, managed by people with underworld ties, and frequented by members of the Mafia. The owners and management of Rancho La Costa sued *Penthouse* for $522 million, and the case went through six years of costly and complex legal maneuvers before it even went to trial. Twice the case was appealed to the U.S. Supreme Court, which refused to hear it either time.

When the case eventually did go to trial, the trial dragged on for nearly six months. In the end, the jury declared that no one was libeled by the article because the charges were substantially accurate. But the trial judge—a man who had been the lawyer for at least one alleged underworld figure before he became a judge—simply overturned the jury's verdict and ordered a new trial. *Penthouse* had repeatedly asked this judge to resign from the case because of his alleged prejudice—to no avail. *Penthouse* then appealed the judge's refusal to step down, further complicating the legal issues involved. By that time, *Penthouse* reportedly had spent $6 million on legal expenses, and the case was nowhere near being resolved.

Meanwhile, several other libel cases made headlines with their million-dollar verdicts against the media. Actress Carol Burnett won a $1.6 million libel judgment against the *National Enquirer* for an item alleging she was ill-mannered in a restaurant. Jurors are supposed to be impartial, but one juror hugged Burnett and others got her autograph after the verdict.

The trial judge reduced the damages to $800,000 ($750,000 of it punitive damages), and a California appellate court ordered Burnett to either accept an additional five-fold reduction in the punitive damages (to $150,000 from $750,000) or start over and go through a new trial. She chose the latter, and her case, too, was years away from being resolved at this writing.

But not all big-dollar libel cases involve controversial publications such as *Penthouse* or the *National Enquirer*.

Another well-publicized libel case pitted the president of Mobil Oil Corporation against the *Washington Post*. In 1982, Mobil President William P. Tavoulareas won a $2.05 million jury verdict against the *Post* and other defendants for reporting that he used Mobil's money and influence to set up his son in the shipping business. Although some media critics questioned the *Post*'s objectivity in covering the story, Tavoulareas' son in fact did go into the shipping business—and did receive lucrative contracts with the help of Mobil and its business associates.

In 1983, the trial judge overturned the jury's verdict against the *Post*, ruling that as a matter of law Tavoulareas had not proved the elements of libel that one must prove to win such a case. However, that ruling did not mean the *Post* could recover the thousands of dollars it spent defending the case.

In short, big-ticket libel suits have become a major problem for the media—regardless of whether they publish something that turns out to be false and libelous. Trial juries often award large sums of money in libel cases without seeing proof that the person suing suffered any real harm.

Like doctors fighting malpractice charges and insurance companies defending claims of fraud and bad faith, the mass media are finding it very difficult to win jury trials, regardless of the facts of a particular case. Although these huge libel judgments are usually set aside on appeal, the litigation process itself causes so much anguish and expense that many media organizations are avoiding controversial stories that deserve to be covered. The chilling effect on First Amendment freedoms that results from these big libel judgments has many journalists deeply troubled.

As we will explain shortly, the U.S. Supreme Court has sometimes intervened in libel suits to protect the First Amendment rights of the media. The court has made it more difficult for both public and private libel plaintiffs to prove that they were libeled. However, trial juries tend to ignore the rules, forcing the media to go through the long and costly appeals process before they finally win justice.

Unfortunately, the Supreme Court has not seen fit to impose limits on these huge damage awards (or on the high cost of defending a libel suit). In fact, most of the Supreme Court's recent libel decisions have made the media an even easier target. In two 1984 rulings, for instance, the high court invited libel plaintiffs to sue the national media anywhere their publications or broadcasts are disseminated. This allows plaintiffs to shop around for the state whose libel laws are most favorable for them—and least favorable for the media.

Moreover, the mere right to sue for libel gives people with real or imagined grievances an unparalleled opportunity to harass the mass media, regardless of whether they actually have a valid complaint. A person suing for libel has the right to ask all sorts of questions during the pretrial "discovery" process (described in Chapter One), and those who have received unfavorable publicity sometimes sue for libel merely as a means of identifying a "whistle-blower" who helped a reporter gather inside information. Because the refusal to name a news source may be deemed an admission that no source exists, the media sometimes must choose between identifying confidential sources and losing costly libel suits that by all rights they should win.

LIBEL DEFINED

Just what are libel and slander?

They are legal actions to compensate the victims of defamatory communications—communications that tend to injure their reputations. Libel is a lawsuit based on a *written* defamatory statement; slander is a similar suit but stemming from a *spoken* defamation. The differences between the two are less important today than they once were, as a result of recent Supreme Court decisions. Because libel is a far more common lawsuit than slander, we will often say "libel" when referring to both kinds of defamation.

Libel and slander suits are almost as old as the English common law from which they emerged. Even before this country was colonized, libel and slander were recognized legal actions. In fact, the concept that a person's good name is something of value, and that anyone who damages it has committed a wrong, can be traced back at least to the time of the ancient Romans.

Most libel cases today are handled as civil tort actions, private disputes between two parties in which the courts merely provide a neutral forum. In earlier times, libel was often treated as a criminal matter: the prevailing view was that defamatory words might lead to a breach of the peace and should be regarded as a crime. This was especially true in the case of seditious libel (the crime of criticizing the government), for reasons explained in Chapter Two. Many states still have criminal libel laws on their statute books, but they are rarely enforced. Some have been ruled unconstitutional. Thus, the bulk of this chapter will be devoted to civil rather than criminal libel.

Libel suits are ordinarily state cases, not federal ones. The U.S. Supreme Court has intervened in some state libel cases in recent years, reminding the states that their libel laws can have a chilling effect on freedom of the press. But aside from the Supreme Court's role in setting Constitutional limits for libel suits, this remains a field of law reserved for the states.

However, that doesn't mean that libel suits are never tried in federal courts. State libel cases are sometimes heard in federal courts when the two parties live in different states, but even then, the federal courts apply state law rather than federal law.

Although libel is a matter of state law, its basic principles are much the same all over the United States, as is true of many kinds of law that grew out of the English common law. Moreover, the Supreme Court's rulings have tended to make libel law more uniform in the various states. Nevertheless, there are still state-to-state variations; you may wish to supplement this national overview by learning the principles of libel in your state, using the legal research methods detailed in Chapter One.

AN OVERVIEW OF LIBEL

In studying a complex legal subject such as libel, it is easy to get lost in the details, overlooking some of the major principles. To help you develop a general understanding of the basics, this section provides an overview of libel law.

A libel occurs whenever the *elements* of libel are present. As you look at the list of these elements, you will realize that many libelous statements are published and broadcast every day. But that doesn't mean numerous libel suits are filed against the mass media every day. Instead, most libelous publications and broadcasts are unlikely to produce lawsuits because they are covered by one or more of the legal *defenses* that apply in libel law. Thus, to decide whether a given item is likely to produce a libel suit, you have to analyze the situation not only to see if the elements of libel are present but also to determine whether there is a viable defense.

For a libel to occur, at least four elements must be present—with a fifth one required in many cases. The elements are these:

1. the statement must actually be *defamatory*—it must tend to hurt someone's reputation;
2. the statement must *identify* its intended victim, either by name or by some other designation that is understood by persons other than the victim;
3. the statement must actually be *communicated*—it must be published or broadcast in such a fashion that at least one person other than the victim and the perpetrator hears or sees it;
4. the U.S. Supreme Court has ruled that in addition to defamation, identification, and publication there must be proof of *fault*, at least in cases involving the mass media. That means a falsehood must have been published (or broadcast), and the publisher must have been either negligent or guilty of actual malice in publishing it;
5. in cases where the victim cannot prove the publication resulted from actual malice, the Supreme Court has also said that the victim of the libel must prove damages (losses that may be compensated in money). Previously, state courts sometimes held the media strictly accountable for libelous statements, and *presumed* that damages existed without proof of any actual injury.

Once these elements are present, a libel has occurred. It doesn't matter whether the defamatory statement is in a direct quote, a letter to the editor, an advertisement, a broadcast interview, or wherever. With few exceptions, anyone who contributes to the libel's dissemination may be sued for it, even if the libel was originated by someone else. That means the reporter who writes a story, the editor who reviews it, and everyone else in the production process may be named as a defendant in a libel suit. Of course, the normal legal strategy is to go after the "deep pocket"—the person with enough money to make it worthwhile. Therefore, the prime defendant is usually the owner or publisher, not the hired hands who actually processed the libelous material. If you were defamed in a letter to the editor, you might want to sue the letter writer and the editor who chose to print it, but your prime defendant would probably be the owner. In this era of corporate and chain ownership of the mass media, this is more true than ever before.

After you determine whether the elements of libel are present in a given situation, the next crucial question is whether any of the defenses apply. What are the defenses? Three major ones developed under the common law and have been recognized for many years. In addition, a few defenses of lesser importance are also recognized at least in some states, and these will be noted later. The major defenses are these:

1. *Truth:* any statement that is substantially truthful is protected. Truth is the oldest common law defense in libel cases, but a 1974 Supreme Court decision made it even stronger. That decision requires those who sue the media to bear the burden of proving either negligence or actual malice, which involves showing that a falsehood was published negligently, recklessly, or knowingly.
2. *Privilege:* any statement that represents a fair and accurate account of what occurred during certain proceedings and speeches in legislative bodies, the courts, and the executive branch of government is protected, even if it is libelous.
3. *Fair comment:* a statement of *opinion* about the performance of a person who places himself in the limelight (e.g. a politician, actor, sports celebrity, etc.) is protected under the common law fair comment defense. In addition, expressions of opinion are generally protected by the First Amendment.

If one or more of these defenses is present, the mass media may publish libelous material without fear of losing a libel suit. However, many lawsuits are filed by people who know they have little chance of ultimately winning. The mere opportunity to force a newspaper or broadcaster into court may seem inviting to someone who feels he or she has been subjected to unfair publicity. Thus, the cost of defending a libel suit is in itself a deterrent to publishing some stories that may be controversial, no matter how strong the defenses are—a problem mentioned earlier.

In addition to the classic defenses of truth, privilege, and fair comment, the Supreme Court's new requirement that libel plaintiffs prove negligence or actual malice has sometimes been referred to as the "constitutional privilege" or "First Amendment" defense. This concept would more correctly be viewed as an element of the plaintiff's case than as a libel defense, but it is occasionally called a defense and is mentioned here in the interest of completeness.

With this overview as an introduction, we will now discuss the law of libel in more detail. In so doing, we will present the material in the order in which you should proceed in deciding if any particular item you wish to publish or broadcast may be libelous.

Who May Sue for Libel

The first step in analyzing any potentially libelous item is to determine whether there is a *plaintiff*—a party who may sue for libel. Generally, the rule is that any living individual or other private legal entity (such as a corporation or an unincorporated business) may sue for libel. The right to sue for libel is what is called a "personal" right, not a "property" right. This means that the right dies with the individual: the heirs cannot sue on his or her behalf in most cases.

On the other hand, corporations are not limited by the life span or tenure in office of any individual: they may pursue a law suit for decades, regardless of the departure of individual officers. But for a corporation to sue for libel, the organization itself must have been defamed, not just an individual officer.

It may seem surprising that a big company can sue for libel. Nevertheless, the courts have repeatedly ruled that a corporation has the much same right as an individual to sue for libel when its reputation is besmirched by a false and defamatory statement. However, special rules apply when the defamation is directed at a product rather than the company itself: that is a special legal action called "disparagement," or "trade libel." In a trade libel suit, the suing company has to prove that the libelous statement actually damaged its business, something that tends to be difficult to prove, given the large number of variables that may influence business trends.

What about nonprofit associations and other unincorporated organizations? They, too, may sue for libel in some states, but the rule on this point varies somewhat around the country.

And what about government agencies? On this question, there is no dispute among the states: governments may not sue for libel anywhere. However, government officials may sue as individuals if their personal reputations are damaged by a libel.

What about a libel of a group of people? May the individuals sue? A long-recognized rule of law is that individuals may sue for libel when a group to which they belong has been defamed, but only if one of two conditions is met: (1) the group must be small enough that the libel affects the reputations of the individual members; or (2) the libelous statement must refer particularly to the individual who is suing.

A libel of a five-member city council could very well hurt the reputations of all the individual members. But what about a libel directed against a big organization, such as the United States Army? Would it be legally safe to say, "all soldiers are stupid"?

The courts settled that sort of group libel question long ago. No individual may sue for libel when the libelous statement was directed toward that large a group. The cutoff seems to be somewhere between five and 100 people, depending on which court you listen to. A court once allowed individual football players to sue when the University of Oklahoma football team was libeled. But other courts have refused to allow individuals to sue when groups considerably smaller than a college football team were libeled. In general, the bigger the group is, the less the chance an individual may be able to sue for libel.

To summarize: any living individual may sue if he or she is libeled, as may any corporation. Unincorporated organizations may sue in some states but not in others. Government agencies may not sue for libel. However, individuals may sue for libel if they belong to a sufficiently small group that has been libeled.

In analyzing an item for possible libel, the next step after you decide there is a potential plaintiff is to run through the elements of libel and see if all are present. If so, then you should check off the defenses and see if any will protect you. Next we discuss the elements of libel and the defenses to assist in such an analysis.

THE ELEMENTS OF LIBEL

Defamation

Of the various elements of a libel case, the one that is sometimes the hardest to remember is the most obvious: the requirement that a statement actually be libelous (i.e., defamatory). Without defamation there is no libel, so the first step in analyzing a statement for potential libel is to decide whether there really is a defamation.

Over the years the courts have recognized a wide variety of statements as defamatory, dividing them into two categories: libel *per se* and libel *per quod*. Libel per se is the classic kind of defamation where the words themselves will hurt a person's reputation. Words such as "murderer," "rapist," "communist," and "extortionist" are obvious examples, but there are thousands of others. Any word or phrase is likely to be libelous if it accuses a person of a heinous crime, public or private immorality, insanity or infection by some loathsome disease (e.g., leprosy), or professional incompetence. Even words that don't fall into any of these categories can be ruled libelous if they cause other people to shun and avoid the person.

When the words themselves communicate the defamation with no additional explanation necessary (as would the words in the categories just cited), you have libel per se. But when, on the other hand, it is not immediately apparent that the words are libelous, or when one must know additional facts to understand that there is a defamation, it is called libel per quod. The classic example of libel per quod—but one that may not be as viable in today's tolerant society as it once was—is that of the unwed mother. To publish birth announcements (as many papers do) is not ordinarily libelous. But when the mother is not married (or wasn't married nine months prior to the birth), and a number of readers are aware of this fact, the result can be libel per quod. Libel per quod is libel created by the context of the situation when the words themselves might not otherwise be libelous.

The distinction between libel per se and libel per quod is becoming less important now. For many years, the courts generally ruled that libel per se was automatically actionable; that is, the plaintiff didn't have to prove any damages. Instead, the courts would *presume* damages from the fact of the libel per se having occurred. But on the other hand, if it was only a matter of libel per quod, the plaintiff would have to prove that he or she suffered damages.

However, the *Gertz v. Welch* (418 U.S. 323) Supreme Court decision, a landmark ruling we will return to later, prohibited presumed damages in many libel suits against the media. The plaintiff today must be prepared to prove that he or she suffered actual damages whether the defamatory statement was libel per se or libel per quod. The only time damages may be presumed today in cases involving the media is when the plaintiff proves actual malice (i.e., that a falsehood was published knowingly or with reckless disregard for the truth). Some states have even eliminated presumed damages in non-media cases.

As a result, there is little practical difference between libel per se and libel per quod today when the mass media are involved. If a statement is libelous (either on its face or because of unique circumstances in the context of the statement) the media may have to defend a libel suit, provided the victim of the libel can prove the rest of the elements of libel.

Several types of subject matter result in disproportionate numbers of libel suits. For instance, the reporting of crime news has probably produced more libel suits than any other kind of journalism. In the American system of justice, a person is presumed innocent until proven guilty: stories that label people as "burglars" or "murderers" before they are convicted by a court are particularly dangerous. The best way to avoid lawsuits is to be as accurate and specific as possible in reporting the news. If someone has been detained for questioning in connection with a certain crime, say that much and nothing more. If the person has been formally charged, report that, but don't go beyond what the facts will support. If the person has been arraigned, indicted, bound over for trial, released on bail, or whatever, be careful to report only what has actually happened and no more. If the police are seeking someone for questioning, be wary of a story that identifies him as a suspect prematurely.

Several other areas of journalism produce more than their share of libel suits. In recent years a number of libel suits have resulted from stories accusing someone of having "Mafia" or organized crime connections. Another dangerous area—because of the ease with which damages can be proven—is any statement that reflects upon a professional person's competence. Professionals such as physicians, psychologists, and attorneys rely on public confidence for their continued livelihood to a greater extent than most other persons. Should the local paper publish a story questioning a doctor's or lawyer's integrity or competence and his business thereafter declines he can probably prove special damages. A false or misleading statement (or even an innuendo) about a professional person invites a libel suit.

Those seeking public office are another group of people who generate a lot of libel suits. Although the media now have strong Constitutional safeguards when sued by a public official or public figure, public officials are frequently inclined to file libel suits, as a means of saving face if nothing else. Even if there is little chance that the politician will ultimately win in court, the cost of defending a libel suit may force some publishers and broadcasters to think twice about carrying a story that reflects upon the character or competence of a politician.

Another problem area is gossip about the private lives of the famous. Some publications that deal in this sort of "news" as their basic commodity expect (and are prepared for) frequent libel suits as a result. Of course, many celebrities would prefer to let the matter drop and thus avoid the cost and additional publicity a libel suit would bring, rather than sue a supermarket scandal sheet. But those who do sue may have a good chance of success: tales about the private lives of celebrities that a publisher knew or should have known to be false are beyond the First Amendment's protection.

These, then, are some of the areas where defamatory statements are a special risk; of course there are others.

The Dissemination Element

Once there is a defamatory statement, the next element required for a libel suit is that it be published or broadcast. The rules in this area are quite liberal: any time someone besides the party making the defamatory statement and the victim sees or hears it, there has been a publication. Actually, the plaintiff in a lawsuit may have a tough time proving he or she suffered any damages if only a few people saw or heard the defamatory statement. Nevertheless, there have been cases where communicating a libel to only a handful of people resulted in a lawsuit for the perpetrator of the libel.

In most instances, of course, what produces a libel suit for the mass media is a statement that actually appears in print (or is broadcast), so proving the dissemination element presents few difficulties for the plaintiff in a resulting law suit.

It should be reiterated that everyone who furthers the dissemination of a libel can be sued. Even though the defamation first appeared in a letter to the editor, or in a public speech, or even in a wire service dispatch, with a few exceptions every publisher and broadcaster who further disseminates it can be sued (as can the originator of the libel or slander). Unless one of the defenses is available, the media can be sued for accurately reporting what someone else said. The speaker may be sued—but the media that report it can be sued too. You need not be the originator of a libel to be sued for it.

The Identification Element

The third element the plaintiff must prove in a libel suit is identification: at least some of the readers or listeners must understand to whom the defamatory statement refers.

Where a person's name is used, there is usually little difficulty in proving identification. However, there are a great many ways a person may be identified other than by name. Any reference—no matter how oblique—is sufficient if the plaintiff can produce witnesses who testify convincingly that they understand the libelous statement to refer to him or her.

Perhaps the classic example of an oblique reference producing a libel suit is the situation that led to the famous *New York Times v. Sullivan* (376 U.S. 254) decision of the Supreme Court. As Chapter One indicated, the plaintiff in that case was a city commissioner in Montgomery, Alabama. What prompted the lawsuit was a *New York Times* ad that alleged police misconduct in the South (including Montgomery) but never mentioned Sullivan either by name or as a city commissioner. He was able to convince a jury that the criticism of the conduct of the local police injured his reputation because many people knew that one of his responsibilities as a city commissioner was to oversee the police. In reversing the judgment years later, the U.S. Supreme Court expressed doubt that the ad really referred to Sullivan. But in the meantime, the case had gone all the way up through the American legal system at a cost of thousands of dollars.

In short, don't expect to escape a libel suit by using a vague identification. If even a few of your readers understand whom you are talking about, the identification requirement for a libel suit has been met.

Another problem that leads to many libel suits is an identification so vague that it can refer to more than one person. A famous libel case more than half a century ago proved this point. Two lawyers in the Washington, D.C., area were named Harry Kennedy. One used his middle initials; the other did not. The one who normally used his middle initials was arrested for a serious crime. The *Washington Post* reported the fact, but omitted the middle initials. The other Harry Kennedy sued for libel, claiming that his reputation had been damaged, and he won (*Washington Post v. Kennedy*, 3 F.2d 207, 1924).

The moral of this story is an obvious one: when you publish or broadcast a libelous statement, be sure to identify the person or persons involved as completely as possible, lest you inadvertently also identify an innocent party. This is one of the reasons it is good journalistic practice to identify people by full name, address, and occupation whenever the story involves potential libel.

Some publishers go so far as to make a special note of who is *not* involved in a libelous story. When news broke of the 1978 Jonestown massacre, in which several hundred followers of the Rev. Jim Jones were murdered or committed suicide in a South American jungle, one of the persons implicated was a young man named Larry Layton. Thousands of miles away in Los Angeles another man named Larry Layton was a prominent lawyer. One Los Angeles newspaper published a separate news story to tell its readers that the Larry Layton involved in Jonestown was not the same person as the prominent local attorney—even though none of the news stories about Jonestown had in any way suggested otherwise.

Beyond the dangers inherent in publishing a story with libelous content when more than one person has the same name, there are pitfalls to avoid when two people have similar names, given that journalists do make errors. A notable example is the case of Ralph A. Behrend and R. Allen Behrendt, two medical doctors who had worked at the same hospital in Banning, Calif. The *Los Angeles Times* reported that Dr. Behrendt had been arrested for theft and using narcotics. Sure enough, it was really Dr. Behrend who was arrested— and Dr. Behrendt had a great libel suit against the *Times* as a result of this copy desk error (*Behrendt v. Times Mirror Co.*, 30 C.A.2d 77, 1939).

If newspapers of the stature of the *Los Angeles Times* and the *Washington Post* have identification problems and face libel suits as a result, you can see why this sort of thing is a serious problem.

The Element of Fault

Until 1974, our summary of the things a plaintiff has to prove to win a libel suit would have been basically complete at this point. However, in that year the U.S. Supreme Court handed down its *Gertz v. Welch* decision, revising the basic law of libel in all 50 states. The *Gertz* case will be discussed in the section on Libel and the Constitution, but in the interest of offering a logical presentation of the elements of libel its major holding will be summarized here.

In *Gertz,* the Supreme Court clarified the mass media's constitutional safeguards in libel suits. The court ruled that the First Amendment precluded awarding a libel judgment against the media unless the plaintiff proved the media guilty of some "fault." No longer would the media face libel suits under a legal doctrine called "strict liability," a doctrine assuming that whenever a wrong occurs its perpetrator will be held strictly responsible (no matter whose fault it was). Without this protection, the Supreme Court ruled, the fear of libel suits would unduly inhibit the media in covering controversial stories that should be reported in a free society.

The Supreme Court set up two levels of fault for the media: *negligence* and *actual malice.* The court said the states could not entertain libel suits by public figures and public officials unless they could prove actual malice, something the court had said in several earlier decisions. But the court also said (for the first time) that private citizens could not sue for libel without proving some fault on the part of the media. The court ruled that states could allow private citizens to sue by showing a lower level of fault than actual malice, perhaps just negligence. Alternately, any state that wished to do so could also impose the tough actual malice requirement on private citizens who sued the media for libel. The Gertz case raised two legal problems:

1. What is negligence, and how does it differ from actual malice?
2. Who is a public figure, and who is a private person?

Negligence is a term that has a long legal history in other kinds of tort actions, but it had not previously been used in libel cases. It refers to a party's failure to do something that he has a duty to do and that a reasonable person would do. More will be said later of the way courts have interpreted negligence in applying the concept to the media, but at this point let's just say it means failing to adhere to the standards of good journalism in double-checking the facts.

Malice is another old legal term, but the Supreme Court had already given it a special meaning in connection with libel suits ten years before the *Gertz* case in the *New York Times v. Sullivan* decision. The court had said malice meant publishing a falsehood either with knowledge of its falsity or with "reckless disregard for the truth." "Reckless disregard" is another term that requires additional explanation later, but generally it would mean publishing a false story when you strongly suspect it to be false—or should entertain such suspicions.

Thus, the states were invited to set up a double standard in which it would be much tougher for public officials and public figures than for private persons to win libel suits against the media. The court's rationale for this approach was twofold. First, public officials and public figures have much greater access to the media to reply to libelous charges than do private persons. Second, those who place themselves in the limelight have to expect some adverse publicity, while private persons should not be unduly subjected to publicity they did not seek.

Since winning a libel suit is now much easier for a private person than a public figure, almost everyone who files a libel suit wants to be classified as a private person. The media, of course, want most plaintiffs classified as public figures. In the last few years, the question of who is and is not a public figure has often been litigated. The public figure question will be discussed later in this chapter.

Proving Damages

Another way in which the Supreme Court's *Gertz* decision changed libel law was that, as mentioned earlier, it abolished what were called "presumed" damages except in those cases where the plaintiff was able to prove actual malice.

Under the old presumed damage rules, many states allowed plaintiffs in libel suits to simply skip the sticky matter of proving they had really been injured by the libelous publication or broadcast. If there was a libel, the courts would simply presume there were damages, without any proof.

The Supreme Court's *Gertz* decision changed all that. Now all plaintiffs who cannot prove the media guilty of actual malice must prove damages to win their cases. Plaintiffs can win special damages by proving their out-of-pocket losses, of course. But in addition, the Supreme Court ruled that plaintiffs may also collect general damages for such intangibles as embarrassment and loss of reputation. Obviously, no dollar amount can be placed on such losses, but the plaintiff can prove he or she was injured and the court (i.e., the judge or a jury) may then decide how many dollars the plaintiff should be given as compensation.

How is this different from presumed damages? It's subtle, but the difference is this: under the old presumed damages doctrine, plaintiffs didn't even have to offer any proof of their loss of reputation in the community. The court would just assume the bad publicity must have had a bad effect. Now plaintiffs must prove their reputations were damaged. How can this be proved? For example, a plaintiff may bring in witnesses to testify about the effect the defamatory statement had on his reputation. Or he might testify himself, saying his former friends shunned him after the libel occurred.

In the *Gertz* decision, the Supreme Court went a step further in placing limits on damages in libel suits: it also held that punitive damages should not be awarded—even to private persons—without proof of actual malice (i.e., knowing or reckless publication of a falsehood) by the media. Previously, the courts in some states allowed punitive damage awards (which can involve huge amounts of money) on proof of a different sort of malice. That kind of malice involved showing that the publisher or broadcaster harbored ill will or evil intentions toward the plaintiff. Under that rule, a publisher could face a massive punitive damage award without being guilty of actual malice as the Supreme Court had defined the term for libel cases.

As indicated earlier, punitive damage awards have not disappeared in libel cases since the Gertz decision, but at least all plaintiffs now must prove actual malice under the new definition to win punitive damages.

LIBEL DEFENSES

In analyzing a given news item (or advertisement, press release, or whatever) for libel, the next step after determining if the elements are present is to decide whether any of the recognized libel defenses applies. At this point, however, the analysis must be approached a little differently. We didn't tell you to be particularly concerned about whether the evidence would stand up in court when we took you through the elements of libel. It's the plaintiff's job to convince a court that the elements of libel are present, not the mass media's. The plaintiff bears the *burden of proof* in that part of the case. But when it comes to building an affirmative defense against a libel suit, it's often the other way around: the defense bears the burden of proof. Thus, in many cases it isn't enough for publishers or broadcasters to believe they have a libel defense: they may have to prove it under a court's rules of evidence.

That can be a problem. The rules of evidence make it difficult to prove many things that are discovered through investigative journalism. A reporter may be absolutely convinced of the correctness of a story: his sources may be completely reliable and he may have extensively double-checked his facts. But that doesn't mean he can prove those facts in court. For example, under a court's rules of evidence, hearsay (statements made by one person to another, with the second person testifying about what he was told) is often inadmissible. A good deal of the information a reporter gathers would be considered hearsay.

Another problem arises when journalists promise to keep the identities of sources confidential. Many important stories could not be developed without the use of such sources, but in a libel suit, a journalist may have to choose between revealing his sources and losing the case. A judge won't take his word that the source exists; the source may have to be identified during the discovery process, or may even have to testify. If the source cannot be produced without compromising journalistic ethics, the case may be forfeited. This difficult problem is discussed later.

With these problems in mind, you should check off the defenses that might apply to a potentially libelous item. Only if there is a defense—and it could be proved in court—should the item be considered safe. There may be times when it is necessary to take a chance and publish an important story without the certainty that it could be defended in court, but the decision to gamble in that way should only be made intelligently, after calculating the risks.

Truth

The oldest of all libel defenses—and certainly the most obvious—is truth (sometimes called "justification"). Since the early days of American independence, courts have been allowing publishers to prove the truth of what they printed as a means of defending against civil libel suits.

For many years, there was a catch: in some states the proof of truth had to be accompanied by proof that the publisher's motives were not improper. For instance, a journalist sometimes could be sued for libel for engaging in a character assassination of a political adversary, even if the charges were true.

And, of course, there was the additional catch that only those truthful facts that could be proved under a court's rules of evidence would be considered true in deciding the case. As just suggested, that has been a serious problem for journalists.

However, the U.S. Supreme Court has lately revised the rules on truth as a libel defense, leading many states to shift the burden of proving the truth or falsity of an allegedly libelous item from the media to the plaintiff. As indicated earlier, in its *Gertz* decision the Supreme Court said it was not Constitutionally permissible to allow a libel judgment against the mass media unless the plaintiff could prove fault, with fault meaning the publication of a false statement of fact due to negligence or malice. Thus, a libel plaintiff almost always has to prove the falsity of a statement as a part of proving fault. A plaintiff who can't do that hasn't proved the elements of a libel and the lawsuit is supposed to be dismissed. In a later decision, the Supreme Court had this to say about the effect of the *Gertz* decision on this burden of proof question:

> The plaintiff's burden is now considerably expanded. In every or almost every case, the plaintiff must focus on the editorial process and prove a false publication attended by some degree of culpability on the part of the publisher. (Herbert v. Lando, 441 U.S. at 175, 1979).

Gradually, state and federal courts all over America have recognized this significant change in libel law and have begun requiring plaintiffs to prove the falsity of a published or broadcast statement. In 1981, a U.S. Court of Appeals ruled that even a private person must prove falsity to win a libel suit (see *Wilson v. Scripps-Howard*, 642 F.2d 371).

As a result of all of this, not only is truth an excellent defense, but most states recognize that the burden is on the plaintiff to prove falsity, not on the defendant to prove truth. Furthermore, the old requirement of truth plus good intentions is no longer valid. The general rule today is that there can be no successful libel suit against the media unless the material was false—period. If the publication is truthful, the publisher's motives no longer matter in a libel suit. Some states have not yet revised their statutory libel laws to comply with the Supreme Court's new Constitutional standards, but that seems certain to change in the coming years. In the meantime, the media are sometimes forced to defend—and appeal—libel cases that shouldn't be in court in the first place, but making changes in the laws of 50 states as fundamental as those mandated by Gertz takes time.

If the publisher's motives are now irrelevant when a publication is truthful, they are very relevant if a publication turns out to be false. In that circumstance, the key issue may be whether the publisher was guilty of either negligence or actual malice. Proving either level of fault may involve inquiring into the publisher's motives and thought processes, a point that will be discussed later.

In flatly stating that the First Amendment does not permit libel judgments against the media for truthful publications, we should emphasize that libel is not the only potential legal problem for the mass media. For example, a publisher or broadcaster may also be sued for invasion of privacy. As Chapter Five explains, truth is not necessarily a defense in a privacy suit. The fact that a statement is truthful may preclude a successful libel suit, but not an invasion of privacy lawsuit. There are circumstances in which the media may be sued for an invasion of privacy involving the publication of truthful (but embarrassing) facts.

Privilege

The legal concept of "privilege" is an old one, and it creates a strong libel defense for the media.

A privilege is an immunity from legal liability, and the term is used in a variety of legal contexts. Chapter Eight discusses "reporter's privilege," the concept that a journalist should be exempt from testifying about his sources of information and unpublished notes. Other privileges excuse lawyers and doctors from testifying about much of what their clients and patients tell them in confidence.

As the term is used in libel and slander law, privilege means an immunity from a lawsuit. The concept was recognized in Article I, Section 6 of the U.S. Constitution, which created an absolute privilege for members of Congress engaged in debates on the floor of Congress. They may never be sued for anything they say there: they have absolute freedom of speech during Congressional debates.

Over the years, this concept of absolute privilege has been broadened to encompass many other government officials and government proceedings. Today, there is a broad privilege for local, state, and national legislative bodies, and it extends to major officials in the executive branch of government and to court proceedings. When performing their official duties, many government officials now have an absolute privilege; they cannot be sued for libel or slander as a result of what they do while conducting their official duties.

As this privilege for government officials was developing, the courts also recognized that in a democracy the news media need to be free to report to the public on what their elected leaders are doing and saying. This led to the concept of *qualified privilege,* sometimes called conditional privilege.

Qualified privilege is a libel defense that allows the media to report on government proceedings and records without fear of a libel suit, provided they give a fair and accurate account. A biased account or one that pulls a libelous quote out of context may not be protected by the qualified privilege defense. In addition, a story that can be shown to have been prompted by improper motives rather than by a desire to cover the news would not qualify for the defense in some states.

However, that limitation on the qualified privilege defense is contrary to several recent Supreme Court decisions, starting with *Cox Broadcasting v. Cohn* (420 U.S. 469). That decision protects the media when they truthfully report information obtained from public records. At first, it wasn't entirely clear that *Cox* applied to libel cases: it is an invasion of privacy case, and it has some language that seemed to suggest it might not apply universally.

However, later Supreme Court decisions (e.g., *Time v. Firestone*, 424 U.S. at 457) indicated that it does apply in libel cases. The Cox case is discussed in Chapter Five.

However, even if the *Cox* ruling renders a publisher's or broadcaster's motives irrelevant to his or her right to assert a privilege defense, the requirement that the account be fair and accurate remains in force in most states.

The qualified privilege defense also raises at least two other major legal issues:

1. What officials and what records does it apply to?
2. Under what circumstances does it apply—when are officials conducting official business and when are they doing something else?

It would take a detailed state-by-state summary to describe which officials and what records are covered by the qualified privilege defense, but some general rules have developed over the years. First of all, this defense clearly applies to official legislative proceedings from the local level to Congress, but not necessarily to informal and unofficial functions. What a local government official says during a meeting of a city council or commission is privileged, but what the official says at a service club meeting or a campaign appearance (or writes in a press release, as will be explained shortly) may be a different matter.

In the executive branch of government, most states apply the privilege to the official conduct of senior elected officials, but not necessarily to lesser officials or appointees. The state attorney general's remarks on an official occasion may be privileged, for example, but not the statements of his deputies. In general, the less official the occasion and the lower the status of the executive making the statement, the less likely it is to be privileged. However, there is a growing trend toward courts applying the privilege defense even to unofficial public events where matters of public concern are discussed.

In the judiciary, the privilege applies to public court proceedings and official records. It may not apply to proceedings and records that are not open to the public, however. If a particular type of proceeding is routinely closed to the public (as divorce and juvenile proceedings are in some states), the reporter who surreptitiously covers such a proceeding or publishes information taken from the secret records of the proceeding probably cannot assert a privilege defense. Also particularly dangerous are false charges appearing in non-public documents that are "leaked" to the press.

Another problem in reporting court news involves documents that have been filed but have not yet received any review by a judge. A number of states recognize a rule that court documents are not privileged (even though they may be available to the public) until they are in some way acted upon by a judge.

One of the most serious privilege problems involves reporting the police beat. Law enforcement officials sometimes let journalists see police files that are not public records. A story based on such reports may not be protected by the qualified privilege defense: if the police privately suspect someone of a crime and they're wrong (i.e., guilt isn't proven in court), there is a danger of libel. Beware of undocumented charges leveled against a potential suspect, charges that may never be substantiated or placed in a public record. Arrest and booking information is almost always privileged; stories quoting police hunches usually aren't.

This is not to suggest that journalists should never report the progress of a law enforcement investigation against someone suspected of a serious crime until charges are formally filed or an arrest is made. There are occasions when such a story is important news. At times, it may be necessary to report information that will not be covered by the qualified privilege defense. But when that step is taken, it should be done with a full awareness of the potential for libel that may exist. At that point, the precise wording of the story may be crucial. To qualify a story by saying someone is only an "alleged" murderer probably won't help, but to say he was "detained for questioning in connection with" a crime may—if that is really what has happened.

Equally troubling is the problem of government officials who engage in activities beyond the scope of their official duties. A 1979 U.S. Supreme Court decision provided a classic example of a United States senator engaged in a thoroughly newsworthy activity in which he was not—the court ruled— protected by privilege. The case, *Hutchinson v. Proxmire* (443 U.S. 11), involved the "Golden Fleece of the Month Awards," presented to various individuals and organizations who Sen. William Proxmire (D-Wis) felt were wasting the taxpayers' money in a conspicuous way.

One of the winners of this tongue-in-cheek award was Dr. Ronald Hutchinson, a mental health researcher who had received nearly a half million dollars in government grants to study such things as the teeth-clench- ing habits of monkeys under stress. Dr. Hutchinson sued, claiming this satirical award damaged his professional reputation. Inasmuch as Senator Proxmire regularly issued a press release publicizing his selection for the "Golden Fleece" award, Hutchinson was able to show the elements of libel, including a publication beyond the limits of Proxmire's absolute privilege. The Supreme Court said this privilege covered the senator's remarks in the *Congressional Record* but didn't cover the press release even though it was almost a verbatim copy of those remarks.

This Supreme Court decision is mainly remembered for its ruling that Hutchinson was not a public figure and thus did not need to prove actual malice. That aspect of the decision will be discussed later. But, in addition, the Supreme Court agreed that the privilege defense did not protect Proxm- ire. The senator had gone beyond his official capacity in issuing a press release, even if it said the same thing he had said on the floor of Congress.

If a U.S. senator who pokes fun at what he considers wasteful govern- ment spending is not protected by the privilege defense, it should be apparent that this libel defense has its limitations. However, it should be noted that the libel suit was against the senator and not against the media that reported the award. Probably no state would entertain (nor would the First Amendment allow) a libel suit against a news medium that accurately reported the contents of the Congressional speech in which Proxmire announced the award. The senator's mistake was republishing his own remarks off the floor of Congress.

The *Proxmire* decision troubles many journalists, because the "golden fleece" awards are not only newsworthy but also deal with a matter of great public concern (wasteful government spending). For better or worse, the Supreme Court has chosen to restrict the scope of the Constitutional absolute privilege of members of Congress. But that has little effect on the qualified privilege of the media to report on issues of public concern, which has been expanding in recent years. Nor does it affect the right of other public officials to issue press releases: at least two other court decisions have extended public officials' common law privilege to their press releases. All *Proxmire* really does is limit the Constitutional privilege of those who serve in Congress.

As a means of protecting the media when they fairly and accurately report public records and public proceedings, qualified privilege represents an important safeguard. When a public official engages in slander during a government proceeding, or when an official public document carries a libelous charge, the privilege defense enables the media to report this newsworthy item to the public.

In addition to the qualified privilege defense, there is one circumstance under which the mass media are afforded an absolute privilege defense. Under Section 315 of the Communications Act, broadcasters are required to provide equal opportunities for air time to all candidates for a given public office. And the act denies the broadcaster any control over the content of a candidate's remarks made on the air under this provision. Thus, the broadcaster has no way to prevent a politician from defaming someone during such a broadcast. In fact, the rhetoric of a political campaign invites defamation.

In a 1959 decision (*Farmers Educational and Co-operative Union v. WDAY*, 360 U.S. 525), the U.S. Supreme Court afforded broadcasters an absolute immunity from libel and slander suits under these circumstances. Since they are forbidden to censor or otherwise control the content of political speeches required under Section 315, broadcasters are powerless to prevent a defamation and should not be held accountable if one occurs, the court ruled.

Some states carry this logic a step further: they exempt broadcasters from liability for defamatory statements made as a part of network programming they are not allowed to edit locally (although the network remains liable).

Fair Comment and Criticism

Another of the classic common law libel defenses is called "fair comment." Although it has been partially superseded by the constitutional protection for the media created by the Supreme Court in recent years, it remains important in some states and should be described here.

The fair comment defense protects expressions of *opinion* about the public performances of those who voluntarily place themselves before the public: persons such as entertainers, politicians and sports figures. The courts recognized long ago that reviewing public figures' performances is a legitimate function of the press and should be protected, even if it sometimes means excusing defamation.

As the defense developed, it protected even hostile expressions of opinion as long as two qualifications were met: the expression had to be based on facts that were correct and accurate, and it had to be a critique of the person's public performance rather than his or her private life.

In recent years, many states have eliminated these requirements, extending libel protection to all expressions of opinion that are clearly labeled as such, while allowing libel suits only for items that could be taken to be false statements of fact. This trend was greatly encouraged by the majority opinion in the Supreme Court's *Gertz* decision, which said:

> Under the First Amendment there is no such thing as a false idea. However pernicious an opinion may seem, we depend for its correction not on the conscience of judges and juries but on the competition of other ideas.

That language seemingly ruled out libel suits for expressions of opinion, but some states are still entertaining libel suits based on charges that could hardly be considered anything but expressions of opinion. And where a given libelous statement could be either an allegation of fact or an expression of opinion, some states are asking juries to decide which the statement is, with a libel award only permitted if the jury decides it is a false allegation of fact.

Nevertheless, the fair comment defense has been afforded something very close to Constitutional status in many states. As a result, fair comment often protects the media from liability even for vitriolic political rhetoric, social commentary, and criticism of the arts. This defense allows the media to use intemperate language and get away with it, as long as it is clearly an expression of opinion. For instance, during a recent year, courts allowed the media to: accuse a church of "Nazi-style anti-Semitism," call someone the "worst" sports announcer in town, and refer to a newspaper publisher as a "near-Neanderthal" whose paper is published "by paranoids for paranoids." (See *Holy Spirit Assn. v. Sequoia Elsevier*, 426 N.Y.S.2d 759, 1980; *Myers v. Boston Magazine*, 403 N.E.2d 376, 1980; and *Loeb v. New Times*, 497 F.Supp. 85, 1980.)

Minor Defenses

In addition to these generally recognized libel defenses, there are several other defenses that have been recognized by some courts. Two purely technical defenses should also be noted here.

Perhaps the most interesting of these less-recognized defenses is one called "neutral reportage." It got its main impetus from a 1977 federal appellate court decision in the case of *Edwards v. National Audubon Society* (556 F.2d 113, 2d.cir. 1977). That case involved a *New York Times* story reporting a heated dispute between the National Audubon Society and a group of scientists the society had accused of being "paid to lie" by pesticide companies. The paper attempted to cover both sides on this controversy and was sued by some of the scientists for reporting the charge against them, even though the reporter attempted to present their side of the story too. The appellate court recognized a special libel defense for this situation, pointing out that the paper was attempting to be neutral in reporting both sides of a controversial issue.

Although the idea of a "neutral reportage" defense is highly appealing to those who believe the mass media should be able to cover all sides of a controversy without risking a libel suit, the concept has not been widely accepted by other courts. For instance, shortly after the *Edwards* decision another federal appellate court declined to follow the precedent and refused to recognize the defense in a seemingly similar situation. Some state courts (in Florida, for instance) have recognized "neutral reportage," while others (in New York and Michigan, for example) have not. In Illinois, one appellate court recognized "neutral reportage" but another appellate court rejected the concept. In short, while neutral reportage has been accepted as a new libel defense in some jurisdictions, it has not yet gained the broad acceptance that many journalists hoped it would.

Another occasionally recognized defense is called "right of reply." It should not be confused with the broader concept of a right of reply to mass media attacks, discussed later in this text. In libel cases, it involves a situation in which two parties—often two publishers—have been exchanging libelous charges. Finally one sues the other, and the defendant responds by pointing out that he was merely replying in kind to a previous attack the plaintiff had directed against him. It has sometimes been accepted as a valid libel defense by state courts, but it is not generally recognized today.

Among the technical (as opposed to substantive) libel defenses, two should be mentioned here: consent and the statute of limitations. Where it can be proved that a plaintiff gave an actual consent to a libelous publication, he cannot thereafter sue for libel. If the consent was voluntarily and intelligently given, it precludes a libel suit. Likewise, where the statute of limitations (the time limit during which a law suit must be filed) has run, the defendant is entitled to an easy dismissal without the trouble and expense of a trial.

LIBEL AND THE FIRST AMENDMENT

The extent to which the U.S. Supreme Court has shaped American libel law in recent years is probably best shown by the number of times we have already mentioned the Supreme Court in this chapter.

Until 1964 we could have concluded our discussion of libel law without hardly mentioning the Supreme Court. For almost 200 years of American jurisprudence, the nation's highest court took the position that civil libel suits were purely a state matter, and none of its business. But in 1964 the historic *New York Times v. Sullivan* decision was handed down, establishing once and for all that there are Constitutional limits to what the states may do in awarding libel judgments.

What prompted this landmark Supreme Court decision was a half-million-dollar libel judgment against the *New York Times*. In making this award, an Alabama jury was allowed to presume that a massive injury had occurred simply because it found the wording of an advertisement libelous to L. B. Sullivan, a Montgomery city commissioner. The ad never mentioned Sullivan, and in fact only a handful of copies of that issue of the *Times* were ever distributed in Sullivan's community.

What did the advertisement say to produce such a large libel judgment? A reproduction of the ad appears in this chapter as Fig. 4-1. It said, among other things, that the Montgomery police had taken certain steps against civil rights demonstrators that they in fact had not. We could devote several pages of this chapter to the charges contained in the ad and the means by which Sullivan's lawyers convinced a jury that the ad defamed him even though he wasn't mentioned. However, Chapter One discussed this case to illustrate court procedures, so we'll not repeat the details here. But Sullivan won at the trial level, and the Alabama Supreme Court affirmed the judgment in its full amount.

Meanwhile, other Montgomery public officials filed additional libel suits against the *New York Times*, seeking total damages of $3 million. The *Times* was going to pay dearly for publishing a pro-civil rights advertisement that contained some factual errors and then distributing a few dozen copies of the paper in Montgomery, Ala.

Had the U.S. Supreme Court not chosen to review the case—instead maintaining its long tradition of leaving civil libel law completely up to the states—the threat of censorship via libel suits would have been a serious one. The Supreme Court agreed to hear the case precisely because of this threat to First Amendment freedoms.

Writing for a unanimous court, Justice William Brennan ruled that the huge libel judgment against the *Times* could not stand—for three reasons. He said to allow such a judgment would in effect sanction a new form of government censorship of the press via civil libel suits. To avoid lawsuits by local officials in various communities to which the nation's major newspapers are mailed, the major papers would have to steer clear of controversial subjects. Moreover, Brennan wrote, the mass media need some "breathing space" in their handling of controversial issues—including some protection when errors inevitably occur during the "robust" debate of these issues.

Finally, Brennan pointed out that public officials voluntarily move into the public arena when they seek office, subjecting themselves to much more scrutiny than private citizens should have to face. Criticism is something they

THE NEW YORK TIMES, TUESDAY, MARCH 29, 1960.　　　　　　L　　25

*"The growing movement of peaceful mass
demonstrations by Negroes is something
new in the South, something understandable. . . .
Let Congress heed their rising voices,
for they will be heard."*

—*New York Times* editorial
Saturday, March 19, 1960

Heed Their
Rising Voices

As the whole world knows by now, thousands of Southern Negro students are engaged in widespread non-violent demonstrations in positive affirmation of the right to live in human dignity as guaranteed by the U. S. Constitution and the Bill of Rights. In their efforts to uphold these guarantees, they are being met by an unprecedented wave of terror by those who would deny and negate that document which the whole world looks upon as setting the pattern for modern freedom. . . .

In Orangeburg, South Carolina, when 400 students peacefully sought to buy doughnuts and coffee at lunch counters in the business district, they were forcibly ejected, tear-gassed, soaked to the skin in freezing weather with fire hoses, arrested en masse and herded into an open barbed-wire stockade to stand for hours in the bitter cold.

In Montgomery, Alabama, after students sang "My Country, 'Tis of Thee" on the State Capitol steps, their leaders were expelled from school, and truckloads of police armed with shotguns and tear-gas ringed the Alabama State College campus. When the entire student body protested to state authorities by refusing to re-register, their dining hall was padlocked in an attempt to starve them into submission.

In Tallahassee, Atlanta, Nashville, Savannah, Greensboro, Memphis, Richmond, Charlotte, and a host of other cities in the South, young American teenagers, in face of the entire weight of official state apparatus and police power, have boldly stepped forth as protagonists of democracy. Their courage and amazing restraint have inspired millions and given a new dignity to the cause of freedom.

Small wonder that the Southern violators of the Constitution fear this new, non-violent brand of freedom fighter . . . even as they fear the upswelling right-to-vote movement. Small wonder that they are determined to destroy the one man who, more than any other, symbolizes the new spirit now sweeping the South—the Rev. Dr. Martin Luther King, Jr.—world-famous leader of the Montgomery Bus Protest. For it is his doctrine of non-violence which has inspired and guided the students in their widening wave of sit-ins; and it this same Dr. King who founded and is president of the Southern Christian Leadership Conference—the organization which is spearheading the surging right-to-vote movement. Under Dr. King's direction the Leadership Conference conducts Student Workshops and Seminars in the philosophy and technique of non-violent resistance.

Again and again the Southern violators have answered Dr. King's peaceful protests with intimidation and violence. They have bombed his home almost killing his wife and child. They have assaulted his person. They have arrested him seven times—for "speeding," "loitering" and similar "offenses." And now they have charged him with "perjury"—a *felony* under which they could imprison him for *ten years*. Obviously, their real purpose is to remove him physically as the leader to whom the students and millions of others—look for guidance and support, and thereby to intimidate *all* leaders who may rise in the South. Their strategy is to behead this affirmative movement, and thus to demoralize Negro Americans and weaken their will to struggle. The defense of Martin Luther King, spiritual leader of the student sit-in movement, clearly, therefore, is an integral part of the total struggle for freedom in the South.

Decent-minded Americans cannot help but applaud the creative daring of the students and the quiet heroism of Dr. King. But this is one of those moments in the stormy history of Freedom when men and women of good will must do more than applaud the rising-to-glory of others. The America whose good name hangs in the balance before a watchful world, the America whose heritage of Liberty these Southern Upholders of the Constitution are defending, is *our* America as well as theirs . . .

We must heed their rising voices—yes—but we must add our own.

We must extend ourselves above and beyond moral support and render the material help so urgently needed by those who are taking the risks, facing jail, and even death in a glorious re-affirmation of our Constitution and its Bill of Rights.

We urge you to join hands with our fellow Americans in the South by supporting, with your dollars, this Combined Appeal for all three needs—the defense of Martin Luther King—the support of the embattled students—and the struggle for the right-to-vote.

Your Help Is Urgently Needed . . . NOW ! !

Stella Adler
Raymond Pace Alexander
Harry Van Arsdale
Harry Belafonte
Julie Belafonte
Dr. Algernon Black
Marc Blitstein
William Branch
Marlon Brando
Mrs. Ralph Bunche
Diahann Carroll

Dr. Alan Knight Chalmers
Richard Coe
Nat King Cole
Cheryl Crawford
Dorothy Dandridge
Ossie Davis
Sammy Davis, Jr.
Ruby Dee
Dr. Philip Elliott
Dr. Harry Emerson Fosdick

Anthony Franciosa
Lorraine Hansbury
Rev. Donald Harrington
Nat Hentoff
James Hicks
Mary Hinkson
Van Heflin
Langston Hughes
Morris Iushewitz
Mahalia Jackson
Mordecai Johnson

John Killens
Eartha Kitt
Rabbi Edward Klein
Hope Lange
John Lewis
Viveca Lindfors
Carl Murphy
Don Murray
John Murray
A. J. Muste
Frederick O'Neal

L. Joseph Overton
Clarence Pickett
Shad Polier
Sidney Poitier
A. Philip Randolph
John Raitt
Elmer Rice
Jackie Robinson
Mrs. Eleanor Roosevelt
Bayard Rustin
Robert Ryan

Maureen Stapleton
Frank Silvera
Hope Stevens
George Tabori
Rev. Gardner C. Taylor
Norman Thomas
Kenneth Tynan
Charles White
Shelley Winters
Max Youngstein

We in the south who are struggling daily for dignity and freedom warmly endorse this appeal

Rev. Ralph D. Abernathy
(Montgomery, Ala.)

Rev. Fred L. Shuttlesworth
(Birmingham, Ala.)

Rev. Kelley Miller Smith
(Nashville, Tenn.)

Rev. W. A. Dennis
(Chattanooga, Tenn.)

Rev. C. K. Steele
(Tallahassee, Fla.)

Rev. Matthew D. McCollom
(Orangeburg, S. C.)

Rev. William Holmes Borders
(Atlanta, Ga.)

Rev. Douglas Moore
(Durham, N. C.)

Rev. Wyatt Tee Walker
(Petersburg, Va.)

Rev. Walter L. Hamilton
(Norfolk, Va.)

I. S. Levy
(Columbia, S. C.)

Rev. Martin Luther King, Sr.
(Atlanta, Ga.)

Rev. Henry C. Bunton
(Memphis, Tenn.)

Rev. S. S. Seay, Sr.
(Montgomery, Ala.)

Rev. Samuel W. Williams
(Atlanta, Ga.)

Rev. A. L. Davis
(New Orleans, La.)

Mrs. Katie E. Whickham
(New Orleans, La.)

Rev. W. H. Hall
(Hattiesburg, Miss.)

Rev. J. E. Lowery
(Mobile, Ala.)

Rev. T. J. Jemison
(Baton Rouge, La.)

Please mail this coupon TODAY!

Committee To Defend Martin Luther King
and
The Struggle For Freedom In The South

312 West 125th Street, New York 27, N. Y.
UNiversity 6-1700

I am enclosing my contribution of $_____
for the work of the Committee.

Name _____
　　　　　PLEASE PRINT

Address _____

City _____ Zone ____ State ____

☐ I want to help　　☐ Please send further information

Please make checks payable to:
Committee To Defend Martin Luther King

COMMITTEE TO DEFEND MARTIN LUTHER KING AND THE STRUGGLE FOR FREEDOM IN THE SOUTH
312 West 125th Street, New York 27, N. Y. UNiversity 6-1700

Chairmen: A. Philip Randolph, Dr. Gardner C. Taylor; *Chairmen of Cultural Division:* Harry Belafonte, Sidney Poitier; *Treasurer:* Nat King Cole; *Executive Director:* Bayard Rustin; *Chairmen of Church Division:* Father George B. Ford, Rev. Harry Emerson Fosdick, Rev. Thomas Kilgore, Jr., Rabbi Edward E. Klein; *Chairman of Labor Division:* Morris Iushewitz

Fig. 4-1 *This is the controversial advertisement that led to the landmark* New York Times v. Sullivan *Supreme Court decision.*

must expect. In return, public officials gain more access to the media to present their side of the story than a private citizen enjoys. Thus, public officials need less libel protection than do other citizens.

Under this rationale, the Supreme Court ruled that public officials could no longer win libel judgments against the mass media unless they could prove *actual malice*:

> The Constitutional guarantees require, we think, a federal rule that prohibits a public official from recovering damages for a defamatory falsehood relating to his official conduct unless he proves that a statement was made with "actual malice"—that is, with knowledge that it was false or with reckless disregard of whether it was false or not.

This language is among the most important ever written on mass media law in America. If you remember any single concept from this discussion, you should remember that public officials must prove actual malice to win libel suits, and you should remember how actual malice is defined. First, actual malice means *publishing a falsehood*. Second, it means publishing that falsehood either with *knowledge* that it was false, or with *reckless disregard* for whether it was false or not.

Malice is a legal term that has other meanings in other contexts, often referring to bad intentions. But in libel law it was given a special meaning in the *New York Times v. Sullivan* decision.

When a landmark Supreme Court decision is handed down, there are often unanswered questions—issues that must be clarified by additional Supreme Court rulings. The *New York Times* case had exactly that result. First of all, what public officials are included in its coverage? Does it apply only to elected officials or does it also apply to public figures who hold no office? And does it apply to all public servants or just to certain prominent ones? And equally important, exactly what does "reckless disregard for the truth" mean?

Post-*Sullivan* Rulings

In the years that followed the *New York Times* decision, the Supreme Court attempted to resolve these ongoing questions by handing down a series of additional libel rulings. First, in a 1966 case (*Rosenblatt v. Baer*, 383 U.S. 75) the court dealt with the extent to which the actual malice requirement would apply to minor public officials. A. D. Rosenblatt, a New Hampshire newspaper columnist, had accused the former supervisor of a county skiing and recreation area of mishandling public funds. The Supreme Court said even a public employee of that rank would henceforth have to prove actual malice to win a libel suit. The "public official" designation would apply to all who have "substantial responsibility for. . . the conduct of governmental affairs," the court ruled. More recent rulings have cast doubts on the applicability of the actual malice requirement to minor public employees, but for the moment the rule was that almost anybody who was on the public payroll and made policy decisions would have to prove actual malice.

Then in 1967 the high court applied the actual malice rule to public figures who hold no office and also offered guidance on the meaning of the "reckless disregard" concept in two cases it decided together, *Curtis Publishing Co. v. Butts*, and *Associated Press v. Walker* (388 U.S. 130).

The *Curtis* case arose when the *Saturday Evening Post*, published by Curtis, carried an article entitled, "The Story of a College Football Fix." The article claimed that Wally Butts, athletic director at the University of Georgia, had given Alabama coach Paul "Bear" Bryant information in advance about Georgia's game plans for an upcoming football game between the two schools. The story was based on information provided by an insurance agent in Atlanta who said he had overheard a telephone conversation between Butts and Bryant through an electronic error.

Although there was no deadline pressure and the article was published some time after the game, the *Post* did not double-check the story with anyone knowledgeable about football to see whether the information the insurance man claimed he overheard would in fact have helped Alabama or hurt Georgia. Athletic Director Butts was not a public official; his salary was paid by the Georgia Athletic Association, a private corporation.

The *Walker* case differed in several respects. It resulted from an AP dispatch detailing the activities for former U.S. Army General Edwin Walker, who resigned his command and engaged in conservative political activities, often speaking out against school desegregation. Walker was present at the University of Mississippi during the initial desegregation of the campus. A group of whites attacked the federal marshals who were protecting the first black student enrolled at the university. Walker had addressed the crowd of whites. The AP dispatch, moved over the wires within minutes after the fast-breaking events occurred, said ex-General Walker led the charge of the whites.

Walker admitted being present and addressing the gathering of whites, but he claimed he had called for a peaceful protest and counseled against violence. He denied leading the charge.

Butts and Walker won libel judgments totaling about half a million dollars each, and both Curtis Publishing and the Associated Press appealed the judgments to the U.S. Supreme Court. The Supreme Court voted 5-4 to affirm Butts' libel judgment against the *Saturday Evening Post*, but unanimously overruled Walker's judgment against the AP. The court took the occasion to compare the two situations as a way of illustrating what reckless disregard for the truth means.

But first, a majority of the Supreme Court justices agreed that both men were public figures and should be subject to the *New York Times v. Sullivan* rule, although neither was a public official at the time of the respective libel suits. Both were involved in issues "in which the public has a justified and important interest." The court was not unanimous in deciding that the *New*

York Times rule as such should apply to public figures as well as public officials, but the precedent has held up in the years since, and is now settled law. Thus, both men had to show reckless disregard for the truth to win their libel suits.

Why, then, did Butts win while Walker lost? The Supreme Court pointed out that there was a big difference between the kind of reporting that went into the two stories. The AP was under intense deadline pressure and had no time to double-check its information; the *Post* was not. The AP had a reporter with a good reputation for accuracy on the scene; the *Post* relied on the uncorroborated statements of a non-journalist, who was in fact an ex-convict, and never checked with anyone who had special expertise in football. Further, the conduct AP's reporter attributed to Walker was consistent with Walker's previous statements on the issue of school desegregation.

In short, because the Supreme Court found a substantial difference between the *Saturday Evening Post*'s reporting practices and AP's, the libel judgment against the *Post* was affirmed while the one against AP was reversed.

After the 1967 *Curtis* and *AP* rulings, the Supreme Court handed down several libel decisions that continued the trend toward protecting the media, almost to the point of abolishing libel as a legal hazard for journalists. Some of these decisions are considered to be relatively unimportant, for instance *St. Amant v. Thompson* (390 U.S. 727), decided in 1968, and *Greenbelt Publishing Assn. v. Bresler* (398 U.S. 6), a 1970 case. *St. Amant* overruled a libel judgment where a series of false charges had not been fully investigated; the case is remembered mainly because the court said reckless disregard means something more than merely failing to investigate: it means there must be evidence the publisher "in fact entertained serious doubts as to the truth of his publication." *Greenbelt* disallowed a libel judgment where the word "blackmail"—traditionally a word that constitutes libel per se—had been used during spirited public debates before a city council. The court felt the word was not used in a sense that connoted actual malice.

The Supreme Court continued its trend of reversing libel judgments against the media with three cases it handed down on the same day in early 1971, *Monitor Patriot Co. v. Roy* (401 U.S. 265), *Ocala Star-Banner v. Damron* (401 U.S. 295), and *Time, Inc. v. Pape* (401 U.S. 279). The *Monitor-Patriot* case stemmed from a syndicated column that branded a candidate for the U.S. Senate as a "small time bootlegger" because of a conviction in the 1920s. The plaintiff contended the publisher was vulnerable to a libel judgment because the conviction involved his private life long ago and had nothing to do with his public performance. The Supreme Court ruled the actual malice requirement had not been met and the libel case could not be sustained, to no one's surprise.

In *Ocala*, the Supreme Court overruled a libel judgment where a newspaper had confused two brothers, identifying a candidate for office as having been convicted of perjury when in fact it was his brother who had been convicted. The Supreme Court said there was no reckless disregard for the truth in this copy desk error. At the time, this seemed to free the media from liability when a public official or public figure is the victim of an accidental misidentification problem such as the ones discussed earlier in this chapter.

The *Time v. Pape* case involved a libel contained in a U.S. Commission on Civil Rights report, disseminated in a *Time* magazine article. *Time* had changed the reported information somewhat, but the Supreme Court found no reckless disregard for the truth in *Time*'s reporting of a statement charging a Chicago police officer with brutality—even though the story did not make it clear these were mere allegations. *Time*'s imprecise reporting was forgiven in large part because the report itself was ambiguous and subject to more than one interpretation.

The theme in all three of these 1971 cases seemed clear: the traditional rules of libel must give way when a public official is the plaintiff, lest the threat of libel suits unduly inhibit the reporting of public affairs.

The *Rosenbloom* Plurality Ruling

Moreover, later in 1971 the Supreme Court handed down a decision that was heralded by some as the ultimate victory for the mass media over the threat of libel: *Rosenbloom v. Metromedia* (403 U.S. 29). Although there was no majority opinion, the three-justice plurality opinion seemed to foreclose libel judgments against the media whenever the plaintiff was involved in an issue of public interest, no matter how private a citizen he or she might be.

George Rosenbloom, a Philadelphia magazine dealer, was arrested during a police campaign against obscenity, and he was called a "smut distributor" and a "girlie-book peddler" on radio station WIP. He was never convicted, and a court granted an injunction ordering the police to leave him alone, since the books were not legally obscene. Rosenbloom sued the station and won a $275,000 libel judgment. An appellate court reversed the judgment, although he contended that he was a private citizen rather than a public figure and should not have to prove actual malice to win a libel suit.

The U.S. Supreme Court agreed on a 5-3 vote that he should not win a libel judgment, but only three justices (Brennan, Burger, and Blackmun) joined in the plurality opinion. Justices Black and White concurred in the result, but on a different rationale. What made *Rosenbloom* memorable was the sweep of the language in that plurality opinion. Justice Brennan, writing for the court, said the distinction between public officials and public figures on the one hand and private citizens on the other "makes no sense." He said that in the future the criterion for applying the actual malice requirement should be whether the plaintiff was involved in a matter of "public or general interest." Thus, the court seemed to be saying the media could bootstrap themselves out of libel suits by publicizing a private person's activities so as to generate public interest, and then avoid a lawsuit because of that public interest.

After *Rosenbloom*, it seemed that virtually everyone whose name appeared in a newspaper or in a radio or television newscast was going to have to prove actual malice. And because proving actual malice turned out to be so difficult, it appeared for a time in the early 1970s that the media were at last virtually free from their most troubling legal problem, the libel suit.

The *Gertz* Precedent

However, three years later this hope was shattered when the Supreme Court handed down its famous *Gertz v. Welch* decision in 1974. Much has already been said of this decision, which profoundly changed the law of libel in all 50 states—and thus laid the foundation for modern libel law when private persons are involved.

Elmer Gertz, a Chicago lawyer, represented the family of a young black man who had been killed by a Chicago police officer (who was later prosecuted for the act). With Gertz's help, the family was seeking civil damages in a tort action called "wrongful death."

An article appeared in *American Opinion*, the magazine of the ultra-conservative John Birch Society, that claimed Gertz was part of a communist conspiracy to discredit law enforcement. Gertz was called a "communist-fronter" and a "Leninist." The article also falsely accused Gertz of various subversive activities.

Gertz sued Robert Welch, Inc., publisher of *American Opinion*, and initally won a $50,000 jury verdict against Welch. However, the trial judge set aside the verdict and ruled that Gertz was a public figure who could not win a libel judgment without proving actual malice, something he had not proved during the original trial. Then the Supreme Court's *Rosenbloom* decision was announced, and an appellate court upheld the trial judge's decision that Gertz would have to prove actual malice to win a libel judgment against Welch. Gertz asked the Supreme Court to review the determination that he was a public figure.

In a narrow 5-4 decision that Justice Blackmun said he joined only because the country needed a clear-cut majority opinion on an issue as important as libel law, the Supreme Court backed away from the *Rosenbloom* decision and reinstated the distinction between private persons and public figures. The court said that Gertz, although he was a prominent Chicago lawyer, had done nothing to seek public figure status in this context. Thus, he should not be Constitutionally required to prove actual malice to win a libel suit.

Instead, the court said the states should feel free to allow private persons such as Elmer Gertz to win libel suits against the media by proving a level of fault short of actual malice. However, in no case could the media be held on the "strict liability" (or "liability without fault") basis that had been the prevailing rule of law for at least 200 years. The court said the media had to be guilty of something beyond merely publishing a falsehood—there had to be some level of fault. Still, the Supreme Court didn't say every state had to allow private persons to prove mere negligence. The court just said the states could allow this lesser standard of proof for private plaintiffs if they wished. But the court also said any state that wished to could still require private persons to prove actual malice.

As a result, public figures still have to prove actual malice in all 50 states. But this is not always true for private persons. The required level of fault private persons must prove varies considerably among the states today. A few states require private persons to prove actual malice just as public figures must. On the other hand, most states allow private persons to prove simple negligence. At least one state (New York) requires gross negligence, which falls between negligence and actual malice, in many instances.

Now all of these terms—malice, negligence, gross negligence—have special meanings in law that have developed over hundreds of years. There is no way we can define them in a way that would be applicable in all states. We already indicated that negligence is a less serious breach of the standards of good journalism than reckless disregard for the truth. Negligence may well mean nothing more than publishing a falsehood as a result of sloppy reporting, or perhaps even because an innocent error slipped past the copy desk. Some states say it means failing to do the kind of checking a "reasonable man" would do under the circumstances. Obviously, it will take many years of case law to clarify precisely what negligence means as applied to libel.

In addition to its ruling that private persons could be allowed to sue for libel without proving actual malice, the *Gertz* case had an important effect on the award of damages in libel suits, as already mentioned. In the interest of continuity and completeness, that aspect of *Gertz* will be reiterated here.

The *Gertz* ruling required most private libel plaintiffs to prove actual damages. The court said that in the absence of a showing of actual malice, there could be no punitive or presumed damages. Instead, plaintiffs who could only prove negligence and not actual malice could win only damages they could prove, although those damages would not be limited to just out-of-pocket losses.

As a result of these sweeping changes in American libel law, a new period of reassessment occurred, as the courts and legislatures tried to adapt their rules to the new Constitutional boundaries. It quickly became apparent that the crucial issue in future libel suits would often be whether the plaintiff was a public figure or a private person. To assist in resolving this question, the *Gertz* ruling offered this observation about public figures and private persons:

> For the most part those who attain this status (public figure) have assumed roles of especial prominence in the affairs of society. Some occupy positions of such persuasive power and influence that they are deemed public figures for all purposes. More commonly, those classed as public figures have thrust themselves to the forefront of particular public controversies in order to influence the resolution of the issues involved. In either event, they invite attention and comment.

Thus, the Supreme Court was saying that many public figures are so classified only because they have thrust themselves into the "vortex" of a particular controversy. These people might be called "vortex public figures," and the courts were to look mainly to a libel plaintiff's own conduct in deciding whether the definition applied.

Despite this guidance, in the five years following the *Gertz* decision, the U.S. Supreme Court found it necessary to render three more rulings to clarify the issue of who is a public figure and who is not.

There is one ironic footnote to the *Gertz* case: after the landmark Supreme Court decision, Elmer Gertz patiently waited as his case meandered through pretrial procedures and finally went to trial again. Although the Supreme Court decision emphasized that non-public figures such as Gertz didn't necessarily have to prove actual malice, during the second trial a jury agreed that he *did* prove actual malice, and awarded him $400,000 in damages (including $300,000 in punitive damages). The new judgment was affirmed by a federal appellate court in 1982—eight years after the Supreme Court decision and 14 years after the police shooting that led to the original libel (*Gertz v. Welch*, 680 F.2d 527).

Decisions after *Gertz*

The first of the post-*Gertz* cases was *Time, Inc. v. Firestone* (424 U.S. 448), a 1976 case involving a divorce in a wealthy and socially prominent Florida family. Russell Firestone, an heir to the tire company, sued his wife Mary Alice for divorce on the grounds of extreme cruelty and adultery, and the case received extensive publicity. When the divorce was granted after a trial in which there was considerable evidence of marital infidelity on both sides (enough evidence "to make Dr. Freud's hair curl," the judge said), *Time* magazine reported that one of the grounds for the divorce was adultery.

However, the judge was vague about the legal grounds for the divorce, and in fact a provision of Florida law would have prohibited the award of alimony if adultery had been the ground for a divorce. Since Ms. Firestone had been granted alimony, adultery couldn't have been one of the grounds for the divorce. This fine point of Florida law escaped the *Time* correspondent— but that could hardly be called publishing a falsehood with reckless disregard for the truth. (Was it negligent reporting?)

Obviously, if Ms. Firestone were ruled a public figure she would have less chance to win a libel judgment. And there was some evidence that she was indeed a public figure and even sought publicity: she held two press conferences to discuss the divorce with the media and subscribed to a press clipping service. The story was covered in no fewer than 45 articles in one local newspaper.

However, the Supreme Court ruled that she was *not* a public figure. She had not voluntarily thrust herself into any public controversy, the court said: "Dissolution of marriage through judicial proceedings is not the sort of 'public controversy' referred to in *Gertz*, even though the marital difficulties of extremely wealthy individuals may be of interest to some portion of the reading public." The court said Ms. Firestone had really done nothing more than she was required to do—avail herself of the courts to terminate a marriage.

The Supreme Court seemed to be saying that, aside from the case of a few persons who are so pervasively famous they are all-purpose public figures, a person does not become a public figure unless he voluntarily injects himself into a public debate on a controversial issue. As a result, some entertainment celebrities may not be considered public figures should they sue for libel based on a reference to their personal lives. And when it comes to persons involved in a crime, the Supreme Court's *Firestone* ruling made it clear they will not ordinarily be classified as public figures:

> While participants in some litigation may be legitimate "public figures," either generally or for the limited purpose of that litigation, the majority will more likely resemble respondent (Ms. Firestone), drawn into a public forum largely against their will in order to attempt to obtain the only redress available to them or to defend themselves against actions brought by the state or by others. There appears little reason why these individuals should substantially forfeit that degree of protection which the law of defamation would otherwise afford them simply by virtue of their being drawn into a courtroom.

After the Supreme Court ruled that Ms. Firestone was not a public figure, she chose not to pursue her lawsuit further, and the case was eventually dismissed.

It would be difficult to overemphasize the extent to which the thinking in the *Firestone* case is a retrenchment from the libel protection the media enjoyed in the late 1960s and early 1970s. However, the Supreme Court continued the same trend away from classifying newsworthy persons as public figures in a pair of 1979 decisions, *Hutchinson v. Proxmire* (443 U.S. 111) and *Wolston v. Reader's Digest Association* (443 U.S. 157). The *Hutchinson* case (involving Senator Proxmire's Golden Fleece Award) was discussed earlier in this chapter in connection with its adverse effect on the privilege defense. At this point, we will simply add that it offered the media little comfort on the issue of who is a public figure, either. The court said that Dr. Hutchinson was not a public figure, despite the fact that he was the research director of a major state-controlled mental health facility—and had won massive grants from tax monies. In looking back over the Supreme Court's libel rulings in the 1960s, can you think of any plaintiffs who were classified as public officials or public figures then who might not be under this 1979 decision? What about Athletic Director Butts? Or Baer, the ski resort manager? How about Pape, the Chicago policeman?

The *Wolston* case followed the same policy of narrowing the definition of a public figure, thus freeing more individuals to sue for libel without proving actual malice. Ilya Wolston had an aunt and uncle who had pleaded guilty to charges of spying for the Soviet Union, and he had been cited for contempt himself when he failed to comply with a Congressional subpoena. Other than that contempt citation, he was never convicted of any offense. Many years later, a *Reader's Digest* publication included his name in a list of "Soviet agents" in the United States. He sued for libel, and a lower court dismissed his case, ruling that he was a public figure who could not prove actual malice. The Supreme Court reversed, finding that he had done nothing to inject himself into a public controversy.

At this point, it is apparent that the heyday of First Amendment protection from libel suits has ended. To be sure, the mass media still have extensive and valuable Constitutional safeguards in libel cases that they lacked only a generation ago, but courts all over America are following the Supreme Court's lead in classifying more and more plaintiffs as private persons who need prove nothing more than negligence to win libel suits against the mass media. It is true that private plaintiffs didn't even have to prove negligence or damages to win their libel suits for hundreds of years; the media were held strictly accountable for what they published, regardless of whether there was any fault or any real injury. However, at one point in the early 1970s it appeared that just about everyone who sued the media would have to prove actual malice in order to win. That era is over.

The Supreme Court and Libel in the 1980s

If the Supreme Court was less than sympathetic to the mass media in libel cases during the late 1970s, that trend continued in the 1980s. In fact, several media organizations have recently settled libel suits to avoid the risk of an adverse Supreme Court decision that might further erode the protection established by *New York Times v. Sullivan* and the cases that followed it.

In 1984, the Supreme Court handed down three major libel decisions. Two of them represented more bad news for journalists, but the third was the first clear victory for the media in a Supreme Court libel ruling in many years. The three 1984 decisions were *Calder v. Jones* (104 S.Ct. 1482), *Keeton v. Hustler* (104 S.Ct. 1473), and *Bose v. Consumers Union* (104 S.Ct. 1949). Both the *Calder* and *Keeton* cases involved what is called "long-arm jurisdiction." In both cases the Supreme Court told journalists that they may have to defend lawsuits in places thousands of miles from where they live and work. Those cases are discussed in the next section.

However, the *Bose v. Consumers Union* case was a reaffirmation of the Constitutional safeguards journalists enjoy under the *New York Times v. Sullivan* rule, a decision handed down almost exactly 20 years before the *Bose* ruling. The case began when the Bose Corporation, a manufacturer of high-fidelity speakers, sued *Consumer Reports* magazine for a product review that commented negatively and hyperbolically about the performance of Bose speakers. In a 1970 article, the magazine said that with these speakers music "tended to wander about the room." A Consumers Union engineer had written a report that said the speakers made violins seem "about ten feet wide."

The manufacturer sued for product disparagement and won a six-figure damage award. During the trial, the judge concluded that the engineer should have said Bose speakers made music sound as if it wandered "along the wall," not "about the room." This, he said, was evidence of actual malice. On appeal, the first circuit U.S. Court of Appeals reversed that judgment, ruling that the magazine was not guilty of actual malice in its product review even if some of the engineer's words and conclusions were debatable.

Normally, appellate courts are not supposed to second-guess a trial court's assessment of the evidence in deciding factual issues (such as whether there was actual malice in this *Consumer Reports* article), but that is exactly what the Court of Appeals did in this case. The Supreme Court upheld that decision, ruling that the media need the additional protection of being able to appeal a trial court's determination of actual malice. To rule otherwise, the court said, would unduly erode First Amendment freedoms by denying the media the right to challenge some libel judgments that are improperly awarded by trial judges or juries.

In concluding that there was no actual malice in this case, Supreme Court Justice John Paul Stevens, writing for the majority, said, ". . .we agree with the Court of Appeals that the difference between hearing violin sounds move around the room and hearing them wander back and forth fits easily within the breathing space that gives life to the First Amendment."

Thus, the *Bose* case represents a significant expansion of the protection the mass media enjoy under the *New York Times v. Sullivan* rule. When a judge or a jury finds actual malice in a publication or broadcast where there was little or no evidence of "reckless disregard for the truth," the media now have a second shot at that verdict.

LIBEL AND PROCEDURAL RIGHTS

The details of courtroom procedure often seem to be arcane and irrelevant technicalities—certainly not issues that should concern journalists. However, on three occasions in recent years the Supreme Court has ruled against the mass media on procedural issues that can be vitally important in libel cases.

In the first of those three rulings, the Supreme Court held in 1979 that libel plaintiffs have the right to inquire into journalists' thought processes at the time when an allegedly libelous story was being prepared.

Ruling in the case of *Herbert v. Lando* (441 U.S. 153), the Supreme Court said that since libel plaintiffs often have to prove actual malice or at least negligence on the part of journalists, they are entitled to use the pre-trial "discovery" process (explained in Chapter One) to check on journalists' attitudes and thought processes.

The *Herbert* case caused considerable alarm among journalists when the Supreme Court ruled that the First Amendment does not excuse journalists from providing state-of-mind evidence to libel plaintiffs who are looking for proof of actual malice. Actually, though, the decision did little more than to uphold a long-recognized principle of discovery: each party is permitted to use discovery to gather information about the other side's case. Where the plaintiff must prove actual malice to win his case, the rules have allowed plaintiffs to seek evidence of malice.

The *Herbert* case arose when a military officer sued the producers of the CBS television program, "60 Minutes," for libel and then sought state-of-mind evidence during the discovery process. The show's producers refused to cooperate, citing the First Amendment, but the high court ruled that the First Amendment provides journalists with no special immunity from the normal rules of discovery.

Where does the *Herbert* case leave the mass media? Technically, it leaves the media in the same position they were in before this Supreme Court decision: required to cooperate in the discovery process even if it means responding to questions designed to determine whether there really was actual malice present when an allegedly libelous story was prepared.

However, the *Herbert* decision appears to have had an important psychological impact on libel cases. The Supreme Court has in effect endorsed and encouraged the aggressive use of discovery procedures by libel plaintiffs as a means of ferreting out evidence of actual malice or negligence. In the years since *Herbert*, discovery has been an increasing burden for the media in libel cases.

Long-Arm Jurisdiction

Another growing burden for the media—albeit once again not really a new burden—is the cost of defending libel suits in courts thousands of miles from home.

The law has long said persons and companies that engage in interstate commerce may be sued in any state where they have "minimum contacts." The Supreme Court so ruled in 1945, in a case called *International Shoe v. Washington* (326 U.S. 310).

However, some journalists have argued that they should not be forced to defend a libel suit in a faraway state merely because copies of their newspaper or magazine are distributed there or their material is broadcast there. In 1984, the Supreme Court ruled that the First Amendment should not be considered in such cases. Instead, the court said, lawsuits against journalists should have to meet only the same test of fairness as would a lawsuit against another kind of business. In short, if it would be fair for a company that makes cars or lawnmowers to be hauled into court in a distant state where its products are sold, it is also fair for the mass media to be sued in that state if their "product" is sold there.

In two cases decided on the same day—*Calder v. Jones* and *Keeton v. Hustler*—the high court unanimously rejected the argument that forcing journalists to defend themselves in faraway courts would have any chilling effect on freedom of the press.

That means the national media and their employees may be sued in any state—and a libel plaintiff is entitled to engage in "forum shopping." A plaintiff can select the state with the most favorable laws and file a libel suit there, regardless of where any of the prospective defendants live or maintain offices.

The *Calder v. Jones* case arose when the *National Enquirer* published a story claiming that producer Marty Ingels had driven his wife, actress Shirley Jones, to drink. ". . .(B)y 3 o'clock in the afternoon she's a crying drunk," the *Enquirer* said. Jones and Ingels both sued the sensational tabloid in California, where they live. Although headquartered in Florida, the *Enquirer* itself did not challenge the California court's jurisdiction. However, John South, the writer of the story, and Iain Calder, editor of the *National Enquirer*, both argued that they should not have to defend themselves in a courtroom nearly 3,000 miles from home.

The Supreme Court unanimously ruled that the writer and editor were subject to California jurisdiction even though neither one went to California to research or write the story. Justice William Rehnquist, who wrote the court's opinion, pointed out that the *Enquirer* was selling about 600,000 copies of each issue in California—twice as many as in any other state. "An individual injured in California need not go to Florida to seek redress from persons who, though remaining in Florida, knowingly cause the injury in California," Rehnquist wrote.

Shortly after the Supreme Court's *Calder v. Jones* decision, Jones and Ingels reached a settlement with the *National Enquirer* to terminate the case. The paper agreed to print a retraction and an apology, and to pay a large cash settlement. Neither side would reveal the amount of the settlement, but Ingels released a statement that said the amount took into account the fact that he and his wife had spent $300,000 in attorney's fees by then.

Although the Supreme Court's decision in the *Jones* case was troubling to some journalists, the *Keeton v. Hustler* case seemed far more so. At least Jones and Ingels had filed suit in the state where they lived and worked: they could hardly be accused of "forum shopping." But in *Keeton*, neither the plaintiff nor the defendant seemed to have any particularly good reason for suing in New Hampshire, the state where the suit was filed. Rather, the choice of New Hampshire was clearly a matter of forum shopping: it was apparently the only state whose deadline for filing libel suits had not passed when the suit was filed.

Kathy Keeton, an executive at *Penthouse* magazine, sued for libel after *Hustler* ran a cartoon suggesting that she had contracted a venereal disease from *Penthouse* Publisher Robert Guccione. She initially sued in Ohio (where *Hustler* was then headquartered), but her case was dismissed because she missed the Ohio filing deadline. By then, it was apparently too late to sue for libel anywhere but New Hampshire, which permitted libel suits as much as six years after publication (that deadline has since been shortened to three years).

When this case was filed, *Hustler* was selling about 10,000 copies of each issue in New Hampshire, but it had no other ties to the state. And Keeton had no ties to the state at all: she lived and worked in New York. Both the federal district court in New Hampshire and the first circuit U.S. Court of Appeals ruled that the jurisdictional requirements were not satisfied. The appellate court suggested that libel cases should be subject to tougher jurisdictional standards than other kinds of lawsuits in order to protect First Amendment freedoms.

The Supreme Court overturned that ruling and reinstated Keeton's lawsuit. ". . .(T)here is no unfairness in calling (*Hustler*) to answer for the contents of that publication wherever a substantial number of copies are regularly sold and distributed," Justice Rehnquist wrote for the court.

The Supreme Court ordered both of these cases back to lower courts. In both instances, the media defendants were trying to get the proceedings dismissed prior to trial, something the Supreme Court has been reluctant to allow in recent libel cases.

Libel and Summary Judgment

Like several earlier Supreme Court decisions on libel, the *Calder* and *Keeton* cases involved attempts by the media to terminate libel suits before trial, a process based on a motion for summary judgment or a motion to dismiss on other procedural grounds. As explained in Chapter One, a summary judgment is a ruling in which the court decides the case without trial, saving the expense and trouble of a prolonged lawsuit.

However, because a pretrial dismissal denies the plaintiff his or her day in court, it is only supposed to be granted when it is absolutely certain he couldn't win.

In recent years, the courts have recognized that many libel suits against the media are filed not in the hope of winning but as a means of harassment. Thus, libel suits have often been thrown out of court under summary judgment proceedings. This procedure was particularly applicable in situations where a public official or public figure was suing and was obviously unable to prove actual malice. But unfortunately, as more and more plaintiffs are classified as private persons who need only prove negligence, this remedy is becoming less available to the mass media. Many judges who were willing to grant summary judgment when a plaintiff had to prove malice are more inclined to let the case go to a jury when all the plaintiff has to prove is negligence.

Moreover, the prospects of winning summary judgments are now even dimmer in view of a footnote Chief Justice Burger appended to the majority opinion in the 1979 *Hutchinson* decision. In that footnote, Burger challenged this trend toward dismissing libel cases on summary judgment. (*Hutchinson* and *Wolston* both reached the Supreme Court on appeals of summary judgments in which judges had ruled that the plaintiffs were public figures who could not prove actual malice and thus had no right to take their cases to trial.)

Burger's footnote issued a warning that proving actual malice requires an inquiry into the state of mind of the defendant—something difficult to do without a full trial. This kind of case "does not lend itself to summary disposition," Burger wrote.

Discovery and News Sources

The discovery process has produced a new dilemma for the media in more and more libel suits. If a plaintiff must prove fault on the part of the media, that means he or she must inquire into a journalist's reporting methods to see if there was negligence or actual malice.

As a result, more and more libel plaintiffs are demanding to know where a reporter got the information that appeared in an allegedly libelous story. That means the plaintiff wants to identify the reporter's news sources so they can be interviewed and possibly called as witnesses in a libel trial. However, one of the strongest ethical standards of journalism is the principle of keeping confidential sources confidential (see Chapter Eight for further discussion of this point). In recent years a number of journalists facing libel suits have refused to reveal their sources during the discovery process.

This has sometimes caused serious problems for the media. Under the normal rules of discovery, if one party to a lawsuit refuses to cooperate in turning over requested evidence to the other side, that evidence may be presumed not to exist. Some judges have responded to a reporter's refusal to reveal his sources in a libel suit by simply ruling that there were no sources. Consequently, the story in question appears to have been published with reckless disregard for the truth—no matter how reliable the sources actually were. The result is almost certain defeat in a libel suit.

Many states have shield laws that exempt reporters from having to reveal their sources. However, these laws often protect the reporter only from a contempt of court citation; such laws may not override the rules of discovery in civil litigation. In some instances, there is simply no way a publisher or broadcaster can defend a libel suit without revealing confidential sources, so he or she must choose between violating a promise to a news source and losing a big libel suit.

A good illustration of this problem is the $60 million libel suit that former Iranian hostage Jerry Plotkin filed against the Los Angeles *Daily News*. Shortly after the hostages were released, the paper reported that Plotkin—the only American captured in the U.S. embassy takeover who was not there on government business—was in Iran to conduct large-scale drug purchases.

The two reporters who wrote the story relied on secret sources. During pretrial discovery, Plotkin demanded to know the identity of the sources, and the paper at first refused to name them. The trial judge ordered a default, clearing the way for Plotkin to win a big libel judgment without proving the story was libelous or false.

At that point, the newspaper replaced original lawyers and adopted a new legal strategy: the paper ordered the reporters to reveal their sources and asked the judge to set aside the default against the publishing company, in effect leaving the reporters on their own.

The judge eventually reinstated the case—but ruled that "as a matter of law" no sources existed for the story other than those who were named. The reporters eventually identified their sources: an FBI agent and an official of the Drug Enforcement Agency. At this writing, the case still had not gone to trial, but this sequence of pretrial events left many journalists alarmed and outraged.

While the Plotkin case has not yet produced any legal precedent, it (and numerous similar cases that have arisen from coast to coast) illustrates the very serious problem facing journalists who use confidential sources for investigative stories.

This problem is so severe that some libel insurance policies are invalid unless the publisher or broadcaster agrees to reveal his confidential news sources should a libel suit occur. It may cost a publisher thousands (or possibly millions) of dollars to maintain source confidentiality; the result could even be bankruptcy for some. How this very serious ethical quandary can be solved remains to be seen.

LIBEL AND FICTION

Another legal quandary for the mass media in the 1980s is the problem of libel and fiction. Although libel judgments have been based on works of fiction before, most publishers and broadcasters didn't worry very much about libel suits resulting from works of fiction until recently. A more serious legal problem has been the threat of lawsuits for invasion of privacy by those who recognized themselves—or thought they did—in fictitious works.

However, in the late 1970s and early 1980s that began to change. Courts started finding sufficient identification in works of fiction to support libel judgments. The result for the media has become a vicious circle: to avoid identifying any real person, those who write novels, short stories and scripts must carefully fictionalize their characters. However, if a real person nevertheless can convince a court he has been identified in the fictitious work, every respect in which the fictional character differs from the real person is a "falsehood" and thus exacerbates the libel. The *New York Times v. Sullivan* rule has been applied—some say misapplied—in these situations with disastrous results for the media. In a work of fiction, the characters necessarily differ from real people, but some courts have ruled that fictionalization equals knowing or reckless falsehood, thus proving actual malice and opening the door to punitive damages.

The case that initiated this trend toward libel judgments for fictionalization was *Bindrim v. Mitchell* (92 C.A.3d 61, 1979; cert. den. 444 U.S. 984), a California appellate court ruling. As a decision of an intermediate appeals court in a single state, it carries little weight as a precedent, but it encouraged other fiction-based libel cases, including the Wyoming judgment against *Penthouse* mentioned in the introduction to this chapter.

In *Bindrim*, novelist Gwen Davis Mitchell described a fictitious "nude encounter" marathon similar to those conducted by Dr. Paul Bindrim, a psychologist. In fact, Mitchell had attended one of Bindrim's sessions and signed an agreement not to write about it. But in Mitchell's book, entitled *Touching*, the psychologist who conducted the sessions had a different name and did not physically resemble Bindrim. The main thing the real man and the fictional character had in common was that they both conducted nude encounters.

Nevertheless, a jury found that Bindrim was identified and libeled by the fictional account in the novel, and awarded Bindrim $75,000 in total damages against Mitchell and her publisher, Doubleday and Company. The award was later reduced to $50,000.

Both the California and U.S. Supreme Courts refused to review the lower appellate decision, which affirmed the judge's determination that Bindrim was sufficiently identified for a libel suit. "The test is whether a reasonable person, reading the book, would understand that the fictional character was, in actual fact, the plaintiff," the appellate majority wrote.

The *Bindrim* ruling was widely criticized by writers and publishers, and the Writers Guild of America filed a brief urging the U.S. Supreme Court to review the case. The guild reminded the justices that many previous literary works have been based on fictionalizations of real people. The guild cited the classic movie, *Citizen Kane*, as a work that could not be produced under the *Bindrim* precedent. In that movie, the fictional Charles Foster Kane was far more similar to William Randolph Hearst, the newspaper publisher, than the character in *Touching* was to Bindrim. If a movie like *Citizen Kane* were done about a person living today, it would invite a *Bindrim*-type libel suit. To allow libel judgments for works of fiction will severely inhibit literary freedom, the guild warned.

Those arguments notwithstanding, no higher court was willing to review the *Bindrim* decision. This was by no means the first time a libel judgment had ever been based on a work of fiction: as early as 1920 the New York Court of Appeals had ruled similarly (see *Corrigan v. Bobbs-Merrill*, 228 N.Y. 58). Several other courts reached similar conclusions later, but none with quite the impact of *Bindrim*, which caused widespread alarm among writers and publishers.

However, fiction writers could take some comfort in the ultimate decision in the "Miss Wyoming" (*Pring v. Penthouse*) case, mentioned earlier. The tenth circuit U.S. Court of Appeals reversed the multimillion-dollar jury verdict and the Supreme Court declined to hear a further appeal.

The case stemmed from a *Penthouse* article describing a fictitious "Miss Wyoming" who competed in the Miss America Pageant, a champion baton twirler who had an even more interesting talent: oral sex. The story said she performed an act of oral sex at the pageant before a national television audience, and the recipient of her favors was levitated—he rose up in the air in defiance of the laws of gravity. Kim Pring, a champion baton twirler who once represented Wyoming in the Miss America Pageant, claimed the story was about her and damaged her reputation, so she sued. A Wyoming jury agreed and awarded $26.5 million in damages ($25 million of it in punitive damages).

The appellate court overturned the jury verdict because it found the story to be "physically impossible in an impossible setting," and therefore not something the reader could reasonably understand as describing actual events involving Pring.

The court called the *Penthouse* story "gross, unpleasant, crude," but said the First Amendment "is not limited to ideas, statements or positions. . . which are decent and popular. . . ." The court also offered some guidance on the murky issue of libel and fiction:

> The test is not whether the story is or is not characterized as "fiction," "humor," or anything else in the publication, but whether the charged portions in context could be reasonably understood as describing actual facts about the plaintiff or actual events in which she participated. If it could not be so understood, the charged portions could not be taken literally.

Thus, the court said the *Penthouse* story was too incredible and obviously false to be libelous to Kim Pring or anyone else. However, this decision offers little comfort for serious fiction writers. If a story is an accurate portrayal of life, it may be a more powerful (and artistically sound) literary work—but it is also more likely to be the basis for a libel suit. In effect, the *Pring v. Penthouse* decision says fairy tales are immune to libel judgments, but realistic literature is not.

LIBEL AND BROADCASTING

In summarizing the principles of libel law, we made little distinction between the print and electronic media. We did that in the interest of clarity and simplicity—and because it is generally justified. There are, however, some special libel problems when the broadcast media are involved.

Not the least of these problems is the question of whether a broadcast defamation is really a libel at all or is in fact a slander. Before broadcasting came along, slander (a spoken defamation) was a limited legal action for the obvious reason that an oral statement was a fleeting thing, while a printed one might be read by thousands of people over many years. In view of slander's limited nature, the courts generally ruled that one could only win a slander suit by proving special damages unless the slander fell into one of several particularly offensive categories that were sometimes called *slander per se.* Because of these restrictions, successful slander suits were relatively rare.

But when broadcasting developed, the potential for harm in a spoken defamation became every bit as great as in a written one. Recognizing the pervasiveness of a broadcast defamation, some states simply declared that broadcast defamation would be regarded as libel, not slander. Other states classified broadcast defamation as slander, but liberalized the requirements for a successful slander suit so there was little difference between libel and slander. Some states even adopted the rule that a defamation contained in a script would be treated as a libel (since it was written down, after all), while an ad-libbed one would be treated as slander. In the 1980s, few states still adhere to this rule.

These variations in broadcast defamation law may seem quaint, and perhaps they are today. Whatever its name, broadcast defamation is a viable legal action in all states. As noted earlier, some states exempt local broadcast-ers from liability for defamation occurring during network programs they have no power to edit, but even then the network remains liable. And, as already noted, the Supreme Court has exempted broadcasters from liability for defamation occurring during political speeches mandated by Section 315 of the Communications Act.

Aside from these exceptions, a defamation that is broadcast is just as actionable as a printed one, and perhaps more so because of the massive audiences the electronic media attract. In evaluating a libel that was broadcast rather than published, the same rules normally apply.

However, there are other practical problems in broadcasting. If broad-casters are going to be held accountable for libels by all the various people whose voices are broadcast, how can defamations by all these people ever be controlled? Various solutions have been developed in the industry, among them the practice of putting as much programming as possible on tape or film to expedite pre-broadcast review. Talk shows have produced problems for broadcasters in this respect; those who call in can hardly be expected to obey (or even know about) the rules of libel. One common solution, of course, is the use of a short time delay to allow the broadcaster to bleep out potentially offensive remarks.

The larger issues of broadcasting and the law are discussed in Chapter 11. In the libel area, much the same rules apply to all of the mass media.

THE ROLE OF RETRACTIONS

In at least 31 states, publishing (or in some cases broadcasting) a retraction or correction of a libelous item reduces the likelihood of a successful lawsuit against the mass media. If you plan a career in one of those states, one of the important aspects of libel law for you to understand is your state's rule on retractions.

In most states that have retraction laws, publishing a timely retraction of a libel (and placing the retraction in as prominent a place as the original libel) limits the damages that may be won. In many states, a retraction restricts the plaintiff to special damages (which, as noted earlier, are often difficult to prove). Therefore, publishing a retraction may effectively preclude a lawsuit in many instances.

The provisions of the retraction laws vary widely from state to state. Some of the strongest ones are found in midwestern and western states, such as Arizona, California, Idaho, Nevada, and Nebraska. These states all have laws that require a potential plaintiff to demand a retraction within a fixed period of time (usually 20 days after learning of the libel), and give the media another 21 days to publish or broadcast the retraction. Nevada, however, allows plaintiffs 90 days to demand a retraction.

Under these retraction statutes, if the plaintiff fails to demand a retraction, or if a suitable retraction is published or broadcast, the plaintiff is limited to special damages—provable out-of-pocket losses.

On the other hand, some states have retraction laws that simply say a libel defendant can show that a retraction was published as a way to "mitigate" damages, or perhaps to defend against charges of malice.

Not all retraction laws are equally comprehensive in their protection of the mass media, however. Of the 31 states that had retraction laws at this writing, only 15 specifically included broadcasters within their coverage. Another nine states had laws that covered "all libel suits" or "all media." Seven states had retraction laws that applied only to the print media or, more specifically, only to newspapers.

California's retraction law is unusual in another respect: it protects newspapers and radio and television stations but not magazines. That was a crucial factor in actress Carol Burnett's libel suit against the *National Enquirer* (mentioned earlier in this chapter): the trial court ruled the *National Enquirer* a magazine and not a newspaper—thus denying it the protection of the retraction statute. An appellate court affirmed that ruling (*Burnett v. National Enquirer*, 144 Cal.App.3d 991, 1983).

Montana's retraction law, on the other hand, was once so comprehensive that it was ruled unconstitutional. The Montana Supreme Court ruled that the law violated the state constitution because it in effect denied libel plaintiffs any reasonable remedy for the wrongs they might have suffered (see *Madison v. Yunker*, 589 P.2d 126, 1978).

The Montana legislature responded to that decision by rewriting the state retraction law in 1979. As it stands today, Montana's retraction law is weaker than those found in many neighboring states: it requires a demand for a retraction prior to a libel suit only if the plaintiff is going to seek punitive damages. And publishing a retraction prevents only punitive damages.

Retraction statutes are obviously useful in situations where the media have made an honest error, but they do little good in many of the circumstances that produce lawsuits—situations in which the publisher does not feel he made an error and is in no mood to back down. Moreover, there is a natural human tendency to believe the original charge—not anyone's later denial. To accuse someone of a crime in print, and then retract, saying it was all a mistake, is certain to leave some readers with a strong suspicion that it really wasn't a mistake. For this reason, some people question whether retraction statutes are really fair to libel victims.

Nevertheless, many states have such laws, and they have an important impact on libel litigation in those states.

CRIMINAL LIBEL

At the beginning of this chapter we said many states still have criminal libel laws on their books, but that these laws are rarely used. Thus the entire discussion so far has been devoted to civil libel.

The reason we can touch criminal libel so lightly in a text such as this is that it has become an obsolete legal action because of both common law traditions and a pair of U.S. Supreme Court decisions in the 1960s.

Criminal libel laws generally cover situations in which civil libel law is inapplicable. For instance, some states still make it a crime to libel a dead person—a form of libel that is almost never actionable in civil suits. In addition, some state laws still forbid distributing literature so defamatory that it might cause a breach of the peace.

The Supreme Court once upheld an Illinois criminal libel law that was used to prosecute a man who distributed racist literature. In a 1952 ruling (*Beauharnais v. Illinois*, 343 U.S. 250), the court said the First Amendment didn't protect the anti-black literature in question. Few legal scholars believe this case would be decided the same way now, given the more liberal interpretation of the First Amendment today.

Shortly after handing down its landmark *New York Times v. Sullivan* civil libel ruling in 1964, the Supreme Court rendered another important criminal libel decision: *Garrison v. Louisiana* (379 U.S. 64). That case arose when New Orleans prosecutor Jim Garrison severely criticized a group of judges, calling them sympathetic with "racketeer influences" and "vacation-minded." Prosecutor Garrison was himself prosecuted under a Louisiana law that made it a crime to defame public officials.

The Supreme Court said Garrison's prosecution was not permitted by the First Amendment, unless it could be proved that he made false statements either knowingly or with reckless disregard for the truth. In short, the court said the same tough standards that apply in civil libel suits by public officials also apply in criminal prosecutions for defamation of public officials.

That decision was perhaps the final blow for seditious libel laws in this country. Some states still have such laws, but they are almost never used. Such laws are likely to be overruled on constitutional grounds by the state courts when they are used.

The U.S. Supreme Court dealt another blow to criminal libel in the 1966 case of *Ashton v. Kentucky* (384 U.S. 195), a decision stemming from circulation of a pamphlet that attacked various local officials. The circulator was prosecuted for criminal libel because the pamphlet allegedly threatened to cause a breach of the peace. The Supreme Court unanimously reversed the conviction, ruling the law overbroad and in violation of the First Amendment.

As a result of these Supreme Court decisions and parallel rulings by a number of state courts, criminal libel prosecutions are extremely rare in modern America. Those criminal statutes that remain in force constitute a minimal legal threat to the mass media today. If the remaining criminal libel laws were vigorously enforced, few of them would withstand a Constitutional challenge at this point in our history.

LIBEL INSURANCE POLICIES

Because a single libel suit can be disastrous, many publishers and broadcasters carry libel insurance, just as they carry insurance to protect them from other business calamities.

However, private libel insurance is difficult to secure in some states. Moreover, few insurance carriers are willing to underwrite certain high-risk media.

To solve these problems, both the American Newspaper Publishers Association and the National Association of Broadcasters, the major trade associations in the two fields, have arranged libel insurance protection for their members through private carriers.

At this writing, the NAB plan, for instance, offered two different policies, one covering libel and invasion of privacy suits, with a second plan covering other First Amendment problems for a 50 percent additional fee. Significantly, the plan did not require the broadcaster to agree to reveal confidential sources as a condition of insurance coverage. But the plan did include surcharges in certain high-risk states, such as California, Oklahoma, and South Carolina. (These states were apparently so classified not because their libel laws are especially unfavorable to the media but because juries there have awarded large judgments.) The policy would pay judgments as high as $2 million and cover lawyer's fees as well as the judgment.

How much does libel insurance cost? The NAB's plan required radio stations to pay an annual premium of ten times their highest rate for a one-minute spot advertisement. Television stations were assessed the rate they received for carrying one hour's prime time network programming. The one-hour rate ranges from a few hundred dollars for stations in small markets up to sums in excess of $5,000 for stations in cities such as New York, Los Angeles, and Chicago.

When this package was introduced in 1980, the NAB estimated that nearly half of all commercial broadcasters still lacked libel insurance.

Libel insurance can be costly, but at least it helps protect publishers and broadcasters from catastrophic libel judgments. However, libel insurance often does not cover punitive damages, and large punitive damage awards are becoming increasingly commonplace, as explained at the beginning of this chapter. In fact, some states have laws forbidding insurance companies to cover punitive damages: the idea is that punitive damages are a punishment, and they should *hurt*.

Another serious shortcoming of many libel insurance policies is that they cover only libel *judgments* and not the prohibitive cost of defending a libel suit. The major cost of libel litigation is not paying off the few judgments that are ultimately upheld by appellate courts, but rather the very high cost of the protracted litigation that precedes the final judgment.

Nevertheless, insurance plays an important role in protecting the media from libel judgments—for those media that can afford it. Ironically, the small-market publishers and broadcasters who are the most vulnerable to libel suits are also the least likely to be able to afford to carry libel insurance.

A Summary of Libel Law

WHAT IS LIBEL?

Libel is a legal action designed to compensate someone whose reputation has been wrongfully damaged. Traditionally, a libel was a written defamation and a slander was a spoken defamation, but the distinction between the two became blurred as the influence of the broadcast media expanded.

WHO MAY SUE FOR LIBEL?

Individuals and corporations—but not government agencies—may sue. Unincorporated associations may sue in some states but not in others. An individual may sue for "group libel" if the group is very small and the libel refers particularly to the individual who wishes to sue.

WHO MAY BE SUED FOR LIBEL?

Usually anyone who contributes to the publication—or republication—of a libelous statement may be sued, even if the libel appears in a direct quote, a live interview, an advertisement or a letter to the editor.

TO WIN A LIBEL SUIT, WHAT MUST A PLAINTIFF PROVE?

To win, the plaintiff (the person who initiates the lawsuit) must prove all of the elements of libel, which are:

1. defamation
2. identification
3. publication
4. fault on the part of the publisher or broadcaster (i.e., dissemination of a falsehood due to either negligence or actual malice)
5. in many instances, actual damages.

WHAT DEFENSES ARE THERE?

Even though all of the elements of libel may be present, the plaintiff will not prevail if the defendant (a newspaper or broadcaster, for example) can prove that any of the recognized defenses apply. The major ones are:

1. truth
2. fair comment and criticism
3. privilege.

WHAT DOES PUBLISHING A RETRACTION ACCOMPLISH?

In many states publishing a retraction—in as prominent a place as the original libel and within a specified time period—limits the plaintiff to special damages (i.e., provable out-of-pocket losses).

5

PRIVACY AND PUBLICITY

The legal concepts called "right of privacy" and "right of publicity" have much in common with libel and slander. Like libel, invasion of privacy is a tort action—a civil lawsuit in which an injured party sues for monetary compensation. Moreover, privacy, like libel, is basically a state legal matter, although the U.S. Supreme Court has sometimes stepped in to place constitutional limits on state actions in this area just as it has in libel law. In fact, some of the major Supreme Court decisions on libel are cited in privacy lawsuits—and Supreme Court decisions on invasion of privacy are sometimes cited in libel cases.

Invasion of privacy and libel are so similar that persons aggrieved by media publicity may sue for both—hoping to win on at least one of the two legal theories. Libel and invasion of privacy overlap enough to invite this sort of double-lawsuit strategy, particularly because the two actions have slightly different defenses. It is entirely possible to have an excellent libel defense in a given situation—but a weak defense against an invasion of privacy suit.

However, there are important differences between libel and invasion of privacy, most notably their histories. Libel and slander were incorporated into the English common law hundreds of years ago, but invasion of privacy is a very new legal action. It was not widely recognized by courts or legislatures until the twentieth century.

THE HISTORY OF PRIVACY LAW

The concept of a "right of privacy" developed only when social institutions began to threaten individual privacy. It wasn't until the United States became an urban society dominated by mass media, large corporations, and big government agencies armed with sophisticated technology that Americans began to worry much about preserving their privacy.

Thus, it wasn't until near the end of the 1800s that invasion of privacy became an issue. But as the twentieth century approached, the biggest newspapers built up their circulations to nearly a million copies a day—and they did it with a heavy emphasis on stories about crime and scandal, stories that were not always truthful and tasteful. It became obvious that the media could destroy someone's reputation, sometimes in a way that did not lend itself to a libel suit. Suppose, for instance, that a sensational newspaper revealed intimate (but truthful) details of a person's private life. The truth defense might preclude a successful libel suit, but shouldn't there be some other way for the injured party to win some justice from the court system?

In what has become one of the most famous law review article of all time, Samuel D. Warren and Louis D. Brandeis addressed this issue in 1890. (Brandeis later served on the U.S. Supreme Court and wrote several well-known opinions on freedom of expression in America.) Their article in the *Harvard Law Review* contended that there should be a right of privacy either under the common law or state statutory law. Such a right, they felt, should protect prominent persons from gossipy reporting of their private affairs. The article was prompted at least in part by the experiences of Warren's family, which had occasionally found its name mentioned in unflattering ways in the Boston press.

Influential as that law review article became later, it did not create an overnight legal revolution. In fact, it was a dozen years later when a case based on the Warren-Brandeis theory finally reached a New York appellate court—and the court didn't buy the idea. The case (*Roberson v. Rochester Folding Box Co.*, 64 N.E. 442, 1902), was brought by Abigail Roberson, whose picture was used without her permission in a flour advertisement. She sued, but the court ruled that "the so-called 'right of privacy' has not yet found an abiding place in our jurisprudence. . . ."

However, Ms. Roberson's defeat in court quickly was turned into a victory in the New York legislature, which responded to the public outcry over the court decision by passing the nation's first statutory law on privacy. Acting in 1903, the legislature enacted what are now Sections 50 and 51 of the New York Civil Rights Law, which read in part:

> . . .(T)he name, portrait or picture of any living person cannot be used for advertising purposes or for purposes of trade, without first obtaining that person's written consent.

Obviously, this was not a sweeping law: it failed to address the sort of invasion of privacy Warren and Brandeis had in mind. All it did was outlaw commercial exploitation of a person's name or likeness without consent—a separate legal right that we call the "right of publicity" today. It said nothing about situations in which the media reveal intimate details about a person's private life in a news story.

Two years after the New York privacy law was enacted, a state supreme court judicially recognized a right of privacy in connection with the media for the first time. In that 1905 case (*Pavesich v. New England Life Insurance Co.*, 50 S.E. 68), the Georgia Supreme Court upheld the right of an artist named Paolo Pavesich to sue New England Life for using his likeness in an advertisement without permission. The ad included an unflattering photo of Pavesich and a testimonial implying that he endorsed the company's insurance.

Another famous early privacy case raised a different question, one that has plagued the courts (and journalists) ever since: can a public figure return to a private life and then sue for invasion of privacy if the press does a "where-is-he-now" story years later? In *Sidis v. F-R Publishing Co.* (113 F.2d 806, 1940), William J. Sidis sued the publisher of the *New Yorker* magazine for doing an article about him. He was a one-time mathematical genius who graduated from Harvard University at age 16. The article, published some 20 years later, revealed that he was living in a shabby rooming house and working as a low-salaried clerk. It ridiculed him and even included a cartoon with a caption calling him an "April fool."

Should someone like William Sidis be able to sue the *New Yorker* for invading his privacy? A federal appellate court ruled that the case should be dismissed, pointing to the newsworthiness of the story. The court said that someone who has become even an involuntary celebrity (as Sidis had) could not completely avoid publicity later in his or her life.

The *Sidis* case did not settle this issue, of course. As we will see later, old-but-true-facts cases continue to arise—and the media try to justify their coverage of such stories by citing the continued public interest in the subject. Publicity-shy plaintiffs, of course, argue that they should not be forced to have their past deeds revealed to people who have forgotten (or never knew) about them.

However, two legal concepts were emerging from these early privacy cases. First, there is the idea that the news media do not need anyone's consent to do stories about *newsworthy* subjects. But on the other hand, when a person's name or likeness is used for commercial purposes (as in advertising), it must be with the person's permission. By the early 1980s, almost every state had recognized at least these aspects of the right of privacy, either by statute or court decision.

Meanwhile, the U.S. Supreme Court began to recognize that there is also a Constitutional right of privacy, although none of the early Supreme Court decisions actually involved the mass media. The high court acknowledged the right of privacy in a law enforcement context as long ago as 1886, in *Boyd v. U.S.* (116 U.S. 616). In that case, the court said the Fourth and Fifth

Amendments provide protection against governmental invasions of the "sanctity of a man's home and the privacies of life."

Then in 1928, Louis Brandeis—by then a Supreme Court justice—wrote a famous dissenting opinion in which he urged recognition of the right of privacy in *Olmstead v. U.S.* (277 U.S. 438). That case involved government eavesdropping to gain evidence against suspected bootleggers in the prohibition era, and the majority opinion held that there was no violation of any right of privacy unless the federal agents committed a physical trespass in order to listen in. But in his dissent, Brandeis called for a "right to be let alone." He said the framers of the Constitution intended "to protect Americans in their beliefs, their thoughts, their emotions and their sensations. . . . They conferred, as against government, the right to be let alone—the most comprehensive of rights and the right most valued by civilized man."

Since then, the Supreme Court has more specifically recognized the right of privacy, both in media cases and in other areas. For instance, the *Olmstead* majority opinion—which allowed electronic eavesdropping as long as there was no physical trespass—was reversed some 40 years later in *Katz v. U.S.* (389 U.S. 347). In that 1967 case, federal agents had used monitoring devices atop a public telephone booth to gather evidence against alleged bookmakers. The Supreme Court said one's right to privacy extends to all areas where there is a justifiable expectation of privacy. Unauthorized eavesdropping need not involve a physical trespass to constitute a violation of the Fourth Amendment, the court ruled.

The Supreme Court also relied largely on a privacy rationale in reaching its famous decisions on birth control and abortion. In the 1965 ruling that overturned state laws against contraceptive devices (*Griswold v. Connecticut*, 381 U.S. 479), Justice William O. Douglas said the various rights listed in the Bill of Rights, taken together, add up to a right of privacy that bars the state from involving itself in individuals' sexual relations in marriage. Although other justices based their judgment on a different rationale, Douglas' view was widely quoted later.

In the 1973 Supreme Court decisions that overturned state laws against abortions (*Roe v. Wade* and *Doe v. Bolton*, 410 U.S. 113), the majority focused on concepts related to personal privacy in reaching the decision that abortions were a private matter between a woman and her physician, at least during the early months of pregnancy.

In recent years, the Supreme Court has also recognized a right of privacy in connection with the activities of the mass media, but we will defer the discussion of those important cases until we have provided an overview of the various kinds of privacy rights recognized by the courts and legislatures around the country.

AN OVERVIEW OF PRIVACY LAW

In 1960 William L. Prosser, one of the nation's great legal scholars, published an analysis of privacy law in which he said the concept of invasion of privacy really breaks down into four different legal rights. His classification has been very widely accepted and provided the basis for many of the court decisions in this field that have followed.

Prosser wrote:

The law of privacy comprises four distinct kinds of invasion of four different interests of the plaintiff, which are tied together by a common name, but otherwise have almost nothing in common except that each represents an interference with the right of the plaintiff, in the phrase coined by Judge Cooley, "to be let alone." Without any attempt to (write an) exact definition, these four torts may be described as follows:

1. Intrusion upon the plaintiff's seclusion or solitude, or into his private affairs;

2. Public disclosure of embarrassing private facts about the plaintiff;

3. Publicity which places the plaintiff in a false light in the public eye;

4. Appropriation, for the defendant's advantage, of the plaintiff's name or likeness. (48 Calif. Law Review 383, 1960)

Courts in a number of states had recognized some of these four kinds of invasion of privacy before Prosser wrote his classic analysis; many others have done so in the years since.

Even today, though, not all states recognize any kind of invasion of privacy as a legal wrong that may be remedied in a civil lawsuit, and a few states recognize some but not all of Prosser's four kinds of invasion of privacy. For example, in 1984 the North Carolina Supreme Court declined to recognize Prosser's third kind of invasion of privacy, holding someone before the public in a false light (*Renwick v. News and Observer*, 10 Med.L.Rptr.1443). Nevertheless, Prosser's breakdown of privacy law is generally accepted in most states, and this chapter is organized accordingly, discussing the four legal actions separately.

Thus, mass communicators may face lawsuits stemming from four different kinds of wrongful acts. The *intrusion* concept is based on the reporter's conduct as a newsgatherer. The reporter—and especially the photographer—who pursues someone too aggressively may face this kind of lawsuit.

Private facts cases usually result from the dissemination of intimate or embarrassing information about a person's private life or past—information that may be factually correct, thus precluding a successful libel suit.

Lawsuits based on holding a person before the public in a *false light* most closely resemble libel suits, because there must be an element of falsity in the presentation. Often a misleading photo caption produces this sort of lawsuit.

The fourth kind of invasion of privacy occurs most often in advertising and entertainment-related activities. Alternately called *misappropriation* or the *right of publicity*, it protects a person whose name or likeness has been used for commercial gain without permission.

As in libel law, there are defenses that the media may assert to escape liability in lawsuits for invasion of privacy. The two most widely recognized ones are *newsworthiness* (or *public interest*) and *consent*. If the media show that the subject matter of a news story or news broadcast is newsworthy, the plaintiff in a private facts lawsuit will normally lose in court. However, the newsworthiness defense is of little help when the alleged invasion of privacy involves an intrusion or holding a person before the public in a false light. Nor is it helpful when the issue is an unauthorized commercial use of a person's name or likeness (in an ad, motion picture, or poster, for instance).

The consent defense is most applicable in misappropriation cases: celebrities regularly give their consent to commercial uses of their names and likenesses, for a fee. However, the consent defense is also useful in other kinds of privacy lawsuits, provided it can be shown the person suing actually gave consent.

In addition to these two common law defenses, the U.S. Supreme Court has created Constitutional defenses in privacy cases, just as it has in libel cases. In fact, the *New York Times v. Sullivan* principle has been transplanted from libel to privacy law, and applies in certain kinds of privacy cases. In addition, the Supreme Court has also recognized a Constitutional right of the media to publish the contents of public records that are lawfully obtained, notwithstanding anyone's claim that publishing the information is an invasion of privacy.

Having briefly surveyed the kinds of invasion of privacy and the defenses, we will now present a more detailed summary of privacy law as it has developed over the last century in America.

INTRUSION

The first of the four kinds of invasion of privacy focuses more on the conduct of a reporter or photographer than on the content of the media. It is a legal action to compensate victims for intrusions into their "physical solitude or seclusion" or into their "private affairs." It often involves snooping, eavesdropping, or simply being in the way when someone has a reasonable right to expect a little peace and quiet. In an era of miniaturized electronic listening devices and long telephoto lenses, technology has created a variety of new threats to personal privacy—threats that have produced new legal protection against unauthorized persons who engage in high-technology snooping.

Perhaps the best way to illustrate the various kinds of invasion of privacy is to describe a few court decisions in each area. Many of these cases are included only as examples, and should not be considered as important as the few Supreme Court rulings we discuss in this chapter.

The case of *Dietemann v. Time, Inc.* (449 F.2d 245, 9th cir., 1971) is a good example of an intrusion by journalists that violated someone's privacy. Two reporters for *Life* magazine investigated a man suspected of practicing medicine without a license by posing as a patient and her husband. They visited the man at his home—where he practiced his craft—and surreptitiously took photographs. They also carried a hidden transmitter so law enforcement personnel nearby could monitor and record the conversation. The result was a criminal prosecution and an article in *Life* called "Crackdown on Quackery."

The man accused of medical quackery sued for invasion of privacy and ultimately won $1,000 in general damages, but only after several years of litigation and an appeal to the U.S. Circuit Court of Appeals. In a 1971 decision the appellate court agreed that the pictures and story were newsworthy but said the reporters had intruded upon Dietemann's privacy in gathering the information. The magazine had a right to publish the story but it did not have the right to use hidden electronic devices in the man's home to get the information.

If the news media may not surreptitiously enter a private home to get a story, may journalists go into a private home that was the scene of a fire and take pictures at the invitation of a public official? The Florida Supreme Court addressed that question in a 1976 case, *Fletcher v. Florida Publishing Co.* (340 So.2d 914). A photographer had taken a picture of a silhouette left on the floor by a girl's body after a fire, and the girl's mother sued, claiming a trespass and an invasion of privacy, among other things. The Florida Supreme Court found no actionable trespass or invasion of privacy in the photographer's actions, particularly because a fire marshal had asked the photographer to take the picture. The court said, "The fire was a disaster of great public interest and it is clear that the photographer and other members of the news media entered the burned home at the invitation of the investigating officers." The U.S. Supreme Court refused to review the case in 1977.

However, under some other circumstances journalists who go onto private property without permission may be sued successfully. A notable example is *Le Mistral, Inc. v. CBS* (402 N.Y.S.2d 815, 1978), in which a New York court partially affirmed a trespass judgment against WCBS-TV. The case arose because news cameramen photographed the interior of a swanky French restaurant over management objections in covering a story on health code violations.

The *Fletcher* and *Le Mistral* cases raise questions about the rights of photographers under privacy law. It is difficult to generalize on this subject because the rules vary somewhat from state to state, but in most states a photographer who trespasses to get a picture may face both civil and criminal sanctions, unless he has consent to be there from someone authorized to give it. On the other hand, photographers in public places may generally shoot any subject within view for news purposes—but not for commercial or advertising purposes, for reasons that will be explained later in this chapter. There are occasional exceptions, but the general rule is that anything within camera range of a public place may be photographed for news purposes. If the picture has even a little newsworthiness, and if you don't create a false impression with a misleading caption, you're usually safe.

Nevertheless, even in public places a photographer may not be so offensive in taking pictures that he seriously interferes with his subject's right to be left alone. The classic example of harassment by a photographer is the case of *Galella v. Onassis* (487 F.2d 986, 2d cir., 1973). Ron Galella, a free-lance photographer who made something of a career of photographing Jacqueline Kennedy Onassis and her children in the late 1960s and early 1970s, ultimately was ordered by a federal appellate court to stay 25 feet away from Ms. Onassis and even farther from her children. This was by no means a typical case: Galella's conduct prior to the court order had been outrageous. He had engaged in a variety of offensive activities, some of which actually endangered the safety of Ms. Onassis and her children.

In fact, a decade after the original lawsuit Ms. Onassis again hauled Galella into court for invading her privacy. She contended that he had repeatedly violated the original court order by failing to stay far enough away, among other things. The court agreed, and found Galella in contempt (*Galella v. Onassis*, 533 F.Supp. 1076, 1982). The court emphasized—again—that Galella had a right to photograph Ms. Onassis (or any other celebrity) in public places, or to write articles about her if he wished. But Galella's conduct was so outrageous as to justify some restrictions on his activities, the court said.

In more typical circumstances, there is little that celebrities can do about those who photograph them in public places, except perhaps to surround themselves with bodyguards whose job is to make it impossible for anyone to get an unobstructed shot. Occasionally, in fact, those who try to photograph the famous actually encounter violence from bodyguards. In those cases, the photographer may well have grounds for a lawsuit of his own—against the celebrity and his or her protectors. But that does little to salvage the pictures the guards may either prevent the photographer from taking or destroy afterward.

Like photographers, reporters sometimes intrude upon someone's privacy to get a story. The problem is more often ethical than legal, but there are circumstances under which reporters may face lawsuits for their newsgathering activities, as the *Dietemann* case illustrates.

DISCLOSURE OF PRIVATE FACTS

The second widely recognized kind of invasion of privacy is the public disclosure of private facts. This legal action provides a remedy for a person who has been embarrassed by a publication but may have little chance to win a libel suit because the facts revealed are accurate. In many states this is the type of invasion of privacy that causes journalists the most problems, because it is often hard to anticipate which stories will be troublesome. What may seem clearly newsworthy to journalists may seem to be a flagrant instance of revealing private facts to someone else. It is hard to generalize in this area, but perhaps a survey of some of the situations that have led to lawsuits will illustrate the problem.

In some states, publishing or broadcasting information about a person's shady past may lead to litigation, especially if the person has changed his way of life. Over the years California courts have entertained lawsuits in a number of instances where details of a person's embarrassing past were revealed. The earliest—and perhaps still the best known—of these true-but-old-facts cases is a 1931 California Appellate Court ruling, *Melvin v. Reid* (112 C.A. 285). The case resulted from a motion picture that revealed the past activities of a former prostitute, using her name in the advertising. The woman had moved to another town, married, and adopted a new life-style. The court said she was entitled to sue for the invasion of privacy inherent in this situation. Actually, the movie producer was guilty of two different kinds of invasion of privacy: revealing private facts and commercially exploiting a person's name without permission. The latter type of invasion of privacy is discussed later.

In two more recent cases, California courts have reiterated their position that one's privacy can be invaded by the republication of old news. In the 1971 case of *Briscoe v. Reader's Digest* (4 C.3d 529), the California Supreme Court allowed a lawsuit to proceed where the *Reader's Digest* had published the name of a man convicted of truck hijacking 11 years earlier. The man had been rehabilitated and started a family in another place. His family and new friends first learned of his past from the magazine article. The man ultimately lost his case, but the state Supreme Court said there was a legal basis for a lawsuit under such circumstances.

In 1978, a California appellate court handed down a similar ruling in a case called *Conklin v. Sloss* (86 C.A.3d 241). That one involved a small newspaper's "Twenty Years Ago. . ." column. The paper republished the story of a local man's murder conviction, and the man sued, contending that he had paid his debt to society and acquired new friends unaware of his past. The appellate court said he, too, had a right to pursue his contention that his privacy had been invaded. Like Briscoe, he lost at the trial court level, but the precedent from both cases—that a person in this situation has a right to sue— may still be valid, at least in California. However, even in that state, this principle doesn't necessarily apply to anyone except rehabilitated criminals, according to a 1980 state Supreme Court ruling (*Forsher v. Bugliosi*, 26 C.3d 792).

Moreover, these decisions have been followed in few other states. Most state courts have not been willing to entertain invasion of privacy lawsuits based on factually accurate revelations of a person's past misdeeds. In fact, the *Cox Broadcasting v. Cohn* (420 U.S. 469, 1975) decision of the U.S. Supreme Court ruled that it is unconstitutional for the media to be held accountable under privacy law for an accurate publication of information contained in a court record open to the public.

The *Cox* decision, one of the most important discussed in this chapter, resulted from a news broadcast that identified a rape victim in Georgia. A

Georgia law prohibited publishing or broadcasting the identity of rape victims, but a reporter was given a copy of the court records during criminal proceedings against several young men accused of the rape. The victim, Cynthia Cohn, was identified in these public records, and Cox Broadcasting used the name in its coverage of the trial. The victim's father, Martin Cohn, sued Cox Broadcasting, contending that the broadcasts identifying his daughter invaded his privacy.

The Georgia Supreme Court upheld the law against publishing rape victims' names and also ruled that the father could sue under common law invasion of privacy principles. However, in 1975 the U.S. Supreme Court reversed that decision. Writing for an 8-1 majority, Justice Byron White ruled that a state may not impose sanctions against the media for accurately reporting the contents of public records such as those involved in this case. Quoting an earlier opinion by Justice William O. Douglas, Justice White said: "A trial is a public event. What transpires in the courtroom is public property."

At the time, this decision was widely viewed as a victory for the mass media, and in the years since, it has become evident that this decision has implications far beyond privacy law. As noted in the last chapter, the Supreme Court has since made it clear that the *Cox v. Cohn* principle also applies in libel law, for example. Also, a later Supreme Court decision made it clear that the *Cox* rule was not limited to court records:

> Our holding there (in *Cox*) was that a civil action against a television station for breach of privacy could not be maintained consistently with the First Amendment when the station had broadcast only information which was already in the public domain. (*Landmark Communications v. Virginia*, 435 U.S. at 840, 1978)

A widely respected summary of tort law, the *Restatement (Second) of Torts*, takes the same position on this point, declaring, "The case (*Cox*). . .holds that under the First Amendment there can be no recovery for disclosure of and publicity to facts that are a matter of public record."

If the *Cox v. Cohn* decision invalidated a Georgia law against publishing the names of rape victims, does that mean state laws against publishing the names of juvenile offenders are also invalid? The U.S. Supreme Court has also addressed that issue.

Publication of Juveniles' Names

Obviously, there are ethical as well as legal issues involved in publishing the names of rape victims and juvenile offenders. But in both areas, many of the legal issues have now been resolved in favor of the media. Going beyond its ruling in *Cox*, the Supreme Court in 1979 ruled that no state may impose criminal sanctions where the media have disseminated the names of juvenile offenders, even if the information was secured from sources other than public records. The high court didn't rule out civil invasion of privacy lawsuits where such information is secured from unofficial sources, but at least criminal prosecution of journalists was forbidden.

This case (*Smith v. Daily Mail Publishing Co.*, 443 U.S. 97) was a test of a West Virginia law making it a crime for a newspaper to publish the name of any young person involved in juvenile court proceedings. The case arose when several journalists were indicted after they identified a 14-year-old boy charged with fatally shooting a schoolmate. The shooting occurred at a junior high school, and journalists learned the name from eyewitnesses. They also heard the name by monitoring a police band radio.

After the indictments, the West Virginia Supreme Court invalidated both the indictments and the law, and the U.S. Supreme Court agreed. Chief Justice Warren Burger wrote:

> At issue is simply the power of a state to punish the truthful publication of an alleged juvenile delinquent's name lawfully obtained by a newspaper.

In voiding this West Virginia law, the court said that the magnitude of the state's interest in protecting the anonymity of juvenile crime suspects is not sufficient to justify imposition of criminal penalties on the newspapers.

However, Burger warned that the court might uphold a similar law if there were an issue of "unlawful press access to a confidential judicial proceeding" or an issue of "privacy or prejudicial pretrial publicity," or if the publication were false.

Still, this represented another instance when the Supreme Court felt it necessary to intervene to protect the right of the media to disseminate lawfully obtained information. The *Cox* decision flatly ruled out invasion of privacy lawsuits for publishing information derived from public records, in effect creating a new invasion of privacy defense. The *Smith v. Daily Mail* case didn't create a new privacy defense, but it did make it clear that criminal prosecution of the media is not an appropriate way to prevent the dissemination of juvenile names (and presumably other kinds of information that could be embarrassing).

An important point to remember about the *Smith* case is that it did not prohibit invasion of privacy lawsuits after publication of personal information that is not part of a public record. The Supreme Court only banned criminal sanctions. Moreover, the Supreme Court has not yet created any special right of access to the names of rape victims and juvenile offenders. It is still constitutionally permissible for a state to keep that kind of information secret. But if the media do obtain the information, it may be published without fear of criminal prosecution.

One unresolved issue in this area is whether it is still constitutionally proper for a state to allow lawsuits for the publication of information taken from old public records. As noted earlier, California, for instance, has continued to allow such lawsuits despite the *Cox* decision. If the Supreme

Court has said state courts may not impose liability for any publication of information obtained from public records, shouldn't that apply to old as well as new public records?

In 1979, the U.S. Supreme Court may have provided a hint about the way it might answer that question should an appropriate case arise. The court declined to overrule a state court order that had nothing to do with the mass media, but was relevant to this issue. A Louisiana court had prohibited a coin-operated laundry owner from "publicizing in any manner whatsoever" the conviction of a man who pleaded guilty of burglarizing the laundry, even though the conviction was a matter of public record. In this case (*Norris v. King*, 355 So.2d 21, 1978), Brian King, the laundry owner, installed a hidden security camera. The camera photographed a man named Michael Norris breaking into a soft drink machine and stealing money. This incident was one of a series of thefts at King's laundromat, and the crimes continued after Norris pleaded guilty and was given probation.

King posted a large handbill entitled "Caught in the Act" on a bulletin board in an attempt to discourage further thefts. The poster also said: "These are actual photographs taken by a hidden camera of a theft in progress." It also identified Norris and listed his address. Several months later, after completing his probation, Norris sued King for damages and for a permanent order prohibiting him from publicizing the incident, claiming it was an invasion of his privacy. King argued that the First Amendment prohibited prior restraints against publishing accurate information about criminal convictions that are on the public record. Moreover, he argued, there was public benefit to his posters because thay had eliminated his theft problem.

Nevertheless, a trial court ruled against King, awarding Norris $500 damages and a permanent injunction against future publication of the information. The Louisiana Court of Appeals affirmed the judgment, saying:

> One of the premises of the rehabilitative process is that the rehabilitated offender can rejoin that great bulk of the community from which he has been ostracized for his anti-social acts. In return for becoming a new man, he is allowed to melt into the shadows of obscurity.

The Louisiana Supreme Court refused to review the case and King appealed to the U.S. Supreme Court, which also declined to review the case.

By itself, this decision proves little, but combined with the fact that California still allows old-but-true-facts lawsuits, it suggests a trend. For the moment, at least, it appears that a state may still entertain invasion of privacy lawsuits by rehabilitated criminals whose past has been revealed, the *Cox Broadcasting* case notwithstanding.

Private Facts: Other Contexts

In addition to the kinds of cases discussed so far, there is another type of situation that produces private facts lawsuits: situations where the facts are contemporaneous but simply embarrassing because they portray a person as a violator of social norms. In these cases, the crucial issue is usually whether the facts fall within the newsworthiness defense.

There have been many such cases litigated over the years, and most of them were ultimately won by the mass media. However, the litigation is often protracted and costly, and the threat of such a lawsuit is often a deterrent to publishing stories containing embarrassing personal information. A good example of such a lawsuit is *Virgil v. Time, Inc.* (527 F.2d 1122, 9th cir., 1975), a case that produced a federal appellate court ruling in 1975. It involved Mike Virgil, a surfing enthusiast who was profiled in an article in *Sports Illustrated*. The writer of the article had interviewed Virgil at great length and had also received Virgil's permission to photograph him. However, before the article was published, Virgil revoked all consent for publication of the article and photographs because he feared the article would focus on bizarre incidents in his life that were not directly related to surfing.

The fact that Virgil revoked his consent for the publication didn't mean the article could not be published. The news media routinely publish and broadcast stories about people who don't want publicity. When an item is published or broadcast without the subject's consent, it merely means the publisher or broadcaster must be certain it is newsworthy enough to prevent a successful lawsuit for invasion of privacy.

The article about Mike Virgil was published over his objections, and it contained this quotation:

> Every summer I'd work construction and dive off billboards to hurt myself or drop loads of lumber on myself to collect unemployment compensation so I could surf at The Wedge.

The article also said he had extinguished a cigarette in his mouth and had eaten spiders and insects.

Virgil sued for invasion of his privacy, and his lawsuit reached the Ninth Circuit Court of Appeals on a motion to dismiss the case before trial. The appellate court said that unless a subject is newsworthy, the publicizing of private facts is not protected by the First Amendment. The court said:

> In determining what is a matter of legitimate public interest, account must be taken of the customs and conventions of the community, and what is proper becomes a matter of the community mores.

The U.S. Supreme Court refused to review the circuit court's ruling that Virgil had a right to take his case to trial. The case went back to a federal district court, which ruled that *Sports Illustrated* published a "newsworthy" article that in fact generally portrayed Virgil in a positive way in the context of prevailing social mores (424 F.Supp. 1286, D.C.Cal., 1976).

Thus, the magazine eventually won the *Virgil* case, but only after a protracted and expensive legal battle. Moreover, the appellate court's ruling left much room for uncertainty about which stories are legally newsworthy and which do not fall within this broad but vague defense.

The newsworthiness defense also was used successfully by the *Des Moines Register* in a 1979 case of an entirely different sort, *Howard v. Des Moines Register* (283 N.W.2d 289). This case was filed by Robin Howard after a news story disclosed that she had been involuntarily sterilized while a resident in a county facility. Howard said that the newspaper had invaded her privacy by giving unreasonable publicity to her private life. She said that friends and acquaintances were not aware of her surgery and that such publicity humiliated her, causing mental pain and anguish.

The trial court granted summary judgment in the case on the grounds that the information in its context was newsworthy. The article focused on the facility's alleged poor care and lax administration. The Iowa Supreme Court affirmed the trial court and ruled that "the disclosure of plaintiff's involuntary sterilization was closely related to the subject matter of the news story." The court went on to say: ". . .they had a right to treat the identity of victims of involuntary sterlizations as matters of legitimate public concern. The subject is one of grave public interest." The court also said:

> The article is an example of investigative journalism. Its obvious purpose was to bring the problems of the Jasper County Home to public attention. In chronicling alleged abuses in the home, defendants portrayed a pattern of incidents which cumulatively established more reason for public concern about management of the home than would any one incident viewed in isolation. This journalistic technique is basic and legitimate.

Another private facts case where the newsworthiness or public interest defense prevailed for the media involved stories in the University of Maryland *Diamondback* and the *Washington Star* reporting that six University of Maryland basketball players were in academic trouble. The university newspaper even published the players' grade point averages.

The six players sued the newspapers, seeking $72 million damages for an invasion of privacy or mental duress. Both a lower court and the Maryland Court of Special Appeals agreed that the players had sought the "limelight" by joining the team. Therefore, they "will not be heard to complain when the light focuses on their potentially imminent withdrawal from the team." The court, in putting the facts in perspective, said basketball in Maryland was a big-time sport and information about team members was a matter of legitimate public interest (*Bilney v. Evening Star*, 406 A.2d 652, 1979).

But what about the people who aren't basketball players, champion surfers, or patients in a state institution? Suppose an ordinary citizen happens to be in the right place at the right time to do something heroic, and as a result the whole world hears intimate details of his or her life. Has that person's privacy been invaded?

A very good example of this problem is the case of Oliver Sipple, who may have saved President Gerald Ford's life during an assassination attempt in 1975. When Sara Jane Moore, the would-be assassin, took aim at the president, Sipple struck her arm and caused her shot to miss. He was hailed as a hero, but soon the media also revealed the fact that he was a homosexual, an active member of the San Francisco gay community. He sued for invasion of privacy, but the California Court of Appeals ruled that the stories about his sexual preferences were newsworthy, given all of the circumstances (*Sipple v. Chronicle Publishing Co.*, 10 Med.L.Rptr. 1690, 1984).

However, the court ordered that its decision in the *Sipple* case not be published in the official reports of California appellate court decisions. Under California law, unpublished decisions may not be cited as legal precedents. This is, nonetheless, an interesting case that raises difficult ethical and legal issues.

To summarize, the private facts area of privacy law is by no means clearly defined. Usually the media win such lawsuits by asserting the newsworthiness defense, but protracted litigation may precede the ultimate victory. No one—not the courts, not legal scholars, and indeed not even journalists—can precisely define newsworthiness. Also unresolved is whether the media may still be sued for revealing true but old facts about rehabilitated criminals, given the *Cox* case's strong statements about the Constitutional protection for news reporting based on information obtained from public records.

The conflict between the individual's right to keep private facts private and the media's right to report the news raises a number of ethical questions. For instance, should the media be able to make a person a celebrity by intensive coverage and then defend against a privacy lawsuit by citing that celebrity status? Does mere publicity make a person newsworthy, or must one already be newsworthy before publicity is permitted? Moreover, when the media make the judgment that someone is newsworthy and publicize his or her activities, should the First Amendment permit the courts to second-guess that judgment?

FALSE LIGHT AND FICTIONALIZATION

The third area of privacy law which has produced litigation for the media is sometimes referred to as false light invasion of privacy. It involves publicity that places the plaintiff in a false light before the public. This kind of privacy case might be described as a libel case but without the defamation. It allows a person to sue when portrayed falsely, but not necessarily in a way that tends to damage his or her reputation.

Photographers (or more correctly those who write captions for photographs) are especially vulnerable to this kind of lawsuit, but other journalists should also be aware of the pitfalls in this area. In fact, two different false light privacy cases stemming from inaccurate reporting have reached the U.S. Supreme Court in recent years.

The first of these false light Supreme Court decisions came in 1967. The case, *Time, Inc. v. Hill* (385 U.S. 374), involved the James J. Hill family, which gained notoriety when it was taken hostage in its own home by three escaped convicts in 1952. The incident, of course, was newsworthy, especially because two of the three convicts were eventually killed in a shoot-out with police.

One year after the event, novelist Joseph Hayes published *The Desperate Hours*, a story about a family taken hostage by escaped convicts. Later the novel was made into a play and a motion picture. The story line differed in significant ways from the Hill family's experiences, although there were similarities.

An invasion of privacy suit was filed by the Hill family in 1955 after an article was published in *Life* magazine reviewing the play based on Hayes' book. *Life* directly stated that the play was based on the Hill family incident. The Hills sought damages on grounds that the magazine article "was intended to, and did, give the impression that the play mirrored the Hill family's experience, which, to the knowledge of defendant. . . was false and untrue."

The Hill family won a $30,000 judgment in the New York state courts, but Time, Inc., appealed the case to the U.S. Supreme Court, which in 1967 reversed the New York judgment.

Justice William Brennan, writing for the court, applied the *New York Times v. Sullivan* libel rule to this kind of situation in privacy law. Thus, Brennan said, a false light privacy suit cannot be won by a public figure unless he can show the falsehood was published either knowingly or with reckless disregard for the truth (something the Hills could not show). Brennan indicated the *Times* rule was to be applied only in the "discrete context of the facts of the *Hill* case." Nevertheless, Brennan's opinion has often been applied by state courts and was cited in a later U.S. Supreme Court ruling on false light invasion of privacy.

That later ruling, *Cantrell v. Forest City Publishing Co.* (419 U.S. 245, 1974), presented the U.S. Supreme Court with the chance to abandon the *Time v. Hill* requirement at a time when the court was narrowing the application of the *New York Times* rule to public figures in libel cases, but it didn't address that issue. Instead the court upheld an invasion of privacy judgment against a newspaper by saying the paper was guilty of "calculated falsehoods" and "reckless untruth." The court didn't say what would have happened if the paper had been guilty of only negligence.

This case resulted from newspaper coverage of the consequences of the collapse of a bridge across the Ohio River. A man named Melvin Cantrell was among 43 victims, and a *Cleveland Plain Dealer* reporter followed up the tragedy with a feature story about how the man's death affected his family. Several months after the accident, the reporter and a photographer visited the Cantrell residence to gather information for the follow-up story. Cantrell's widow was not home, so the reporter talked to the children and the photographer took many pictures. The resulting feature appeared as the lead story in the *Plain Dealer*'s Sunday magazine. It stressed the family's abject poverty and contained a number of inaccuracies including a description of the widow's attitude, with statements that clearly implied that the reporter had talked to her.

Mrs. Cantrell brought an action for invasion of privacy against the publisher of the newspaper. When the U.S. Supreme Court reviewed the case in 1974, it upheld a $60,000 judgment in her favor. The Supreme Court said the evidence showed that the newspaper "had published knowing or reckless falsehoods about the Cantrells." The court also said much of what was published consisted of "calculated falsehoods and the jury was plainly justified in finding that. . . the Cantrells were placed in a false light through knowing or reckless untruth."

Interestingly enough, the Supreme Court ruled that the photographer who took the pictures should not be held liable since there was no misrepresentation inherent in his pictures. In comparison, there was an obvious misrepresentation in the feature story itself.

The *Hill* and *Cantrell* cases are notable because they reached the U.S. Supreme Court—but they are not necessarily representative of all false light privacy lawsuits. As indicated earlier, another common source of false light privacy lawsuits is misleading photo captions. Two California Supreme Court decisions in the 1950s nicely illustrate the problem in this area.

Both lawsuits were initiated by John and Sheila Gill, a couple who operated a candy and ice cream store at a tourist attraction in Los Angeles. Noted photographer Henri Cartier-Bresson caught them sitting side by side at the counter in their shop. John had his arm around Sheila, and they were leaning forward with their cheeks touching. The photo, taken without permission on private property that was open to the public, was published in both *Harper's Bazaar*, a Hearst publication, and *Ladies Home Journal*, a Curtis publication.

The Hearst publication used the photo to illustrate an article entitled, "And So the World Goes Round." The couple was described as "immortalized in a moment of tenderness." However, the Curtis publication used the photo in a different context. There, it illustrated an article on the dangers of "love at first sight," with statements such as this one: "publicized as glamorous, love at first sight is a bad risk." Further, the article went on to condemn this sort of thing as love based on "instantaneous powerful sex attraction—the wrong kind of love."

The Gills sued both publishers, but the two lawsuits produced opposite results. In *Gill v. Hearst Corporation* (40 Cal.2d 224, 1953), the couple lost. The California Supreme Court found no misrepresentation of their status, and thus no basis for an invasion of privacy lawsuit. But in *Gill v. Curtis Publishing* (38 Cal.2d 273, 1952), the couple won: the court found that the Gills had been held up before the public in a false light, since there was no basis for saying their relationship was "love at first sight" or based merely on "instantaneous. . .sex attraction."

The two *Gill* cases are typical of many others that have been filed since. If there is a general rule in these situations, it is that a photograph is reasonably safe if the caption is not misleading, provided it was taken in a public place and is used in a manner that falls within the newsworthiness defense. However, if the caption creates a false impression about the people in the picture, or if it is used for commercial (i.e., non-editorial) purposes, the risk of a lawsuit for invasion of privacy is much greater.

APPROPRIATION/RIGHT OF PUBLICITY

The fourth kind of privacy law, variously called appropriation (or misappropriation) and *right of publicity*, protects people from commercial use of their names and likenesses without consent. Because of that, it is very different from the other three. In the first place, the other three kinds of privacy law most often protect people who want to avoid publicity and would prefer to be left alone to live their lives quietly. Right of publicity lawsuits are sometimes filed by private persons whose names or photographs were for some reason used for someone else's commercial gain, but more commonly the plaintiff in these lawsuits is a celebrity—someone whose name or likeness has commercial value. The problem usually isn't that the celebrity objects to the publicity; what he or she objects to is not being adequately paid. An endorsement or an appearance by a celebrity may be worth thousands (or even millions) of dollars, and the celebrity's lawyers want to make sure their client collects.

The right of publicity is the oldest kind of privacy law. The 1902 *Roberson* case, discussed in the section on the history of privacy, would be called a right of publicity case if it were decided today. The New York statutory privacy law that was enacted in response to the *Roberson* decision is fundamentally a right of publicity law—it protects a person's name and likeness from unauthorized commercial exploitation.

In the years since that pioneering New York case, many states have recognized the right of publicity in some form, either by statute or court decision. The concept was given its contemporary name in a 1953 U.S. Court of Appeals decision, *Haelan Laboratories v. Topps Chewing Gum* (202 F.2d 866, 2d cir., 1953). The case involved the right of baseball players to control the commercial use of their names and photos on baseball trading cards, and the court said this:

> We think that in addition to an independent right of privacy. . .a man has a right in the publicity value of his photograph, i.e., the right to grant the exclusive privilege of publishing his picture. . . .This right might be called a "right of publicity."

A variety of state laws and court decisions have reiterated the point made in the *Haelan* case: one cannot commercially exploit a person's name, public personality, or likeness without consent. Various courts have said the right protects sports figures, entertainment celebrities, and even people who would be classified as public figures only because of their involvement in controversial public issues.

Nor does the right of publicity just protect a person's name and likeness. A number of courts have ruled that the right extends to the commercial exploitation of other aspects of an individual's identity and public personage. A memorable illustration of this point is the 1983 federal appellate court decision in a case called *Carson v. Here's Johnny* (698 F.2d 831).

The case arose after Here's Johnny Portable Toilets, Inc. began marketing its products in 1976. Entertainer Johnny Carson, host of NBC's long-running "Tonight Show," has been introduced to viewers with the phrase "here's Johnny" ever since the show began in 1962. Carson was obviously not amused when the toilet company not only called its product "Here's Johnny" but also added the phrase, "the world's foremost commodian." Carson sued for the violation of his right of publicity, among other things.

Overruling a trial judge who had dismissed Carson's lawsuit, the appellate court held that the use of "Here's Johnny" as a brand name did violate Carson's right of publicity. The court emphasized that a person's full name need not be used for his right of publicity to be violated, especially in a case involving a celebrity as well known as Johnny Carson. Clearly, the phrase "here's Johnny" is associated with Carson in the minds of millions of television viewers. In fact, at one point in the case the company had conceded that it was trying to capitalize on Carson's reputation.

In deciding the *Here's Johnny* case in this way, the appellate court cited another case the same court had heard almost a decade earlier: *Motschenbacher v. R. J. Reynolds Tobacco* (498 F.2d 821). In that case, the court held that a race car driver's right of publicity was violated by an advertisement in which R. J. Reynolds used a photo of his car, even though the driver's face was not visible. The car's markings were so distinctive that the car fell within the driver's right of publicity, the court ruled.

Thus, the right of publicity protects celebrities and others from the commercial use of far more than just their names and likenesses. Catch phrases and even tangible objects that are closely associated with a celebrity in the public mind may be out of bounds for advertisers (unless permission is negotiated and paid for).

However, there are limits to this rule. Another federal appellate court decision permitted a tire company ad to use actresses dressed in miniskirts and boots, a style that singer Nancy Sinatra had popularized, even though the ad also featured a revised version of "These Boots are Made for Walkin'," one of her hit songs. In *Sinatra v. Goodyear* (435 F.2d 711), the court said it was clear that Nancy Sinatra was neither singing the song nor appearing on camera in the ad, which promoted Goodyear's "Wide Boots" tires. The court said Sinatra's right of publicity had therefore not been violated. (Note that the use of the song itself was not an issue. As Chapter Six explains, under the concept of "compulsory licensing," anyone may perform a copyrighted song upon payment of the proper royalty).

The *Sinatra v. Goodyear* case raises the question of how far an advertiser can go in using celebrity look-alikes. Traditionally, the rule has been that celebrity imitations did not violate the celebrity's right of publicity as long as the public was not deceived into thinking the celebrity was actually appearing in the ad or endorsing the product. However, in 1984 a New York judge ruled that the use of a celebrity look-alike in an ad did violate Jackie Onassis' right of publicity, and he ordered an ad agency to stop using an Onassis look-alike to promote Christian Dior clothes. The judge issued this order without finding that anyone was actually deceived into thinking Ms. Onassis was appearing in the ad or endorsing the product. Although a trial judge's ruling normally sets no legal precedent, it remains to be seen what long-term effect this one may have on either the law or advertising industry practices.

If celebrities have a right to prevent the unauthorized commercial use of their names and likeness—and possibly even some limited right to prevent others from doing imitations—where does that leave the journalist who wants to write news stories about the famous?

That is an important issue, and the answer is relatively clear: the right of publicity does not apply to news situations, even though the media are commercial enterprises. The print and broadcast media are free to use a person's name and likeness whenever the situation creates newsworthiness— and the courts have tended to be very liberal in defining newsworthiness for these purposes. Even if a news medium engages in advertising to promote its own product, and reproduces a photograph of someone famous that appeared in print, that advertisement does not fall within the right of publicity.

However, if a newspaper, magazine, or radio or TV station uses the name or photograph of a celebrity in a way that implies an *endorsement,* it is a different matter. Cher, the singer and actress, was involved in a case that illustrated this point in 1982.

In *Cher v. Forum International* (692 F.2d 634, 1982), Cher had granted an interview to a free-lance writer who hoped to write an article for *Us* magazine. The article was rejected by *Us,* and the writer then sold it to the publishers of two other magazines, *Star* and *Forum.* Both published it. *Star* carried the article with a headline that offended Cher. The headline read, "Exclusive Series. . .Cher: My life, my husbands, and my many, many men."

Cher disliked the idea that the interview ended up being published in *Star* instead of *Us,* and she disliked the headline even more. But what apparently offended Cher the most was that *Forum* not only ran the article but also used her name and likeness in advertising that implied she endorsed and read the magazine. One ad in the *New York Daily News* included Cher's photograph and the words, "There are certain things that Cher won't tell *People* and would never tell *Us.* She tells *Forum.* . . So join Cher and *Forum's* hundreds of thousands of other adventurous readers today."

In deciding the legal issues raised by this series of events, the ninth circuit U.S. Court of Appeals overturned a trial verdict against the free-lance writer and the publisher of *Star.* They did not violate Cher's right of publicity by writing and publishing a newsworthy article, the court decided. The writer, for instance, had never promised Cher any control over where the article would be published. If the writer had made such promises and then published the article elsewhere, Cher could have sued him for breach of contract. But in the absence of any contractual commitment, the writer had the same right to freely publish his article as would any other journalist.

However, what *Forum* did was another matter: that magazine promoted the article in a way that clearly implied an endorsement by Cher. Although *Forum*'s publication of the article did not violate Cher's right of publicity, the advertising for it did, the court ruled.

This case, then, illustrates the principle that the media may freely publish stories about newsworthy people—but not advertisements that imply an endorsement—without violating their right of publicity. On the other hand, if the ad had simply promoted the story by saying something like "Read an interesting article about Cher in *Forum*," it would probably have been safe.

Nevertheless, almost all other forms of commercial advertising do fall within the restrictions of the right of publicity. In most advertising, you cannot include photographs of recognizable people, be they famous or unknown, unless you get their consent. This rule applies equally to the print and electronic media: you can be sued if you use a street scene in a television ad without getting the consent of everyone recognizable on the street.

The right of publicity also applies to the entertainment media. When someone produces a motion picture, all of the people appearing on the screen who are recognizable must give their consent—which is why producers commonly use "extras" who are on the payroll instead of just photographing whoever happens to be walking past for use in scenes showing public places. These rules do not apply, of course, to most news, news-documentary, and public affairs productions. But in movies produced for entertainment purposes, the unauthorized use of a person's likeness under any circumstances invites a lawsuit.

Even a news presentation may lead to a lawsuit for invasion of the right of publicity under some circumstances. An excellent example is a case that produced a U.S. Supreme Court decision—the only one to date dealing with the right of publicity.

The case was *Zacchini v. Scripps-Howard Broadcasting* (433 U.S. 562, 1977), and it involved Hugo Zacchini, who called himself "the human cannonball" and had an "act" in which he was shot from a cannon into a net at fairs and other exhibitions. His entire "act" was filmed and broadcast as news by Scripps-Howard Broadcasting despite his objections to the filming. He sued for invasion of his right of publicity under Ohio law, but the state Supreme Court said the First Amendment precluded any recovery by Zacchini because the newscast covered a matter of "legitimate public interest."

However, in 1977 the U.S. Supreme Court modified the Ohio ruling by declaring that the First Amendment did not protect a broadcaster who took a performer's entire act and showed it without consent as news. The Supreme Court didn't rule that Zacchini's rights had necessarily been invaded: that was a matter for the Ohio state courts to decide. But the high court did say that Scripps-Howard was not constitutionally exempt from being sued if the state courts cared to entertain such a suit.

The case was returned to the Ohio courts, and Zacchini won his lawsuit. To deny him a right to sue when his entire act was broadcast without his consent would deny him the economic value of his performance, the state court said.

The *Zacchini* decision is troubling to many journalists, particularly because it seems to suggest that other people whose ability to earn money is somehow damaged by a news story could also sue. Also, the court didn't really consider whether Scripps-Howard actually profited from the telecast at Zacchini's expense.

There is obviously a fine line between news coverage of a celebrity's activities and the commercial exploitation of the person's name and likeness. Normally the courts give the news media considerable leeway in this area, but the rule is different in a situation such as the *Zacchini* case where all or most of a performer's act is broadcast without consent. The test of what is improper commercial exploitation and what is legitimate news coverage would seem to be somewhat like the test used to determine what is a fair use under copyright law (discussed in Chapter Six). Thus, a purported news story or news broadcast that seriously impairs a celebrity's ability to make a profit by exercising his or her right of publicity is less likely to be considered proper than one using only a small portion of a performance and having little effect on the celebrity's profit opportunities.

Even news coverage of people who aren't celebrities sometimes produces right of publicity lawsuits. A number of people whose photographs have been used in newspapers and news programs without their consent have sued for an alleged invasion of their right of publicity, but they have almost always lost in court if the photograph was taken in a public place and the use was even minimally newsworthy. The news media clearly have the right to use people's names and show their likenesses in covering the news—without violating anyone's right of publicity. However, there is still the danger that the combination of a photograph and text matter may place someone in a false light. If that happens, a false light invasion of privacy lawsuit may result, even though there may be no basis for a right of publicity lawsuit.

A Personal or Property Right?

One particularly unsettled point about the right of publicity is whether it is a "personal right" or an inheritable "property right." Courts in various regions of the United States have taken conflicting positions on this question.

In a widely noted case involving Bela Lugosi, the star of the original *Dracula* film, the California Supreme Court ruled that the right dies with the person. The case, *Lugosi v. Universal Pictures* (25 Cal.3d 813), was decided in 1979.

The California court had to mediate a long-standing dispute between Universal and the widow and son of the late actor. The Lugosis contended that Universal was violating their inherited publicity rights by marketing tee shirts and other "Dracula" souvenirs using the actor's likeness after his death. The state Supreme Court said they had no right to sue, because the right of publicity could not be inherited. Even if a person builds a business marketing his name or likeness during his lifetime, the court said the most his heirs could inherit would be monies from the use of his name or likeness during his lifetime—not the right to control the commercial exploitation of his right of publicity after his death.

However, the death of an even more famous deceased celebrity, rock and roll musician Elvis Presley, produced conflicting federal appellate court decisions. One of them is contrary to the California Supreme Court's "Dracula" ruling. Almost as soon as Presley died, unauthorized commercial exploitation of his name and likeness began. In a 1978 decision (*Factors v. Pro Arts*, 579 F.2d 215), the second circuit U.S. Court of Appeals ruled that Presley's right of publicity was a property right and survived his death. Moreover, the court said that the right could be transferred to a business, which could maintain its exclusive right to exploit Presley's name after his death.

However, two years later another federal circuit court ruled in just the opposite way regarding Elvis Presley. The sixth circuit ruled, in *Memphis Development Foundation v. Factors* (616 F.2d 956, 1980), that Presley's right of publicity did not survive his death. Thus, Factors did not have an exclusive right to exploit the rock and roll star's name and likeness. At issue was the foundation's right to sell $25 pewter replicas of a statue of Presley it planned to erect in Memphis. The court said, "after death, the opportunity for gain shifts to the public domain, where it is equally open to all."

Further confusing matters, after the *Memphis Development Foundation* decision was published, the court that decided *Factors* (the second circuit U.S. Court of Appeals) reversed itself. In a 1981 ruling (*Factors v. Pro Arts*, 652 F.2d 278), the court followed the sixth circuit's lead, concluding that Presley's right of publicity did *not* survive his death. The second circuit made this abrupt switch because it felt obligated to follow the law of Tennessee, Presley's home state, as it had been interpreted by a court in that region (the sixth circuit U.S. Court of Appeals).

As a result of this ruling, those desiring to exploit Presley's name or likeness commercially were apparently left free to do so. However, these court decisions do not affect the *copyright* on Presley's recordings and motion pictures. As the next chapter explains, copyrights are always property rights rather than personal rights, and they do NOT terminate at the artist's death. The inheritability of the right of publicity, not the inheritability of copyrights, is unclear at this point.

What is clear is that a living person's name and likeness may not be used for advertising or other commercial purposes without consent.

PRIVACY DEFENSES

Throughout this chapter we have repeatedly talked about the legal defenses available to the mass media in various kinds of privacy cases, but in the interest of completeness we should separately reiterate them here.

In most cases where the mass media are defendants, the best defense is newsworthiness, often called public interest. If it is possible to convince a court that a given story, broadcast, or photograph is newsworthy, the plaintiff will not win a private facts lawsuit. The trend just about everywhere is for the courts to define news liberally, recognizing that even sensational reporting is permissible as long as it is not inaccurate. Therefore, the media do not often lose private facts cases, although the cost of defending a lawsuit alone may deter coverage of some kinds of stories.

However, if there are inaccuracies, it is a different matter. False light privacy cases against the media are more often successful, with the Constitutional standards first established in libel cases often used to evaluate the media's conduct. The Supreme Court created a First Amendment defense for false light privacy cases in its *Time, Inc. v. Hill* decision. That defense protects the media from false light privacy suits for nonmalicious but erroneous publications involving public figures. If a journalist has not been guilty of actual malice, a public figure has just about as little chance of winning a false light privacy suit as a libel suit. If, on the other hand, there has been wrongful conduct by the media, plaintiffs fare about as well in false light privacy cases as in libel cases.

Much the same is true in intrusion cases. The inquiry focuses on the conduct of the media when a court tries to decide if someone's right of privacy has been invaded. Unfortunately, the newsworthiness of a story is not a defense for unscrupulous reporting methods. A journalist who resorts to unlawful acts in gathering a story (or otherwise intrudes upon someone's right to be let alone) may face a privacy lawsuit.

In areas other than news-editorial journalism, the best (and often the only) privacy defense is consent. Persons who consent to a use of their names or likenesses have no recourse when the use to which they consented occurs. However, we should point out a couple of legal technicalities about consent.

First, the consent must be in a form that is legally enforceable, and that means there must be a contract that complies with the formalities of contract law. The person who enters the contract must be of age, and the contract must be supported by some form of consideration. Consideration is often thought of as another way of saying money, but it can be other things, even intangibles. Any time the person who is giving the right to use his or her likeness commercially gets something of value in return, that is consideration enough. For instance, photo release forms are one of the most common kinds of contracts granting consent, and they sometimes simply say that the person posing gives his or her consent for publication of a picture in return for the free publicity that may result. Publicity is a valid form of consideration.

To be valid, the consent must be voluntarily entered into. And it must be given in a manner that lends itself to proof in court, if necessary. For that reason, a written consent is much better than an oral one, and infinitely better than the implied consent a photographer tries to establish when he says, ". . .but he posed willingly."

Another caution is that the consent must be all-encompassing enough to apply to all situations in which a person's name or likeness is likely to be used. A consent for one commercial use may not imply any consent for subsequent uses of the same photograph, for example. And a consent to use a picture at one time may not be a consent to use it later. All of these kinds of problems are contract law problems, and the solution lies in writing a contract that leaves no loopholes.

In addition to the newsworthiness and consent defenses, the Supreme Court has, in effect, created another separate Constitutional defense for publication of information lawfully obtained from public records. The *Cox v. Cohn* ruling included some strong language assuring the media a right to report on public affairs. That right may not include a right to report on rehabilitated criminals' past activities—additional decisions will be needed to clarify that issue—but in other respects the right to report the contents of lawfully obtained public records appears to be almost absolute.

This, then, is an overview of the defenses in privacy law. Because they differ slightly from the defenses in libel cases, it is possible to publish something that is safe from a libel standpoint, but risky under privacy law (or vice versa). In evaluating stories that may defame or embarrass someone, you must keep that point in mind. Once you have analyzed any sort of material that you plan to publish or broadcast for potential libel and concluded it is safe, you must also run through the possible invasion of privacy problems. At a time when many lawyers routinely append allegations that there was an invasion of privacy to almost any libel suit they file, mass communicators must also think in terms of both of these legal actions.

PRIVACY ACT OF 1974

After years of debate, a comprehensive federal privacy law was passed by Congress in 1974. The new law recognized the individual "right to be left alone." The act gives all citizens the right to inspect most of the government files maintained on them, to prevent improper distribution of those records, and to challenge their accuracy. The act flatly prohibits indiscriminate government snooping and prying. Federal agencies are now under orders to streamline their files and to stop accumulating information that has no relevance to the job they were set up to do.

Meanwhile, many states have enacted similar laws forbidding activities by state and local government agencies that improperly impinge upon individual privacy.

These laws have sometimes interfered with the work of journalists seeking to gather news because they place many records containing personal information off limits. The conflict between the journalist's struggle for access to information and the growing body of statutory privacy law is one of the major challenges for journalists today.

A Summary of
The Right of Privacy

WHAT IS INVASION OF PRIVACY?

Invasion of privacy is a legal action designed to compensate someone whose right of privacy has been interfered with. There are four generally recognized types of invasion of privacy:

1. intrusion upon a person's physical solitude
2. publication of private facts, causing embarrassment
3. placing a person before the public in a false light
4. unauthorized commercial exploitation of a person's name or likeness.

ARE THESE RIGHTS UNIVERSALLY RECOGNIZED?

No. Some states have recognized all four kinds of invasion of privacy, while others allow lawsuits for only some of them. However, statutory laws or court decisions in virtually all states recognize that a person's name or likeness may not be used in commercial advertising without permission.

WHAT DEFENSES ARE THERE?

The courts have recognized several defenses as applicable to one or more of the four kinds of invasion of privacy. The primary ones are:

1. newsworthiness or public interest
2. consent
3. the *New York Times* rule (applicable only under limited circumstances)
4. the *Cox v. Cohn* public record defense.

6

MASS COMMUNICATIONS AS PRIVATE PROPERTY

How can someone own an idea?

Shouldn't information and ideas belong to everyone in a free society? Why should creative people be able to lock up their creations and treat them as private property, denying their use to others? Isn't a copyright an abridgment of First Amendment freedoms?

These are difficult philosophical questions, and there really isn't a completely satisfactory answer to some of them. But the fact remains that ideas, inventions, creative works, and trademarks are sometimes treated as private property. Collectively, the law governing this kind of property is called "intellectual property law." It includes copyrights, trademarks, unfair competition, and patent law.

Intellectual property law exists to encourage creativity by protecting the creator's right to make a profit from his or her works. The basic rationale for it is that creative people are just as entitled to profit from their labors as are the people who make consumer goods. Nevertheless, it is true that copyrights and patents create monopolistic controls on knowledge. For that reason educators, librarians, scientific researchers and even newsgatherers sometimes find copyrights and patents to be a major annoyance.

Even antitrust lawyers for the U.S. government have been known to oppose copyright laws because of their monopolistic tendencies. For instance, during the Congressional debate over a comprehensive revision of the U.S. Copyright Act in the mid-1970s, the Justice Department lobbied to weaken the proposed copyright law in an effort to minimize the restraints on competition inherent in copyright protection.

Though this kind of law may be monopolistic and an abridgment of free expression, it has a long history in the United States. It is unlikely this form of monopoly will soon disappear, the First Amendment notwithstanding.

Intellectual property law originally evolved within the English common law, but the framers of the U.S. Constitution considered it so important that they specifically recognized it, making both copyrights and patents federal matters right from the time the Constitution was ratified.

Article I, Section 8 of the Constitution includes this language:

> The Congress shall have the power to promote the progress of science and the useful arts, by securing for limited times to authors and inventors the exclusive right to their respective writings and discoveries.

Shortly after the Constitution was ratified, Congress accepted that invitation and enacted the first federal copyright law, the Copyright Act of 1790. That law has been revised several times since, as technology created new problems that could not have been anticipated by the framers of the Constitution. The most recent of these major revisions occurred in 1976, and, as we shall see shortly, it attempted—not always successfully—to deal with such troublesome new problems as photocopying, audio and video recording, satellite communications, and cable television.

Whatever the unresolved problems in copyright law, the history of Congressional involvement makes copyright law fundamentally different from some of the other areas of mass media law: it is an area of federal statutory law, not primarily a form of state statutory or common law. If the problems of copyright law are to be solved at all, they must be resolved mainly by Congress, with help from the federal courts.

There is another way in which copyrights and other kinds of intellectual property law differ from such areas of law as libel and invasion of privacy. As Chapters Four and Five point out, the right to sue for libel, slander, and most kinds of invasion of privacy is a purely personal right; it dies with the aggrieved party. That person's heirs have no basis for a lawsuit unless they were also personally injured. Copyright, trademark law and unfair competition are entirely different in this respect. They create property rights rather than personal rights, rights that may be passed on to one's heirs. In fact, copyright law is specifically written to provide legal rights many years after the death of a work's creator.

AN OVERVIEW OF COPYRIGHT LAW

What It Covers

The Copyright Act of 1976 continues a tradition begun in the earlier copyright laws, setting up a system under which people may protect their creative works from unauthorized commercial exploitation by others, but only for a limited time.

What sort of things may and may not be copyrighted under this law?

Generally, all kinds of creative endeavors may be copyrighted. That includes literary works (fiction and non-fiction, prose and poetry), musical works (and any accompanying words), dramatic works (including music), choreographic works and pantomimes, pictorial, graphic, and sculptural works (including both photographs and paintings), recordings, motion pictures, and radio or television productions (whether dramatic or news/documentary in nature). Just about everything that is printed or broadcast may be copyrighted.

However, there are some very important exceptions to that rule. Probably the most important one for the mass media is that the news itself cannot be copyrighted, although a description of a news event can be. The first reporter to reach the scene of a plane crash, for instance, cannot prevent others from reporting the fact that the plane crashed or the details of how it happened. All he can deny to others is his account of the event. Others may tell the story in their own words.

Thus it is commonplace for journalists to rewrite and use each other's stories. Whenever one reporter scores an important "scoop," others quickly pick up the story, carefully putting it in their own words and perhaps giving credit to the original source. Even though this is permissible under copyright law, it should be emphasized that one news medium cannot systematically purloin all of its news from a competitor to avoid having to employ its own news staff. To do that is called "unfair competition," and on several occasions courts have awarded damages for this kind of wrongdoing even though it may not be a copyright infringement. Systematic "news piracy," as it is called, is not permissible. More will be said of unfair competition later in this chapter.

There are several other important categories of material that cannot be copyrighted. Like news, other forms of factual information cannot be copyrighted. Historical and scientific information, for instance, are available to everyone. (However, remember that a particular description of the facts can be copyrighted.) And ideas, processes, and inventions may not be copyrighted, although they may be protected under the federal patent laws. Copyright law protects the style of presentation, not the underlying facts.

Another kind of material that cannot be copyrighted is the words and short phrases that constitute "trademarks" and "service marks." As will be explained later, they may be protected under state and federal trademark registration laws, but they cannot be copyrighted. You cannot be sued for copyright infringement for using (or misusing) someone's trademark, although you may face a trademark infringement suit if you wrongfully exploit a protected trademark as if it were your own.

Securing a Copyright

Once you have a creative work that is eligible for copyright, obtaining copyright protection is easy. Basically, you secure a copyright by claiming it: you insert a notice in a prominent place that says the work is copyrighted.

The notice must say something like this: "Copyright © 1985 by John Author." The little "c" with a circle around it is the standard symbol to indicate that a work is copyrighted.

The 1976 Copyright Act is much more flexible than its predecessor, the 1909 Copyright Act, regarding the insertion of this copyright notice. Under the older law, the failure to include the notice—or even putting it in the wrong place—would generally mean forfeiture of copyright protection. The new law allows somewhat broader latitude on this point. Even if you should fail to insert the notice, you can retrieve for yourself some copyright protection by registering the work under procedures described later. Registration without including the copyright notice doesn't protect you from innocent infringers (people who don't know the work is copyrighted), but once you notify an infringer that your work is copyrighted, the infringement must stop.

On the other hand, if you do include the copyright notice, you don't even have to register the copyright for it to be valid, although the law contains some incentives to encourage copyright owners to register. These incentives will be described shortly.

What happens to a work if you neither insert the copyright notice nor register the copyright? Then the work falls into the "public domain." That means the work belongs to everyone, and anyone who wishes may reproduce or perform it as if he owned the copyright.

How do you register a copyright? First, you secure the proper forms from the U.S. Copyright Office, Library of Congress, Washington, DC 20559. For works that are primarily text, you will need Form TX. For films, broadcast works, and the like, request Form PA. For visual arts works, Form VA is required. The Copyright Office also has a free package of copyright information that will be sent on request.

To complete registration, you fill out the forms, pay a $10 registration fee, and send in two copies of the work for deposit in the Library of Congress (there are some exceptions to this two-copy deposit requirement for bulky works such as motion pictures and some works of art). You have to complete these steps for each edition you want to register.

As already indicated, the 1976 Copyright Act specifically says that completing this registration procedure is "permissive;" failure to do it does not affect the validity of the copyright. The requirement to deposit copies with the Library of Congress is not "permissive," but there is no penalty for failure to comply unless you are specifically asked by the Library of Congress to make the deposit (something that rarely happens), and even then you have 90 days to do it. Failure to comply with a request for deposit after that could result in criminal sanctions, but it does not invalidate the copyright.

This flexibility in registration and deposit requirements is another change brought about by the new Copyright Act. Over the years, some people (particularly the publishers of small newspapers and magazines) began inserting the copyright notice in their works without following through with registration.

Although this violated the 1909 Copyright Act, it became commonplace to include a copyright notice but do nothing more unless an infringement occurred. The new law legitimized this practice by eliminating copyright registration as a precondition to the validity of a copyright. However, registering promptly (i.e., within 90 days of publication) still has advantages. If you register within 90 days, or before an infringement occurs, you have more legal remedies available than you have if you don't register before there is an infringement.

Remedies for Infringements

Copyright protection would mean little if the law had no enforcement provisions. Thus, the Copyright Act provides a variety of legal remedies for copyright owners to use against infringers. When a copyright *is* registered, the remedies available include the right to seek an injunction (a court order to stop the infringement), court-ordered impounding of all pirated copies, court-ordered payment of the copyright owner's attorney's fees by the infringer, and either actual or statutory damages. Owners of unregistered copyrights retain some (but not all) of these rights, as will be explained shortly.

Statutory damages are an arbitrary sum of money a court may award where actual damages are either hard to prove or very nominal (perhaps because the infringer made little or no profit). The amount of statutory damages provided for each infringement may range from $250 to $10,000 at the judge's discretion, although awards as low as $100 are authorized where an infringement was an innocent one, with amounts as high as $50,000 permitted in the case of a flagrantly wrongful infringement.

Of course, if the infringer made a great deal of money, the copyright owner would seek actual damages rather than statutory damages.

When a copyright is unregistered at the time of an infringement, the copyright owner may still seek several remedies. First, however, he or she must register the copyright, following the procedures described earlier. Only then may a lawsuit for copyright infringement be initiated. After registering the copyright, the owner may sue the infringer for actual damages—but not statutory damages. He or she may also seek an injunction or court-ordered impoundment of the pirated copies.

Thus, if your copyright is unregistered when an infringement occurs, you lose the right to sue for your attorney's fees and statutory damages. This means owners of unregistered copyrights are protected from large-scale infringements in which there may be substantial damages. But small-scale infringements—those where actual damages are minimal and the lawyer's fees would be disproportionately high—are more likely to go unchallenged if a copyright is unregistered.

Nevertheless, the viability of an unregistered copyright should not be overlooked. Actual damages alone can be a substantial deterrent because of the manner in which they are calculated. To collect actual damages, the copyright owner sues for both his losses and the infringer's gross profits. The infringer then must prove all of his or her expenses in order to get them deducted from that gross profit figure. Thus, actual damages are supposed to take away all of the net profit from an infringement.

However, this provision can be so harsh to an infringer that courts have been known to refuse to enforce it fully. For instance, there was a famous 1940 U.S. Supreme Court decision involving a pirated script that was made into a major-studio motion picture, complete with high-priced promotion and big-name stars.

After deducting all costs, the profits for the movie came to nearly $600,000—a very large sum for the time. A trial court complied with the Copyright Act and awarded that full amount to the author of the pirated script. However, the Supreme Court set aside the provisions of the Copyright Act and apportioned the profits, awarding the author only about $120,000. Much of the profit was attributable to factors other than the script, the high court held (*Sheldon v. MGM*, 309 U.S. 390).

Despite the Sheldon decision, large actual damage awards do occur. Moreover, the infringer could face criminal sanctions. The law was designed to make copyright infringements painful and expensive, whether the copyrighted work is registered or not.

The Copyright Owner's Prerogatives

Once you have a valid copyright, you own a variety of property rights that are protected by federal law. First of all, the copyright owner has the exclusive right to reproduce the work or sell it for a profit. In addition, the copyright owner may abridge, expand, revise, or rearrange the copyrighted work. And the copyright owner has the right to perform the copyrighted work. The owner can sell (or give away) these rights.

In many of the performing arts areas, it is customary to grant others the right to arrange and perform a work in return for payments called "royalties." In fact, the law requires copyright owners in the music field to grant such rights to others. This process is called "compulsory licensing." It gives anyone the right to perform copyrighted musical works by merely paying the prescribed royalty for each performance (or for each copy of a recording sold).

There is no similar compulsory licensing system for most other kinds of copyrighted works, such as written materials, audiovisual works, and works of art. However, the 1976 Copyright Act did establish a compulsory licensing system in some new areas, notably cable television. The problems of cable television and copyright law will be discussed later.

Works for Hire

Returning to the prerogatives of copyright owners, it should be noted that in many instances those who create artistic and literary works sell some or all of their rights to others instead of retaining those rights themselves. In free-lance writing, for example, it is not unusual to sell first reprint rights on an article while retaining ownership of the copyright itself so the work may later be published in book form.

However, there are some potential hazards in copyright law that may trap unwary authors. One is the Copyright Act's "works for hire" provisions. The law says that the copyright on works for hire belongs to the employer, not to the creator of the work. If you are a staff writer for a newspaper and you write a news story that your publisher decides to copyright, the copyright belongs to the publisher, not to you.

Few people would question the fairness of that principle, but what about writers who do free-lance work? Or what about the composer who accepts a commission to write the score for a new musical production? The law says that such a person is presumed to be on his own and not creating a "work for hire." However, contracts offered by publishers and others who buy creative works are sometimes written to offset this presumption. If your contract says you are doing a "work for hire," someone else may end up owning all rights to your creative efforts rather than just the first reprint or performance rights you intended.

In addition, a free-lance writer should be aware of the difference between selling a publisher "all rights" and merely selling "first North American rights." A contract that specifies the former means the writer cannot later include the work in an anthology, for instance, without the original publisher's permission. If you sell "all rights," the publisher thereafter owns your work.

The Duration of Copyrights

One of the major changes resulting from the 1976 Copyright Act was an extension and simplification of the duration of a copyright. Under the 1909 law, a copyright was valid for 28 years and could be renewed for another 28 years. The new law changed that: the basic term now is the author's life plus 50 years. For works created anonymously or for hire, the term is now 75 years from the date of publication or 100 years from the date of creation, whichever causes the copyright to expire sooner.

An interesting twist to the author's-life-plus-50-years rule is that when a work is co-authored, the copyright term runs for the lifetime of the last surviving author plus 50 years. An elderly novelist writing the work that could be the crowning achievement of his literary career could increase the earnings of his descendants several generations later by taking in a young collaborator.

What about works copyrighted before the new law went into effect? For most of these works, the copyright term was extended to a straight 75-year period from the date of publication.

The new law also simplifies the bookkeeping on copyright terms in another way: all copyrights end on December 31 of their expiration year, not on the exact date the 50- or 75-year period terminates.

Federal Copyright Law Preemption

One of the most significant changes in copyright law that resulted from the passage of the 1976 Copyright Act is that now both published and unpublished works are protected under the federal system. Previously, the federal law covered only published works, leaving unpublished materials protected only by the varying state laws that developed from what was called "common law copyright." That meant there were different rules and sometimes two different copyright offices with which to deal because some states set up their own registration systems to protect the copyright on unpublished works.

That dual system of state and federal copyright protection also caused both state and federal courts to stretch their definitions of the word "published" to protect authors. If someone handed out 100 copies of a short story to friends or potential publishers, was it published? If the author remembered to put in the copyright notice, federal courts tended to rule that it was published, so the federal copyright system could be used to protect the work from would-be infringers. But if, on the other hand, the author failed to insert the notice, the work would fall into the public domain if "published." Thus, state courts tended to bend the rules to find that such works were really unpublished so they could provide common law copyright protection to otherwise unprotected authors.

The new system eliminates this sort of double standard. As soon as a work is "fixed in a tangible form," it is protected by the federal law. This means that as soon as a work is written down on paper, recorded on film or tape, or placed almost anywhere else outside the creator's mind, it can be copyrighted under the federal law. One need not wait until the work is published to secure protection—federal copyright protection is immediately available. To secure this protection, you merely include a copyright notice in the draft of the work—and you may register the unpublished work if you want the strongest possible protection.

In short, the 1976 Copyright Act completely abolished the state common law copyright system for works published after January 1, 1978 (the effective date for the new law). After that date all state laws relating to copyrights were "pre-empted." That is, all such laws were superseded by the federal law and ceased to be valid for new works. Congress always had the authority to abolish state common law copyright protection and assume complete jurisdiction in this field; in the 1976 Copyright Act Congress finally did so, thus greatly simplifying the American copyright system.

Proving an Infringement

Suppose someone publishes a magazine article that you feel was pirated from one you wrote. What can you do about it?

As already pointed out, there are many remedies available if you sue the infringer and win your lawsuit. But to win a copyright infringement lawsuit, there are several things you have to prove. One is that the alleged infringer had some access to your work. And, of course, you have to prove that you in fact owned a valid copyright on a legitimate original work.

In the case of a verbatim copy of your copyrighted work, proving these things is not very difficult, but what happens if the infringer was skillful enough to modify the original work? At that point, you must prove there is "substantial similarity" between your work and the allegedly infringing work—and that is not always easy. Where literary works are involved, authorities on literature have sometimes been called as expert witnesses to testify about the subtle similarities of plot, character development, and theme. However, the original copyright owner ultimately has to convince a judge or jury that the average person (not just an expert) would see the new work as similar enough to have been pirated from the original.

Not only is substantial similarity sometimes difficult to prove where a pirated work isn't an exact copy of the original, but there can be problems in proving access to the original work. If someone who has never seen nor heard of your copyrighted work creates a very similar work, that is not a copyright infringement. If you cannot prove the alleged infringer had some opportunity to learn of your work, you can't prove he copied it. If the second work is truly an independent creation by someone who had no access to your original work, he or she can copyright it and go into business reproducing and selling it, as far as copyright law is concerned. (However, he or she may have other legal problems in the unfair competition and trademark areas, to be discussed shortly).

How do you prove that your work is independently created and original when you plan to submit it to someone else for possible publication? How do you prevent an editor, for instance, from taking the work and using it without payment? There are various ways to amass evidence that could be used in court to prove your original authorship, should a lawsuit be necessary. The classic advice was to mail a copy to yourself before submitting the work to anyone else, retaining the copy in the sealed (and postmarked) envelope. However, the 1976 Copyright Act provides a much more dependable approach: you may now copyright the unpublished work under federal law and register it with the U.S. Copyright Office. Then your copyright is protected, prior to the work's submission to anyone who might be tempted to claim it as his or her own.

COPYRIGHTS AND MUSIC

Mass communicators are finding themselves increasingly involved in the copyright problems of the music industry, whether they want to be or not. As indicated earlier, there is "compulsory licensing" in the music field, which means anyone can play or perform copyrighted music upon the payment of a fee. But the manner in which those fees are computed and collected has created a number of problems, particularly for broadcasters.

How can a composer or songwriter ever keep track of all the different radio stations and night clubs, for instance, that are using his copyrighted material? Wouldn't it be impossible to monitor every single radio station?

To solve this sort of practical problem, various organizations have been established to represent the interests of music composers, lyricists, and publishers. The most important ones in the United States are the American Society of Composers, Authors and Publishers (ASCAP) and Broadcast Music, Inc. (BMI). Using sampling techniques, these organizations keep track of whose music is being played on the air all over the country. Then ASCAP and BMI both charge each broadcaster for a "blanket license" to cover the royalties for the station's use of all copyrighted music whose owners they represent.

Given the large amount of money involved, there are recurring disputes (and lawsuits) over the collection and distribution of royalties for copyrighted music. But in the end, most broadcasters have little choice but to pay up: music is essential to their programming, and ASCAP and BMI between them control the copyrights to more than 90 percent of the copyrighted music they want to play on the air.

ASCAP and BMI also send representatives out to collect royalties from the owners of night clubs and other business establishments where copyrighted music is played or performed. These agencies have formulas based on such things as the size of the establishment and its business volume to determine the amount that each business has to pay for its "blanket license."

All but the smallest retail stores must pay royalties for the music played in their establishments—even if it involves nothing more than playing a radio. The Supreme Court once ruled that very small businesses are exempt from the obligation to pay royalties to music composers if they simply leave a radio running. That happened in *Twentieth Century Music Corp. v. Aiken* (422 U.S. 151, 1975), a case involving a carry-out fried chicken store with about 1,000 square feet of floor space. However, more recently a federal appellate court ruled that the same exception does not apply to a chain of clothing stores that averaged 3,000 to 4,000 square feet per store (*Sailor Music v. The Gap Stores*, 668 F.2d 84, 1981).

More than one merchant has been forced to stop his employees from playing the radio in order to avoid having to pay royalties to ASCAP and BMI—much to the chagrin of a local broadcaster who was more than happy to have the extra listeners, and who wouldn't receive any of the royalty money collected by ASCAP and BMI anyway. How can it be, some broadcasters wonder, that they have to pay for the right to play music themselves, and then local merchants have to pay again for the right to listen to the same music on the radio?

Rather than pay royalties for the privilege of listening to music on the radio, of course, many business establishments instead buy a "canned" music service, which provides background music on tape for a flat fee that includes the cost of royalty payments to ASCAP and/or BMI.

One irony in this system is that the money collected by ASCAP and BMI goes only to those who write and publish the songs—not to the recording artists who play or sing the songs. Congress has repeatedly declined to give performers a share of the royalties from the use of their music by broadcasters. Congress' rationale is that the on-the-air exposure helps sell more records and tapes, thus benefiting the recording artists.

Once ASCAP, BMI, and other licensing agencies have collected the royalties from broadcasters, business establishments, and others, the money is distributed to copyright owners on the basis of formulas that take into account the amount of air time each copyright owner's material has been receiving. It is assumed that each song's popularity in night clubs and other businesses parallels the song's popularity on the nation's radio stations.

CABLE TELEVISION COPYRIGHT PROBLEMS

Another major feature of the 1976 Copyright Act is a section dealing with the special problems created by cable television (CATV) systems. In fact, one of the major reasons Congress finally passed a new copyright law after years of stalemated deliberations was a pair of U.S. Supreme Court decisions on cable television and copyright law.

In the 1968 case of *Fortnightly v. United Artists* (392 U.S. 390), the Supreme Court had ruled that a cable television system is really nothing more than a sophisticated receiving antenna. Thus, CATV systems were not "performing" the copyrighted programming they picked up off the air, amplified, and delivered to their subscribers' homes for a fee. In so ruling, the Supreme Court exempted CATV systems from any obligation to pay royalties.

Then in a 1974 decision, *Teleprompter v. CBS* (415 U.S. 394), the Supreme Court went even further. It held that CATV systems were still not performing the programming even if they retransmitted it over great distances via microwave relay. Only if they video taped the material rather than delivering it "live" would they be liable to pay royalties to copyright owners, the court ruled.

Alarmed by these two Supreme Court decisions, motion picture and television producers, broadcasters, and others with a stake in the protection of copyrighted works banded together and began lobbying Congress for legislation to establish copyright royalties for cable television systems. They prevailed, and the 1976 Copyright Act was written to require cable systems to pay royalties for all distant signals they import, even if they were already paying a distant station directly for its programming. This particularly affected stations such as WTBS in Atlanta and other "superstations" that offer programming for a nationwide cable audience via satellite. However, the law did not require cable systems to pay royalties for amplifying local television and radio signals and delivering them to their subscribers' homes.

Shortly after the new law went into effect, the new Copyright Royalty Tribunal began its job of setting royalty rates for cable television systems. But broadcasters and program producers quickly became dissatisfied with the rates being established by the tribunal. The rates, they contended, were far too low, and they began lobbying Congress to eliminate compulsory licensing for cable systems altogether. If that were to happen, cable systems would have to negotiate individually for the right to pick up each distant signal, paying whatever royalty the copyright owner wanted to charge. Most cable operators opposed this change in the rules.

Eventually the Copyright Royalty Tribunal drastically increased the rates cable systems had to pay for each distant signal, and the cable systems turned to Congress for relief. They were particularly outraged because the tribunal was lumping all the royalties it collected into a general fund and then apportioning the money among all copyright owners. The money did *not* go directly to the stations whose signals were being picked up by cable systems.

Many cable operators called this arrangement unfair and demanded an end to the so-called "must carry" rules that require them to include all local television stations among their offerings for viewers. That would give them the freedom to offer any mixture of broadcast and non-broadcast programming they wished, simplifying the copyright problem. Broadcasters were as bitterly opposed to that move as cable operators were to the new higher royalties. And, as Chapter 11 explains, this controversy was further complicated by the fact that in 1980 the Federal Communications Commission deregulated cable television, deleting all of its old rules that once restricted the importation of distant signals.

The result of all this was a bitter industry-wide battle over cable television and copyright royalties in the halls of Congress. At this writing, the dispute was far from resolved; the warring parties were far apart on several key issues. Meanwhile, the Copyright Royalty Tribunal was continuing to collect substantial royalties for each distant signal a cable system carried, and many cable systems were cutting back on the number of distant "superstations" they offered to viewers.

NEW TECHNOLOGIES AND COPYRIGHT LAWS

While cable interests, broadcasters, and program producers were battling over cable TV royalties in Congress, another equally intense battle over copyright protection was also being waged on Capitol Hill: the fight over copyrights and new technologies, such as home tape recording. And like the cable copyright dilemma, this battle for new copyright legislation to set up a royalty system for at-home video taping was triggered by a controversial Supreme Court decision.

When video cassette recorders (VCRs) began to gain popularity, motion picture and television producers became alarmed by the ease with which the public could tape programs off the air for later viewing. The producers saw the sale of home video tapes as a lucrative new market, and they felt that market would be jeopardized if consumers could simply tape movies and TV shows off the air for free.

In one of the most eagerly awaited Supreme Court decisions in many years, the court ruled in 1984 that home video taping is *not* a copyright infringement. In *Sony Corp. of America v. Universal City Studios* (104 S.Ct. 774), the court split 5-4 in ruling in favor of the estimated 20 million Americans who had VCRs in their homes at the time of the decision.

Writing for the Supreme Court's majority, Justice John Paul Stevens pointed out that nothing in the Copyright Act specifically prohibits consumers from taping TV shows for later viewing, a practice commonly called "time shifting." Instead, such noncommercial video taping is a "fair use" of copyrighted programming, Stevens wrote in his majority opinion. (The Fair Use Doctrine will be discussed shortly.) Stevens said:

> One may search the Copyright Act in vain for any sign that the elected representatives of millions of people who watch television every day have made it unlawful to copy a program for later viewing at home, or have enacted a flat prohibition against the sale of machines that make such copying possible.

Forecasting the legislative battle that he knew would follow the Supreme Court's decision, Stevens conceded that Congress could "take a fresh look at this new technology just as it so often has examined other innovations in the past. But it is not our job to apply laws that have not yet been written," he added.

In so ruling, the Supreme Court reversed a federal appellate court decision that held private at-home video taping to be a copyright infringement. The lower court suggested that a flat royalty fee could be added to the price of each blank tape and each video recorder to compensate the entertainment industry for the copying that consumers would do.

Critics of the lower court decision pointed out that not all VCRs and blank tapes are used to tape copyrighted TV shows. Thus, they said, a blanket royalty would force many VCR owners to pay for copyright infringements they do not commit. As a result, such a royalty should more accurately be called a "tax" to support the entertainment industry, not a royalty, some contended.

Program producers replied by pointing to the potential for the sale of video tapes that would not be realized if consumers could freely tape TV shows. The industry needs those revenues to produce new and better shows, they said.

In the end, the Supreme Court merely passed the buck to Congress by ruling that at-home video taping was not a copyright infringement, critics suggested. Predictably, both sides launched major lobbying efforts in Congress after the Supreme Court's 1984 decision. But Congress was not anxious to get involved in this politically touchy dispute in an election year. At this writing, proposed legislation to establish a royalty system for private, at-home video taping seemed to be bogged down.

Thus, it remains to be seen whether Congress will ultimately step in and require consumers to pay royalties for blank tapes and VCRs or leave intact the high court's ruling that home video taping is a "fair use."

Meanwhile, other groups of copyright owners were also at work in Congress, seeking to protect their economic interests. A group called "The Coalition to Save America's Music" was lobbying for royalties on blank audio tapes and audio taping equipment—on the ground that consumers are taping copyrighted music from friends' records and tapes (and also taping it directly off the air) instead of buying their own recordings. To no one's surprise, consumer groups responded by pointing to the many other uses for audio recorders besides taping copyrighted music, and argued that flat royalties on audio tapes would be unfair to everyone who uses a tape recorder for other purposes.

Representatives of some book publishers were also lobbying Congress, seeking the right to charge extra fees when books are placed in libraries where many people can read them instead of buying their own personal copies. Like home audio and video taping, the use of libraries cuts into the profits that copyright owners would otherwise realize, they contended.

Librarians, of course, replied that their budgets are hopelessly strained already, and that such added royalties would be a burdensome new tax on knowledge. Libraries, they noted, are not exactly a new invention. The nation's founding fathers knew about libraries when they drafted the first American copyright law in 1790, and they could have set up a royalty system if they thought the fact that libraries let people read books without buying them was unfair to copyright owners.

As all of these issues were debated in the courts, in Congress, in college classrooms, and probably in thousands of other places, some critics of the moves by copyright owners to enhance their profits began wondering where it would all end. Since photocopying machines are also used to copy copyrighted materials, some suggested that it would be just as logical to impose a flat royalty on reams of blank paper as it is to place such a royalty on blank audio and video tapes.

As each new technology develops, it creates new copyright problems, forcing the courts and Congress to adapt age-old legal concepts to situations the founding fathers could never have imagined. It is not easy to balance the rights of copyright owners against the rights of consumers as each new technology tips the scales one way or the other.

Copyright Law and Computers

The mushrooming growth of the personal computer business created still another difficult copyright dilemma in the 1980s. In 1975, a "video display terminal" (VDT) was a gadget that journalists were beginning to see in their newsrooms and that computer professionals used for esoteric applications that the public didn't understand—and didn't want to understand. But by 1985 nearly ten million personal computers had been sold to the general public, and copyrighted computer software was being traded openly at almost every high school in the land. Like video tapes of movies and TV shows, "floppy disks" containing computer programs were being copied by consumers on an enormous scale, prompting copyright owners to look for new ways to control what they saw as a flagrant copyright infringement by the public.

At first, it was not even clear that certain types of computer software could be copyrighted. A computer's "operating system," for example, is a complex pattern of binary numbers (ones and zeros) stored inside an electronic component known as a "read-only memory" (ROM) chip. Because these operating instructions for computers are readable only by the machines themselves and not by humans, some copyright experts questioned whether they could even be covered by copyright law (as opposed to patent law, which is normally what protects the designs of electronic and mechanical devices from infringement).

However, securing a patent is a difficult and time-consuming process, while registering a copyright is easy, as indicated earlier in this chapter. Thus, many computer manufacturers wanted to copyright their computer operating instructions rather than waiting and hoping to secure a patent eventually.

What brought this esoteric legal dilemma into focus was the emergence of the Apple II computer as a popular commodity, a computer for which thousands of programs were written. Few people questioned the rightness of extending copyright protection to these "application programs," programs that make it possible to play video games, do word processing, or solve complex mathematical problems on a personal computer. However, the Franklin Computer Company began making "Apple-compatible" computers, computers that used a basic operating system so similar to the Apple II operating system that the Franklin Ace computers would run programs written for the Apple.

Meanwhile, a number of companies in the Far East also began making Apple-compatible computers, some of them blatant copies of the Apple II's styling and electronic circuitry. Since some of these competing computers were sold for less than half the price of an Apple computer, the Apple Corporation began an aggressive legal campaign to halt the sale of Apple-compatible computers.

The legal rationale for this campaign was that Apple's operating system was a legitimately copyrighted product that no one else could duplicate without permission. Franklin and others defended themselves by pointing out that copyright law had not previously covered "useful devices" like a ROM chip containing computer code. To apply the Copyright Act to such things would be about like letting General Motors copyright the designs of the parts in its cars so no one else could make tires or carburetors that would fit on GM cars. Such things should be patented if they are really novel inventions, but if they are not novel enough to be patented, competitors should be free to copy the designs without fear of a lawsuit, Franklin and other Apple-compatible computer makers argued.

The question of whether a computer's encoded "operating system" could be copyrighted was resolved in two federal appellate court decisions—both decisive victories for Apple. In *Apple Computer, Inc. v. Franklin Computer Corp.* (714 F.2d. 1240), a 1983 ruling of the third circuit U.S. Court of Appeals, the validity of Apple's copyright on its computer operating instructions was upheld. Writing for the court, Judge Dolores Sloriter rejected the argument that a pattern of ones and zeros embedded in a computer chip was not copyrightable. She said copyright protection "is not confined to literature in the nature of Hemingway's *'For Whom the Bell Tolls'*."

The ninth circuit U.S. Court of Appeals ruled in much the same way in a 1984 case, *Apple Computer, Inc. v. Formula International* (725 F.2d 521). In this case, Judge Warren J. Ferguson wrote:

> The Copyright Act extends protection to "original works of authorship fixed in any tangible medium of expression. . . ." The computer program when written embodies expression; never has the Copyright Act required that expression be communicated to a particular audience.

Thus, the federal courts have ruled that Apple can use the Copyright Act to prevent others from making a computer that uses the same basic operating instructions as the Apple II. It remains to be seen whether other companies can write different basic computer operating instructions and still come up with computers that will run all of the same games, educational software, and business programs as the Apple II.

After the *Apple v. Franklin* decision, Franklin entered into a multi-million-dollar settlement with Apple that allowed it to sell its existing inventory of Franklin Ace computers. Franklin chief executive R. Barry Borden responded to the adverse court decision by pointing out that some other personal computer manufacturers—notably IBM—have actually published their basic computer operating instructions and in effect invited others to develop computers that are compatible with theirs. Borden added:

> (Because of IBM's open policies toward its operating system) software companies can be assured a large market for their products and cannot be frozen out by IBM. Computer stores can find alternative sources of products should they not be an IBM dealer or if the product is in limited supply. And the consumer can find variety, such as portable computers and lower-cost versions.

However, later in 1984 the Franklin company filed for the protection of a federal bankruptcy court. Although the Apple lawsuit may not have been the sole cause of Franklin's impending bankruptcy, it was surely a contributing factor.

Whatever eventually happens in the booming and volatile personal computer business, the courts have made it clear that, like a novel, a movie, or a work of art, the pattern of ones and zeros that tell a computer how to compute can be copyrighted and thus denied to competing manufacturers. Once again, the courts have had to adapt the Copyright Act to a technology not envisioned when the Copyright Act was written. Given that the present Copyright Act was written in 1976, it is amazing how many times the courts have had to do this to cover technologies not envisioned way back then.

THE FAIR USE DILEMMA

As new technologies have abruptly appeared on the scene to confound copyright lawyers and consumers alike, the traditional Fair Use Doctrine has been repeatedly called on to help resolve these new copyright problems. The Fair Use Doctrine itself deserves some explanation at this point.

Basically, the Fair Use Doctrine is a legal concept that was originally created by the courts to allow some copying of copyrighted works in spite of the seemingly absolute rules against it in the 1909 Copyright Act. The courts recognized that such things as quoting brief passages for scholarly criticism (or satire) were reasonable and did not interfere with the copyright owner's financial return.

The 1976 Copyright Act specifically recognized the Fair Use Doctrine and established guidelines for determining which uses of copyrighted works are fair ones. Congress even addressed the tough issue of photocopying and attempted to establish some basic rules in that area.

To decide if a given use of a copyrighted work is a fair use, the Copyright Act says these four factors must be considered:

1. the purpose and character of the use, including whether it is for profit or for a nonprofit educational purpose;
2. the nature of the copyrighted work;
3. the percentage of the total work that is used;
4. the effect the use will have on the value or profitmaking potential of the original work.

These guidelines are vague and general; a number of court tests will be needed to determine just what constitutes a fair use in various areas. Meanwhile, there have been some voluntary agreements between representatives of copyright owners and various other interests (such as education) on what constitutes a fair use.

For instance, as Congress was completing its revision of copyright law in 1976, representatives of educators, authors, and publishers met to decide what would constitute a fair use of a copyrighted work in a classroom. Under their agreement, teachers are permitted to photocopy as much as a chapter of a book, an article from a newspaper or magazine, a short story, essay, or poem, and charts, graphs, drawings, or similar materials—but only for their own use.

For classroom use, teachers are permitted to reproduce one copy per student provided the work copied is sufficiently brief (usually under 2,500 words for prose, 250 words for poetry) if the original copyright notice is retained, and if the copying is a spontaneous one-time activity. The teacher is required to ask for permission (or buy copies of the copyrighted work) before using it a second time. There are also limits on how many times during a single semester a teacher may distribute classroom sets of copyrighted works, and such copying may not ever be a substitute for requiring the students to buy either an anthology or a "consumable" item (such as a workbook or a test).

This agreement does not carry the force of law; a court would be free to rule that more (or less) copying than this constitutes a fair use. These guidelines are mentioned in the legislative history of the 1976 Copyright Act, but not in the act itself. The act itself vaguely acknowledges that teachers have a right to make copies for their classes under the Fair Use Doctrine. However, another provision of the law exempts teachers from copyright liability when they perform or display copyrighted works as part of their teaching activities—unless the copy they perform or display was itself pirated (as it would be if a teacher showed an illegally copied motion picture or television program).

The Copyright Act is somewhat more specific in dealing with the question of photocopying by libraries because an important court decision had allowed wholesale reproduction of copyrighted works by libraries—something Congress wished to curtail. That case (*Williams and Wilkins v. U.S.*, 487 F.2d 1345, 420 U.S. 376) was initiated by a publishing house whose medical journals were being photocopied on a massive scale by federally-funded medical libraries so the libraries could avoid purchasing additional copies. The publishing house lost its case: a federal court said the dissemination of medical knowledge was so important that this copying was a fair use. The case was appealed to the U.S. Supreme Court, but because the high court divided 4-4 (with one justice not participating), the judgment of the lower court stood.

Alarmed at the *Williams and Wilkins* case, publishers lobbied in Congress to win restrictions on library photocopying in the new Copyright Act. The result was another compromise, with the rules for photocopying by libraries spelled out in considerable detail. Basically, the law says it is a fair use for a librarian to make copies of damaged or deteriorating works that cannot be replaced at a reasonable cost, and to provide single copies to those who request them, provided the request is for only a small portion of a work. An entire work that cannot be purchased at a reasonable price may also be copied at a patron's request.

These rules contain a number of other qualifications and restrictions that will not be summarized here. Significantly, however, they apply only to copying done by library staff members, not copying by members of the public who use coin-operated machines. The Copyright Act exempts librarians from liability for copyright infringements by unsupervised library patrons, as long as a warning about infringements is posted near the self-service copy machine.

Obviously, the law on photocopying was written in this fashion in tacit recognition that there is simply no way to prevent private individuals from engaging in coin-operated infringements—just as there is no way to prevent private audio or video taping of copyrighted materials that are broadcast.

In several other areas, the rules on fair use are equally complex, unsettled, and in some instances unenforceable. And for the mass media, another important problem is the clash between copyright law and the public's right to know. Two court decisions on the application of the Fair Use Doctrine in such situations will illustrate the issues involved.

One of the best-known tests of the Fair Use Doctrine came in a 1966 federal appellate court decision, *Rosemont Enterprises v. Random House* (366 F.2d 303). In that case, Rosemont (a company set up by billionaire industrialist Howard Hughes) was trying to prevent publication of a biography about Hughes, who intensely disliked publicity.

Rosemont learned that the biographer was relying heavily on information gleaned from several old *Look* magazine articles about Hughes. The company quickly bought the copyright on those articles and then sought an injunction to prevent publication of the new biography as an infringement of the copyrighted articles.

A trial court ruled in Rosemont's favor, but the federal appellate court reversed that decision, holding that a copyright owner has no right to, in effect, copyright history. The appellate court noted that the magazine articles were only a fraction of the length of the book and that there had been extensive independent research for the book. The court brushed aside the argument that the book, like the original copyrighted magazine articles, was aimed at a popular market and was not merely an instance of scholarly criticism (something that earlier court decisions had recognized as a fair use).

Ultimately, the court ruled that there is a legitimate public interest in the doings of the rich and powerful, and that this interest outweighs the copyright consideration in a case such as this one. Random House was allowed to publish its book about Howard Hughes without incurring liability for a copyright infringement.

Another fair use case involving an issue of even greater public interest arose a few years later, *Time, Inc. v. Bernard Geis Associates* (293 F.Supp. 130, S.D.N.Y. 1968). That case involved an amateur photographer's film of the assassination of President John F. Kennedy in 1963. The highly unusual and revealing film was purchased by Time, Inc., and published in *Life* magazine—and, of course, it was copyrighted.

Later, author Thomas Thompson was publishing a book advocating a new theory about the assassination, *Six Seconds in Dallas*. Bernard Geis, the book publisher, offered to pay *Life* a royalty equal to the entire net profits from the book in return for permission to use *Life*'s still photographs made from the copyrighted film, which was central to Thompson's theory. *Life* refused.

The book publisher then hired an artist to make charcoal sketches from the copyrighted photographs, and these appeared in the book. Time, Inc., sued for copyright infringement. The federal court said the use of charcoal drawings instead of the photographs themselves did not eliminate the copyright infringement, but the court also pointed to the legitimate public interest in the assassination of a president and said this was a fair use of the copyrighted pictures. To rule otherwise would prevent a full public discussion of the controversial issues raised by President Kennedy's assassination.

Despite these and other court decisions, the Fair Use Doctrine remains a vague and unsettled aspect of copyright law. At one extreme, there is little question that journalists may make use of information in copyrighted works to develop news stories, as long as they do not plagiarize the copyrighted description and do conduct some independent research.

On the other hand, it is clearly not a fair use when someone takes a work that is primarily intended as entertainment rather than news and heavily borrows from it, cutting into its market potential. But between these two extremes, there are a variety of uses of copyrighted works that may or may not be fair uses and must be adjudicated on a case by case basis.

UNFAIR COMPETITION: AN ALTERNATIVE TO COPYRIGHT

Earlier in this chapter we pointed out that news, factual information, and ideas cannot be copyrighted. However, we also noted that there is another kind of law that may prevent one news medium from systematically pirating its news from another. That legal action is called "unfair competition" or "misappropriation," and it has often been used as a supplement to copyright law. Unlike copyright, which is now exclusively governed by a federal statutory law, unfair competition is a tort action that has developed primarily through court decisions. There is no federal unfair competition statute and few states have enacted statutory laws in this field even today.

Unfair competition was recognized as a separate legal action largely as a result of a 1918 U.S. Supreme Court decision that came to be regarded as a classic ruling: *International News Service v. Associated Press* (248 U.S. 215). The case arose because INS, owned by the Hearst newspaper chain, consistently appropriated AP stories (this was possible because some Hearst papers were also AP members) and distributed them to INS customers as if they were INS stories. The Supreme Court acknowledged that the news cannot be copyrighted, but it ruled that no business may purloin its basic commodity from a competitor, "reaping where it has not sown," to use the court's language, which was a paraphrase of a passage from the Bible.

Following this Supreme Court precedent, a number of other courts have ruled similarly in similar situations, creating a new common law legal action for misappropriation. For instance, in 1963 the Pennsylvania Supreme Court decided a very similar case in the same way. In that case (*Pottstown Daily News Publishing Company v. Pottstown Broadcasting*, 192 A.2d 657), the court found unfair competition where a radio station had been pirating its news from the local newspaper on an ongoing basis.

However, serious doubts were raised about the continuing usefulness of unfair competition as an alternative to copyright law by two 1964 U.S. Supreme Court decisions, *Sears, Roebuck and Co. v. Stiffel* (376 U.S. 225) and *Compco v. Day-Brite Lighting* (376 U.S. 234). These were unfair competition cases involving mechanical designs that could not be patented rather than news that could not be copyrighted, but the court's language was alarmingly sweeping.

The Supreme Court said the states simply could not create alternative forms of protection to fill in the gaps left by copyright and patent law. "When an article is unprotected by a patent or a copyright, *state* law may not forbid others to copy that article," the Supreme Court said (emphasis added).

In effect, what the Supreme Court seemed to hold was that the federal government had preempted the entire field of patent and copyright law, denying any role in this area to the states. And as already noted, even if the federal government did not preempt copyright law then, the new Copyright Act makes it clear that Congress intended to preempt copyright law in 1976.

Thus, some legal scholars have concluded that there is simply no such thing as unfair competition law as an alternative to copyright protection any more. However, other legal scholars disagree, contending that unfair competition protects subject matter that is so far beyond the scope of copyright law that it was not preempted by the new Copyright Act. To back up their contention, these scholars point to a 1973 U.S. Supreme Court decision (*Goldstein v. California*, 412 U.S. 546) that upheld a California law against record piracy at a time when copyright law did not cover sound recordings, despite the defendant's contention that the federal government had preempted the field under the *Sears* and *Compco* decisions.

Moreover, the record of Congress' deliberations on unfair competition during the revision of the Copyright Act seems to imply that Congress did not intend to abolish unfair competition, but the record is so ambiguous that no one is really certain.

This is an issue on which thousands of words have been written in legal journals, and yet it is still far from being resolved. Obviously, additional court decisions are needed to clarify the role of unfair competition, if any, as a legal action in the 1980s. However, it seems likely a state court would be willing to entertain an unfair competition suit today, given an outrageous case of systematic news piracy that would otherwise go unpunished. Journalists should continue to assume that they may not consistently purloin their news from a competitor, regardless of the very muddled state of unfair competition law today.

TRADEMARKS

Another area of intellectual property law that fills a gap in copyright protection is trademark and tradename law. Unlike unfair competition, however, the law of trademarks unquestionably remains viable today—on both the state and federal level.

There is a federal trademark law, the Lanham Trademark Act. But unlike the Copyright Act, it is nonexclusive. That is, it does not preempt state trademark laws. In fact, many states have their own trademark statutes, and all states recognize at least some kind of inherent right of a business to adopt a name and deny that name to imitators.

All of these laws govern the short phrases, logos, and names under which businesses operate and market their products. An understanding of this area of law is especially important for a student planning a career in advertising or public relations.

Basically, the Lanham Act sets up a first-come, first-served registration system for trademarks. When a business wants to begin using a trademark, the first step is to conduct a search to see if any competitor or potential competitor is using a similar name. Before seeking a federal trademark, most businesses (or their lawyers) pay a commercial research firm to find out whether their chosen name is available by searching the voluminous files of past trademark registrations (and other sources of information on trademark usage). If no one else has registered the name, the business initiates a registration and filing procedure not unlike that set up by the Copyright Act. As part of the registration process, proposed trademarks are published and rival businesses may challenge the registration of a new trademark if they wish.

What sort of names may and may not be registered under the Lanham Act? Generally, any name, phrase, or symbol that distinguishes a firm's goods or services may be registered, but there are some exceptions. Flags and symbols for cities, states, and countries cannot be registered, for instance. Nor may the name, portrait, or signature of a living person be registered—except under circumstances where the name or likeness has already become distinctively associated with a firm.

In addition, purely geographic names and descriptive terms (for instance "first rate," "high quality," "blue ribbon," and "A-1") are often unregisterable. One reason for this rule is that most popular names, descriptive terms, and geographic names are so widely used that no one may gain a monopoly on their use nationally in connection with trade. This is not to say you can't open a business and call it "A-1 Auto Repair" or "Blue Ribbon Trophy Company," but you'll have a tough time getting it registered nationally as your exclusive trademark. And if there is already another firm using the same or a similar name in your area, you may also face a lawsuit under the common law or equity procedures to be described shortly.

Because there have been so many different businesses seeking distinctive trademarks for so many years, the surest way to get a new trademark registered nationally is to come up with a new coined word. Several firms have done that over the years: Exxon, Citgo, and Kodak, for example.

Assuming a business gets its proposed trademark past the hurdles of registration, the firm may use the trademark in various ways. The name may appear on products, in advertising, and on the corporate letterhead. The fact that the trademark is registered under the Lanham Act is indicated by the little "R" in a circle after the word or phrase. However, trademarks may also be indicated in other ways. For instance, when registration has not yet been secured, a firm may indicate that it claims a word or phrase as a trademark by placing "TM" in small letters after the name.

Once registered under the Lanham Act, a trademark must be renewed after five years. Thereafter, a renewal every 20 years is required. There is no limit to the number of times a trademark may be renewed. Unlike a copyright, a trademark can be maintained as private property indefinitely.

However, a trademark may also be abandoned or lost. Under the Lanham Act, failure to use a trademark for two years creates a presumption that it has been abandoned. Acquiescence in allowing others to use your trademark in a generic way can also result in its loss, which explains why trademarks such as "Xerox" and "Coca-Cola" are so vigorously defended by their owners. Should those words be allowed to become generally descriptive of all photocopying or all cola-type beverages, the owners could lose their exclusive rights to these names, as did the former owners of ex-trademarks such as "aspirin" and "linoleum."

Companies do various things to avoid losing their trademarks through common usage as generic words. For instance, some companies buy advertising in magazines read by journalists to admonish writers and editors about the correct usage of their trademarks. The Xerox Corporation, for example, reminds journalists to capitalize "Xerox," and to use it only as a noun referring to a Xerox-brand product. Never use the word as a verb, the company insists. And journalists who fail to heed this sort of advice may receive pointed letters from a trademark owner's lawyers—all as part of the company's effort to demonstrate that it is not acquiescing or accepting the generic use of its trademark.

Although federal registration of a trademark is obviously desirable if it can be secured, a person or business that has used a name over a period of time acquires some special rights with or without federal registration. In fact, Lanham Act registration is unavailable to purely local businesses, although most states have their own registration systems under which local trademarks may be protected. But as already noted, the courts will step in to prevent a new business from creating public confusion by imitating the name or trademark of an old, established one, whether the trademark is registered or not.

Under the principles of common law and equity trademark protection, the key issue in such a lawsuit is whether a word or phrase has acquired a "secondary meaning" in connection with a certain product or service. There is a secondary meaning if the words connote something more than their dictionary definition because of the commercial usage. For instance, the word "playboy" has one meaning in the dictionary, but when applied to a magazine or a chain of nightclubs, it has a special meaning beyond that.

If a word or phrase is found to have a "secondary meaning" to a substantial number of people, no one else may use the name for a similar kind of business in that locality without creating confusion and misleading the public. With or without a trademark registration under federal or state law, the courts will act to protect such a tradename. No business is entitled to pass off its product or service as someone else's. In fact, the principles of trademark law stand in sharp contrast to copyright law on this point. If a literary work is published but not copyrighted, it falls into the public domain—it thereafter belongs to everyone. But the mere use of a tradename, without any registration or claim of a registration, gradually gives one ownership rights. Even if someone else comes along and registers the name as a trademark first, the original user of the name may prevail in court. The goal is to prevent a newcomer from fraudulently trading on the goodwill of an established business. This is the overriding objective of the common law of trademarks, of state trademark laws, and of the federal Lanham Act.

A Summary of Copyright Law

WHAT MAY BE COPYRIGHTED?

All types of literary and artistic works, including fiction and non-fiction prose, poetry, scripts, musical scores and lyrics, photographs, motion pictures, television and radio productions, recordings, maps, paintings, sculptures, advertising layouts, etc. may be copyrighted.

WHAT MAY NOT BE COPYRIGHTED?

Factual and historical information (including news) may not be copyrighted, although a *description* of a news event (or a news production) may be copyrighted. In addition, typeface designs, ideas, processes, inventions, and trademarks may not be copyrighted (but note that inventions may be patented and trademarks may be protected under state and federal trademark laws).

HOW DOES ONE SECURE A COPYRIGHT?

To secure a copyright simply include the copyright notice (e.g., "© 1985 by John Author") in a prominent place in the work. Whether the work is published or unpublished, doing that invokes the protection of the Copyright Act.

IS IT NECESSARY TO REGISTER A COPYRIGHT?

No, your copyright is valid without registration. However, if you register before an infringement occurs, you have more legal rights in the event of an infringement than you would otherwise—including the right to win statutory damages and your lawyer's fees should a lawsuit be necessary. And in any case, you must register before filing a lawsuit.

HOW DOES ONE REGISTER A COPYRIGHT?

To register a copyright, secure the proper forms from the U.S. Copyright Office, Washington, DC 20559, complete the forms, and then return the forms with two copies of the work and the $10 filing fee.

WHAT DOES A COPYRIGHT GIVE YOU?

The copyright owner has the right to reproduce, perform, rewrite, or display the work for the duration of the copyright, which normally runs for the author's life plus 50 years. He/she may sell any or all of these rights. In some fields (notably music) anyone may perform the copyrighted work upon payment of the prescribed royalties (this is called compulsory licensing).

WHAT ABOUT FAIR USES?

The Fair Use Doctrine allows anyone to make certain limited uses of copyrighted works, such as quoting from or photocopying a small portion of the work. Whether a given use is a fair one is determined by weighing several factors, including the effect of the use on the owner's profits and whether the purportedly fair use is for commercial or for nonprofit educational purposes.

7

FAIR TRIAL-FREE PRESS CONFLICTS

The Sixth Amendment guarantees a person accused of a crime the right to a speedy and public trial *before an impartial jury.* However, the First Amendment gives the mass media the right to report the news, including crime news that may well prejudice an entire community against a person who has not yet stood trial and is still presumed innocent by the law.

In the last three decades there have been many confrontations between the nation's courts and the news media over this problem. In attempting to control prejudicial publicity and assure fair trials for defendants in sensational cases, the courts have taken a variety of steps that seemingly interfere with the media's First Amendment freedoms. One of the most important legal problems for the mass media in recent years has been this conflict with the nation's courts.

On the one hand, some judges and attorneys contend there is an overabundance of crime news in the media—and that such news is so sensationalized that celebrated defendants may be denied an impartial jury. The jury is supposed to consider only the defendant's guilt or innocence in the specific case before the court, not whether he or she is of high moral character generally. Thus, a suspect's past record is not ordinarily considered relevant evidence. But sometimes the media report inflammatory information about a suspect's past, information that will never be admissible as evidence when the trial actually occurs. Moreover, the media may report unsubstantiated details of an arrest or unverified test results. Or they may reveal the existence of a "confession" that will not be admitted into evidence in court because it was given under duress. As a result, it may be very difficult to find unprejudiced jurors. Lawyers and judges sometimes feel that drastic measures are necessary to control what they see as irresponsible journalism that interferes with criminal defendants' Constitutional rights.

On the other hand, representatives of the news media cite the important role of the press in keeping the public informed about modern society—a society with a high crime rate. In addition, the press performs an important watchdog role in monitoring the administration of justice. Covering the criminal justice system is an important function of the mass media, journalists point out.

Moreover, the media's right to cover the news is constitutionally protected. When the courts attempt to curtail the reporting of crime news by the media, the result is a conflict between two Constitutional rights: freedom of the press and the right of the accused to a trial before an unprejudiced jury.

This chapter examines several aspects of the free press-fair trial controversy, discussing the various ways the courts have attempted to protect defendants' rights and the resulting constitutional conflicts.

PUBLICITY AND PREJUDICE

The first question raised by the fair trial-free press conflict is whether media publicity really influences jurors. Does the judiciary really have any empirical evidence to prove that jurors who read news accounts of a case cannot be impartial?

Social scientists have attempted to study this question, but it is not easy to research. For one thing, it is difficult to duplicate an actual trial under controlled conditions. There are numerous variables that may render mock trial experiments invalid. And it is difficult to study the behavior of participants in actual trials without interfering with the judicial process. Because of these and other problems, the results of research on jury prejudice are inconclusive. Findings have gone both ways: some studies have found that media publicity does have a significant prejudicial impact on jurors while other studies have found that it does not.

Although the research on how media publicity affects jurors is inconclusive, judges often assume that intense news coverage does produce jury prejudice. Certainly the media have covered some criminal cases in a sensational fashion, lending credibility to those who argue for restrictions on the media in this area. A look at several major cases will illustrate the problems and show how the U.S. Supreme Court has dealt with them.

EARLY CASES

One of the early cases that dramatized the problem of prejudicial publicity was the 1935 trial of Bruno Hauptmann, the alleged kidnapper and murderer of celebrated aviator Charles Lindbergh's young son. Although Hauptmann's trial didn't take place until nearly two and one-half years after the kidnapping, the courtroom was so jammed with reporters and photographers that it was impossible to conduct orderly proceedings at times. There was a great deal of inflammatory publicity.

After Hauptmann was convicted and executed for the crime, a Special Committee on Cooperation between Press, Radio and Bar was established to recommend standards of publicity in judicial proceedings. In its final report, the committee said the Hauptmann trial was "the most spectacular and depressing example of improper publicity and professional misconduct ever presented to the people of the United States in a criminal trial."

At least partly in response to the Hauptmann trial, the American Bar Association in 1937 added Canon 35 to its recommended Canons of Judicial Ethics. That rule prohibited broadcasting and taking photographs in the courtroom:

> Proceedings in court should be conducted with fitting dignity and decorum. The taking of photographs in the courtroom, during sessions of the court or recesses between sessions, and the broadcasting of court proceedings are calculated to detract from the essential dignity of the proceedings, degrade the court and create misconceptions with respect thereto in the mind of the public and should not be permitted.

Canon 35 was later amended to specifically prohibit television coverage and also made applicable to areas adjacent to courtrooms. In the early 1970s, it was revised again and incorporated into Rule 3A(7) of the ABA Code of Judicial Conduct, which replaced the old ABA Canons. At that point it permitted some television coverage of court proceedings, but only with the consent of all parties, and only then for use in educational institutions after all direct appeals were exhausted (which could be years later). As we will explain shortly, Rule 3A(7) was eventually rewritten to allow much more extensive television coverage, but before that happened, journalists fought a long and frustrating battle for access to the nation's trial courtrooms.

These ABA rules, of course, were merely recommendations to the state and federal court systems; they were not mandatory. However, by the 1960s every state except Colorado and Texas had adopted rules forbidding most camera and broadcast coverage of its court proceedings. And in 1946, radio broadcasts and photography were prohibited in federal courts by Rule 53 of the Federal Rules of Criminal Procedure. That rule was also later expanded to forbid television broadcasting and to prohibit photography or broadcasting in the "environs of the courtroom."

THE *ESTES* DECISION

Stunned by these rules, broadcast journalists and photographers wondered why the First Amendment shouldn't protect their right to cover trials. If the rules permit print journalists to bring their notebooks into court while prohibiting the basic tools used by electronic journalists, isn't that a form of discrimination? The U.S. Supreme Court addressed these issues in an important 1965 decision, *Estes v. Texas* (381 U.S. 532).

The case involved a Texas grain dealer with political connections, Billie Sol Estes. Estes was convicted of swindling a group of investors, but his conviction was reversed by the U.S. Supreme Court because two days of the preliminary hearing and part of the trial were televised under Texas' highly unusual court rules permitting it.

The television coverage of the pretrial hearing was obtrusive: there were bright lights, bulky cameras, and cables trailing around the courtroom. Before the actual trial, the judge imposed some restrictions on the media, and the TV cameras were confined to a booth in the back of the room. However, it was still obvious to everyone in the courtroom that the cameras were there.

In reversing Estes' conviction, five Supreme Court justices said the television coverage had denied him a fair trial. Four of them seemed to be saying a fair trial was never possible if television is permitted in a criminal trial. However, the fifth member of the majority, Justice John Marshall Harlan, wrote a separate opinion in which he agreed that Estes had been denied a fair trial but suggested that television might not always prevent a fair trial in cases less celebrated than this one.

Thus, the *Estes* case is remembered for the holding that television coverage is prejudicial in certain cases—but not necessarily in all criminal cases.

Justice Tom Clark, writing for the court, said that televising trials most likely would have an impact on jurors, witnesses, lawyers, the judge, and the defendant. Therefore, he concluded, television injected an irrelevant factor into court proceedings that might increase chances of prejudicing the jurors.

As for the argument that the electronic media were being unfairly discriminated against, Chief Justice Earl Warren pointed out that print journalists were not permitted to bring their typewriters or printing presses into court. He said the rules were fair and nondiscriminatory as long as broadcasters were free to have their reporters cover the proceedings and report back to viewers.

However, Justice Clark recognized that future technological advances might permit less obtrusive coverage of a trial. In the years since the *Estes* decision, broadcast technology has indeed advanced. Thanks to solid-state electronics, cameras have become far more compact than they were in 1965. Moreover, modern cameras are sensitive enough to permit television coverage with less light than was required then.

By 1984 at least 40 states had recognized these technological changes and authorized some form of television or still photographic coverage of court proceedings. However, a number of these states permitted television coverage of criminal trials only with the consent of the defendant, something that was rarely given. For instance, in Colorado—a state that allowed broadcast coverage of court proceedings long before most other states—about 80 percent of all requests for live coverage were denied in the 1970s, usually because of objections from the defense. Nevertheless, at least 10 states permitted television coverage of criminal trials without the defense's consent by 1980. Clearly, it was time for a new Supreme Court decision applying the *Estes* standards to the new circumstances.

THE *CHANDLER* DECISION

In 1981 the Supreme Court responded to the changing circumstances and handed down a new rule on television coverage in the nation's courtrooms in *Chandler v. Florida* (449 U.S. 560).

The *Chandler* case resulted from the convictions of two police officers accused of a restaurant burglary in which they allegedly used their squad car and two-way radios. At the time of their trial in 1977, Florida was engaged in a one-year experiment with cameras in the courtroom, and much of the trial was videotaped by a television camera crew. The defendants objected to the television coverage, but their objections were consistently overruled. (The Florida rule permitted television coverage even if the defense objected.)

The defendants, Noel Chandler and Robert Granger, appealed their conviction, contending that the television coverage denied them a fair trial. The Florida appellate courts rejected their appeals, but the U.S. Supreme Court agreed to hear the case.

The Supreme Court ruled against Chandler and Granger. Voting 8-0, the justices held that the presence of television cameras does not inherently violate a defendant's Constitutional right to a fair trial, although they left open the possibility that a defendant could show that his or her rights were violated in a specific case. Thus, the Supreme Court refused to overturn Florida's rules allowing television coverage of trials even without the defendant's consent. The court said that the states were free to adopt such rules if they wished.

Writing for the majority, Chief Justice Warren Burger said:

An absolute Constitutional ban on broadcast coverage of trials cannot be justified simply because there is a danger that, in some cases, prejudicial broadcast accounts of pretrial and trial events may impair the ability of jurors to decide the issue of guilt or innocence uninfluenced by extraneous matter.

However, the Burger opinion made it clear that criminal defendants are entitled to challenge their convictions if they can show that media coverage actually prejudiced the jury:

(The) appropriate safeguard against such prejudice is the defendant's right to demonstrate that the media's coverage of the case—be it printed or broadcast—compromised the ability of the particular jury that heard the case to adjudicate it fairly.

Chief Justice Burger cited the dramatic changes in broadcast technology between the time of the *Estes* trial and 1981. Burger made it clear that *Estes* had not prohibited all experimentation with cameras in the courtroom. He noted that Chandler and Granger had not shown that their right to a fair trial was actually jeopardized by the broadcast coverage.

As a result of the *Chandler* decision, the states that already allowed television coverage or still photography in their courtrooms were free to continue doing so, and a number of additional states authorized electronic and photographic courtroom coverage after that. Some of the states that previously permitted cameras in their courtrooms only with the consent of defendants dropped that requirement after the *Chandler* ruling was announced.

Obviously, the *Chandler* decision was a victory for the media, but it is important to remember what it did and did not say. It simply said there is no Constitutional prohibition on cameras in the courtroom. It did *not* say the broadcast media have any special right of access to the nation's courts. Rather, *Chandler* said that the states are free to allow cameras in court if they choose to do so. Even then, when a particular defendant can show that media coverage denied him a fair trial, he is entitled to a new trial.

As we said earlier, in 1982 the American Bar Association recognized the new trend and revised Rule 3A(7), which had urged the states to impose severe restrictions on broadcast and photographic coverage of criminal trials.

As rewritten, the rule says judges may allow photographic coverage if certain safeguards are met. It specifies that the coverage must be "consistent with the right of the parties to a fair trial" and must be handled so that cameras "will be unobtrusive, will not distract trial participants, and will not otherwise interfere with the administration of justice."

The ABA's policy change had no effect in federal courts, where camera coverage was still barred at this writing. In 1983, 28 media organizations joined to petition the U.S. Judicial Conference to reconsider its ban on broadcast and photographic coverage in federal courts. In 1984, the Judicial Conference rejected this petition and reaffirmed the ban.

In the meantime, a U.S. Court of Appeals has rejected a First Amendment-based challenge to the ban on cameras in federal courts. In *U.S. v. Hastings* (695 F.2d 1278, 1982), the appellate court held that the Supreme Court's rulings on public access to the courts, which will be discussed shortly, in no way invalidated the federal rules. The *Hastings* case involved a federal judge who was on trial for bribery, and who asked for broadcast coverage of his own trial. His wish was not granted.

Nevertheless, the mass media are gradually winning the right to take cameras and television equipment into state courtrooms from coast to coast, and will most likely gain access to the federal courts eventually. The media have made great progress in this area since their defeat in the *Estes* case two decades ago.

PREJUDICIAL PUBLICITY AND FAIR TRIALS

Just as the Supreme Court has recognized that televising court proceedings may sometimes interfere with a defendant's rights, the high court has also

acted against sensational news reporting in cases where it seemingly prevented a fair trial.

As the ABA's ethical guidelines on media publicity gained acceptance in
the 1950s, various state and federal courts began to take new precautions on
behalf of defendants in highly publicized cases. Finally, the U.S. Supreme
Court took the drastic step of reversing a state court murder conviction on the
grounds of prejudicial publicity in the 1961 case of *Irvin v. Dowd* (366 U.S.
717). The nation's highest court had previously expressed concern about the
effect of publicity on trials (see *Shepherd v. Florida*, 341 U.S. 50, and *Stroble
v. California*, 343 U.S. 181) and it had reversed a federal conviction due to
prejudicial publicity in the 1959 case of *Marshall v. U.S.* (360 U.S. 310), but
Irvin is especially remembered because of the seriousness of the crime
involved, the dramatic nature of the publicity, and the fact that this was the
first state conviction reversed mainly due to prejudicial publicity.

The case involved Leslie Irvin, who was convicted of murdering six
people in the vicinity of Evansville, Indiana. Irvin had been arrested on
suspicion of burglary and writing bad checks about one month after the
murders. However, the county prosecutor—under political pressure to come
up with a suspect—issued press releases asserting that "Mad Dog Irvin" had
confessed the murders. Since the murders themselves had received extensive
news media coverage, the "confession" led to a barrage of publicity. Other
stories focused on Irvin's criminal past, revealing much information that
would never be admitted into evidence at the trial.

The defense was granted a change of venue (a change in the location of
the trial), but only to a nearby county where there had also been extensive
publicity about the crimes and "confession." A second request for a change of
venue was denied because Indiana law allowed only one change of venue.
Subsequently, of 430 prospective jurors examined by the prosecution and
defense attorneys, 370 admitted they had formed some opinion about Irvin's
guilt. And of the 12 jurors finally seated to hear the case, eight admitted they
believed Irvin was guilty before hearing any evidence in court but said they
could be impartial anyway. Because they claimed they would be impartial,
the defense could not show cause to have them discharged as jurors, and
Irvin's lawyer had long since used up all of his peremptory challenges
(requests to discharge prospective jurors without having to prove they would
not be impartial).

With this backdrop, the U.S. Supreme Court reviewed the case more
than five years after Irvin was originally convicted and sentenced to death.
The court found that Irvin had not received a fair trial and thus set aside his
conviction. Irvin was eventually retried, convicted, and sentenced to life in
prison.

Two years later, pretrial publicity again resulted in the U.S. Supreme
Court reversing a murder conviction. Wilbert Rideau was arrested and
charged with robbing a bank and killing a bank employee in Louisiana.
During a jailhouse interrogation session conducted by the local sheriff, he
confessed the crimes. The session was filmed and the film was later shown on

local television three times. The Supreme Court held that it was a denial of Rideau's right to a fair trial not to grant him a change of venue after the people "had been exposed repeatedly and in depth to the spectacle of Rideau personally confessing in detail to the crimes. . . ." The court said his real trial occurred on television, not in the courtroom (*Rideau v. Louisiana*, 373 U.S. 723, 1963).

The *Sheppard* Decision

Finally, in 1966 the U.S. Supreme Court handed down the ruling on prejudicial media publicity that has come to be regarded as the landmark decision in this area, *Sheppard v. Maxwell* (384 U.S. 333). Dr. Sam Sheppard, a socially prominent Cleveland, Ohio, osteopath, was involved in one of the most famous criminal trials of his generation, a case that was the subject of a television documentary and a long-running fictionalized television series.

Sheppard's pregnant wife was murdered at their lakefront home in 1954, and "Dr. Sam" said he struggled in the darkness with the assailant, a hairy figure who escaped to the lake. Within a few weeks, the local papers were editorially demanding Dr. Sam's arrest and conviction. The media literally took over the courtroom during his trial, and at one point the jurors' home telephone numbers were published in a gesture certain to build pressure on them for a guilty verdict. The press reported all sorts of "evidence" that was not admitted at the trial.

Sheppard was convicted, and his conviction was affirmed by the Ohio courts. The U.S. Supreme Court declined to review the case at that point.

However, when the Supreme Court took a new interest in the free press-fair trial problem in the 1960s, Sheppard's lawyers again asked the Supreme Court to review the case. This time the Supreme Court did so, and in 1966—12 years after his original trial—Dr. Sam had his conviction reversed and was granted a new trial (at which he was later acquitted).

In an 8-1 opinion written by Justice Clark, the court ruled that "the state trial judge had not fulfilled his duty to protect Sheppard from the inherently prejudicial publicity which saturated the community." The Supreme Court went on to instruct trial judges as to what they must do to ensure a fair trial. The court warned that failure to follow these safeguards would result in more reversals of convictions.

The Supreme Court's *Sheppard* decision suggested a number of specific things the nation's trial judges could do to protect defendants from sensational media publicity. The court said judges should do some or all of the following things to control publicity and protect defendant's rights:

1. adopt rules to curtail in-court misconduct by reporters;
2. issue protective orders (sometimes called "gag" orders) to control out-of-court statements by trial participants;
3. grant a "continuance" to postpone the trial until community prejudice has had time to subside;

4. grant a change of venue to a place where there has been less prejudicial publicity;
5. admonish the jury to disregard the media publicity about the case; or
6. sequester the jury (i.e., confine them in a place where they will not be able to read about the trial in newspapers or hear about it on radio or television).

In the years following *Sheppard,* judges tried all of these things to control publicity. Some also began to do things the Supreme Court didn't recommend in the Sheppard case, such as closing their courtrooms to the press and public and holding preliminary proceedings—or entire trials—in secret. These judicial actions raised new Constitutional issues.

"Gag" Orders and the First Amendment

Of all these remedies for prejudicial publicity, the one that generated the most controversy involved the suppression of information about the trial. Justice Clark wrote:

> Neither prosecutors, counsel for defense, the accused, witnesses, court staff nor enforcement officers coming under the jurisdiction of the court should be permitted to frustrate its function. Collaboration between counsel and the press as to information affecting the fairness of a criminal trial is not only subject to regulation, but is highly censurable and worthy of disciplinary measures.

Responding to this mandate, jurists all over the country began issuing these controversial orders that they called "protective orders" and the media called "gag orders." These orders generally fell into two categories: those directed against only the participants in the trial, ordering them not to reveal prejudicial information to the media, and those directed against the media, ordering them not to publish prejudicial information even if they somehow learn of it. The first category—orders intended to dry up the media's sources of prejudicial information—have been consistently upheld when challenged on First Amendment grounds. But the second kind—those purporting to exercise prior restraint of the media—have not fared as well.

In fact, in a television interview nine years after the *Sheppard* decision, Justice Clark said he did not mean that the media should be prohibited by judges from publishing information in their possession. Instead, gag orders were to be imposed only on those who might give prejudicial information to the press. Yet many judges imposed protective orders directly on the press after the *Sheppard* decision, citing the mandate to protect the rights of defendants as justification for doing so. More will be said of these orders shortly.

Other Remedies

The protective or gag order is just one of the remedies for prejudicial publicity recommended in the *Sheppard* decision, but it has surely been the most viable and controversial one. All of the others have limitations that sometimes render them impractical.

For example, a change of venue is expensive: it means all parties to the case, including witnesses, must travel a long distance for the trial, and it abridges the defendant's right to be tried in the place where the crime was committed, another Constitutional right. Moreover, with today's pervasive mass media, the new community may be just as aroused about the case as was the community where the trial was originally scheduled.

Ordering a postponement of the trial also has major disadvantages. For one thing, it denies defendants their Constitutional right to a speedy trial. For another, witnesses tend to become unavailable after a period of time. And finally, there is no assurance that the prejudicial publicity will not resume as the date of the long-delayed trial finally approaches. The community may harbor prejudices against a suspect for many years, and if anything a long delay may leave many persons more convinced than ever of the suspect's guilt.

Likewise, sequestering the jury has its drawbacks, although some states do sequester juries routinely in cases where the death sentence may be imposed. Nevertheless, many prospective jurors are unwilling to serve in a case where they will be isolated from the modern world for weeks or months. Moreover, sequestering a jury is expensive—the jurors must be provided food, lodging, and entertainment. And finally, it has proved virtually impossible to completely insulate jurors from the mass media. The celebrated trial of Charles Manson and his followers for the murder of actress Sharon Tate and her friends provides a good illustration of the problems involved with sequestration. In the Manson trial the jury was sequestered, but on various occasions newspapers containing prejudicial stories appeared in the courtroom, in the rest rooms used by the jurors, and on newsracks the jurors saw during the bus ride from their hotel to the court.

At one point, Manson himself held up a newspaper in court so that the jurors could see the main headline, which proclaimed, "Manson Guilty, Nixon Says." The judge immediately stopped the proceedings and asked the jurors if seeing that headline would influence their verdict, and they all said it would not, but no one will ever know for sure if that was true.

Among the other ways to protect the defendant from prejudicial publicity are closing the trial or pretrial proceedings and directly questioning the jurors about their potential prejudices. The problems of closing the trial or pretrial hearings will be treated later in this chapter.

The limitations of questioning the jurors about their prejudices (a process called "voir dire") were already cited in connection with the *Irvin* case. As already noted, jurors may say they can be impartial when in fact they harbor strong prejudices based on the media publicity. Each side in a criminal trial is allowed to dismiss a certain number of jurors without actually showing they are prejudiced. This kind of challenge to a juror is called a "peremptory" challenge. However, as the *Irvin* case illustrated, in a sensational case the defense may use all of its peremptory challenges and still be stuck with jurors who cannot be shown to be prejudiced but who nevertheless will not be impartial.

Furthermore, admonitions to the jury to disregard publicity they may see or read—another of the means of protecting the defendant's rights suggested in *Sheppard*—can hardly be expected to ensure that the jurors will not base their "guilty" or "not guilty" verdict on what they read in the papers as well as what they heard in court. Jurors being human, it is likely that most will consider everything they know about the case in reaching a verdict, regardless of the source of that information.

This brings us back to protective (or "gag") orders, the most controversial but probably also the most practical means of controlling prejudicial publicity.

The *Nebraska* Case

Protective orders were in the center of a bitter debate between the media and the judiciary from the time of the *Sheppard* decision until the U.S. Supreme Court finally clarified the Constitutional issues involved a decade later in a case called *Nebraska Press Assn. v. Stuart* (427 U.S. 53, 1976).

These orders were widely used all over the country in the early 1970s. A judge who believed an upcoming case might generate extensive publicity would almost routinely issue an order forbidding all parties in the case to make statements to the media. Such orders usually prohibited disclosing a defendant's prior criminal record, discussing the merits of the evidence in the case, and revealing the presence or absence of any confession. In many instances, this kind of information would be excluded as evidence at the trial, something that does little good if the jurors already know about it from watching television or reading the newspapers. But some judges went beyond these restrictions, actually attempting to censor the media by ordering publishers and broadcasters not to disseminate information they already had.

The Reporters Committee for Freedom of the Press kept records on the issuance of protective orders in the 1967-75 period. That organization identified 174 instances in which such orders were issued, including 63 that prohibited statements by court participants, 61 closing court proceedings or records to the press and public, and 50 involving direct prior restraint of the media.

After a number of state and lower federal court decisions on the validity of gag orders, the U.S. Supreme Court finally ruled on the issue in the 1976 *Nebraska Press Association v. Stuart* decision. That ruling all but eliminated gag orders that directly restrained the press (as opposed to orders that merely prohibited trial participants from giving prejudicial information to reporters).

The case involved Erwin Charles Simants, an unemployed handyman with a purported IQ of 75. Simants borrowed his brother-in-law's rifle, walked to the house next door, and murdered six members of the James Henry Kellie family. Simants turned himself in the day after the murders.

At the preliminary hearing, Lincoln County Judge Ronald Ruff ordered the media not to report any of the testimony. This gag order was appealed to District Court Judge Hugh Stuart by Nebraska news organizations. Stuart replaced Judge Ruff's order with his own.

Stuart's order prohibited the publication of certain kinds of prejudicial information. Later, the Nebraska Supreme Court modified the order to prohibit publishing only confessions made by Simants and any other facts "strongly implicative" of the suspect. The press was ordered not to mention the existence of a confession.

The news organizations appealed the order to the U.S. Supreme Court. The high court ruled unanimously that this order was a violation of the First Amendment in that it imposed a prior restraint on publication. In striking down the order, Chief Justice Warren Burger, writing for the court, referred to previous prior restraint cases and wrote:

> A prior restraint, by contrast and by definition, has an immediate and irreversible sanction. If it can be said that a threat of criminal or civil sanctions after publication "chills" speech, prior restraint "freezes" it at least for the time.

The Chief Justice continued, "The thread running through all these cases is that prior restraints on speech and publication are the most serious and the least tolerable infringements on First Amendment rights."

But the court did not totally rule out the possibility of protective orders being directed against the media in future cases. It said that in "extraordinary circumstances" such an order might be imposed. However, there must be sufficient evidence to reasonably conclude that:

1. there will be intense and pervasive publicity concerning the case;
2. no other alternative measure—such as a change of venue or continuance or extensive voir dire process—is likely to mitigate the effects of the pretrial publicity; and
3. the restrictive order will in fact effectively prevent prejudicial material from reaching potential jurors.

Thus, the *Nebraska Press Association* case severely limited the power of judges to restrain the press, but it did not limit their power to impose such an order on trial participants. For now, protective orders against the media are nearly dead, although "extraordinary circumstances" may arise to permit them at some future time.

Since the *Nebraska* decision, gag orders have often been imposed on trial participants, but almost never on the media. The few imposed on the media have been reversed or set aside. "Gag" orders that apply only to trial participants obviously make a reporter's job more difficult, but at least the reporter is entitled to disseminate whatever information he can secure from a news source, even if the order is applicable to that source.

Of course, if a judge is able to identify a trial participant who violates the order, that person most likely will be found in contempt of court. A whole new legal problem arises when the judge attempts to force the reporter to reveal his source of information so the source can be punished. Chapter Eight discusses shield laws (which excuse reporters from revealing their sources) and the problem of contempt of court citations for reporters who refuse to reveal their sources when no shield law is applicable.

CLOSED COURTROOMS

Before the mass media could long enjoy the victory over gag orders contained in the Supreme Court's *Nebraska Press Association* decision, a new conflict with the nation's trial courts assumed crisis proportions. This conflict stemmed from judges' efforts to bar the press and the public from preliminary hearings, hearings on motions to suppress evidence, and sometimes even from trials.

In the late 1970s there were increasingly frequent instances of preliminary criminal proceedings being closed to the press and the public in an effort to curtail prejudicial publicity. Gag orders directed against trial participants do not always stop the flow of prejudicial information to the press, and the *Nebraska* case imposed limits on judges' power to gag the press directly. Therefore, judges increasingly saw closed pretrial hearings as a good way to limit prejudicial publicity in sensational cases.

In order to understand the judges' viewpoint, we should explain why pretrial hearings occur and what happens at these proceedings. A preliminary hearing is intended as a check on law enforcement officers and prosecutors. It is a hearing where the case against the accused is reviewed by a judge, not to determine guilt or innocence but merely to decide whether there is enough evidence to justify a full trial. It's supposed to be a shortcut out of the criminal justice system for defendants who should never have been charged with a crime in the first place. The purpose is *not* to decide if the accused is guilty beyond a reasonable doubt (the standard of proof required in a criminal trial) but instead to see if there is enough evidence to justify a trial.

As a result, only the prosecution presents evidence at most preliminary hearings. If there is enough evidence, a trial is scheduled, almost without regard to the strength of the defense's case. Thus, as a matter of strategy, the defense often waits until the full trial before presenting its side of the case. As a result, news coverage of a preliminary hearing is necessarily imbalanced in most instances since only one side has been heard. The defense does have the right to cross-examine prosecution witnesses. Even so, if the hearing is covered by the media, most of the news generated there is going to be unfavorable to the defendant, who may have to stand trial before jurors who read about the preliminary hearing in the papers.

Pretrial hearings on motions to suppress evidence are even more likely to produce prejudicial publicity. At these hearings, the defense asks a judge to throw out damaging evidence, often because it was obtained by an unlawful search or seizure. Or perhaps the challenged evidence is a confession that was secured through coercion. In any event, what good does it do to have the tainted evidence suppressed (i.e., ruled inadmissible at the trial) if prospective jurors learn about it on the evening news? For these reasons, many judges and lawyers feel strongly that hearings on motions to suppress evidence should be closed to the press and public.

In addition to preventing jury prejudice, closing preliminary court proceedings protects the reputations of defendants who have been charged with a crime but are not held for trial because the hearing reveals that the prosecutor has little evidence.

Few journalists would deny that there are powerful arguments for secrecy at the pretrial stage in criminal proceedings, except for one thing: more than 80 percent of all criminal prosecutions in America are resolved without the case ever reaching a full trial. Because the judge's ruling on a motion to suppress crucial evidence is the decisive step in many criminal cases, serious plea bargaining usually occurs after these pretrial proceedings. If key evidence is barred, the prosecutor may be inclined to accept a guilty plea to a lesser charge or even drop the charges. If the evidence is ruled admissible, on the other hand, the defendant may plead guilty as charged at this stage, perhaps in return for a promise of a light sentence. In the vast majority of criminal proceedings, the last chance the public will have to monitor the justice system is at the pretrial hearing stage.

As a trend toward closed pretrial hearings developed in the late 1970s, a Constitutional challenge to this practice reached the U.S. Supreme Court in the 1979 case of *Gannett v. DePasquale* (443 U.S. 368).

The Supreme Court upheld a judge's order barring a newspaper reporter from a pretrial evidentiary hearing in upstate New York. The case arose when two young men were charged with murdering a former New York policeman. They reportedly confessed the crime and were later indicted by a grand jury.

Because of the intense publicity surrounding the incident and the arrest, the defense and prosecution concurred in closing the pretrial hearing. When Judge Daniel DePasquale barred the press and public, the Gannett newspapers appealed the ruling. The state's highest court affirmed the order and Gannett asked the Supreme Court to hear the case.

In affirming the closure, Justice Potter Stewart, writing for a 5-4 Supreme Court majority, acknowledged that "there is a strong societal interest in public trials." His opinion also noted, "there is no question that the Sixth Amendment permits and even presumes open trials as a norm." However, Stewart continued, the Sixth Amendment right to a public trial belongs to the defendant and not the public, and it is a right the defendant may waive.

Justice Stewart agreed with the trial judge's decision that the press' right of access to this particular hearing "was outweighed by the defendant's right to a fair trial. . .because an open proceeding would pose a reasonable probability of prejudice to these defendants."

Justice Stewart's opinion was joined by Justices John Paul Stevens, Lewis Powell, William Rehnquist, and Chief Justice Burger. The latter three also wrote separate concurring opinions. Justices Marshall, Brennan, Blackmun, and White joined in a dissent, which said, "Secret hearings. . .are suspect by nature. Unlike any other provision of the Sixth Amendment, the public trial interest cannot adequately be protected by the prosecutor and judge in conjunction or connivance with the defendant."

Justice Powell's concurring opinion was noteworthy in that it said the press and public should have a right to contest proposed courtroom closures. In the years since *Gannett,* many journalists have done precisely that, sometimes successfully. Many reporters who regularly cover the courts carry a card with them containing the correct legal phrasing of a motion to object to a courtroom closure.

Nevertheless, the *Gannett* decision stood as a precedent permitting judges to close at least pretrial hearings when they felt the danger of prejudicial publicity would outweigh the public's right to observe the proceedings.

As a result of this decision, there was an avalanche of closed hearings— and even trials—in late 1979 and early 1980. The Reporters Committee for Freedom of the Press counted 21 courtroom closures ordered or upheld on appeal in the first 30 days after the *Gannett* ruling was announced. Within the year, there were at least 100 more such courtroom closures around the nation.

The *Richmond* Decision

Apparently alarmed at the reaction to *Gannett* by trial judges, several Supreme Court justices made public statements condemning the trend. And the high court quickly agreed to review another related case, this one involving a closure of a full trial in Virginia.

In this case (*Richmond Newspapers v. Virginia,* 448 U.S. 555), a county judge had cleared his courtroom of reporters and spectators before the fourth trial of a man who was charged with murdering a hotel manager. His first trial had been invalidated on a technicality, and the next two resulted in mistrials. Relying on a Virginia statute that allowed "the removal of any persons whose presence would impair the conduct of a fair trial," the judge simply closed the trial. The defendant was acquitted after a two-day closed trial because there were "too many holes" in the prosecution's case, the judge said.

Two jointly owned Richmond, Va., newspapers challenged the courtroom closure. Just a week after the *Gannett* ruling of the U.S. Supreme Court, the Virginia Supreme Court upheld the ruling closing this trial.

Ruling in 1980—a year to the day after its controversial *Gannett* decision—the U.S. Supreme Court voted 7-1 to overrule this trial closing, a decision that was widely seen as a major victory for the mass media. Not only did the high court invalidate the closing of this particular trial, but Chief Justice Burger's opinion for the court recognized for the first time that there is a Constitutional right of access to information inherent in the free press guarantees of the First Amendment:

> We hold that the right to attend criminal trials is implicit in the guarantees of the First Amendment; without the freedom to attend such trials, which people have exercised for centuries, important aspects of freedom of speech and of the press could be eviscerated.

Moreover, Burger's opinion went to some trouble to make it clear that this public right to attend trials, although only an implied right and not one specifically stated in the Constitution, was nonetheless legitimate. Burger pointed to a variety of other Constitutional rights the Supreme Court has recognized over the years, although those rights too were only implied in the Constitution. Burger noted that the rights of association and privacy, the right to travel, and the right to be judged by the "beyond-a-reasonable-doubt" standard of proof in criminal cases were only implied and not stated in the Constitution.

Although this opinion was joined by only two other justices, at least two additional justices recognized a right of the public to attend trials in their opinion in the *Richmond* case. However, Justice Rehnquist (the only dissenter) said the states should be free to set their own standards on the administration of justice and found no provision in the federal Constitution that prohibited the Virginia judge from doing what he did.

In overturning the closure of a trial in the *Richmond* decision, the Supreme Court avoided reversing its year-old *Gannett* ruling, apparently leaving judges free to conduct closed pretrial hearings in instances where a closed trial would not be permitted. In fact, on the same day the Supreme Court handed down its *Richmond* decision, the court declined to review a lower court decision authorizing another closed pretrial hearing in New York.

Moreover, the Supreme Court did not even flatly forbid closed trials in the *Richmond* case. Instead, the high court said trials could still be closed under certain extraordinary circumstances. "Absent an overriding interest (in closing the trial) articulated in the (judge's) findings, the trial of a criminal case must be open to the public," Burger's opinion held. The Supreme Court did not set forth any guidelines for determining when a trial should be closed, but the court did make it clear that a judge must pursue alternative means of ensuring the fairness of a trial before barring the press and public.

In short, the *Richmond* decision limits a judge's discretion in barring the press and public from a trial, while permitting trial closures in extreme circumstances if the judge can set forth valid reasons for his action. This decision may not have gone quite as far as many journalists hoped it would, but it nonetheless sharply curtailed the nationwide trend toward closed courtrooms that had developed in the year between the *Gannett* and *Richmond* decisions.

Courtroom Closures After *Richmond*

The *Richmond* decision was a vindication of the principle of open courtrooms in America. While there have been a number of controversial courtroom closures since that bellwether 1980 Supreme Court decision, the trend toward closed trials has been reversed. In fact, the Supreme Court has since handed down several more decisions overruling courtroom closures.

In 1982, the Supreme Court invalidated a Massachusetts law that automatically closed the courtroom whenever a juvenile victim of a sex crime was to testify. In *Globe Newspaper Company v. Superior Court* (457 U.S. 596), the court said judges must evaluate each trial closure on a case-by-case basis rather than automatically closing a trial whenever a young sex crime victim is testifying.

In a 6-3 decision, the high court found the Massachusetts law unconstitutional because it made the closure mandatory. The court took pains to point out that judges could exclude the press and public in individual cases where they found that a minor's well-being would be in jeopardy if the trial were open.

Writing for the majority, Justice William Brennan took note of the court's ruling in *Richmond Newspapers* that the public has a Constitutional right of access to criminal trials. However, Brennan pointed out that this right is not absolute: a trial may be closed if a state can show two things: (1) a "compelling governmental interest" that requires the closure and (2) that the law requiring closure is "narrowly tailored to serve that interest."

Weighing the Massachusetts statute—as interpreted by that state's highest court—the Supreme Court concluded that it failed this two-part test because a case-by-case determination of whether a criminal trial should be closed would be sufficient to protect young victims. The mandatory closure provision was overbroad, the court held.

The case arose when a judge closed a rape trial in which the victims were three girls under age 18. The *Boston Globe* challenged the closure, and after several preliminary decisions the state Supreme Court upheld the mandatory closure provision of the Massachusetts law. The *Globe* appealed, setting up the U.S. Supreme Court's decision.

The gist of the *Globe Newspaper* decision is nicely summarized by one of the footnotes in the majority opinion:

> We emphasize that our holding is a narrow one: that a rule of mandatory closure respecting the testimony of minor sex victims is constitutionally infirm. In individual cases, and under appropriate circumstances, the First Amendment does not necessarily stand as a bar to the exclusion

from the courtroom of the press and general public during the testimony of minor sex-offense victims. But a mandatory rule, requiring no particularized determinations in individual cases, is unconstitutional.

The ruling produced dissents from Chief Justice Warren Burger and Justice William Rehnquist, who felt the mandatory closure rule was not unconstitutional, and from Justice John Paul Stevens, who felt the case should not have been heard.

In 1984 the Supreme Court took another step to assure public access to the criminal justice system when it ruled that the jury selection process must also normally be open to the public. In the case of *Press-Enterprise Co. v. Superior Court* (104 S.Ct. 819), the court unanimously overturned a Riverside, Calif., judge's decision to close almost six weeks of jury selection procedures during a 1981 murder trial.

The judge not only closed the jury selection process, but also refused to make a transcript of the proceeding public after the defendant was tried, convicted, and sentenced to death for raping and killing a 13-year-old girl. The effect of the judge's decision was to ensure that the public would never know how the jury was selected for a trial that ended with a death sentence.

Writing for the Supreme Court, Chief Justice Warren Burger emphasized that the jury selection, like other aspects of criminal trials, has traditionally been open to the public—and should continue to be open in all but very unusual circumstances. He wrote:

> Proceedings held in secret would. . .frustrate the broad public interest; by contrast public proceedings vindicate the concerns of the victims and the community in knowing that offenders are being brought to account for their criminal conduct by jurors fairly and openly selected.

However, Burger said there might be rare occasions when prospective jurors could be questioned in private in the judge's chambers to protect their privacy during discussions of "deeply personal matters." However, even then a transcript of the proceedings should be made available within a reasonable time unless that would further invade a juror's privacy. But to close the entire process for "an incredible six weeks" (as Burger put it) was going much too far.

Although the decision that the judge should not have closed the jury selection in this case was unanimous, three justices wrote separate opinions. Justice Thurgood Marshall said the jury selection and "all aspects of criminal trials" should be open, regardless of whether open jury selection procedures might embarrass a prospective juror. Justices Harry Blackmun and John Paul Stevens wrote a separate opinion emphasizing the importance of jurors' privacy rights.

A few months after the *Press-Enterprise* decision, the Supreme Court again reiterated that criminal proceedings other than the trial itself must normally be open. In *Waller v. Georgia* (104 S.Ct. pg. 2210, 1984), the high court overturned a judge's decision to close a lengthy pretrial evidence suppression hearing in a case where the police had searched numerous homes and conducted telephone wiretaps to gather evidence of gambling. The defendants argued that much of the evidence was unlawfully obtained, and they wanted it suppressed. Moreover, they demanded that the evidence suppression hearing be open to the public, but the judge refused to open the hearing. Then he admitted most of the evidence and convicted several defendants of various crimes.

The Supreme Court ruled that most if not all of this evidence suppression hearing, like the jury selection proceedings in the *Press-Enterprise* case, should have been open to the public. Only a little of the 7-day hearing involved material that might invade anyone's privacy, the court noted. Once again in the *Waller* case, the court emphasized the right of the public—as well as defendants—to have criminal trials and pretrial proceedings held in open court under most circumstances. The court reiterated its rule about judicial openness from the *Press-Enterprise* decision:

> The presumption of openness (in court proceedings) may be overcome only by an overriding interest based on findings that closure is essential to preserve higher values and narrowly tailored to serve that interest. The interest is to be articulated along with findings specific enough that a reviewing court can determine whether the closure order was properly entered. (10 Med.L.Rptr. at 1717)

In short, the Supreme Court was saying that when judges abridge the open-courtroom rights of the press, public, and criminal defendants, they must have a compelling reason for doing so, they must explain that reason clearly, and they must close no more of the proceeding than is really necessary.

While the Supreme Court was repeatedly reaffirming the public's right to attend criminal trials during the 1980s, state courts and lower federal courts were generally ruling in much the same way, although there were exceptions.

A good example of a lower court ruling that affirms the right of access to court proceedings (and documents) is the ninth circuit U.S. Court of Appeals decision in a 1983 case, *Associated Press v. District Court* (705 F.2d 1143). The case arose when a federal judge closed some of the pretrial proceedings and also sealed many pretrial court documents in the celebrated case of automaker John DeLorean, who was accused of arranging a multimillion dollar cocaine deal to save his failing auto company.

In this case, the appellate court ruled that the judge's secrecy orders violated the public's First Amendment right of access to court documents and proceedings that have traditionally been open.

The ruling in *Associated Press v. District Court* is especially noteworthy because of the appellate court's specific recognition that the First Amendment includes a right of access to court documents. However, the court said this right must be balanced against other rights, mainly the defendant's right to a fair trial. Reiterating an earlier decision, the court said a three-part test should be used in deciding whether pretrial secrecy is justified. Before sealing documents or barring the public from the courtroom, the judge must determine that:

1. allowing public access would cause "a substantial probability that irreparable damage to (a defendant's) fair trial right will result";
2. there are no alternative ways to protect the defendant's right to a fair trial; and
3. there is "a substantial probability" that the secrecy would actually prevent the defendant's rights from being violated.

In ordering the DeLorean records opened, the appellate court noted that there had been extensive publicity about the case in spite of the court records being sealed. Thus, the secrecy wasn't working and could not be justified.

While this decision is a major victory for the news media, it carries the force of law only in federal cases within the federal ninth circuit (a map on page 10 shows which states fall in the various federal circuits). In 1982 the third circuit U.S. Court of Appeals handed down a ruling that said much the same thing as the *Associated Press* case, but not quite as emphatically (see *U.S. v. Criden,* 675 F.2d 550).

In short, the right of the press and the public to attend criminal trials and many of the preliminary proceedings has been repeatedly vindicated since the Supreme Court put those rights in question with its *Gannett v. De-Pasquale* decision in 1979.

Federal Open-Trial Policy

Shortly after the *Richmond* decision, the U.S. Justice Department issued new rules ordering government attorneys not to request or consent to trial closures except under very limited circumstances, and only then with the permission of a deputy or associate attorney general.

The new federal guidelines, approved in October, 1980, apply to all federal trials, pretrial evidentiary hearings, and certain other proceedings. They order government attorneys not to seek or consent to closed judicial proceedings unless the closure is "plainly essential to the interests of justice." Courtroom closures are permitted only: (1) to prevent imminent danger to someone's safety; (2) to protect a defendant's right to a fair trial when there is a "substantial likelihood" it would otherwise be threatened; or (3) to avoid seriously jeopardizing an ongoing investigation.

The guidelines say that government attorneys may not seek or approve trial closures even then if there is any alternate way to safeguard the rights that are endangered. "There is. . .a strong presumption against closing proceedings or portions thereof, and the Department of Justice foresees very few cases in which closure would be warranted," the guidelines say.

Nevertheless, media organizations questioned the need for some of the provisions, particularly the one permitting trial closures to protect ongoing investigations. Even the Supreme Court's *Gannett v. DePasquale* decision didn't mention that ground for closing a courtroom.

VOLUNTARY GUIDELINES

As the media and the judiciary engaged in legal battles over the problems of prejudicial publicity and cameras in the courtroom in the 1960s and 1970s, another more cooperative effort to solve some of the fair trial-free press problems was under way in many states: groups of lawyers, judges, and journalists were attempting to agree on voluntary guidelines for media coverage of sensational criminal cases.

This process was an indirect result of the 1964 report of the Warren Commission, the body set up to investigate the circumstances surrounding the assassination of President John F. Kennedy. As one of its findings, the Warren Commission noted that throngs of news reporters tied up facilities and interfered with normal police operations after the assassination. The commission placed some of the blame for the circumstances that allowed the shooting of assassination suspect Lee Harvey Oswald on the media.

The Warren Commission report led to a new interest in the problems created by media coverage of sensational events. This produced a variety of voluntary and not-so-voluntary efforts to alleviate these problems.

Many representatives of the press resisted the calls for voluntary restraint that were heard in those days, but others began to work on the local level to establish guidelines for coverage of major crimes. Meanwhile, in 1965 U.S. Attorney General Nicholas Katzenbach issued rules restricting the release of prejudicial information to the media by federal prosecutors. These rules limited information released to basic facts about the crime itself and the suspect's identity, barring the release of such information as reports of confessions, comments about the evidence, and specific details of the defendant's past.

At about the same time this was happening on the federal level, the American Bar Association responded to the Warren Commission's findings by creating a committee under Massachusetts Supreme Court Justice Paul C. Reardon to recommend similar guidelines for the nation's state courts and law enforcement officers.

The Reardon Report—as it came to be known—was adopted by the ABA House of Delegates in 1968. It urged that all parties to a criminal prosecution refrain from releasing prejudicial information to the press. Moreover, the report urged judges to use their contempt power against those who release inflammatory statements to the media. The report also endorsed the idea of closed preliminary hearings when the information revealed at such hearings might interfere with a defendant's right to a fair trial. Finally, the Reardon Report urged local groups of lawyers, judges, and journalists to develop voluntary guidelines for press coverage of criminal trials.

Like the federal guidelines, the Reardon proposals were widely opposed (and ignored) by reporters. Nevertheless, a 1974 ABA study found a majority of both local bar association leaders and newspaper editors claiming the Reardon guidelines were generally being followed. However, a 1976 study by three University of Texas researchers who actually analyzed the content of pretrial crime news stories found violations of the Reardon guidelines in two-thirds of all such stories.

Despite their limitations, the Reardon guidelines did provide the basis for many local agreements among journalists, lawyers, and judges. By 1975 some kind of voluntary guidelines had been agreed upon in no fewer than 23 states. These local agreements vary widely from place to place, but they generally prohibit publishing the kinds of prejudicial information cited in the Reardon Report. Such guidelines may well be ignored at times, but at least they have produced a dialogue between the judiciary and reporters about the problems of prejudicial publicity.

However, the whole concept of voluntary bench-bar-press guidelines was thrown into controversy by a series of events that unfolded in the state of Washington during the early 1980s. In a 1981 Washington case that was an offshoot of the celebrated "hillside strangler" murders, a judge forced journalists to promise to obey the "voluntary" guidelines as a condition of attending some of the proceedings. Any reporter who refused to make this pledge would not be admitted to the courtroom, he decreed. That meant reporters would be unable to report things they heard in an open courtroom—and it sounded very much like the kind of prior restraint the Supreme Court's *Nebraska Press Association* decision was intended to prevent.

The result was outrage among journalists from coast to coast, and the order was appealed to the Washington Supreme court in the case of *Federated Publications v. Swedberg* (633 P.2d 74, 1981). The state high court said the order was simply a reasonable means of avoiding a closed hearing while protecting the defendant's right to a fair trial. The court distinguished this case from the *Nebraska* case, contending that no prior restraint was involved. Rather, the reporters' promise was merely a "moral one. . . and not enforceable in a court of law."

Nevertheless, requiring journalists to promise not to report some of the information they obtained in an open court sounds a lot like a prior restraint. Even if reporting forbidden information doesn't get a journalist jailed, there could be other sanctions. Couldn't an offending reporter be barred from attending similar proceedings in the future—while others whose stories pleased the judge were admitted?

In response to the *Swedberg* decision, journalists all over the country began rethinking the wisdom of entering into voluntary bench-bar-press agreements on courtroom coverage. The Washington state guidelines were rewritten, and journalists made it clear that they would no longer cooperate if the guidelines were anything but voluntary.

Meanwhile, in 1982 the Washington Supreme Court handed down another ruling that seems to ameliorate the effect of *Swedberg*. In *Seattle Times v. Ishikawa* (640 P.2d 716), the court said trial judges must weigh a number of factors before closing pretrial hearings or sealing the records of such hearings. For instance, judges must first consider alternative means of protecting the defendant's rights and also allow anyone present to object to the closure. Moreover, if the justification for the secrecy is anything other than a defendant's fair trial rights, there must be a much stronger justification for any secrecy.

Ishikawa was a murder-for-hire case in which Judge Richard Ishikawa sealed the record of closed pretrial proceedings, and ordered it kept secret even after the trial ended in a conviction. At that point, the *Seattle Times* challenged the continuing secrecy on the ground that it was no longer necessary to protect the defendant's fair trial rights (since the trial was over). At first the judge refused to open the records, but after the state Supreme Court ordered him to reconsider his ruling under these stringent new standards, he unsealed the records.

CONCLUSION

After several decades of controversy, the fair trial-free press dilemma is by no means resolved, but several recent Supreme Court decisions offer journalists some encouragement. The Supreme Court's *Chandler* decision helped open some courtroom doors to the electronic media, but judges continue to occasionally issue gag orders to limit the media's access to information about sensational criminal cases. At least these orders rarely attempt to censor the press directly, thanks to the *Nebraska* decision of the Supreme Court. However, judges also continue to close pretrial hearings (and an occasional trial) in a further attempt to limit prejudicial publicity, but that practice was discouraged by the Supreme Court's *Richmond* decision.

Nevertheless, the conflict persists today, and probably will as long as we have a First Amendment that guarantees a free press and a Sixth Amendment that guarantees defendants a trial before an impartial jury.

Moreover, the fair trial-free press controversy has generated several related legal problems, chief among them the threat of contempt of court that arises when a judge demands—and a journalist declines to reveal—the source of information that was somehow leaked to the press in violation of a gag order. The next chapter addresses these issues, detailing the growth of shield laws and the increasing use of contempt of court citations against reporters in the years since gag orders became popular.

A Summary of Fair Trial-Free Press Problems

WHAT IS THE PROBLEM?

On the one hand, the First Amendment guarantees freedom of the press—and that includes the right to cover crime news. On the other, a person charged with a crime has a Sixth Amendment right to a trial before an impartial jury—a jury made up of people who have formed no prejudices before the trial and will base their decision solely on what they hear in court.

WHY SHOULDN'T JURORS LEARN ABOUT A CASE IN THE MEDIA?

Much of the information that may be published in the media will never be admitted into evidence in court and is not supposed to be considered by a jury.

DOESN'T THAT MEAN THE COURTS IGNORE RELEVANT EVIDENCE?

A court may only hear evidence that was gathered by lawful means, not evidence secured in violation of the Constitutional ban on illegal searches and coerced confessions. Any other policy would reward law enforcement agencies for ignoring the Constitution. In addition, a jury is only supposed to decide whether a defendant is guilty of the particular crime charged—not whether he is a bad fellow in general. Information about a person's criminal record may be reported in the media, but it is not admissible at many trials.

WHAT HAS BEEN DONE ABOUT THIS PROBLEM?

The Supreme Court has urged trial judges to take a variety of actions to control inflammatory publicity, such as "gagging" participants in trials so they will not reveal prejudicial (and inadmissible) evidence to the media. However, the Supreme Court has also ruled that closing the courtroom is not usually the solution. The court has held that trials and pretrial proceedings should be open to the press and public unless the trial judge determines that a closed session is absolutely necessary to protect the defendant's rights. Also, the Supreme Court has ruled that broadcast coverage of trials is not inherently prejudicial, although it may be in specific instances.

HOW DO JOURNALISTS FEEL ABOUT THIS?

Many journalists oppose the judiciary's attempts to control publicity, contending that these efforts interfere with the public's right to know about the administration of justice. They warn of the dangers to democracy inherent in any kind of secret court proceedings.

8

NEWSGATHERER'S PRIVILEGE AND CONTEMPT OF COURT

To an unprecedented extent, journalists have become participants instead of spectators in the legal system in recent years. Journalists have been jailed for refusing to reveal their news sources, newsrooms have been ransacked by law enforcement officials in search of evidence, and contempt of court—a legal threat that seemed to be disappearing only a few years ago—has reemerged as a major problem.

At one time, journalists had relatively few brushes with the law over their newsgathering activities. But the turbulent 1960s changed that. Within the militant social movements of that era, some journalists were afforded special privileges. Often a trusted journalist was given inside information that no law enforcement officer could hope to obtain. Reporters at times witnessed unlawful activities—and then wrote about them. Long gone was the day when journalists just interviewed the police and thought they had adequately covered crime news. Reporters were covering both sides and increasingly questioning what they were told by law enforcement authorities or prosecuting attorneys. As a result, reporters not only had access to more information of interest to the authorities than ever before, but reporters came to be viewed less as allies than as adversaries.

The Watergate era in the early 1970s intensified these trends. Investigative journalists unearthed confidential information of great social and political importance, and often published it without revealing their sources. In many of these circumstances law enforcement officials, grand juries, and the courts began demanding information from journalists.

This inevitably produced conflicts because most journalists believe they have an ethical duty not to identify their confidential news sources. Without confidential sources, journalists contend, many important news stories could never be reported. It is commonplace for "whistle-blowers" (people with inside information about wrongdoing in government or big business) to come forward and talk to a reporter in secret, something they could not do without a pledge of confidentiality. If reporters had to reveal their sources, many people with important information would not talk to them out of fear of the recriminations that might result.

For this reason, journalists often find themselves ethically obligated to protect the confidentiality of news sources. On the other hand, judges want all relevant information to be made available in court, and they are increasingly using their contempt of court power to enforce orders requiring journalists to supply confidential information. Judges often feel that journalists are no different from other citizens, and should be obligated to comply with subpoenas. Why, they ask, should journalists have special privileges? But many journalists feel their moral and ethical responsibilities in this area are so compelling that they would rather go to jail than break a promise of confidentiality.

In treating this difficult problem, this chapter discusses two separate but intertwined legal issues: contempt of court as a legal sanction and the "newsgatherer's privilege"—the right of reporters to keep their sources and unpublished materials confidential. The chapter also addresses another related issue: the legality of law enforcement raids on newsrooms in search of evidence.

CONTEMPT OF COURT

Contempt of court is a very old—and very new—legal problem for journalists. Basically, it originated with the idea that a judge should be able to control the decorum of the courtroom, and should have the authority to summarily punish those who violate that decorum. American judges have had contempt powers ever since the founding of the republic, and English and colonial judges exercised the power considerably before that.

There are several different kinds of contempt of court, and the distinctions among them are sometimes crucial in cases involving the media. First, there is *direct contempt*, which involves an act that violates the decorum of the court or shows disrespect for the legal process. A citation for direct contempt usually results from either misconduct in or near the courtroom, or from the refusal to obey a judge's order. A photographer who surreptitiously takes a picture in a courtroom where cameras are not permitted risks a citation for direct contempt of court. Similarly, a reporter who refuses to reveal a source of information when ordered to do so by a judge may be cited for direct contempt.

In addition to direct contempt, there is *indirect contempt* (sometimes called "constructive contempt" or "contempt by publication"), which involves a disrespectful act remote from the courtroom. From the early 1800s until the 1940s, one of the major legal threats to journalists was indirect contempt. Journalists were frequently cited for contempt because of what they wrote about a judge or the justice system. Unlike other public officials, judges had the power to punish journalists—immediately and directly—for publishing things they didn't like, and some judges used that power freely. Surprisingly, the First Amendment wasn't recognized as a limit on judges' contempt powers until a 1941 Supreme Court decision, to be discussed shortly.

Still another distinction may be drawn between types of contempt of court. Contempt may be either criminal or civil in nature. *Criminal contempt*, as the name suggests, is a punishment for an act of disrespect for a court. That disrespect might be in the form of a photographer taking unauthorized pictures in court or a lawyer violating the rules of the court in his zeal to win his case. In either case, the offense would be an example of direct contempt of court and would lead to a criminal sanction. The punishment might be a fine or a jail sentence, or both. Indirect contempt is also treated as a criminal matter at times, as it often was in the days when journalists were punished for writing stories that judges found offensive.

Civil contempt, on the other hand, is not a punishment at all, although it may lead to a term in jail. Civil contempt is a form of coercion: a person who is disobeying a court order is locked up until he or she decides it would be better to obey the court order. Thus, it can result in an indefinite sentence. The contemnor (the person cited for contempt of court) is free to leave any time—if he or she obeys the court order. But if this person stands on principle and steadfastly refuses to obey the order, the jail term could theoretically last for a lifetime in some states. Reporters who refuse to reveal their sources are often cited for civil contempt, and thus run the risk of an extended stay in jail if no compromise can be reached.

One thing particularly troubles many journalists about contempt of court: often the judge unilaterally defines the offense, determines that there has been a violation, tries and convicts the guilty party, and sets the sentence—all within a few minutes. Contempt citations may be appealed, and many involving journalists are, but the fact remains that judges have enormous power in this area. Unfortunately, that power is sometimes abused.

Nevertheless, a judge's contempt power has limits other than the recourse to a higher court. For example, if a criminal contempt sentence is to exceed six months, the judge is no longer permitted to decide the case unilaterally: the U.S. Supreme Court has ruled that those accused of contempt have a right to a jury trial if the sentence is to be that long (see *Bloom v. Illinois*, 391 U.S. 194, 1968). Of course, this Constitutional limit doesn't necessarily affect civil contempt, which has no fixed term in many instances.

By the early days of this century, contempt of court had become a major problem for journalists. Anyone who criticized a judge or gave unsolicited advice about the handling of a pending case risked a jail sentence, so the media were often reluctant to subject the judiciary to the same kind of criticism as other officials.

The *Bridges* Decision

In 1941 the U.S. Supreme Court handed down a landmark decision on contempt of court, a decision that stripped judges of their vast power to use indirect contempt against the media. The case, *Bridges v. California* (314 U.S. 252), resulted from two unrelated contempt citations, one against Longshoremen's Union leader Harry Bridges and another against the *Los Angeles Times*. Bridges sent a telegram to the secretary of labor threatening to call a massive West Coast dock strike if a court ruling unfavorable to him was enforced. Meanwhile, the *Times* published several editorials that judges disliked, including one entitled "Probation for Gorillas?" that admonished a judge to impose tough sentences on a group of Teamsters Union organizers.

Both Bridges and the *Times* were cited for indirect contempt, or contempt by publication. Deciding the two cases together, the Supreme Court ruled that these contempt citations violated the First Amendment. The court prohibited contempt citations for public statements in the future, unless it could be shown that the publication created a *clear and present danger* to the administration of justice. The court rejected an older test, under which any publication with an "inherent tendency" or "reasonable tendency" to interfere with the orderly administration of justice could be punished. As a result, an indirect contempt citation of a journalist became vastly harder for a judge to defend.

A few years later, the Supreme Court overturned two more indirect contempt citations against newspapers in *Pennekamp v. Florida* (328 U.S. 331, 1946) and *Craig v. Harney* (331 U.S. 367, 1947). In *Pennekamp*, the Florida Supreme Court upheld a contempt citation based on *Miami Herald* editorials criticizing local judges for being soft on criminals. The *Craig* case arose when a Corpus Christi, Texas, newspaper criticized a judge for his handling of a minor landlord-tenant dispute. In both cases, the Supreme Court reversed the contempt citations, reiterating that the clear and present danger test applied to indirect contempt citations. In neither case could the judge who issued the citation meet this test, the Supreme Court said.

In *Craig*, the court said the contempt power should not be used to punish newspapers for what they print "unless there is no doubt that the utterances in question are a serious and imminent threat to the administration of justice."

After those decisions, the use of indirect contempt against the media almost disappeared. For a time, about the only sort of contempt threat journalists faced was the kind that arises when a photographer is caught taking illicit courthouse pictures. To be cited for contempt, one almost had to advocate marching on the courthouse (see *Cox v. Louisiana,* 379 U.S. 559, 1965). In short, contempt of court resulting from publications ceased to be a major legal problem for the media.

However, after the *Sheppard v. Maxwell* decision in 1966 (see Chapter Seven), judges began to exercise more control over the conduct of the media in and around their courtrooms. Moreover, the *Sheppard* case encouraged judges to issue "protective orders" (or "gag" orders) directing trial partici-pants not to reveal prejudicial information to the media. Naturally, when a reporter somehow secured such information anyway, the judge wanted to know who had violated his court order. Thus, judges began to summon journalists and demand to know their sources, citing them for direct contempt when they refused to answer such questions. The modern press-judiciary conflict over contempt and reporter's privilege had begun.

In the decade following *Sheppard,* hundreds of journalists were sum-moned before judges and questioned about their sources. In addition, grand juries and both prosecutors and defense attorneys began to view journalists as sources for useful information. During the discovery process in civil cases, journalists were called on to reveal their sources ever more frequently (see Chapter Four). In 1969 and 1970 alone, at least 166 subpoenas were issued seeking notes, tapes, and film outtakes from the three national television networks. In the same two years, the *Chicago Daily News* and *Chicago Sun-Times* faced more than 30 subpoenas seeking information.

What journalists needed more than ever before was a viable reporter's privilege, preferably at the federal level and in all states.

REPORTER'S PRIVILEGE

The term "privilege," as used in this chapter, means an exemption from a citizen's normal duty to testify when ordered to do so in court or in other official information-gathering proceedings. The concept is an old one that developed under the English common law, but the idea of a journalist's privilege emerged much more recently; the common law traditionally did not recognize journalists as among the people who could invoke privilege.

Several kinds of privilege were recognized under the common law, including the doctor-patient, the lawyer-client, the priest-penitent, and the husband-wife privileges. Each of these was established to protect a relation-ship that needed to be kept confidential for socially important reasons. These privileges have numerous exceptions, but all still remain viable today, at least under some circumstances.

The journalist's privilege, on the other hand, is largely a twentieth century idea. Maryland adopted a "shield law" (a statutory law shielding a reporter from the duty to reveal sources of information) in 1896, but it was some 30 years before the next such law was enacted anywhere in the United States. By 1980, shield laws had been enacted in at least 25 more states, and these statutory laws are discussed later. However, some journalists began to argue that, even in the absence of a statutory shield law, the First Amendment protected their right to keep their sources confidential.

Is the First Amendment a Shield?

An appellate court first ruled on the argument that the First Amendment constitutes a shield law in a 1958 libel decision, *Garland v. Torre* (259 F.2d 545). Columnist Marie Torre made some unflattering statements about actress Judy Garland and attributed them to an unnamed CBS network executive. Garland sued for libel and demanded the identity of the source during the discovery process. Torre refused to comply and a federal trial court cited her for contempt. She appealed, and the U.S. Court of Appeals upheld the citation Torre was sentenced to 10 days in jail.

In an opinion by Potter Stewart (later a Supreme Court justice) the appellate court conceded that this case required a difficult balancing of two rights, but the information sought went to the heart of Garland's claim, Stewart said. Thus, the reporter's right to keep a source confidential had to give way to the right of a court to require the disclosure of relevant information.

After that decision, the idea of a Constitutional privilege for journalists remained in limbo until the late 1960s. At that point the argument began to be seriously reconsidered in view of the flood of contempt citations of journalists. In 1970 and 1971, three court rulings on the issue were appealed to the Supreme Court. In one of these cases a court recognized a Constitutional privilege, while in the other two courts declined to do so. To resolve this conflict, the Supreme Court agreed to hear the three cases together.

The result was *Branzburg v. Hayes* (408 U.S. 665), an important 1972 decision that denied the existence of a journalist's Constitutional privilege in cases such as the ones before the court. However, the ruling was confusing because the vote was 5-4, with only four justices rejecting a Constitutional shield outright while another four (the dissenters) said there should be a qualified Constitutional shield. The swing vote was provided by Justice Lewis Powell, who said the First Amendment should not excuse journalists from revealing their sources in these cases. However, Powell also suggested that it might under some other circumstances.

The three cases that were consolidated in *Branzburg* involved widely varying circumstances, but all had one thing in common: reporters had refused to answer grand juries' questions about potential criminal activity they allegedly witnessed. The case where a court recognized a Constitutional shield, *U.S. v. Caldwell*, involved Earl Caldwell, a black reporter for the *New*

York Times. Caldwell had interviewed leaders of the militant Black Panther movement. In California, a federal grand jury investigating black groups subpoenaed Caldwell to testify and to bring along his notes and tapes.

Caldwell refused even to appear. Not only would testifying breach his confidential relationships with his news sources, he said, but merely appearing would undermine that confidential relationship. Since grand jury proceedings are secret, the Panthers might never know for sure whether he kept his promises of confidentiality if he appeared.

Caldwell and the *Times* asked a federal district court to quash (set aside) the grand jury subpoena. The court granted the request only in part, and Caldwell appealed. The ninth circuit U.S. Court of Appeals ordered the subpoena quashed, ruling that Caldwell had a First Amendment right to keep his sources confidential. The U.S. government appealed to the Supreme Court.

In the second case of the *Branzburg* trilogy, *In re Pappas,* television journalist Paul Pappas was invited to a Black Panther headquarters in Massachusetts. He also promised not to disclose any information he was given in confidence. A county grand jury summoned him and asked what he had seen at Panther headquarters. He refused to answer many of the grand jury's questions, citing the First Amendment (Massachusetts had no statutory journalist's privilege). The state Supreme Court rejected his argument and he appealed to the U.S. Supreme Court.

In the *Branzburg* case itself, *Louisville Courier-Journal* reporter Paul Branzburg observed two young men processing hashish and wrote a bylined story about it. The article included a tightly cropped photo of a pair of hands working with what the caption said was hashish. Later, Branzburg wrote an article about drug use in Frankfort, Kentucky. The article said he spent two weeks interviewing drug users. Branzburg was twice subpoenaed by grand juries, but he refused to testify, citing both a Kentucky shield law and the First Amendment. He appealed both cases, but the Kentucky Court of Appeals ruled against him, declaring that neither the First Amendment nor the Kentucky shield law applied to his situation. The shield law, the court said, only applied to the identities of informants; it did not excuse a reporter from testifying about events he personally witnessed. Branzburg also appealed to the U.S. Supreme Court.

Consolidating the three cases, the Supreme Court said all three reporters had to comply with the grand jury subpoenas. Thus, the high court affirmed the lower court rulings in *Branzburg* and in *In re Pappas* while reversing the *Caldwell* decision. Four Supreme Court justices said flatly that a journalist has the same duty as any other citizen to testify when called upon to do so. However, Justice Powell, who provided the crucial fifth vote to reject a reporter's privilege in these cases, didn't go that far. He left open the possibility that the First Amendment might excuse a reporter from revealing confidential information under other circumstances. Powell said:

The asserted claim to privilege should be judged on its facts by striking of a proper balance between freedom of the press and the obligation of all citizens to give relevant testimony with respect to criminal conduct. The balance of these vital Constitutional and societal interests on a case-by-case basis accords with the tried and traditional way of adjudicating such questions.

In short, the courts will be available to newsmen under circumstances where legitimate First Amendment interests require protection.

Thus, Powell felt a balancing process was necessary, with a constitutional shield for journalists available in some cases. One dissenter (Justice Douglas) took the absolute position that no restriction on freedom of the press, including the requirement that reporters testify in a court, was Constitutional. The other three dissenting justices (Stewart, Brennan, and Marshall) said they thought there should be a qualified journalist's privilege, based on the Constitution. These three justices said that, to justify requiring a journalist to reveal his sources, the government should have to show:

1. that there is probable cause to believe the journalist has clearly relevant information regarding a specific probable violation of law;
2. that the information cannot be obtained in some way that doesn't so heavily infringe on the First Amendment;
3. that there is a compelling and overriding interest in the information.

Even though these guidelines appeared in a dissenting opinion, they have been used by several lower federal and state courts in deciding journalist's privilege cases in recent years. The *Branzburg* decision, it turns out, was not quite the defeat for the media that it first appeared to be. The high court refused to create a Constitutional shield law, but five of the nine justices (the four dissenters plus Powell) did say that the Constitution gives journalists at least a limited right to withhold confidential information. Since then, a number of lower courts have undertaken the balancing process suggested by Powell, often ruling that journalists' confidential information is privileged in situations different from the ones that led to the *Branzburg* ruling (grand jury investigations). In so ruling, courts have often looked to the guidelines in the *Branzburg* dissent.

Federal Rulings after *Branzburg*

Perhaps foreshadowing things to come, it was only a few months after *Branzburg* that a federal appellate court refused to follow it as a precedent. Late in 1972, the second circuit U.S. Court of Appeals ruled that a case was sufficiently different from *Branzburg* to justify a different result. In *Baker v. F & F Investment* (470 F.2d 778), the court said a journalist has a Constitutional right not to reveal his sources, at least under certain circumstances.

In *Baker*, the author of an article exposing the "blockbusting" practices of real estate agents (i.e., tactics calculated to panic white homeowners into selling out at low prices) in all-white neighborhoods was asked to reveal his source—but in a civil lawsuit between black home buyers and real estate firms. Since the source was in the real estate business, he would be subjected to harassment and economic harm if identified, the writer said. The appellate court allowed this writer to keep his source confidential, noting that unlike *Branzburg* (which involved grand jury investigations) this was a civil lawsuit to which the journalist was not a party. In this instance, the U.S. Court of Appeals said the First Amendment protected the author's right to keep his source confidential.

In addition to the Constitutional argument for a reporter's privilege, some federal courts have recognized a limited federal common law journalist's privilege within the Federal Rules of Criminal Procedure, the Federal Rules of Civil Procedure and the Federal Rules of Evidence. None of these rules actually mentions a reporter's privilege, but several federal courts have held that a qualified reporter's privilege is inherent in them. For instance, Rule 17(c) of the Federal Rules of Criminal Procedure authorizes courts to set aside subpoenas that are "unreasonable or oppressive." Rule 501 of the Federal Rules of Evidence recognizes the concept of evidentiary privileges. It doesn't specifically cite a reporter's privilege, but the Congressman most responsible for drafting Rule 501 said in Congress: "The language of Rule 50l permits the courts to develop a privilege for newspaper people on a case-by-case basis."

By 1984, federal courts from coast to coast had recognized a limited reporter's privilege under various rationales, including the First Amendment, the federal rules of procedure, federal common law, or a combination of these. However, none of the federal courts had recognized the sort of absolute privilege journalists seek. Instead, the courts have weighed reporters' privilege claims against other considerations, often ruling that the privilege must give way—or at least that the media must let a judge examine the purportedly confidential information to determine whether it should be disclosed. In such cases, difficult confrontations between the press and the judiciary often result.

For example, in 1980 the third circuit U.S. Court of Appeals ruled against the producers of the CBS television program, "60 Minutes," on a reporter's privilege issue. In *U.S. v. Cuthbertson* (630 F.2d 139, 1980), a federal judge in New Jersey ordered CBS to submit confidential materials to him for an in-chambers review. The judge hoped to determine whether the materials should be released to the defendants in a criminal case that stemmed from a "60 Minutes" story.

The *Cuthbertson* case resulted from a story entitled "From Burgers to Bankruptcy." It questioned the franchising practices of an East Coast fast-food chain, Wild Bill's Family Restaurants. A grand jury later indicted several Wild Bill's executives on various criminal charges. The executives subpoenaed CBS' outtakes and other unpublished information before their trial. The judge ordered CBS to provide much of the requested material for an in-chambers inspection. When CBS refused, the judge cited the network for contempt, and CBS appealed. The U.S. Court of Appeals affirmed the judge's order. The judge would have to see the materials in order to adequately weigh the defendants' need for them against the network's qualified privilege to keep them confidential, the appellate court ruled. Thus, the appellate court affirmed the contempt citation against CBS.

CBS asked the U.S. Supreme Court to review the lower courts' rulings, but the petition was denied. In 1981, CBS reluctantly allowed the judge to review the requested materials.

Cuthbertson notwithstanding, the federal third circuit is among the leaders in recognizing a reporter's privilege judicially. That circuit has ruled that the privilege covers not only sources but also unpublished materials, and that it applies in both criminal and civil cases.

A year before *Cuthbertson*, the third circuit Court of Appeals affirmed a reporter's right to keep her sources confidential in a civil case, *Riley v. Chester* (612 F.2d 708, 1979). A lawsuit was filed by a police officer who contended he was harassed by the police chief and others in the department when he ran for mayor. He wanted to know the source of a news story he considered unfavorable, but the reporter, Geraldine Oliver of the *Delaware County (Pennsylvania) Daily Times*, refused to disclose it at a court hearing. Oliver was cited for contempt, but the appellate court overturned the citation because the identity of the source was not relevant enough to the case to override the qualified reporter's privilege. In so ruling, the court said that three requirements had to be met before a reporter should be required to disclose confidential information: (1) the information had been sought elsewhere; (2) the information could not be obtained from other sources; and (3) the information was clearly relevant to the case.

On the other hand, the third circuit refused to uphold the reporter's privilege in another 1980 decision, *U.S. v. Criden* (633 F.2d 346). In that case, Jan Schaffer, a Philadelphia *Inquirer* reporter, refused to testify about her conversations with a U.S. attorney during the "Abscam" case, in which many public officials were charged with bribery. The U.S. attorney admitted the conversations had occurred, and Schaffer was eventually cited for contempt. The third circuit Court of Appeals affirmed a contempt citation, noting that the issue here was not confidentiality (the source had already waived his right to confidentiality) but the conduct of the U.S. attorney in allegedly "leaking" word of the investigation to the press. In this criminal proceeding, the defendants were seeking a dismissal by alleging prosecutorial misconduct and sought Schaffer's testimony to show such misconduct. The appellate court ruled that the reporter's testimony was crucial to the case and thus affirmed the civil contempt citation. In so ruling, the court noted:

> When no countervailing Constitutional concerns are at stake, it can be said that the privilege is absolute; when Constitutional precepts collide, the absolute gives way to the qualified and a balancing process comes into play to determine its limits.

The third circuit then applied the three-part test it enunciated in *Riley*, and found it satisfied. Thus, the court said the reporter's privilege had to yield to the defendants' Sixth Amendment right to a fair trial in this particular case.

In 1981 the U.S. Supreme Court refused to hear an appeal of the third circuit decision, in effect forcing Schaffer to choose between testifying and going to jail. However, all four of the Philadelphia "Abscam" defendants either were acquitted or had the charges against them dismissed. The contempt citation against Schaffer was dropped after she agreed to reveal whether she had in fact interviewed the U.S. attorney in the case, without revealing the content of the conversation. Nevertheless, the case was closed only because the defense attorneys said they no longer needed Schaffer's testimony—not because of any victory for the reporter's privilege.

Meanwhile, other federal appellate courts across America have also recognized a qualifed reporter's privilege in the years since *Branzburg*. But like the *Criden* decision, these other decisions have emphasized the limited nature of the privilege, insisting that it must be balanced against other rights. For example, in *Silkwood v. Kerr-McGee* (563 F.2d 433, 1977), the tenth circuit Court of Appeals recognized the reporter's privilege and said it applied to a documentary filmmaker. The court overturned a trial judge's order requiring the filmmaker to reveal his confidential information because the party seeking it (the Kerr-McGee Corporation) had not diligently tried to secure it elsewhere first. In any future request for the filmmaker's (or any other journalist's) confidential information, the trial court was ordered to weigh: (1) the relevance and necessity of the information; (2) whether it went "to the heart of the matter"; (3) its possible availability elsewhere; and (4) the type of case involved. The *Silkwood* case attracted wide attention because Karen Silkwood was killed in an auto accident en route to testify to the Atomic Energy Commission about allegedly dangerous practices of her employer, the Kerr-McGee Corporation. This civil lawsuit by her estate and others charged the company with violating her civil rights.

In a civil libel case, the first circuit U.S. Court of Appeals handed down yet another decision recognizing the existence of a journalist's privilege. In *Bruno & Stillman v. Globe Newspaper Co.* (633 F.2d 583, 1980), the court ruled on a dispute over pretrial discovery of a reporter's confidential sources by emphasizing the balancing of rights necessary in such cases. The court reaffirmed the existence of the privilege, but said the trial court had to balance the First Amendment interests involved against the plaintiff's need for the information. The case was remanded, with instructions for the trial judge to follow in deciding whether to order the newspaper involved (the *Boston Globe*) to disclose its sources for a series of stories criticizing the plaintiff's products (fishing boats).

The federal fifth circuit Court of Appeals also recognized the existence of a reporter's privilege in 1980, in *Miller v. Transamerican Press* (6 Med.L.Rptr. 1599). But in that case, the Court of Appeals said the privilege had to give way to a libel plaintiff's need for confidential information without which he could not prove actual malice. Thus, that appellate court allowed the discovery of a magazine's confidential sources. The case resulted from an article in *Overdrive* magazine (a specialty magazine for truck drivers) alleging mishandling of the Teamsters Union's Central States Pension Fund. The appellate court upheld a lower court ruling that the identity of a source for the article "went to the heart of the matter" in the libel suit, since the plaintiff could probably not prove actual malice without checking on what the source told the article's author.

On the other hand, a federal district court in Washington, D.C., decided not to require a reporter to reveal his sources in a situation somewhat like the *Silkwood* case. In a 1979 decision, *U.S. v. Hubbard* (493 F.Supp. 202), the court recognized a *Washington Post* reporter's qualified privilege, and evaluated the Church of Scientology's demand for the reporter's notes about an FBI investigation of the church. The court decided the privilege protected the reporter, since the church could obtain the same information from FBI sources.

The U.S. Court of Appeals for Washington, D.C., followed up the *Hubbard* ruling with a 1981 decision that strongly endorsed the concept of a reporter's privilege, *Zerilli v. Smith* (656 F.2d 705). The case arose after U.S. Justice Department officials allegedly leaked wiretapped telephone conversations of Detroit underworld leaders to the *Detroit News*. Two reputed underworld figures sued the Justice Department and sought a court order requiring a reporter to reveal his sources.

The judge refused to issue such an order, and his decision was appealed. The appellate court affirmed the refusal, noting that the plaintiffs had not exhausted alternative means of securing the information. They had not queried Justice Department employees who had access to the tapes, for instance. In civil cases to which the reporter is not a party, a reporter is exempt from revealing his or her sources "in all but the most exceptional cases," the appellate court held.

The court said that to overcome the reporter's privilege, a civil litigant must show that: (1) the lawsuit is not frivolous; (2) the information sought is crucial to the case; and (3) all alternative sources for the information have been exhausted.

Technically, these federal decisions are binding only in the regions of the country where they were decided, but there is a growing national trend toward the federal courts' judicially establishing at least a limited journalist's privilege. The consensus of the federal courts seems to be that journalists must sometimes reveal confidential information, but only if a party to a lawsuit clearly needs it and cannot obtain it anywhere else.

State Rulings on Privilege

In addition to the rulings by federal courts, at least seven state supreme courts have recognized a journalist's privilege even in the absence of a statutory shield law. For instance, in 1977 the Iowa Supreme Court recognized a qualified First Amendment privilege for reporters. In a libel case, *Winegard v. Oxberger* (258 N.W.2d 847), the court roughly followed the three-part test in the *Branzburg* dissent, indicating that a reporter could refuse to reveal confidential information, at least in a civil proceeding, unless: (1) the information sought "goes to the heart of the matter" before the court; (2) other reasonable means of obtaining the information have been exhausted; and (3) the lawsuit in which the information is sought does not appear to be "patently frivolous." However, the Iowa Supreme Court weighed the case at hand and decided that three-part test was met, so the reporter was not excused from revealing her sources for several stories about a protracted divorce case that led to a libel suit.

A number of other state courts have also found a Constitutional basis for a journalist's privilege, sometimes even in criminal proceedings when a defendant contended the information was needed for his or her defense. In so doing, some state courts have ruled that a qualified reporter's privilege is inherent in their own state constitutions as well as the federal Constitution. The Wisconsin Supreme Court so ruled in a murder case (*Zelenka v. Wisconsin*, 266 N.W.2d 279, 1978), although the court emphasized that the journalist's right to withhold confidential information had to be balanced against the defendant's need for the information. The case stemmed from a drug-related murder, and the defendant sought the identity of the source for an underground newspaper story that claimed the victim had been cooperating with narcotics officers. The state Supreme Court said the defendant had not shown that the privileged information would have helped him in his defense. Thus, the court upheld the reporter's right to keep his source confidential.

In 1982, the New Hampshire Supreme Court ruled in much the same way in another murder case: *New Hampshire v. Siel* (8 Med.L.Rptr. 1265). In that case two student journalists at the University of New Hampshire refused to release documents that would have revealed their sources for a story about the murder victim's alleged drug dealings. The state Supreme Court affirmed a judge's ruling that the materials sought from the student journalists would not have affected the outcome of the case.

Similarly, the supreme courts of Kansas, Vermont, Virginia, and Washington have recognized at least a limited reporter's privilege in the absence of a state shield law (see *Kansas v. Sandstrom*, 581 P.2d 812, 1978; *Vermont v. St. Peter*, 315 A.2d 254, 1974; *Brown v. Virginia*, 204 S.E.2d 429, 1974; *Clampitt v. Thurston County*, 9 Med.L.Rptr. 1206, 1983; and *Senear v. Daily Journal-American*, 641 P.2d 1180, 1982).

On the other hand, some state supreme courts have flatly refused to recognize any journalist's privilege, even a qualified one. The Idaho Supreme Court, for instance, once refused to recognize any sort of First Amendment privilege for journalists, even in a civil libel suit (*Caldero v. Tribune Publishing*, 562 P.2d 791, 1977), although that court has more recently moderated its stance on this issue. The *Caldero* case was particularly notable for the stridency of the court's language in condemning the concept of a reporter's privilege:

> In a society so organized as ours, the public must know the truth in order to make value judgments, not the least of which regard its government and officialdom. The only reliable source of that truth is a "press". . . . which is free to publish that truth without government censorship. We cannot accept the premise that the public's right to know is somehow enhanced by prohibiting the disclosure of truth in the courts of the public.

Caldero was a libel case in which the plaintiff, a police officer, was criticized by a newspaper for shooting a suspect fleeing a minor crime. The officer, Michael Caldero, sought the identity of a source for the newspaper article during pretrial discovery, but the paper refused to reveal it. The Idaho Supreme Court affirmed a contempt citation against a reporter, flatly refusing to recognize any journalist's privilege.

However, three years after *Caldero,* the Idaho Supreme Court back-pedaled on the privilege issue in *Sierra Life v. Magic Valley Newspapers* (6 Med.L.Rptr. 1769, 1980), another libel case in which the plaintiff demanded the identity of confidential sources during pretrial discovery proceedings. Here the *Twin Falls Times-News* published stories reporting on various legal actions taken against a life insurance company by other western states. The company never alleged that anything in the stories was false, but nonetheless a trial judge ordered the paper to name its sources during the pretrial discovery process. The paper refused, maintaining that the information was taken from public records and was accurate, and that sources within the company merely told reporters where to look to find these public records. When the paper refused to reveal the sources, the judge stripped the paper of all its normal libel defenses and entered judgment in the amount of $1.9 million for the plaintiff—still without any proof of the elements of libel (such as the negligent or malicious publication of a falsehood).

The Idaho Supreme Court was forced to retreat from its refusal to recognize a reporter's privilege, reversing the judge's action and reinstating the paper's defenses. The court acknowledged that a journalist's confidential information has to be shown to be *relevant* before it could be discovered. The court said the plaintiff had not shown that knowing the identity of the sources would help prove its libel case. This time, the Idaho Supreme Court was at least a little more sympathetic to the needs of the media:

> We recognize that the news media rely upon confidential sources in the preparation of many stories. . . . The ability to keep the identity of those sources confidential is not infrequently a prerequisite to obtaining information. This interest, while legitimate, is not so paramount that legitimate discovery needs of a libel plaintiff must bow before it. But by the same token a trial court can be expected to exercise caution when it

orders these sources be revealed. As the Supreme Court of the United States has suggested, the first question to be answered is whether the identity of the sources is relevant.

Thus, the Idaho Supreme Court afforded limited protection to journalist's sources in *Sierra Life*. Still, Idaho journalists enjoy far less protection from indiscriminate discovery or subpoenas than do journalists in many states. In states such as Idaho, journalists need a statutory shield law far more than they do in states where the courts have given them more Constitutional protection. In such states a journalist still has little choice but to reveal confidential sources or go to jail. Perhaps the best solution to this problem on a nationwide basis would be a federal shield law that applied to all state and federal proceedings.

STATUTORY SHIELD LAWS

Immediately after the *Branzburg* Supreme Court decision, a number of bills were introduced in Congress in an attempt to establish a federal statutory shield law. The plurality opinion in *Branzburg* emphasized that Congress would be free to enact a shield law, even though the high court was declining to create one by judicial decree. However, Congress became hopelessly bogged down in the details of the proposed federal shield laws, and none was ever approved.

Two of the major problems that stymied Congress were the tough problem of deciding who should be covered and the "prescient witness" question. A prescient witness is someone who actually witnesses a crime, such as reporter Branzburg. There was a strong feeling in Congress that someone like Branzburg should have to testify about the unlawful activity he witnessed. But others in Congress felt such an exception would fatally weaken a shield law.

Moreover, Congress could never completely agree on the definition of a journalist. A shield law applicable only to "establishment" journalists would have been politically acceptable, but it would have created serious new First Amendment problems. How could a federal law single out some journalists and give them a reporter's privilege without affording the same privilege to journalists working for less middle-of-the-road publications? On the other hand, many in Congress were simply unwilling to vote for any shield law that also protected "underground" journalists because such a law might help them develop even stronger ties to radical groups than they already had.

Also, Congress was unable to decide whether the federal shield law should be a strong one with few exceptions or a much weaker one with many exceptions. In addition, there was no consensus on the question of protecting reporters' notes and film outtakes as well as the identities of sources.

As a result of these unresolved issues, no federal shield law was enacted, leaving the question to the state legislatures and the courts to decide.

State Shield Laws

In the 26 states that had enacted statutory shield laws at this writing, there was a wide variation in philosophy and approach. Moreover, some state shield laws have been significantly altered by judicial interpretation. The highest court in one state (New Mexico) has gone so far as to overturn a statutory shield law as an unconstitutional encroachment on the information-seeking authority of the judiciary (see *Ammerman v. Hubbard Broadcasting, Inc.*, 551 P.2d 1354, 1976). Another state (California) placed its shield law in the state constitution, where it would presumably be safer from attacks on its constitutionality in the courts.

Here are the 26 states that had adopted statutory shield laws at this writing, with the years of their adoption: Maryland (1896), New Jersey (1933), Alabama (1935), California (1935), Arkansas (1936), Kentucky (1936), Arizona (1937), Pennsylvania (1937), Indiana (1941), Montana (1943), Michigan (1949), Ohio (1953), Louisiana (1964), Alaska (1967), New Mexico (1967), Nevada (1967), New York (1970), Illinois (1971), Rhode Island (1971), Delaware (1973), Nebraska (1973), North Dakota (1973), Minnesota (1973), Oregon (1973), Tennessee (1973), and Oklahoma (1974). Many of these statutory laws have been extensively revised since their original enactment and, as just noted, many have been heavily modified by judicial interpretation.

In view of the widely varying judicial interpretations, it is difficult to generalize about state shield laws. Some appear very strong but have been fatally weakened by court decisions. Others have been upheld and even strengthened by court decisions. Generally, shield laws fall into three groups: (1) absolute privilege laws, which seemingly excuse a reporter from ever revealing a news source in a governmental inquiry; (2) laws that only apply the privilege if information derived from the source is actually published or broadcast; and (3) qualified or limited privilege laws, which may have one or many exceptions, often allowing the courts to disregard them under certain circumstances. Any list of which states' shield laws fall into each category could well be outdated before it is printed, in view of the frequent court decisions in this area.

Perhaps the best way to summarize state laws is to provide a checklist of things a good one should cover. You may wish to review your state's shield law (if any) and particularly the court decisions (listed after the law itself in your state's annotated statutes), using the research method described in Chapter One. In evaluating your state's statute and court decisions, determine if the law includes these provisions:

1. coverage for all journalists, including newspaper, wire service, magazine, broadcast, free-lance, and foreign reporters;
2. coverage of all communications media, including newspapers, magazines, sporadically published newspapers and magazines (some "underground" publications are published only irregularly), wire services, broadcasters, book publishers, cable systems, documentary film producers, etc.;

3. applicability to all sources of information, regardless of whether the information is ultimately published or broadcast;
4. applicability to journalists' "work product", i.e., notes, unpublished photographs and tapes, film outtakes, rough drafts, etc.;
5. applicability to all official proceedings, including grand jury investigations, legislative and administrative proceedings, criminal and civil court proceedings (including the discovery process, even if the reporter is a litigant as in a libel suit);
6. applicability even if the confidential source waives confidentiality by revealing his or her identity to a third party;
7. the absence of any exceptions that would create loopholes to exclude some reporters or some proceedings.

Obviously, few state laws include all of these provisions, but many journalists believe their needs would be best served by one that does. Still, state shield laws mean little until they are interpreted by the courts.

THE COURTS AND SHIELD LAWS

Sadly, the reality about shield laws is that many lawyers and judges don't like them. Judges sometimes find themselves dealing with reporters who possess important information—information that might well affect the outcome of a case—but who simply refuse to fulfill what judges see as a civic responsibility by disclosing it. How can a court seek the truth under those circumstances, judges ask. Some judges view shield laws as obstacles to justice, laws made by people who are, after all, politicians. Shield laws, they feel, strip the courts of some of their authority to do an important job. Many judges seem perfectly willing to weigh a journalist's privilege against other interests; some are willing to create such a privilege judicially in the absence of a statutory law, as already explained. However, when a legislature makes the decision for them—and makes the privilege absolute under all circumstances—judges tend to look for loopholes.

Perhaps the sentiment of the legal establishment was best summarized many years ago by John Wigmore, the preeminent scholar on the law of evidence. Speaking in 1923 about the nation's first shield law, enacted in Maryland in 1896, he said: "the (Maryland) enactment, as detestable in substance as it is in form, will probably remain unique."

Wigmore's prediction was wrong, of course, but the sentiment has been shared by generations of lawyers and judges. For years judges have been whittling away at the older common law evidentiary privileges of doctors, lawyers, and clergymen, and they have shown great ingenuity in interpreting the language of state shield laws to reduce their impact.

For sheer judicial gall, certainly the most notable court decision on a shield law is *Ammerman v. Hubbard Broadcasting*, the New Mexico case cited earlier. In that decision a state supreme court said the legislature doesn't have the power, under the state constitution, to restrict a judge's authority in this way. Thus, the court simply invalidated the whole shield law as it applied to the state's judiciary. The New Mexico shield law is still valid in connection with legislative and administrative proceedings, but not in court proceedings (including grand jury investigations). That means the New Mexico shield law is nearly useless, since reporters are rarely required to reveal confidential information except in court proceedings. To justify its decision, the New Mexico Supreme Court declared that a shield law is a *procedural* rule. The legislature has no authority to dictate procedural rules to the judiciary, the court said.

No other state's highest court has gone quite that far, but several other courts have handed down decisions narrowing the scope of state shield laws or broadening their exceptions. For instance, New York courts repeatedly carved out judicial exceptions to that state's shield law in the early years after its enactment in 1970. By 1973, the courts had created a prescient witness exception and ruled that the law didn't apply unless a reporter had promised confidentiality to a source. They also ruled that the law didn't apply if the information came to a reporter unsolicited (see *WBAI-FM v. Proskin*, 344 N.Y.S.2d 393, 1973). In New York, more than a dozen reported court decisions have gone against journalists who were seeking to keep sources or information confidential under the state's shield law.

Across the continent in California, the pattern is much the same. State courts repeatedly narrowed the scope of a seemingly absolute shield law during the 1970s. First, an appellate court said the law simply didn't apply when a judge was trying to find out who violated a judicial "gag" order. The legislature doesn't have the authority to pass a law that makes it impossible for courts to investigate violations of their orders, the court held (*Farr v. Superior Court*, 22 Cal.App. 3d 60, 1971). Later, another California appellate court said the shield law didn't apply when the information might help exonerate someone charged with a crime, because the defendant's Constitutional right to a fair trial was paramount. Thus, the reporter would be required to bring in the requested information for a judge's inspection in his chambers, with the judge entitled to release the information if he deemed it significant to the case (*CBS v. Superior Court*, 85 Cal.App.3d 241, 1978). In 1980 the people of California voted to place the shield law in the state Constitution, where it would presumably be somewhat safer from judicial modification.

However, in the 1980s judges continued to carve out exceptions to the California shield law, despite its Constitutional status. For instance, in a 1982 case, *KSDO v. Superior Court* (136 Cal.App.3d 375), a California appellate court ruled that the shield law protects journalists only from contempt of court citations and not from other legal sanctions (such as the loss of otherwise valid defenses in libel cases). The problem of shield laws and libel cases is also discussed in Chapter Four.

In New Jersey, an equally large loophole was created in the state shield law by a state Supreme Court decision. In the celebrated Myron Farber case (discussed later), the court said the shield law must give way when a criminal defendant seeks evidence held by a journalist. At the very least, the journalist must submit the material to a judge, who is to make an in-chambers evaluation and decide whether to release the information (*In re Farber*, 394 A.2d 330, 1978).

In the aftermath of the *Farber* decision, both the New Jersey Legislature and the state Supreme Court have acted to *strengthen* that state's shield law. In *Maressa v. New Jersey Monthly* (8 Med.L.Rptr. 1473) and *Resorts International v. New Jersey Monthly* (8 Med.L.Rptr. 1487), the state Supreme Court ruled that the shield law is virtually absolute in libel cases. In the *Maressa* ruling, the court said:

> Twice in recent sessions, the legislature has made evident its intent to preserve a far-reaching privilege in this state. And twice in recent terms, this court has construed the shield law to protect confidential information to the extent allowed by the United States and New Jersey Constitutions. Absent any countervailing Constitutional right, the newsperson's statutory privilege not to disclose confidential information is absolute. (8 Med.L.Rptr. at 1476)

Another state in which the courts have not only affirmed but strengthened a shield law is Pennsylvania, where the state Supreme Court significantly expanded the shield law's scope in *In re Taylor* (412 A.2d 32, 1963).

The Pennsylvania law specifically protected only "sources of information," but the court interpreted that language to include notes and other unpublished materials, even if they didn't reveal the news source. Moreover, Pennsylvania state courts have liberally interpreted a phrase in the law that exempts reporters from revealing their sources "in any legal proceeding." "Any legal proceeding" really means what it says, the Pennsylvania courts have ruled.

Furthermore, a federal court deciding a case that arose in Pennsylvania chose to observe the state shield law in *Steaks Unlimited v. Deaner* (623 F.2d 264, 1980). That decision is neither surprising nor unique, inasmuch as federal courts are supposed to apply most types of state law in "diversity of citizenship" cases (i.e., cases decided in federal rather than state courts only because they involve citizens of two different states). The Pennsylvania shield law did not apply in the federal case from Pennsylvania discussed earlier (*Riley v. Chester*) because it was not a diversity case. *Riley* was a federal civil rights case.

To summarize, journalist's privilege is in a state of change and uncertainty. Many states have shield laws, but even in these states reporters are often called upon to reveal their sources or confidential information. On the other hand, in some states without shield laws the courts have judicially recognized a limited reporter's privilege, but the courts in other states have refused to take that step. On the federal level, a number of courts have recognized a qualified privilege as a matter of federal common law in the years since the Supreme Court's *Branzburg* decision.

FARR AND *FARBER*: TWO NOTABLE CASES

Given the wide variety of laws and court decisions on shield laws, perhaps the best way to illustrate how this legal problem can affect a journalist is to describe two famous cases in which reporters went to jail to avoid revealing confidential information. The cases involve Bill Farr, a former *Los Angeles Herald Examiner* reporter (more recently with the *Los Angeles Times*), and Myron Farber, a *New York Times* reporter.

In 1970 Farr was covering the trial of Charles Manson and his counter-culture "family" for the sensational murders of actress Sharon Tate and a number of other persons. A protective ("gag") order was in effect, but two of the six attorneys in the case gave Farr a copy of a statement by a prospective prosecution witness who said Manson planned to torture and murder several more show business celebrities. Farr published the story, and the trial judge, Charles Older, demanded to know who had violated the court order by giving Farr the information. Invoking the California shield law, Farr refused to name his sources. Judge Older accepted Farr's response at the time.

However, Farr later left the *Herald Examiner* and became a special investigator for the Los Angeles County District Attorney. Judge Older summoned Farr after the trial and again demanded the names of the sources, contending that the shield law applied only to currently employed reporters. Farr still refused to comply and was cited for contempt of court.

At this point there began a complex series of legal maneuvers that lasted for a decade. Farr faced an indefinite jail sentence for civil contempt of court, but he was released pending appeal. In the first of four appellate court decisions involving Farr (*Farr v. Superior Court*, cited earlier), a California appellate court in 1972 carved out a giant exception to the state shield law. The court said the legislature had no power to enact a law that would prevent a judge from finding out who had violated a court order. Thus, the shield law was invalid in Farr's situation. The court sidestepped the question of whether the shield law should apply to former reporters, but the legislature quickly closed that loophole.

Still, Farr had to reveal his sources or go to jail. He chose jail, and began serving a potential life sentence for civil contempt after the California and U.S. Supreme Courts declined to review the appellate ruling. However, after 46 days Farr was released by order of U.S. Supreme Court Justice William O. Douglas, pending still another appeal.

After almost two more years of legal maneuvering, another California appellate court decision was handed down: *In re Farr* (36 Cal.App.3d 577, 1974). In that case, the court recognized the possibility that Farr might spend the rest of his life in jail rather than obey the court order and reveal his sources.

A procedure had to be created to allow the release of civil contempt prisoners whose violation of a court order was based on "a clearly articulated moral principle." The appellate court said a hearing should be held to decide if: (1) Farr was refusing to obey the court order because of a moral principle;

and (2) continued incarceration would not induce him to obey the court order. If Farr was obeying such a principle and was committed to stand firm regardless of the prospect of continued jailing, the trial court had to change the contempt citation from civil contempt (which has no time limit) to criminal contempt (with a maximum sentence of five days in this case).

At Farr's "moral principle" hearing, an array of media celebrities testified on Farr's behalf. A judge agreed that Farr was obeying such a moral principle and ended the civil contempt citation. The next day, however, Judge Older (the original judge who cited Farr for contempt) initiated a new criminal contempt proceeding and eventually sentenced Farr to five more days in jail and a $500 fine. That sentence was delayed while Farr again appealed. The U.S. Court of Appeals rejected Farr's challenge to the constitutionality of his contempt citation, deciding that the court's need to find out who violated the original court order outweighed Farr's journalistic privilege (*Farr v. Pitchess*, 522 F.2d 464, 1975). Ultimately, a California appellate court set aside the new contempt citation on the ground that it constituted a multiple prosecution for the same event (*In re Farr*, 64 Cal.App.3d 605, 1976).

However, even then Farr's legal troubles were not over. Two of the six Manson trial lawyers filed a $24 million libel suit, contending that he had libeled them by saying two of the six lawyers had given him the information for the story that started the whole escapade. A trial judge dismissed the libel suit in 1979, but the two attorneys appealed the dismissal. In 1981—a decade after Farr's legal troubles began—an appellate court finally affirmed the dismissal of the libel suit.

In addition to enduring a decade of litigation, Farr was left with another problem: paying a huge bill for legal expenses. The *Los Angeles Times* covered Farr's legal fees after he became a *Times* employee, but not the legal expenses he incurred before that time.

Compared to Bill Farr's legal battle, Myron Farber's troubles were short-lived, but nonetheless painful, both for Farber (who eventually spent 40 days in jail) and the *New York Times* (which was assessed $285,000 in fines). The case arose from stories Farber wrote for the *Times* in 1976, investigating a series of mysterious deaths at a New Jersey hospital some ten years earlier. The stories were largely responsible for the indictment of Dr. Mario Jascalevich for murder.

About halfway through the doctor's six-month trial in 1978, his attorney got a subpoena ordering Farber and the *Times* to release information from interviews with witnesses at the trial. Farber and the *New York Times* refused and were cited for criminal and civil contempt of court. Farber was fined $1,000 and ordered jailed until he chose to provide the subpoenaed information. The *Times* was fined $100,000 plus $5,000 a day until the court order was obeyed.

Farber and the *Times* appealed the orders to the New Jersey Supreme Court, contending that both the First Amendment and the New Jersey shield law, a seemingly absolute one, protected them. The state Supreme Court denied their appeal, in the process carving out an exception to the shield law where a criminal defendant needs information from a journalist for his defense. The court ordered Farber and the *Times* to submit the requested material to the trial judge to examine in his chambers so the judge could decide whether the material was necessary to the defense or if it should be kept confidential.

Both Farber and the *Times* refused to comply. Farber went to jail and the *Times* continued paying $5,000 a day until the trial was concluded and the case was given to the jury, which eventually acquitted Dr. Jascalevich. After that, all of the other civil and criminal contempt citations were dropped. Eventually the governor of New Jersey pardoned both Farber and the *Times* and refunded the fines paid by the *Times*.

Some journalists were critical of Farber's and the *Times'* handling of this dispute, particularly because Farber struck up a lucrative book-publishing deal involving the Jascalevich case and because the whole confrontation might well have been avoided, given a little more diplomacy on all sides. Nevertheless, both Farber and the *Times* paid a high price for their principles, as did Bill Farr. Myron Farber's legal troubles didn't last nearly as long as Farr's, but he missed breaking Farr's record for jail time by only a few days.

Fortunately, the *Farr* and *Farber* cases are unusual, but that is of little comfort to journalists. Few journalists have paid as high a price as Farr and Farber for protecting their sources. In fact, jail sentences for journalists are still rare. But, on the other hand, numerous journalists lacking the resources available to papers such as the *Los Angeles Times* and *New York Times* have been forced to reveal confidential sources, simply because the money to fight such a costly legal battle just wasn't available.

Moreover, it is becoming increasingly commonplace for journalists to have to either reveal confidential information or go to jail. James C. Goodale, a New York lawyer who specializes in press law, reported a study of the problem at the 1983 Communications Law Symposium of the Practising Law Institute. He said he had identified 67 instances in which a reporter was ordered to reveal confidential information between September, 1982 and September, 1983. Although journalists eventually avoided revealing any confidential information or going to jail in 37 of the 67 cases, Goodale said the 67 cases represented about twice as many confrontations between reporters and the courts as occurred only a year earlier. He said more and more lawyers—both prosecutors and defense attorneys—are viewing journalists as likely prospects for subpoenas.

The mass media have a tough struggle ahead of them if the fight for an effective reporter's privilege is ever to be won.

NEWSROOM SEARCHES

A related legal problem produced a crisis for journalists in the 1970s: searches of print and broadcast newsrooms. In a disturbing 1978 decision, the U.S. Supreme Court ruled that the First Amendment does not create any privilege that would protect the media from newsroom searches (*Zurcher v. Stanford Daily*, 436 U.S. 547).

The case began in 1971 when a large group of demonstrators occupied the Stanford University Hospital and were forcibly ejected by Santa Clara County (California) sheriff's deputies and Palo Alto police. The *Stanford Daily*, the student newspaper at Stanford University, covered the incident, which was marked by considerable violence. A number of persons, including several law enforcement officers, were injured. Two days later, the *Daily* ran a special edition with a number of photographs of the disturbance.

The Santa Clara County district attorney's office got a search warrant, and four police officers searched the *Daily*'s office in the presence of several staff members. No member of the staff was suspected of any involvement in the violence, but the police searched the offices for additional photographs or relevant information. They found none.

The *Daily* staff sued the local officials in a federal civil action, alleging violations of the First, Fourth, and Fourteenth Amendments. Both the federal district court and the ninth circuit Court of Appeals ruled in the student journalists' favor, but the Supreme Court reversed those rulings.

In a 5-3 decision, the Supreme Court said the Constitution does not prevent an unannounced search of a newspaper, even where no member of the staff is suspected of any crime. The court said that such a search is Constitutional, as long as the requirements of specificity and reasonableness are satisfied by the search warrant. Police would not be permitted to go rummaging through a newspaper's files indiscriminately, but if a warrant described specific evidence, the police could conduct a newsroom search in an attempt to obtain that evidence, the court ruled.

However, the Supreme Court made it clear that Congress or state legislatures could act to forbid newsroom searches; the high court merely said it wasn't going to forbid them judicially. Within days of the *Zurcher* decision, anti-newsroom search bills were introduced in a number of state legislatures and in Congress. Several states passed such laws within a few months, among them Illinois, California, Alaska, New Jersey, and Virginia.

The Privacy Protection Act of 1980

Two years later, Congress passed a comprehensive federal law against newsroom searches, the Privacy Protection Act of 1980. This far-reaching federal law effectively overruled the *Zurcher* decision, outlawing most newsroom searches by federal, state, and local law enforcement officials.

Under the Privacy Protection Act, law enforcement officials are prohibited from conducting searches and seizures involving "documentary materials" (photographs, tapes, films, etc.) held by newsgatherers except under very limited circumstances. The law allows such searches and seizures only when: (1) the person holding the information is suspected of a crime; (2) there is reason to believe the materials must be seized immediately to prevent someone's death or serious bodily injury; (3) there is reason to believe giving notice and seeking a subpoena would result in the materials being destroyed, changed, or hidden; or (4) the materials were not produced as a result of a court order that has been affirmed on appeal.

The rules regarding a journalist's "work product" (e.g., notes and rough drafts) are even tougher. These materials cannot be seized except when the journalist is suspected of a crime or when necessary to prevent someone's death or bodily injury.

Anyone who is searched in violation of the Privacy Protection Act may sue the federal government and most state and local governments, but evidence secured in violation of the bill may nonetheless be used in court.

The law also directed the U.S. Justice Department to prepare guidelines for searches by federal officers involving evidence held by someone not suspected of a crime but also not working in a First Amendment-related area.

Perhaps the major virtue of the Privacy Protection Act is that it usually requires law enforcement officials to get subpoenas instead of search warrants if they wish to obtain information from journalists.

Why is this distinction important? Search warrants are ordinarily authorized by judges unilaterally; the person who is the object of the search has no chance to argue against the issuance of the warrant. He or she first learns of the warrant's existence when law enforcement officers show up and enter the premises (by force, if necessary).

Subpoenas, on the other hand, are merely court orders directing someone to produce information. They can be challenged on legal grounds, and their issuance can be appealed. Granted, subpoenas are a major problem for journalists; some large newspapers and television stations have attorneys working nearly full time on the job of resisting subpoenas. Nevertheless, most journalists would much rather face a subpoena than have their offices raided by law enforcement officers armed with a search warrant.

At the very least, the Privacy Protection Act is an improvement over the situation in which journalists found themselves after the *Zurcher* decision. However, many journalists wish the law had been made even tougher: evidence secured during illegal newsroom searches should not be admissible in court, they contend. In the area of newsroom searches, as in the broader area of reporter's privilege, the major legal problems are not completely resolved.

A Summary of Contempt and Reporter's Privilege

WHAT IS CONTEMPT OF COURT?

Judges have the authority to punish those who show disrespect for a court or disobey a court order by citing them for contempt. Criminal contempt is a punishment for a past misdeed: it results in a fine or jail sentence. Civil contempt is coercive: the person cited (the "contemnor") is often jailed only until he chooses to obey a court order that he previously refused to obey.

WHY IS CONTEMPT A PROBLEM FOR JOURNALISTS?

When a journalist promises to keep certain information (such as the identity of a news source) confidential, he/she has an ethical obligation to keep that promise, even if a court asks for the information. Thus, an ethical journalist may risk a contempt of court citation—and perhaps a jail sentence.

WHAT IS REPORTER'S PRIVILEGE?

Because many important stories could not be researched without promising confidentiality to key news sources, journalists believe they should have a right to keep their film outtakes, unpublished notes, and sources' names confidential. Reporter's privilege is the concept that a newsgatherer has a right to withhold this information, even when asked to reveal it by a court.

WHEN DOES THIS PRIVILEGE APPLY?

Reporter's privilege is recognized in states with "shield laws". Some 26 states have enacted shield laws, but some of them have so many exceptions that they provide a reporter little protection from a contempt of court citation. Also, courts have sometimes declined to observe shield laws, instead ruling that they unconstitutionally abridge the authority of the judiciary.

WITHOUT A SHIELD LAW, DOES THE PRIVILEGE EXIST?

In *Branzburg v. Hayes*, a majority of the Supreme Court justices said a limited Constitutional reporter's privilege exists under certain circumstances, but not under the circumstances that led to the *Branzburg* case (grand jury investigations where reporters allegedly knew of unlawful activity). A number of lower federal and state courts have recognized a qualified privilege for reporters to withhold confidential information unless the information:

1. Goes to the heart of the matter at hand;
2. Is clearly relevant and necessary to the case; and
3. Is unavailable from non-journalistic sources.

ARE NEWSROOM SEARCHES LAWFUL?

Under the Privacy Protection Act of 1980, most newsroom searches by federal, state, and local law enforcement agencies are unlawful.

9

FREEDOM OF INFORMATION

Of the various legal battles modern journalists must fight, one of the most difficult and frustrating is the struggle for "freedom of information." Without the freedom to gather the news, the freedom to publish is little more than a right to circulate undocumented opinions—a right to editorialize without any corresponding right to report the facts.

In recent years, the media have made significant gains in the battle for access to government meetings and records, but there have also been defeats. As governments have expanded in size, their sheer vastness has made it easy for them to conceal important information from public scrutiny. Moreover, the tendency of the federal government to keep secrets in the name of national security has grown dramatically in recent years. By 1980 a Congressional subcommittee estimated that no fewer than 4.5 million documents a year were being declared secret for reasons of national security alone.

If democracy is to work, the public must be well informed about the activities and policies of government. How can the people intelligently compare the policies of rival candidates unless there is freedom of information? How can the people decide if government policy toward countries such as El Salvador or Lebanon, for example, has been misguided unless they know what the official policy is and how it was formulated?

Moving closer to home, the same principle applies. How can the voters know if the city budget is reasonable or the school board is following sound educational policies unless the public can know what those budgets and policies actually are and how they were determined?

Recognizing these needs, journalists and public interest groups have launched a massive campaign for openness in local, state, and national government in recent years. That crusade has produced dramatic improvements in public access to official records and proceedings. Today, all 50 states have laws requiring most agencies of state and local government to hold open meetings, as well as laws guaranteeing public access to government records. A generation ago, very few states had such laws.

On the federal level, hundreds of thousands of documents have now been released to members of the public under the Freedom of Information (FoI) Act, a law that wasn't enacted until 1966. In addition, many federal agencies that once treasured their privilege of holding private meetings to shape their policies are subject to the 1976 federal Government in the Sunshine Act. That law has many loopholes, but at least it has opened some formerly closed meeting room doors.

How significant are these laws? The number of requests for information under the federal FoI Act will probably exceed one million per year by the time it is 20 years old. Moreover, it would take a book as long as this one just to summarize all of the litigation that occurred during the first 15 years of the FoI Act's existence. But is the information that is ferreted out of once-locked government files under the FoI Act really important?

Using the FoI Act, researchers learned that the Central Intelligence Agency spied on Martin Luther King, Jr. and other pioneer civil rights leaders, and that longtime FBI Director J. Edgar Hoover used the FBI in efforts to discredit King. Other FoI Act inquiries revealed government experiments with mind-controlling drugs that killed at least two persons in the 1950s. Meanwhile, still other researchers using the FoI Act learned of the CIA's efforts to overthrow a government in Chile and to use journalists as foreign agents.

The list of socially important government secrets uncovered because of the FoI Act is nearly endless. The FoI Act was used to discover long-concealed health hazards caused by radiation and the dangers of Agent Orange to Vietnam War veterans. It was also used to unearth important details of America's unsavory role in the Bay of Pigs invasion of Cuba and President Nixon's plans for military action in Cambodia.

Moreover, the federal FoI Act is just one law among many intended to open closed doors and unlock secret files, although it is a very important one. This chapter summarizes these freedom of information laws, and then surveys other problems journalists encounter in their quest for information.

THE FEDERAL FREEDOM OF INFORMATION ACT

When Congress enacted the federal FoI Act in 1966, many observers felt that its primary users would be journalists. Certainly journalists who were alarmed at the growing trend toward government secrecy took the lead in lobbying for its passage. But ever since it was passed, its main users have been businesses and individuals seeking government information. Thus, most of those actually filing formal requests for information are lawyers representing private clients, not journalists representing the public interest. In fact, historians and other academic researchers may well file more requests under the FoI Act than journalists. FoI Act requests take time, and journalists tend to need information too quickly to wait for a formal request to be honored by a slow-moving bureaucracy. The act naively orders government agencies to honor FoI requests quickly, but the courts have gone along when agencies argued that promptness was out of the question.

What are the basic provisions of the FoI Act? It declares that a vast number of records kept by administrative agencies of the federal government shall be open for public inspection, and that copies are to be provided at a reasonable cost. Unless these "agency records," as they are called, fall within one or more of nine specific exemptions, they must be opened to the public on request.

To facilitate this process, a 1974 amendment to the FoI Act requires agencies to publish lists of their records and even their fee schedules for making copies in response to FoI requests. Agencies are permitted to charge only for finding and copying a record, not for reviewing or editing it so it can be released. Fees may be waived or reduced when an agency feels that releasing a document would benefit the general public.

That provision has caused some controversy, since it allows agencies to charge one requester more than another for the same information. The FBI once charged the major wire services $9,000 for material that it provided free to one writer whose work was a public service (in the FBI's opinion). A requester need not justify his FoI Act request, but those who can convince an agency they are serving the public interest have a big advantage at the agency's cash register.

In an effort to avoid complying with the law, federal agencies have sometimes claimed that honoring a given FoI Act request would be prohibitively expensive. The courts have generally not heeded that argument, instead compelling agencies to comply despite the alleged cost. For instance, in a 1980 decision (*Long v. Internal Revenue Service*, 596 F.2d 362, cert. den. 446 U.S. 917), a federal appellate court held that the IRS had to supply requested information even if it would cost $160,000, as the agency claimed.

For FoI purposes, the term "agency" is defined to include executive departments, military departments, government corporations, government controlled corporations, other executive agencies, and independent regulatory agencies. In short, it covers just about the entire federal government, except for Congress and the courts.

Once an agency receives a formal request for a particular record, it is supposed to respond by either providing the record or denying the request (and explaining why it did so) within ten working days. However, the courts have repeatedly excused government agencies from this very short time limit, ruling that the deadline is "directory" rather than "mandatory." Thus, FoI Act requests may take a year or more, although a court once ruled that a four-year delay was too long when the law requires a response in ten days.

If a request is denied, the requester has a right to appeal the denial, first through the agency's appeals procedures and then to the federal courts. Thousands of lawsuits have been filed in the federal courts under these provisions of the FoI Act. As a result of amendments to the FoI Act in 1974 and 1976, federal judges are empowered to review the requested documents in private in their chambers and then rule on the rightness of an agency's decision to deny the request. The judge must decide if the documents properly fall within one of the nine exemptions, thus justifying government secrecy.

Thus, much of the controversy surrounding the FoI Act involves the nine exemptions. Briefly they are:

1. documents that have been properly classified as confidential or secret to protect national security;
2. documents relating to "internal personnel rules and practices" of federal agencies;
3. matters that are specifically exempted from public disclosure by some other statutory law;
4. trade secrets and certain other financial and commercial information gathered by government agencies;
5. interagency and intra-agency memoranda that involve the internal decision-making process (e.g., working papers and tentative drafts);
6. personnel and medical files and similar documents that should be kept confidential to protect individual privacy;
7. investigatory files compiled for law enforcement purposes, but only when such files must be kept secret to prevent interference with law enforcement, to protect someone's right to a fair trial, to avoid invading someone's personal privacy, to avoid disclosing the identity of a source of confidential information, to avoid disclosing investigative techniques or to protect the safety of law enforcement personnel;
8. reports used by agencies regulating banks and other financial institutions;
9. oil and gas exploration data, including maps.

Obviously, many of these exceptions are so broad and all-encompassing that they can be used to justify massive government secrecy. In addition to the millions of government documents that are classified for national security reasons, millions more are confidential for other reasons. The exceptions for law enforcement files and internal memoranda, for example, have been widely used to withhold information from the public.

Using the FoI Act

Anyone seeking information under the FoI Act should make it clear in writing that he or she is making an FoI Act request, perhaps mentioning the act by its official citation: Title 5 of the United States Code, Section 552 (or simply 5

U.S.C. 552). The request should be as specific as possible, identifying the desired record exactly as the agency identifies it. Each agency is required to publish its record-keeping scheme in *The Federal Register*, available in most law libraries, to assist FoI Act users in properly identifying the records they seek.

An FoI request should first be directed to the official designated to handle FoI requests within a particular agency. If that fails, the request should next go to the agency head, unless the agency has specified a different appeals procedure.

If that too fails, a journalist has little recourse except to go to court—or perhaps cultivate "sources" within the agency who may be willing to "leak" the material surreptitiously.

For anyone who plans to use the FoI Act, an extremely valuable booklet is available from the Reporters Committee for Freedom of the Press, 800 18th St., N.W., Room 300, Washington, DC 20006. Titled *How to Use the Federal FoI Act*, it includes government agency FoI directories and fee schedules, plus general instructions and samples of request letters, appeals letters, fee waiver requests, and the legal documents needed to file a lawsuit.

FoI Lawsuits

If the time comes when an FoI Act lawsuit is necessary, the act includes a provision allowing a court to require the government to pay the requester's attorney's fees and court costs if the lawsuit is successful. And if the court finds that agency personnel acted capriciously in denying the original request, the Civil Service Commission is required to hold a proceeding to decide if the government employees who denied the request should be disciplined.

Of the numerous lawsuits filed under the FoI Act, a few should be summarized to illustrate the typical workings of the act and the role of the courts in interpreting it. The first exemption (for national security) is a broad one that the courts have tended to uphold. In fact, judges have sometimes declined to even look at classified material in their chambers if an agency submits a convincing affidavit (a statement made under oath) to justify the need for keeping the document secret. In a 1977 ruling (*Bell v. U.S.*, 563 F.2d 484), a federal appellate court said such an affidavit should be given "substantial weight."

However, other courts have ruled that documents must have been properly classified for the national security exception to apply. In a 1974 case (*Schaffer v. Kissinger*, 505 F.2d 389), a federal appellate court held that Red Cross reports on South Vietnamese prison camps had not been classified under proper procedures and thus had to be released.

Nevertheless, the national security exception remains a gigantic and very troublesome loophole in the FoI Act. Numerous abuses of the national security classification system have been revealed over the years, among them instances where it was used to conceal corruption, government waste, and bureaucratic bungling.

The Pentagon's preoccupation with secrecy is at times even amusing. In his book, *Without Fear of Favor: The New York Times and Its Times*, Harrison Salisbury told a story about the Pentagon Papers case (discussed in Chapter Three). The government was trying to prove that publishing the Pentagon Papers would cause irreparable harm to national security, so an official communique from the National Security Agency's director was brought into a Washington courtroom in a double-locked briefcase. Inside the briefcase were three envelopes of diminishing size, each inside the next larger one. Inside it all was a very sensitive secret message. At the crucial moment of its unveiling, a *Washington Post* reporter pulled from his pocket a Congressional document that included the identical message, published long ago for all the world to read.

Another notable illustration of the same point was the government's attempt to censor *The Progressive* magazine when it planned to publish an article on the hydrogen bomb, an article prepared from readily available public information (that case is also discussed in Chapter Three). It has been suggested more than once that foreign spies in America should spend their time reading popular newspapers and magazines and browsing in public libraries rather than snooping around the Pentagon.

Nevertheless, the national security exception to the FoI Act must be taken seriously because it allows the government to withhold many important documents from public inspection, thus concealing much information that should be public in a democracy.

Among the other exceptions, several have stirred considerable controversy. The trade secrets and private business information exception, for instance, has prompted a number of double lawsuits with federal agencies caught in the middle. On one side, someone (often a competitor) is seeking information that may be covered by the trade secrets exception. On the other, the private company that originally submitted the information is suing to compel the government to keep the material confidential. The latter kind of lawsuit is called a "reverse FoI" suit.

Of more interest to journalists and scholars, however, have been the exceptions for law enforcement information, internal personnel rules, and internal working documents. The federal courts have shied away from compelling law enforcement agencies to disclose information that they contend is essential to their investigatory functions. However, the courts have been somewhat less inclined to let federal agencies broadly interpret the exception for internal agency materials. On a number of occasions, agency efforts to maintain internal confidentiality have failed.

One notable case of this sort is a 1976 Supreme Court decision, *Department of the Air Force v. Rose* (425 U.S. 352). That case arose when legal researchers sought records of honors and ethics code violation hearings at the Air Force Academy, with the names of alleged violators deleted. The Supreme Court ruled that where there is a genuine and significant public interest in an agency's policies, those policies should be disclosed unless their revelation would jeopardize an investigation or prosecution. The court noted the clear Congressional intent that such information be made public as long as no individual's personal privacy rights are threatened.

Many other practical problems have become evident as federal agencies, information seekers, and the courts have attempted to live under the FoI Act. One of the most important of these problems is the fact that agencies can escape the law by either destroying or concealing sensitive records, and public officials can sometimes circumvent it by simply taking their records home with them. There may be no way for anyone outside an agency to prove that a given document ever existed, if the agency steadfastly maintains that it didn't.

Moreover, in a 1980 decision (*Kissinger v. Reporters Committee for Freedom of the Press*, 445 U.S. 136), the Supreme Court ruled that former Secretary of State Henry Kissinger could keep his diary of official telephone calls secret because he took the diary home with him, unless the government itself should compel him to return it. In response to Justice William Rehnquist's majority opinion, the dissenting justices warned that this ruling would give major government officials freedom to completely escape the reach of the FoI Act by simply taking their important papers home.

In another major 1980 decision (*Forsham v. Harris*, 445 U.S. 169), the Supreme Court also made it clear that private organizations doing research under government grants need not make their data public. The court ruled that such research data simply doesn't fall within the definition of "agency records" and is thus not covered by the FoI Act.

In 1982, the Supreme Court handed down two more decisions that further restricted public access to government information under the FoI Act: *FBI v. Abramson* (456 U.S. 615) and *U.S. Department of State v. Washington Post* (456 U.S. 595).

In *Abramson*, the high court ruled that some of the information compiled by the Nixon administration about its critics was exempt from disclosure under the FoI Act. The FBI had originally gathered the information for investigatory purposes, and the court said the information was covered by the law enforcement investigatory exemption even though it was eventually recompiled and put to partisan political uses.

The *Abramson* decision produced dissents from four Supreme Court justices (Blackmun, Brennan, Marshall, and O'Connor). In two separate opinions, they said the majority was in effect amending the FoI Act by its broad interpretation of the law enforcement investigatory exception. Justice O'Connor's opinion pointed out that the records in questions were clearly not compiled in their present form for law enforcement purposes and therefore should not fall within the exemption.

The *Washington Post* case expanded the scope of the exemption for "personnel, medical and similar files." The court held that records indicating whether an individual holds a U.S. passport are a "similar file" that falls within the exemption if the individual's interest in privacy outweighs the public interest in disclosure.

The case began when the *Post* sought to find out if two Iranian nationals living in Iran were also U.S. citizens with American passports. The State Department refused to provide that information, contending that to provide it would "cause a real threat of physical harm" to both men. The *Post* sued under the FoI Act. In deciding the case, a virtually unanimous court said:

> Although Exemption 6's language sheds little light on what Congress meant by "similar files," the legislative history indicates that Congress did not mean to limit Exemption 6 to a narrow class of files containing only a discrete kind of personal information, but that "similar files" was to have a broad rather than a narrow meaning.

Eight justices signed the majority opinion. Justice O'Connor concurred without joining in the court's opinion. The Supreme Court sent the case back to a lower federal court to determine if the privacy rights of the two Iranians outweighed the public interest in disclosure, thus justifying the government's nondisclosure of their citizenship status.

Taken together, these Supreme Court decisions clearly sent a message to the federal bureaucracy: when in doubt, withhold the requested information.

Other FoI Act Problems

Users of the FoI Act also encounter other practical problems with the act. One of them, as already noted, is the problem of delays in compliance. Many federal agencies have large backlogs of FoI requests, and the courts have not chosen to enforce the time limits contained in the act. This poses a particular problem for journalists as opposed to other users of the FoI Act. While a historian or a business enterprise may well be prepared to wait a year or two for important information, that kind of a delay is often fatal for a journalist working on a timely news story.

Long delays in securing information are one problem for those who attempt to use the FoI Act. Another is the problem of court costs and attorney's fees. The act says those who sue the government for the release of documents and "substantially prevail" in court are entitled to have the government pay their costs and attorney's fees. The FoI Act doesn't say anything about those who seek documents having to pay the government's expenses if they lose. However, the general rules governing federal appellate court proceedings say that the winner is entitled to recover court costs (but not lawyers' fees) from the loser in any lawsuit that reaches the U.S. Courts of Appeals.

On the basis of these appellate rules, the U.S. Justice Department sought—and eventually won—an order from a federal appellate court requiring singer Joan Baez to pay $365 of the government's court costs in an FoI Act appeal. Baez gained the release of about 1,500 pages of FBI records about her, but she sued to obtain additional files the government had kept secret.

Although she lost, at first the appellate court refused to order her to pay the government's court costs. Then the court reconsidered and ruled that she had to pay (*Baez v. U.S. Justice Department*, 684 F.2d 999, 1982).

This case was troubling to many civil libertarians—not because they felt the well-known recording artist could not afford the $365 but because of the precedent it established.

Still another problem encountered by those who use the FoI Act is the legally sanctioned censoring of documents. The act permits agencies to delete portions of documents that fall within an exemption while releasing the remainder of the document. The result is sometimes a document with page after page of blank space, interrupted only by conjunctions and prepositions.

Perhaps most serious of all, the federal bureaucracy has made a concerted effort to weaken the FoI Act in recent years. As this was written, the FBI and the CIA were both lobbying Congress for a blanket exemption from the act, and efforts were under way to have Congress broaden the exceptions. Citing the cost of complying with FoI Act requests and alleged breaches of national security, some officials were arguing that public access rights should be sharply curtailed.

As of mid-1984, none of the proposed amendments to weaken the FoI Act had cleared Congress. However, in 1982 Congress did pass another law that restricted freedom of information involving the CIA: the Intelligence Identities Protection Act. That law made it a crime to engage in a "pattern of activities" with the "intent to identify and expose covert agents." While the law was apparently aimed at former CIA agents who reveal agency secrets— a troubling instance of prior censorship in and of itself—some journalists feared that the law was written so broadly that it could be used against the mass media as well.

Also, in 1981 Attorney General William French Smith issued new guidelines on FoI Act compliance by federal agencies, and these new policies made it much easier for bureaucrats to withhold information. Smith's new guidelines said the Justice Department was prepared to defend almost all lawsuits challenging a federal agency's decision to withhold information. Under an earlier set of guidelines, the Justice Department had expressed reluctance to defend FoI Act lawsuits, and instructed agencies to routinely release requested material unless "demonstrable harm" would result.

Despite all of these difficulties, the FoI Act remains a valuable tool for information gathering. In its short history, this law has opened thousands of files to public scrutiny, files that otherwise would have remained locked indefinitely.

FOI LIMITATIONS

Executive Privilege

Ever since the days of George Washington and Thomas Jefferson, American presidents and sometimes others in the executive branch have asserted a right to withhold information from Congress and the courts under a concept called "executive privilege." The legal foundation for executive privilege is vague; chief executives won the right to keep many of their working papers confidential mostly because no one was really in a position to challenge this kind of secrecy.

Executive privilege has also been claimed by some executive officers of state and local governments. As it developed, the privilege generally covered not only military and diplomatic secrets but also many of the internal documents generated within the executive branch of government.

The executive orders issued by Presidents Harry Truman and Dwight D. Eisenhower in the 1950s to govern the rapidly growing national security classification system were justified largely by the concept of executive privilege. Those orders allowed military and diplomatic secrets to be classified on three levels: confidential, secret, and top secret. Only persons who had been granted an appropriate security clearance were to be given access to this kind of information.

As the national security classification grew, it became a complicated bureaucratic operation that annually locked up millions of documents, as mentioned earlier. The Pentagon Papers case involved attempts by newspapers to publish classified documents that the editors felt were of significant concern to the American public. The editors believed that the classification system had been used not to protect important national secrets but rather to conceal the diplomatic errors of several presidents and their administrations.

In resolving the case, the Supreme Court allowed the papers to be published but did not generally rule on the concept of executive privilege itself. (see *N.Y. Times v. U.S.* in Chapter Three) The FoI Act in effect recognized executive privilege by exempting from disclosure two kinds of information that executive privilege had covered: matters affecting national security and the internal working documents of federal agencies.

However, executive privilege was carried a step too far by the Nixon administration during the Watergate scandal, and the result was a U.S. Supreme Court decision that severely restricted its scope. As the scandal drifted nearer to the president himself, Nixon sought to invoke executive privilege to avoid releasing some very incriminating tape recordings to a court. The tapes included a number of conversations between Nixon and his aides, and Nixon realized how damaging some of them would be if made public. The Watergate special prosecutor contended that the tapes were needed in the prosecution of several Nixon aides.

Nixon's refusal to release the tapes, which he justified by citing executive privilege, was challenged by the special prosecutor, and the case reached the Supreme Court. In the resulting 1974 decision (*U.S. v. Nixon*, 418 U.S. 683), the scope of executive privilege was drastically curtailed.

In a unanimous decision, the Supreme Court ruled that executive privilege is absolute only in connection with military and diplomatic information that must be kept secret to protect national security. In other areas, the high court said, the privilege has to be balanced against other interests, such as the obligation of every citizen (including the president) to step forward with evidence of a crime that may be in his possession. Like the reporter's privilege, executive privilege has its limits.

The Supreme Court ordered the president to release the Watergate tapes. That, of course, accelerated the amazing chain of events that led to Nixon's resignation from the presidency later in 1974.

Thus, executive privilege is a less formidable justification for government secrecy today than it once was. However, these new restrictions on executive privilege are of little help to the press and public, since the FoI Act still exempts so much of the information that was once kept secret under the justification of executive privilege.

Nevertheless, some of the internal government information that was once hidden by executive privilege is now available at least to the courts. That provides limited public access, since evidence presented in many court proceedings becomes part of the public record. The problem of public access to court records is discussed later in this chapter.

The 1974 Privacy Act

Journalists and civil libertarians—normally allies on First Amendment issues—find themselves on opposite sides of one of the most troubling problems in the freedom of information area. When the public's right to know and the individual's right to personal privacy conflict, the two groups often sharply disagree. Organizations such as the American Civil Liberties Union (ACLU) argue strongly for laws assuring the secrecy of personal information collected by government agencies, even at the expense of journalists' access to information.

The controversy reached a climax during the debate leading to the enactment of the 1974 Privacy Act, the first comprehensive federal law intended to protect individuals from improper disclosure of personal information by government agencies. The Privacy Act was a response to the growing public alarm over the massive amount of personal information government agencies were placing in computerized data banks. Groups such as the ACLU argued that these data banks constituted a major threat to individual freedom. If the private information kept in these data banks were to fall into the wrong hands, flagrant abuses could occur, they pointed out. Journalists, on the other hand, feared that a strong privacy protection law would be misused by government officials as an excuse for needless secrecy. Bureaucrats could avoid public scrutiny of their own deeds (and misdeeds) in the name of protecting individual privacy.

As it was finally enacted, the 1974 Privacy Act (5 U.S.C. 552a) represents something of a compromise on this issue. The act applies to all information contained in hundreds of government record-keeping systems, placing strict limits on the manner in which the records are used. The act forbids federal agencies to release personal data from these record-keeping systems, or even transfer it to another federal agency without the permission of the person the information concerns.

The Privacy Act grants private citizens a right to inspect their own records in government data banks, with provisions for citizens to correct errors they discover. In addition, federal officials who improperly release personal records may be sued for damages, attorney's fees, and court costs.

The Privacy Act includes a number of exceptions, allowing government agencies to release personal information without the affected person's permission for law enforcement purposes, for use by the census bureau and Congress itself, and for similar purposes. Significantly, the Privacy Act also allows the release of personal data that is defined as public information under the FoI Act. The Privacy Act was written this way to minimize its effect on the FoI Act.

In its first few years of operation, the Privacy Act appeared to be a relatively minor threat to the needs of journalists, but a threat nonetheless. One of the exceptions to the FoI Act excludes "personnel and medical files and similar files the disclosure of which would constitute a clearly unwarranted invasion of personal privacy."

That language is broad enough to give federal officials considerable leeway in deciding what personal information they must release under the FoI Act, and what they may withhold. Furthermore, the Privacy Act tends to discourage officials from releasing information in borderline cases because of the disparity between the consequences of violating the two laws.

The FoI Act allows those seeking information to sue officials who balk at releasing information, but only for attorneys fees and court costs. The Privacy Act, on the other hand, provides penalties for violations as well.

Thus, although the Privacy Act was written in such a way as to minimize restrictions on the release of information that would otherwise be accessible under the FoI Act, it does discourage openness in some cases. An official who errs in the direction of disclosing too little information faces no monetary penalty and only a vague threat of disciplinary action under the FoI Act; the official who errs in the direction of disclosing too much information faces monetary penalties under the Privacy Act.

Perhaps the most controversial data bank to which the Privacy Act has provided citizen access is the one maintained by the Federal Bureau of Investigation. The FBI is frequently slow in releasing individual files, and the files that are released are often censored (file censoring is permitted by the Privacy Act because these are, after all, law enforcement investigatory files). But nevertheless, the act gives citizens their first opportunity to learn something about the records the FBI may be keeping on them.

The FBI's handling of personal information under the Privacy Act has stirred criticism from both civil libertarians and journalists. On at least one occasion, the FBI piously refused to release to journalists any background information on a well-known murder suspect. However, the FBI did issue 15,000 "wanted" posters to post offices, and these posters contained much of the information journalists were seeking.

At about the same time as the enactment of the 1974 Privacy Act and the 1974 amendments to the FoI Act, Congress also approved "The Buckley Amendment," more formally known as the Family Educational Rights and Privacy Act (20 U.S.C. 1232g). That federal law is often confused with the more general 1974 Privacy Act, and in fact the two have similar provisions. The Buckley Amendment was so designated because Senator James Buckley of New York led the effort to add it to the 1974 Elementary and Secondary Education Act amendments, a major federal-aid-to-education bill.

The Buckley Amendment gives parents the right to see their children's school records and forbids the release of these school records to outside parties without the parents' consent. Similarly, it allows students over age 18 to see their own school records, and requires their consent before these records may be released to outside parties. School systems that fail to obey the Buckley Amendment may be denied federal funds.

This law has some impact on the newsgathering activities of the media, at times in absurd ways. Overzealous school officials have sometimes used it as an excuse to withhold newsworthy and nonsensitive information about students involved in athletics or other newsworthy extracurricular activities. But perhaps the Buckley Amendment's most serious effect on newsgathering has been to increase the secrecy of school disciplinary records. That has sometimes made it difficult to report on newsworthy disciplinary actions, such as those involving student athletes or political activists. Fearful of losing federal money, some school officials have tended to avoid risking any appearance of non-compliance with the Buckley Amendment.

Criminal History Information

For working journalists, a much greater problem than the Buckley Amendment has been the effect of state and federal privacy laws on access to information about those accused of crimes. In 1976, the federal Law Enforcement Assistance Administration (LEAA) issued a controversial set of guidelines intended to restrict the release of personal information by law enforcement agencies. They required state and local police agencies receiving federal aid to develop policies governing the release of information about persons arrested or charged with crimes. The guidelines were prompted at least in part by the LEAA's efforts to establish a new nationwide computerized law enforcement information network. LEAA officials feared that the vast amount of personal information available through this new system would lead to abuses such as the indiscriminate release of individual criminal history information (i.e., records of past arrests and convictions).

Originally, the LEAA guidelines were intended to seal all criminal history records in the interest of individual privacy. But those rules produced strenuous objections by journalists. In their final form, the guidelines did not specifically tell local police agencies what their information policies had to be, but did require these agencies to develop consistent policies.

As a result of the LEAA recommendations, some law enforcement agencies stopped releasing criminal history information to the press. Even current police blotter information that had traditionally been available was sometimes denied to the press. In many states, all records of arrests that do not lead to convictions—and even some records of arrests that do lead to convictions—are now sealed or simply destroyed. By 1980, at least 47 states had restricted access to criminal history "rap sheets," at least under some circumstances.

This is the area in which the disagreement between information-seeking journalists and privacy-oriented civil liberties groups tends to be the most clear-cut. ACLU leaders and other civil libertarians argue vehemently that a person should not be permanently stigmatized by public access to his or her police arrest record, particularly if the arrest does not lead to a conviction. When a record of an arrest has been legally expunged (erased), ACLU leaders are particularly emphatic in their contention that making information about it public is an injustice.

Many journalists, on the other hand, feel that while closing these records does protect individual privacy, it also allows wholesale abuses by law enforcement agencies. To support that assertion, they cite the dangers to civil liberties inherent in secret arrests and secret police activities. Also, they argue that society needs protection from persons with criminal records. They cite instances when privacy laws prevented employers from discovering their employees' criminal records, with the result that ex-convicts were placed in positions where they could commit similar crimes again. For instance, they point to a 1980 case in Texas where an employee of a mental institution allegedly raped a patient, and officials had been denied access to his criminal record (including a previous rape conviction) when they hired him.

This ongoing conflict will not soon be resolved. As Chapter Seven points out, there has been a long-term trend away from easy access to information about criminal suspects' past deeds, a trend prompted by the fair trial-free press dilemma at least as much as by the concern for personal privacy.

FEDERAL OPEN MEETING LEGISLATION

Another aspect of the struggle for freedom of information involves access to the meetings of government agencies. This is one of the oldest and most difficult information-gathering problems encountered by journalists. In theory, all public agencies should conduct the public's business openly, with citizens invited to listen in. But in practice, many public officials find it tempting to make their decisions behind closed doors, announcing them in carefully worded press releases afterward. Obviously, if the press is to serve as a watchdog on behalf of the public, reporters must have a right to attend the meetings where public officials make their important decisions. To ensure this right, journalists have campaigned for open-meeting laws for many years—with some success.

In fact, at least 46 states had enacted open-meeting laws before Congress finally enacted such a law in 1976. That 1976 federal law, the Government in the Sunshine Act (5 U.S.C. 552b), requires about 50 administrative agencies to conduct some of their meetings in public.

The policy-making boards and commissions of these agencies must meet at announced times and places, with the public generally invited to attend. However, closed sessions are still permitted for ten different reasons; the legal officer of the agency must specify the basis for each closed meeting.

The first nine grounds for secret meetings closely parallel the nine FoI Act exemptions, listed earlier in this chapter. They include such things as matters affecting national security, personnel matters, law enforcement investigations, discussions of trade secrets, and the like. The tenth subject that may be discussed in a closed meeting is pending litigation and similar adjudicatory matters.

Whatever the reason for a closed meeting, the board or commission must vote to close a meeting before the public may be excluded, and the vote must be recorded. The agency must then keep accurate and complete records of what goes on during the closed meeting. In most instances, that record must be either a verbatim transcript or a tape recording of all proceedings. In some instances, however, detailed minutes are permitted instead.

When an agency holds a closed meeting, it must quickly publish the results of any votes, including a record of how each commissioner or board member voted.

Any person may initiate a lawsuit against an agency that appears to be violating the Government in the Sunshine Act, and federal district courts are authorized to issue injunctions ordering federal agencies to comply with the law. When a complaining party wins such a lawsuit, the federal court is authorized to require the federal government to pay his or her attorney's fees and court costs. However, the act contains no civil or criminal penalties for government officials who violate its provisions. In addition, the law specifically orders federal courts not to invalidate actions taken by agencies during illegal secret meetings. Thus, the federal open meeting law has virtually no "teeth" in it. As we shall see shortly, it is much weaker than many state open meeting laws in this respect.

The Government in the Sunshine Act covers a number of well-known agencies, including the Federal Communications Commission, Federal Trade Commission, Interstate Commerce Commission, Nuclear Regulatory Commission, Consumer Product Safety Commission, Equal Employment Opportunity Commission, National Transportation Safety Board, Civil Service Commission, Securities and Exchange Commission, U.S. Postal Service board of governors, and Federal Reserve Board. The act applies to the central policy-making board of each of these agencies, but not to local or national staff meetings, even if those meetings involve important policy matters.

The law also covers some not-so-well-known government agencies, such as the Harry S. Truman Scholarship Foundation. However, the law does not apply to cabinet-level departments, nor does it apply to some of the advisory bodies closest to the presidency, such as the National Security Council.

The Government in the Sunshine Act excludes most informal gatherings and unofficial meetings held by members of federal boards and commissions. In a 1984 decision, the U.S. Supreme Court ruled that it was proper for a majority of the members of the Federal Communications Commission to meet in private with communications leaders from other countries at an international conference. The court said the gathering in question was not a "meeting" and the international body itself was not an "agency" within the meaning of the law (*FCC v. ITT World Communications*, 104 S.Ct. 1936).

In short, the federal open meeting law leaves a lot to be desired. It allows closed meetings for a wide variety of dubious reasons. Moreover, its enforcement provisions are notably weak, and it fails to cover many of the federal bodies that make the most important decisions. Nevertheless, it is a first step toward openness in the gigantic federal bureaucracy, a bureaucracy that once felt it had an absolute right to do the public's business in private without interference from meddlesome reporters or private citizens.

STATE OPEN MEETING AND RECORD LAWS

Although the federal FoI Act and Government in the Sunshine Act are important, most journalists find their own state FoI laws even more relevant than the federal laws. On a daily basis, thousands of journalists rely on state open meeting and public record laws to provide access to many of their most important news sources.

But while state public record and open meeting laws are of paramount importance to so many journalists, they are difficult to summarize in any detail in a national media law textbook. Not only do these laws vary considerably from state to state, but they are so often amended that no survey text can long remain accurate for all states. Anyone preparing for a career as a general assignment reporter should become familiar with the current open meeting and public record laws of his or her state. To do that, you should check the index volumes of your state's statutes or codes, available in any law library and larger city libraries. You can locate your state's public record law or laws by looking under "records and recording" and finding the sublisting for "public records," "open records," "access to records," or perhaps "freedom of information." The open meeting law or laws are usually indexed under "meetings" or "open meetings."

Most state open meeting and public record laws resemble the federal laws in many respects. In fact, many of the state open meeting laws were either adopted or extensively revised at about the time the federal law was enacted. The mid-1970s saw a dramatic growth of such laws all over the

United States. In 1974, the Freedom of Information Foundation at the University of Missouri published a study of open meeting laws by John Adams, a University of North Carolina professor.

Adams rated the various laws on an 11-point scale. Nine states were given especially low ratings for openness in Adams' study, either because they had no comprehensive open meeting law or because the law was notably weak. But by 1980, every one of Adams' low-ranked states had significantly strengthened its open meeting law or enacted a new one. Thus, in 1980 every state had at least one comprehensive open meeting law on its books.

State open meeting laws typically apply to the agencies of both state and local government. They usually require state boards and commissions, city councils, school boards, and county governing boards to hold open meetings at regularly announced times and places. Any person is permitted to attend most of these open meetings, although some state laws have provisions authorizing public officials to remove anyone who creates a disturbance.

Virtually all state open meeting laws provide for closed or "executive" sessions. Most state laws spell out the circumstances under which these closed sessions are permitted, authorizing private meetings for matters affecting national security, personnel matters, discussions of pending law-suits, and usually various other subjects. Some states allow closed meetings for only a few reasons, while others allow them for many more. Probably the nation's weakest open meeting law in this respect is the one in Mississippi, which gives government agencies carte blanche to exclude the press and public whenever the body's members vote to do so, regardless of the subject matter to be discussed.

An increasing number of state open meeting laws provide specific legal remedies for violations, allowing any citizen to sue the offending government body for an injunction to halt further illegal secret meetings. In addition, a number of state open meeting laws authorize the courts to invalidate any action taken at an unlawful closed meeting, a provision the federal Govern-ment in the Sunshine Act lacks. Such provisions are important, because the possibility of having a major action overturned in court is a strong deterrent to holding secret meetings.

Another provision missing in the federal law—but present in many state open meeting laws—is criminal sanctions for knowing violations. In many states it is a misdemeanor for government officials to participate in a closed meeting if they know the subject at hand should be discussed only during an open meeting. However, criminal prosecutions remain rare, since it is difficult to prove that a government body actually discussed an illegal subject behind closed doors or that the officials involved knew they were violating the law.

Perhaps the nation's strongest enforcement provisions are found in Connecticut, where a state Freedom of Information Commission serves as a watchdog agency. The Connecticut FoI Commission conducts seminars for government officials to make them aware of their legal responsibilities under

244 FREEDOM OF INFORMATION

the state's open meeting and public record laws. In addition, the FoI Commission enforces the two laws, acting against offending government agencies on the basis of citizen complaints.

New York has a state committee to oversee compliance with that state's FoI laws, but at this writing it lacked the enforcement powers provided in Connecticut. Some states place the responsibility for enforcement of FoI laws in the hands of the state attorney general, denying citizens any private enforcement rights.

Some states have a variety of open meeting provisions scattered through their statutory laws. In these states, it is possible to locate some of the open meeting laws and overlook others, erroneously concluding that some government agencies are exempted from open meeting requirements. For example, California has four different open meeting laws, and several national surveys of such laws have missed some of them, underreporting the comprehensiveness of the state's open meeting requirements. One California law requires local government agencies to hold open meetings, a second law imposes similar requirements on state-level agencies, and a third applies to the legislature itself. The University of California Board of Regents is required to hold open meetings under still another statute. Further complicating matters, the four laws have differing exceptions and enforcement provisions.

For comparison, Pennsylvania has a single comprehensive open meeting law that covers government agencies ranging from the legislature itself to local cities and school boards. It even applies to the boards of state and state-aided universities and colleges, some of which still hold charters as private institutions. The Pennsylvania law permits executive sessions only for personnel matters and labor negotiations, includes criminal penalties for violations, and declares actions taken at illegal closed meetings invalid.

However, before you conclude that Pennsylvania has a very good open meeting law and California has four very bad ones, you should know that the Pennsylvania law applies only to formal meetings at which official actions are taken; at this writing it does not apply to work sessions or the informal meetings at which government officials typically conduct so much of their real business. In California, on the other hand, the various laws apply to informal "work sessions" as well as formal meetings, giving the press access to far more of the actual deliberations of government agencies than is true in Pennsylvania.

Across the nation, the same kinds of state-by-state comparisons could be made. New York's open meeting law comprehensively covers state and local government agencies, and it doesn't have the loopholes found in Pennsylvania, but it lacks criminal penalties for violations.

In Texas, the open meeting law is comprehensive in covering state and local agencies, it defines meetings broadly enough to include informal as well as formal sessions, and it has enforcement provisions. However, it allows closed sessions for more reasons than the Pennsylvania law and it lacks provisions authorizing the courts to invalidate actions taken at illegal closed meetings.

Ohio's open meeting law includes another novel feature: a provision for the courts to remove officials from office if they participate in an illegal closed meeting after once being ordered not to do so by a court. A prosecuting attorney or the attorney general must initiate such an action to remove a public official from office.

Many of the other state open meeting laws have unusual features. It would be impossible to describe all of them without making this chapter unreasonably lengthy. The only way to be certain of your rights as a reporter is to learn the provisions of your own state's open meeting law or laws.

State Public Record Laws

Likewise, the provisions of public record laws vary widely around the country. All 50 states have laws in this area. Most state public records laws define the term "public records" broadly enough to encompass a wide variety of documents maintained by agencies of state and local government. And most such laws allow general public access to these records without requiring that the person inquiring demonstrate any special interest or "need to know."

State public record laws consistently exempt certain kinds of records from public disclosure, most often personnel records, law enforcement investigatory records, and records of juvenile courts, adoptions, parole matters, etc.

Most state public record laws specifically provide for judicial review in instances where public access is denied, and about two-thirds of the states provide criminal sanctions for officials who improperly deny public access. About one-third of the states cover the attorneys' fees of those who successfully sue for access to public records.

In all states the comprehensive public record laws supplement other statutory provisions for public access to government records. Long before it was fashionable to enact statutory open records laws, various records were open to the public under the common law, and many of these miscellaneous common law provisions for public access have also been codified.

In some instances, lawmaking in this area has occurred by vote of the people. For example, the people of Washington state enacted a public record law by popular vote in 1972. Meanwhile, in California the voters were approving a state Constitutional amendment establishing an "inalienable" right of privacy in that same year.

As on the federal level, state public record laws have had to be reconciled with privacy laws. By 1984, about half the states had privacy statutes that limited public access to personal information in state data banks. These laws, sometimes given euphemistic titles such as "Information Practices Act", usually forbid state officials to release personal information without the individual's permission. Some of them go much further than the federal Privacy Act in sealing records that would otherwise be open under public records laws. California, for instance, enacted a voluminous Information Practices Act in 1977, and it prohibited the release of "disparaging" information about any individual. The result was a massive freeze-up of public information, and the problem was only partially solved when the media succeeded in getting the reference to "disparaging" information deleted two years later. Such laws have become a major obstacle for journalists, limiting disclosure of everything from hospital patients' records to errant motorists' driving records.

As in the area of open meeting laws, it is impossible to describe all of the state record laws in detail. If you will need access to public records as a journalist—or if you will be responsible for controlling the release of personal information (as a hospital public relations officer, for instance)—there is no substitute for looking up and learning your own state's public records and privacy statutes.

ACCESS TO OTHER PLACES AND PROCEEDINGS

Having a strong public records or open meeting statute solves some of a journalist's information-gathering problems, but in a number of circumstances these laws are of little help. For instance, public records laws rarely govern the release of court records, and open meeting laws do not guarantee access to either the courts or the scene of a news event. These laws are of little value when a journalist seeks to cross police lines and reach the scene of a disaster. Nor are they of any assistance when a journalist wishes to cover a controversial criminal trial or visit a prison where inmates are allegedly mistreated.

In the absence of a statutory law assuring journalists access to these places and proceedings, is there any Constitutional right of access to the news? In several cases involving access to prisons, the U.S. Supreme Court has said there is no such right.

The high court decided two such cases, *Saxbe v. Washington Post* (417 U.S. 843) and *Pell v. Procunier* (417 U.S. 817), the same day in 1974. The court said rules against interviewing individual prison inmates were not a violation of the First Amendment. The *Pell* case arose in California when a policy that gave journalists freedom to interview specific prisoners was eliminated. That happened after an escape attempt in which several persons were killed. Thereafter, the media were only allowed to interview inmates selected more or less at random, not the inmates they wished to interview. Prison officials contended that media interviews had made celebrities of certain prisoners and helped provoke the escape attempt. The *Saxbe* case was a challenge to federal rules that similarly prohibited media interviews with inmates.

The Supreme Court said these anti-interview rules do not violate the Constitutional rights of journalists since journalists have no special right of access to prisons. The court said neither journalists nor ordinary citizens have a right to freely visit prisons and interview inmates.

However, lower federal courts in California tried to avoid following this precedent, and the result was another Supreme Court ruling on prison access in 1978, *Houchins v. KQED* (438 U.S. 1). In that case, television journalists wanted to visit a portion of a jail where an inmate had committed suicide, a place where a psychiatrist said conditions were so bad that inmates could suffer psychological damage. Jail authorities denied access to the reporters, and they sued, contending that prison conditions were a matter of legitimate public concern. A federal district court agreed, ordering authorities to let journalists see and photograph the controversial area of the jail. In the meantime, public tours of the jail had been initiated, but they did not include that area. The ninth circuit U.S. Court of Appeals affirmed the decision, but the Supreme Court reversed.

Writing for the majority, Chief Justice Warren Burger reiterated the Supreme Court's view that journalists have no Constitutional right of access to prisons. He acknowledged that prison conditions are a matter of public concern, but he said, in effect, that the subject is none of the media's business:

> The media are not a substitute for or an adjunct of government, and like the courts, they are "ill-equipped" to deal with the problems of prison administration.

Burger said that if journalists wanted to find out about prison conditions, they should interview former inmates, prisoners' lawyers, prison visitors, and public officials. In short, he said, the press has no Constitutional right of access to places not accessible to the general public.

The *Houchins* decision was alarming enough, but the next year the court handed down its *Gannett v. DePasquale* ruling (discussed in Chapter Seven), allowing even pretrial courtroom proceedings to be closed to the press and public. However, in 1980 the Supreme Court seemingly backed away from these denials of First Amendment protection for newsgathering activities. As noted in Chapter Seven, the *Richmond Newspapers v. Virginia* majority opinion included language suggesting that the court recognized a First Amendment right to gather news. "Without some protection for seeking out the news, freedom of the press could be eviscerated," the court said, quoting its 1972 *Branzburg v. Hayes* decision (see Chapter Eight).

In a concurring opinion in the *Richmond* case, Justice John Paul Stevens put it even more strongly:

> This is a watershed case. Until today the court has accorded virtually absolute protection to the dissemination of ideas, but never before has it squarely held that the acquisition of newsworthy matter is entitled to any Constitutional protection whatsoever.

Many journalists saw *Richmond Newspapers v. Virginia* as a great victory for the right to gather the news. However, the majority opinion was somewhat less enthusiastic on this point than Justice Stevens' concurring opinion, and subsequent court decisions have not generally extended the concept beyond its original application (access to courtrooms).

Whatever the Constitutional status of the right to gather the news, Congress, state legislatures, and local governments have often acted to grant journalists access to many sources of information. In fact, journalists have been granted access to prisons in many states; the Supreme Court was simply saying in *Houchins* that there is no *Constitutional right* of access to prisons. If state or local authorities choose to let journalists in, that's fine.

Another related access problem involves journalists' rights to cross police and fire lines to reach the scene of an accident or natural disaster. In virtually all states, journalists are afforded at least some special privileges of this kind, but they are usually treated as privileges, not rights. They can be denied by authorities.

However, when law enforcement authorities grant access to some favored journalists while denying it to others, another problem arises. May authorities play favorites among journalists without violating the First Amendment?

In a case involving access to police press passes, the California Supreme Court once allowed such favoritism. The *Los Angeles Free Press*, an "underground" newspaper with a paid circulation of nearly 100,000 at the time, sought the same press pass privileges as were routinely granted to other newspapers. The *Free Press* was turned down by local police, and that denial was upheld by the state Supreme Court in a 1970 decision, *Los Angeles Free Press v. City of Los Angeles* (9 Cal.3d 448). In so ruling, the court accepted the police contention that the *Free Press* didn't regularly cover police beat news except when it involved social issues. Thus, the police were able to convince the court that the *Free Press* didn't have the same need or justification for press credentials as more conventional kinds of newspapers. The court refused to recognize that the *Free Press* had any First Amendment right to hold police press credentials, even if they were routinely given to papers of which the police approved.

However, a federal district court in Iowa reached the opposite conclusion in a 1971 case, *Quad-City Community News Service v. Jebens* (334 F.Supp. 8). Local police there denied an "underground" paper access to police blotter information that was routinely available to other newspapers, but the court overruled the practice. The court pointed out that there were no written guidelines for determining who should be given access to police records and who should not. The police standards were too vague to be valid, the court said.

A few years later, a federal appellate court ruled on a similar question involving the granting of White House press credentials. In that case (*Sherrill v. Knight*, 569 F.2d 124), the Secret Service had denied press credentials to two "underground" newspaper reporters on the grounds that they had been convicted of crimes. Ruling in 1978, the appellate court refused to accept the Secret Service's argument that it had complete discretion in granting or denying White House press credentials. The court said the agency had to establish procedures for granting press passes. Reporters were to be told the reason for any denial and given an opportunity to reply.

Thus, these cases suggest that the police may grant information-gathering privileges to some journalists and not to others, but only if there are defensible guidelines to govern the awarding of these privileges. The decision cannot be arbitrary.

Access to Judicial Proceedings

Another difficult problem of access to information in recent years has involved the nation's judiciary. As Chapter Seven indicates, there has been a nation-wide trend toward closed preliminary courtroom proceedings, a trend encouraged by the Supreme Court's *Gannett v. DePasquale* decision.

In many states, preliminary hearings are routinely closed when a judge feels that prejudicial publicity would result if the hearing were open. Similarly, pretrial hearings where motions to suppress evidence are made are often closed, again to prevent publicity about evidence that may never be presented to a jury. The *Gannett* case certainly encouraged these practices. However, in more recent decisions the Supreme Court has repeatedly overruled judicial orders that closed courtrooms. At this point, access to even pretrial proceedings is much more rarely denied than it was in the immediate aftermath of *Gannett*.

When a trial itself is closed, the press has a very good chance to overturn the judge's action. A year after *Gannett*, the Supreme Court ruled that trials must usually be open. In *Richmond Newspapers v. Virginia* the high court said trials could be closed to the press and public only under very unusual circumstances. The judge who closes a trial must be able to show compelling reasons for doing so if his decision is appealed.

The problem of closed courtrooms is discussed more fully in Chapter Seven and is mentioned here only in the interest of comprehensiveness.

Another related problem for journalists is access to grand jury proceedings. Grand juries are bodies that hear evidence and decide whether to charge persons with a crime. All major federal criminal prosecutions begin with a grand jury indictment, and many of the most politically sensitive—and newsworthy—state cases are initiated in the same way. (The Fifth Amendment to the U.S. Constitution requires grand jury indictments in major federal cases but not in state cases.)

Grand jury proceedings are almost always closed, in part to keep suspects from learning what's happening and fleeing before they can be charged and arrested. Grand jury transcripts are also closed in many states, although a few states make some transcripts public after all of those to be charged with crimes are actually arrested. Even in these states, however, the transcripts are likely to be sealed in the cases that command the greatest public interest, such as those involving wrongdoing by public officials. If a grand jury transcript is sealed, there is little a journalist can do to learn its contents, aside from engaging in such investigative reporting techniques as inquiring of persons who were present at the closed proceedings. Judges sometimes object to that kind of newsgathering, but what grand juries do is often very newsworthy.

Other records kept by the judiciary are usually open under an old common law tradition, but there are important exceptions. Much news can be gleaned from the filings that occur in both civil and criminal lawsuits. The complaints and responses filed by those involved in lawsuits are usually public, and may reveal newsworthy details about individuals' and businesses' plans, finances, and past deeds (or misdeeds). One thing to remember about these documents is that they may not be protected by the qualified privilege libel defense until they are acted upon by a judge; reporters must be especially careful about reporting potentially libelous information contained in court records up to that point.

Some court records that involve personal matters are sealed in many states. For instance, probation department reports that recommend either jail terms or probation for persons convicted of crimes may be kept secret because they contain very personal information.

In addition, certain entire categories of court information may be off limits to reporters. For example, juvenile court proceedings are almost always closed, and the records that result are usually confidential. And some states have laws requiring the confidentiality of proceedings and records involving rape victims. As Chapter Three notes, some states even have laws that forbid the media to publish the names of rape victims and juvenile suspects, although those laws are now being challenged on First Amendment grounds. The Supreme Court has said repeatedly that the states may keep such records confidential, but the press may not be prevented from publishing the information once it becomes public.

Access to Private Organizations

Everything we have discussed so far in this chapter involves access to *government* information. However, many newsworthy things happen in private business enterprises. For instance, when a corporation decides to open or close a plant, the economy of an entire city can be dramatically altered. What right of access, if any, does a reporter have to investigate this kind of news?

Unfortunately, the answer is often disappointing. Private businesses need not admit reporters to their policy-making board meetings, and private business records are rarely open for public inspection. However, there are ways private corporate information can be researched.

Perhaps most important, almost all corporations whose stock is publicly traded are subject to very specific disclosure requirements under federal securities laws. The federal Securities and Exchange Commission is responsible for enforcing two important depression-era laws that require honesty and openness in the release of corporate information. These laws, the Securities Act of 1933 and the Securities Exchange Act of 1934, were passed to correct some of the abuses that led to the stock market collapse in 1929.

The Securities Act requires most corporations to file detailed reports on their management and business prospects with the SEC before they may offer their stock for public sale. The Securities Exchange Act requires publicly traded corporations to continue providing current information on their business and financial conditions even when they are not issuing new stock. A publicly held company cannot conceal either good news or bad news to defraud the investing public. Nor may a corporation's officers use what the securities laws call "insider information" to profit at the expense of unwary investors. For instance, when an oil company discovers a promising new field, its executives cannot quietly buy up a lot of stock at low prices before they publicly announce the discovery.

As a result of these laws and the SEC's traditionally vigorous enforcement, major corporations must disclose a great deal of corporate information to the public. The 1934 Securities Exchange Act is no freedom of information law, but at least it does provide the press and public with far more information about corporate doings than might otherwise be available. In compliance with these laws, major corporations provide a steady stream of news releases that must be frank and forthright in describing the company's business prospects.

When it comes to businesses that are operated as purely private entities (i.e., sole proprietorships, partnerships, and non-publicly traded corporations), there are few legal requirements for public release of information. Such companies may adhere to an enlightened information policy on a voluntary basis, or they may not.

However, even the smallest and most secrecy-prone private firm has to deal with federal, state, and local governments, and often its government filings can provide valuable information. The federal FoI Act and virtually all state public records laws exempt trade secrets and proprietary information from disclosure, but private businesses must file a variety of other documents that an inquiring reporter may be able to see and copy. For instance, often a private land developer will file detailed reports and plans in an effort to win local approval for a new construction project, generating public records that an alert reporter can use to learn many details about what would otherwise be a hush-hush deal. In addition, when a private company is involved in litigation, it must often disclose information in court records that it would never otherwise release. Such information also provides many an insightful story about a private business enterprise.

Access to Private Property

Another problem for journalists is the need to go onto private property to cover the news. When a disaster occurs on private property, for instance, journalists routinely go to the scene of the event along with law enforcement, fire, and other emergency personnel. However, journalists have to be aware that they may be sued for trespassing or invasion of privacy for doing so. When there is no event as clearly newsworthy as a major disaster, the potential liability of reporters who trespass to get a story may be even greater. This problem is discussed in Chapter Five.

PRACTICAL SUGGESTIONS FOR JOURNALISTS

The procedures for using the federal FoI Act were discussed earlier, and the procedures under state public records laws are generally similar, but how does one gain access to a government meeting that is closed when it shouldn't be? In fact, how do you know for sure what is really happening behind closed doors?

The first step is to be absolutely sure what your rights are under the applicable open meeting law. Many journalists carry a copy of their state's open meeting and public records laws with them whenever they're on an assignment. When an agency you are covering goes into a closed session, demand to know the specific legal basis for the closure. Make it clear that you understand the open meeting law too—and are prepared to assert your rights.

If a public agency still insists on going into a closed session when you doubt its legality, you have a dilemma. You should make it known that your employer is prepared to challenge any unlawful closed meeting in court, if in fact your employer will back you. If not, you have to decide if you are prepared to go it alone. Many state laws (and the federal Government in the Sunshine Act) provide for the government to pay your attorney's fees if you win, but if you lose, you may be out a lot of money. Moreover, you will probably have to put a substantial amount of money up front before a court will award you any repayment of your attorney's fees. Are you prepared for that?

There is, of course, a second problem: reporting what happens in a closed meeting. In many states and under the federal law, government bodies are required to keep either detailed minutes or a transcript of closed proceedings. Find out what the requirements are in your state, and make it clear you want to see the transcript or minutes at the earliest possible time. Failing that, many journalists simply wait out the closed meeting and then interview some of the participants, perhaps double-checking by separately interviewing others who attended the meeting.

For many readers of this text, the problem may be just the opposite of the one facing the reporter. You may be a public relations representative of the agency that is holding a closed meeting. Your responsibility as a professional is twofold: (1) you must make sure the officials of your agency are aware of their responsibilities under the applicable open meeting (and public records) laws; and (2) you must take steps to be sure that reporters have access to you and others in your agency so they can be accurately informed about what occurred during the closed meeting.

When there is secrecy, the information-gathering process places special demands on both the journalist and the public relations representative. Fortunately, in recent years more and more states have enacted strong open meeting and public records laws—laws that call for openness in government and seek to curtail the government secrecy that creates these problems.

A Summary of
Freedom of Information Laws

WHAT ARE FREEDOM OF INFORMATION (FoI) LAWS?

Taken as a group, FoI laws are state and federal statutory laws that assure public access to the documents generated by government agencies and to the meetings of government bodies. While granting general public access, virtually all such laws also contain numerous exceptions, limiting public access to certain meetings and records.

WHAT IS THE FEDERAL FoI ACT?

The federal FoI Act is an act of Congress requiring many federal agencies to open their records for public inspection and copying. Government agencies must publish lists of their records to assist FoI Act users in identifying the records they wish to see. Agencies have 10 working days to respond to FoI requests, but that deadline is often ignored. Information falling into any of nine specified categories is exempted from public disclosure.

HOW DOES THE PRIVACY ACT AFFECT THE FoI ACT?

Theoretically, the 1974 federal Privacy Act does not limit public access to government records. Instead, it allows an individual to inspect many of his own records in government data banks, and protects personal records from misuse. However, its practical effect is to restrict access to much information about individuals that might otherwise be accessible to journalists.

WHAT IS THE GOVERNMENT IN THE SUNSHINE ACT?

The Sunshine Act is a law requiring the governing boards of about 50 federal administrative agencies to hold open meetings. These boards must announce their meetings in advance and must allow the public to attend unless any of 10 specified subjects is being discussed.

DO THE STATES HAVE FoI LAWS?

As of 1984, all 50 states had laws requiring government agencies to hold open meetings. In addition, all states had public records laws as well. These laws generally apply to both state and local government agencies, but they usually limit or deny public access to meetings and records dealing with certain subjects, most commonly personnel matters (e.g., the hiring and firing of employees).

WHAT CAN A CITIZEN DO IF AN FoI LAW IS VIOLATED?

The federal FoI Act and Sunshine Act both authorize private citizens to sue offending government agencies, with the agency required to pay attorney's fees and court costs if the citizen wins the lawsuit. Many state laws have similar provisions, although some do not.

10

OBSCENITY AND THE FIRST AMENDMENT

Probably there is no more controversial problem in First Amendment law than the conflict between free expression and the right of the majority to set standards of sexual morality for everyone. The Supreme Court has made it clear that legally obscene materials are not protected by the First Amendment and may be suppressed by local, state, or federal authorities. But if, on the other hand, a work is not obscene, it is constitutionally protected. Thus, it is essential to define obscenity—and yet that task has stymied the Supreme Court for many years.

The nation's highest court has had to intervene in this field repeatedly, sometimes reviewing specific works to decide if they are obscene on a case-by-case basis. It's an onerous and thankless task for a court whose other responsibilities are so lofty. In a moment of utter frustration, former Supreme Court Justice Potter Stewart once admitted he couldn't define obscenity, but added: "I know it when I see it."

Even if the Supreme Court has had trouble defining it, many people besides judges and professional pornographers need to know what is and isn't legally obscene. Print and broadcast journalists, cinematographers, photographers, and advertising people, for instance, need to know the ground rules. Journalists are often accused of publishing something obscene when, in fact, the material in question comes nowhere near the legal definition of obscenity.

All 50 states have at least some legal provisions to control obscenity, and federal law prohibits both the importation and the mailing of obscene works. Federal law allows fines of up to $10,000 and prison terms of up to 10 years for importing, mailing, privately shipping, transporting for sale or broadcasting obscene works (18 U.S.C. 1461-1465). Transporting as few as five obscene items creates a legal presumption that they are for sale. A separate law allows customs agents to seize and destroy obscene materials (19 U.S.C. 1305).

Many state laws make producing, performing, or selling obscene works a crime and also allow their seizure. But when these state and federal laws are enforced, the result is often a difficult conflict between individual liberty and society's purported right to dictate moral standards for everyone.

Both sides in these controversies have turned to the courts, and ultimately to the Supreme Court, for help. But in the years since the Supreme Court first tried to define obscenity in 1957, its pronouncements on the subject have shed more confusion than light, partly because the court itself vacillated so much.

Given the difficulty of coming up with a legally sound definition of obscenity, many states and cities have looked for alternate ways to control the sale or exhibition of sexually oriented books, magazines, and films. For example, many cities have attempted to zone adult businesses out of residential neighborhoods. And some communities have used nuisance laws against these businesses—with varying degrees of success.

This chapter traces the development of American obscenity law from its English and colonial roots to its current uncertain status.

EARLY PRECEDENTS

In colonial America and Victorian England, there were fervent but inconsistent efforts to eradicate literature that those in power considered obscene. As early as 1712, the Massachusetts colonial legislature passed a law that made it a crime to publish "any filthy, obscene, or profane song, pamphlet, libel or mock sermon."

Meanwhile, the English common law on obscenity was evolving through court decisions, and colonial courts and legislatures looked to the common law for guidance. The common law foreshadowed things to come in this field by failing to define obscenity and instead focusing on the alleged corruption of youth and threats to order.

By the mid-1800s, however, England and America were moving toward specific statutory laws aimed at obscene works. The Tariff Act of 1842 was the first federal law in America designed to restrict the flow of obscenity. It prohibited the "importation of all indecent and obscene prints, paintings, lithographs, engravings, and transparencies." In 1857, it was expanded to include printed matter as well. The U.S. Post Office entered the field in 1865, when Congress enacted a law that made mailing obscene materials a crime.

Meanwhile, what was happening in England continued to shape American law. Lord Campbell's Act of 1857 and the first case tried under it produced a standard for obscenity that was followed in America as well as England for many years. Adopted as the Victorian period was beginning, the act prohibited obscene books and prints. It was tested in 1868 when a judge seized copies of an anti-Catholic pamphlet by a man named Henry Scott. Scott appealed to Benjamin Hicklin, recorder of London, and Hicklin ruled in Scott's favor. However, Chief Justice Alexander Cockburn reversed Hicklin's decision and ruled thus:

> The test of obscenity is whether the tendency of the matter charged as obscenity is to deprave and corrupt those whose minds are open to such immoral influences and into whose hands a publication of this sort may fall.

In short, Scott's work was held obscene because of how certain passages in the work might affect the most susceptible readers. And that concept came to be known as the "Hicklin" rule because the case was named *Regina v. Hicklin* (L.R. 3 Q.B. 360, 1868).

The Hicklin test was enthusiastically adopted by American courts in the late 1800s and early 1900s. The Hicklin test allowed a work to be ruled obscene based on isolated passages taken out of context, and it defined obscenity in terms of its effect on the *most susceptible* members of society. As a result, all sorts of once-respected classical literature became suspect. The country was in the mood for a moral crusade.

It wasn't long until a crusader came along to meet the need. His name was Anthony Comstock, and he developed a following as he campaigned for morality. He and his supporters spent four months in 1873 lobbying Congress, and the result was what came to be known as the Comstock Law, or more officially the federal Anti-Obscenity Act of 1873. This act went far beyond the 1865 law, giving the U.S. Post Office the power to banish from the mails any "obscene, lewd, lascivious, or filthy book, pamphlet, picture, paper, letter, writing, print, or other publication of an indecent character."

Conspicuously absent was any definition of obscenity; that would be left up to the people at the post office who would enforce the law. And who would that be?

None other than Anthony Comstock became the post office's special agent to ferret out obscenity and banish it from the mails. He pursued his new duties with a passion, and once boasted that he had "destroyed 160 tons of obscene literature."

Not content to bar dirty books from the mails, Comstock organized citizens groups to suppress "immoral" books even if they weren't mailed anywhere. Two of the most famous of these groups were the New York Society for the Suppression of Vice and the New England Watch and Ward Society.

These organizations cared little about the distinctions between great literature and pure pornography; anything "immoral" was fair game. Anthony

Comstock and his followers made the word "Victorian" mean prudish. For 70 years, almost any sort of material depicting or referring to any kind of sex was likely to be censored.

What about the First Amendment? Apparently it never even occurred to the Victorians that freedom of the press included any protection at all for erotic expression. But somehow, both literature and human life survived— and the Hicklin rule drifted out of style in the twentieth century.

THE END OF THE HICKLIN TEST

By 1920, times were changing, and so was the law. In that year a New York appellate judge ruled that a book must be evaluated as a whole rather than being banished because of isolated passages. Further, the judge said the opinions of qualified critics should be considered before a book is ruled obscene. That happened in *Halsey v. New York Society for the Suppression of Vice* (180 N.Y.S. 836).

Finally, in 1933 federal judge John Woolsey refused to follow the most basic part of the Hicklin Rule, the idea that a work was to be judged by its effect on the most susceptible members of society. In reviewing James Joyce's great work, *Ulysses*, he refused to follow the Hicklin Rule, under which he would have had to rule it obscene. He said a work must be judged by its effect "on a person with average sex instincts" rather than by its influence on the most corruptible members of society. Moreover, he said the work had to be judged as a whole, not by looking at isolated parts.

In 1934 the U.S. Court of Appeals upheld that decision (*One Book Entitled 'Ulysses' v. U.S.*, 72 F.2d 705). The appellate court—with Augustus and Learned Hand, two famous jurists who were cousins, in the majority— handed down a ruling that all but abolished the Hicklin test. The appellate court affirmed Judge Woolsey's view that the work should be judged as a whole and weighed by its effect on the average person.

THE *ROTH* DECISION

By the 1950s, many state and federal courts had abandoned the Hicklin Rule in favor of the more liberal one suggested in the *Ulysses* decision, but the U.S. Supreme Court had not attempted to write a definition of obscenity that would square with the First Amendment.

In 1957 the Supreme Court reviewed a series of obscenity prosecutions and finally dealt with this issue. In *Butler v. Michigan* (352 U.S. 380), the court overturned a Michigan law that prohibited the sale of any book that might incite minors to commit depraved acts or corrupt their morals. In so doing, the court said that states cannot quarantine "the general reading public against books not too rugged for grown men and women in order to shield juvenile innocence." If that were allowed, the court said, the result would be "to reduce the adult population of Michigan to reading what is only fit for children."

Thus, the Supreme Court had taken its first step toward the ultimate elimination of the Hicklin Rule: it had said material cannot be forbidden to adults just because it may be considered bad for children.

Four months later, the Supreme Court handed down another obscenity decision, and this one has been viewed as the court's landmark ruling in the field. The case was *Roth v. U.S.* (354 U.S. 476, 1957). The case arose when a man named Samuel Roth was convicted under federal law for mailing circulars, a book, and advertising material that were considered obscene. It was decided together with another case, *Alberts v. California,* in which David Alberts had been convicted of violating a California law against possessing obscene materials for sale.

The Supreme Court upheld both convictions, deciding that the laws under which they were convicted did not violate the Constitution. In fact, the court specifically ruled that obscene materials are not protected by the First Amendment.

However, Justice William Brennan's majority opinion also adopted a definition of obscenity that some lower courts had been following in lieu of the Hicklin Rule. Under this new definition, a court determines whether a work is obscene by asking:

> whether to the average person, applying contemporary community standards, the dominant theme of the material taken as a whole appeals to prurient interest.

Thus, the Supreme Court specifically disavowed the Hicklin test, partly because it allowed judging obscenity "by the effect of isolated passages upon the most susceptible persons." The Hicklin test violates the First Amendment, the court ruled. However, the courts that tried Roth and Alberts both used proper definitions of obscenity, so their convictions were affirmed. Still, *Roth* is a very important case, because it officially adopted a new definition of obscenity and made it binding everywhere in America.

The *Roth* case produced the first of a series of dissenting opinions on obscenity law by Justices Hugo Black and William O. Douglas. These two jurists took an absolutist position about the First Amendment. They said the First Amendment protects even obscenity. Thus, they argued that criminal prosecutions based on the content of the materials—or the bad thoughts they allegedly inspire—should be unconstitutional.

For years these two justices consistently maintained that obscenity laws are unconstitutional, a position free expression advocates heartily endorsed. However, on several crucial occasions their absolutist stance created problems: it enabled the high court to reverse obscenity convictions, but made it impossible for a majority of the court to agree on the reason for the reversal. The result was a series of plurality decisions that left the nation unsure what the law really was.

Shortly after the *Roth* decision, the Supreme Court was called on to review a number of other cases involving sexually explicit material. Soon a trend began, as the Supreme Court repeatedly overturned lower courts' determinations that various works were obscene. In 1958 and 1959 alone, the high court reversed obscenity rulings involving a collection of nudist and art student publications, a magazine for homosexuals, and another nudist magazine. The court also overturned a state statute prohibiting movies depicting adultery and reversed a ruling that held bookstore owners responsible for the content of all the books they offered for sale.

Obviously, these decisions represented a trend toward liberalism on obscenity. The Supreme Court continued to consider obscenity beyond the protection of the First Amendment, but fewer works were being adjudged obscene, while more and more works were being given First Amendment protection.

REFINING THE ROTH TEST

The *Roth* case was a landmark decision, but it left several questions unanswered. For instance, what is the definition of a community for "community standards"? Does it encompass a local area, or is it something larger than that? And just what does it take for something to violate those community standards?

The Supreme Court addressed the latter issue in a 1962 decision, *Manual Enterprises v. Day* (370 U.S. 478). The case involved the post office's attempts to ban from the mail several magazines intended mainly for homosexuals. Although the majority opinion branded the magazines "dismally unpleasant, uncouth and tawdry," the court said they were not obscene and thus upheld their right to use the U.S. mail.

Under the federal obscenity law in force at the time, a work had to be both "patently offensive" and appealing to "prurient interest" before it could be banned. The court said these publications were not "patently offensive," and ruled that a work had to be "patently offensive" to be obscene. The court also affirmed a position it had previously taken that mere nudity is not obscene.

That case left "community standards" undefined, but a 1964 Supreme Court decision, *Jacobellis v. Ohio* (378 U.S. 184), addressed that problem. Nico Jacobellis, a theater manager, was convicted of violating an Ohio law by showing an allegedly obscene French film, *Les Amants*. The court reversed Jacobellis' conviction, ruling the film was not obscene. It had been shown in about 100 cities, including at least two others in Ohio.

Justice Brennan, writing for the court's plurality, said the Constitution requires *national* standards on obscenity. "The federal Constitution would not permit the concept of obscenity to have a varying meaning from county to county or town to town," he said.

However, Brennan's reference to national standards attracted a strenuous protest from Chief Justice Earl Warren, who argued that local standards
are precisely what was intended in *Roth*. ". . .(C)ommunities throughout the
nation are in fact diverse, and it must be remembered that, in cases such as
this one, the court is confronted with the task of reconciling conflicting rights
of the diverse communities within our society and of individuals," Warren
wrote.

As we shall see, Warren's view rather than Brennan's eventually prevailed, but for nearly a decade most judges assumed there should be national
standards of obscenity, with local juries obliged to follow them no matter how
much those standards differed from prevailing local sentiment.

"FANNY HILL" AND "SOCIAL VALUE"

The developing Constitutional law of obscenity was further expanded in
1966, when the Supreme Court ruled that a classic erotic work, *Memoirs of a
Woman of Pleasure* (often called "Fanny Hill"), was not obscene. In *Memoirs
v. Massachusetts* (383 U.S. 413), the Supreme Court was again unable to reach
enough of a consensus for a majority opinion, but the plurality opinion
authored by Justice Brennan suggested a three-part test for obscenity: the
original Roth test, plus "patent offensiveness" and a requirement that the
work be "utterly without redeeming social value."

In *Roth*, Brennan had said works that are obscene lack any "redeeming
social importance," but the *Roth* decision did not specifically make the
absence of "social importance" a part of the test for obscenity. However,
lower courts began to consider that factor, and Brennan referred to it again in
Jacobellis. Finally, in *Memoirs* Brennan said a liberalized version of the
"redeeming social importance" concept was a constitutionally required part
of the test for obscenity. He said a work could not be considered obscene if it
had "social value." However, Brennan's opinion in *Memoirs* was still only a
plurality opinion.

But despite its lack of majority support on the Supreme Court, the "social
value" test was very widely accepted after 1966. Like Brennan's concept of
national standards, the "social value" test would eventually be abandoned by
the Supreme Court, but for a time it made obscenity prosecutions extremely
difficult. Proving that a work is "utterly without redeeming social value" is by
no means easy. Almost any obscenity defendant could find an expert witness
somewhere who would testify that the work in question has some sort of social
value.

The *Memoirs* case involved what some would consider a classic bit of
erotica. Written about 1750 by a man named John Cleland, it attracted the
book censors of Massachusetts as early as 1821. By the 1960s, "Fanny Hill"
had been translated into braille, placed in the Library of Congress and
purchased by hundreds of other libraries, but the Massachusetts attorney
general tried to have it "banned in Boston" again, nearly 150 years after the

first such effort. This final attempt to ban "Fanny Hill" in Boston failed, of course, when the nation's highest court ruled that the book was not legally obscene.

A NEW APPROACH

After the *Memoirs* decision, the Supreme Court moved away from attempting to define obscenity and looked to other factors in deciding three important obscenity cases.

In *Ginzburg v. U.S.* (383 U.S. 463), the court upheld the federal obscenity conviction of a well-known pornographer, Ralph Ginzburg. In so ruling, the court avoided dealing with the question of whether the publications he was convicted of marketing were inherently obscene and instead took note of the way he promoted his works. The court said there was abundant evidence of pandering, "the business of purveying textual or graphic matter openly advertised to appeal to the erotic interest of their customers."

Ginzburg originally tried to mail his publications from Intercourse and Blue Ball, Pennsylvania, but the post offices in those small towns couldn't handle the volume, so he settled for Middlesex, New Jersey. The court concluded that those mailing points were selected only for the effect their names would have on his sales.

Thus, the court affirmed an obscenity conviction based on the conduct of the seller rather than the content of the works.

The next year in *Redrup v. New York* (386 U.S. 767, 1967), the Supreme Court reversed three state obscenity convictions. In all three cases, a state court had assumed the material was "obscene in the Constitutional sense," but the Supreme Court said those decisions were wrong. However, the justices could not agree on any one standard by which to judge obscenity.

As a result, the court backed away from defining obscenity and simply listed three categories of marketing that might justify state prosecutions without any finding that the works themselves are obscene. The three were: (1) the sale of sexually titillating material to juveniles; (2) the distribution of such materials in a manner that is an assault on individual privacy because it is impossible for unwilling persons to avoid exposure to it; and (3) sales made in a "pandering" fashion.

The result of *Redrup*, apparently, was that only hard-core pornography could be banned. The court seemed to be extending Constitutional protection to materials that, though possibly obscene, were neither pandered nor forced upon unwilling recipients. The impact of the *Redrup* decision is shown by the fact that it was cited as a basis for the reversal of 35 reported obscenity convictions in the next year and a half. Some of these reversals came in additional Supreme Court rulings that were decided without formal opinions, with others in decisions of lower state and federal courts.

The Supreme Court affirmed its suggestion in *Redrup* about obscenity and juveniles a year later, in *Ginsberg v. New York* (390 U.S. 629, 1968).

There, the court upheld the conviction of Sam Ginsberg (not to be confused with Ralph Ginzburg) for violating a state law against selling to minors materials defined to be obscene on the basis of its supposed effect on them. In affirming Ginsberg's conviction, the court accepted the concept of "variable obscenity"—that is, that a state could punish someone for selling a work to juveniles that might not be obscene to adults.

Thus, the sum effect of these three decisions is to allow obscenity prosecutions under special circumstances, even though it had become almost impossible to prove a work was legally obscene to adults.

THE END OF THE LINE

In 1969 the Supreme Court handed down the last major obscenity decision of the liberal Warren era (Chief Justice Warren retired later that year). But that last decision went a long way toward protecting the private possession of obscene matter from government scrutiny.

In *Stanley v. Georgia* (394 U.S. 557), the court overturned an obscenity conviction that resulted from an amazing law enforcement "fishing expedition." Police searched Robert Eli Stanley's home in quest of bookmaking materials, but instead they found some interesting films in a dresser drawer in his bedroom. They set up his projector, watched the films, and then arrested him for possessing obscene matter in violation of a Georgia law.

In Justice Thurgood Marshall's majority opinion, said this:

Whatever may be the justification for other statutes regulating obscenity, we do not think they reach into the privacy of one's home. If the First Amendment means anything, it means that a state has no business telling a man, sitting alone in his own house, what books he may read or what films he may watch.

The court said, in effect, that there is a Constitutional right to possess and use even obscene materials in the privacy of one's home. Also, Marshall wrote, the First Amendment protects the "right to receive information and ideas, regardless of their social worth."

However, the court warned that this ruling was not intended to abolish "*Roth* and the cases following that decision." This was a unique set of facts, and two years later the Supreme Court refused to extend *Stanley* to other situations.

In two cases decided the same day, *U.S. v. Reidel* (402 U.S. 351, 1971) and *U.S. v. Thirty-Seven Photographs* (402 U.S. 363, 1971), the court backed away from the *Stanley* principle. In *Reidel*, the court upheld the constitutionality of the federal obscenity law's ban on mailing obscene matter even to consenting adults. Thus, the court avoided following the "right to receive" concept from *Stanley*. In *Thirty-Seven Photographs*, the court said customs officials could still seize obscene materials from a returning traveler's luggage, even if they were intended for private use.

Two years later, in *U.S. v. Twelve 200-foot Reels of Super 8mm Film* (413 U.S. 123, 1973), the Supreme Court was even more emphatic in saying the First Amendment doesn't give a private individual any right to bring allegedly obscene materials back from abroad. Thus, once a person makes it home with his obscene materials, he's safe, but if officials catch him en route, it's a different matter.

These decisions were widely criticized as inconsistent with the language of *Stanley*. The *Stanley* decision was only "distinguished" and not reversed, but it was obvious by 1973 that the Supreme Court's view of obscenity was changing. Richard Nixon had by then appointed four new justices to the Supreme Court, and he made it clear that one of the things he was looking for was justices who would crack down on pornography. A new and more conservative majority on obscenity matters was coalescing.

MILLER AND ITS AFTERMATH

The new Supreme Court majority had an opportunity to make its own mark on obscenity law in 1973, and the result was a new landmark decision that revised much of what the Warren court had done, *Miller v. California* (413 U.S. 15). The four Nixon appointees and Justice Byron White made up a five-justice majority in this case, and Justice Brennan, long the author of important majority and plurality opinions on obscenity, began writing dissents.

In *Miller* and four other cases decided at the same time, the court revised the *Roth-Memoirs* test, saying "community standards" would henceforth be local rather than national, and abandoning the "redeeming social value" concept.

The case arose when Marvin Miller conducted a mass mail campaign to sell "adult" material. Five of his brochures were sent to a Newport Beach, Calif., restaurant, and the recipients complained to police. Miller was convicted of violating California obscenity law and appealed to the U.S. Supreme Court.

The high court took the occasion to write a specific new test for obscenity. The new test said a work is obscene if:

1. an average person, applying contemporary community standards, would find that the work, taken as a whole, appeals to the prurient interest;
2. the work depicts or describes, in a patently offensive way, sexual conduct specifically defined by the applicable state law;
3. the work, taken as a whole, lacks serious literary, artistic, political, or scientific value.

Thus, the court reaffirmed the first two parts of the test set forth in *Memoirs*, although the community standards would now be local. Also, the term "patently offensive" would have to be defined in statutory law. However, the third part of the *Memoirs* test, the "redeeming social value" concept, was abandoned in favor of "serious literary, artistic, political or scientific value," something much easier to prove in a criminal proceeding.

It was still only a 5-4 decision, but the *Miller* decision marked the first time since 1957 that a majority of the Supreme Court had been able to agree on "concrete guidelines to isolate 'hard core' pornography from expression protected by the First Amendment."

In abandoning national standards, Chief Justice Warren Burger emphasized the diversity of the communities of America. "It is neither realistic nor constitutionally necessary to read the First Amendment as requiring that the people of Maine or Mississippi accept public depiction of conduct found tolerable in Las Vegas, or New York City," Burger said.

One of the court's goals in returning to local standards, certainly, was to reduce the workload of the federal courts. The Supreme Court had been asked to review hundreds of obscenity cases, and it had been forced to accept far more than any of the justices would have preferred. But if the court was seeking to get out of the obscenity business, it failed. In the years after *Miller,* the high court had to accept a number of additional obscenity cases.

In one of them, *Pinkus v. U.S.* (436 U.S. 493, 1978), the Supreme Court said that children should not be a part of the "community" when jurors determine "community standards," if the work was intended for adults. However, the court said adults with varying degrees of susceptibility to obscene materials should be considered in the determination.

There were other unresolved issues in allowing local standards, too. For instance, what happens when a local jury somewhere decides a serious literary work that is clearly not obscene violates the local standards?

The answer, of course, is that the Supreme Court has to step back into the picture. In *Jenkins v. Georgia* (418 U.S. 153, 1974), a jury convicted Billy Jenkins, a theater manager, of violating the Georgia obscenity statute by showing an Academy Award-nominated R-rated film, *Carnal Knowledge.* The film had occasional scenes of nudity and non-explicit scenes suggesting that sexual intercourse occurred.

The Supreme Court said the film did not depict sex in a patently offensive way and was thus not outside the protection of the First Amendment. Local juries must consider all parts of the Miller test, including the "patent offensiveness" factor, in determining obscenity, the court said.

But more to the point, perhaps, was the obvious fact that the court was hedging on its commitment to local standards. If a jury in an isolated community somewhere decides a work that is considered a serious one everywhere else violates the local standards there, isn't that exactly what the court invited in *Miller?*

In the 1974 case of *Hamling v. U.S.* (418 U.S. 87), Justice Brennan dissented when the court affirmed a federal obscenity conviction, warning:

> National distributors choosing to send their products in interstate travels will be forced to cope with the community standards of every hamlet into which their goods may wander.

This threat is not just an academic one. In a 1978 case, an Oregon distributor of sexually explicit materials was forced to defend a federal obscenity prosecution in Wyoming because postal authorities thought the conservative community standards there would make a conviction easier to secure. At the request of an Oregon postmaster, a Wyoming postmaster solicited materials from the distributor, using a false name and address. Other than mailing the materials, the Oregon man had no contact with Wyoming, and he mailed materials to no one else in the state. But he was charged with violating the federal obscenity law in Wyoming and was forced to defend himself there. He eventually pleaded guilty to one count, and a federal appellate court felt it had no choice but to uphold the judgment, although the justices vigorously protested this "venue shopping" by federal officials.

The appellate court said, ". . .publishers and distributors everywhere who are willing to fill subscriptions nationwide are subject to the creative zeal of federal enforcement officers. . . ." (*U.S. v. Blucher*, 581 F.2d 244, 1978). The decision was eventually vacated by the Supreme Court, but the fact that Blucher was prosecuted at all raises serious questions about the community standards issue.

For those who produced or appeared in nationally distributed books or films, the problem became very serious in the late 1970s. For example, Harry Reems, male star of the widely known explicit movie, *Deep Throat,* was prosecuted for violating federal obscenity laws in Memphis, Tenn.

Aside from the problem of varying "community standards," doesn't this sort of thing also raise issues of fundamental fairness? Is a publisher or actor afforded "due process of law" when forced to defend himself hundreds or thousands of miles from where he lives and works, just because a copy of his allegedly obscene material made its way there?

While the courts were wrestling with the problems of community standards, the 1970s and 1980s marked another trend in obscenity law: a nationwide crackdown on the production and distribution of films and other works depicting minors in sexually explicit roles. By the early 1980s at least 20 states had passed laws forbidding the use of minors in such roles even if the work was not legally obscene.

In 1982, the Supreme Court ruled on the constitutionality of these laws in *New York v. Ferber* (458 U.S. 747). The high court carved out an exception to the normal rules on obscenity, upholding a New York law that permitted criminal prosecutions for those who produce or sell printed matter or movies in which minors perform sex acts, without any proof of obscenity.

The court ruled that the states have the right to prohibit children from appearing in sexually explicit scenes regardless of the literary merit or non-obscene character of the work. Where such a scene is needed for literary or artistic reasons, the court said "a person over the statutory age who looked younger could be utilized."

In urging the high court to find the New York law unconstitutional, civil libertarians and the book publishing industry warned that such laws could be used to prosecute those who produce many socially important works, including motion pictures such as *Taxi Driver*. The Supreme Court did not heed their arguments, choosing instead to give the states a relatively free hand to regulate the use of minors in sexually explicit roles.

POSTAL CENSORSHIP

From the Comstock era to the *Blucher* case, many federal efforts to suppress allegedly obscene materials have centered on the postal service. However, postal censorship has its limits.

A classic example is the time when the Post Office tried to censor *Esquire* magazine, which was then more sexually oriented than it is today but not exactly hard-core pornography. The case arose in 1943 when the postmaster general refused the magazine second class mailing privileges.

A federal appellate court reversed that postal decision, and the Supreme Court agreed. Justice William O. Douglas, writing for the court, said, "Congress has left the postmaster general with no power to prescribe standards for the literature or the art which a mailable periodical disseminates" (*Hannegan v. Esquire*, 327 U.S. 146, 1946).

After that adverse ruling, the postal service backed away from most efforts to censor popular publications, but it was given a new role in obscenity law enforcement in 1968. At that point Congress passed the Pandering Advertisement Act (39 U.S.C. 3008), a law allowing postal patrons to demand that their names be removed from objectionable mailing lists after they receive material they consider sexually offensive. The post office is required to force mailers to remove names from their lists in compliance with these requests.

The Supreme Court upheld that law in 1970, in *Rowan v. Post Office* (397 U.S. 728). Congress strengthened the law in 1971, allowing postal customers to have their names removed from offensive mailing lists even before the first sexually objectionable item arrives in the mail.

The U.S. Post Office has also engaged in various other forms of censorship. For example, for many years it was unlawful to mail unsolicited advertisements for contraceptive devices. However, *Bolger v. Young Drug Products*, a 1983 Supreme Court decision that is discussed in Chapter 12, overturned those regulations on First Amendment grounds.

FILMS, OBSCENITY, AND CENSORSHIP

Motion pictures have created special censorship problems ever since the cinema emerged as a form of entertainment and art. From the early days of magic lantern shows to the modern era of X-rated adult films, irate citizens have demanded censorship to protect public morals.

The movies have been criticized for irrelevant escapism—and for being too relevant. From the 1920s until the 1960s, it was commonplace for cities and states to operate film censorship boards that blatantly engaged in prior restraint of motion pictures, something that would have been unconstitutional if applied to almost any other communications medium. More recently, some newspapers have refused to carry ads for movies of which they disapproved, and cities have tried to zone offensive theaters out of town.

Meanwhile, of course, films of all kinds have appealed to the millions, often while bureaucrats were trying to shut them down. At one point in the 1970s, more than half a million Californians had paid to see the controversial X-rated film, *Deep Throat*, in Los Angeles County, while local authorities were on a crusade to censor it in neighboring Orange County.

But censorship crusades by no means began when films were first given "X" ratings in the 1960s. Amidst a furor, Ohio authorities censored a film and then won the Supreme Court's blessing in 1915. In fact, that case (*Mutual Film Corp. v. Industrial Commission of Ohio*, 236 U.S. 230) set a precedent that stood up for 37 years: movies weren't protected by the First Amendment, the court said.

Justice Joseph McKenna, writing for a unanimous Supreme Court, said, "The exhibition of motion pictures is a business pure and simple." Thus, movies should not be regarded as part of the press. Instead, they were mere entertainment and did not purvey ideas or public opinion. Moreover, movies had a special capacity for evil, the court said.

The *Mutual Film* decision was both a cause and the result of mediocrity in the film industry. Because early films were unsophisticated and often lacking in artistic qualities, the Supreme Court had no problem dismissing them as frivolous entertainment and not a vehicle for significant ideas. But at least in part because of the Supreme Court's ruling, American films remained a frivolous form of entertainment for many years.

It was not until 1952 that the Supreme Court finally said films were a vehicle for important ideas, and it took an Italian film to make the high court change its mind. New York authorities attempted to ban a film called *The Miracle*, in which a peasant girl encounters a stranger she believes to be the Biblical Joseph and gives birth to a child she imagines to be the Christ child.

The New York film censorship board ruled the film sacrilegious, but the ruling was appealed. In *Burstyn v. Wilson* (343 U.S. 495), the Supreme Court said for the first time that films are "a significant medium for the communication of ideas," and afforded them First Amendment protection.

The court said *The Miracle* could not be banned, but the ruling did not preclude future prior censorship of films. Unfortunately, no specific guidelines for review boards were provided, and the licensing of films continued in many states.

Several more film censorship cases followed. In *Times Film Corp. v. Chicago* (365 U.S. 43, 1961) the Supreme Court upheld the constitutionality of a film pre-censorship system, but in 1965 in *Freedman v. Maryland* (380 U.S. 51) the court demanded procedural safeguards of film censors. In the meantime, however, both the Supreme Court and lower courts reviewed a number of other film censorship cases, often overruling specific instances of prior restraint.

Times Film involved a challenge to Chicago's licensing system by the producer of a movie that obviously would have been granted a license: a movie version of a Mozart opera. But Times Film refused to submit the film to the licensing board and instead challenged the system. The Supreme Court upheld the city's power to license films, finding films beyond the scope of the *Near v. Minnesota* ruling on prior censorship (see Chapter Three).

However, four years later in *Freedman v. Maryland* the Supreme Court backed away from giving carte blanche to film censors. The case arose from a challenge to Baltimore's censorship system, which was much like Chicago's. As in the Chicago case, the film in question (*Revenge at Daybreak*) was not sexually explicit, but it still had to be licensed.

However, this time a movie exhibitor made a more convincing case: he argued that the procedures were unfair and slow. In fact, it could take so long to get a license, he argued, that everyone who wanted to see the film would have gone somewhere else to see it before it was legal to show it in Baltimore.

The Supreme Court agreed, and overturned the Maryland system because it lacked adequate procedural safeguards for movie exhibitors. The court said any licensing system would be required to: (1) operate very quickly; (2) assure prompt judicial review, with any final censorship order made only by the court; and (3) place the burden of proof on the censor rather than the film exhibitor.

Maryland rewrote its licensing procedures in an effort to comply with the *Freedman* decision, and in 1974 the Supreme Court affirmed a federal court ruling upholding the new procedures (*Star v. Preller*, 419 U.S. 956). The new procedures gave the censorship board five days to grant or deny a license. Denials had to be submitted to a court for review in three days, and an appeal of a court decision allowing censorship was given top priority on the appellate calendar. Also, the licensing board had the burden of proof to show that the film was obscene.

Thus, Maryland was able to retain its movie licensing system. However, most other cities and states abandoned their movie censorship systems rather than devise procedures that would meet the requirements of the *Freedman* decision. Several more licensing systems were overruled by lower courts after *Freedman*.

From a filmmaker's point of view, it was a good riddance. Local censorship boards were notorious for banning films that were by no means obscene, but simply offended the moral, religious, or racial sentiments of the censors.

However, film censorship is still constitutionally permissible if adequate procedural safeguards are provided. And that, of itself, alarms many who believe movies should have the same First Amendment protection afforded to other mass media. Of all of the major mass media, only motion pictures may be routinely subjected to government prior restraint based on their content. Granted, the broadcast industry faces other forms of government control that are intended to prevent the airing of sexually explicit material and offensive language. In fact, broadcasters are forbidden to carry much material that is perfectly legal in the nation's motion picture theaters (this problem is discussed in Chapter 11). However, even broadcasters do not face prior restraints: government censors could not lawfully preview their programs for decency before they are aired. Only motion picture exhibitors have had to deal with the problem of direct prior censorship by the government.

Meanwhile, the motion picture industry has attempted to ward off even more heavy-handed government control with a vigorous policy of self-regulation. Beginning in the 1920s, the Motion Picture Association of America maintained a tough code governing movie content, and a code committee exercised censorship powers over movies. Critics attributed the irrelevance and frivolity of early American movies more to the influence of this industry body than to direct government controls.

In 1968 the MPAA finally shifted to a more permissive approach. Rather than attempting to censor movies, the MPAA introduced a rating system that would simply advise theatergoers about the content of each movie in advance. The rating system, with its ubiquitous G, PG, R, and X ratings, has largely accomplished its objective of protecting unwilling persons from offensive material while allowing others to see more explicit movies.

OTHER APPROACHES TO OBSCENITY

Given the difficulty of defining obscenity and winning criminal convictions, many communities have attempted to control bookstores and theaters they consider offensive in other ways.

One method used by local governments is to ask a court to declare an adult-oriented business a "public nuisance." In such a civil action, a city may be able to win a court-ordered closure by meeting a lower standard of proof than is required in criminal cases.

However, the U.S. Supreme Court placed Constitutional limits on this approach in a 1980 decision, *Vance v. Universal Amusement* (445 U.S. 308). The case involved a Texas nuisance law that was construed to authorize closing down adult movie theaters because they had shown obscene films in the past. It was not necessary to prove that any film currently showing was obscene. The court said the Texas law lacked adequate procedural safeguards to protect the movie exhibitor's rights and that it posed an unconstitutional prior restraint.

The California Supreme Court said somewhat the same thing in a 1976 case, *People ex rel. Busch v. Projection Room Theatre* (17 Cal.3d 42). In that case, the court said local authorities could not use nuisance law against a bookstore until specific works were adjudged obscene by a court, and then only those works could be seized. The store itself could not be closed down.

In the mid-1980s several cities were attempting to act against obscenity by declaring that its existence violates the civil rights of women. At this writing, city officials in both Minneapolis and Indianapolis were considering such laws. In effect, these laws would give women the right to complain of civil rights violations when literature that they found offensive was offered for sale at local stores or shown in local theaters. However, the American Civil

Liberties Union, among other groups, was strenuously objecting to these laws as having the potential for flagrant First Amendment violations. If material that is not legally obscene under the *Miller* test were censored as a result of civil rights complaints, the result would be an unconstitutional denial of freedom of expression, they contended.

Various communities have also attempted to control adult-oriented businesses through their zoning powers, and they have enjoyed some success. The use of zoning to control such businesses was encouraged by a 1976 U.S. Supreme Court decision, *Young v. American Mini-Theatres* (427 U.S. 50). That case arose in Detroit, where city officials attempted to limit the number of adult-oriented businesses that could exist in a given neighborhood. The Supreme Court said this was constitutionally permissible, even if the city didn't define obscenity with great precision, since the city wasn't forbidding adult materials altogether but simply controlling the time, place, and manner of their distribution.

Encouraged by that ruling, hundreds of other American cities have adopted zoning restrictions on adult businesses, sometimes zoning them out of town altogether. However, in 1981 the Supreme Court made it clear that communities could not use zoning to banish all adult entertainment without violating the First Amendment. That ruling came in the case of *Schad v. Mt. Ephraim* (101 S.Ct. 2176).

In that case, the Supreme Court overturned a New Jersey community's ban on live entertainment as a violation of the First Amendment. Under its zoning powers, the city attempted to outlaw nude dancing and other forms of live entertainment. Overruling the local ordinance, the court said that mere nudity does not make entertainment obscene. The majority said the city could ban all forms of entertainment (including motion picture theaters), but that local officials could not use their zoning powers to forbid nude dancing while allowing other forms of entertainment. The court pointed out that this case was different from the Detroit case, in which adult-oriented businesses were merely dispersed around town and not banned altogether.

The *Schad* decision had a far-reaching impact on the use of local zoning ordinances against adult businesses. While it remains constitutionally permissible to bar adult businesses in residential areas—or near churches and schools—most courts are now ruling that a city cannot use its zoning powers to force all adult-oriented businesses to get out of town. To completely banish a particular business (or type of business), local officials must prove that it is engaged in producing, exhibiting, or selling legally obscene works. In some states, even that isn't enough: the most local authorities can do is to have each legally obscene work banned on a case-by-case basis—a very costly and cumbersome process.

Thus, local officials again face the task of defining obscenity, the age-old dilemma that has made this such a difficult and controversial aspect of First Amendment law. The Supreme Court has spent hundreds of hours of its valuable time trying to define obscenity, without ever really solving the problems inherent in laws that dictate moral standards for all Americans.

A Summary of Obscenity and the First Amendment

DOES THE FIRST AMENDMENT PROTECT OBSCENITY?

The Supreme Court has consistently held that the First Amendment *does not* protect materials that are legally obscene. Thus, the crucial issue is defining obscenity. If a work is legally obscene, it may be censored and its producers prosecuted. If it isn't obscene, it is protected by the First Amendment and may not be censored.

WHAT WAS THE HICKLIN RULE?

For many years, obscenity was defined by the Hicklin Rule, which looked to a work's effect on the *most susceptible* members of society to determine if it was obscene. Also, the Hicklin rule permitted classifying a work as obscene if only isolated passages were obscene, regardless of the literary merit of the work taken as a whole.

WHAT HAPPENED TO THE HICKLIN RULE?

The Hicklin Rule was followed in both the United States and England through much of the Victorian era, but it was abandoned in the twentieth century. The key turning point was the *Ulysses* decision, in which a federal court refused to follow the Hicklin Rule and instead viewed James Joyce's classic work as a whole and weighed its effect on average persons.

WHAT WAS THE ROTH TEST?

Handed down by the Supreme Court in 1957, the Roth test defined obscenity by asking, "whether to the average person, applying contemporary community standards, the dominant theme of the material taken as a whole appeals to prurient interest." The result was that First Amendment protection was extended to many works that might have been classified as obscene in an earlier era.

HOW WAS THE ROTH TEST INTERPRETED?

In a series of decisions during the 1960s, the Supreme Court amplified its Roth decision. For a time, it appeared that "community standards" were national standards, and that a work could not be censored unless it was "patently offensive" and "utterly without redeeming social value."

WHAT WAS THE MILLER v. CALIFORNIA DECISION?

In 1973, a new conservative majority on the Supreme Court redefined obscenity, abandoning both the idea of national standards and the "social value" test. In its place, the Supreme Court said a work is legally obscene if: (1) it meets the original Roth test; (2) it describes sexual conduct in a "patently offensive" way; and (3) the work, taken as a whole, lacks serious literary, artistic, political, or scientific value. The court made it clear that community standards could be local, and could vary from place to place.

11

SPECIAL PROBLEMS OF BROADCASTING AND CABLE TELEVISION

In many ways, the broadcasting and cable industries are unique among the mass media. They face almost all of the same legal problems as the print media, but they must deal with a variety of special legal problems, too. Like publishers, broadcasters may be sued for libel, invasion of privacy, or copyright infringement. Likewise, they share the problems of advertising and antitrust regulation, and of restrictions on their access to information.

However, the electronic media must also contend with direct government regulation. A broadcaster must get a license from the federal government before going on the air, and must renew it periodically. Cable systems are not formally licensed by the federal government, but they are subject to other federal regulations as well as rules imposed by the local governments that grant their franchises. In between license or franchise renewals, broadcasters and cable system operators must comply with hundreds of government regulations covering everything from the content of their programming to the technical quality of their signals. The print media face no similar rules.

Furthermore, as some broadcasters and cable operators have learned, a license (or franchise) renewal is by no means automatic. As this is written, a legal action is under way that could strip a single company, RKO General, of 13 radio and television licenses that are worth several hundred million dollars on the open market. RKO has already lost its license to operate a television station in Boston—a license worth at least $150 million.

Can you imagine the government ordering the *Boston Globe, New York Post*, and *Los Angeles Times* to stop publishing forever? Although that kind of thing happens in some countries, it would be unthinkable in America. And yet, that is very much like what is happening to RKO General, whose broadcast licenses in Los Angeles and several other cities may be revoked, as the one in Boston was in 1980.

How did the federal government acquire such life-and-death power over the broadcast industry? The answer lies in the nature of the "radio spectrum." Only a limited number of frequencies are available, and the number of stations that may transmit at one time without causing intolerable interference is also limited. The idea that this justifies government regulation of broadcasting is called the "scarcity rationale." Early in the twentieth century Congress relied on this rationale when it decreed that the entire radio spectrum would be used to serve "the public interest, convenience and necessity."

As a result, the Federal Communications Commission was established to regulate broadcasting and other non-governmental uses of the radio spectrum. Over the years, the FCC assumed broad authority over the electronic mass media under the scarcity rationale. However, today there are many new technologies of mass communication, and the entire philosophy of broadcast regulation—including the scarcity rationale itself—is being reexamined by the FCC, Congress, and the courts. This point will be discussed later in this chapter and in Chapter 15, which describes some of the legal and policy questions raised by the new technologies.

As things stand now, the FCC has two primary functions: authorizing various individuals and organizations to transmit in the radio spectrum (the licensing function) and regulating those licensees (a supervisory function). Although cable television systems do not use the radio spectrum, the FCC has also assumed some jurisdiction over the burgeoning cable industry. How the FCC acquired its regulatory powers and how it exercises those powers are the major topics of this chapter.

For many years, the FCC tended to collectively sit back and believe it was fulfilling its mandate if it issued licenses and wrote ever more complex rules to regulate the conduct of licensees. That has all changed in recent years, as the FCC took a series of far-reaching and controversial steps to deregulate the broadcast and cable industries.

Instead of trying to ensure public service through government regulation, the commission is increasingly looking to marketplace forces to achieve that goal. The FCC has adopted the philosophy that competition is healthy, and that more competition equals better public service. To foster competition, it has moved aggressively to juggle its frequency allocations, endeavoring to make room for more broadcasters. At the same time, the FCC has authorized a variety of new broadcast-like services that it hopes will offer the public new alternatives in programming. All of these new steps have created new problems, both in the United States and overseas. For that reason, the international regulation of mass communications has become increasingly important in recent years.

INTERNATIONAL REGULATION OF BROADCASTING

Although this fact is not widely known, American broadcasting is subject not only to national but also to international regulation, at least indirectly. What the print media publish may well have international implications, but what one country's newspapers say isn't supposed to be any other country's business. In broadcasting, it's entirely a different matter. Radio and television signals freely cross international boundaries, and broadcasters cannot operate with blatant disregard for the interference they might cause in other countries.

Thus, many basic issues in telecommunications policy are decided on a worldwide basis. By treaty, the International Telecommunications Union (ITU), headquartered in Geneva, Switzerland, has overall responsibility for international administration of radio and television matters. Its approximately 150 member nations hold plenary sessions every four or five years to discuss major international issues. In 1979, the ITU's members held a World Administrative Radio Conference (WARC), an event that occurs only once every 20 years, and made policy decisions significantly affecting telecommunications around the world. For instance, the conference agreed to allocate more frequencies to amplitude modulation (AM) radio broadcasting, creating room for more stations worldwide.

Allocating frequencies is the primary function of conferences such as the 1979 WARC. No nation may simply place its radio and television stations on whatever frequencies it wishes; frequency assignment policies must be set on a global basis to avoid incompatible uses. Each country is free to decide which station transmits on a given channel in the AM, FM, or television bands, for instance, but the decision about how much of the radio spectrum is set aside for broadcasting (as opposed to other uses) is made on an international basis.

In addition to worldwide telecommunications policy-making, there is regional coordination. For communications purposes, the world is divided into three regions. Region I encompasses Europe, Africa, and the Soviet Union. Region II includes North and South America, and Region III covers Asia and the Pacific (except for the Soviet Union). The United States regularly meets with its neighbors at Region II conferences to agree on radio and television frequencies in this hemisphere.

However, those meetings are not always amicable. In recent years the United States and its neighbors have experienced severe difficulties in coordinating broadcast channel assignments. For example, at such a conference in 1980, the United States urged other Region II governments to approve a reduction in the width of AM radio channels so more stations could go on the air. But by late 1981, the FCC had reversed its position on that issue, so the United States delegation lobbied against it at the next regional conference, leaving America's neighbors a little bewildered.

Meanwhile, the Reagan administration announced intentions to create a powerful radio station named "Radio Marti," which would beam news (and the American version of world events) to Cuba. Cuba viewed this as a blatant attempt to propagandize its people, so the Cuban delegation retaliated by walking out of an international conference on western hemisphere frequency coordination. Then Cuba turned on a number of powerful AM radio stations on frequencies used by American stations. The result was interference (some called it deliberate "jamming") to stations thousands of miles away from Cuba. For instance, one station in Des Moines, Iowa, saw its reliable nighttime range drop from a 700-mile radius to a mere 25 because a high-powered Cuban station showed up on its frequency.

When that happened, American broadcasters began lobbying in Congress to stop the Radio Marti project. Congress finally passed a law requiring the Reagan administration to make Radio Marti a part of the Voice of America—with ground rules requiring that it provide objective news, not propaganda.

As the Radio Marti controversy illustrates, broadcasting has political and diplomatic ramifications that reach far beyond any country's borders. As a result, international cooperation is vital, particularly at a time when many nations are moving into new technologies such as broadcasting directly to home viewers from satellites. A single satellite positioned 22,000 miles above the equator can transmit a signal powerful enough to be received in an enormous area; a satellite transmitter may have a radio "footprint" that can cover half a continent, ignoring all boundary lines.

Broadcasters and other users of the radio spectrum have always engaged in bloody battles for more turf, but today more than ever before those battles are becoming volatile international feuds.

THE RADIO SPECTRUM

Most of these feuds occur, of course, because of one simple fact about the radio spectrum: there isn't enough of it to go around, either in the United States or abroad. Everyone is clamoring for more frequencies.

The Federal Communications Commission has recently launched a major effort to modernize its spectrum allocation policies—in the hope that room can be found for many new broadcasters (and for more non-broadcast users of the radio spectrum). At this writing, the FCC is engaged in a major effort to open not only AM and FM radio but also the television channels to more stations. Hoping to increase the number of programming choices available and also to expand minority group ownership of the electronic media, the FCC is taking a very hard look at the radio spectrum.

Because Congress declared long ago that the spectrum is to be used in the "public interest, convenience and necessity," the FCC's job is to allocate a limited resource so as to maximize public benefits.

When FCC policymakers discuss the radio spectrum, they must use technical jargon. It's hard to avoid running into terms such as "Hertz," "megaHertz," "AM," "FM," "VHF," "UHF," "grade A contours," etc. Here are a few definitions that will make the rest of this chapter more comprehensible.

A Hertz (abbreviated Hz) is a unit of measurement, just as a foot, an inch or a pound is a unit of measurement. However, a Hertz is a measurement of frequency instead of distance. One Hertz equals one electrical cycle per second, All radio and television signals are measured by their electrical frequency, in cycles per second, or Hertz. A "kiloHertz" (abbreviated kHz) is 1000 Hertz, a "megaHertz" (mHz) is one million Hertz. The term Hertz, by the way, was chosen to honor Heinrich Hertz, a German scientist whose early research proved the existence of radio waves. Thus, the term Hertz is usually capitalized.

A station's frequency, expressed in kiloHertz or megaHertz, is its home address in the radio spectrum. Only one station can transmit on each frequency in a given geographic area; if two or more stations transmit on the same frequency, interference will result, and neither station can be heard by many listeners. Therefore, each radio and television station has an assigned frequency on which no one else is allowed to transmit in that station's service area.

A station's service area is defined by measuring or calculating the strength of its transmitted signal at various locations and then plotting the measurements on a map. For example, a TV station's "primary service area" is based on its "grade A contour," which is nothing more than a circular plot showing where the station's signal drops below a given strength. The FCC has to know how strong a station's signal is at various points in order to decide how far away other stations must be before they can be allowed to use that frequency. If two stations too close together share the same frequency, harmful interference will result.

Obviously, these plots are different for different kinds of radio and television stations. AM radio signals propagate (i.e. travel from the transmitting antenna to listeners' receivers) differently than FM (frequency modulation) radio and television signals. Similarly, VHF (very high frequency) television contours usually differ from UHF (ultra high frequency) television contours.

In its all-important frequency allocation decisions, the FCC must decide how the public interest may best be served by weighing these factors of propagation in various parts of the radio spectrum.

Figure 11-1 is a chart of the radio spectrum, showing only the most important highlights because the spectrum is so large. Looking at the area AM radio stations occupy is a little like looking at your home town on a world map. You can see where it is, but there isn't much detail.

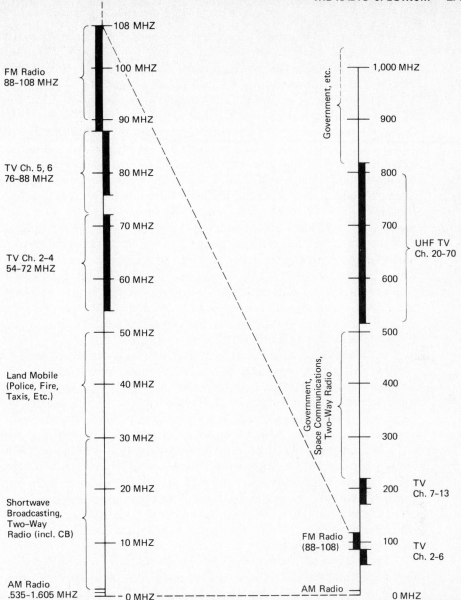

Fig. 11-1 *The Radio Spectrum. This chart shows how the radio spectrum is allocated to various uses. The right side shows the frequencies from zero to 1000 megaHertz, which is only about 5 percent of the total spectrum usable with today's technology. The left side shows one tenth of the right side, or the frequencies from zero to 100 megaHertz. Altogether, television broadcasting is allocated about one third of this part of the spectrum, but only about 1.5 percent of the total usable spectrum. For comparision, AM radio is allocated a total of one tenth of 1 percent of the space on the left-hand line, or about one two-hundredth of 1 percent of the space that is usable with today's technology. Obviously, broadcasters wonder if more room couldn't be made for them. The vast majority of the usable spectrum is allocated to government, military, and space communications.*

When radio first developed, the equipment was very primitive by today's standards and would only work on the low frequencies at the bottom of the spectrum. Generally, as the frequency goes up, so does the complexity of the equipment required to transmit and receive signals.

The frequencies below what came to be known as the AM broadcast band were occupied by ocean-going ships for ship-to-shore communications even before broadcasting developed, and those frequencies are still used for certain kinds of navigation. The standard (AM) broadcast band starts at 535 kHz (or .535 mHz) and goes to 1605 kHz (1.605 mHz). At first, that seemed like a huge amount of space, but today we consider it very small. AM radio signals are very narrow in "bandwidth," which means they take very little space in the spectrum. The AM band is only about one megaHertz wide, but that small area is divided into 106 different channels, each ample for an AM radio station. At the 1979 worldwide radio spectrum conference that we mentioned earlier, the delegates from various nations agreed to move the top of the AM radio band from 1605 kHz up to 1705 kHz. When this change is fully implemented (and radios that will tune the new frequencies become widely available), there will be space for 10 more AM radio channels—and the FCC will surely receive hundreds (or thousands) of applications from those who would like to put a station on one of them.

In the AM band, there are propagation characteristics that cause the FCC no few headaches. Signals propagate differently in the daytime than they do at night. In the daytime, propagation is mainly by "groundwave," which means signals literally travel along the surface of the earth. Stations with high-power transmitters have a reliable groundwave range (i.e., a "primary service area") of roughly 100 miles, depending on the terrain.

At night, this local groundwave propagation still occurs, but AM radio signals also travel by "skywave" propagation. That means signals leave the earth's surface and travel out toward space, with some of the radio energy reflected back to the earth by a layer in the ionosphere (the Earth's upper atmosphere) about 150 miles up. AM radio signals also travel out toward space during the daytime, but the ionosphere absorbs most of the energy and almost none is reflected back.

As a result of this skywave propagation, high-powered AM radio stations can sometimes be heard well at distances of 1000 miles or more at night. In the early days of radio, this was a tremendous advantage, because it allowed persons far away from any station to hear some radio broadcasts. However, as the spectrum filled up it became a major problem; one powerful station can interfere with all others over an enormous area. The FCC had to require many radio stations to either reduce their power or go off the air altogether at night. Today, about 2,300 AM radio stations are licensed to transmit during the day only; they must shut down at night to avoid interfering with stations in other cities that share their frequencies.

Of course, this phenomenon of long-distance night-time propagation explains why an extremely powerful transmitter in Cuba can cause such havoc all over North America, as we indicated earlier.

The region above the AM broadcast band is called the "shortwave" spectrum. It runs from about 2 megaHertz to 30 megaHertz (see Fig. 11-1), and it too has unique propagation characteristics. Groundwave propagation deteriorates as the frequency increases, but at any given time of the day or night some of the shortwave bands offer worldwide skywave propagation. Beginning in the 1920s, they were used for international "shortwave broadcasting" as well as other commercial, government, and military communications where long distances had to be spanned. Even long-distance telephone services used shortwave radio in the days before microwave technology and communications satellites were developed.

Because a station half a world away can cause interference, the shortwave spectrum was never of much commercial value for strictly local communications. However, it continues to be used for worldwide broadcasting, much of it political propaganda. More than a hundred nations operate shortwave broadcast services. On any given day or night, an American shortwave listener can hear such stations as Radio Moscow, Radio Peking, Radio Tokyo, Radio Australia, the British Broadcasting Corporation, and our own Voice of America. Some, like the BBC and VOA, operate under government rules requiring that they practice objective journalism, but others do not. All of these organizations broadcast in English (as well as many other languages and dialects), often on several different frequencies at once to cover different parts of the world.

Radio Moscow, one of the world's most extensive shortwave broadcasting operations, runs something of a worldwide talk show, with American and other foreign listeners invited to send in questions about Soviet policy and life in the U.S.S.R. The questions are purportedly answered by top Soviet officials, and announcers read the replies in perfect English with an American accent (or a British one, when the signal is beamed to Europe).

However, relatively few people own receivers capable of tuning in shortwave broadcasts. Had the Reagan administration's Radio Marti proposal merely involved shortwave broadcasting, the Cuban government would probably not have been so outraged by the idea. What is unique about Radio Marti is that it was to be placed right in the middle of the AM radio dial, where almost everyone could listen in. Florida and Cuba are so close together that it was not necessary to use the esoteric shortwave bands for Radio Marti: an AM station in Florida can be heard in much of Cuba even during the daytime.

Above the shortwave spectrum is the VHF region, spanning 30 to 300 megaHertz. At these frequencies, there is little skywave propagation, so a broadcaster's service area extends only a little beyond the visual horizon. Stations with antennas on high towers, buildings, or mountaintops achieve much better coverage than those with less favorable antenna sites. Because of both the large amount of spectrum available here and the local nature of propagation, the VHF region is ideal for FM radio and television broadcasting.

The VHF region became technologically usable prior to World War II, which was fortunate in view of the vastly escalating demand for space in the radio spectrum in those days. As noted earlier, the AM band is only about one megaHertz wide, but that is enough space for 106 different channels. When FM radio and television developed, the demand mushroomed. Each FM radio station occupies 200 kiloHertz—20 times the bandwidth of an AM station. In order to provide even 100 FM radio channels, the FCC had to allot 20 megaHertz (88 to 108 mHz) to FM radio.

If AM radio stations use so much less space than FM stations, why did the FCC allow FM to develop instead of creating a new and bigger AM broadcast band? FM has some important advantages, such as greater immunity to noise and the potential for higher sound quality. Perhaps if the decision were made today, the FM channels would be made narrower than they are, because good high fidelity FM sound is technically feasible with about one-fourth the bandwidth of the existing FM channels. But that decision was made many years ago when the demands for spectrum space were far fewer than they are today. To change it today would render obsolete millions of dollars worth of FM equipment.

Also, many FM broadcasters today are using the extra spectrum around their main broadcast signal for other purposes, such as data transmission. Some stations make nearly as much money from these "subsidiary communications authorizations," or SCAs, as the FCC calls them, as they do from broadcast advertising.

When television broadcasting began, the demand for spectrum space escalated again. A single television station needs six megaHertz of bandwidth to transmit its picture and sound. That means one TV station takes up almost six times the space of the entire AM radio band. You could fit 600 AM radio channels or 30 FM radio channels into one TV channel, give or take a little. Thus, a huge amount of the spectrum had to be set aside for television. Five TV channels (channels 2-6) were tucked in below the FM radio band. Channels 7 through 13 are located higher in frequency than FM radio, between 174 and 216 megaHertz.

Why isn't there a channel 1 for television? Originally there was, but its six megaHertz of radio spectrum were desperately needed for other things. Channels 2 through 13 are referred to as VHF television, but there is also a very large television allocation in the UHF spectrum, a vast region running from 300 to 3000 megaHertz.

The frequencies from 470 to 890 megaHertz were originally set aside for UHF television channels 14 through 83. However, that tied up a large amount of space that other users (such as two-way police and fire communications) needed too. The FCC finally took back channels 70 through 83 and reallocated them to various two-way radio services and other uses. Still, a vast part of the radio spectrum is allocated to UHF television, and other users of the spectrum continue to look longingly at all that space. In some large cities, the FCC has also allowed other services to use UHF channels 14 through 20, simply as a means of meeting urgent needs for more two-way communications frequencies.

As we continue to go up in frequency, there is a great deal of space still available in the microwave region (i.e., frequencies above 3000 megaHertz), but the equipment cost escalates and the communication range on the Earth's surface declines. However, those frequencies are ideal for satellite and space communications. Satellite television and computerized data communications take a huge amount of spectrum space, and it's just not available anywhere else. As direct satellite-to-home broadcasting develops in the coming years, the demand for UHF and even microwave spectrum space will continue to grow faster than our ability to design the ever-more-sophisticated equipment required.

When radio broadcasting was in its infancy, the major rationale for government regulation was that there just wasn't enough room for everyone. Even though we've learned how to use hundreds of times more spectrum space than we were using then, there still isn't enough room to go around.

One of the greatest concerns of the FCC today is finding ways to accommodate more radio and television stations within the limited amount of space available. The need to accommodate new broadcast voices is great, but the radio spectrum, like so many of our other natural resources, is limited.

THE BIRTH OF BROADCASTING

When the pioneers of radio were conducting their experiments in the 1890s, they had no idea they were developing a new mass communication medium. Rather, they were looking for a way to send Morse code messages from one point to another without telegraph wires. In fact, for many years radio was called "wireless."

The first serious users for wireless radio communications were the world's navies and commercial shipping lines. By the early 1900s, Europe and North America were criss-crossed with telegraph wires, so the early inventors saw only one obvious need for wireless communication: at sea.

The first major legislation governing radio in the United States, the Radio Act of 1912, recognized this reality. It did not anticipate the development of commercial radio broadcasting, but it did provide for the licensing of shipboard and shore stations.

The 1912 act was prompted in part by the disastrous sinking of the luxury liner, the Titanic. The fact that the Titanic had a wireless station was credited with saving hundreds of lives, but many more might have been saved had the wireless stations of that era been better organized. There was a ship much closer to the Titanic than the one that came to its rescue, but that ship's wireless operator was off duty when the disaster struck, so no one aboard knew what was happening. Consequently, the 1912 Act required all large ships to be equipped with wireless, and to have operators on duty full time. Also, the act established qualifications for the operators themselves.

After World War I, radio broadcasting developed almost overnight, and almost by accident. Westinghouse and other equipment manufacturers supported stations such as Dr. Frank Conrad's widely noted Pittsburgh station, KDKA, mainly to promote the sale of more equipment, not to establish a new mass medium of communications.

However, in 1921 and 1922 radio broadcasting suddenly caught on much as personal computers caught on in the early 1980s. Hundreds of stations rushed in to fill the available space in what is now the AM band. By the mid-1920s, there were so many stations that conditions were, at best, chaotic. Interference, not all of it accidental, reached intolerable levels.

The 1912 Radio Act had authorized the Department of Commerce to issue radio station and operators' licenses, but federal courts repeatedly ruled that Secretary of Commerce Herbert Hoover had no authority to stop issuing licenses when the AM broadcast band became overcrowded. Nor did Hoover have the authority to tell broadcasters what frequencies they could use. Some stations jumped from frequency to frequency in a frantic effort to avoid interference.

The AM broadcast band in 1926 or 1927 might be compared with the "Citizens Band" (CB radio) today in terms of interference. Like modern CB, the AM band then had layer upon layer of signals, with the louder ones covering up weaker ones and with signals suddenly disappearing and showing up elsewhere on the dial.

In a move that some in the industry have regretted ever since, the nation's broadcasters demanded government action to bring order out of that chaos. For five consecutive years in the 1920s, national radio conferences were held to make these demands. Most industries dread government regulation, but here was an industry asking for government regulation.

Congress responded with the Radio Act of 1927, which set up a separate regulatory body for radio communications, the Federal Radio Commission. The FRC was composed of five commissioners, appointed by the president to serve as a policy-making board. Significantly, the FRC was given the authority to assign broadcasters to specific frequencies and to deny license applications when there was no room for additional stations. The FRC's staff was still housed within the Department of Commerce, but the commission nonetheless had wide authority.

The FRC quickly went to work creating order on the AM broadcast band. There were simply too many stations on the air, so the commission began gradually reducing the number. In deciding who should get a license, the commission had several goals (listed in their order of priority):

1. to assure that everyone in America could receive at least one radio station;
2. to provide service to as many persons as possible from as many diversified sources as possible;
3. to provide outlets for local self-expression.

Within a few years, the AM band was an orderly place, with each station assured an interference-free frequency, at least in its local area. The commission created several classes of stations to serve different purposes. First, certain powerful stations were designated as "clear channel" stations—

stations that shared their frequencies with no one else anywhere in the country at night. These assignments went to stations that already had wide listening audiences and high-power transmitters. Their mission was to serve their metropolitan areas in the daytime and vast regions of the country at night.

Other stations were restricted to lower transmitter power and forced to share their frequencies with other broadcasters. At the bottom of the pecking order were daytime-only stations that had to leave the air at nightfall to make way for the clear channel giants.

Although the FRC was effective in achieving its major goals, it was replaced during President Franklin D. Roosevelt's "New Deal" administration. Roosevelt set out to systematically reorganize the federal government, and he felt the FRC should have both broader authority and a separate administrative staff.

To effect those changes, the Communications Act of 1934 was passed, establishing the basic regulatory structure that exists today. The FRC was replaced by a seven-member Federal Communications Commission. The FCC was given a separate staff, making it a fully independent regulatory agency. In addition to radio broadcasting, its jurisdiction was extended to include long-distance telephone service as well as virtually all non-governmental uses of the radio spectrum.

The FCC was specifically forbidden to "censor" broadcasting, but it was given extensive authority to regulate broadcasters in other ways. The most important power given the FCC, of course, was the power to grant or deny licenses. Broadcasters were required to renew their licenses periodically, an onerous burden they still must bear. The FCC was authorized to assure that broadcasters served "the public interest, convenience and necessity," a mandate the FCC has used to impose various programming requirements on broadcasters.

The FCC's authority was based on the Interstate Commerce Clause in the U.S. Constitution. For a time after the 1927 Radio Act was passed, some broadcasters contended that they were exempt from Federal Radio Commission regulation because their signals did not cross state lines. However, the FRC claimed jurisdiction over all broadcasters as "ancillary" to the regulation of interstate broadcasting: even purely local broadcasting could interfere with stations whose signals did cross state lines, the FRC said. The U.S. Supreme Court upheld the FRC on this point (*U.S. v. Nelson Brothers.*, 289 U.S. 266, 1933).

A few years later, the Federal Communications Commission moved far beyond its original role as a traffic cop of the airwaves. The commission began not only saying who could use what frequency, but also issuing detailed rules to govern broadcasters' content and business practices. When the FCC adopted a package of "Chain Broadcast Regulations" (described in Chapter 13), the major networks said the agency had gone beyond its authority. The networks went to court to test the commission's right to make such rules. In a landmark 1943 decision, the Supreme Court relied on the scarcity rationale to uphold the FCC's authority. The court said the agency was entitled to regulate broadcasting comprehensively, going far beyond its role as a traffic cop (*NBC v. U.S.*, 319 U.S. 190).

These early court decisions gave the FCC broad authority over all radio and television broadcasting as well as many other telecommunications services. As we shall see later, however, the FCC is seeking to shed some of its authority today, and a 1984 Supreme Court decision suggests that the scarcity rationale may no longer justify extensive government control over broadcast content.

The FCC's authority is limited in some other respects. For example, the commission has little authority over government and military uses of the radio spectrum. About half of the entire useful radio spectrum is reserved for federal government and military uses, including an enormous chunk of the VHF, UHF, and microwave regions. Government uses of the spectrum are coordinated by the National Telecommunications and Information Administration. Earlier, the authority now exercised by the NTIA was exercised by various offices in the executive branch of government. For a time, an Office of Telecommunications Policy directly under the president had final say over federal government uses of the spectrum. The FCC consults with the NTIA on many spectrum use questions, but the NTIA has the final say over most federal government telecommunications.

Some critics of this two-headed system sometimes feel it is not the ideal one for serving the public interest. If federal government and military radio uses were subject to FCC jurisdiction, the radio spectrum would surely be allocated differently than it is now. Commercial users of the spectrum chronically face severe frequency congestion. And they sometimes look longingly over the electronic fence, as it were, to the uncrowded green pastures of radio space where a few government users lazily graze.

The FCC has only a limited amount of the radio spectrum to work with. The best it can hope to do is allocate scarce resources as fairly as possible, accommodating as many of the various services' needs as it can.

AN OVERVIEW OF THE FCC

The Federal Communications Commission's basic mandate has remained much the same for half a century, although the commission itself was reconstituted as a five-member body in 1982. The five commissioners serve as the agency's policy-making body. They are appointed by the president, with the consent of the Senate, for seven-year terms. Only three of the five members may come from one political party.

The commission has the power to adopt administrative regulations that have the force of law, so it is a lawmaking body. But it is a law enforcement and executive body as well. It makes judgmental decisions—often crucially important ones to broadcasters—in selecting among competing applicants for an available frequency. Moreover, it functions somewhat as a court would in weighing evidence in proceedings to penalize those who violate its rules. In short, the agency makes the rules, it enforces them, and it judges alleged violators.

However, its powers are limited. It must afford all parties who appear before it "due process of law," and it must obey the First Amendment. Moreover, its jurisdiction is limited by the Communications Act of 1934, and its decisions may be appealed to the U.S. Circuit Courts of Appeals, and from there to the Supreme Court. On numerous occasions the federal courts have overturned decisions of the FCC.

When an FCC decision is appealed, the court must determine if the FCC exceeded its statutory authority or violated the Constitution, or if the agency "abused its discretion" by reaching a decision that was not justified by the facts.

FCC Procedures

As a rulemaking body, the FCC must follow specific procedures, as must other federal administrative agencies such as the Federal Trade Commission (see Chapter 12). When the commissioners need information on a particular subject, they may issue a *Notice of Inquiry.* Then they will await responses from interested parties. Or they may propose new regulations by issuing a *Notice of Proposed Rulemaking.* These notices are published in the *Federal Register*, a daily publication of the federal government that announces actions by many federal agencies. After a rulemaking proposal is announced, interested parties are invited to respond with comments. Then anyone who wishes may react to the comments by submitting "reply comments."

After receiving written comments, the commissioners may also conduct a hearing at which oral arguments are presented. Finally, the commissioners vote on the proposed rule. If it is approved, the new rule becomes a part of the agency's official regulations, which appear in Title 47 of the *Code of Federal Regulations.*

If you have a special interest in any particular FCC rule, you can look up both the rule and the commission's detailed statement about the rule in the *Federal Register*, which you will find in any well-equipped law library and many large city libraries. The *Federal Register* is a huge publication, running to some 75,000 pages each year. However, FCC actions are indexed by subject and are thus easy to find.

Although the major policy decisions are made by the five commissioners, the bulk of the FCC's work is carried out by the agency's administrative staff. The agency does most of its work through four "bureaus," each of which has a separate area of responsibility. These are the bureaus:

1. The *Mass Media Bureau* is of primary concern to broadcasters and cable system operators. It is responsible for licensing and supervising about 10,000 commercial radio and television stations. The bureau handles the paperwork of licensing and other administrative matters, only referring the

most controversial questions to the commission itself. However, the commissioners and ultimately the federal courts may review the bureau's decisions.

The Mass Media Bureau also supervises the burgeoning community antenna television (CATV or just "cable") industry. The FCC's authority over cable has been challenged in the federal courts, and the commission has now "deregulated" cable, dropping a great many of its former rules governing the industry. Nevertheless, this bureau has the responsibility for supervising cable systems that now serve more than one-third of all American homes.

In addition to cable and broadcasting, the Mass Media Bureau oversees the new television-like technologies through its Video Services Division. These technologies are discussed more fully in Chapter 15.

For many years there were separate "broadcasting" and "cable television" bureaus. The two were merged in 1982 in order to provide better coordinated regulation of all television-like services for the public.

2. The *Common Carrier Bureau* regulates interstate telephone and other "common carrier" communications. A common carrier is a utility-like operation that must serve everyone who seeks service and is prepared to pay for it. The states regulate these services within their boundaries through their public utilities commissions; the FCC regulates interstate services and rates. The American Telephone and Telegraph Company (AT&T) is the biggest common carrier within this bureau's purview, but there are about 1,600 others, including wire, radio, and satellite common carrier systems. With overlapping federal and state rate-setting authority, and with the complexity of deciding exactly what is an intrastate communication and what is interstate, this bureau's duties are highly complex.

3. The *Private Radio Bureau,* formerly called "safety and special services," has one of the broadest but least known areas of responsibility within the FCC. It supervises virtually all of the non-broadcast radio services, including the land-mobile service (police and fire communications and many other public and private two-way radio services), the marine radio service, aeronautical radio, amateur (or "ham") radio, and the enormous but seemingly ungovernable citizens band radio service (CB radio). Even though called the "private radio bureau," it regulates many public agencies: it has authority over the radio activities of government agencies that share the two-way radio bands with non-government users.

4. The *Field Operations Bureau* provides field engineering services for the other bureaus, monitoring and policing the radio spectrum and providing technical support all over the United States. The country is divided into districts for FCC administrative purposes, and each has a field office. Several also have field monitoring stations. If a broadcaster violates FCC technical standards by allowing his transmitter to drift off its proper frequency or by running the audio level too high, for instance, this arm of the FCC is responsible for detecting the violation.

In addition to these four specialized bureaus, the FCC has a central administrative staff, a science and technology office, a large legal staff, and a plans and policies office.

This, then, is an overview of how the Federal Communications Commission is organized and operates. Obviously, the FCC has vast responsibilities beyond the regulation of radio and television broadcasting. Even in the broadcasting field, only a small percentage of the FCC's regulatory energy is directed toward such high-visibility activities as enforcing the Fairness Doctrine and the Equal Time rule, two controversial broadcast requirements that are sometimes thought of as the FCC's main interests aside from issuing and renewing licenses.

In recent years, in fact, a number of the FCC's highest priorities in the broadcasting field have been in other areas. As noted earlier, two of the commission's main endeavors have been efforts to create room in the crowded radio spectrum for more broadcasters and to deregulate the industry.

MORE BROADCAST VOICES

In the early 1980s, the FCC was moving on several fronts in its efforts to open up the radio and television bands for new stations, the first major expansion in many years.

In the AM radio field, the commission had taken two major steps to create room for newcomers:

1. It sought and got a decision at the 1979 World Administrative Radio Conference to expand the size of the broadcast band by 100 kiloHertz, making room for ten new channels; and
2. The commission stripped the last of the old high-power clear channel stations of their status, clearing the way for other stations to be assigned to their once-exclusive frequencies.

The 1979 world conference decision to expand the AM band was a major victory for the United States, but it will be a number of years before the new frequencies can be occupied by broadcasters. This is because the previous users of those frequencies must be given time to relocate. Even then, the new band segment will be of little value until AM radio receivers are mass produced to cover it, as we pointed out earlier.

Nevertheless, this step opens up virgin territory for AM broadcasters for the first time in five decades. It has to be considered a major step forward in the FCC's effort to create more diversity in programming and foster minority ownership.

In terms of its immediate impact on the AM band, the second change was more far-reaching. When abolishing the last clear-channel stations was proposed, the FCC was flooded with letters from faithful listeners to such shows as the "Grand Ole Opry," carried live for many years on WSM in Nashville, Tenn. As a high-power clear channel station, WSM had nighttime listeners all over the eastern two-thirds of the United States. Many of the other clear channel stations also had large and loyal regional audiences, the FCC learned.

Altogether, there were 25 clear channels, 11 of which were still assigned to just one station each in the 48 contiguous states. Stations on these channels were classified as "Class I-A" stations. In addition to these 25 frequencies, 22 other frequencies were designated as "Class I-B" channels, meaning that a single station had national priority on each frequency, with other broadcasters required to avoid interfering with that station. As a result of these policies, the great majority of America's AM radio stations had to be crowded onto only about half of the available frequencies in the broadcast band.

In opening up these channels, the FCC nevertheless agreed to protect the former clear channel stations from interference in both their "primary service areas" and their "secondary service areas," which extend out to a distance of about 750 miles in all directions. Beyond this distance, reception is less reliable anyway, and the FCC felt few listeners would really be harmed by the change.

But on the other hand, the change created room for about 100 new AM radio stations nationally, an improvement the FCC felt was worthwhile.

Meanwhile, the FCC has also taken steps to create new access to the FM radio and VHF television bands in the 1980s. The commission's FM plan involves changing its traditional classifications of FM stations and reducing the required geographic separation between stations sharing adjacent channels.

Previously, the FCC classified all commercial FM stations as Class A (low power for local coverage), Class B (medium power for urban coverage), and Class C (high power for regional coverage). The 80 commercial channels in the FM band had been allocated to various cities for specific classes of stations. There are also 20 FM channels reserved for noncommercial stations.

The new plan, approved in 1983, created two new intermediate classes of FM stations, and also allows Class A stations to occupy Class B or C channels if no Class A channel is available locally. Also, the new plan substantially reduces the mandatory geographic separation.

Taken together, these steps made room for about 600 new FM radio stations in the United States. However, most of the new allocations turned out to be in smaller communities. All of this rule juggling produced only a handful of new assignments in the nation's 100 largest markets.

Television Expansion

The FCC's television expansion plans are perhaps the most visionary of all of its changes in over-the-air broadcasting. In 1982, the commission created a brand new form of television broadcasting: low power television (LPTV).

These LPTV "mini-stations" face minimal regulation and will need much less expensive equipment than normal television stations. The commission's idea was to create a purely local TV service for communities that have previously had no television service either because no frequency was available or because the cost of a conventional station was too great. Many rural communities have been served only by low-power "translator" stations, which pick up a distant commercial station and retransmit its signal on a different frequency. In effect, this new policy allows these translators to originate their own local programming, as well as opening the door for entirely new stations. However, when the FCC began accepting applications for these LPTV stations, the staff was quickly overwhelmed by more than 10,000 applications—most of them from big cities, not rural areas. Many of the applicants were large corporate interests, not the low-budget operators the FCC seemed to have in mind when LPTV was first proposed.

To handle the crush of applications, the FCC decided to process them in three groups, starting with those in rural areas having little existing television service. Later, the staff will use a lottery system to award LPTV licenses in more competitive markets. By the time the entire screening process is completed, the FCC estimates that there will as many as 4,000 new television stations in the United States, roughly eight times the total number of TV stations on the air in 1980.

These new stations will operate on a "secondary," non-interfering basis with existing stations. That means the new stations are responsible for correcting any interference problems that result when they go on the air.

The new low-power stations will be free of many technical and program-ming rules that apply to other TV stations. The Equal Opportunity provision of the Communications Act and the Fairness Doctrine (which are discussed later in this chapter) will apply, but only to the extent that a station has the staff and resources to comply with these rules. Most other programming rules will not apply, although LPTV stations will be subject to the ban on lottery advertising (explained in Chapter 12) and obscenity. These stations will even be allowed to offer pay TV programming. There are no low-power TV ownership restrictions: networks, conventional broadcasters, cable systems, and newspapers will all be eligible. Moreover, there is no limit to the number of these stations that one person or company may own. However, the FCC will favor minority applicants and those who hold no other licenses in choosing among competing applicants for a given channel. Thus, anyone who holds one or more licenses (either conventional or low power) will have little chance to win additional licenses if there are competing applicants who own no broadcast properties.

Although the LPTV program is a dramatic departure from past FCC policies and may fundamentally alter the nature of American television, it is not the FCC's only effort to create more TV stations. The commission is also adding VHF television "drop-ins," in effect authorizing new stations on channels where the commission's old allocation policy, established in 1952, would have prohibited it. The FCC hoped to eventually find space for 100 more stations to augment service in communities with few existing stations.

In addition, the FCC has authorized a plethora of new television-like services with alphabet-soup names: MDS, ITFS, SMATV, DBS, and STV, to name a few. These new technologies are discussed in Chapter 15.

While pursuing these long-range goals, the FCC has continued to exercise its regular functions, the most important being licensing.

BROADCAST LICENSING

Certainly the FCC's most intimidating power is its licensing authority, and particularly its power to revoke or refuse to renew an existing license that could be worth a fortune on the open market.

However, in the 1980s the FCC has dramatically simplified the license renewal process, eliminating a great deal of the paperwork and red tape that once made a license renewal such a bureaucratic headache for broadcasters. The process has been so greatly streamlined that most broadcasters can now take advantage of what has become known as "postcard renewal." Instead of a detailed report, broadcasters fill out a renewal application that is really an oversized postcard. The FCC requires about five percent of all broadcast licensees to go through an "audit" in which the long renewal application form is still required.

Thousands of pages of paperwork—forms that some critics of the process said the FCC staff didn't have time to read anyway—have been eliminated as a result of postcard renewal. However, a coalition of minority groups went to court to challenge the FCC's authority to eliminate the more detailed application form. They contended that the short renewal form really excused most broadcasters from having to show any record of public interest programming at all. But in a 1983 ruling, the U.S. Circuit Court of Appeals in Washington, D.C., upheld the postcard renewal process (*Black Citizens for a Fair Media v. FCC*, 719 F.2d 407). The court said occasional "audits" were sufficient to ensure that broadcasters would meet their obligations.

Even Congress acted to ease the license renewal burden for broadcasters, dramatically lengthening the license terms for both radio and TV stations in 1981. Radio stations now must renew their licenses only every seven years, while TV stations must renew every five years. Previously, all broadcast licenses came up for renewal every three years.

In granting licenses, the FCC has two different processes, one for new license applicants and another for renewals of existing licenses. For an applicant seeking a new license, the process is considerably more involved than just filling out a postcard. In fact, the first step is to determine if a frequency is available.

The FCC has a variety of rules to determine whether a frequency is available for a new station in a given community. An applicant for a new license must either identify a frequency that has been assigned to an area but is not in use or convince the FCC to make a new assignment. The FCC will not consider the request unless it can be shown that the new station will not interfere with any existing station. Every station has a defined service area in which it is protected from interference.

Once a new applicant has identified an available frequency, the next step is to initiate the lengthy application process by applying for what is called a "construction permit."

For many years broadcast applicants had to complete an elaborate study called *ascertainment* in which community needs were identified. This process involved interviews with perhaps hundreds of community leaders representing all segments of society. The senior management had to do much of the study personally; it could not all be farmed out to a research organization.

The FCC approved a major deregulation of radio broadcasting in 1981, and eliminated the formal ascertainment requirements along with a number of other rules that are discussed later. The commission extended this deregulation to commercial television stations in 1984.

To return to the licensing process, applicants must eventually file a complete license application. In it, they must convince the FCC that they qualify for a license in terms of character, financial standing, technical capability, programming plans, non-discrimination in employment, and non-ownership of conflicting media. Applicants must be U.S. citizens.

The character requirement is rather straightforward: the applicant must have a clean record, although occasionally the FCC will overlook a minor criminal record in areas unrelated to the station's likely performance. For instance, once an applicant who had been convicted of gun-running in Israel was awarded an FCC license years later. However, any record of dishonesty is likely to be fatal to the applicant. As we shall see, the FCC has sometimes severely penalized broadcast licensees for misrepresentations on their application forms. The commission is now reevaluating its character qualification policies in the light of the *RKO General* case (discussed later).

The financial requirement can be a tough one. Many applicants have been required to have enough resources to buy the needed equipment and run the station for a year. Sometimes an applicant may count anticipated advertising revenue if affidavits can be obtained from potential advertisers to prove their willingness to support the new station. This rule, of course, means that only those with substantial money behind them have a good chance of getting licensed. At this writing, the FCC was considering a relaxation of this financial requirement for radio licensees, recognizing that it deters otherwise qualified applicants (especially members of minority groups). Rather than having to show they could bankroll the station for a year, applicants would only need to show they have enough money for three months under the proposed policy.

The technical qualifications are probably the easiest of all to demonstrate, since this merely requires applicants to show that they plan to use appropriate equipment and employ qualified engineers.

The ownership question reflects the FCC's interest in fostering local ownership and in-resident management of radio and television stations. But in addition, the FCC will not grant a radio or television license to the owner of a daily newspaper in the same market area, nor will the commission license someone who already holds the maximum number of radio or television stations allowed (see Chapter 13).

The programming part of an application is sometimes a pie-in-the-sky fairy tale, and the FCC gives the applicant's plans in this area relatively little weight unless they call for something drastically out of the ordinary in the way of programming.

There is an equal employment opportunities requirement: the applicant must present a plan for assuring that women and minorities will be fairly represented in the station's work force. It doesn't have to involve racial quotas that match the demographic makeup of the community, but the licensee must promise to affirmatively seek minority employees. If the license is granted, the applicant must be prepared to prove that this promise was kept if asked to do so at license renewal time.

Once an applicant satisfies the FCC that all of these requirements have been met, the license is usually granted if a frequency is available—unless the application is opposed, either by an existing licensee or a public interest group, or perhaps by another applicant for the same frequency.

License Opposition: The Carroll Doctrine

Another licensee may oppose the application, fearing that the new station will cause excessive interference with reception of his station. If that can be proved, it effectively kills the proceeding unless the interference problem is solved. A licensee may just fear new economic competition, however. In that case the FCC is not permitted to consider the objection unless the established licensee can show that the station's economic standing will be so badly damaged that its ability to serve the public will be substantially reduced. That concept is called the Carroll Doctrine, because it resulted from a federal appellate court decision by that name (*Carroll Broadcasting Co. v. FCC*, 258 F.2d 440, 1958).

When there is a rival applicant for the same frequency (as there often is), the FCC holds a full *comparative proceeding* in which it weighs the merits of the two applicants. If one applicant's qualifications are clearly superior, that applicant gets the license. However, if the applicants are about equally qualified, the commission applies an elaborate set of rules for evaluating the competing applications. The commission considers a number of factors, including these: (1) the need for a first broadcast facility in communities that have none; (2) the need for competition in a community with only one broadcaster; (3) the desirability of having every frequency efficiently used, which means the applicant offering to serve a larger area would probably be preferred.

The commission also gives a preference to minority group members and may soon grant a similar preference to women in these comparative proceedings, a step designed to help correct the traditional underrepresentation of women and minorities in broadcasting.

Given the difficulty of choosing between equally qualified applicants for a license, Congress authorized the FCC to use a lottery system to award new licenses in 1982. This luck-of-the-draw system would be less arbitrary than any judgment based on the promises made by rival applicants, Congress concluded. At this writing the FCC had not yet implemented a lottery system except for low-power TV licenses, although the commission had ruled that members of minority groups and persons who hold no other broadcast licenses will be given a preference in future lotteries.

Eventually, the entire licensing process is completed and one of the applicants is granted a construction permit. After the conditions of the construction permit have been met, the license is granted and the new station goes on the air.

Almost as soon as the new station is licensed, it must begin preparing for the next crisis in the relationship between broadcaster and government: renewal time. At that point, the broadcaster has to show good stewardship in its use of its assigned frequency.

However, as a result of deregulation (discussed later), many of the things broadcasters had to show to justify renewal are no longer required. For example, the rules that once required community ascertainment, set specific standards for public affairs programming, and recommended limits for advertising time no longer apply in most instances.

LICENSE RENEWAL PROBLEMS

For many years, broadcasters assumed that once they had a license from the FCC, it was theirs indefinitely. A license to broadcast in a big city (without any station equipment or any of the other accoutrements of a going business) came to be worth millions of dollars. This is true despite the fact that the licensee technically has nothing more than a right to use his or her frequency for the balance of the license term. The Communications Act says a license never becomes a vested right. In fact, broadcasters have to sign an agreement acknowledging that their frequencies will remain public property indefinitely.

However, in actual practice the FCC virtually rubber-stamped most renewals for many years. To lose a license, one had to commit a serious crime or try to deceive the FCC (by falsifying a license application, for example). The FCC did occasionally refuse to renew a license for that kind of misconduct, as it did in a case that reached the U.S. Supreme Court, *FCC v. WOKO, Inc.* (329 U.S. 223, 1946).

In the *WOKO* case, a CBS executive secretly received stock in WOKO, an Albany, New York, radio station, in return for his help in getting WOKO a

CBS affiliation. The station filed false ownership statements with the FCC for 12 years in an effort to conceal this arrangement. When the FCC learned of the falsification, it refused to renew the station's license, even though the majority stockholders didn't know about the deal. A federal appellate court reversed the FCC's decision, but the Supreme Court overturned the appellate ruling and said such a decision was within the commission's discretion, despite its harsh consequences for innocent parties.

Aside from situations such as the *WOKO* case, broadcasters came to assume they were guaranteed a license in perpetuity: if you didn't get caught lying, cheating, or stealing, you didn't have to worry about getting your license renewed. You certainly wouldn't lose your license to someone else who came out of the blue and promised to do a better job of serving the community. However, that changed somewhat in the 1960s and 1970s. Both the FCC and the courts began taking a new look at the licensing process.

A key turning point in this process was a federal court ruling, *Office of Communications of the United Church of Christ v. FCC* (359 F.2d 994, 1966; 425 F.2d 543, 1969). In that case, a public interest group requested a hearing to protest the renewal of a Mississippi television station's license on the ground that its programming evidenced blatant racial prejudice. The FCC refused to grant the group any standing to challenge the license renewal, but a federal appellate court ordered the FCC to hold a new hearing and allow the group to appear. Next, the FCC held such a hearing but placed the burden of proof on the citizen group. The federal court overruled the FCC again, declaring that the burden of proof should have been on the broadcaster to justify his performance. Then the court set aside the license renewal, and the station eventually lost the license.

After that decision, citizens' groups demanded and won standing to oppose a number of other license renewals, and sometimes rival applicants demanded a comparative hearing so they could attempt to show that they could make better use of the frequency. This was a new element in the renewal process; no longer could a broadcaster merely fill out the forms and rest assured that renewal would be a routine matter. The risk that an opponent might file a "petition to deny" a license renewal came to be a fact of life for broadcasters.

Further breaking the rubber-stamp tradition, the FCC shocked the broadcast industry by denying renewal to an incumbent television licensee in Boston in 1969. A rival group challenged the renewal of WHDH, and the FCC eventually decided the challenger could do a better job than the incumbent.

The policy of holding a comparative hearing when a renewal is challenged was not new, but the rules had so favored the incumbent licensee that challengers had little chance to win. If the incumbent licensee had provided even average service, that record was supposed to be given preference over the mere promises of a challenger. But in this case, the FCC ignored the broadcaster's record of average service and granted the license to a challenger who promised better things. In so ruling, the FCC noted that the incumbent licensee, also the owner of the Boston *Herald-Traveler* newspaper, had shown little interest in the active management of the television station. Really, the station was little more than a source of revenue for the newspaper. A federal appellate court affirmed the FCC decision in 1970 (*Greater Boston Television Corp. v. FCC*, 444 F.2d 841).

The idea that an incumbent licensee could lose his or her license to a challenger at renewal time, thus forfeiting a piece of property worth millions of dollars, frightened the broadcast industry. The industry quickly had legislation introduced in Congress to strip the FCC of authority to hold comparative hearings unless it first decided the incumbent broadcaster had done an unacceptable job. But before Congress could act, the FCC abruptly abandoned its policy of holding comparative hearings in most challenged license renewal cases.

However, a citizens' group took the FCC to court over that change in policy, and in 1971 a federal appellate court reversed the FCC, ordering the agency to hold comparative hearings in most instances when a renewal was challenged (*Citizens Communications Center v. FCC*, 447 F.2d 1201). The court said that only broadcasters with service records "far above average" should be exempted from comparative hearings if their license renewals were challenged. Thus, the FCC resumed its practice of holding comparative hearings when licensees faced renewal challenges, although perhaps the agency did so halfheartedly.

Over a period of years, the FCC gradually refined its comparative renewal policy. Eventually the commission reached the point of saying that a licensee who had a "substantial" record of service (as opposed to a "far above average" record) was entitled to a renewal almost regardless of what a challenger might promise. Although that change may have been an exercise in semantics more than anything else, it led to more lawsuits.

In 1982, the U.S. Court of Appeals in Washington, D.C., affirmed this new policy on license renewals in *Central Florida Enterprises v. FCC* (683 F.2d 503). The court agreed that the FCC is entitled to give considerable weight to an incumbent licensee's "renewal expectancy" if the licensee has a "substantial" record of service. In essence, the FCC policy now says this: The better the incumbent's record, the greater should be his or her "renewal expectancy." A licensee with a record of minimal service would get no preference over a challenger in a comparative hearing, while someone with a superior record would get a very strong preference.

The *Central Florida* case began in the mid-1970s when Central Florida Enterprises challenged the Cowles Broadcasting Company's right to continue operating WESH-TV on channel 2 in Daytona Beach, Fla. Cowles had moved its studios to a different town without getting the FCC's permission, and there were allegations of fraud on the part of a subsidiary of Cowles. Also, Cowles was a multi-station owner with little integration between ownership and local management (the FCC normally prefers for ownership and management to be in the same hands). Despite all of these factors, the commission initially seemed not to take the challenger seriously, almost routinely renewing Cowles' license. However, the Court of Appeals then ordered the commission to reconsider the matter. The commission responded by again deciding to renew the license—but with a much more detailed rationale for the decision the second time.

In its earlier ruling on this complex case, the court had said the FCC was acting as if there were an "irrefutable presumption in favor of renewal" and overturned the renewal. But in its second ruling, the court reluctantly upheld the renewal, accepting the commission's rationale this time. In so doing, the court affirmed the FCC's new policy of considering a licensee's "renewal expectancy" whenever there is evidence of "substantial" service.

This FCC policy makes it very difficult for a challenger to take a license away from an established broadcaster, a point that troubled the Court of Appeals when it decided the *Central Florida* case. Nevertheless, the fact is that broadcasters are just about assured of license renewals—unless they flagrantly violate the law or the commission's rules. What does a broadcaster have to do to lose a license? The *RKO* case is a good example.

The *RKO* Case

One of the most dramatic license non-renewal cases in the FCC's history became a controversial issue in 1980. In that year the commission decided to strip RKO General, one of the nation's largest broadcasting corporations, of major-market television stations in New York, Boston, and Los Angeles. At the same time, the FCC made it clear that RKO's other radio and television licenses would also be in jeopardy at renewal time.

This case did *not* arise because someone challenged RKO's right to a renewal and used a comparative hearing to promise better service. Rather, the FCC took the initiative to terminate RKO's licenses because RKO and its parent company, General Tire and Rubber, were allegedly guilty of various kinds of fraud and other illegal activities. Nevertheless, the *RKO* case is important because of its potential impact on broadcasting.

RKO claimed the three television licenses in question were worth at least $400 million, and immediately appealed the FCC's decision. In 1981 the U.S. Court of Appeals affirmed the FCC's non-renewal of the Boston license (*RKO v. FCC*, 670 F.2d 215), and the Supreme Court declined to hear the case in April of 1982. Thus, RKO reluctantly went off the air in Boston and handed the channel over to a new licensee.

However, the Court of Appeals sent the actions to terminate the Los Angeles (KHJ-TV) and New York (WOR-TV) licenses back to the FCC for further consideration because the commission had not yet provided a "principled explanation for RKO's disqualification" to operate those two stations. In upholding the FCC decision to take away the Boston license, the appellate court said:

> The denial of a license renewal to a major licensee in a major market is of manifest moment and financial impact. The FCC's decision has not

been reviewed callously, and we have tried not to lose sight of the difficult issues in this case by sweeping the reasoning of the Commission under a rug of agency expertise or administrative convenience. The record presented to this court shows irrefutably that the licensee was playing the dodger to serious charges involving it and its parent company. (7 Med.L.Rptr. at 2331)

Of all the evidence presented in the case, apparently the most persuasive to the court was the FCC's documentary proof that RKO provided information to the commission in the early stages of the proceeding that the company itself contradicted in later filings. The commission cited an "egregious lack of candor" on RKO's part.

After the *RKO v. FCC* court ruling, RKO managed to make a deal with Congress to rescue its New York license. Congress passed special legislation that overruled the FCC and renewed WOR-TV's license on condition that it move its studios from New York to New Jersey. Given New Jersey's proximity to both New York and Philadelphia, the state had not had even one commercial VHF TV station within its borders. For years, New Jersey residents (and their legislators) had been demanding a VHF television station of their own. Congress decided to solve that problem—and let RKO partially off the hook at the same time—by trading a guaranteed renewal for a move across the Hudson River. But even after WOR's move to Secaucus, N.J., some New Jersey leaders were still unhappy about the VHF TV problem: WOR was allowed to keep its actual transmitter site in New York (atop the World Trade Center), and the station continued to maintain an advertising office in New York. Many New Jersey residents felt that WOR was still primarily a New York station, though it had a New Jersey mailing address.

Meanwhile, the FCC accepted some 160 competing applications for RKO's other 13 licenses and declared that the ultimate fate of those stations will depend on the outcome of the non-renewal proceeding involving KHJ-TV in Los Angeles. At this writing no one can be sure what the FCC will ultimately do with RKO General's remaining broadcast properties.

Whatever the outcome of this amazing case, the fact that it happened illustrates the major contradiction in broadcast regulation. In theory, every frequency belongs to the public: the broadcaster has nothing more than temporary authorization to use it, a permit that may be revoked at any time. But in practice, broadcast licenses are immensely valuable pieces of property, items that can be sold for huge sums of money. Thus, on those rare occasions when the FCC does what the Communications Act clearly authorizes it to do and decides the public interest would be better served by not renewing a license, the result is an economic catastrophe for someone.

For this reason, the FCC has developed sanctions short of non-renewal to punish broadcasters for wrongdoing. Probably the most viable of these sanctions is a short-term renewal. The commission may renew a license for as little as one year instead of the usual five or seven. When that happens, a broadcaster knows he is on probation and had better improve his performance.

BROADCAST CONTENT REGULATION

Aside from its frequency allocation and licensing functions, the FCC's main job is to supervise the ongoing operations of its licensees. Much of that supervision involves technical matters. Broadcasters and other FCC licensees must comply with detailed requirements in such areas as frequency stability, modulation percentage, power level, and record keeping. Although complying with FCC rules in these areas occupies much of both the FCC's and broadcasters' time, this sort of regulation is of little concern to the public or even to most non-engineering broadcast employees. Perhaps for that reason, the FCC was considering rule changes that would deregulate many of these technical standards in the mid-1980s.

What is of far more concern to most people is the FCC's regulation of broadcast content. Although Section 326 of the Communications Act specifically forbids the FCC to "censor" broadcasters, over the years the commission has adopted a number of rules governing broadcast content. Also, the Communications Act itself and other federal laws set forth rules governing broadcast content.

One of the FCC's major efforts in the 1980s has been to disentangle itself from the problem of content regulation. No government agency has the authority to tell newspaper and magazine publishers to print a specific amount or kind of material, or to open their columns to those with whom they disagree. Why, the FCC has been asking, should broadcasters be second-class citizens when it comes to First Amendment freedoms? Some consumer groups reply to that question by arguing that broadcasters are given a government-sanctioned monopoly and should have to provide some mandatory public service in return.

Whatever the pros and cons by deregulation, by 1981 the FCC had decided most of the government controls on broadcast content were inappropriate if not unconstitutional. In that year the commission voted to seek the elimination of the two most significant content controls, the Fairness Doctrine and the Equal Time provision of the Communications Act. Since both are at least recognized in acts of Congress, the FCC initially assumed that they could be eliminated only by Congress. The FCC urged Congress to drop these content controls (as did many broadcasters themselves), but Congress seemed hopelessly divided on the issue, with many members of Congress strongly opposed to any deregulation in this area.

In 1983 the FCC initiated its own review of the validity of the Fairness Doctrine. The commission sought public comments on the possibility of revising or abolishing it. Even that move stirred the ire of some members of Congress, and it appeared that Congress might resist any move to significantly weaken either the Equal Time Rule or the Fairness Doctrine. However, in 1984 the Supreme Court seemed to invite the FCC to go ahead and revise or eliminate the Fairness Doctrine and other broadcast content restrictions on its own. That Supreme Court decision is discussed later in this chapter.

For the moment, however, there are still a number of important restrictions on broadcast content, restrictions that do not apply to most other communications media. Thus, we will describe this aspect of broadcast regulation in some depth.

The Law of Political Broadcasting

Probably the most important statutory content requirement for broadcasters concerns political broadcasting. The basic law is contained in Section 315 of the Communications Act, and it has come to be known as the Equal Time Rule or "equal opportunity provision."

Section 315 requires broadcasters to provide equal access to the airwaves to all legally qualified candidates for a given public office during election campaigns. It reads:

> If any licensee shall permit any person who is a legally qualified candidate for any public office to use a broadcasting station, he shall afford equal opportunities to all other such candidates for that office in the use of such broadcasting station. . . .

The Equal Time Rule has a number of provisions, some of them troublesome for broadcasters. Section 315 specifically exempts "bona fide" newscasts, news interviews, news documentaries, and, significantly, live coverage of news events such as political conventions and most debates between candidates. That means a broadcaster can cover news stories involving one candidate without having to include all other candidates.

In 1984, the FCC extended the exemption for news and public affairs programs to the Donahue Show, a talk show hosted by Phil Donahue. Presumably, the same rule would apply to other shows having similar formats, thus allowing them to host political candidates during election campaigns without having to give equal time to all other candidates for the same office.

Section 315 doesn't give politicians free air time. Rather, it merely requires that all candidates be treated equally. If one is sold airtime for a certain fee, the Equal Time Rule merely requires that others be sold equal time for the same price. If Section 315 were the only applicable provision of the Communications Act, a station could comply with the law by simply excluding all political advertising. That would, after all, be giving all candidates *equal* time—none.

In federal elections, however, another provision of the Communications Act places an additional requirement on broadcasters. Under Section 312(a)(7), broadcasters may have their licenses revoked if they fail to provide reasonable access to candidates in federal elections. That means a broadcaster cannot avoid the Equal Time provision by simply turning away all candidates.

In addition, although 312(a)(7) applies only to federal elections, the FCC has made it clear that broadcasters have an obligation to cover state and local political campaigns too, although they need not necessarily provide access to the candidates for every office.

Only in federal elections are broadcasters obliged by Section 312(a)(7) to provide access to candidates for each office contested in their service area. Even then, they need not give or sell the candidates as much time as they might like, although they must provide some time, and it must be provided to all candidates on an equal basis.

During the 1980 presidential election campaign, the Constitutionality of Section 312(a)(7) was tested in court. The Carter-Mondale presidential campaign asked to purchase 30 minutes of airtime on each network in late 1979, about a year before the election. All three networks refused to honor the request, despite the provisions of Section 312(a)(7). CBS offered only five minutes during prime time, while NBC and ABC flatly rejected the request. The FCC then ruled that the networks had failed to meet their legal obligations under Section 312(a)(7). The networks challenged the FCC's ruling in federal appellate court.

In early 1980, the U.S. Court of Appeals in Washington, D.C., upheld the Constitutionality of Section 312(a)(7), and said the FCC acted properly in ruling that it applied to the networks and not merely to local stations. The court upheld the FCC's determination that the campaign had begun, even though the general election was nearly a year away.

The networks appealed this ruling to the U.S. Supreme Court, and the result was an important 1981 decision upholding the FCC, *CBS v. FCC* (453 U.S. 367). Voting 6-3, the high court affirmed the commission's authority under Section 312(a)(7) to order broadcasters to air federal candidates' political statements. The decision came far too late to help the Carter-Mondale campaign, of course, but it represented a major victory for future candidates and a defeat for broadcasters.

The Supreme Court majority ruled that the First Amendment rights of candidates and the public outweighed the First Amendment rights of broadcasters in this particular context. Writing for the court, Chief Justice Warren Burger pointed out that the FCC need not (and does not) honor all requests for air time by federal office seekers, but Burger said the FCC was well within its statutory authority in ordering the networks to air the Carter-Mondale campaign statements in late 1979. In fact, Burger noted that the FCC had set forth specific guidelines for broadcasters to follow in determining when candidates would have a right of access to the airwaves under Section 312(a)(7). In this case, the FCC was justified in concluding that the three major networks had violated those guidelines, Burger said.

However, this Supreme Court decision had no effect on the networks' policies of charging candidates' for airtime. Neither the Equal Time Rule (Section 315) nor Section 312(a)(7) requires broadcasters to give free airtime to any candidate. If one candidate is sold 30 minutes of prime time for a certain price, his rivals must be allowed to buy comparable time for a comparable price. But if one of the rivals can't afford the time, broadcasters need not give it away free. A broadcaster is allowed to give candidates free airtime if he wishes, but only if it is free to all candidates.

On the other hand, Section 312(a)(7) requires broadcasters to charge federal candidates their "lowest unit rates" for advertising within 45 days of a primary election and 60 days of a general election. That means the candidates get the rate charged the largest volume advertisers, even if that discounted rate isn't normally offered to one-time or short-term advertisers. Earlier in the campaign, candidates may be charged rates "comparable" to those charged other advertisers, which means that a candidate doesn't get the quantity discount then unless he buys enough advertising to qualify for it.

The Equal Time Rule only applies to candidates in the same election. Thus, a station may provide airtime during a *primary election* only to those running for the Democratic and Republican nominations and not to those seeking minor party nominations. In the primary, the minor party candidates aren't actually running against the Democratic and Republican candidates. However, during the general election campaign all candidates have to be treated equally. A federal appellate court provided this interpretation of Section 315 in 1970 (*Kay v. FCC*, 443 F.2d 638).

As a result, broadcasters must sell airtime to all candidates who can afford it in federal general elections. And a broadcaster cannot give time away free to some candidates without doing others the same favor.

For many years, that rule created messy problems for broadcasters who wanted to cover presidential debates. In 1960, when John Kennedy and Richard Nixon held the first nationally televised presidential debates, Congress had passed a law temporarily setting aside Section 315 to make the debates possible. This was necessary because the networks were unwilling to provide national prime time for all the minor candidates for the presidency and thus could not have televised the debates otherwise.

In several subsequent presidential elections, no nationally televised debates occurred because Congress would not act to set aside Section 315 again. In 1964, for instance, the polls indicated that Lyndon Johnson was far ahead of his Republican challenger, Barry Goldwater. Johnson's strategists felt he had nothing to gain and a lot to lose if he debated Goldwater, so the Democratic majority in Congress refused to set aside Section 315. For various reasons there were no nationally televised debates during the 1968 and 1972 campaigns, either.

However, in 1975, the FCC reinterpreted Section 315 to say that a debate sponsored by a non-broadcast organization would be considered a bona fide news event, and hence exempt from the requirements of Section 315 (*In re Aspen Institute and CBS*, 55 F.C.C.2d 697). That new interpretation, which came to be known as the *Aspen Rule*, was quickly challenged by Shirley Chisholm, a minor candidate in the 1976 presidential election, but a federal appellate court upheld the rule (*Chisholm v. FCC*, 538 F.2d 349, 1976).

Thus, in both 1976 and 1980, presidential debates were sponsored by the League of Women Voters and dutifully covered as bona fide news events by the networks. Had the debates been staged by a broadcaster or network, it would have been necessary to include (or give equal time to) perhaps 30 lesser-known candidates for president.

Finally, the FCC ruled in 1983 that broadcasters could sponsor debates directly instead of having them sponsored by third parties such as the League of Women Voters. At the same time, the FCC dropped rules that had restricted the use of debates or segments of debates in news programs.

The League of Women Voters challenged the FCC's new rule on debates, but in 1984 the U.S. Court of Appeals in Washington rejected the League's appeal. (*League of Women Voters v. FCC*, 731 F.2d 995). Since it does not violate the Equal Time Rule for a civic organization to sponsor a debate and exclude lesser-known candidates, it doesn't violate the rule if a broadcaster is the sponsor, the commission had contended in defending its new policy. As a result of this decision, broadcasters are permitted to organize their own debates and invite only the major candidates to participate.

Whether candidates' debates are sponsored by broadcasters or civic organizations, ethical questions arise when only certain candidates are invited to take part. Given the great influence of television, some would argue that any debate that excludes some candidates for an office violates the spirit, if not the letter, of the Equal Time provision. A particularly strong argument for this position can be made in state and local elections, where there may be only three or four candidates running (as opposed to the 30 or so who usually become legally qualified candidates in a presidential election).

There are other ethical problems in political broadcasting. For example, the fact that news events are excluded from the Equal Time Rule allows incumbents to get extensive media coverage without other candidates having any similar opportunity. When Senator Edward Kennedy was challenging Jimmy Carter for the 1980 Democratic presidential nomination, he asked the FCC to require the networks to give him equal time to reply to one of Carter's nationally televised news conferences. The FCC turned Kennedy down, and a federal appellate court upheld that decision (*Kennedy for President Committee v. FCC*, 636 F.2d 432, 1980).

Another problem with the Equal Time provision involves non-political appearances by candidates for office. The FCC has steadfastly refused to define what is a political appearance, and the result is that candidates' appearances as actors in dramatic roles have been subjected to the Equal Time Rule. In view of Ronald Reagan's long career in Hollywood before he entered politics, this caused problems for broadcasters: airing old movies in which Reagan appeared created an obligation to give other candidates equal time during election campaigns. A federal appellate court upheld the FCC on this interpretation of Section 315 in a 1974 ruling, *In re Paulsen v. FCC* (491 F.2d 887).

Section 315 forbids the broadcaster to censor a political broadcast. That means a candidate may libel someone on the air, and there is nothing the broadcaster can do to stop it. However, the Supreme Court has exempted broadcasters from any liability for defamatory remarks on such occasions (see *Farmers Educational and Cooperative Union v. WDAY*, discussed in Chapter Four).

This ban on censorship of political broadcasts also poses other dilemmas for broadcasters. For example, what happens if a candidate chooses to include language the broadcaster considers distasteful? Occasionally a candidate insists on including vulgar or offensive language in a political statement—language that a broadcaster could not ordinarily air without incurring the wrath of the FCC. In 1984, the FCC issued a statement declaring that the no-censorship provision of Section 315 can be set aside when it is necessary to prevent a candidate from using language that is not normally permitted on the airwaves. The general problem of restrictions on language use on the air is discussed later.

The Fairness Doctrine

Probably the Fairness Doctrine is the most controversial aspect of the FCC's regulation of broadcast content. Originally established by a commission report in 1949, the Fairness Doctrine requires commercial broadcasters to keep their public affairs programming reasonably balanced: when they cover one side of a controversial issue, they must balance that presentation by airing opposing viewpoints. Another part of the Fairness Doctrine is called the "Personal Attack Rule." That rule simply says that individuals who are personally attacked (in a broadcast editorial or commentary, for instance) must be notified of the attack and given an opportunity to reply over the air.

The Personal Attack Rule does not apply to news coverage, to personal attacks on foreign groups or individuals, or to personal attacks made by candidates for office or their spokespersons.

Obviously, the Fairness Doctrine is a broad, vague, and general policy. It has led to relatively few disciplinary actions against broadcasters and almost no license non-renewals. One notable exception to that generalization involved a conservative religious radio station. The owner promised fairness to all religious faiths when he sought FCC permission to purchase the station, but then he followed a policy of presenting only one viewpoint. The license was not renewed, a decision a federal court upheld (*Brandywine-Main Line Radio v. FCC*, 473 F.2d 16, 1972).

However, in most instances complaints of Fairness Doctrine violations aren't even passed along to broadcasters by the FCC. The FCC receives thousands of Fairness Doctrine complaints each year, and only a small percentage of them lead to any FCC inquiry, let alone a formal action against the broadcaster. This is true because the party claiming a violation must prove the accusation under strict documentation requirements. Few persons can amass the detailed information about a station's programming practices needed to satisfy these requirements. Nevertheless, virtually all Fairness Doctrine proceedings that do occur result from outside complaints; the FCC's Mass Media Bureau doesn't have the staff to monitor radio and TV stations in search of Fairness Doctrine violations.

Some critics of the Fairness Doctrine think it has survived for so long only because it rarely leads to enforcement actions. Were it vigorously enforced, the result would be such severe abridgements of the First Amendment that the courts—or perhaps Congress—would quickly abolish it, these critics suggest.

Comparing Section 315 and the Fairness Doctrine

The Fairness Doctrine is often confused with the Equal Time provision, but it shouldn't be. The Equal Time Rule is a specific provision of the Communications Act, the basic statutory law governing telecommunications in the United States. The Fairness Doctrine had its origins in a regulation of the FCC, although Congress seemingly endorsed it by adding language to the Communications Act in 1959 that required broadcasters to "afford reasonable opportunity for the discussion of conflicting views on issues of public importance."

Moreover, the Equal Time Rule applies only to legally qualified candidates for public office. The Fairness Doctrine applies to all sorts of controversial public issues, not just election isues. And in addition, the Equal Time Rule creates specific broadcast access rights for specific persons: if a broadcaster gives or sells one candidate airtime, equal time must be offered to rival candidates on the same basis. The Fairness Doctrine ordinarily creates no such rights: it requires broadcasters to provide overall balance in covering controversial issues, but it doesn't require broadcasters to grant airtime to any particular spokesperson for any viewpoint. The only time the Fairness Doctrine creates access rights for a specific person is when that person has been the victim of an on-the-air attack to which the Personal Attack Rule applies.

In short, while the Equal Time Rule requires broadcasters to give rival political candidates specific dollar-for-dollar and minute-for-minute equality of access, the Fairness Doctrine merely says broadcasters must provide overall balance in their programming by presenting varied opinions on controversial issues.

While the Fairness Doctrine is unpopular with broadcasters, many of whom feel it abridges their First Amendment rights and actually stifles free expression rather than fostering it, some consumer and media watchdog organizations see it as the public's only hope of assuring that broadcasters serve the public interest and not just their own private commercial interests.

The *Red Lion* Decision

These conflicting viewpoints were weighed by the U.S. Supreme Court in 1969, when it handed down a landmark decision upholding the Fairness Doctrine, *Red Lion Broadcasting v. FCC* (395 U.S. 367). The case arose at the end of the 1964 presidential election when a radio evangelist named Billy James Hargis attacked Fred Cook, the author of a book that criticized Republican candidate Barry Goldwater. The attack was aired over Red Lion's radio station in Pennsylvania, and Cook demanded reply time under the Personal Attack Rule.

Red Lion replied by telling Cook, in effect, to buy an advertisement. Instead, Cook complained to the FCC, which ordered the station to give Cook reply time. Red Lion appealed, charging that it violated a broadcaster's First Amendment rights to be forced to provide airtime to someone like Cook. A federal appellate court upheld the FCC order, ruling that the First Amendment does not free broadcasters of their duties under the Fairness Doctrine.

Meanwhile, a broadcast industry group that was alarmed by the *Red Lion* decision, the Radio and Television News Directors Association, filed a lawsuit in another federal appellate court challenging the FCC on the Fairness Doctrine. The court there overturned the doctrine as a violation of the First Amendment.

Given opposite rulings on the Fairness Doctrine in two different federal appellate courts, the Supreme Court agreed to hear the two cases together. And in its 1969 decision, the nation's highest court upheld both the Fairness Doctrine and the Personal Attack Rule. The court agreed that the First Amendment was an important issue here, but it said the First Amendment rights of the general public took precedence over the rights of broadcasters. A broadcaster, the court said, has a responsibility to respect the First Amendment rights of the public. Thus, the Supreme Court said people such as Fred Cook must be given a chance to reply to broadcast personal attacks. Broadcasters, then, must present diverse opinions on controversial issues, and they must give free airtime to the victims of personal attacks. This is one of the key examples of broadcasters and print journalists being subject to differing interpretations of the First Amendment: there is no comparable right of reply or obligation to cover all sides in the print media. In the landmark case of *Tornillo v. Miami Herald*, which is discussed in Chapter 12, the Supreme Court ruled that newspaper publishers have a First Amendment right to publish only one side of controversial issues and to attack people without granting them space for a reply, if they so choose. Newspapers and magazines may be as biased or unbiased as they wish: there is neither a Fairness Doctrine nor a Personal Attack Rule for the print media.

Many broadcasters feel this disparity in editorial freedom makes them second-class citizens under the First Amendment. The ramifications of this issue are further discussed in the next chapter.

The Fairness Doctrine and Advertising

The Fairness Doctrine had little specific impact on most broadcasters until 1967, but in that year the commission decided that cigarette advertising raised controversial issues. Therefore, the FCC required stations carrying cigarette advertising to broadcast counter-advertising urging people not to smoke. In *Banzhaf v. FCC* (405 F.2d 1082, D.C. Cir. 1968), a federal appellate court upheld that ruling. Although the court tried to make it clear its ruling was specific to cigarette advertising and did not necessarily make the Fairness Doctrine applicable to other advertising, the result of *Banzhaf* was an avalanche of other demands for air time to reply to controversial advertising.

Meanwhile, Congress stepped into the controversy about cigarette counter-advertising by banning radio and television cigarette advertising, effective in 1971. However, by then federal courts were finding possible Fairness Doctrine violations in other advertising. In one notable case, the same federal appellate court that decided *Banzhaf* ruled that the Fairness Doctrine applied to television ads for cars with large engines requiring high-octane gasoline. The FCC had rejected an environmental group's request for time to reply to those ads. The court overruled the FCC and said the ads indeed raised Fairness Doctrine issues. The FCC was ordered to reconsider whether the environmentalists would have to be given airtime or whether the broadcaster's other programming adequately covered the other side on the issues raised by the ads (*Friends of the Earth v. FCC*, 449 F.2d 1164, D.C. Cir. 1971).

In another case, the federal appellate court said much the same thing about a department store's advertising during a strike. In that case, *Retail Store Employees Union v. FCC* (436 F.2d 248, 1970), a labor union tried to broadcast ads urging shoppers not to patronize the store, in response to the store's ads urging the public to ignore a union's boycott. The store had run hundreds of ads on one radio station, but the station wouldn't accept ads from the union.

The union challenged the station's license renewal, charging a Fairness Doctrine violation, and the appellate court overturned the commission's refusal to hear the union's complaint. The court did not flatly rule that the Fairness Doctrine applied in this situation, but it did order the FCC to reconsider the matter. The commission ultimately got out of this dilemma by issuing new rules reinterpreting the Fairness Doctrine in 1974. Those new rules eventually took some of the sting out of the Fairness Doctrine for broadcasters by excluding commercial advertising from the doctrine's scope.

But before that happened, the U.S. Supreme Court handed down another important decision in this area, ruling that the First Amendment does not create a right to advertise on controversial subjects. This 1973 decision, *CBS v. Democratic National Committee* (412 U.S. 94, 1973), resulted from an appeal by the Democratic National Committee for assurances that it could buy network airtime to solicit money and argue the Democratic viewpoint on controversial issues. Another group, the Business Executives Move for Vietnam Peace, was appealing a radio station's rejection of its issue-oriented advertising. A federal appellate court had held that broadcasters' policies flatly prohibiting issue advertising were unconstitutional.

The U.S. Supreme Court, voting 7-2, reversed the lower court ruling and said unequivocally that broadcasters may reject idea ads if they wish. Neither the First Amendment nor the Fairness Doctrine gives any individual or group a right of access to the broadcast media (except in response to personal attacks), the Supreme Court ruled. Affirming the concept that a broadcaster is not a common carrier, the high court said the station owner has broad discretion in deciding what issues and what people to put on the air. No broadcaster has to accept a given group's ads unless it voluntarily chooses to do so. A broadcaster may have to seek out someone to present a view contrary to that espoused by the station in an editorial, for example, but the station has the right to choose who will present the opposing view. No individual or group has a right to demand reply time (again, except in personal attack situations).

In the aftermath of the *Democratic National Committee* decision, the FCC finally backed out of the dilemma involving the Fairness Doctrine and advertising. As noted earlier, the commission reinterpreted the Fairness Doctrine in 1974, declaring that the doctrine would no longer apply to purely commercial advertising.

The 1974 FCC report went so far as to disavow the commission's earlier decision on cigarette advertising. Under this new policy, the FCC has steadfastly refused to apply the Fairness Doctrine to advertising for products, no matter how controversial someone claims the ad may be. For instance, a television station in Maine carried ads for snowmobiles, and environmentalists demanded reply time to argue against the use of snowmobiles, but both the FCC and a federal court rejected the appeal (*Public Interest Research Group v. FCC*, 522 F.2d 1060, 1975). Thus, the court upheld the FCC's new policy of excluding commercial advertising from the scope of the Fairness Doctrine.

Another federal appellate court decision reaffirmed the FCC's new approach to the Fairness Doctrine, rejecting a group's argument that the doctrine should require broadcasters to address a certain number of major issues each year (*National Citizens Committee for Broadcasting v. FCC*, 567 F.2d 1095, 1977). This case should not be confused with a Supreme Court decision of the same name that affirmed the FCC's rules on cross-ownership of newspapers and radio or television stations (see Chapter 13).

When does the Fairness Doctrine still apply? For one thing, it still applies to advertising that specifically addresses controversial issues. In 1978, a federal appellate court affirmed an FCC ruling that eight television stations had violated the Fairness Doctrine by carrying pro-nuclear power commercials without presenting the anti-nuclear power viewpoint (*Public Media Center v. FCC*, 587 F.2d 1322, 1978).

This means broadcasters who carry ads taking a stand on a public issue must present the other side of the issue or risk violating the Fairness

Doctrine. Rather than assume that responsibility, many broadcasters and particularly the national networks have refused to carry most issue advertising. Fewer than 10 percent of all TV stations were accepting such ads in the early 1980s. The ABC network had begun to accept a few advocacy ads, particularly for late night placement, but for the most part the networks continued their tough stance against idea advertising. Some critics charge that as a result the Fairness Doctrine actually has the opposite of the desired effect. Instead of encouraging discussion of controversial issues, it leads many broadcasters to avoid them as much as possible in order to keep from having to provide time for opposing views.

Whether they accept issue advertising or not, broadcasters are still required to cover some public issues of importance as part of their news and public affairs programming. In its deregulatory actions of the early 1980s, the FCC relaxed the requirement that broadcasters carry specific types and quantities of public affairs programming. However, broadcasters are still subject to the general rule that they must provide some public affairs programming to meet the needs of their service areas.

Normally, the broadcaster has wide latitude in deciding what issues are important enough to cover, but not always. In 1976, the FCC ruled that WHAR, a radio station in a West Virginia coal mining region, had violated the Fairness Doctrine by failing to provide any local programming on the controversial issue of strip mining. All the station had done with this issue was to carry wire service news stories on it as a part of the regular newscasts. Patsy Mink, a Congresswoman who was sponsoring an anti-strip mining bill, asked WHAR to air an 11-minute tape regarding her bill, but the station refused.

The FCC ordered the broadcaster to come up with a plan for covering this topic (but not necessarily by airing Mink's tape) because of its very great importance in the station's service area (*Patsy Mink*, 59 F.C.C.2d 984, 1976). However, this is an unusual case. Here a particular issue was overwhelmingly important in a community and had not been covered in public affairs programming. The FCC almost never specifically requires a broadcaster to cover a particular subject. In fact, such an order smacks of a First Amendment violation.

Today, it is doubtful that this issue would be decided as it was in 1976. As noted earlier, broadcasters are no longer subject to specific news and public affairs programming requirements. In addition, the commission has been reluctant to enforce the Fairness Doctrine under any circumstances during most of the last decade.

Not only does the FCC normally afford broadcasters considerable latitude in deciding which issues to cover and which ones to ignore, but the FCC is also supposed to avoid second-guessing a broadcaster's judgment that a particular issue isn't a controversial one. In 1974, the FCC was told by a federal appellate court to respect the National Broadcasting Company's judgment in deciding that a program it aired on retirement plans did not involve a controversial issue. A conservative media monitoring group accused NBC of focusing on bad retirement plans, thus unfairly giving the impression that employee pension plans are generally inadequate. By presenting that perspective, NBC violated the Fairness Doctrine, the group contended. NBC said this wasn't a controversial issue, and a federal court eventually ruled that the FCC had to respect the network's judgment on that point (*NBC v. FCC*, 516 F.2d 1101, D.C. Cir. 1974).

The Cullman and Zapple Rules

One of the more controversial and often-misunderstood features of the Fairness Doctrine is a concept known as the *Cullman Rule*. Also, the Cullman Rule is often confused with another concept known as the *Zapple Rule*. (For the origin of these rules, see *Cullman Broadcasting*, 40 F.C.C. 576, 1963, and *In re Nicholas Zapple*, 23 F.C.C.2d 707, 1970).

The Cullman Rule, sometimes called the "Cullman Doctrine," flatly declares that broadcasters must air both sides of controversial issues, even if those representing one side cannot afford to buy any airtime. If a broadcaster accepts advertising expressing a particular viewpoint on a controversial issue, it is quite possible that the broadcaster may end up having to give free time to the opposition under the Cullman Rule.

The Zapple Rule, on the other hand, says almost the opposite of Cullman, but it applies under different circumstances. The Zapple Rule, often called the "quasi-equal time" rule, says that when supporters of political candidates (as opposed to the candidates themselves) buy airtime during an election campaign, those who support opposing candidates must be given the right to buy equal time for the same fee. Thus, Zapple applies the principles of the Equal Time Rule (Section 315) to candidates' supporters and campaign committees—organizations that do a lot of political advertising these days. Like Section 315 itself, the Zapple Rule merely requires that each side be sold airtime at the same price. It never requires broadcasters to give away free time to one side when the other side has paid for its time. Only if one side was given free time would the opposition be entitled to free time under the Zapple Rule.

However, the Zapple Rule applies only during election campaigns, not at other times. Outside of election campaign periods, only the Cullman Rule is applicable. So what happens when a political action committee, for example, buys airtime to attack public officials it doesn't like when there isn't any election campaign under way? Does the other side get free reply time under the Cullman Rule, whereas the time would have to be paid for under the Zapple Rule if an election campaign were under way?

This issue became controversial with the dramatic increase in the popularity of political action committees in the early 1980s. At one point, the National Conservative Political Action Committee began purchasing airtime on radio and TV stations in many areas of the country to criticize liberal public officials. Many of the victims of these attacks demanded free reply time, and in 1982 the FCC said they were entitled to it (*National Conservative Political*

Action Committee, 89 F.C.C.2d 626). To reach that conclusion, the commission said the Cullman Rule and not the Zapple Rule applied to advertising by political organizations outside of campaign periods.

Some 18 broadcast organizations, including the CBS network, asked the FCC to reconsider this ruling. They warned that many broadcasters would turn down political advertising during non-campaign periods rather than risk having to give free time to the opposition. They urged the FCC to declare that the Zapple Rule rather than the Cullman Rule applies to all advertising by political organizations, regardless of whether an election campaign is under way. However, in late 1983 the FCC refused to change its position on this issue (*In re Request of CBS Inc. et al.*, FCC 83-528). Thus, broadcasters who accept political advertising outside of a campaign period may have to give free time to those with opposing views under the Cullman Rule. Only during election campaigns does Zapple, with its quasi-equal-opportunity provisions, apply.

However, a federal appellate court decision in 1983 took some of the sting out of this FCC ruling. In *Democratic National Committee v. FCC* (717 F.2d 1471), the court said broadcasters did not have to give free time to the Democrats to reply to ads purchased by the Republican National Committee to support the Reagan administration's economic policies. The ads ran during a non-election period, and the situation was quite similar to the National Conservative Political Action Committee case—except for one thing: the court ruled that the networks had covered the Democrats' views on Reagan's economic policies adequately during their normal news and public affairs programming. The Fairness Doctrine does not require minute-for-minute equal time, the court pointed out. Instead, if there is overall balance in the presentations of various views, that is sufficient.

Thus, if a broadcaster can show that all sides have been adequately covered during a station's programming without anyone being given free airtime, there appears to be no obligation to give free time—despite the Cullman Rule.

Broadcast Deregulation

In 1981 the FCC dropped many of its regulations governing radio content, and the commission extended this deregulation to television in 1984.

These deregulatory moves were widely applauded by broadcasters but criticized by some consumer, minority, and public interest groups. Commercial radio and television broadcasters were relieved of formal community ascertainment requirements, under which they had been compelled to go out into their communities and interview various people about the problems and needs of their listeners or viewers. In addition, the rules requiring a specific amount of news and public affairs programming and the suggested limits on advertising time were deleted.

In acting to deregulate radio in 1981, the FCC noted that there are more than 8,000 commercial radio stations in the United States. The FCC was saying, in effect, that competitive forces in the marketplace would assure that broadcasters operate in the public interest, making detailed federal content guidelines unnecessary. Thus, broadcasters are now free to make their own decisions about how much news and public affairs programming (and advertising) they will carry, given the realities of the marketplace.

Previously, broadcasters were expected to prove at license renewal time that they devoted specific portions of their total programming to such things as public affairs. Under the new rules, they do not need to show any particular amount of programming in public affairs—or in a number of other specific categories—to justify a license renewal. They do, nevertheless, have to be prepared to show that they have continued to serve the needs of their listeners and viewers, should the commission ask for documentation.

The deregulation did not eliminate either the Equal Time provision or the Fairness Doctrine: both still apply to all broadcasters.

The FCC's decision to deregulate radio, reached six days before Ronald Reagan was inaugurated, produced emotional responses on all sides. The National Association of Broadcasters called it "a turning point in the history of broadcast regulation," but several public interest groups criticized it. The television deregulation in 1984 produced much the same reaction from broadcasters and their critics.

In 1981, the Office of Communication of the United Church of Christ, the group that won the landmark court decision giving citizens' groups the right to challenge license renewals, appealed the FCC's radio deregulation in the U.S. Court of Appeals.

This group and other critics of deregulation predicted that marketplace forces would not adequately assure good public service, particularly in small communities with little media competition. Many broadcasters, on the other hand, pointed out that newspaper publishers have never been required to answer to the government for the quality or quantity of their news and public affairs coverage. This was only a first step toward ending the second-class status of broadcasters, they said.

In a 1983 decision, the U.S. Court of Appeals in Washington, D.C., affirmed virtually all of the FCC's radio deregulation. Of all the provisions of the 1981 deregulation, the only one the court overturned was the relaxation of program log-keeping requirements. Before deregulation, radio stations had been required to maintain fairly detailed records of their programming and to make those records available for public inspection. The court said that without these program logs it would be very difficult for someone challenging a license renewal to show that the station's public service programming had been inadequate. Thus, the court ordered the FCC to reconsider what rules might be needed to ensure that stations keep good records of their programming (*Office of Communication of the United Church of Christ v. FCC*, 707 F.2d 1413).

Given the appellate court's blessing for its radio deregulation, the FCC extended most of the same deregulatory provisions to most commercial television stations in 1984, as noted earlier.

Thus, the FCC moved closer to abandoning the traditional "scarcity principle" that said broadcast regulation was needed because there weren't enough frequencies available to provide sufficient competition to assure good public service. The idea that the government must act to compel broadcasters to provide public service has largely been abandoned by the FCC.

FCC Chairman Mark Fowler, in urging the commission to deregulate television as well as radio broadcasting, pointed out that 65 percent of the nation's households now can receive seven or more TV signals, compared to only 26 percent two decades earlier. Also, the commission relied on the rapid growth of cable television, low-power television, and the new television-like technologies (discussed in Chapter 15) to ensure sufficient diversity and competition that marketplace forces will guarantee that television broadcasters serve the public.

While deregulation was on the FCC's agenda, Congress continued to debate a variety of bills that would write radio and TV deregulation into the Communications Act itself. The Senate passed a deregulation bill in 1982, but the bill died when it failed to clear the House before the end of the 97th Congress. In 1983 the Senate passed another deregulation bill (S.55 by Senator Barry Goldwater, R-Ariz.). That bill would have eliminated comparative license renewal proceedings and codified many of the deregulatory acts of the FCC.

However, the deregulation bill again became bogged down in the House in 1983. Several key House leaders strongly advocated broadcast license renewal standards based on "quantification." That is, each broadcaster would have to produce a specific number of hours of local programming of various types to qualify for a license renewal. If approved, this plan would have undone many of the deregulatory actions of the FCC, which were intended to eliminate the formal rules that once told broadcasters how much time they had to devote to various kinds of programming. At this writing, it seems unlikely that any comprehensive deregulation bill will win the consensus needed for Congressional approval.

Editorializing by Public Broadcasters

Public radio and television stations are noncommercial broadcasters, and most receive federal government funding through the Corporation for Public Broadcasting. These stations are subject to a number of special rules, including a federal law that has forbidden them to broadcast editorials expressing their own views.

The ban on editorializing by public broadcasters produced an important U.S. Supreme Court decision in 1984—a decision that marked the first time the high court has ever overturned a federal content restriction on broadcasters on First Amendment grounds. In this ruling, the court seemed to invite a review of the validity of many other broadcast content restrictions, including the Fairness Doctrine.

In *FCC v. League of Women Voters of California* (104 S.Ct. 3106), the high court struck down the ban on editorializing as much too sweeping a restriction on the freedom of public broadcasters. The Public Broadcasting Act of 1967 prohibited editorializing by stations receiving federal funds on the theory that if they editorialized these stations would feel obligated to support the government's policies. In effect, these stations could become propaganda organs for the government, Congress feared.

The court disagreed with that rationale and said there were many ways public broadcasters could be insulated from political pressures that might influence their editorial policies without simply forbidding them to speak out on the issues.

The case began when the League of Women Voters, a California Congressman, and the Pacifica Foundation, a noncommercial broadcaster, joined in an effort to challenge the law against editorializing by stations receiving federal funds. The League contended that the rule denied it the freedom to seek support for its own policies from public broadcasters. Representative Henry Waxman, a Democrat, argued that the ban denied him the right to listen to the editorial views of public broadcasters, and Pacifica said the law directly interfered with its freedom to express its opinions on the major issues of the day.

Although the Supreme Court's decision came on a narrow 5-4 vote, the majority agreed with the League, Waxman, and Pacifica, declaring the law unconstitutional. In fact, the majority opinion in the *League of Women Voters* case was so sweeping in overturning the anti-editorializing law that it raised doubts about the continuing validity of the entire range of broadcast content controls. Writing for the majority, Justice William J. Brennan included a footnote that said the court may be prepared to reexamine the scarcity rationale that has justified the restrictions on broadcast content. Brennan seemingly invited the FCC to begin a wholesale review of broadcast content regulation when he wrote:

> The prevailing rationale for broadcast regulation based on spectrum scarcity has come under increasing criticism in recent years. Critics, including the incumbent Chairman of the FCC, charge that with the advent of cable and satellite television technology, communities now have access to such a wide variety of stations that the scarcity doctrine is obsolete. We are not prepared, however, to reconsider our long-standing approach without some signal from Congress or the FCC that technological developments have advanced so far that revision of the system of broadcast regulation may be required. (52 U.S.L.W. at 5011)

It may be some years before it is clear whether this case represents an isolated ruling by the Supreme Court to expand the First Amendment rights of public broadcasters or is in fact a major step toward a complete overhaul of the philosophy under which broadcasters have been regulated for more than half a century. For now, rules such as the Fairness Doctrine remain in force, but it is by no means certain that they will be retained indefinitely.

Other Content Controls

In addition to the equal time provision and the Fairness Doctrine, radio and television stations must still observe a variety of other restrictions on the content of their broadcasts.

For instance, under federal obscenity law (see Chapter 10), broadcasters may not air material that is obscene, profane, or "indecent." Federal criminal prosecutions for on-the-air obscenity are rare, but occasionally the FCC penalizes a broadcaster for airing material considered inappropriate.

A famous 1978 Supreme Court decision resulted from such an FCC action. In *FCC v. Pacifica Foundation* (438 U.S. 726), the Supreme Court voted 5-4 to uphold a mild FCC sanction against the foundation that operates a noncommercial radio station in New York City, WBAI. The station aired a program on contemporary attitudes toward language, and it included a 12-minute monologue by comedian George Carlin entitled "Filthy Words." In it, Carlin named seven words "you couldn't say on the public. . .airwaves" and ridiculed society's taboos about words such as "shit," "fuck," "cocksucker," and "motherfucker." The program was broadcast at 2 p.m., preceded by a warning that some of the content might be offensive to some persons.

A man who said he and his son inadvertently stumbled on the monologue while listening to their car radio complained to the FCC, and the FCC eventually placed a notice in the station's license renewal file about the incident. The FCC did not find the language obscene, but did decide it was "patently offensive."

Pacifica Foundation appealed to the courts, and the Supreme Court eventually ruled on this controversial issue. The majority conceded that the language in question might not be obscene, but insisted it was nonetheless inappropriate for broadcasting, at least during the daytime. The court said the words were "indecent" and didn't belong on the air, even if they might be Constitutionally protected under other circumstances.

The court cited nuisance law as part of its rationale and quoted an earlier decision defining a nuisance as "merely a right thing in the wrong place—like a pig in the parlor instead of the barnyard." Then the court concluded: "We simply hold that when the Commission finds that a pig has entered the parlor, the exercise of its regulatory power does not depend on proof that the pig is obscene."

Thus, the traditional limits on broadcast speech were affirmed by the Supreme Court. The FCC was upheld in its insistence that broadcasters not use language that would be Constitutionally protected in print or even in a motion picture (the high court had previously ruled that Carlin's most offensive words were protected speech in other contexts).

The *Pacifica* decision was a controversial one, but it was not inconsistent with the FCC's earlier sanctions on language and subject matter that would be Constitutionally protected in other media.

On one occasion, an FM radio station was fined $100 for carrying an interview with a rock musician who used various four-letter-words that the FCC found to be "indecent" (*In re WUHY-FM*, 24 F.C.C.2d 408). On another occasion, the FCC fined a broadcaster $2,000 for airing a daytime "Topless Radio" talk show on which female callers explicitly described their experiences with oral sex. The commission decided the material was titillating enough to meet the *Roth* test of obscenity, which was then in effect, in addition to being "indecent" (*Sonderling Broadcasting*, 41 F.C.C.2d 777, 1973). A federal appellate court later affirmed that FCC decision (*Illinois Citizens Committee for Broadcasting v. FCC*, 515 F.2d 397, 1975).

The FCC has acted to limit broadcast content in a number of other controversial areas, including drug-oriented music and children's programming. In 1971 the FCC issued a public notice in which it said licensees would be held accountable if they broadcast drug-oriented music. The result was a panic reaction in the industry; hundreds of stations hurriedly developed long "don't play" lists in an effort to avoid the FCC's wrath. Many popular songs were blacklisted, sometimes more because station managers didn't understand them than because they had any real references to illegal drugs. Among the songs blacklisted by many stations were "Puff (the Magic Dragon)," "Hey Jude," "Lucy in the Sky with Diamonds," and even "Yellow Submarine."

Facing widespread charges of blatant censorship, the FCC backed down a few weeks later and said it would not penalize broadcasters at license renewal time for playing any particular song, although licensees would be held responsible for the overall content of their broadcasts. The FCC's actions in this area were challenged in court, and in 1973 a federal appellate court affirmed the commission's rules (*Yale Broadcasting v. FCC*, 478 F.2d 594).

Programming and advertising targeted for children have been another controversial issue. In 1974, the FCC issued a policy statement calling on broadcasters to discontinue certain practices, such as allowing children's show hosts to advertise products. The commission also urged broadcasters to voluntarily upgrade their offerings for children.

In the late 1970s, the FCC considered imposing much stricter children's programming requirements on broadcasters. However, in 1983 the FCC voted to discard the 1974 policy statement and to reject any formal children's television programming requirements. The new policy says that broadcasters must provide programs for children, but the commission declined to establish any specific requirements for the amount of such programming that must be offered. Instead, broadcasters were given wide discretion to determine what kind of children's programs would be most appropriate.

Action for Children's Television, a group that favors mandatory standards for children's television programming, challenged the FCC decision in the U.S. Court of Appeals in Washington, D.C. The court had not ruled on the case at this writing.

Earlier, the Federal Trade Commission also terminated an inquiry into children's television without taking any action (see Chapter 12).

Another controversial issue in television content regulation has been the "family hour," or "family viewing policy," under which the content of programs aired in the early evening has been limited to protect children. Although the policy was voluntarily adopted by the networks, the move followed considerable arm-twisting by the FCC.

The family hour policy resulted in program restrictions and sometimes outright censorship by the networks. This angered many television writers and program producers, and the writers went to court. They charged that the government pressured the industry into adopting the family hour. This coercion violated the First Amendment, they contended. A U.S. District Court judge in California agreed, finding Constitutional violations by the commission and the networks. However, his decision was appealed and a federal appellate court set aside the district court ruling on the ground that the writers should have gone to the FCC before taking the case to court (*Writers Guild of America, West v. FCC*, 609 F.2d 355, 1979).

Broadcasters are also subject to content control in several other areas. One of the most controversial—and least successful—government controls has been the Prime Time Access Rule, an FCC regulation that generally limited the networks to three hours of evening programming during the four-hour period from 7 to 11 p.m. (6 to 10 p.m. in the central time zone), with exceptions for news events and special occasions. The rule only applies in the 50 largest metropolitan areas. It went into effect in 1971 and was repeatedly amended. The FCC's stated objective was to create new opportunities for local programming by limiting the portion of the evening hours the networks would lock up. Instead, what happened in many instances was that local stations relied on syndicated programming rather than doing local public affairs programs. (A syndicated program is one produced independently and then sold directly to broadcasters rather than to a network.)

Among the other FCC regulations governing content are rules governing sponsorship identification. Broadcasters must identify the sponsors of ads and disclose the fact if someone has paid for the airing of non-advertising material. Also, FCC rules forbid broadcast promotions and contests that are in any way "rigged." And both federal law and FCC regulations forbid the broadcasting of material that promotes "lotteries" (i.e., gambling), with some exceptions (see Chapter 12).

Finally, broadcasters are subject to many other laws that govern advertising in general. For example, the federal Truth-in-Lending Act requires the full disclosure of credit terms if any of the terms of a loan are mentioned in an ad, as explained in Chapter 12. Almost no one would quarrel with the wisdom of having laws requiring credit advertising to be truthful and complete. However, the required disclosures are sometimes so detailed that they cannot all be squeezed into a short broadcast advertisement.

Broadcasting and the Hearing-Impaired

Do broadcasters, or at least noncommercial public broadcasters, have an obligation to provide special programming for the hearing-impaired?

In 1983, the Supreme Court decided they do not. The court ruled that the FCC need not consider whether public television stations have provided special programming for the hearing-impaired at license renewal time. In *Community Television of Southern California v. Gottfried* (103 S.Ct. 885), the Supreme Court ruled that the Rehabilitation Act of 1972, which forbids discrimination against the handicapped by federally funded activities and institutions, imposes no special license renewal obligations on the FCC.

The court pointed out that the FCC does not dispense funds to public television stations. There is no question that the Rehabilitation Act does not apply to commercial broadcasters, the court said. And if anything, public broadcasters are less able to afford special services for the hearing-impaired than are their commercial counterparts. Thus, they should not be singled out for scrutiny on this point. The Supreme Court concluded that it is simply not the FCC's job to evaluate broadcasters' efforts to serve the handicapped in their programming.

Format Changes and the *WNCN* Case

The FCC has also become involved in content regulation on some occasions when a radio station proposed to change a unique programming format. During the 1970s, the only classical music stations in several cities tried to abandon that format, spurring protests by classical music lovers. The FCC originally refrained from getting involved in these controversies. However, the federal courts began ordering the FCC to review format changes when a station abandoned a unique format and the change produced widespread protests. For instance, that happened in Atlanta (*Citizens Committee to Preserve the Voice of the Arts in Atlanta v. FCC*, 436 F.2d 263, 1970).

Then in 1974 the federal appellate court that serves Washington, D.C.— the court that has heard so many FCC appeals over the years—decided *Citizens Committee to Save WEFM v. FCC* (506 F.2d 246). The court, ruling *en banc* (i.e., with all judges of the court instead of the normal panel of three participating), ordered the FCC to hold a hearing whenever a unique format is being abandoned and a substantial number of persons object.

However, two years later, the FCC issued a policy statement calling for the court to reverse itself and let the commission stay out of such disputes. The FCC said, ". . .the public interest in diversity of entertainment formats is best served by unregulated competition among licensees."

But the federal appellate court in Washington refused to back down when it decided a 1979 case, *WNCN Listeners Guild v. FCC*. In that case, also decided *en banc*, the court reiterated its belief that some format abandonments deserve FCC review because of the scarcity of radio frequencies and because some listener interests may not be served if all broadcasters target their programming for the largest possible audience. However, the FCC appealed that ruling to the U.S. Supreme Court and won a reversal of the appellate court decision.

Ruling in 1981, the Supreme Court affirmed the FCC's right to stay out of broadcast format disputes. The court said entertainment programming was within the broadcaster's discretion. The seven-justice majority wrote: "We decline to overturn the commission's policy statement, which prefers reliance on market forces to its own attempt to oversee format changes at the behest of disaffected listeners."

The Supreme Court decision was thus a major victory for the broadcast industry, which has strongly supported the FCC's moves to deregulate the field, but a defeat for classical music lovers and others who fear that minority tastes will not be served if all broadcasters are free to target their programming for the audiences that are most attractive to advertisers. The decision was criticized by a wide variety of minority and consumer groups.

The *WNCN* decision was an endorsement of the FCC's desire to get out of the business of regulating broadcast content wherever possible. However, it was not an unqualified victory. Justice Byron White, writing for the majority, cautioned that the FCC should "be alert to the consequences of its policies and should stand ready to alter its rule if necessary to preserve the public interest more fully" (*FCC v. WNCN Listeners Guild*, 450 U.S. 582).

Thus, the court upheld the FCC's decision to let marketplace forces regulate broadcast content, but the court also made it clear that broadcasters still have an obligation to act in the public interest. Deregulation notwithstanding, broadcasters still do not have the freedom from government regulation that newspaper, magazine, and book publishers, and even motion picture producers, take for granted.

CABLE TELEVISION REGULATION

Just as radio was the growth medium in the 1920s and television boomed in the 1950s, cable has been a growth leader in the 1980s. At the decade's beginning, something like one-fourth of all American homes were served by cable television systems; by the decade's end, forecasters think as many as three homes out of every four will be on cable.

Cable began in the 1950s as something called "community antenna television" or CATV. In its early days, it was literally what its name implied: a fancy antenna system serving a whole community. Because it offered little more than improved television reception, CATV first developed in rural areas far from the nearest television transmitters. By pooling their resources, the people of a community could afford a large antenna system and signal boosters to receive the weak signals from distant television stations. Each home was connected to this central receiving system via coaxial cable, a special kind of wire that will efficiently carry television signals a considerable distance.

Thus, cable television got its start in the countryside and had little appeal in big cities where reception was good. However, in the 1960s and 1970s that began to change because of two trends. First, a growing number of people were forbidden to put up TV antennas at condominiums, apartment complexes, and even some tracts of single family homes. Instead, they were offered cable hookups for a fee. But even more important, cable systems began offering a lot more than clear television reception: they began providing many additional channels of programming, including out-of-town "superstations," original made-for-cable programming, and such special attractions as music videos, current movies, and sports events (for an additional fee).

Because cable systems don't actually transmit an over-the-air signal, they aren't users of the radio spectrum and hence need no FCC license to operate. Also, the number of channels that may be offered via coaxial cable is limited mainly by the number of channels a television receiver or cable converter can cover. A local cable system can put programming on every one of those channels without interfering with other cable systems or over-the-air broadcasters.

For these reasons, cable television was able to develop without much federal regulation—at first. However, by the late 1960s, broadcasters became alarmed at the growth of cable television systems. So did the producers of motion pictures and television shows, which cable operators picked up off the air and then delivered to their subscribers for a fee. Two U.S. Supreme Court decisions held that cable operators did not have to pay copyright royalties for the material carried over their systems, since the court viewed CATV as nothing more than an adjunct of the television receiving function (see Chapter Six). The owners of copyrighted programming felt they were being deprived of a fair profit by these Supreme Court decisions, and Congress enacted the 1976 Copyright Act in part to remedy this situation. Cable systems now must pay royalties for the copyrighted programming they pick up off the air from non-local stations and deliver to their subscribers.

When cable started winning copyright victories, broadcasters became more alarmed about this new medium. If a cable system imported distant signals, that could mean economic losses for local broadcasters. At least some of the cable subscribers would watch distant stations instead of local ones, especially if a cable system offered subscribers high-budget stations based in large cities along with nearby low-budget stations. Also, of course, the added non-broadcast programming represented new competition for broadcasters.

Given the embryonic status of CATV in the 1950s, the FCC had refused to assume jurisdiction over cable in 1958, since CATV didn't involve a use of the spectrum and the commission had no specific statutory authority to regulate it. But by 1966, the FCC had changed its mind. To protect broadcasters and program producers, the FCC then issued regulations for cable television systems. The new regulations had many very technical provisions, but one of the most important was a strict limit on distant signal importation. For instance, cable systems were required to carry the nearest station affiliated with each network rather than more distant ones. The rules also spelled out the relationship between cable systems and local governments, which had been granting franchises (i.e., government-sanctioned monopolies) to CATV operators.

The FCC claimed the authority to make these rules by arguing that cable affected on-the-air broadcasters, and that regulation was necessary to carry out the commission's regulatory responsibilities to broadcasters. Legally, this was called "ancillary jurisdiction."

The FCC's cable rules were quickly challenged in court, and in 1968, the Supreme Court affirmed the FCC's authority to regulate cable television in *U.S. v. Southwestern Cable Co.* (392 U.S. 157). The high court found authority for the FCC's regulation of cable not only in the concept of ancillary jurisdiction but also in a provision of the Communications Act that places wire and telecommunications in general under FCC control.

Given this mandate, the FCC repeatedly expanded its cable rules, placing more and more restrictions on cable systems. Many cable operators felt these rules were intended to protect the FCC's major clientele, the over-the-air broadcasters, not to promote the public interest. By the early 1970s, cable systems were required to do these things: (1) provide local public and government access channels if they had more than 3500 subscribers; (2) originate a minimum amount of local programming, again if they had 3,500 subscribers; (3) refrain from importing distant signals or "leapfrogging" over the nearest network affiliate in providing each network's programming (these were called the "non-duplication" and "signal carriage" requirements); and (4) respect syndication agreements by not carrying a distant station's syndicated shows if a local station had exclusive rights to the show.

In addition, each system had to get sort of a de facto license called a "certificate of compliance" from the FCC before it could conclude its franchise agreement with local government officials, and cable systems had to comply with most of the other requirements imposed on broadcasters, such as the Equal Time Rule, the Fairness Doctrine, and equal employment opportunity policies.

Faced with these comprehensive (and costly) federal regulations, a cable system again challenged the FCC's authority to issue such orders. But in 1972 the Supreme Court voted 5-4 to affirm the commission's program origination requirements (*U.S. v. Midwest Video Corp.*, 406 U.S. 649). Ironically, the FCC had dropped many of its access and programming requirements during this lawsuit and did not immediately reinstate them afterward, although cable systems were still required to provide equipment to those who wanted to do programming on such public access channels as remained available.

During most of the 1970s the FCC continued to regulate cable systems heavily in an effort to keep them from doing anything to upset the commission's policy of defining television service in terms of local markets. In 1976, the commission issued new rules on public access and also required cable systems with over 3,500 subscribers to eventually provide at least 20 channels.

However, Midwest Video, the company that lost the narrow 1972 Supreme Court decision, again challenged the commission's rulemaking authority.

This time, Midwest Video won. In 1979 the Supreme Court overturned the FCC's new public access and channel capacity requirements (*FCC v. Midwest Video*, 440 U.S. 689). The court said these rules, in effect, made common carriers of cable systems, placing them under obligations the Communications Act forbids the FCC to impose on broadcasters. Moreover, the court said the rules went far beyond what was reasonably ancillary to the FCC's lawful responsibilities in broadcast regulation. In effect, the Supreme Court told the FCC to go back to Congress and get the specific authority to do these things if they were really in the public interest:

> The Commission may not regulate cable systems as common carriers, just as it may not impose such obligations on television broadcasters. We think authority to compel cable operators to provide common carriage of public originated transmissions must come specifically from Congress.

While this Supreme Court decision overturned the FCC's nationwide rules requiring public access to cable systems, that did not mark the end of public access. First of all, some cable systems continue to provide public access channels on a voluntary basis. In addition, many cable systems' franchise agreements with state and local governments require public access. Some states have even enacted laws in this area.

After its setback in the second *Midwest Video* decision, the FCC decided it was time to undertake a major deregulation of the cable industry. As noted earlier, cable operators had long argued that the FCC's rules were more intended to protect broadcasters by stunting the growth of cable than to serve the public interest.

In 1980 the FCC heeded the cable systems' arguments and approved a major deregulation of the cable industry. In particular, the FCC abandoned the restrictions on distant signal importation. This allowed cable systems to offer their subscribers a much wider choice of programming—but at the probable expense of small-market television stations whose viewers may prefer to watch metropolitan stations via cable.

In the deregulation plan, the FCC also deleted the requirement that cable systems black out syndicated programs shown by distant stations when another station has an exclusive agreement to show the program locally.

In deciding to drop these regulations, the FCC noted that the syndication rules were intended to protect producers when they had no copyright protection from cable systems. With cable systems by then required to pay copyright royalties for distant signals, the FCC majority felt the rules were obsolete. The commission chairman at the time, Charles D. Ferris, said the FCC action "removed the regulatory debris of a previous decade."

However, the FCC did not eliminate the one rule many cable operators were most anxious to get rid of: the must-carry rule. Cable systems are required to include all local television stations in the package they offer their subscribers. In 1980, the Turner Broadcasting System, headed by cable pioneer Ted Turner, petitioned the FCC to drop the must-carry rules. His proposal was vigorously opposed by broadcasters.

Turner argued that the must-carry rules violate the First Amendment and unduly inhibit marketplace forces that would otherwise encourage cable operators to offer their subscribers whatever programming they wanted most. Broadcasters replied by pointing out that in many places it is not possible to receive local television signals directly, often due to the terrain or restrictions on outdoor antennas. Thus, the only way to receive local TV stations may be via cable. This puts cable operators in a position of being able to unfairly eliminate competition, and in the process thwart the FCC's goal of providing local broadcast service, they argued.

After repeated delays, the FCC denied Turner's petition to eliminate the must-carry rules in late 1983, and Turner sued the FCC in the U.S. Court of Appeals in an attempt to get its decision overturned. The court had not ruled on Turner's lawsuit at this writing.

While broadcasters and cable operators were debating the merits of the must-carry rules, they were also in court battling over the FCC's 1980 decision to deregulate cable. Broadcasters challenged the cable deregulation plan in federal court, a move that some media critics saw as ironic in view of most broadcasters' staunch support for deregulation in their own industry. In 1981, a federal appellate court rejected the challenge to cable deregulation, holding that the FCC had followed proper procedures and was justified in doing what it did. The Supreme Court declined to review the appellate court's decision in this case (*Malrite Television v. FCC*, 652 F.2d 1140), leaving cable operators free of the old restrictions on importing distant signals.

However, in 1984 the Supreme Court did rule on another aspect of the FCC's cable rules, and sharply curtailed the power of local governments to control cable content. In *Capital Cities Cable Inc. v. Crisp* (104 S.Ct. 2694), the court overturned an Oklahoma law that prohibited cable systems from carrying advertising for wine and hard liquor, even if the advertising in question was legal where it originated.

The Oklahoma law directly conflicted with the federal must-carry rules. Several cable systems near other states' borders were required by FCC regulations to carry television signals from out of state, including the advertising content (some of it alcoholic beverage advertising).

As a result, cable operators were in a classic Catch-22 situation. If they obeyed the federal must-carry rules, they faced prosecution under Oklahoma law. If they obeyed the state law, they risked punishment for violating federal regulations.

The high court resolved this conflict by ruling decisively in favor of the federal rules. The court said that the FCC, like Congress, clearly has the authority to preempt (i.e., invalidate) state and local laws that conflict with federal purposes. In essence, the court said cable content was a federal matter, not subject to local rules that conflict with federal policies.

However, the court did not rule that liquor advertising per se violates the First Amendment, although both broadcasters and cable operators had urged the court to address the Constitutional issue. Rather, the high court based its decision to overturn the Oklahoma law solely on the concept of federal preemption, not the First Amendment.

But the *Capital Cities* decision did make it clear that state and local governments may not impose rules on cable systems that conflict with federal rules, thus raising doubts about some other aspects of state and local cable television regulation. As cable television develops its own identity as a medium, the *Capital Cities* decision will surely contribute to the industry's effort to eliminate the varying and contradictory local rules under which it now operates.

New Cable Legislation

Even before the *Capital Cities* decision, local governments and cable operators were lobbying in Congress, seeking a clarification of the roles of federal, state and local governments in regulating cable. Meanwhile, in 1984 the FCC joined the Supreme Court in curtailing local authority over cable: the commission declared that cities may regulate only basic cable service, not the premium services that are offered for additional fees. In effect, the FCC stripped local governments of the power to control both content and fees charged for such things as movie and sports channels. The FCC said that cable systems are "free to add, delete or realign service offerings as long as all must-carry signals (i.e., local TV stations) are retained" (see *Community Cable of Las Vegas*, 4 *Communications Daily* 136, pg. 1).

As local governments saw their right to regulate cable being eroded by the Supreme Court and the FCC, their leaders decided they needed cable legislation from Congress—even if it wasn't exactly what they had originally hoped for. They worked out a compromise with the cable industry; the two rival groups jointly endorsed an amended version of a cable bill that had been bogged down in Congress for two years. Called the *Cable Communications Policy Act of 1984,* the compromise bill was approved late in that year.

While it is too early to predict the long-term effects of the new cable law, it is clear that Congress has reaffirmed the right of local governments to maintain some limited control over cable systems. The new law deregulates many cable subscription fees after a two-year transition period, and it bars local governments from charging franchise fees in excess of five per cent of a cable system's gross revenues. In return for this rate deregulation, the law authorizes local governments to require public access, government and educational channels—something the second *Midwest Video* Supreme Court decision had prohibited in the absence of an act of Congress.

The new law affirms the right of local governments to award franchises, but it also protects cable operators from arbitrary franchise nonrenewals. The law also excludes telephone companies from the cable business except in rural areas, and it prohibits TV stations from owning cable systems in their service areas (although the FCC can grant waivers of these restrictions). And the law requires cable operators to wire their entire franchise service areas, not just the most affluent neighborhoods where the potential for profit might be greatest.

But at the same time, the new law gives a Congressional sanction to the *Capital Cities* decision and the FCC's *Las Vegas* ruling, leaving cities with little say over cable content. In short, the 1984 Congressional cable legislation recognizes and codifies the FCC and Supreme Court rulings that freed cable systems of local government content controls, while reaffirming the basic right of local authorities to regulate cable.

While this far-reaching and long-awaited legislation will affect cable-government relations for many years to come, it does not resolve all of the unanswered questions about cable.

Perhaps the most fundamental unresolved question is still cable's Constitutional status. Will cable always be regarded primarily as a hybrid form of broadcasting, subject to government controls not applicable to the print media? Or will cable operators eventually gain recognition as "electronic publishers," free of most broadcast-like content controls? Certainly no newspaper or magazine publisher needs the permission of a local government to publish. And no government can force the print media to carry "public access" columns against their wishes.

For cable systems, on the other hand, mandatory public access (and government access) channels are a fact of life. However, it is clear at this point that local governments may not censor the content of cable systems as they once did. Even before the 1984 Supreme Court and FCC rulings, lower courts were overturning local attempts to censor cable. For instance, in 1982, a federal court intervened when movies that would not be obscene under the *Miller* standard were forbidden on cable systems in Utah (see *Home Box Office v. Wilkinson*, 531 F.Supp. 987).

In short, local governments may still require cable systems to carry programming of which public officials approve (e.g., public access and government channels), but they may not ban programming of which they disapprove (except, of course, for subject matter that is always unlawful such as legally obscene material).

Nevertheless, it may be many years before all of the uncertainties and inconsistencies of cable television regulation are resolved. This is an area of mass media law that will likely remain in transition for some time.

A Summary of Broadcast Regulation

WHY ARE BROADCASTERS TREATED DIFFERENTLY THAN OTHER MEDIA?

Broadcasters do not own their frequencies. The radio spectrum is a valuable and limited resource; Congress has declared that those who are given the privilege of using it must serve "the public interest, convenience, or necessity." Thus, broadcasters must answer to the Federal Communications Commission for the way they use their frequencies. They must secure licenses and then renew them periodically. In addition, they are subject to numerous controls on the content of their broadcasts.

WHY IS THE SPECTRUM SO LIMITED?

The radio spectrum can accommodate a large number of different users at the same time. As a policy judgment, an international regulatory body has allocated only a limited portion of the spectrum to broadcasting. Radio (as opposed to television) broadcasting has been given a particularly small part of the spectrum. Recently, however, the FCC has taken steps to make more AM, FM, and television frequency assignments available.

ARE LICENSE RENEWALS AUTOMATIC?

No. However, if the broadcaster's service record is considered "substantial," a renewal is almost a certainty. License renewal challenges by citizens' groups and others have become much more commonplace in recent years, but non-renewals are still rare.

WHAT IS THE FAIRNESS DOCTRINE?

The Fairness Doctrine is a Congressionally-recognized policy of the FCC that requires broadcasters to provide overall balance in their programming. The doctrine includes a "Personal Attack Rule," which requires broadcasters to provide airtime to victims of editorial attacks. The Fairness Doctrine should not be confused with the Equal Time Rule, a provision of the Communications Act that requires broadcasters to make equal time available to rival political candidates—at comparable rates. Recently, the FCC has backed away from regulating broadcast content and looked more and more to market place forces and creative spectrum management to ensure that broadcasters serve the public interest.

HOW IS CABLE TELEVISION REGULATED?

Cable television systems need no FCC license as such, since they do not broadcast over the air. However, cable systems are subject to many FCC rules because their operations affect on-the-air broadcasting. The FCC acted to deregulate cable television in 1980. Cable systems are also subject to state and local regulation, particularly through franchising agreements. Local governments usually grant a single CATV system the right to serve a particular area in return for a fee and promises of good public service. Congress has passed legislation to further deregulate cable television.

12

ADVERTISING AND ACCESS

Like broadcasting, the advertising industry has specialized legal problems not shared by other mass communications industries. In addition to all of the legal problems other communicators face, advertisers—like broadcasters—have a federal agency assigned to look after them. For advertisers, the special legal problem is to get along with the Federal Trade Commission.

In recent years the advertising industry has fought many battles with the FTC and even won a few. However, advertisers' victories in the regulatory arena seem minor compared to the dramatic triumphs they have achieved before the U.S. Supreme Court, which has completely rewritten the Constitutional law of advertising and commercial speech since 1975.

THE FIRST AMENDMENT AND ADVERTISING

For many years, the prevailing rule was that advertising had no First Amendment protection. If a particular expression of fact or opinion could be dismissed as "commercial speech," it could be arbitrarily suppressed by law. The "commercial speech doctrine," as it came to be known, simply said advertisers were at the mercy of every arm of government, without the guarantees of freedom the Constitution afforded to most other kinds of speech and publishing.

That all changed in the late 1970s, as the U.S. Supreme Court handed down a series of decisions establishing new First Amendment protection for commercial speech. The cases that produced this dramatic change represent one of the best examples of American law growing through judicial precedent to be found anywhere in the mass communications field.

The starting point for this summary is a 1942 Supreme Court decision that denied First Amendment protection to commercial speech, a landmark ruling that stood for many years. That case is *Valentine v. Chrestensen* (316 U.S. 52). It stemmed from a bizarre situation. Just before World War II, a man named F.J. Chrestensen acquired a surplus U.S. Navy submarine, and tried to dock it at a city-owned wharf in New York City. City authorities wouldn't let him, so he had to arrange for other dock facilities. Next, he started advertising guided tours of the submarine, but city officials wouldn't let him distribute his handbills on city streets because an anti-litter ordinance banned all but political leaflets. So he added a note criticizing city officials for refusing him dockage to the back of the handbill. Then he took the city to court for denying his right to distribute literature. The Supreme Court had just ruled in favor of that right in the first of the *Jehovah's Witness* cases (see Chapter Three).

When his case reached the Supreme Court, Chrestensen was in for a surprise. The high court said his back-of-the-handbill political statement was really a ruse to justify a purely commercial advertisement. And that was different from the *Jehovah's Witness* cases. Where purely commercial advertising is involved, the First Amendment does not apply, the court ruled. For many years, *Valentine v. Chrestensen* was regarded as the prevailing judicial precedent on commercial speech. In fact, when the landmark *New York Times v. Sullivan* libel decision was announced in 1964, the court went to some length to explain why the *Valentine* rule didn't apply (the *Sullivan* libel suit was based on an advertisement). The court said the ad involved in the *Sullivan* case was an idea ad supporting the civil rights movement, not an ad for a purely commercial product or service as in *Valentine*. Thus, the *Valentine* rule still denied First Amendment protection to commercial advertising for another decade, despite *New York Times v. Sullivan*.

In 1973, the Supreme Court again denied First Amendment protection to commercial advertising, this time in a case involving the "help wanted" ads in a large newspaper. In *Pittsburgh Press v. Pittsburgh Commission on Human Relations* (413 U.S. 376), the Human Relations Commission ordered the newspaper to stop classifying its employment ads as "Jobs—Male Interest" and "Jobs—Female Interest." The newspaper contended that there were editorial judgments inherent in the decision to classify job openings that way, and that those judgments were protected by the First Amendment.

The Supreme Court disagreed, and ruled that the classified ads are not only commercial speech, but commercial speech promoting an illegal form of discrimination as well. The court had no difficulty in ruling that whatever First Amendment considerations might be involved were secondary to the city's right to outlaw advertising for an illegal commercial activity.

An interesting follow-up note to this case is that in 1979 the Pennsylvania Supreme Court ruled against the Human Relations Commission when it tried to stop the *Pittsburgh Press* from accepting "help wanted" ads from individuals who indicated the age, sex, race, or religion of the job seeker. The commission objected to such language as "salesman age 30," "born again Christian seeks work in Christian business," or "white woman seeks domestic work." The state high court said the job seeker had a First Amendment right to communicate such information as this, even though an employer isn't supposed to consider these factors. The U.S. Supreme Court declined to review this second *Pittsburgh Press* decision.

The *Bigelow* Decision

Only two years after the original *Pittsburgh Press* decision, the Supreme Court handed down the first of its major decisions extending First Amendment protection to commercial speech (*Bigelow v. Virginia*, 421 U.S. 809, 1975). The case began in 1971 when Jeffrey Bigelow published an ad in The *Virginia Weekly* for an abortion service in New York, where abortions were legal at that time. The Supreme Court's decision allowing abortions in all states did not occur until 1973, and both abortions and abortion advertising were illegal in Virginia at that point.

Bigelow was prosecuted for violating the Virginia law, and he appealed his conviction to the U.S. Supreme Court. The result was a dramatic shift in the Commercial Speech Doctrine. The high court emphasized that the service in question was not illegal where it was offered, and said the readers had a First Amendment right to receive this information. The court distinguished this case from *Pittsburgh Press* by pointing out that the commercial activity in question there was illegal. But above all, the Supreme Court in *Bigelow* decided the mere fact that this information appeared in the form of an advertisement did not deprive it of the First Amendment protection it would otherwise have. The high court said that in the future there would have to be a *compelling state interest* to justify laws prohibiting any form of commercial speech that has a legitimate purpose.

Then in 1976, the Supreme Court took a giant additional step toward protecting commercial speech under the First Amendment. In *Virginia State Board of Pharmacy v. Virginia Citizens Consumer Council* (425 U.S. 748), the Supreme Court overturned Virginia's state laws against advertising the prices of drugs. Many other states had similar prohibitions on drug price advertising, but the Supreme Court again emphasized the First Amendment right of consumers to receive information as it overturned the state regulations.

Again, the court said the information in question was protected by the First Amendment, despite its commercial nature. At this point, it seemed clear that the old *Valentine v. Chrestensen* doctrine was dead: commercial speech did have Constitutional protection. However, while the court recognized the importance of price advertising to the free enterprise system, it also emphasized that this ruling in no way affected the right of governments to control false and misleading advertising.

In 1977, the Supreme Court handed down three more decisions strengthening the First Amendment protection of commercial speech. First, in *Linmark Associates v. Willingboro* (431 U.S. 85), the Supreme Court said homeowners have a First Amendment right to place "for sale" signs in front of their homes. The town of Willingboro, New Jersey, had outlawed "for sale" signs at a time when the area's racial composition was changing. There was considerable "white flight," and city officials wanted to discourage panic selling by white homeowners. One way to do this, the city felt, was to keep it from appearing that entire neighborhoods were for sale. A real estate firm challenged the constitutionality of the ordinance.

In defending the ordinance, city officials pointed to the social importance of racial integration and the evils of "white flight." Also, they said, homeowners who really need to sell their homes have other ways to advertise (by listing their homes with realtors or using newspaper classified ads, for instance). Nevertheless, the Supreme Court ruled against the city. In an opinion written by Justice Thurgood Marshall, the only Black on the high court, the majority said the city could not Constitutionally deprive its residents of the information that a for sale sign offers. "If the dissemination of this information can be restricted, then every locality in the country can suppress any facts that reflect poorly on the locality. . .," Marshall wrote.

Next, the Supreme Court handed down a commercial speech decision that was not at all surprising in view of its ruling in *Bigelow v. Virginia*. In *Carey v. Population Services International* (431 U.S. 678), the court overturned a variety of New York laws that restricted advertising of contraceptive devices. Even though these devices were not illegal in New York, state laws prohibited advertising, in-store displays and even sales of these products except by licensed pharmacists. Even pharmacists could not sell these devices to anyone younger than age 16. The Supreme Court found First Amendment violations in these laws, and said there was no *compelling state interest* to justify them, as required in *Bigelow*.

In mid-1977, the Supreme Court handed down one of its most far-reaching commercial speech decisions, *Bates v. Arizona State Bar* (433 U.S. 350). That case overturned Arizona's ban on advertising by lawyers, a rule similar to those found in nearly every other state. The case involved a legal clinic run by two young lawyers. The lawyers were disciplined by the State Bar for advertising the prices of routine legal services, prices that were far below the "going rate" charged by other lawyers. In ruling against the state bar, the Supreme Court again emphasized the First Amendment right of consumers to receive commercial information. The court said advertising by lawyers (and presumably other professionals) could not be prohibited unless it was misleading or fraudulent. However, the court expressed reservations about ads that say something about the quality of the services offered ("we're the best lawyers in town"), because such ads could well be misleading.

That warning about misleading advertising by professionals foreshadowed two more Supreme Court rulings, *Ohralik v. Ohio State Bar Association* (436 U.S. 447, 1978) and *Friedman v. Rogers* (440 U.S. 1, 1979). In

Ohralik, the Supreme Court affirmed sanctions against a lawyer for soliciting new clients in a manner that is sometimes called "ambulance chasing." The court said the First Amendment does not prevent a state bar association from adopting rules against that sort of conduct.

In *Friedman,* the court went a step further, upholding a Texas ban on the use of trade names by optometrists. The court said a trade name could be misleading, and that it did not provide consumers important information—as did the commercial advertising in question in earlier cases. The court said a trade name could be misleading because there could be a change of optometrists (and thus a change in the quality of service offered) without the name changing. Therefore, a state is not violating the First Amendment when it requires an optometrist to practice under his own name rather than a trade name, the court ruled. This case was viewed as a slight retreat by some, and critics pointed out that it was customary and completely legal for law firms, for instance, to continue to use the names of the founding partners long after their deaths. Isn't such a name really a tradename at some point? Wouldn't that also be misleading? The court didn't address that issue.

However, the Supreme Court continued to expand the First Amendment protection for commercial speech in other respects. In fact, the court took an important new step to protect commercial speech in 1978, ruling that corporations also have First Amendment rights. In *First National Bank v. Bellotti* (435 U.S. 765), the court overturned a Massachusetts law that forbade corporate advertising for or against ballot measures except when such a measure might "materially affect" a company's business. In reaching this conclusion, the court emphasized the importance of a free flow of information, even when some of that information comes from corporations rather than individuals. The decision raised doubts about the Constitutionality of limits on corporate political advertising in about 30 other states.

Massachusetts tried to defend its ban on corporate political advertising by arguing that corporations have so much money they could drown out other viewpoints if allowed to advertise. However, there was no evidence presented to prove that, and the court wasn't persuaded. Another problem with the Massachusetts law was that it allowed corporations engaged in mass communications (newspapers, television stations, etc.) to say anything they pleased on political issues, but that freedom was denied to other corporations. The Supreme Court said that, if anything, banks and other financial institutions might be better informed on economic issues than the mass media.

Thus, *First National Bank v. Bellotti* was a major victory for corporate advertising. It didn't guarantee corporations any special right of access when the media refuse to accept their issue-oriented advertising (a problem we discuss later in this chapter), but it did say that, where the media are willing to publish or broadcast advertising from corporations, a state cannot prohibit it just because it comes from a company instead of an individual or a campaign committee.

Corporate Freedom of Speech

In 1980, the Supreme Court handed down two more decisions that expanded the First Amendment protection of corporate speech, upholding the right of large utility corporations to advertise for more business or to enclose promotional material with utility bills. The cases were *Central Hudson Gas and Electric v. Public Service Commission of New York* (447 U.S. 557) and *Consolidated Edison v. Public Service Commission of New York* (447 U.S. 530).

Both cases stemmed from rules the Public Service Commission adopted in 1977. The commission prohibited advertising that encouraged more consumption of utility services, a rule intended to foster energy conservation. Second, the commission told utilities not to insert any written material in billing envelopes that discussed "political matters" or "controversial issues of public policy." The two large utility companies challenged the new rules, but the companies lost in the New York state courts. The state's highest court found the ban on inserts with bills to be a reasonable regulation of the time, place, and manner of speech, and said the ban on pro-consumption advertising was justified because the need to conserve outweighed the slight free speech issue involved.

The U.S. Supreme Court reversed the New York courts on both points. The majority said the ban on promotional advertising would have only a "highly speculative" effect on energy consumption or utility rates, and thus a total ban was going too far. The court said the ban on bill inserts was an excessive restriction of corporations' First Amendment rights.

These two decisions would appear significant for several reasons. First, they attracted the support of at least seven of the nine Supreme Court justices. The *First National Bank* decision, by comparison, came on a narrow 5-4 vote. But in addition, the court set forth legal guidelines that can be used to determine whether future restrictions on commercial speech are valid. The court said commercial speech is Constitutionally protected if it concerns "lawful activity" and is not misleading or fraudulent.

When commercial speech is lawful and truthful, the Supreme Court said that government restrictions are permissible only if: (1) the claimed government interest that justifies the restrictions is substantial; (2) the regulation directly advances the governmental interest in question; and (3) the regulation is not more broad than needed to fulfill the governmental interest.

In the *Central Hudson* and *Consolidated Edison* cases, the Supreme Court also made a distinction between *commercial speech* and *noncommercial corporate speech*. In essence, commercial speech is advertising of products and services. Noncommercial corporate speech, on the other hand, involves statements on political or social issues by companies, often in the form of an idea-oriented or "editorial" advertisement.

Where noncommercial corporate speech is involved, the Supreme Court suggested an even tougher scrutiny of government restrictions. In this case, government restrictions are justified only if one of these three conditions is met: (1) the restriction in question is a "precisely drawn means of serving a compelling state interest"; (2) the restriction is required to fulfill a "significant government interest" and merely regulates time, place, and manner, leaving open "ample alternate channels for communication"; or (3) there is a narrowly drawn restriction on speech under a few special circumstances where disruption of government activities must be avoided, such as at a military base.

What does all of this mean? It means the standards are slightly different for commercial advertising than they are for noncommercial corporate speech. Commercial advertising seems to have slightly less Constitutional protection than idea-oriented or "editorial" advertising. However, it may require years of additional court decisions to clearly spell out the rights of corporations and others engaged in commercial speech under the new rules. What is clear is that commercial and noncommercial advertising now enjoys substantial Constitutional protection, something that was not true until recently.

In 1981 the Supreme Court further expanded its Commercial Speech Doctrine in a case involving the right of local governments to outlaw roadside billboards, *Metromedia v. San Diego* (453 U.S. 490). The court overturned a San Diego, Calif., city ordinance banning both political and commercial billboard messages. However, the court was deeply divided in deciding the case, and Justice William Rehnquist called the decision a "virtual Tower of Babel from which no definitive principles can be drawn."

Nevertheless, a majority of the justices did agree that San Diego's billboard ban was too broad because it banned all billboards containing political messages as well as purely commercial ones. The court left open the possibility that a narrower ordinance forbidding only commercial but not political billboards would be Constitutionally permissible. But beyond that, the court's five different opinions seemed to shed more confusion than light.

In 1984, the Supreme Court again addressed the Constitutionality of a local ordinance restricting political signs, but this time the court decided that such an ordinance did not violate the First Amendment. In *Los Angeles City Council v. Taxpayers for Vincent* (104 S.Ct. 2118), the court said the city of Los Angeles has the right to ban political posters on public property. The court ruled that forbidding posters on city-owned utility poles and buildings was not an excessive restriction on First Amendment freedoms. The court said this decision was not inconsistent with the *Metromedia v. San Diego* decision, in which a ban on all billboards (including those placed on private property with the owner's consent) was overturned as a First Amendment violation. In contrast, the Los Angeles ordinance only prohibited attaching posters to public property, not placing signs and billboards on private property.

In upholding the Los Angeles ordinance, the high court said a city has the right to prevent the "visual assault on the citizens. . . presented by an accumulation of signs posted on public property."

The Supreme Court also decided two other commercial speech cases in the early 1980s. In 1982, the court released another decision on advertising by attorneys, *In Re R.M.J.* (102 U.S. 929). The case involved regulations that severely restricted lawyers' advertising in Missouri. The rules allowed lawyers to use only certain words to describe the kinds of law that they practiced, and the approved words were in legalese, not layman's terms. A lawyer could not advertise that he or she handled personal injury or real estate cases, for instance. An unnamed lawyer violated these rules and was disciplined. The Supreme Court overturned the disciplinary action, holding that the attorney's advertising was protected by the First Amendment. However, the court again re-emphasized the point that only nondeceptive advertising—by lawyers or anybody else—is protected by the First Amendment.

In view of the earlier commercial speech rulings, the Supreme Court surprised no one when it decided *Bolger v. Young Drug Products Corp.* (103 S.Ct. 2875) in 1983. The court overturned the post office's ban on mailing unsolicited ads for contraceptive devices. The court said such a ban denies consumers access to important information that the public has a Constitutional right to receive. In the majority opinion, Justice Thurgood Marshall emphasized the importance of family planning and the prevention of venereal disease as social issues, and said the post office had not adequately justified the ban on mailing this material.

ADVERTISING AND MEDIA ACCESS

Is there a Constitutional right to advertise? Or may one place an advertisement only if those who control the media are willing to accept it? To put it another way, is there any right of access to newspapers or radio and television stations?

The answer to these questions has traditionally been simple and straightforward: there is no right of access to the media for either editorial or advertising purposes. However, it took several U.S. Supreme Court decisions in the early 1970s to settle that question. Even so, under certain unusual circumstances, a right to advertise may exist—particularly if the rejected advertiser can show that the refusal to place his material fell within a pattern of unfair or monopolistic business practices. Also, under certain circumstances government-sponsored media cannot deny public access.

A good starting point in summarizing the principles of advertising and access is a 1933 Iowa Supreme Court decision. It's ancient history, but it was a pioneering court decision in favor of a newspaper's right to accept or reject advertising from whomever it pleases. The case, *Shuck v. Carroll Daily Herald* (247 N.W. 813), simply ruled that a newspaper is a private enterprise, and its management has no duty to be a public utility that serves everyone who may come along.

In the decades since, courts have repeatedly ruled the same way when would-be advertisers demanded space in commercial newspapers. For instance, in 1970 a federal appellate court turned down a labor union's appeal for access to the advertising columns of the *Chicago Tribune*. In that case (*Chicago Joint Board, Amalgamated Clothing Workers of America v. Chicago Tribune,* 435 F.2d 470), the court rejected the union's claim that major newspapers should be public forums. The union wanted to run ads protesting a department store's sale of imported clothing, but no daily newspaper in Chicago would accept the ads. The union argued that there should be a First Amendment right of access under those circumstances. Nevertheless, the federal court affirmed the publisher's right to reject advertising even if it means one side of a controversial issue will not be heard. The U.S. Supreme Court declined to review the decision.

In 1971, another federal appellate court ruled against a movie producer who objected to censorship of his ads by the *Los Angeles Times*. In *Associates & Aldrich v. Times Mirror* (440 F.2d 133), the court declined to rule that the newspaper had any obligation to publish the ads at all, much less any duty to publish them exactly as submitted.

These decisions were setbacks for advocates of public access to the press, but an even greater defeat came in 1974, when the U.S. Supreme Court handed down its landmark decision on access to the print media. The decision, *Miami Herald v. Tornillo* (418 U.S. 241), overturned a Florida state law creating a limited right of access.

The case arose when Pat Tornillo, a Miami teacher's union leader, ran for the state legislature. The *Miami Herald* twice editorially attacked Tornillo. Tornillo demanded space for a reply. The law seemed to be on his side when he made this demand: Florida had a right-of-reply law requiring newspapers to publish replies when they editorially attacked candidates for office. The *Herald* turned Tornillo down and he sued, invoking the Florida law. The state Supreme Court ruled in his favor, and the newspaper appealed to the U.S. Supreme Court. The Supreme Court unanimously reversed the Florida ruling, affirming the newspaper's First Amendment right to control its content without government interference. Thus, the court invalidated Florida's right-of-reply law.

Of course, this case involved a state's attempt to control editorial content rather than advertising, but the decision affirmed the publisher's right to control the content of his entire publication; the ruling was not limited to the news side. In the years since *Tornillo*, courts have continued to reject any right of access to the editorial and advertising columns of newspapers and magazines except when there was evidence of unfair or monopolistic business practices (see Chapter 13).

What sort of monopolistic business practices would cause a court to force a newspaper to accept unwanted advertising? A good example is provided by a series of lawsuits challenging the classified advertising policies of the *Providence Journal* and *Providence Evening Bulletin*. These papers did not accept ads from rental referral services, a policy they defended as necessary to prevent fraud.

In a complex series of lawsuits, several rental referral services challenged this policy. They claimed it violated federal antitrust laws because the Providence papers enjoyed a virtual monopoly in their market, and were in fact competitors of the rental services (both newspaper ads and rental referral services help people find housing).

At first the federal courts upheld the Providence papers' policies as reasonable anti-fraud measures: they said the referral service challenging the policies was guilty of deceptive practices. However, in 1983 a federal appellate court ruled that there was no evidence of fraud by another referral service. Thus, the court said the Providence papers were violating the Sherman Act by denying advertising space to this would-be competitor. However, by then this referral service had gone out of business, and a federal judge awarded just $3 as token damages. (See *Home Placement Service v. Providence Journal*, 682 F.2d 274, 1982, and 9 Med.L.Rptr. 2518.)

The point: a newspaper that enjoys a virtual monopoly in its service area (as many papers do) risks an antitrust lawsuit if it denies advertising space to someone whose business might be viewed as being in competition with the paper.

One other kind of allegedly unfair business practice has produced a number of lawsuits: charging similar advertisers different rates. Some state laws forbid discriminatory pricing, and the Federal Trade Commission has also acted against such practices. The role of the states and the Federal Trade Commission in regulating advertising is discussed later in this chapter.

In the electronic media, the rules on access are much the same, as a result of a 1973 Supreme Court decision, (*CBS v. Democratic National Committee*, 412 U.S. 94). Under the Fairness Doctrine (see Chapter 11), broadcasters were at one time required to air advertisements expressing specific viewpoints in order to balance other ads they had accepted. Under this rule, broadcasters had been obliged to air anti-cigarette smoking commercials, for example. At one point in the early 1970s, it appeared that the Fairness Doctrine created something of a right of access to broadcast advertising, thus denying broadcasters one of the basic prerogatives enjoyed by the print media.

However, that trend came to an abrupt halt in the *CBS v. Democratic National Committee* decision. The case arose when two different groups demanded that the FCC assure them a right to advertise on radio or television. One, the Business Executives Move for Vietnam Peace, had been turned down in its quest for airtime. The Democratic National Committee merely wanted a declaration that it had a right to buy airtime. The FCC rejected the arguments of both, but a federal appellate court reversed the FCC decision. The Supreme Court then reversed the lower court's ruling, holding that neither the First Amendment nor the 1934 Communications Act created any right of access to broadcast advertising time. If a broadcaster chooses to carry no advertising of a certain type, that's his prerogative, the high court said.

The court emphasized that the Fairness Doctrine requires broadcasters to offer overall balance in their programming. If a radio or TV station chooses to air issue-oriented advertising for one viewpoint on a controversial issue, it may be obligated to air opposing views. However, that does not mean any particular group or individual has a right of access. Commercial radio and television stations are simply not public utilities running common carrier operations, the Supreme Court said. A common carrier such as a telephone company must provide service to everyone who can pay for it; a broadcaster is under no such obligation.

Thus, the privately owned print and broadcast media are usually treated alike when it comes to access: neither medium is under any Constitutional obligation to carry any particular person or group's advertisements or editorial material in most instances. However, remember that the Personal Attack Rule of the Fairness Doctrine (discussed in Chapter 11) does require broadcasters to grant reply time to anyone who is personally attacked in a broadcast editorial. The *Tornillo* principle allows the print media to publish personal attacks without giving the victim any right of reply, but the rule on that point is different in broadcasting. Under *Red Lion Broadcasting v. FCC*, a broadcaster must provide airtime for replies to personal attacks that occur under most circumstances other than news coverage.

Broadcasters are also required to accept advertising from candidates in federal elections under the Federal Election Campaign Act (see Chapter 11). Again, the print media are subject to no similar requirement. Newspapers may accept no political ads at all or even carry ads favoring just one candidate, if they wish. There is neither a Fairness Doctrine nor an Equal Time Rule for the print media. In the narrow areas of personal attacks and federal election campaigns, broadcasters must provide access while the print media have no such obligation.

Under some other circumstances, however, advertisers feel they have more access to print than to the broadcast media. Many broadcasters voluntarily exclude ads espousing controversial ideas, a point discussed in the section on "self-regulation" later in this chapter. A number of major corporations have attempted to place issue-oriented ads on television, only to be rebuffed. Several of them, notably Mobil Oil and the Kaiser Corporation, have purchased newspaper and magazine ads to protest their denial of advertising space in the electronic media. For whatever practical reasons, the print media have been much more willing to carry idea ads than broadcasters, although neither medium is ordinarily under any legal obligation to do so.

The print media are also more receptive to a number of other kinds of ads. For example, many broadcasters voluntarily reject hard liquor ads, and federal law has prohibited broadcast advertising of cigarettes since 1971. The print media routinely carry ads for these products.

Other Access Questions

If neither the print nor the broadcast media must ordinarily carry ads to which the management objects, does that settle the matter of public access to all media?

Not necessarily. One communications medium that has provided considerable public access is cable television. In fact, for many years cable public access rights were mandated by FCC regulations. The Supreme Court's *FCC v. Midwest Video* decision eventually overturned those regulations, saying the FCC exceeded its authority by adopting what amounted to common carrier requirements for cable systems.

However, state and local governments that issue franchises to CATV systems may still have the authority to impose public access requirements as part of the franchising process, and some state and local governments have done so. Also, some cable systems voluntarily provide public access channels as a community service. Thus, many cable systems represent exceptions to the general rule that there is no mandatory public access to the mass media in America.

Another exception to that rule, at least to some extent, involves government-run communications media. In the years prior to the *Tornillo* decision, state and federal courts began recognizing a right to advertise on city buses and in public school newspapers. When state action is involved, as it is with these media, courts for a time ruled that the authorities were Constitutionally required to accept controversial advertising. During the 1960s, a federal court in New York and a state court in California both prohibited public transportation systems from flatly denying space to advertisers whose ideas they disliked. (See *Kissinger v. New York City Transit Authority*, 274 F.Supp. 438, and *Wirta v. Alameda-Contra Costa Transit District*, 68 Cal.2d 51.)

Similarly, federal courts in New York and Wisconsin overturned state-supported school and college administrators' efforts to keep student newspapers from accepting ads espousing controversial ideas (see *Lee v. Board of Regents*, 441 F.2d 1257, and *Zucker v. Panitz*, 299 F.Supp. 102).

However, the idea that there should be a right of access to state-run media was dealt a severe blow by another U.S. Supreme Court ruling, *Lehman v. Shaker Heights* (418 U.S. 298, 1974). In that decision, handed down the same day as the *Tornillo* ruling, the Supreme Court denied a political candidate's appeal for access to the advertising space on a city-run bus line. The bus line's policy was to accept only commercial ads, not political ads, and the Supreme Court denied that the First Amendment creates any right to advertise even in government-run media such as this. Although the Supreme Court has repeatedly said city streets and parks, for instance, are "public forums" protected by the First Amendment, it refused to rule that ad space on city-run buses is necessarily a public forum.

On the other hand, if a state-run communications medium rejects one candidate's ads while accepting others, the person whose ads were rejected might have a case under the Fourteenth Amendment's "equal protection" clause, the court said. But in the *Lehman* case, all political ads were rejected; there was no discrimination.

As a result of the *Lehman* decision, courts in recent years have usually refused to order access to ad space even in government-run media, let alone privately owned media. Today there appears not to be any right of access to this kind of advertising, provided those in charge follow their advertising acceptance policies consistently.

However, the problem of public access to a state-run communications medium takes a different perspective when the management creates a public forum by accepting some political and social issue ads, but then rejects ads from those whose ideas it dislikes. That was illustratred in *Gay Activists Alliance v. Washington Metropolitan Area Transit Authority* (5 Med.L.Rptr. 1404), a 1979 federal district court ruling. As a district court decision, its precedent-setting impact is not great, but it does illustrate an exception to the *Lehman* rule. Here a government-sponsored transit system rejected a gay rights group's ads even though it accepted other controversial ads. The court said state action was clearly present here, and accepting other issue-oriented ads made the bus line a public forum, where the one in *Lehman* was not. Thus, transit officials could not refuse the gays' ads, the court held.

On the other hand, two years after the *Tornillo* and *Lehman* decisions, a federal appellate court rejected an appeal for access to the ad columns of the Mississippi State University newspaper in *Mississippi Gay Alliance v. Goudelock* (536 F.2d 1073). The Gay Alliance wanted to place an announcement of its services and was turned down by the staff. The court said this case was different from the previous public school advertising access cases because here the staff, as opposed to the administration, rejected the ad. Hence, the court said there was no state action in this decision to reject advertising from a gay organization. But in addition, the court said *Tornillo* gave the editors final say over the content anyway. (As Chapter 14 explains, the First Amendment protects public school newspaper editors, particularly when an administrator attempts censorship. The staff appears to have the final say over both news and advertising content.)

It is not easy to reconcile all of the varying court decisions involving the right to advertise in state-run media, but the prevailing rule since *Lehman* seems to be that there is no such right unless a state agency accepts some ads of a certain type and then arbitrarily rejects other similar ads.

In the commercial media, on the other hand, the rules are much more clear. Commercial advertising is almost always a privilege, not a right. Neither the print nor the electronic media are public utilities: they may accept ads to their liking and reject the rest.

However, broadcasters do have certain special obligations not shared by the print media. The Fairness Doctrine requires that they present all sides of controversial issues (which means *someone* must be allowed to reply to ads that express opinions on such issues). Also, broadcasters must provide opposing political candidates with equal opportunities to advertise.

FEDERAL ADVERTISING REGULATION

Beyond the issues of advertising access and commercial speech, advertising law is a field dominated by the Federal Trade Commission and, to a much lesser extent, state and local agencies that regulate advertising.

Unquestionably, the FTC is the most important regulatory agency for advertisers. Created by the Federal Trade Commission Act in 1914, this independent federal agency is responsible for overseeing many kinds of business activities in America. The 1914 act said: "Unfair methods of competition in commerce are hereby declared unlawful; the Commission is hereby empowered and directed to prevent persons, partnerships, or corporations from using unfair methods of competition in commerce."

Thus, the FTC's initial mandate was to prevent unfair business practices—but only for the protection of other businesses. It was not at first given the job of protecting consumers from fraudulent business practices.

Perhaps this was because of a very old tradition in American advertising. The prevailing attitude was "caveat emptor" (roughly translated, "let the buyer beware"). For several centuries, that meant advertisers were free to flagrantly exaggerate the merits of their products. Newspapers in the 1800s were full of fraudulent advertising, most notably ads for patent medicines. These medicines were trumpeted as cures for everything from colds to cancer, although many of them had no medicinal value at all.

The consumer who was deceived by this false advertising had few legal remedies under the common law; the only remedies available involved complicated lawsuits that were difficult to win. Most victims of advertising fraud had no choice but to accept their losses and vow not to be fooled again.

However, the Federal Trade Commission quickly made false advertising one of its main concerns. By the 1920s, the majority of its enforcement actions involved advertising. The FTC contended that false advertising was unfair to other businesses. For instance, in a famous case that went all the way to the Supreme Court, the FTC challenged a company that advertised clothing as "natural wool" when it was really only 10 percent wool. In *Federal Trade Commission v. Winsted Hosiery Co.* (258 U.S. 483, 1922), the court agreed that false advertising is a form of unfair competition, since it diverts customers from honest merchants' products.

However, a few years later the Supreme Court curtailed the FTC's crusade against false advertising by ruling that the agency had no authority to act on behalf of consumers in the absence of evidence that the false advertising was unfair to a competing business. That happened in 1931, in *FTC v. Raladam* (283 U.S. 643).

As a result, the FTC's powers were sharply reduced, but only temporarily. In 1938, Congress enacted the Wheeler-Lea Amendment, authorizing the FTC to act against "unfair or deceptive acts or practices" that might mislead the consumer. The Wheeler-Lea Act also expanded the FTC's enforcement powers.

The FTC operated under this enabling legislation until 1975, when its powers were again expanded by the Magnuson-Moss Act. That law specifically empowered the commission to act against fraudulent practices all the way down to the local level. No longer would it be limited to practices involving interstate commerce as it had been; now the FTC could pursue businesses that merely "affected" interstate commerce. In addition,

Magnuson-Moss authorized the FTC to issue "Trade Regulation Rules," orders carrying the force of law that mandate fair trade practices for entire industries.

Under these broad new powers, the commission entered an unprecedented period of activism in the late 1970s, and some of its actions were so unpopular that Congress refused to grant it a budget for a time in 1980. The agency had to briefly lock its doors and cease all operations. Finally, it was given an operating budget, but with severe restrictions on its authority, in the Federal Trade Commission Improvements Act of 1980.

Before summarizing the provisions of that law, we should describe the FTC's basic structure and enforcement powers, and explain what it did to abuse those powers—in the opinion of Congress.

FTC Enforcement Tools

The Federal Trade Commission, like the Federal Communications Commission, is an independent regulatory agency. It is governed by a five-member commission, with an administrative staff of nearly 2,000 persons. The five commissioners, appointed by the president with Senate ratification, have seven-year renewable terms.

The FTC uses a variety of enforcement tools against fraudulent and anti-competitive business practices. Although most are purely legal actions, the FTC's most effective single means of controlling fraudulent advertising is publicity. Since an advertiser's whole purpose is to persuade a segment of the public to buy or believe something, one of the worst things that can happen to an advertiser is to have the same media that carry the ads also publish news stories reporting that a government agency thinks the ads are false.

But beyond the clout of its press releases, the FTC has a variety of enforcement powers. The agency often acts on the basis of complaints from consumers or other businesses, but whatever the source of a complaint, the first step in an enforcement action is usually to notify an advertiser that it considers his or her ads deceptive or misleading. The advertiser may be provided a copy of a proposed *cease and desist order*, along with supporting documents. Rather than face the lengthy and costly proceedings that lead to the issuance of such a decree, the advertiser may well choose to sign a consent order, agreeing to discontinue the challenged advertising without admitting any wrongdoing and without any official proceeding.

In some cases, the FTC is willing to let an advertiser merely sign an affidavit called an *assurance of voluntary compliance*. But under either this procedure or the more official consent decree, the FTC usually negotiates with the advertiser to reach a settlement. The agency prefers to avoid its more formal proceedings when possible, not only to save staff time but also to halt the misleading advertising quickly enough to protect the public. A typical advertising campaign runs for only a few months, and the entire campaign may be over long before the FTC can complete its formal proceedings.

However, if the advertiser refuses to sign a consent order, the agency may initiate formal proceedings. Those proceedings involve bringing the advertiser before an administrative law judge, who will hear both the commission's and the advertiser's arguments and issue a ruling. The commission has the right to review the judge's decision, and may issue a formal cease and desist decree, which the advertiser may then appeal to a federal appellate court. These are civil proceedings, and the defending advertiser isn't afforded the full rights available in criminal trials. For instance, an administrative law judge may decide the FTC is wrong and the challenged ads are perfectly legal. In a criminal trial, that would be an acquittal and would end the proceeding. But here, the FTC can rule that the ads are illegal and issue a decree anyway, ignoring the judge's findings. The advertiser has no recourse then, except to appeal the FTC decision to a federal appellate court.

Once a consent order or cease and desist decree is in effect, the advertiser faces massive civil penalties—sometimes up to $10,000 a day—for violating its terms.

In addition to these enforcement tools, the FTC uses several other procedures. One is to publish purely advisory *Guides*. These pamphlets tell advertisers how the FTC interprets the law on a given point, such as the use of testimonials in advertising or product pricing. Violating a Guide is not a violation of law, but Guides are very valuable to advertisers because they provide insight into the FTC's current thinking on various advertising practices. Another similar FTC action is to issue *Advisory Opinions*. Like Guides, they are voluntary, but they differ in that they are issued in response to inquiries from advertisers rather than on the commission's own initiative.

A similar policy guideline—but carrying the force of law—is called a Trade Regulation Rule, or "TRR." These rules generally apply to an entire industry, requiring certain specific advertising practices and forbidding others. As we'll explain shortly, the liberal use of TRRs was largely responsible for the Congressional action against the FTC in 1980.

In the 1970s, the FTC also launched another major effort to control advertising fraud, this one through an *Advertising Substantiation Program*. In this program, the FTC required certain industries to document all of the claims in their ads, something that produced voluminous and highly technical reports in some cases. This also led to controversy, because the reports were often so complicated they were of no value to the consumer, and critics charged that the FTC staff didn't even read some of them. A U.S. senator once complained that such a report cost a tobacco company $800,000 to prepare and the FTC never made any legitimate use of it.

In 1984, the FTC—under the guidance of James C. Miller, a new chairman who disagreed with many of the agency's earlier regulatory efforts—revised its advertising substantiation policies. Instead of demanding that entire industries substantiate their ad claims, the new policy called for the FTC to demand substantiation mainly from individual companies.

Two more of the FTC's most controversial approaches to enforcement have been *Affirmative Disclosure Orders* and *corrective advertising*. Affirmative disclosure involves requiring the advertiser to reveal the negative as well as the positive aspects of a product. In a pioneering case of this sort, a federal appellate court upheld an FTC order aimed at the makers of Geritol. Geritol was advertised as a "tired blood" cure for the elderly, and the manufacturer was ordered to reveal that it did little to help people with certain kinds of anemia (*J.B. Williams Co. v. FTC*, 381 F.2d 884, 1967).

The FTC required hundreds of advertisers to reveal similarly negative facts about their products after this decision. Banks and savings institutions were obliged to advertise that there were "substantial interest penalties" for early withdrawal of money, and automakers who quoted mileage ratings from government tests had to tell customers, "your mileage may vary."

Many advertisers found these requirements onerous and embarrassing, but corrective advertising angered the business community even more. Probably the most famous FTC corrective advertising order was one aimed at Warner-Lambert Company, maker of Listerine mouthwash. For nearly a century, Listerine had been advertised as a cure for colds and sore throats, a claim that medical research did not support.

The FTC ordered Warner-Lambert not only to spend $10 million on advertisements admitting that Listerine would not cure sore throats, but also to preface the correction with the phrase, "Contrary to prior advertising." Warner-Lambert appealed the FTC ruling, but the federal appellate court affirmed the corrective order—although the court did agree that saying "contrary to prior advertising" was just too much penance. Warner-Lambert was allowed to run its corrective ads without that confession of past sins (*Warner-Lambert Co. v. FTC*, 562 F.2d 749, 1977). Warner-Lambert asked the Supreme Court to review this ruling, but the high court declined to do so.

The FTC issued a number of other corrective advertising orders in the 1970s, including one that required the makers of STP oil additive to publish ads telling the public its claims that STP would reduce auto oil consumption were based on unreliable road tests.

Examples of FTC Rulings

In addition to these cases involving various forms of penance by advertisers, the FTC has acted in thousands of other instances of what it considered to be false, misleading, or deceptive advertising. A few examples will illustrate the FTC's philosophy on advertising regulation.

Perhaps the best-known FTC case for many years, in part because it produced a U.S. Supreme Court decision, was the "sandpaper shave case," *FTC v. Colgate-Palmolive Co.* (380 U.S. 374, 1965).

In one of the most famous television ads of the era, Colgate-Palmolive Rapid Shave was shown shaving the sand off of sandpaper. The only problem was that what the viewer really saw was sand being scraped off a sheet of plexiglass. The FTC contended that this was deceptive and ordered the ads halted. Colgate-Palmolive chose to fight the order, and set out to prove that the sand really could be shaved off a sheet of sandpaper. The company did it, but it took a little longer in real life than in the ads: about 90 minutes.

The Supreme Court eventually upheld the FTC, ruling that the ad was deceptive. In so ruling, the Supreme Court did not say that all television mockups are deceptive. But, the court said, mockups that are central to the point of the ad or enhance the product are deceptive. A common industry practice was to use mashed potatoes in place of ice cream because of the heat generated by television lighting. The court used that mockup to explain its point. Perhaps showing actors eating ice cream that was really mashed potatoes would not be deceptive if the point of the ad was to promote something else, but it would be deceptive if the point was to sell the ice cream by showing its rich texture and full color, the court said.

In the years since that decision, the FTC has acted against a wide variety of advertising practices. The FTC has gone after advertisers who used a number of other mockups, mockups that hardly seem as flagrantly deceptive as the Rapid Shave commercial. In one Lever Brothers commercial for All detergent, an actor was shown standing in a huge washing machine with a stain on his shirt. The water rose to his neck and then receded—and the stain vanished. The FTC said it was deceptive, since the whole process couldn't really happen that fast.

On another occasion, the FTC went after the makers of Prestone Anti-Freeze for a commercial showing the "magnetic film" in Prestone protecting a strip of metal from acid. The FTC objected because the acid used in the demonstration was not the same kind encountered in auto radiators and because certain other test conditions didn't duplicate what really happens in a car.

Often the FTC has based its complaints on ads that were literally true but nonetheless deceiving. As early as 1950 the commission acted against a cigarette manufacturer for advertising that a study found its brand lower in tar and nicotine than others tested. That was true, but the study also concluded that all brands tested were dangerously high in tar and nicotine. The ads were literally true, but still misleading, the FTC said.

On other occasions, the FTC has acted against advertising claims that were controversial and dealt with issues on which there was scientific disagreement. In 1974, the commission filed a complaint and sought an injunction against the National Commission on Egg Nutrition for publishing ads that said, "there is no scientific evidence that eating eggs increases the risk of heart and circulatory disease." A federal appellate court upheld the FTC's action to halt this advertising claim, although the court overruled an FTC order requiring future egg ads to say the health issue was controversial and that experts differed.

The FTC has also expressed considerable interest in misleading testimonials. The commission requires that celebrities who endorse products actually use them, and that "experts" who give endorsements must really be experts. Moreover, the claims users make in endorsements must in fact be verifiably true. A grass-roots or "plain folks" ad cannot have someone saying he gets 50 miles per gallon from his Guzzlemobile Diesel when tests indicate it won't deliver over 40. In fact, an ad in which "Mrs. Holly Hollingsworth" of "Guzzle Gulch, Nevada" endorses a product must actually show Mrs. Hollingsworth, not an actress portraying Mrs. Hollingsworth.

In 1978, the commission even acted against entertainer Pat Boone for what the FTC considered to be a misleading endorsement of a skin-care product. The FTC accused the manufacturer, the advertising agency, and Boone of participating in false and misleading advertising. The FTC charged that the product would not cure acne as the ad implied it would. The commission sought a $5,000 penalty from Boone, and he signed a consent order agreeing to pay the $5,000 into a fund to compensate customers who were misled by the ad.

This action, the first to hold a celebrity accountable for a misleading endorsement, was a major shock to other celebrities who endorse products. After the Boone incident, virtually all celebrities demanded *indemnification clauses* in their endorsement contracts. (Indemnification means the advertiser has to pay any penalty the celebrity might incur because of the ad.)

Like testimonials, comparison advertising attracted the FTC's attention in the late 1970s. Traditionally, advertisers have hesitated to criticize each other's products, partly out of fear of lawsuits and partly because industry self-regulation codes discouraged the practice. But in 1979, the FTC issued a policy statement demanding that the advertising industry and broadcasters drop their restrictions on comparative ads and calling on advertisers to compare their products "objectively" against competing brands by name.

If the 1970s saw the FTC push aggressively into new areas such as advertising substantiation, corrective advertising, and comparative advertising, the 1980s were an era of retrenchment. In fact, in the mid-1980s, there was growing uncertainty about the FTC's basic rules defining what constitutes deceptive advertising. In 1983, FTC Chairman Miller released an "enforcement policy statement" that said the commission would henceforth only regard advertising as deceptive if it harmed a hypothetical "reasonable consumer." However, it was not clear what legal weight this new statement would carry, and it was widely criticized in Congress as inadequate to protect the public from false and misleading advertising.

FTC Actions Against "Unfair" Practices

In the 1970s, the commission increasingly looked beyond advertising that was merely deceptive or misleading and began to act against ads it considered unfair even though they were truthful. Critics came to call this policy the "Unfairness Doctrine," an obvious reference to the Federal Communications Commission's Fairness Doctrine in broadcasting.

The FTC's authority to act against ads that are merely "unfair" was affirmed by the U.S. Supreme Court in a 1972 decision, *FTC v. Sperry*

Hutchinson Co. (405 U.S. 233). The court said the FTC has the power to act against "business practices which have an unfair impact on consumers, regardless of whether the practice is deceptive. . .or anti-competitive in the traditional sense."

After that ruling, the FTC initiated a series of controversial actions against "unfair" advertising. In 1979, for instance, the commission acted against bicycle ads in which it felt unsafe riding habits were shown by ordering the advertiser to distribute public service ads on bicycle safety.

In the late 1970s, the FTC also used its authority to issue Trade Regulation Rules to ban allegedly unfair practices in a variety of industries. These campaigns stirred bitter opposition among businesses, and eventually in Congress.

For example, in 1978 the commission initiated a very controversial proposal to severely restrict television advertising aimed at children. The proposed restrictions would have completely banned advertising aimed at young children and prohibited ads for sugared food products targeted to older children. At one point before the commission voted on the matter, the FTC chairman, Michael Pertschuk, made public statements on the issue that were so prejudicial that national organizations in advertising sought—and won—a court order prohibiting him from voting on the matter. The order was reversed by a federal appellate court, but the damage was done.

The FTC also proposed rules forcing funeral directors to list all their prices and service options, as well as rules requiring used car dealers to inspect the cars they sell and post a list of mechanical problems on each car. On other occasions, the commission acted to break up Sunkist Growers, an agricultural cooperative, and launched campaigns against various trademarks, seeking to take them from their owners and have them declared generic words. The FTC also issued rules requiring trade and vocational schools to provide a great deal of information to incoming students, and let them withdraw with a prorated tuition refund during their programs.

The FTC's policy on corrective advertising had angered the advertising profession. The extensive use of the Unfairness Doctrine against advertisers intensified that feeling, as did the move to ban children's television advertising. Chairman Pertschuk's public pronouncements further united the business community against the commission. Finally, the rules aimed at morticians, used car dealers, the Sunkist cooperative, and trade schools were the FTC's undoing.

Responding to nationwide protests about the FTC's regulatory zeal, Congress refused to appropriate a budget for the agency in 1980, and then enacted the restrictive Federal Trade Commission Improvements Act.

That law extended the FTC's funding for three more years, but the price was high. The new act temporarily prohibited the FTC from acting against advertising that is only "unfair" but not deceptive or misleading. Responding in part to the industry's complaints and in part to the Supreme Court's rulings extending First Amendment protection to advertising, Congress declared that FTC actions should not be aimed at truthful advertising.

In addition, the 1980 act halted the FTC proceeding on children's television until the commission published a new specific proposal aimed only at "deceptive" advertising, and ordered the FTC to publish the text of every proposed new rule at the start of the rulemaking proceeding. The FTC staff eventually terminated its study of advertising aimed at children in 1981 without recommending any formal action to the commission.

The 1980 act specifically set aside the FTC's actions involving morticians and agricultural cooperatives such as Sunkist Growers. Moreover, the commission was ordered to give Congress advance notice of new proposed rules. The 1980 law also declared that Congress would have the power to veto future FTC regulations. Finally, the FTC was ordered to reduce the paperwork burden it had imposed on businesses and to stop trying to invalidate businesses' trademarks.

Taken as a whole, these revisions constitute a drastic curtailment of the Federal Trade Commission's power. Business interests lobbied heavily in Congress to harness the FTC, and their campaign happened to fit in with the mood of the times. Certainly popular distaste for government regulation was a factor in Ronald Reagan's decisive victory in the 1980 presidential election.

FTC Chairman Miller, appointed soon after Reagan took office, pledged to reverse many of the commission's policies of the 1970s. Miller, for instance, urged Congress to retain the 1980 FTC Improvement Act's ban on FTC actions against advertising that was merely "unfair" and not deceptive.

During the early 1980s Congress again debated the merits of the Unfairness Doctrine but was unable to agree on any long-term solution. Thus, Congress authorized the FTC to continue operating under a "continuing resolution" that merely provided funding for the agency. At this writing, Congress still had not decided whether to reinstate the commission's power to act against "unfair" advertising or to heed FTC Chairman Miller's request and permanently eliminate the Unfairness Doctrine.

Congress was also deadlocked over the question of allowing the FTC to regulate advertising practices by doctors, dentists, and other professionals. The commission had been acting against alleged abuses in these professions in the 1970s, but in 1982 and 1983 the American Medical Association and other groups of professionals were lobbying Congress to curtail the FTC's authority to regulate them. Consumer groups were lobbying on the other side of this issue.

Congress first exercised its newly created power to veto FTC regulations in 1982, overturning the FTC's long-awaited rules requiring dealers to disclose known defects in used cars. However, later that year a federal appellate court ruled that Congress did not have the right to give itself this veto power. In 1983, the Supreme Court agreed, ruling in an unrelated case: *Immigration and Naturalization Service v. Chadha* (103 S.Ct. 2764). With this one ruling, the high court invalidated some 200 different laws that gave Congress the power to veto actions taken by agencies in the executive branch of the federal government.

Thus, the role of the Federal Trade Commission was a subject of Congressional debate as this book went to press. Just about everyone in Congress agreed that the FTC should continue to have the enforcement tools it needs to act against false and misleading advertising. However, there was no such consensus regarding the Unfairness Doctrine or the commission's authority to act against alleged abuses in the professions.

Other Federal Regulators

Although the Federal Trade Commission has the primary responsibility for regulating advertising on the federal level, a number of other federal agencies also have responsibilities in this general area.

Under the Food, Drug and Cosmetic Act of 1938, the Food and Drug Administration is responsible for assuring the purity and safety of foods, drugs, and cosmetics. One of the FDA's major duties is to act against false and fraudulent packaging and labeling practices. In this respect, its duties overlap those of the FTC, which is empowered to act against false food, drug, and cosmetic advertising. The two agencies generally cooperate in sharing their regulatory responsibilities, with the FTC mainly enforcing the rules on advertising while the FDA enforces the labeling requirements.

The Federal Communications Commission also has authority in the advertising area, although much of it is indirect, derived from the FCC's licensing powers. For many years the FCC had specific guidelines that limited the amount of advertising a broadcaster could carry without risking special scrutiny at license renewal time.

In the early 1980s those guidelines were deleted as part of a comprehensive deregulation package (see Chapter 11). The FCC still has the right to consider the quantity and quality of advertising when it renews broadcast licenses, but there are no longer any specific quotas for broadcasters to follow. In practice, most broadcasters carry less advertising than the old FCC guidelines permitted, anyway.

The FCC also has several other rules that affect broadcast advertising, perhaps the most notable being regulations requiring sponsorship identification.

Another federal agency with authority over some advertising is the Securities and Exchange Commission. As noted in Chapter Nine, the SEC is responsible for preventing the release of incomplete or fraudulent information about corporations whose stock is publicly traded. Thus, the SEC has responsibility for advertising regarding offerings of stock and certain other investment advertising. The agency exercises its authority by acting mainly against the corporation whose advertising is judged false, often by canceling stock offerings. It requires those who advertise stock offerings to make it clear that a media ad is neither an offer to sell nor a solicitation of an offer to buy, since media ads don't lend themselves to the highly detailed reporting of corporate information that is required. That information is provided in a prospectus.

The U.S. Postal Service also has the authority to oversee advertising, especially that of mail-order businesses. If the post office decides a particular advertisement is fraudulent, it has the power to halt all mail addressed to the advertiser, stamp it "fraudulent," and return it to the sender. The post office has an administrative procedure for determining that a business is engaging in mail fraud; its decisions may be appealed to the federal courts.

These federal agencies do exercise control over advertising content, but their collective impact on mass media advertising is small compared to that of the Federal Trade Commission.

STATE ADVERTISING REGULATION

Virtually all states also have laws empowering their officials to act against advertising fraud. At least 45 states have adopted various versions of what has been known as the "Printer's Ink Statute," an anti-advertising-fraud law first proposed in *Printer's Ink* magazine in 1911.

The statute makes advertising fraud a crime, and gives state and local prosecutors the responsibility for enforcement. Because it is a criminal law that must be enforced by officials who often feel they have more serious crimes to worry about, enforcement has traditionally been lax.

Recognizing the shortcomings of this law, about half the states have enacted other laws giving consumers and competitors civil remedies in instances of advertising fraud. In addition, some states have given local and state prosecutors civil enforcement responsibilities much like those the FTC Act gave to the Federal Trade Commission. In a few other states, separate agencies have enforcement responsibilities.

Some of these state laws are strong and vigorously enforced. But in other places, local advertising fraud is largely overlooked. The major problem with these state advertising laws has always been inconsistent enforcement.

Nevertheless, anyone who prepares, publishes, or broadcasts advertisements should be familiar with the local laws on false or misleading advertising. If you plan an advertising career, you should look up your state's laws on the subject. To check your state's annotated codes or statutes, look in the index volumes under "advertising" or perhaps "unfair trade practices."

SELF-REGULATION

Another very important influence on the content of advertising is self-regulation, the voluntary systems the advertising industry and the media have developed to prevent the release of false and distasteful advertising.

In 1971, four major advertising and business groups united to form an organization known as the National Advertising Review Board. The board is a cooperative venture of the American Association of Advertising Agencies, the American Advertising Federation, the Association of National Advertisers, and the Council of Better Business Bureaus.

The NARB is a review board composed of 30 representatives of national advertisers, 10 ad agency representatives, and 10 non-industry or public representatives. It accepts complaints about advertising and asks advertisers to substantiate their ad claims. The board asks advertisers to change their ads if they cannot be substantiated. If they refuse, the board is authorized to present its findings to a suitable government enforcement agency, but that is almost never necessary.

Although the NARB's main tools are persuasion and peer pressure, it has dealt with hundreds of questionable advertisements and represents an excellent example of an industry endeavoring to keep its own house in order without government involvement.

For many years, the National Association of Broadcasters maintained similar voluntary codes for radio and television advertising and programming practices. Broadcasters who subscribed to these codes were allowed to display a "seal of good practice." As of 1980, about 4,500 television and radio broadcasters were code subscribers.

The NAB codes set limits on the number of commercials broadcasters were to carry, and also set standards for the content of both advertising and non-advertising materials. The NAB "Code Authority" and "Code Board" enforced these rules, although their only real enforcement power was the ability to prevent violators from using the "seal of good practice."

However, in 1979 the U.S. Justice Department filed an antitrust lawsuit against the NAB, charging that the codes constituted a restraint of trade. By placing limits on the number of commercials and the amount of commercial time that would be permitted, the NAB codes artificially forced up ad rates, the government contended.

After losing the case in federal district court, the NAB signed a consent decree in 1982, agreeing to drop many of the provisions of the television code. To avoid any further potential antitrust liability, the NAB then decided to eliminate its codes altogether and to disband the Code Authority and Code Board.

Thus, the broadcast industry's major attempt at self-regulation fell victim to a government antitrust lawsuit. As Chapter 13 explains, whenever competitors get together and agree to do anything that might limit competition, they risk running afoul of the nation's antitrust laws—no matter how noble their intentions.

In the print media, there is no industry-wide code of advertising practices. Various organizations have adopted codes of ethics, but they generally deal with editorial matters, not advertising. However, many major newspapers have their own policies on advertising acceptability, and these policies are very influential. The *New York Times* not only has an advertising acceptability policy but also a Department of Advertising Acceptability, which reviews ads prior to publication. That department independently checks advertising claims and bars future ads from those found to have violated the company's standards.

The *New York Times* prohibits ads considered in bad taste, ads proposing marriage, and attacks on individuals or competing products, among others.

Many newspapers prohibit advertising by theaters showing X-rated pictures, a policy that has survived a number of court challenges. The *Los Angeles Times* has such a policy, and has successfully defended lawsuits by movie exhibitors who contended it violated everything from the First Amendment to antitrust laws. Even though theater owners were able to show that a number of other Southern California newspapers banned X-rated movie ads as soon as the *Times* did it, they were never able to convince a court that this constituted any sort of conspiracy to violate antitrust laws (see *Adult Film Association v. Times Mirror*, 97 Cal.App.3d 77, 1979).

AD RATES AND THE LAW

A new legal challenge that confronted the media in recent years was the contention of various organizations including the Federal Trade Commission that discriminatory advertising rates are unlawful.

It is a virtually universal practice in the print and broadcast media to charge different rates for different kinds of ads. Newspapers, for instance, typically have one rate for local advertisers and a different rate (usually much higher) for national advertisers. In addition, most papers grant quantity discounts to high-volume advertisers.

In 1977 the Federal Trade Commission initiated a legal action to stop the *Los Angeles Times* from granting quantity discounts to large advertisers. The FTC contended the policy violated both the FTC Act and the Robinson-Patman Act, a federal law against charging different prices for the same commodity where the result is a restraint of trade. The newspaper defended its differential ad rates before an adminstrative law judge in 1978, and the judge dismissed the FTC's complaint, ruling that the paper's ad rate structure didn't violate the law. The FTC overruled the judge and reinstated the action.

But then an amazing series of events transpired. In 1980 the *Times* and the FTC reached agreement on a consent order under which the paper would reduce its volume discounts substantially. The *Times* was roundly criticized for signing this agreement, which many other publishers and broadcasters feared might jeopardize their own volume discount policies. Then the *Times* had second thoughts, disavowed the agreement, and started working to get it set aside.

Sure enough, before anyone in the industry could get too upset about the *Times* allegedly selling out, the FTC itself rescued the paper from its critics: in 1982 the commission (which by this time included two new members who disagreed with the earlier decision) simply dropped the whole proceeding and tossed out the proposed settlement. As a result, the *Times* and everyone else was free to continue giving volume discounts without the FTC trying to stop the practice.

Meanwhile, a federal appellate court addressed much the same issue in a private antitrust lawsuit against *Time* magazine, the *New York Times,* and several major ad agencies. In that case (*Ambook v. Time, Inc.,* 612 F.2d 604, 2nd cir. 1979), the court said the Robinson-Patman Act simply doesn't apply to advertising rates. Thus, the court said, there's nothing illegal under that law about granting quantity discounts. In so ruling, the court took note of the FTC's action against the *Los Angeles Times,* and said the FTC's interpretation of the Robinson-Patman Act was wrong.

SPECIFIC LIMITATIONS ON CONTENT

In addition to the laws prohibiting fraudulent and monopolistic advertising, there are a variety of federal and state laws prohibiting specific kinds of advertising content.

Many states still have laws on their books forbidding abortion or contraceptive advertising. In view of the Supreme Court's commercial speech decisions, such laws are unconstitutional, but any advertiser who finds himself being prosecuted for violating that sort of law has to be prepared to convince a court of the law's unconstitutionality.

A much more serious problem for advertisers is state and federal laws that prohibit "lottery" advertising. As the term is defined in law, a lottery is any game of chance where three elements are all present: (1) a valuable prize; (2) determination of the winner by chance; and (3) payment of a consideration as a requirement to participate. Significantly, consideration can be many things besides money, such as buying a product.

If those elements are present, you have a lottery. A federal law bars materials advertising or promoting lotteries from the U.S. mail. That affects virtually all newspapers and magazines, since a few copies of nearly every publication are mailed. The federal law also prohibits broadcasting ads or other information that would promote a lottery. The provisions applying to both the print and broadcast media exempt publicity about state-run gambling systems. Also exempted, of course, is news coverage of gambling (e.g., stories about local residents who are big winners).

In addition to these federal laws, a number of states have statutory provisions prohibiting ads that promote gambling.

Other miscellaneous prohibitions on specific advertising content are scattered around the state and federal laws. For instance, federal law prohibits ads featuring either U.S. currency or the American flag, although either may appear incidentally in the background in an ad. Also, it is unlawful to use the name of the Federal Bureau of Investigation for advertising purposes.

In addition, don't overlook the rules on the commercial use of any person's name or likeness in an advertisement, described under the "Right of Publicity" in Chapter Five.

Another specific advertising content rule that is sometimes misunderstood is the federal Truth-in-Lending Act. "Regulation Z," adopted by the Federal Reserve Board to implement this act, requires advertisers to disclose a number of details about credit arrangements if the terms are mentioned at all in an ad. For instance, any quotation of an interest rate must include a declaration of the "annual percentage rate" (APR). Similarly, an ad that quotes a down payment or monthly payment must also disclose additional details of the financing: you cannot merely say a particular car sells for "$500 down and $150 a month" without disclosing the other terms and the APR. Real estate and auto ads often fail to comply with Regulation Z, and the FTC occasionally launches well publicized campaigns to force advertisers to obey the law.

In the 1980s there were several lawsuits challenging the constitutionality of still another kind of advertising content restriction: state laws forbidding alcoholic beverage advertising. A number of states—though a minority—have such laws. In view of the Supreme Court's decisions on the First Amendment and commercial speech, are such laws unconstitutional? If there is a constitutional right to advertise such things as abortions, contraceptives and prescription drugs, is there also a First Amendment right to advertise liquor?

In 1983, two different federal appellate courts addressed this issue, and both ultimately ruled that state laws banning liquor advertising were not unconstitutional. In *Capital Cities Cable v. Crisp* (699 F.2d 490), a case later reversed by the Supreme Court on non-constitutional grounds (see Chapter 11), the tenth circuit U.S. Court of Appeals upheld Oklahoma's law against liquor advertising. The court said it did not violate the First Amendment.

At almost the same time, the fifth circuit Court of Appeals ruled in just the opposite way on this issue, but then changed its mind. In two cases that were eventually combined (*Dunagin v. Oxford* and *Lamar Outdoor Advertising v. Mississippi Tax Commission*, 718 F.2d 738, 1983), the fifth circuit initially ruled that Mississippi's laws against liquor advertising violated the First Amendment.

However, this court then reconsidered and heard the case "en banc" (i.e., with all judges on the court rather than the usual panel of three deciding the case). The court reversed itself and held that the Mississippi law did not violate the First Amendment. That brought the fifth circuit Court of Appeals into agreement with the tenth circuit's *Capital Cities* ruling: both courts were saying that laws against liquor advertising are not unconstitutional.

In the *Dunagin* case the appellate court used the test of Constitutionality formulated by the Supreme Court in the *Central Hudson* and *Consolidated Edison* cases. The court had no trouble deciding that a state has a "substantial interest" in protecting the health and safety of its citizens, and that alcohol can be injurious to health and safety. Then the court considered whether laws against liquor advertising directly advance that interest. The court said:

It is beyond our ability to understand why huge sums of money would be devoted to the promotion of sales of liquor without expected results, or continued results. . . . It is total sales, profits, that pay the advertiser; and dollars go into advertising only if they produce sales. (718 F.2d at 749)

In short, the Court of Appeals concluded that state laws against liquor advertising further a legitimate state goal and are therefore Constitutional, even if restrictions on many other kinds of advertising are not. In 1984, the Supreme Court declined to review this decision.

Although state laws restricting liquor advertising may not be unconstitutional, don't forget that they may still be invalid if they conflict with federal laws or FCC rules. As Chapter 11 explains, when the Supreme Court heard the *Capital Cities* case, it did not rule on the First Amendment question inherent in laws forbidding liquor advertising, but the high court did overturn the Oklahoma law as inconsistent with the federal rules governing cable television.

Perhaps the key difference between the Oklahoma law (which the Supreme Court overturned on federal preemption grounds) and the Mississippi law (which the high court chose not to review) was that the Oklahoma law required cable systems to delete liquor ads from television signals imported from other states. The Mississippi law, on the other hand, did not apply to liquor advertising that was carried on out-of-state media.

The validity of other state and local laws banning liquor advertising may be open to question at this point, depending on their affect on the media in other states and whether they conflict with federal regulatory policies. The status of laws against liquor advertising is a complicated—and unresolved—issue.

These, then, are some of the special legal problems of advertising. Obviously, this is a rapidly changing field: if you anticipate an advertising career, you should be regularly reading one or more of the trade journals in your specialty area to stay up to date. Such publications as *Advertising Age*, *Editor and Publisher*, and *Broadcasting* regularly cover new developments in the regulation of advertising.

A Summary of Advertising Regulation

IS ADVERTISING PROTECTED BY THE FIRST AMENDMENT?

Until 1975 it would have been safe to say that "commercial speech" was not generally protected by the First Amendment. However, in a dramatic series of decisions since then, the Supreme Court extended Constitutional protection to both commercial speech and non-commercial corporate speech.

IS MEDIA LAW GENERALLY APPLICABLE TO ADVERTISING?

Advertising has its own unique body of law, but the general rules of media law also apply to advertising. An advertisement may produce a lawsuit for libel, invasion of privacy, commercial misappropriation, copyright infringement or trademark infringement, for instance.

DO ADVERTISERS HAVE A RIGHT OF ACCESS TO THE MEDIA?

Generally, there is no right of access to the media. A publisher or broadcaster may accept or reject advertising as he pleases, unless the acceptances or rejections fall into a pattern of unfair or monopolistic business practices. However, broadcasters (but not newspaper or magazine publishers) must sell advertising to federal election candidates, and sometimes state-run media are required to grant advertising access.

WHO REGULATES ADVERTISING CONTENT AND WHY?

The most important regulatory agency for advertising is the Federal Trade Commission. To protect the public from false and misleading advertising, the FTC closely monitors major advertisers and acts against practices it considers improper. Until 1980, the FTC also had the authority to prohibit advertising that was "unfair" although not false or misleading.

HOW DOES THE FTC ENFORCE ITS REGULATIONS?

The FTC has a variety of enforcement tools, including publicity, informal letters of compliance, consent decrees, and cease and desist decrees. The FTC may require substantiation of an advertising claim, and it may order corrective advertising if an ad has been particularly false or misleading.

DOES ANYONE ELSE REGULATE ADVERTISING?

A number of other federal agencies have authority over certain kinds of advertising. Also, all 50 states have statutory laws prohibiting fraudulent business practices; some states vigorously enforce these laws against false advertisers, but others are less diligent. The advertising industry has an elaborate system of self-regulation as well.

13

THE MASS MEDIA AND MONOPOLY

Who owns America's mass media? Is local ownership better than chain ownership? Does the public suffer when the same person or company owns several newspapers, magazines, radio stations, television stations, and cable systems—or a combination of these?

Ever since William Randolph Hearst and the Scripps family began building the nation's first newspaper chains nearly 100 years ago, these have been controversial questions. Media critics have viewed the ongoing trend toward centralized ownership of the mass media as a threat to journalistic freedom. Regardless of how well intentioned the management of a large chain may be, central ownership deprives the media of the independence that is so vital in a democracy, some critics say. Others, of course, have defended the growing chain ownership of the mass media, pointing to the efforts of many owners to provide good management and public service to each community they serve.

However, even the defenders of multi-media ownership concede that abuses have occurred, and government agencies have sometimes acted to correct these abuses. The antitrust division of the U.S. Justice Department, for instance, has often acted against monopolistic business practices in the mass media. And at times the Federal Communications Commission has acted to limit both chain ownership in broadcasting and cross ownership of print and broadcast media.

For many years, the way a company conducted its business was no concern of the federal government, but that changed in the late 1800s. Serious government regulation of monopolistic business practices began with the Sherman Act, enacted in 1890 to combat the abuses that were rampant in the post-Civil War era of industrialization. The Sherman Act is the nation's pioneering *antitrust* law; it forbids a wide variety of "contracts, combinations. . . or conspiracies in restraint of trade or commerce."

In 1914 the Clayton Act was adopted, forbidding certain other business practices and expanding the federal government's antitrust enforcement powers. This law was strengthened in 1950 by the addition of the Celler-Kefauver Act, which prohibits one company from buying out a competitor where the result is more monopoly and less competition. Thus, business ownership as well as business practices have come under federal regulation.

Of the many business practices banned by these antitrust laws, a few should be specifically noted. For instance, price fixing and profit pooling are prohibited. That means it is generally unlawful for competing companies to enter an agreement either to share profits and charge non-competitive prices. Rival companies are supposed to keep each others' prices low by competing. They're not supposed to conspire to avoid price competition.

In addition, most tying arrangements and boycotts are illegal. A tying arrangement involves forcing customers to buy something they may not want in order to get something they do want and cannot readily get elsewhere. Boycotts take many forms, but one common type is a refusal to do business with a person or a company as a means of coercing that person or company to do something he wouldn't otherwise be willing to do.

Federal antitrust laws establish three different kinds of legal actions to be used against businesses that engage in monopolistic practices: (1) criminal prosecutions by the U.S. Justice Department to punish wrongdoers; (2) civil actions by the Justice Department to halt monopolistic business practices; and (3) civil actions for "treble damages" by private individuals or other businesses that may have been injured by these practices. "Treble damages" means the victim of monopolistic business practices is entitled to recover three times his or her actual losses. This very strong remedy is intended to discourage violations of the antitrust laws.

All of these are provisions of *federal* antitrust laws. They apply to businesses engaged in interstate commerce and to local businesses whose activities in some way affect interstate commerce. The U.S. Justice Department maintains a large antitrust division to enforce these laws. However, where purely local businesses are involved, the jurisdiction over antitrust matters falls to the 50 states, all of which have at least some laws prohibiting monopolistic business practices within their borders.

All of this may be well and good, but don't these government actions violate the First Amendment when directed against the mass media? Aren't publishers and broadcasters protected from government interference in their business affairs?

For about 150 years, Congress and the federal bureaucracy did assume the business practices of the media were none of their concern, but that all changed in the New Deal era. In that period at least three factors led to a change in policy: the economic depression of the 1930s, the formation of a labor union for journalists, and the Roosevelt administration's willingness to vigorously pursue violations of the law that past administrations had been more inclined to ignore. By 1945, the U.S. Supreme Court had twice ruled that the business practices of the mass media were very much within the government's purview. Both of these pioneering cases involved the Associated Press, the nation's largest news wire service.

MEDIA BUSINESS PRACTICES AND THE SUPREME COURT

The U.S. Supreme Court ruled that the First Amendment does not exempt the mass media from regulations that apply to other industries in a 1937 case involving labor laws, *AP v. National Labor Relations Board* (301 U.S. 130). The case arose when an Associated Press writer was fired for engaging in union organizing activities on behalf of the American Newspaper Guild. The guild complained to the NLRB, which found the AP guilty of an unfair labor practice. The wire service appealed the NLRB ruling, and the Supreme Court affirmed it, brushing aside the AP's argument that union activity was a threat to the agency's editorial freedom. The court said:

> The (National Labor Relations) act does not compel (AP) to employ any one; it does not require that (AP) retain in its employ an incompetent editor or one who fails to faithfully edit the news to reflect the facts without bias or prejudice. The act permits a discharge for any reason other than union activity or agitation for collective bargaining with employees.

Later in its opinion, the court added:

> The business of the Associated Press is not immune from regulation because it is an agency of the press. The publisher of a newspaper has no special immunity from the application of general laws. He has no special privilege to invade the rights and liberties of others.

A few years later, the Supreme Court again ruled against the AP's claims of First Amendment exemption from government regulation in a landmark case involving antitrust law, *Associated Press v. U.S.* (326 U.S. 1, 1945).

This case arose when the *Chicago Sun*'s application for AP membership was vetoed by its primary competitor, the *Chicago Tribune*. Under the AP's bylaws, each member was given what amounted to blackball privileges to prevent competitors from joining the wire service and gaining access to its worldwide news coverage. This policy had been in effect for nearly 100 years, but when it was used by such a prominent newspaper to blackball a well-known competitor, it invited government scrutiny.

The U.S. Justice Department challenged the exclusion of the *Chicago Sun* from AP membership as a violation of federal antitrust laws. The Justice Department pointed out that it was very easy for newspapers that did not directly compete with an AP member to join the organization. However, any potential competitor of an AP member was forced not only to get past the competitor's potential veto but also to pay a very large sum of money to join. Without joining the organization, a paper could not get AP news, since it was also against the bylaws to provide AP news to a non-member.

The case reached the Supreme Court, which ruled that these bylaw provisions indeed violated antitrust law. The high court emphasized that the First Amendment does not exempt the media from obeying laws regulating business practices:

> The fact that the publisher handles news while others (engaged in business) handle goods does not. . .afford the publisher a peculiar constitutional sanctuary in which he can with impunity violate laws regarding his business practices.

Moreover, the court said, what the AP was doing amounted to a denial of the freedom to publish for many would-be members. Its bylaws, far from furthering the goal of freedom of the press, actually inhibited freedom of the press:

> Freedom to publish means freedom for all and not for some. Freedom to publish is guaranteed by the Constitution, but freedom to combine to keep others from publishing is not. Freedom of the press from governmental interference under the First Amendment does not sanction repression of that freedom by private interests.

Once the Supreme Court had twice ruled against the Associated Press on questions involving the government's right to regulate its business practices, the Justice Department brought actions against a number of newspaper publishers who appeared to be violating federal antitrust laws.

NEWSPAPER ANTITRUST CASES

In the 1950s, two antitrust cases involving newspapers reached the U.S. Supreme Court, while several others were decided by lower federal courts.

The first of these cases involved a newspaper accused of refusing to accept advertising from anyone who placed advertising with a local radio station. The case, *Lorain Journal Company v. U.S.* (342 U.S. 143, 1951), resulted in a unanimous Supreme Court ruling in favor of the government and against the publisher. Because the paper reached almost every home in its market area, its threat to refuse advertising from those who advertised on the radio station was a viable one: many merchants needed to advertise in the paper because there was no other way to reach a lot of their customers.

Defending its policies in court, the newspaper cited not only the First Amendment but also the well-recognized principle that a publisher has a right to refuse advertising. The Supreme Court dismissed these arguments, pointing out that antitrust law creates an exception to the publisher's right to refuse advertising. When the refusal to accept advertising is based on a desire to monopolize commerce, that right must give way to the right of other businesses to be free of monopolistic competition, the court said. A lower court injunction against the paper's business practices was affirmed, as was an unusual and slightly humiliating order that the newspaper publish a notice of the ruling every week for six months.

A decade later, the broadcaster that the *Lorain Journal* had tried to drive out of business won a treble damage civil suit under federal antitrust law (*Elyria Lorain Broadcasting v. Lorain Journal*, 298 F.2d 356, 6th cir. 1961), thus recovering three times its losses that resulted from the paper's monopolistic practices.

However, a newspaper publisher fared better in another antitrust lawsuit that reached the Supreme Court in the 1950s, *Times-Picayune v. U.S.* (345 U.S. 594, 1953). In that case, the Justice Department challenged a tying arrangement in which an advertiser had to buy space in an evening paper, the *New Orleans States*, in order to get space in the same company's morning paper, the *New Orleans Times-Picayune*. A competing evening paper, the *New Orleans Item*, was the alleged victim in this tying arrangement.

When the case reached the Supreme Court, the justices voted 5-4 in the Times-Picayune Company's favor. The majority sympathized with the Justice Department's contention that this was a tying arrangement, but said there was insufficient evidence of injury to the other paper to justify an antitrust action in this particular instance. This was true because the *Item* was profitable. In addition, the *Item* was gaining in ad revenue and actually carrying more advertising than its evening competitor, the Times-Picayune company's *States*. In addition, the majority refused to view the *Times-Picayune* as a sufficiently "dominant" product for an unlawful tying arrangement to be effective. In short, the Justice Department failed to prove its case.

Was the Supreme Court right in this decision? Perhaps, but only a few years later the *Item* did fall upon hard times and was taken over by the Times-Picayune Company, forming the *New Orleans States-Item*.

Still another antitrust action against a newspaper arose in the 1950s, one that is remembered because it illustrates all three kinds of antitrust lawsuits permitted under federal law. The case, *U.S. v. Kansas City Star* (240 F.2d 643, 8th cir. 1957), resulted from a variety of questionable practices by the employee-owned Star Corporation, the publisher of Kansas City's only morning and evening daily newspapers and also owner of the leading network-affiliated radio and television stations in town. (A competing daily paper had gone bankrupt before these lawsuits were completed.)

The company engaged in several monopolistic practices. For example, advertisers and subscribers had to buy a combination ad or subscription in both the morning *Times* and afternoon *Star* to get either one. You couldn't advertise in (or subscribe to) just one. In addition, some advertisers who also bought space in the competing paper before it failed were threatened with the cancellation of their ads in the Star-owned papers. Also, some advertisers were forced to buy ads in the *Times* and *Star* to get advertising on the company's radio and TV stations. In one case, a business partly owned by a major league baseball player was threatened with a blackout of news about the player on the sports pages if the business didn't discontinue its advertising in the competing paper.

Overall, it was a flagrant example of abuses by an ownership that wielded too much influence in one city. Critics of the situation suggested that being employee-owned doesn't necessarily make a newspaper more ethical than it might be if controlled by a huge out-of-town chain. Other observers saw irony in the fact that a newspaper founded by one of the most public-spirited publishers of the late 1800s—the great William Rockhill Nelson—would stoop to these depths. The *Star* gained its position of dominance because of Nelson's commitment to his community, only to abuse its power after the founder's death in 1915.

Whatever the *Star's* distinguished past, the Justice Department took an unsentimental look at the present and filed both criminal and civil antitrust lawsuits. The Justice Department sought criminal sanctions against the corporation and some of its executives in addition to a civil order to halt the unlawful practices. A federal court of appeals affirmed criminal convictions of the corporation and the advertising manager in 1957. Shortly later, the company settled the civil suit by agreeing to sell off its radio and TV stations and to stop forcing advertisers to buy space in both papers to get space in either one.

Meanwhile, a variety of private treble damage civil suits were filed against the embattled company. The company eventually settled most of these lawsuits and returned to doing business more in the fashion founding publisher Nelson had in mind. An interesting footnote to this complex litigation is that, some two decades later, the employee owners sold the Star Corporation to Capital Cities Communications (a large media conglomerate) for $115 million, ending one of the last large-scale experiments with employee ownership in American journalism.

An antitrust lawsuit of another sort resulted in the mid-1960s when the Times-Mirror Corporation, publisher of the *Los Angeles Times*, purchased one of the last family-owned daily newspapers in Southern California, the *San Bernardino Sun-Telegram*. The Justice Department sued to force Times-Mirror to resell the *Sun* on the ground that its purchase by Times-Mirror substantially lessened competition in San Bernardino County. The city of San Bernardino is about 60 miles east of downtown Los Angeles and is the county seat of the largest county in America.

In a federal district court proceeding, the Justice Department showed that the only real competition the Sun Company had in much of that huge county came from the *Times*. Moreover, several other papers in the county either ceased daily publication or were sold to chains at about the same time. The court ruled that the *Sun's* purchase violated federal antitrust law and ordered Times-Mirror to resell the paper. The judge's decision was affirmed without opinion by the U.S. Supreme Court in 1968 (*Times-Mirror v. U.S.*, 390 U.S. 712).

In compliance with this court decision, Times-Mirror sold the Sun Company to the Gannett Corporation, a large newspaper chain then head-quartered in Rochester, New York. While Gannett owned far more newspapers than Times-Mirror, it had none in Southern California. Thus, this sale did not violate the law against acquisitions that tend to lessen competition.

This entire sequence of events disturbed observers of Southern California journalism for two reasons. First, in the name of preventing monopolies, the Justice Department forced an absentee owner 60 miles away to sell out to an absentee owner 2,500 miles away. Moreover, at that time Times-Mirror also owned the *Orange Coast Daily Pilot*, another suburban daily even closer to Los Angeles and even more directly in competition with the *Times* than the *San Bernardino Sun.* Certainly Times-Mirror's track record with the *Daily Pilot* had been a good one in terms of both community service and ethical business practices. Perhaps the Justice Department would have opposed Times-Mirror's acquisition of the *Daily Pilot* too, had it not happened before such acquisitions were given close government scrutiny.

Nevertheless, antitrust law is clear on this point: it's perfectly legal to buy newspapers in various markets all over America, but it isn't legal to buy nearby newspapers in overlapping markets. The fact that a management close to home may be better able to meet community needs than one thousands of miles away complicates the ethical issues here, but it doesn't change the law.

JOINT OPERATING AGREEMENTS

The late 1960s also produced another Supreme Court decision on antitrust law that disturbed many publishers and media critics. The case, *U.S. v. Citizen Publishing Co.* (394 U.S. 131, 1969), stemmed from a kind of cooperative arrangement between once-competing publishers that had become commonplace. Under a "joint operating agreement," as these arrangements are called, two newspaper publishers in the same town merge many of their business and printing operations but maintain separate editorial staffs so the two papers retain separate identities. The objective, of course, is to cut costs by only maintaining one expensive newspaper printing plant, for instance, instead of two. Obviously, it works best if one of the papers is a morning paper and the other an afternoon paper, so scheduling conflicts can be minimized. These arrangements often also include joint advertising sales, with advertisers offered a package deal and a discount if they place ads in both papers.

Such an agreement had existed between the *Tucson (Ariz.) Daily Citizen* and the *Arizona Daily Star* since 1940. Not only did it involve a merger of production, advertising, and circulation operations of the two papers, but it also involved profit pooling. In the mid-1960s, the *Star* appeared to be in financial difficulty, but a purchase offer from a large newspaper chain was rejected. Shortly later, the owners of the *Citizen* organized a new company and bought the *Star*. As a result of this series of events, the once-independent news department of the *Star* now found itself working for the owners of the *Citizen*.

The U.S. Justice Department challenged not only the change of ownership but the entire joint operating agreement as a violation of antitrust law. The case reached the U.S. Supreme Court in 1969, and the Supreme Court agreed that much of this cooperative arrangement was illegal. Justice William O. Douglas, writing for the court, said the only defense for acquisition of the *Star* by the *Citizen* was the "Failing Company Doctrine," which allows a company to buy out a competitor on the brink of bankruptcy. The rationale for this judicially created exception to antitrust law is that the rival company's failure would lessen competition anyway. However, Douglas said the Failing Company Doctrine didn't apply here because neither paper was failing at the time the joint operating agreement was initiated.

The decision was shocking to publishers all over America, because joint operating agreements were in force in 22 cities, involving 44 daily newspapers. If this decision were left intact, many other joint operating agreements would also be illegal. Publishers said many of the participating newspapers would be forced to shut down because they could not afford to operate a complete business and printing facility on their own.

The American Newspaper Publishers Association, the major trade organization for the newspaper industry, went to work lobbying for a change in antitrust laws to legalize joint operating agreements. Congress obliged in 1970 with the *Newspaper Preservation Act*. Basically, this law legalized the 22 existing joint operating agreements, including the one in Tucson. In effect, Congress revised the law to overrule the Supreme Court's interpretation of it.

In addition to protecting the existing joint operating agreements, the Newspaper Preservation Act authorized the Justice Department to approve new agreements when it could be shown that at least one of the newspapers involved would fail without a joint operating agreement.

The Newspaper Preservation Act was bitterly opposed by the Justice Department, which contended it would allow publishers to enter anti-competitive arrangements even when they could survive on their own. Publishers of small newspapers also opposed it, fearing that the large papers in their area would offer joint advertising packages so attractive the smaller papers would be squeezed out of the marketplace. Also, labor unions in the newspaper field opposed the act because it authorized consolidations that would certainly eliminate jobs. Nevertheless, the act quickly moved through Congress and was signed by President Nixon.

Once enacted, the Newspaper Preservation Act was challenged on Constitutional grounds by a small San Francisco newspaper, the *Bay Guardian*. This muckraking monthly contended that the joint operating agreement between the *San Francisco Chronicle* and *San Francisco Examiner* resulted in an unconstitutional infringement of its First Amendment rights by encouraging a monopoly that made it difficult for other papers to operate.

In a 1972 decision, a federal district judge rejected the *Guardian*'s arguments, affirming the constitutionality of the Newspaper Preservation Act (*Bay Guardian Co. v. Chronicle Publishing Co.*, 344 F.Supp. 1155). However, the lawsuit against the San Francisco papers continued on other grounds, and was eventually settled for an amount in excess of $1 million.

In the years since its enactment, the Newspaper Preservation Act hasn't exactly produced an avalanche of applications for new joint operating agreements. In fact, the Justice Department approved only two such agreements during the 1970s, although a third pair of newspapers entered an agreement prior to receiving Justice Department approval.

The first application for a new joint operating agreement came in 1974, when the well-entrenched Anchorage (Alaska) *Times* and "failing" Anchorage *Daily News* asked permission to merge their non-editorial operations. The agreement was approved, but under it things got even worse for the *Daily News*: its circulation slipped to 12,000 (compared to 46,000 for the *Times*). Finally, the *Daily News* withdrew from the agreement, sued the *Times*, and sold a controlling interest to C. K. McClatchy, head of a strong newspaper chain in California. Taking over in early 1979, McClatchy poured money into the *Daily News*, modernizing and computerizing its operation. By 1980, its circulation was up to 30,000, while the *Times* had slipped to 44,000.

Whatever ultimately happens in Anchorage, for the time being it seemed clear that a joint operating agreement couldn't do for the town's "failing" newspaper what a good dose of American free enterprise could do.

In 1979 the Justice Department approved one more joint operating agreement, this one involving the "failing" *Cincinnati Post*, owned by the large Scripps-Howard chain, and the *Cincinnati Enquirer*, which was purchased during the approval process by the even bigger Gannett chain. Critics of the whole process wondered whether the *Post* was really failing or if perhaps two large chains simply saw a good way to cut their costs and enhance their long-term profit possibilities.

Meanwhile, a bizarre sequence of events unfolded in Chattanooga, Tenn., in 1980. The "failing" *Chattanooga Times* entered into a joint operating agreement with the *Chattanooga News-Free Press* without first securing the government's permission as required by the Newspaper Preservation Act. The two papers asked for Justice Department approval of their merger, but while the government was considering the issue, the *Times* abruptly fired 102 production employees, shut down its printing press, and in effect merged its printing operations with those of its crosstown competitor. After some embarrassing moments during which the Chattanooga publishers were chastised for their impatience, the Justice Department approved the Chattanooga joint operating agreement.

Perhaps the bitterest battle ever fought over a joint operating agreement unfolded in Seattle, Wash., during the early 1980s. The financially troubled *Seattle Post-Intelligencer* and the *Seattle Times* sought government permission to merge their non-editorial operations in 1981. Under their proposed arrangement, the *Times* would publish weekday afternoons and Saturday mornings. The *Post-Intelligencer* would publish weekday mornings, while the two papers would produce a joint Sunday edition.

The proposal drew strenuous protests from a coalition of suburban newspaper publishers, major retail advertisers, and employee groups, who contended the merger would result in price-fixing, excessively high ad rates, a decline in the editorial quality of both papers, and needless employee layoffs. Nevertheless, the plan was approved by Attorney General William French Smith on June 15, 1982. It was to go into effect shortly thereafter, but a federal judge granted a 60-day delay in the agreement's implementation so the opponents could challenge it in court.

In *Committee for an Independent P-I v. Hearst Corp.*, the foes of the merger won their case in federal district court, mainly because the Hearst Corporation, owner of the *P-I*, had not been willing to sell the paper to any of several qualified buyers who expressed an interest. Opponents of the plan contended that another owner could reorganize the paper and make it profitable as a fully separate newspaper.

However, in a 1983 decision, the ninth circuit U.S. Court of Appeals reversed the district court ruling, holding instead that it is not necessary to offer a failing newspaper for sale to justify a joint operating agreement. The ninth circuit said that Hearst had adequately proved that new management would not be successful in maintaining the paper as an independent entity. Thus, the Justice Department's decision approving the merger was valid (*Committee for an Independent P-I v. Hearst Corporation*, 704 F.2d 467).

In its decision—a key ruling on the right of two newspapers to merge under the Newspaper Preservation Act—the court said that when there is sufficient evidence that a paper will probably fail under any ownership, the owner need not sell the paper to qualify for a joint operating agreement.

After the ninth circuit Court of Appeals ruled against them, opponents of the Seattle merger took their case to the Supreme Court, which refused to hear the case, thus ending the legal battle over the Seattle joint operating agreement.

BROADCASTING, THE FCC, AND MONOPOLY OWNERSHIP

Just before the U.S. Justice Department challenged the Associated Press' exclusionary practices in the early 1940s, the Federal Communications Commission was taking a tough look at the way the networks dominated radio broadcasting in America. Technically, the FCC has no authority over antitrust matters, but as part of its licensing process the commission is empowered to consider all factors that affect the "public interest, convenience and necessity." Thus, the FCC has the right to scrutinize the business practices and ownership patterns of broadcast licensees.

By the late 1930s, the FCC didn't like what it saw in radio broadcasting. Some 97 percent of all night-time transmitter wattage was controlled by three networks, with the vast majority of the most powerful stations affiliated with either the National Broadcasting Company or the Columbia Broadcasting System. In fact, NBC operated two different networks, both of which had affiliates in many major cities.

Even more disturbing, the networks imposed strict contractual controls on their affiliates. For instance, network affiliates were not permitted to carry any programming from another network. Moreover, affiliates were locked into five-year contracts with the networks—something the FCC found alarming in view of the fact that broadcasters were then issued licenses to be on the air for only three years at a time. And the networks tied up virtually all of their affiliates' prime time programming. In addition, affiliates' rights to reject network programs were limited.

To end these abuses, the FCC issued a set of rules known as the "Chain Broadcasting Regulations" in 1941. These rules prohibited many of the questionable network practices. One provision was intended to force NBC to sell one of its two networks. NBC quickly took the FCC to court, charging that these new rules exceeded the FCC's authority and violated the First Amendment.

In *NBC v. U.S.* (319 U.S. 190), an important 1943 case that foreshadowed the *Associated Press v. U.S.* decision, the Supreme Court ruled against NBC on all grounds. The court said the First Amendment does not exempt broadcasters from government regulation of their business practices. Moreover, the court said, the FCC could properly issue rules to curb monopolistic network policies, despite the fact that enforcement of antitrust laws is beyond the commission's authority.

As a result of this decision, NBC had no choice but to sell one of its networks, so it sold the weaker one, the "Blue" network, later in 1943. That network became known as the American Broadcasting Company two years later, joining CBS and NBC to form the big three of broadcasting. The other radio network of the 1930s, the Mutual Broadcasting System, included a large number of affiliates, but most of them were in smaller markets. Mutual remained only a minor force in broadcasting.

In 1953 the FCC made its next major move against monopoly control of broadcasting: it issued new rules limiting the number of radio and television stations any one person or company could own. The FCC had taken steps toward limiting the number of licenses anyone could hold in a given community as early as 1940, but these new "Multiple Ownership Rules" had a far more significant impact on broadcasting. They limited each owner to a nationwide total of seven AM radio stations, seven FM radio stations, and seven television stations (only five of which could be in the VHF spectrum).

The new rule—which came to be known as the "Seven-Seven-Seven Rule" or the "Rule of Sevens"—quickly produced another challenge in court, and in a 1956 decision (*U.S. v. Storer Broadcasting Co.*, 351 U.S. 192) the Supreme Court again upheld the FCC's rulemaking authority.

The commission expanded these rules again in 1970 and 1971, acting to prevent new "duopoly" ownerships. (As the term is used by the FCC, duopoly means one person or firm owning more than one kind of broadcast station in the same market area.) The pre-1971 rules only prohibited one person or firm owning two or more stations of the same kind (e.g., two AM radio stations) in the same market. But under the new rules, the owner of a radio station would not be permitted to acquire a VHF television station in the same market, or vice versa. Existing duopolies were allowed to continue.

For a time the commission also enforced complex rules that restricted regional concentrations of broadcast ownership. In essence, these rules curbed the right of a broadcaster to own three stations in any service area if two were within 100 miles of the third. Even the FCC staff had trouble understanding and administering these rules, and there were few complaints when the commission abandoned them in 1984.

In 1975 the FCC adopted what were perhaps its most controversial rules on media ownership: the commission banned "cross-ownerships" between newspapers and radio or television stations in the same market. The FCC's rules did not require most existing multi-media owners to sell any of their properties, nor did they apply to cable television systems, but the rules did forbid daily newspaper owners from buying new broadcast properties in the same markets. Likewise, broadcast licensees were forbidden to buy daily newspapers in their market areas.

The FCC did require "divestiture" (selling of existing media properties) in 16 small communities where the owner of the only daily newspaper also owned the only television or radio station.

These rules stirred immediate criticism from all sides. Both broadcasters and newspaper publishers attacked the ban on new cross-media combinations. Consumer groups, meanwhile, attacked the FCC for not insisting on the breakup of many more existing cross-ownerships. Lawsuits were filed by both those who felt the FCC had gone too far and those who felt the FCC hadn't gone far enough.

When the resulting case, *FCC v. National Citizens Committee for Broadcasting* (436 U.S. 775, 1978), reached the Supreme Court, the court unanimously affirmed the FCC's cross-ownership rules, thus satisfying neither group of critics. The court said the FCC had acted within its authority and had based its rulemaking on appropriate grounds. Thus, the high court simply declined to second-guess the FCC on such a complex and controversial issue. And once again, the court affirmed the FCC's right to consider antitrust and monopoly ownership factors in its decision-making, despite the fact that the commission is not charged with enforcing the federal antitrust laws.

In 1984 the FCC decided to relax several of its broadcast ownership restrictions, including the Rule of Sevens. The commission first solicited comments from the public and the broadcast industry about the extent to which the limit of seven AM, seven FM, and seven TV stations should be liberalized, if at all.

A number of industry groups, including independent TV station owners, minority groups, and TV program producers, urged the FCC not to make major changes in the Rule of Sevens. Some felt the limit of five VHF TV stations per owner should be retained even if the Rule of Sevens were to be relaxed in other ways. Many in the industry expressed the fear that the three major networks might become even more dominant in commercial television than they are now. Some felt the networks should not be able to own more than seven television stations even if other groups were allowed to buy additional stations.

On the other hand, others in and out of the broadcast industry argued that the Rule of Sevens was an improper restriction on the marketplace. A company should be able to own and operate as many radio and television stations as it can afford, provided each one adequately serves its community, they argued. If an owner should engage in monopolistic business practices, that should be the concern of the antitrust enforcement arm of the Justice Department, they said.

The FCC responded to these arguments by replacing the Rule of Sevens with a "Rule of Twelves" under which one company could own as many as 12 AM, 12 FM and 12 TV stations. However, this decision brought strenuous protests from many quarters, and Congress acted to reinstate the limit of seven TV stations. At this writing, this issue was far from resolved, although the new limit of 12 AM and 12 FM stations remained in effect.

The FCC has also acted against television-cable cross ownerships on several occasions. In 1970, the commission ordered divestiture of broadcast-cable combinations within the same market area, and prohibited new ones. However, the commission granted many waivers of this rule. At the same time, the FCC barred the major networks from owning cable systems. The FCC's 1975 cross-ownership rules basically left existing TV-cable cross-ownerships intact, although the commission said it would require divestiture in "egregious" cases.

However, in 1984 the FCC was reviewing the whole problem of broadcast-cable cross-ownership. The commission was working on standards by which concentration of ownership problems could be evaluated. Meanwhile, Congress enacted comprehensive cable television legislation in 1984 and the new law included a provision barring television broadcasters from buying cable systems in their local service areas.

BROADCAST ANTITRUST CASES

Although the main efforts to regulate broadcast ownerships and business practices have come from the FCC, the U.S. Justice Department has occasionally challenged broadcasters' business practices too. One notable example was a case that reached the U.S. Supreme Court in 1959, *U.S. v. Radio Corporation of America* (358 U.S. 334). In that case, the Justice Department contended that RCA, parent company of NBC, had used NBC's clout as a network to force Westinghouse Broadcasting to trade its Philadelphia television station for NBC's less valuable station in Cleveland.

The case was an indirect result of the FCC's 1953 rules on multiple station ownership. After the FCC limited each owner (including the major networks) to five company-owned VHF television stations apiece, each major network wanted its five network-owned and -operated stations to be in the largest possible market areas. At the time, Philadelphia was the nation's number four market; Cleveland was number ten.

The Justice Department claimed that NBC had threatened to lift the NBC affiliations from Westinghouse's Boston and Philadelphia stations unless Westinghouse agreed to the Cleveland-Philadelphia exchange. Also, the government said NBC had refused to grant Westinghouse an NBC affiliation for its Pittsburgh station until Westinghouse agreed to the unfavorable trade. In short, the Justice Department claimed NBC had exercised monopolistic power to coerce Westinghouse into making a bad deal, even though NBC had paid Westinghouse $3 million to make the trade more even. The two stations had identical frequency assignments: both operated on VHF channel three.

RCA responded by arguing that the FCC had approved the entire transaction, and that the FCC was fully aware of all of the facts when it did so. RCA contended that the Justice Department was barred from bringing the antitrust suit because the FCC had considered the antitrust questions before approving the deal in the first place. A federal district court dismissed the suit, agreeing with RCA's contentions.

The Supreme Court reversed that dismissal. The high court pointed out that while the FCC is permitted to consider antitrust factors in approving or disapproving a change of ownership, it is not a law enforcement agency. The fact that the FCC approved the trade does not bar the Justice Department from later challenging it, the Supreme Court ruled.

The case was sent back to the federal district court for trial, but meanwhile the FCC took a new look at the situation and decided to use its licensing power to straighten things out. Acting in 1964 (eight years after the original station trade), the FCC refused to renew the license of the Philadelphia station unless NBC rescinded the trade with Westinghouse. NBC had attempted to extricate itself from the entire controversy by arranging another trade, this time offering the Philadelphia station to RKO General in return for RKO's Boston station. The FCC disapproved that trade, and instead ordered NBC to return the Philadelphia station to Westinghouse ownership, in turn accepting the Cleveland station back.

This FCC-mandated second exchange occurred in 1965. In the 1980s, Westinghouse continued to operate the Philadelphia station (now KYW-TV), while NBC retained control of the Cleveland station (now WKYC-TV).

On another occasion, the Justice Department accused all three major networks of an antitrust violation. In 1974, it charged the networks with monopolizing the prime time programming of their affiliates. In essence, the Justice Department contended that it was improper for a network to produce entertainment programs and then require affiliates to accept them. In a civil action, the Justice Department sought a court order barring the networks from producing the majority of the programming they provide to their affiliates.

Instead, most entertainment programming should come from independent producers, the Antitrust Division contended. The case dragged on for several years, but NBC broke ranks and signed a consent decree in 1977, agreeing to comply with many of the Justice Department's demands without admitting any wrongdoing. CBS and ABC signed similar consent decrees in 1980. These decrees had no effect on the networks' policies of producing all of their own news and documentary programs, but they did place limits on network production of entertainment shows.

Aside from these cases, there have been only a few Justice Department antitrust actions against the nation's broadcasters—too few, critics say. Fortunately or unfortunately, the Justice Department has often deferred to the FCC on matters of broadcast ownership, despite the FCC's lack of authority to enforce antitrust laws except indirectly through the licensing process.

The Financial Interest and Syndication Controversy

The question of who should own the entertainment programming shown on network television was again being hotly debated in the mid-1980s. Earlier, the FCC had adopted what became known as the "financial interest and syndication rules." They prohibited the networks from acquiring a financial interest in the independently produced shows they aired. Also, the rules barred the networks from controlling the syndication of "reruns."

As a part of its effort to deregulate broadcasting, the FCC proposed to eliminate many of these rules by 1984, with the remainder to be phased out by 1990. However, Hollywood's production industry, led by Jack Valenti, president of the Motion Picture Association of America, began an aggressive lobbying campaign against any change in the rules. If the networks were allowed to own an interest in the shows they aired, Valenti argued, ABC, CBS, and NBC would use their economic clout to force the producers to give up their lucrative syndication business. Valenti found powerful allies in Congress and in the White House, where Ronald Reagan—himself a former actor—personally lobbied the FCC not to change the rules.

Facing enormous political pressure, the FCC backed off, postponing any final action to eliminate the financial interest and syndication rules so the warring factions could try to negotiate an agreement among themselves.

MONOPOLIES AND NEW TECHNOLOGY

As we approach the twenty-first century, new issues of media ownership and monopoly control are emerging that would seem to make the antitrust issues of the 1960s and 1970s almost insignificant by comparison. In concluding our discussion of the media and monopolies, we should briefly note these rapidly developing ethical and legal issues, which are the subject of Chapter 15.

In the 1980s America is undergoing a new revolution in mass communications. The technology already exists to place electronic information terminals in every American home. Experiments in the electronic home delivery of daily newspapers and wire service news are already under way. Instantaneous access to some of the nation's largest newsgathering networks is available to any owner of a video display terminal and a modem (a device for interfacing a terminal and a computer via ordinary telephone lines). Millions of home computer owners already have this equipment.

But as newspapers are moving into this new form of computerized journalism, so are other organizations. Television and radio stations are preparing to offer strikingly similar services, in which news and other kinds of information are also delivered to the viewer's home via a video screen. Television stations in several cities are experimenting with "teletext," a system in which the viewer can call up an on-screen display of text or computer graphics transmitted on the television signal. Teletext systems are well suited for news, sports scores, weather and traffic information, travel timetables, games, emergency service information, and classified advertising. This seeming merger of the print and electronic media has many implications for both the communications industries and the consumer, and the print media are concerned about these developments.

One of the key issues is who will control—and profit from—these new technologies. Newspaper publishers and broadcasters feared that AT&T, still a gigantic corporation even after the historic breakup of 1984, would become the dominant force in the home information business. Alternately, they feared that the newly independent regional phone companies would take over this business.

The mass media were troubled by the phone companies' government-sanctioned monopoly on the nation's local telephone systems, the channel through which these home information systems will most likely operate. And to the alarm of publishers and broadcasters alike, the phone companies were moving rapidly toward a position where they could be ready to offer a full range of information services as well as providing the communications channel itself. Newspaper publishers who opposed the phone companies' entry into the home information business argued that allowing them to provide mass communication services over the phone lines they control would be like letting a trucking company own the nation's highways—and then have everyone else forced to use roads owned and controlled by a competitor.

The consent decree in a federal court that authorized the AT&T breakup required the Bell System to spin off 22 local phone companies. In return, AT&T was specifically authorized to enter new fields. The media won a temporary (seven-year) ban on AT&T's entry into the electronic publishing and advertising business. After the seven years, AT&T may seek to have this restriction lifted.

Newspaper publishers particularly fear that phone company home information systems might take over classified advertising—one of the best and most dependable sources of revenue for most newspapers. Indeed, a computerized home information system may be an ideal substitute for classified ads in a newspaper. With such a system, a potential buyer with a home terminal could call up a directory that lists ads by categories, such as "used cars," "apartments for rent," and "help wanted." Electronic ads could be further broken down into subcategories; a customer could get a list of apartments in a particular price range and geographic area. And from both the advertiser's and buyer's viewpoint, electronic classified ads offer one tremendous advantage over ads in a newspaper: the minute the item is taken, the ad can be canceled. The advertiser would not have to answer phone calls for days afterward, and prospective customers wouldn't have to waste their time and money calling about items that are already sold or rented.

If classified advertising is taken over by electronic information systems—be they run by the phone companies or someone else—the economics of newspaper publishing will change drastically. At this writing, American newspapers were earning an estimated $5 billion a year from classified advertising. Without it, many newspapers would surely go bankrupt.

Meanwhile, other industrial groups also are eyeing the potentially lucrative home information market. Cable television systems, for instance, may be even better equipped to provide these services than the phone companies, because their coaxial cables are capable of carrying much more data into a home at any one time than conventional telephone lines. And, of course, broadcasters are moving forward with teletext systems. Teletext systems are one-way: they do not allow viewers to communicate directly back to the broadcaster. However, an over-the-air teletext system costs far less to set up than a full-blown interactive (two-way) system. Obviously, competition in this new field will be vigorous, at least at the outset.

Satellite Television Ownership Problems

Only a little less perplexing than the problems of home information systems are the questions of satellite television ownership and control. For two decades already, AT&T has been battling the Communications Satellite Corporation (Comsat), the Western Union, and others over control of satellite communications.

As satellite-relayed television broadcasting grows, new problems are emerging. For instance, under what circumstances should viewers be allowed to directly receive satellite television that is intended for cable relay? When cable operators and others are charging a fee for satellite programming, how can bootleg reception by private parties be controlled? Should the FCC engage in the messy business of ferreting out backyard dish antennas? Or should cable and subscription television proprietors do this kind of detective work? Some cable and STV firms are aggressively chasing down "pirates" now. Although the law is on their side, they have a big enforcement problem when thousands of people choose to defy the law. Encoding the signal has not entirely solved these problems, given the fact that so many people have taken it as a personal challenge to break the codes and watch the programs without paying full freight.

Cable: Broadcaster, Publisher, or Common Carrier?

Another difficult ownership and antitrust problem concerns cable television itself. Just what is cable television? Is it a new kind of broadcasting? Or is it more analogous to an electronic newspaper? Chapter 11 discusses the question of whether the Federal Communications Commission—or any other government agency—should have the right to control cable television content in the way that broadcast content is controlled. But cable's identity crisis also has implications for the regulation of the industry's ownership and business practices.

Some cable operators call themselves "video publishers" in an effort to gain the same legal status as newspapers. On the other hand, could cable systems become common carriers—public utilities that state and local governments may freely regulate? And to what extent are there antitrust problems when a city or county awards a cable "franchise" that gives one company a monopoly on cable service?

In 1982 the U.S. Supreme Court had to deal with the problem of franchising and antitrust law. In the case of *Community Communications v. City of Boulder* (455 U.S. 40), the high court said cities are not exempt from antitrust lawsuits when they grant exclusive cable franchises. State governments have long been exempted from antitrust laws, but the court said that exemption does not automatically extend to local governments. However, it appears that the states remain free to grant antitrust immunity to local governments in spite of this decision.

The case involved a situation in which Boulder, Colo., authorized Community Communications to provide cable service in a small part of the city where TV signals were weak. About 13 years later, Community Communications sought permission to serve more of the city. The city passed an emergency ordinance forbidding the firm to expand and then drafted a cable ordinance under which other firms would be invited to apply for a city franchise.

Community sued, charging that this refusal to let it do business in much of the city—and the possibility that another company might be given a government-sanctioned monopoly—violated federal antitrust laws. The high court did not decide whether the city's action was actually illegal. Rather, it held that the city was not inherently exempt from such a lawsuit. The case was sent back to the lower courts for further consideration of the antitrust issues involved. The whole problem of antitrust law and cable franchising is far from resolved at this writing.

In fact, some cable operators zealously avoid the word "franchise" to describe their relationships with local governments, arguing that this concept gives local officials a rationale for imposing excessive control over not only their business practices but also their program content. In 1984, Congress acted to restrict local government control over cable content, but the new law affirmed the right of local governments to award franchises and regulate some cable business practices. (The FCC, however, still has the authority to regulate cable content.)

Cable systems are finding out that it is difficult to separate business regulation from content regulation, at least in the minds of government officials. When cable operators argue that they should have the same legal status as newspapers, they are in effect saying that their business practices should be subject to government regulation (as are newspapers' business practices), while their content should be largely free of government regulation (as is newspaper content). Newspaper interests, on the other hand, fear this may lead to guilt-by-association problems for them: they are concerned that they may find themselves forced to live with content controls that they have never faced before, controls that will substantially erode their traditional Constitutional rights. As the print media go electronic and the electronic media get into the text business, this problem will be increasingly difficult to untangle.

Obviously, the advance of the technical state of the art continues to create new legal problems of mass communications ownership and control faster than the old ones can be resolved. These conflicts between media owners and consumers—and among the various media owners—will continue well into the next century.

A Summary of
Media Monopoly Issues

DO ANTITRUST LAWS APPLY TO THE MEDIA?

For many years, publishers contended that the First Amendment exempted them from antitrust laws, but the Supreme Court ruled otherwise in 1945. Today, the mass media are subject ot the same antitrust laws as other businesses.

WHAT BUSINESS PRACTICES ARE UNLAWFUL?

Antitrust laws forbid a variety of practices, including tying arrangements (where customers are compelled to buy something they may not want to get something they want) and certain boycotts and other coercive practices. Also, mergers that reduce competiton are usually unlawful. The federal government has occasionally acted against the media for violating these laws.

WHAT IS A JOINT OPERATING AGREEMENT?

Under a joint operating agreement, two competing newspapers merge their business, advertising, and printing operations while maintaining separate editorial staffs. Some publishers say they could not stay in business without such arrangements.

DO JOINT OPERATING AGREEMENTS VIOLATE ANTITRUST LAWS?

The Supreme Court once ruled that a joint operating agreement violated antitrust laws, but then Congress passed the Newspaper Preservation Act, legalizing existing agreements and setting up a procedure for the approval of new ones.

WHAT IS CROSS-OWNERSHIP?

Cross-ownership occurs when one party owns a combination of newspapers, broadcast properties, and/or cable systems in the same metropolitan market area.

ARE CROSS-OWNERSHIPS PROHIBITED?

Under FCC rules that have been upheld by the Supreme Court, new newspaper-broadcast cross-ownerships are forbidden, but most existing cross-owners were not required to sell any of their properties. Cable-broadcast combinations in the same market are also forbidden, but some continue to operate under waivers of the FCC rules.

HOW WILL THE NEW TECHNOLOGIES AFFECT MEDIA OWNERSHIP?

As home information systems become more economically feasible, the print and electronic media will be competing more directly than ever, with both (and possibly non-mass media companies as well) offering these services. Also, many new technologies are now competing for the public's video entertainment dollar, including both cable systems served by satellite and direct satellite broadcasting.

14

FREEDOM OF THE STUDENT PRESS

Almost all student publications—no matter how well edited—eventually face the wrath of administrators who don't like something that appears in print. Official reactions vary from telephone calls or irate interoffice memos to attempts at outright censorship.

The student press has been censored for almost as long as there have been student newspapers, but until recent years the staffs and their faculty advisers could do little or nothing about it. However, the era of student unrest in the late 1960s changed that. Students in that period were unwilling to limit their expression to editorials bemoaning the lack of school spirit or attacking the quality of cafeteria food. Instead, many high school and college newspapers focused on issues such as war and peace, civil rights, and later drug use, sex counseling, and other sensitive issues. Amazingly, many of them got away with it, creating a legacy of First Amendment protection for future generations of campus journalists.

Since the U.S. Supreme Court first extended First Amendment protection to students in 1969, at least 125 other court decisions have followed that precedent, repeatedly overturning administrative efforts to censor student publications and other forms of student expression.

In case after case, the courts ruled that public school and college administrators cannot arbitrarily censor student expression as they once did. Whenever there is state action, as there always is when federal, state, and local public officials (including school officials) act, the courts have held that the First Amendment applies, as do the due process and equal protection clauses of the Fourteenth Amendment. At private institutions, on the other hand, courts rarely find state action in the conduct of administrators, and that creates a different problem, which we'll discuss later.

There are dozens—and perhaps hundreds—of confrontations between administrators and college journalists every year, and surely even more occur at the high school level. Although many of these incidents involve blatant prior restraint, these acts of censorship often go unchallenged because no one has the money, the motivation, or the legal resources to haul the powers that be into court. While some of the cases that never make it to court are very interesting, this chapter of necessity concentrates on cases that *did* end up in court—cases that established legal precedents for the future.

THE *TINKER* DECISION

In many areas of media law, the basic principles can be traced to a landmark Supreme Court decision, and student press freedom is one of those areas. In 1969, the Supreme Court ruled on the case of *Tinker v. Des Moines Independent Community School District* (393 U.S. 503), often called the "black armbands case." The case arose when John and Mary Beth Tinker, ages 15 and 13, and a 16-year-old friend were suspended for wearing black armbands at school as a symbolic protest of the Vietnam War. The Des Moines school principals had heard of the pending protest and hurriedly adopted a rule against wearing armbands on campus.

The suspension was challenged on First Amendment grounds. Two lower courts upheld the school officials' action, but the Supreme Court reversed, declaring that their act was symbolic speech, protected by the First Amendment. The court said:

> First Amendment rights, applied in the light of the special characteristics of the school environment, are available to teachers and students. It can hardly be argued that either students or teachers shed their constitutional rights to freedom of speech or expression at the schoolhouse gate.

The court noted that the three students did nothing to disrupt the educational process. The court said, "In our system, state-operated schools may not be enclaves of totalitarianism. School officials do not possess absolute authority over their students."

However, the court did make it clear that the rights of students were not "co-extensive" with the rights of adults off campus. The court said freedom could be suppressed when its exercise "would materially and substantially interfere with the requirements of appropriate discipline in the operation of the school."

Applying the *Tinker* Precedent

Even before the *Tinker* decision, a federal district court had ruled that a student newspaper's advertising columns were protected by the First Amendment (see *Zucker v. Panitz*, cited in Chapter 12). But after *Tinker*, many more cases arose, as students asserted their newly won Constitutional rights. Some of the earliest post-*Tinker* cases were only federal district court decisions and hence of limited value as precedents, but students were winning lawsuits against school officials.

In a 1970 case, *Antonelli v. Hammond* (308 F.Supp. 1329), a federal court in Massachusetts said a college president could not impose prior restraint on a campus newspaper without elaborate procedural safeguards. John Antonelli, a student newspaper editor at Fitchburg State College, resigned rather than submit an article by black activist Eldridge Cleaver to a campus review board. College President James Hammond set up the board to pre-censor the paper for obscenity and to assure "responsible freedom of press in the student newspaper."

Antonelli sued Hammond and won: the court said the campus paper was protected by the First Amendment, and that the review board constituted prior censorship without adequate safeguards. Moreover, the court condemned a threat by Hammond to withhold funding if the paper wasn't "responsible."

The next year, another federal district court overruled the suspension of a student editor because of a cartoon critical of the college president and an editorial criticizing a local judge, in *Trujillo v. Love* (322 F.Supp. 1266). Dorothy Trujillo was an editor of a "laboratory" newspaper produced by the Mass Communications Department at Southern Colorado State College. The faculty adviser and department chair said the editorial and cartoon didn't meet the Canons of Journalism and were potentially libelous. Trujillo challenged her suspension in court and won, because the court felt the paper was still a student forum protected by the First Amendment, despite its in-house "lab" character. The court said that if its status as a teaching tool rather than a First Amendment forum had been clearly spelled out and put into effect, the censorship and suspension might have been Constitutional. However, the lab status wasn't clearly defined, and the paper had become a forum for expression protected by the First Amendment.

Healy, Papish and Campus Decorum

The *Antonelli* and *Trujillo* cases were typical of a number of other student press cases that followed *Tinker*. Meanwhile, a case involving a radical student organization reached the U.S. Supreme Court, resulting in another precedent in favor of student freedom in 1972.

A chapter of the Students for a Democratic Society, a campus organization known for its militancy, sought official recognition as a campus organization at Central Connecticut State College, and was turned down because of

SDS' national reputation for disruptive tactics. Without official status, the group could not use campus facilities for meetings and other functions. The group sued, and in *Healy v. James* (408 U.S. 169), the Supreme Court said the local group couldn't be denied campus privileges merely because of the national organization's reputation. Public colleges "are not enclaves immune from the sweep of the First Amendment," the court said, ruling that the college president's decision abridged the students' Constitutional rights.

A year later the Supreme Court decided another student rights case, this one involving disciplinary action against the editor of an "underground" or alternative campus newspaper. In *Papish v. University of Missouri Curators* (410 U.S. 670), the high court overruled the expulsion of Barbara Papish, a graduate student and editor of the *Free Press*.

Papish had previously angered university officials by distributing her paper when high school students and their parents were on campus, but when she published an issue they regarded as particularly indecent, they took action. The edition that led to the expulsion had a political cartoon depicting a policeman raping the Statue of Liberty and the Goddess of Justice, and a headline entitled, "Mother Fucker Acquitted."

The Supreme Court ruled that neither the cartoon nor the headline was obscene. Nor did Papish's activities "materially and substantially" interfere with campus order, the court said. The court ordered Papish reinstated, citing the *Healy* decision: "We think *Healy* makes it clear that the dissemination of ideas—no matter how offensive to good taste—on a state university campus may not be shut off in the name alone of 'conventions of decency.'"

COLLEGE PRESS FREEDOM CASES

Within two years of the *Papish* decision, three noteworthy federal appellate court decisions on student press freedom were handed down, and each affirmed student rights.

In *Bazaar v. Fortune* (476 F.2d 570, 1973), the fifth circuit U.S. Court of Appeals overruled the prior censorship of a literary magazine at the University of Mississippi. The magazine, edited by Eugene Bazaar, carried two short stories with earthy language, both dealing with racial themes. The magazine was sponsored by the English Department and was to be printed on campus, but the print shop superintendent noticed some of the content and called the university chancellor, Porter Fortune, who ordered it censored.

When hauled into court, university officials acknowledged that the First Amendment protected the Ole Miss student newspaper but argued that this magazine was different because it was produced by a class. The appellate court disagreed and ordered the university to allow its publication, although the court did allow the university to put a disclaimer on the cover ("This is not an official publication. . .").

At almost the same time, another press freedom case with racial overtones was decided by the fourth circuit U.S. Court of Appeals, *Joyner v.*

Whiting (477 F.2d 456, 1973). That case arose when Albert Whiting, president of North Carolina Central University, cut off funds for the *Campus Echo* because editor Johnnie Joyner editorially opposed integration of this formerly all-black school. At one point Joyner also said whites were unwelcome on the paper's staff, and that the paper would not accept ads from white-owned businesses. Whiting said he feared the paper's editorial position would cause the school to lose federal funds.

The court said Whiting's actions violated the First and Fourteenth Amendments. Even though Joyner was using his freedom of the press to speak out against another Constitutionally protected principle, the court said the First Amendment still applied. The court noted that Joyner's editorial stance had not produced any disruption of the campus. A college administration doesn't have to create a student newspaper in the first place, but once a paper is established, it can't be shut down just because the administration doesn't like its content, the appellate court said.

Two years later, the same federal appellate court that decided *Bazaar* overruled the firing of three student editors by a college president in *Schiff v. Williams* (519 F.2d 257, 1975). Kenneth Williams, president of Florida Atlantic University, fired the three editors because "the level of editorial responsibility and competence has deteriorated to the extent that it reflects discredit and embarrassment upon the university." The paper engaged in vilification and rumor mongering "instead of accurately reporting items likely to be of interest to the university community," the president said.

In overturning the firings, the federal appellate court said this was an unconstitutional attempt to impose administrative control on the newspaper. Citing *Tinker*, the court said such control could be justified only under special circumstances where disorder might otherwise result. Even if these editors produced a paper full of poor grammar, spelling, and expression, as Williams claimed, that would not lead to a significant disruption on the campus, the court said. And without the threat of disruption, censorship of student publications is unconstitutional, the court noted.

All of these cases were decided in the years immediately following the era of campus unrest in the late 1960s. In recent years, few disputes involving freedom of the college press have reached the nation's appellate courts. However, in 1983 the eighth circuit U.S. Court of Appeals handed down a ruling that was a major victory for campus press freedom: *Stanley v. Magrath* (719 F.2d 279).

This case arose after the *Minnesota Daily* at the University of Minnesota published a humor issue in 1979. One article purported to be an interview with Jesus Christ, and it described him as a Jewish "cult hero." The article angered many Minnesotans, including more than a few on the campus itself. The university responded by changing its rules to allow students to withhold from their fee payments the amount destined for the paper.

Although the policy change had little effect on its actual income, the *Minnesota Daily* challenged the legality of this action on First Amendment grounds. Reversing a trial judge's decision in favor of the university, the federal appellate court ruled that the change in funding was an attempt to control the paper's content in violation of the First Amendment.

In 1984 the university and the student paper reached a settlement in which the University Regents agreed to pay the paper's legal expenses (a total of $182,000) and restore its funding. The agreement also provided for the university and the paper to set up a $20,000 fund to sponsor seminars on press freedom and responsibility.

Taken as a group, these cases say that student journalists enjoy substantial First Amendment protection. It may be that a campus publication could avoid becoming a First Amendment forum, as the court suggested in *Trujillo*, but that didn't occur in any of these cases, even though several involved publications produced in instructional situations with at least partial university funding. It has been suggested more than once that student newspapers are a little like Dr. Frankenstein's monster: school officials don't have to create one, but once they do, it's very hard to control.

HIGH SCHOOL PRESS FREEDOM

Except for *Tinker* itself, all of the cases discussed so far involved press freedom at colleges, not high schools. While the same principles apply at both the high school and college level, some courts have been more inclined to find threats of substantial disruption in high school publications. Nevertheless, federal courts have also repeatedly overruled administrative efforts to censor the high school press, usually in cases where the language or subject matter in independently produced "underground" or "alternative" publications offended school officials.

Overall, far more high school than college free press cases have been litigated: no fewer than 12 federal appellate court decisions have overturned censorship or discipline of student journalists by high school administrators. In almost all of these cases, administrators attempted to engage in prior restraint, often pointing to profanity or language they considered obscene as their justification. But the courts have repeatedly told school officials that neither profanity nor four-letter words constitute obscenity, and that the prior censorship was unjustified.

In deciding these cases, often the federal courts have focused on school procedures for reviewing student publications. The courts have generally held that prior restraint is permissible on a school campus when it wouldn't be in the community at large, but to justify censorship administrators must bear a heavy burden of proof and provide students with many procedural safeguards—things school officials failed to do in virtually all of the cases that have been litigated.

However, the leading precedent in one federal appellate circuit (the seventh circuit, covering Illinois, Wisconsin, and Indiana) seemingly forbids prior restraint of school publications except when prior restraint of a commercial newspaper would also be constitutional (i.e., almost never). In *Fujishima v. Board of Education* (460 F.2d 1355), the federal court overruled the suspension of two students who distributed a paper called *The Cosmic Frog*. The court said *Tinker* did not permit school officials to merely predict that a disruption would occur and use that as an excuse to engage in censorship:

> *Tinker* in no way suggests that students may be required to announce their intentions of engaging in certain conduct beforehand so school authorities may decide whether to prohibit the conduct. Such a concept of prior restraint is even more offensive when applied to the long-protected area of publication.

In so ruling, the *Fujishima* decision took issue with *Eisner v. Stamford Board of Education* (440 F.2d 803, 1971), an earlier ruling of another federal appellate court that said prior restraint would be acceptable if certain procedural safeguards were provided:

> We believe that the court erred in *Eisner* in interpreting *Tinker* to allow prior restraint of publication—long a constitutionally prohibited power—as a tool of school officials in "forecasting" substantial disruption of school activities.

Nevertheless, most federal courts have taken the *Eisner* view rather than the *Fujishima* view, ruling that prior restraint is permissible if there are sufficient procedural safeguards. But, as it turns out, the courts almost never find that adequate procedural safeguards exist.

Even in the *Eisner* case, the court overturned a Connecticut school system's censorship procedures because they did not provide for a quick administrative review or specify to whom and how literature could be submitted for prior review. Still, under the *Eisner* precedent, decided by the second federal appellate circuit (which includes New York, Vermont, and Connecticut), students have less freedom from prior censorship than they do in several other appellate circuits. Each federal appellate court sets precedents that are binding in its region but not elsewhere, although other courts often follow non-local precedents.

The second circuit Court of Appeals also upheld an administrative censorship action in a 1977 case, *Trachtman v. Anker* (563 F.2d 512). That case isn't a student press case strictly speaking: a group of students wanted to distribute a questionnaire on sexual attitudes at a New York high school, and the court allowed the administration to stop them. However, the court said literature distribution was not the issue here; expert witnesses had testified that responding to the questionnaire could cause psychological harm to some adolescent students. In fact, one of the two justices in the majority joined the dissenting third justice in emphasizing that this should not be viewed as an "unintended" precedent for any future abridgement of student freedom of expression.

Nevertheless, a federal district judge in New York cited the *Trachtman* decision when he upheld a high school principal's decision to censor a student newspaper in 1979. In *Frasca v. Andrews* (463 F.Supp. 1043), a judge said he didn't want to second-guess a principal who predicted that disruptions might result from two items in the paper: a heated exchange between members of the school lacrosse team and the editors, and an article accusing a student body officer of incompetence.

In *Frasca*, a federal judge allowed a school official to forecast a disruption as a justification for prior censorship, precisely what the court prohibited in *Fujishima*. However, *Fujishima* is a seventh circuit case, and *Frasca* was decided in the second federal appellate circuit.

However, even the second circuit has more recently handed down a decision in favor of student freedom, *Thomas v. Granville* (607 F.2d 1043, 1979). In that case, the court overturned a disciplinary action against students who distributed an underground paper near (but not on) school property. The paper offended school officials because it had articles on masturbation and prostitution. However, no disruption resulted and the court said the students' Constitutional rights were violated by the disciplinary action.

Elsewhere around the country, other federal appellate courts have generally fallen somewhere between the stance of the second and seventh federal appellate circuits on issues of student freedom. Courts in the fourth and fifth circuits (covering the Southern states) have almost always reversed school officials' efforts to censor publications or discipline editors, while emphasizing that they were not flatly prohibiting prior censorship of school publications. Fourth and fifth circuit cases that so held include: *Nitzberg v. Parks* (525 F.2d 378), *Baughman v. Freienmuth* (478 F.2d 1345, 1973), *Quarterman v. Byrd* (453 F.2d 54, 1971), *Gambino v. Fairfax County School Board* (429 F.Supp. 731, aff'd 564 F.2d 157, 1977), and *Shanley v. Northeast Independent School District* (462 F.2d 960, 1972).

In a number of these cases, the courts said prior restraint would be constitutionally permissible under something like the procedural safeguards required for motion picture censorship in *Freedman v. Maryland* (see Chapter 10). Thus, the *Baughman* decision emphasized the need for prompt review of any decision to censor, with clearly drawn guidelines describing the kind of material that could be censored. In the *Baughman* case, the court overturned a school policy that allowed prior restraint when material was libelous or obscene. The court said these were terms of art and much too vague to be applied by students and principals in censorship cases. Furthermore, since *New York Times v. Sullivan* and *Gertz v. Welch* (see Chapter Four), much that is seemingly libelous is also privileged, the court pointed out.

The *Nitzberg* case echoed the ruling in *Baughman*, but also said that when school officials want to justify prior censorship by forecasting disruptions, they must have clearly drawn criteria that may be used in predicting that a publication would cause such a disruption.

The seventh federal appellate circuit, which decided the *Fujishima* case, has also ruled on two other student press freedom cases, *Scoville v. Board of Education* (425 F.2d 10, 1970) and *Jacobs v. Indianapolis Board of School Commissioners* (490 F.2d 601, 1973). The U.S. Supreme Court agreed to review *Jacobs* but then set it aside as moot (the students had all graduated). *Jacobs* was especially notable because the appellate court emphasized that the use of earthy language doesn't make a publication legally obscene. In so ruling, the court cited the Supreme Court's *Papish* holding that mere four-letter (or twelve-letter) words do not constitute obscenity.

Another appellate decision worth special mention is *Gambino v. Fairfax* (cited earlier). That 1977 decision is notable because it arose from a situation that must be repeated hundreds of times every year somewhere in America: the editors of an official campus newspaper faced censorship because what they wrote was considered too sensitive and controversial for high school students. Gina Gambino and her staff wanted to publish an article on contraceptive methods in the student paper at a high school in Virginia. It was headlined, "Sexually Active Students Fail to Use Contraceptives." The principal reviewed and decided to censor certain parts of the article, contending that sex eduction instruction was prohibited at the school. Therefore, the student paper shouldn't do something the teachers were forbidden to do in class, the principal contended.

A federal district court overruled the school's censorship, brushing aside the argument that the public forum doctrine shouldn't apply because the paper was part of the school curriculum, produced by a class. Despite its status, the paper was still protected by the First Amendment, the judge ruled. The fourth circuit Court of Appeals affirmed that decision.

However, the same federal appellate court upheld an act of administrative censorship when illegal drug use rather than birth control was the issue. In a 1980 case, *Williams v. Spencer* (622 F.2d 1200), the court affirmed a decision by school officials to halt distribution of an underground newspaper called *Joint Effort* because the paper contained advertising from a "head shop" that officials felt would encourage drug use. Citing the language in *Tinker* that students' rights are not "necessarily co-extensive with those of adults," the court affirmed school regulations under which the publication was banned. The court said a rule against distributing information dangerous to the health and safety of students was not unconstitutionally overbroad even though it did not specify the kind of material that could be censored. The court seemingly gave school officials broad latitude to justify censorship by contending that a story or ad in a publication might encourage drug use or something else allegedly dangerous or unhealthy.

Where does all of this leave us? It is clear that school officials no longer may arbitrarily censor student publications without risking a reversal in court. However, as the era of militant student protest fades into history it is also clear that the schools and the courts are reflecting changing social conditions. In the 1980s, courts should be expected to continue to affirm student editors' constitutional rights in clear cases of arbitrary censorship, but more and more judges may be willing to defer to school officials' judgment when a disruption is forecast or the subject matter may encourage unlawful acts.

Meanwhile, at least one state legislature has gone so far as to enact a statutory law setting ground rules for high school newspapers. In 1977, a law was enacted in Califonia to regulate official as well as underground student publications. The law said the principle of freedom of the press applies to school newspapers, but it also authorized prior censorship for libel, obscenity, and material likely to cause rule-breaking or campus disturbances (see Calif. Educ. Code, sec. 48916). The law not only requires censorship of material falling in these categories, but places the primary responsibility for this censorship on the faculty adviser. This authorization for prior censorship is so broad that the American Civil Liberties Union opposed the law in the state legislature.

The ACLU was particularly annoyed because section 48916 reimposed prior censorship of school newspapers in California only a year after the state's Supreme Court had ruled that prior restraint was not permitted under a previous law guaranteeing free expression for students. The old law afforded students broad free-expression rights, but didn't mention official school newspapers. Interpreting that law, the California Supreme Court overruled the administrative censorship of an underground newspaper in 1976 (*Bright v. Los Angeles Unified School District*, 18 Cal.3d 450). The paper had been censored because an article accused a school principal of lying. The court said prior restraint might be possible in the school setting, but the existing California law didn't authorize it.

The legislature closed that loophole the next year, offering in return provisions covering official as well as unofficial school papers. The new law was supported by groups of high school journalism teachers, who believed some statutory protection was better than none at all. They felt school officials would be more likely to obey a specific statutory law than the broad principles of Constitutional law.

FREEDOM AT PRIVATE SCHOOLS

This entire chapter has been devoted to freedom of expression at public schools and colleges. What about private institutions?

At private schools, the general rule is that freedom only exists if school officials find it in their interest to grant it: in the absence of state action, the First Amendment does not apply. When a private university newspaper is censored or its editors are fired, normally the worst the administration need fear is bad public relations. The school may face condemnation by professional media and journalistic organizations, but there is usually little chance for the aggrieved students to win a lawsuit.

This problem was well illustrated by a 1980 incident at Baylor University, a Baptist church-related institution. *Playboy* magazine was doing a photo feature on "Girls of the Southwest Conference," and a *Playboy* photographer was coming to town. University President Abner McCall warned that any Baylor student who posed nude for *Playboy* would be punished (and presumably expelled). The Baylor newspaper, the *Lariat*, editorially said that Baylor girls should be free to make up their own minds about whether to pose. Then

McCall told the *Lariat* editors not to cover the growing *Playboy* controversy any more. The editors rejected that blatant censorship, and several were fired. Shortly, more staff members and two journalism professors resigned in protest. One faculty member who resigned was abruptly ordered to leave Baylor in mid-semester. Before it was over, the Baylor incident stirred a national controversy, but the *Lariat* staff had no legal recourse. They were out.

Although the issues that provoke censorship aren't often as spectacular as the one at Baylor, similar incidents probably occur every year on other private campuses.

During the era of student activism in the late 1960s and early 1970s, many lawsuits were filed alleging Constitutional violations by private institutions, but the courts consistently ruled in favor of school officials—except in a very few cases where state action could be shown.

To establish state action, it must be shown that a government is deeply involved not only in funding the institution but also in its management. In separate cases (neither involving student press freedom as such), state action has been shown at two major private universities in Pennsylvania: Pittsburgh and Temple. However, in both instances the Commonwealth of Pennsylvania had entered agreements with school officials in which the state provided major funding in return for substantial reductions in tuition for Pennsylvania residents. Moreover, the state was given the power to appoint one-third of each institution's governing board. (See *Isaacs v. Temple University*, 385 F.Supp. 473, 1974; and *Braden v. Pittsburgh University*, 552 F.2d 948, 1977.)

Aside from the two Pennsylvania cases, court decisions establishing state action at private schools and colleges are hard to find. Once a New York court issued a memorandum opinion in connection with a settlement of a student discipline lawsuit against Hofstra University. The opinion discussed the procedural rights of students, but didn't address the basic issue of whether state action was present (*Ryan v. Hofstra*, 324 N.Y.S.2d 964, 1971).

On the other hand, a number of court decisions have held that state action does not exist at various private universities. For instance, in *Furumoto v. Lyman* (362 F.Supp. 1267, 1973), a court failed to find any state action at Stanford University, despite massive federal grants and a state charter. The seventh circuit Court of Appeals reached the same decision in *Cohen v. Illinois Institute of Technology* (581 F.2d 661, 1978).

In a 1982 decision, the U.S. Supreme Court may have settled the question of state action at private educational institutions. In *Rendell-Baker v. Kohn* (457 U.S. 830), the court ruled that state action was not present at a private high school for students with special problems, even though the school received 90 per cent of its revenue from government funds. In a 7-2 ruling, the court made it very unlikely that state action can now be shown at any purely private school or college.

Thus, the conclusion seems clear: in the absence of an arrangement like those at Temple and Pittsburgh, there's no state action, and private school administrators may therefore ignore the First Amendment.

There is, however, one other possible recourse. In a law review article entitled "Common Law Rights for Private University Students: Beyond the State Action Principle" (84 Yale Law Journal 120, 1974), Paul G. Abrams and Peter M. Hoffman urged that the common law principles of private association law be applied to student rights cases. It is well established that a private association must operate in accordance with its own bylaws. When it fails to do that, its members may turn to the courts for help, they pointed out. That principle has not often been used by students, but it could be, given a university policy that guarantees freedom of the press and a clear violation of that policy. Perhaps, in an appropriate case, a court would follow Abrams' and Hoffman's reasoning and recognize that private university students have some rights, at least when the insitution has adopted a policy that says they do.

PRACTICAL CONSIDERATIONS

So far, we've talked mainly about student press freedom in terms of lawsuits and the First Amendment. Because this chapter will certainly be read for guidance by students facing threats of censorship, a few practical observations are in order.

First, it should be emphasized that Constitutional rights are only available to those who are prepared to fight for them—in court, if necessary. School administrators often ignore the First Amendment until forced to recognize that it exists. In the 1980s school officials continue to treat student newspapers as if the *Tinker* decision and all the cases that followed it simply didn't happen. High school and college papers are censored every year without anyone doing anything about it.

It is unfortunate but true that winning one's Constitutional rights can be expensive and time-consuming. Thus, if you experience threatened or actual censorship, you may have some tough choices to make. Ask yourself some questions. How important is the item you've been told you can't publish? Is it worth fighting for, even if you lose your position (and perhaps a scholarship or a salary), and maybe even your status as a student in good standing? Martyrdom may be attractive, but does common sense dictate a compromise? Moreover, is the controversial item something with which a judge would sympathize? Justice Oliver Wendell Holmes' legal maxim, ". . .hard cases make bad law," certainly applies here. Don't pursue a case that invites a bad legal precedent, one that could be used to deny freedom to students elsewhere. A well-documented story about malfeasance by the school administration is one thing; a column that uses four-letter words merely to prove the author knows how to spell them is another.

After weighing these questions, if you feel you have a case worth pursuing there are some specific steps to take. First, go through all available channels. If you have a faculty adviser, consult him or her. If there is a publications policy board, take the case there. Only if all internal remedies fail is it time to consider a lawsuit. But if you reach that point, weigh your options again. Is there a local attorney willing to represent you on a low-cost basis? The American Civil Liberties Union has represented students in numerous First Amendment cases, sometimes with resounding success. The Student Press Law Center in Washington, D.C., may also be able to offer advice—or help you find a volunteer attorney. If legal help isn't available, compromise may again be in order. But if, on the other hand, you really have a clear First Amendment violation involving a defensible story or photograph—and if you find a good lawyer—perhaps the next edition of this textbook will discuss a case in which your name and your institution's name appear on opposite sides of the little "v." in a legal citation.

A Summary of
Student Press Law

DOES THE FIRST AMENDMENT APPLY TO STUDENTS?

In the landmark case of *Tinker v. Community School District*, the Supreme Court extended First Amendment protection to students attending public schools.

ARE THERE LIMITATIONS ON STUDENTS' FREEDOMS?

The Supreme Court said students' rights on campus are not as extensive as those normally available off campus. Students' freedom of expression may be limited when necessary to prevent campus disruptions and maintain an orderly educational process.

ARE STUDENT PUBLICATIONS CONSTITUTIONALLY PROTECTED?

Federal courts have repeatedly held that both "underground" and official student publications are protected by the First Amendment and may not be arbitrarily censored by school administrators. The courts have refused to allow censorship in many cases involving even earthy language or controversial subject matter.

ARE HIGH SCHOOL AND COLLEGE STUDENTS TREATED DIFFERENTLY?

The courts have rarely addressed this issue specifically. But courts have sometimes focused on the age and maturity levels of students in determining whether particular material may be censored by school officials.

ISN'T THE SCHOOL ADMINISTRATION REALLY THE PUBLISHER?

Federal courts have consistently refused to rule that school officials have powers comparable to those of a private newspaper publisher. Instead, courts have often found school publications to be public forums protected by the First Amendment.

ARE PRIVATE SCHOOLS TREATED DIFFERENTLY?

The legal basis for extending First Amendment protection to students is that school officials' acts constitute "state action." The First Amendment protects people from denials of their basic freedoms by governments, not by private citizens. Unless a private school official's conduct constitutes "state action," (which it almost never does), the First Amendment is inapplicable to private institutions.

WHAT IS THE CURRENT TREND IN STUDENT PRESS FREEDOM?

After a decade of consistent victories, students have begun to lose some cases they once might have won. The era of student activism has ended, and judges are beginning to reflect the changing social climate by ruling against students in borderline cases.

15

NEW TECHNOLOGIES AND MEDIA LAW

The growing impact of the new technologies has been a recurring theme of this book: these technologies are forcing us to reevaluate some of the basic assumptions that underlie communications law. The number of times the new media have already been mentioned probably shows how important they are today.

To recap what has already been said, Chapter Six discusses the copyright implications of emerging technologies such as video tape recording, cable television, and the personal computer.

There have been repeated battles in Congress and the courts over the copyright liability of cable systems that import distant broadcast signals and relay them to subscribers. Probably no royalty formula exists that both cable operators and copyright owners would consider fair. For years producers and broadcasters complained that cable systems were paying too little for the product they delivered to their customers. But the Copyright Royalty Tribunal drastically increased the royalties in 1983, and now it is the cable operators who say the system is unfair.

The battle over royalties for home videotaping has also gone on for a decade. To no one's surprise, the Supreme Court's *Sony v. Universal Studios* decision did not end the controversy. Instead, it merely shifted the scene of battle to Congress, where the copyright owners were lobbying for an across-the-board royalty system when this chapter was written.

Chapter 11 also discusses the new technologies, and particularly notes their effect on the rules governing radio and television. The Federal Communications Commission has been overhauling its basic philosophy of broadcast regulation to take into account the growth of alternatives to traditional television broadcasting. The commission has authorized or is considering an alphabet-soup assortment of new broadcast-like services, including not only CATV (cable) but also SMATV, MDS, HDTV, STV, DBS, ITFS, OFS, LPTV, and several others that will be discussed in this chapter.

Finally, Chapter 13 discusses some of the ownership and cross-ownership issues relating to these new technologies. Newspaper publishers, broadcasters, cable system operators, and even the nation's telephone companies see home information services as a promising new business opportunity—one that they all want to exploit. Each, of course, would like to get as large a piece of the action as possible. At the same time, serious questions are being raised about the legal consequences of the merging of print, broadcast, and "common carrier" technologies.

Using all of this as background material, we now look at the new technologies themselves, discussing their characteristics and some of the new legal problems they have created.

THE NEW MEDIA

This chapter primarily talks about new *delivery systems*—new ways of disseminating information and entertainment to consumers. It is a world of strange jargon and acronyms, some of it old but most of it very new.

Actually, many of the new technologies are really nothing more than new approaches to something that has been around for 40 years: television broadcasting. Because of the FCC's regulatory philosophy, several not-so-new adaptations of television have become important as mass communications media only recently. Others, such as direct broadcast satellites, are truly *new* technologies.

Cable Television

Cable television is discussed in Chapter 11; it is mentioned here only in the interest of completeness. Cable has been a major growth industry in the past decade due to a number of factors. One of the important ones was the FCC's decision to deregulate cable, freeing it of rules that kept it from becoming a major communications medium much earlier.

Another important factor was the emergence of "premium" program services and television "superstations" that offer original programming not available elsewhere. The dramatic growth of satellite-relayed programming for cable made many consumers see the value of this medium for the first time. As long as cable offered nothing more than good reception of local television stations, many urban and suburban residents found little reason to pay for cable service instead of receiving TV signals directly with their own antennas. Until the premium services came along, cable was still widely regarded as "community antenna television" (CATV), something that was mainly intended for people living in areas with poor television reception.

One major development that opened the way for the premium services was a 1977 federal appellate court decision, *Home Box Office v. FCC* (567 F.2d 9). This decision overturned an old FCC rule strictly limiting the right of cable systems to offer such features as new movies for an additional fee. The court said the rule was clearly intended to keep cable from becoming a serious competitor for over-the-air broadcasting. The FCC did not have the authority to restrict the premium cable services so severely, the court held.

Given the freedom to offer satellite-relayed original programming and for-pay but commercial-free special features, cable television has become much more popular in recent years. More than one third of all American households are now paying a monthly fee for cable service, and most feel that what they get is worth the money.

But while cable television has been growing rapidly, so have a number of other alternative delivery systems for television programming.

Low Power Television

Low power television (LPTV) is an excellent example of a new adaptation of a very old technology: there is no particular technical innovation in using a low-power transmitter instead of a high-power transmitter. The FCC authorized this new service in an effort to open up television broadcasting to hundreds or thousands of new broadcasters—stations that could not have been licensed or could not have been financially successful under the old rules. The idea was to set up stations that would be inexpensive to operate and local in their service area.

Many LPTV stations are nothing more than deregulated television "translators." For many years small communities have been served by low-power television translators that received a distant television signal and retransmitted it on another channel. Until recently, these translators were not permitted to originate their own local programming. But when these translators are reclassified as low-power television stations, they gain the right not only to produce local programs, but also to use programming received via satellite and on video tape from syndicators.

The FCC hoped LPTV would open up television to small communities and to those who would target programming to specialized audiences in larger communities. The goal was to provide new service to communities and special interests not fully served by the major-market telecasters—the big stations that feel they must reach mass audiences to pay their bills.

At this writing, the FCC faced a backlog of thousands of applications for LPTV licenses. Only a few hundred LPTV licenses had been granted, most of them in rural areas.

Subscription Television

Subscription television (STV) is another very old idea that was given new life by recent FCC policy changes and court decisions, including the *Home Box Office* case mentioned earlier. There were experiments with both over-the-air and cable-based pay-television as early as the 1950s, but these early ventures were plagued by technical problems—and public relations problems. For example, when a major pay-TV venture was launched in California in the early 1960s, the state's theater owners saw it as a serious threat to their financial interests. So they launched a political campaign that eventually placed a proposal to ban pay television on the California ballot in 1964. Campaign advertising warned voters that pay-TV was a threat to their free television service: it said all of the best TV shows, movies, and sporting events would be siphoned off to pay-TV, forcing consumers to pay for programming they had previously received without charge.

This same argument has been heard repeatedly since 1964, and some still say it is true. The California voters apparently believed it, because they overwhelmingly approved the "Free Television Act," thus outlawing pay-TV in California by popular vote. This law prohibited all forms of pay television in the state, no matter how they might be transmitted. There was an exemption for cable systems that charged a flat monthly fee not based on program content.

Had it survived, this law would have prohibited all of the premium services now offered by cable television systems. However, the advocates of pay-TV challenged the constitutionality of the ballot proposition, and in 1966 the state Supreme Court overturned it in the case of *Weaver v. Jordan* (64 Cal.2d 235). The court said the fact that the Free Television Act was overwhelmingly approved by the polls did not guarantee its validity. In fact, the majority said the right to charge a fee for television programs is in effect a Constitutional right that may not be voted out of existence at the polls. To justify that ruling, the state court quoted *West Virginia Board of Education v. Barnette*, an earlier U.S. Supreme Court ruling:

> The very purpose of the Bill of Rights was to withdraw certain subjects from the vicissitudes of political controversy, to place them beyond the reach of majorities and officials and to establish them as legal principles to be applied by the courts. One's right to life, liberty, property, to free speech, a free press, freedom of worship and assembly, and other fundamental rights may not be submitted to a vote; they depend on the outcome of no elections. (319 U.S. 624, 638)

By the time this decision was handed down, the pay-television firm that had been the target of the 1964 ballot proposition was out of business. However, new pay-TV services later appeared in California as they did elsewhere, unhampered by the old Free Television Act's purported ban on pay TV.

By 1982 there were at least 27 over-the-air subscription television stations (as opposed to cable-based systems) in the United States, with about 1.3 million subscribers. Almost all of these stations operate on UHF channels. Many additional people subscribe to pay-TV services delivered by over-the-air multipoint distribution service (MDS) transmitters, direct broadcast satellites (DBS), and cable.

In 1982 the FCC deregulated over-the-air subscription television stations. The commission dropped its "Complement of Four Rule," which restricted STV operations to communities with four or more commercial TV stations. Also, the rules requiring STV stations to do community ascertainment and offer 28 hours per week of free programming were abolished. The elimination of the Complement of Four Rule opened the way for STV stations in about 70 additional cities.

To prevent non-subscribers from receiving their programming, over-the-air STV stations have to "scramble" their signals. As a result, their broadcasts cannot be received without a special decoder unit provided by the company.

However, one of the problems encountered by these STV stations was the manufacture and sale of pirate decoding devices to unscramble the signals. In the late 1970s electronics enthusiasts in several cities began selling unauthorized decoders, enabling viewers to receive the pay-TV programming without paying for it. It should be a citizen's right to receive any signal that is transmitted over the air, they contended.

Pay-TV executives and local law enforcement officials took a different view, however, and a number of pirate decoder entrepreneurs were criminally prosecuted. Some of these prosecutions were challenged in court. In 1980 and 1981 two federal appellate courts affirmed the right to pay-TV firms to deny their programming to unauthorized viewers (see *National Subscription Television v. S & H Television*, 644 F.2d 820, and *Chartwell Communications Group v. Westbrook*, 637 F.2d 459).

In so ruling, the courts relied on Section 605 of the Communications Act, which reads in part, "No person not being authorized by the sender shall intercept any radio communication and divulge or publish the existence, contents, substance, purport, effect or meaning of such intercepted communication to any person." This forbids the unauthorized reception of pay-TV signals, the courts said in the *National* and *Chartwell* cases. Also, the courts noted that the FCC's rules require pay-TV operators to lease rather than sell their decoders to viewers. Thus, the sale of pirate decoders as well as their unauthorized use is illegal, the courts said.

Multipoint Distribution Service

From a consumer's point of view, STV and *Multipoint Distribution Service* (MDS) systems are just about identical: both offer pay-TV programming that is transmitted over the air and can be received only with special equipment.

However, STV and MDS are treated very differently under the FCC rules. STV stations use standard television channels for their broadcasts and try to prevent unauthorized reception by scrambling their signals. MDS stations, on the other hand, use much higher frequencies (above 2000 mHz), not standard VHF or UHF TV channels. And their signals are frequently not scrambled. Because it requires a special "converter" and antenna to receive MDS broadcasts, most MDS systems have not found it essential (or practical) to scramble their signals. Nevertheless, MDS operators, like STV stations, have sometimes taken legal action against electronics buffs who build and sell equipment that will receive their broadcasts.

MDS falls into a different legal category than STV broadcasting. Strictly speaking, MDS isn't even a form of broadcasting. MDS was created by the FCC to permit point-to-point closed-circuit television. The idea was that a school district headquarters, for example, might wish to prepare educational television programs and distribute them to schools all over town. For a fee, an MDS station would transmit the programs to a receiving system at each of the schools. Hence, it was called a *multipoint* distribution system.

Because of its intended use, the multipoint distribution service was officially designated as a *common carrier*. That is, it was *not* to engage in broadcasting. Instead, it was to transmit only to specific receiving locations, delivering programs prepared by someone else. MDS systems do not create their own programs—they only provide a means of delivery. Nor do they have any say over the content of the material they deliver. As common carriers, MDS systems provide transmission services on a first-come, first-served basis, leasing time to program originators.

By the late 1970s, program originators such as Home Box Office and Showtime had begun to lease MDS transmitter time and install receiving equipment at the homes of subscribers. When that happened, MDS systems began to look more like broadcasters than common carriers. However, MDS stations remain classified as common carriers: only the program providers and not the MDS station owners have the right to control the content of the programming. For that matter, the FCC itself has no right to control the content of common carrier communications. As a result, program providers who use MDS systems for their transmissions can deliver movies and other programs to home viewers that would not be permitted by a broadcaster—movies containing explicit sex and earthy language, for example. Sometimes local governments have tried to outlaw this kind of programming. However, the courts have consistently held that they cannot stop it unless the material is legally obscene, which it rarely is.

In fact, one of the major questions about MDS systems is whether the FCC has any legal basis for controlling the programming delivered to the public over MDS. Since the FCC can't control the content of common carrier communications, and also has no direct authority over the program originators (who aren't broadcasters and hold no FCC licenses), this may be a broadcast-like service that has the full First Amendment rights of the print media—for the moment, at least.

Some think MDS offers the best of both broadcasting and cable. It costs far less to set up an MDS system than to wire a city for cable, and the service can be established much more quickly. And yet MDS can offer many of the same programming choices as a pay-cable system.

In 1983, the FCC further expanded MDS by making more microwave channels available. In addition, the commission authorized schools and colleges holding channel assignments in the *instructional television fixed service* (ITFS) to lease surplus channel capacity to program originators for MDS-like services to subscribers. This created something of a bonanza for some educational institutions—and it prompted a flood of new applications for ITFS assignments from schools that planned to lease them out to program providers. This is practical because MDS and ITFS both operate in the same part of the radio spectrum.

New multichannel pay-TV services were being established all over the United States in the mid-1980s, using frequencies assigned to MDS and ITFS. These systems were preparing to offer not only pay-TV programming but also other video services such as teletext and data transmission. Some of the new systems on the drawing boards will offer two-way communication with subscribers by allowing them to communicate back to the program provider via a small computer and telephone lines.

Many of the companies that were moving into MDS-type programming had names that traditional TV viewers might recognize. For instance, in 1983 CBS began leasing ITFS channels so it could offer several channels of pay-TV programming in a number of major cities. Originally, CBS sought permission to offer multichannel MDS programming in five large cities where it also owns television stations, but the FCC refused to allow that. CBS then started leasing ITFS channels as a way to offer pay-TV service anyway.

Despite their attractiveness to large media companies, however, MDS systems do have limitations. For instance, their service area is generally limited to about a 25-mile radius. Also, the receiving antenna and converter are still expensive enough to discourage some potential subscribers, although the price has declined considerably in recent years.

Operational Fixed Service

In the mid-1980s, still another alphabet-soup technology was emerging as a potential competitor to traditional television broadcasting. The *operational fixed service* (OFS), like MDS, is a microwave transmission service. Originally established to provide for the transmission of video programming to hotels and commercial buildings, OFS was opened up for home video services by a 1983 FCC decision.

The result was still another flood of applications in the FCC's in-basket, as hundreds of companies and individuals sought a chance to get in at the start of another new service that might prove lucrative as a video programming delivery system.

Unlike MDS, however, OFS is set up so that those who provide the delivery system must also have an ownership or contractual interest in the programming delivered to subscribers. OFS will not be a common carrier service like MDS: its licensees will apparently be accountable to the FCC for the content of the programming they offer.

Thus, at this writing it appeared that this service might not be able to compete on an equal footing with pay-cable and MDS systems, which are free to deliver programming that may violate the FCC's rules for broadcasters but not common carriers.

OFS also is disadvantaged in comparison to MDS in another way. Only a few of the frequencies that have been allocated for OFS are as good for reliable communication as the ones assigned to MDS. The rest fall in a portion of the radio spectrum where rainy weather severely interferes with reception, causing potential blackouts for hours or days at a time. Unless this problem can be solved by the use of much better equipment, this fact alone may leave OFS systems handicapped in the competition for preeminence in the home video marketplace.

However, OFS systems may also be used to support rather than compete with the other broadcast-like home video services. OFS systems can deliver programming to MDS operators, cable systems, and satellite master antenna television systems in apartment buildings.

Direct Broadcast Satellites

From a technical standpoint, the most innovative video delivery system is the *direct broadcast satellite service* (DBS). Authorized by the FCC in 1982, DBS is the only one of the new technologies that permits direct service to millions of viewers over a large geographic area (sometimes up to half of the North American continent) without any local intermediary at all.

The concept underlying DBS is fairly simple, although the technology to accomplish it is complex and expensive. A number of satellites are positioned above the equator at an altitude of 22,300 miles. To stay in orbit, every satellite must move at a high rate of speed, but at this particular altitude the satellite's speed exactly matches the Earth's rotation speed. The result: a satellite that is positioned over the equator at this altitude appears to remain stationary over one point on the Earth's surface, not moving at all. Such a satellite is said to be *geosynchronous*.

Why does it matter whether a satellite is geosynchronous? The parabolic "dish" antennas used to communicate with these satellites are highly directional; if a satellite were not stationary, very costly tracking hardware, computers, and software would have to be used to keep the dish antennas pointed at the satellite. On the other hand, if the satellite is geosynchronous, both the transmitting and receiving antennas can be adjusted to the correct orientation and locked in place.

Once a geosynchronous satellite is in orbit, transmitting stations on the ground send up signals on an "uplink" frequency. The satellite receives these signals and retransmits them back to earth on a "downlink," which is usually a different frequency.

Geosynchronous satellites are not new. In fact, virtually all of the nation's major cable systems, broadcasters, wire services, and newspapers have used these satellites for years to relay programming or information. However, the earlier communications satellites operated with such low transmitter power that a very sensitive (and therefore large) dish antenna was required to receive the signal.

The new DBS satellites use not only more powerful transmitters but also higher frequencies, allowing good reception with much smaller dish antennas. Television signals from the new broadcast satellites can be received with a rooftop dish antenna only two or three feet in diameter. Most earlier satellites required a dish antenna at least ten feet in diameter for dependable television reception.

Most communications satellites have a "footprint" that can cover a sizable portion of the North American continent, meaning that a viewer in Massachusetts and another in Michigan can receive exactly the same signal at the same time. DBS is a regional broadcasting service, not a local one.

In fact, because DBS threatens to bypass not only local television stations but also cable systems and the other local delivery systems (such as MDS), several industry groups opposed the creation of the satellite broadcasting service when it was proposed. The National Association of Broadcasters went to court to challenge the FCC's authority to establish direct satellite broadcasting.

The NAB contended that allowing direct satellite broadcasting violates Section 307(b) of the Communications Act, which requires the FCC to maintain a "fair, efficient and equitable distribution" of service among the states. NAB contended that the non-local character of DBS made it such a radical departure from traditional broadcast service that it could not be authorized without an act of Congress. The Court of Appeals rejected this argument and upheld the FCC's authority to allow DBS in 1984.

Under the FCC rules authorizing the new service, DBS systems are free to offer either standard television or an enhanced version with a higher quality picture (called "high definition television" or HDTV). The FCC permitted DBS system owners to deliver their own programming or to lease channels to others and serve as common carriers, or do a little of both.

At this writing, the FCC had granted construction permits to eight companies that hoped to offer DBS service. Most of them proposed to offer at least three channels or programming in each region of the country.

While billion-dollar corporations were rushing to get full DBS systems into operation as quickly as possible, they were upstaged by United Satellite Communications, Inc. (USCI), which began marketing a DBS-type service in late 1983. At this writing, the USCI service was available in a number of midwestern states, using leased transmitter time on a Canadian satellite that was originally designed for non-broadcast applications.

To receive the USCI service, a customer was charged a $300 installation fee for the dish antenna and receiving hardware, with a monthly service charge of about $40 after that. Those who preferred could buy the receiving equipment for $1,000 and then pay a smaller monthly service charge. For these fees, the subscriber received two movie channels, a video music channel, and ESPN's predominantly sports channel—plus the satisfaction of knowing that he or she was one of the first to have a brand-new kind of home video service.

Meanwhile, the Satellite Television Corporation, a subsidiary of the giant Communications Satellite Corporation (Comsat), was preparing to launch its DBS service in 1985 with temporary satellite facilities, and then switch over to its own high-powered broadcast satellite in 1986. Some of the other companies that won FCC construction permits in 1982 were also moving quickly to get their DBS systems into full operation. Others, however, were hedging in the mid-1980s, opting not to build their full systems until they have a chance to reassess the profit potential of DBS.

In short, direct satellite broadcasting may join cable, local television broadcasting, and the other broadcast-like technologies in a high-stakes competition for the public's video entertainment dollar. It is too early to tell whether this will lead to revolutionary changes in American mass communications—or merely turn into a multibillion-dollar boondoggle with little consumer acceptance.

Satellite Master Antenna Television

While many people were captivated by the idea of direct satellite broadcasting, another much more mundane television delivery system was winning quiet consumer acceptance. *Satellite Master Antenna Television* (SMATV) systems were being established in large apartment and condominium complexes all over the country, providing residents with a private cable-like service.

SMATV involves nothing more than a good receiving antenna system for over-the-air television reception, plus a large dish antenna to pick up satellite-relayed premium cable services, such as movie, sports, and news channels. The programming is then routed to individual residences by coaxial cable.

SMATV is not really a new technology. Technically, it's nothing more than a private form of cable television. However, it became much more popular after the FCC's 1979 decision to drop its old licensing requirements for receive-only dish antennas. Also, the cost of a satellite television receiving system declined sharply in the early 1980s. This made it much easier for apartment building owners to set up SMATV systems instead of providing access to a local cable system.

Several other legal actions also encouraged the growth of SMATV systems, often at the expense of community-wide cable systems. In 1982, the Supreme Court overturned a New York "cable access" law that forced landlords to permit cable installations in their apartment buildings for a $1 fee. In *Loretto v. Teleprompter Manhattan Cable Corp.* (458 U.S. 419), the court said this was a confiscation of private property without proper compensation. As a result, New York cable operators were required to negotiate with each landlord. And landlords were free to exclude cable from their buildings, offering their own private SMATV systems instead.

A year after the *Loretto* decision, the FCC acted to curb another attempt by local governments to encourage cable television at the expense of private SMATV systems. In New Jersey, the state's Board of Public Utilities tried to prevent the construction of an SMATV system in an apartment complex. The board said the SMATV system would interfere with the viability of the government-sanctioned cable system which was supposed to have a monopoly on cable service in the area.

The FCC overruled the utility board's efforts, declaring that the regulation of SMATV systems is federally preempted. That is, SMATV systems are regulated by the FCC, and the commission was saying the states may not adopt rules that interfere with the federal agency's policies permitting such systems to operate. As a result, SMATV systems may be developed without the approval of local governments—except for such matters as compliance with zoning and building codes.

Video Cassette and Video Disc Systems

Although video cassette recorders (VCRs) and video disc players (VDPs) are not really communication media as such, they deserve some mention in this summary of the new video technologies because of their profound effect on the mass media.

Chapter Six discusses the copyright problems of video recording. However, the impact of VCRs and disc players extends far beyond the Copyright Act. For example, as more and more viewers watch pre-recorded programs instead of live television, the result may be significant changes in the economics of broadcasting and cablecasting. This is especially true if viewers turn to movies and specialized programs. But on the other hand, the "time shifting" capabilities of VCRs enable viewers to see TV programs that they might otherwise miss because of schedule conflicts. This tends to increase the size of the television viewing audience for any particular show.

At a time when at least 20 million Americans live in households equipped with VCRs or disc players, it is apparent that these new kinds of hardware are changing the shape of the mass media. It remains to be seen where those changes will be felt and to what extent.

Electronic Publishing

In addition to the television-like home video services, there has been another aspect of the revolution in communications technology in the 1980s: the growth of electronic publishing in various forms.

The two main technologies are *teletext*, a one-way text delivery system that often utilizes an over-the-air television signal, and *videotex*, a term that describes a number of different "interactive" (i.e., two-way) information services, some of them sponsored by newspapers alone or in cooperation with telephone companies or others.

Because it is often transmitted over the air, teletext is more heavily regulated by government agencies than the various forms of videotex. Some say videotex is a term that was created just to frustrate English teachers: it seems to desperately need another "T" so "text" is spelled correctly. However, the term has become widely accepted—without any final T.

Teletext services have been offered by broadcasters on an experimental basis in a number of U.S. cities, including Chicago, Cincinnati, Los Angeles, Salt Lake City, St. Louis, and Washington, D.C. The service usually includes news, weather, sports scores, and sometimes a variety of other items such as movie listings, stock prices, airline schedules and shopping guides. Teletext can be disseminated by any television-like delivery system, including cable, MDS, and DBS, among others.

To receive a broadcast teletext service, the viewer needs a small command unit, a teletext adaptor, and a television set. The command unit is used to call up a list of the available materials and then to specify the desired item (usually by calling up the "page" on which it appears). The on-screen display may include both text and graphics.

The teletext messages are transmitted along with the TV signal. In most systems, the information is carried in the "vertical blanking interval" between frames of the television picture. When the picture on a TV set rolls, a black bar becomes visible between frames; that is the vertical blanking interval. A considerable amount of information can be placed there in digital form without affecting the picture or sound quality.

In 1983, the FCC adopted rules formally authorizing broadcast teletext services. To the alarm of many broadcasters, the commission declined to set technical standards for teletext, preferring instead to leave that up to the marketplace. As a result, broadcasters feared that several incompatible systems might develop. If so, viewers would have to buy several different adaptors to be able to receive all of the teletext services available. However, at this writing certain major corporations including CBS and AT&T were developing a set of standards that they hoped would prevent the proliferation of incompatible systems.

There was also controversy over the FCC's decision to allow cable systems to delete the teletext messages from television signals they deliver to their customers, inserting their own teletext messages in place of the original material.

The commission's teletext rules allow broadcasters to use teletext not only for messages of general public interest but also to provide specialized non-broadcast data services for business and industry. In adopting these rules, the FCC said broadcasters would be subjected to most of the normal restrictions on broadcast content when the teletext messages are directed to the general public. However, when a broadcaster offers private teletext messages, the common carrier rules apply.

Thus, the FCC was saying that a broadcaster could at times also be a common carrier—a seeming contradiction in terms that illustrates just how much the new technologies are blurring the old distinctions between broadcast and non-broadcast communications services. Another example of this merger of media was the FCC's decision not to apply the Fairness Doctrine and Equal Time Rule to broadcast teletext services. In announcing these rules, the commission acknowledged that teletext is "a unique blending of the print medium with radio broadcasting. . ."

Videotex services are much more varied and unregulated than teletext. In the mid-1980s the Knight-Ridder newspaper group was offering Viewtron, a two-way electronic information service delivered over telephone lines, to subscribers in south Flordia. The system used a standard television receiver with an auxiliary keyboard and adaptor unit. It allowed subscribers to call up news and sports, classified advertising, and a variety of other kinds of information. But because of the two-way nature of the system, subscribers could also order such things as theater and airline tickets through Viewtron.

Viewtron, like most similar electronic publishing ventures, was local and experimental in nature. However, by 1984 two nationwide electronic information services were operating as profitable business ventures: The Source and CompuServe. At this writing, CompuServe was apparently the most successful mass-market electronic publishing venture anywhere, with more than 100,000 paying customers.

Both The Source and CompuServe are services for personal computer owners who purchase a membership and then pay for their on-line access time. Both systems are accessed by telephone, using a "modem" (a device that links a computer to a telephone line for data communications). In addition to the hourly access charges, some members also pay telephone tolls to contact these information services, since neither service has toll-free phone lines for all parts of the country.

Both systems provide market reports, airline reservations, news, and other information. In addition, both offer two-way communication between users, allowing people with special interests to leave messages for each other (this is an example of "electronic mail") and communicate directly with one another by typing on their computer keyboards. These two services are mergers of computer and communication technologies; they may be the first of many such services that will develop as the microcomputer becomes a standard fixture in American homes.

A number of cable systems also offer electronic text services, some of them two-way systems using two cable channels for the exchange of information between subscribers and a central computer.

Whatever their specific arrangements, all of these electronic publishing ventures represent combinations of print and electronic communication techniques. Perhaps the key legal issue they raise is whether they should be regulated by any government and, if so, to what extent and by whom.

POLICY QUESTIONS, THE LAW, AND NEW TECHNOLOGIES

Taken as a group, these new mass communication systems could become a dramatic force for change. They may offer the public an unprecedented variety of viewing and reading alternatives, or they could offer nothing more than the same old product delivered by fancy new hardware.

For the traditional media, the new media represent both a threat and a promise—a threat of new competition (and of extinction for those who do not adapt) and a promise of new opportunities to grow. And above all, these new media challenge our traditional definitions of publishing, broadcasting, and common carrier services.

Perhaps we should conclude this chapter by summarizing some of the difficult unresolved issues that these new technologies have created.

The Demise of the Scarcity Rationale

For more than 50 years broadcasters have been subjected to far more intense government regulation than the print media. The fundamental rationale for this regulation has been that broadcasters are using a scarce public resource, the radio spectrum, and that they must therefore use it in the "public interest, convenience and necessity." Broadcasters have been regarded as "public trustees" who were given the right to use their frequencies only for a short period of time.

The FCC has largely abandoned that philosophy in recent years. With an incredible variety of mass communications choices now available to consumers, it is hard to argue that there is scarcity now. In fact, there are far more alternatives available in the electronic media than in newspapers—which are largely free of government content regulation.

Although a broadcaster still must have a government license while a newspaper publisher does not, in practice it is far more difficult to become a successful newspaper publisher than it is to become a successful broadcaster.

Numerous cities that support only one or two daily newspapers will support dozens of radio and television stations. The economic realities make it virtually impossible to start a new daily newspaper today, while new electronic media of many kinds are emerging regularly.

In view of these developments, the FCC has lately looked almost entirely to marketplace forces to assure that the public receives good service from the regulated media. In this spirit, the commission has repeatedly abandoned rules that were considered sacred for many years, astonishing even some broadcasters and cable operators, people who had come to assume that extensive government regulation, like taxes, was inevitable.

Regulating Functions, Not Means of Delivery

We have repeatedly used the term "delivery systems" in this discussion. We are suggesting that a television program is a television program, regardless of how it gets from a producer's studio to the viewer's screen. The only thing that really differs among all of the television technologies is the means of delivery.

When the video product can be delivered by many different means, the government—and the public—must face up to some of the inconsistencies in the old way of regulating the media. As was pointed out earlier, a motion picture that could never be delivered by over-the-air television because of its content may be perfectly legal if it is delivered by a cable system or MDS, neither of which is subject to all of the content regulations faced by broadcasters.

Because cable systems, unlike broadcasters, do not use the airwaves, it is not difficult to rationalize the greater freedom from government content regulation enjoyed by cable systems. But MDS systems, like broadcasters, use the airwaves as a method of delivering video programming to consumers, and this makes it hard to come up with a logical reason why broadcasters should face strict content regulations that may not apply to the MDS systems.

In fact, to carry the irony a little further, a pay-TV system that uses a UHF TV channel faces stricter government regulation than other pay systems that use the MDS band.

As the rules stand today, we can offer a generalization: if video programming is delivered to consumers on a frequency below 1000 mHz, it is subject to the traditional restrictions on content, but if the broadcast frequency is higher than that, many of the rules may not apply.

Given the absurdity of that kind of double standard, many critics of the system believe it would make more sense to regulate *functions* instead of *delivery systems*. Indeed, the commission has started doing that in some instances. For example, a broadcast teletext system is subjected to the broadcast rules when the transmitted material is intended for the general public, although the same teletext system—operating on a television channel that is reserved for broadcasting—is treated as a common carrier when it transmits certain non-broadcast materials. The commission has shown the same kind of flexibility in its rules for DBS: satellite operators can choose to be either broadcasters (if they originate their own programming) or common carriers (if they lease their channels out to others). DBS licensees will be allowed to select their own regulatory category.

It would seem logical to establish consistent policies for all providers of home video programming. All broadcast-like services should be treated alike, as should all common carrier services, regardless of the bailiwick to which a particular delivery system officially belongs.

Technical Standards, or the Lack Thereof

When television broadcasting began, it was possible for consumers to buy TV sets with confidence that their sets were capable of receiving all of the television signals within range. There was no question of various stations using different and incompatible transmission techniques.

And when color television was introduced a few years later, consumers could be sure that any brand of color TV set would receive the color television programs being transmitted by any broadcaster within range. Those who owned black and white TV sets were not ignored, either: they could receive the color programs (in black and white) on their sets without any special difficulty.

This was all true because the FCC established *technical standards* for television broadcasting, electronic rules of the road that all stations had to obey.

Likewise, when stereophonic FM radio broadcasting was introduced, consumers were assured that any brand of receiver they might buy would be compatible with the type of stereo signal being broadcast by each station that was using stereo. Moreover, those who continued to use monaural FM radios could still receive the programming from stereo stations (though not in stereo, of course).

This, too, was possible because the FCC established and enforced technical standards.

But during the 1980s the commission has repeatedly declined to establish national standards for the new technologies. For example, after years of controversy the FCC simply declared that it would not establish a technical standard for AM stereo broadcasting. That meant a consumer might buy a stereo radio that would correctly receive one AM radio station in town, but not others. It might be necessary to buy four or more AM stereo radios in order to receive all of the AM stereo stations in a given city.

As indicated earlier in this chapter, the FCC also refused to establish technical standards for teletext, leaving that up to the marketplace to determine. And the same thing has happened in several other areas, including high-definition television and the very important area of direct satellite broadcasting.

Perhaps the FCC is correct in saying that the marketplace will set a standard—eventually. But by not establishing uniform technical standards, the commission has surely delayed the development of several worthwhile new technologies.

Why does this cause delays? Because few broadcasters would want to risk investing a large amount of money in equipment that is designed for one set of standards, only to see the industry end up standardizing on something else. And many consumers are also reluctant to buy hardware that may be made obsolete by changing standards.

Until someone somewhere establishes a standard, a new technology cannot really move toward general public acceptance. Given enough time, everyone may come to agree on the standard set by one large company. Many broadcasters predict that a de facto industry standard for AM stereo will be established when General Motors decides which AM stereo format to offer in GM cars. In the past, volunteer industry groups have been organized to set standards when the government would not or could not do the job. However, several recent antitrust lawsuits have made many trade groups reluctant to get together and do anything in concert—even set technical standards.

Perhaps the marketplace will eventually set standards for all of the new technologies. And perhaps some things are better decided in the marketplace than by government fiat. But many observers of the new technologies feel that technical standards are not among those things. The development of several new technologies has already been delayed for years because the FCC has not seen fit to set technical standards.

Electronic Pie in the Sky

While the government's regulatory policies toward the new technologies have been criticized both by those who feel there is too much regulation and by those who think there is too little, those who are pioneering these technologies have not always been above reproach, either.

Entrepreneurs—some of them desperate for a piece of the action—have been promising anything and everything to the regulators—while knowing perfectly well that they could never keep those promises.

The result has been something of a corporate bait-and-switch game in which huge companies promise local governments, state governments, and even the FCC that they will build incredible communications systems and then sell their product at give-away prices. The strategy has often been to outbid the competition and win the necessary government license or franchise at any cost, and then to redesign the whole system once the license or franchise is safely in hand and the competing applicants have disappeared.

Sometimes cable companies have promised cities enormous cash incentives and dream-world service coupled with bargain-basement rates for subscriptions. Some cable operators have actually kept these promises, and the public has benefited as a result. But in too many instances cable promoters have demanded that their contracts be renegotiated even before their systems were put into service. The cable operator would pose a blunt question to local officials: "Do you want a cable system in your city or don't you?"

On occasion this high-stakes poker game would be played out to its conclusion, with local officials refusing to budge and the cable company responding by going out of business before the system was finished. But then the local authorities would often discover that the people who had promised the financial backing had also insulated themselves and their parent companies from their cable subsidiaries. And embarrassed local officials would have to start the cable bidding process all over again—while trying to explain all of this to their impatient constituents.

However, on other occasions local officialdom would avoid that awkward situation by giving in and rewriting the cable contract or franchise—on terms far less favorable to the community.

Nor are all of the victims in this process local government officials. Almost every communications lawyer in Washington can tell stories about the same thing happening at the Federal Communications Commission's headquarters building. Some of the best examples of electronic pie in the sky can be found in the applications for such new services as direct broadcast satellites and cellular mobile telephone systems.

In many instances the rival applicants have promised to build impressive communications systems, systems that they knew perfectly well could never be operated at a profit in the real world. Again, the trick was to win the license. . . and worry later about getting the FCC to allow the system to be scaled down so it would be practical and profitable.

Bait and switch is, after all, a proven (but unethical) way to sell cars and furniture. Why shouldn't it work just as well when the product is a cable or satellite television system and the "customers" are government officials?

Marketing by "Package Deal"

Another thing that troubles some observers of the new technologies is the tendency of both those who run them and those who regulate them to bundle things up and sell them as packages.

Suppose the government established policies forbidding newsstands to sell individual copies of newspapers or magazines. Suppose you could buy only a "consumer reading package" that included a newspaper, two general interest magazines, and an assortment of specialty publications designed to appeal to a variety of individual tastes and preferences. If you wanted just one copy of your favorite newspaper or magazine—or if your chosen specialty magazine wasn't included in the package deal—you would be out of luck. You might have to buy *Newsweek* in order to get *Car and Driver* or take *Seventeen* to get *Playboy*.

That, in essence, is what the policy-makers who regulate the new technologies are requiring in many instances. And in some cases the entrepreneurs themselves are going even further than the rules require in bundling their services. Everyone talks of (and regulators often demand) multichannel capability in new communications systems. That means each new delivery system offers a variety of different channels, but those channels are almost always marketed only in package deals. For instance, at this point it is almost impossible to obtain the premium cable services (movies, sports, etc.) without first purchasing the basic service (local television signals). The FCC's must-carry rules force cable operators to sell their product in this fashion. MDS and DBS operators are also moving toward package deals. If you want everything in the package, it may be a bargain; if not, you have few options.

Some may say that the marketplace will correct this problem—if it is a problem. If consumers really want the freedom to pick and choose, someone will give them that option.

That may well happen someday, but only if the policy-makers really believe in the free enterprise system strongly enough to allow their pet programming schemes to run the risk of failing in the marketplace.

At this point that sort of freedom rarely exists. Most communities have only one franchised cable system operator, for instance, and that operator is required to offer anywhere from 20 to 100 channels of programming. Why shouldn't each channel be available as an individual item, just as each newspaper or magazine can be purchased separately from the rest? Not everyone wants all of the channels, but the premium cable services usually are not (and legally cannot be) sold without the basic service included in the package.

In almost any other kind of business, these package deals would be called a "tying arrangement," a probable violation of the antitrust laws (see Chapter 13). To get a desired product on which the supplier has a monopoly (the premium services), you have to buy another product (the basic service) that you could get for less elsewhere (in this case, at no charge over the air).

While the plethora of new video delivery systems gives consumers many new options, it sometimes also deprives them of options. Perhaps marketplace forces will eventually assure the consumer as many choices in content as there are in hardware.

A Summary of
New Technologies and the Law

WHAT ARE THE NEW TECHNOLOGIES?

The "new technologies" are a variety of new systems for delivering printed matter, illustrations, and television programming, or a combination of these, to consumers' homes.

WHAT IS SUBSCRIPTION TELEVISION?

The term "subscription television" refers to VHF or UHF television stations that "scramble" their signals and then charge viewers a fee to receive their programming, which often includes movies and sports events. In a broader sense, subscription television also refers to cable or microwave transmission systems that offer premium programming for a fee. An example is the multipoint distribution service (MDS), which uses the airwaves but which is legally classified as a "common carrier" rather than a broadcaster.

WHAT IS A COMMON CARRIER?

A common carrier is a service that is available to everyone on a first-come, first-served basis for a standard fee. In the transportation industry, airlines, bus companies, and some trucking companies are common carriers. In communications, the telephone companies are common carriers, as are many satellite and microwave communication systems. The Federal Communications Commission regulates many common carriers, but it has no right to control the content of common carrier communications.

DOES IT MATTER IF A VIDEO DELIVERY SYSTEM IS A COMMON CARRIER?

Broadcasters are subject to many forms of content regulation by the FCC; common carriers are not. Thus, a common carrier can offer television programming that might be illegal on a conventional television station (as do some cable systems).

WHAT OTHER NEW TECHNOLOGIES ARE THERE?

In addition to the growing cable and STV industries, an important new communication technology is *direct broadcast satellites*, which have transmitters powerful enough to deliver programming directly to small rooftop "dish" antennas at viewers' homes. Also, the FCC is now licensing hundreds of new *low power television* (LPTV) stations, which will offer programming to serve communities and special interests that have not been fully served by full-power television stations in big cities.

WHAT ARE VIDEOTEX AND TELETEXT?

Videotex and teletext are two kinds of electronic information systems. The term videotex refers to a variety of two-way information systems that deliver news and other material to consumers' homes and can receive messages from consumers as well, using cable or telephone lines. Teletext is a one-way system that typically uses an unused portion of a television signal to deliver text to consumers for display on a modified TV set.

SIDEBAR TO CHAPTER 15:
A GUIDED TOUR OF
A COMPUTERIZED
INFORMATION SYSTEM

"You have EMAIL waiting."

That sentence may cross your screen just after you sign on to CompuServe Information Service (CIS). It is probably the service's main attraction. Though there are many who buy CompuServe for specialized information—stock quotes, airline reservations, weather data, news reports, reference databases and more—the most popular item CIS sells is people, interaction with other "users."

This two-way computerized information exchange may be a harbinger of things to come not because it promises to change the face of the news business (at least in its present form that's very unlikely) but because it offers something no other medium could until now—a controlled, structured environment in which to communicate with the rest of the world, or at least those who've chosen to subscribe to CIS.

That piece of "EMAIL" (electronic mail) waiting for you could be from almost anyone. It could be from a professor of musicology who's responding to a message you left asking whether anyone can explain why Bach wrote a piece of music a certain way. It could be a fellow computer enthusiast hopelessly snarled in the throes of a program and pleading for your help. It could be from a pal of yours, a space buff, who's found the answer to the nagging question that was bothering both of you: What is NASA going to do about the problems with the payload booster rockets on the Space Shuttle? Probably none of these people have you met in person. They're all acquaintances you've come across by sitting down at your keyboard. And they're surprisingly easy to find.

If you were to walk down a city street and stop people at random in search of someone who shared a specialized interest (sailing or space flight, for instance), it might be a while before you'd find the right person. But because of the way CompuServe is organized, you can find people who share your interests very quickly. Logic, not happenstance, plays the major role in determining who you meet and what you talk about on CompuServe. Once you're familiar with how CompuServe operates, it's not hard to find people of like minds.

CompuServe maintains many Special Interest Groups, called SIGs. You can "log into" any of them by simply typing a few letters and numbers from a directory you receive when you join CompuServe. If you're a writer, for instance, and you have a question about a particular market, just type "G-HOM-136" and you will soon be in the Writers SIG, where you have these options: You may read messages left by others (or leave messages yourself), read poetry or short stories written by others, or "talk" directly to other writers if they're signed on the same time you are. Typing gets fast and furious sometimes when several people get to "talking" at once. The computer puts your name, or a pseudo-nym you select, at the head of each line you type.

Conversation in each of the SIGs generally concerns the topic of that SIG. If you want to get more specific, you can ask for a list of users who have chosen to indicate their particular fields of interest. Finding someone to answer a question or just someone to chat with isn't difficult.

Feeling unstructured? Ready to take on any and all comers on any topic? Then try CompuServe's CB. It's set up to operate much as a Citizens Band radio. The commands are similar to those used in the SIGs, only you're encouraged to adopt a "handle" and not use your real name. Some SIG users regard CB as a zoo and won't go near it; others regard it as a zoo and drop by occasionally anyway. The general level of conversation is usually several notches below the topic-oriented chatter on the SIGs, but that's not to say it can't be just as intellectual when the need arises. Just when you're ready to quit in disgust and head for more fertile regions on the system, you're liable to fall into a chat with "Mr. Postman" and discover that he's a heck of a guy who can fill you in on all the little details he sees as he walks his rounds in Fargo, North Dakota. Though there are far more male than female users of CompuServe, banter between the sexes is common. In fact, the most common ice-breakers on CB are "Where are you from?" and "R U M or F?" (You'll quickly find out that just because some people take shortcuts when they type doesn't mean they're not worth talking to.)

Both on CB and in the SIGs, the scope of CompuServe is largely the scope of its users. Editors of periodicals know that a good letters page is often a popular feature. But it's limited and two-way communication is impossible. Computer systems like CompuServe are breaking down those barriers and introducing people to each other in a new way; their popularity could foreshadow major changes in mass communications.

Will systems like CompuServe provide us with our news in the future? Well, in the very short term, certainly not. CIS offers some news on line right now. But considering that it costs at least $6 an hour to be on line—and that the equivalent of a single newspaper page takes about 15 minutes to transmit at the data rate normally used by CompuServe—other old and new media are a better bargain. To put it charitably, it's an expensive and slow way to keep informed.

Given that CompuServe's news delivery system can and will be improved, there's another consideration: being your own editor, though it may have its advantages, takes a LOT of time. News services transmit hundreds of stories each day. Even if you were able to select a list of topics in advance and use it to filter the day's stream of news for what you want, the chances are you'd miss an unexpected event.

A packaged electronic "newspaper" (such as those offered by Viewtron and some teletext systems) may be a better bet; faster transmission and editors to wade through the huge, repetititious flow of news may make the difference. But consider the speed with which you can get through your newspaper or magazine right now. Then consider the price per unit of information received.

The question is whether an electronic "newspaper" can match the paper version for ease of use and cost.

It's likely that both printed and electronic "newspapers" will flourish for some time.

EPILOGUE: ONGOING ISSUES IN MEDIA LAW

Mass Communications law is complex, and it's easy to lose sight of the main themes among all the details. At this point we should step back from the details for a moment and look at some of the major issues.

This is a time of revolutionary change in mass communications—and in communications law. In fields such as broadcasting, for instance, rules that have been in effect for 50 years are being abandoned in the 1980s, but the new technologies are creating difficult new legal questions. To cite one example, should cable television have the same legal status as over-the-air television? Or is cable a form of "electronic publishing" that should have the same First Amendment rights as the print media? Or should cable be treated as something between the two? Given that kind of fundamental uncertainty, no one can really predict what communications law will be like at the turn of the next century.

LIBEL: LEGAL ISSUES AND BIG JUDGMENTS

Through most of American history, the threat of being sued for libel has been the most serious continuing legal problem for the mass media, and today that threat may be more serious than ever. For a time, it appeared that the libel problem was subsiding. After *New York Times v. Sullivan*, the Supreme Court handed down a series of decisions that made it more and more difficult for plaintiffs to win libel suits. By the time of *Rosenbloom v. Metromedia* in 1971, even private persons involved in public issues were seemingly required to prove actual malice (i.e., that a falsehood had been published with knowledge or with reckless disregard for the truth).

However, the 1974 *Gertz v. Welch* decision reversed that trend. While *Gertz* rewrote the common law of libel in all 50 states by forcing even private plaintiffs to prove at least negligence (something that was not previously required in most states), it also reclassified many of the people whose names appear in the media as private persons. As a result, many persons who would previously have been required to prove actual malice were allowed to win libel cases by proving nothing more than negligence. For this reason, the growing tendency for courts to classify well-known people as private persons is seriously eroding the media's protection in libel suits.

But to talk of negligence, actual malice, private persons, and public figures is to dwell on legal theory. The real problem today is that juries in libel cases tend to ignore the law: they often hand out monstrous damage awards without worrying about whether the material in question was really libelous. Just since the first edition of this book was published, juries have announced no fewer than 20 different million-dollar verdicts in libel cases. Granted, almost all big libel judgments are eventually overturned by appellate courts, but by the time that happens the bill for legal expenses may be almost as big as the judgment was.

Moreover, the high cost of defending a libel suit will surely go even higher in the aftermath of the Supreme Court's *Keeton v. Hustler* and *Calder v. Jones* decisions, which permit "forum shopping" in libel cases. Few people would question the fairness of requiring a major corporation to defend a lawsuit in any state where it injures someone while doing business there. Years ago the Supreme Court authorized the states to exercise what is called "long-arm jurisdiction" over companies having "minimum contacts" with a particular state. But the Supreme Court now says that selling a few thousand copies of a magazine constitutes "minimum contacts."

Many journalists and lawyers disagree with that conclusion, but what is even more troubling about *Keeton* and *Calder* is that they allow individual writers and editors to be sued in courts thousands of miles from where they live and work. Where, one might ask, are the "minimum contacts" to justify a distant state taking jurisdiction over these individuals? It is one thing to force a major corporation to defend itself in the courts of all 50 states, but it is quite another to place that burden on individual journalists whose employers may or may not pay their legal expenses.

Another very troubling issue in libel law is the refusal of some courts to recognize the reporter's privilege concept when a journalist is defending a libel suit. To prove actual malice (or even negligence), the plaintiff must inquire into the reporter's methods and intentions. The reporter's accuracy in processing the information provided by his or her sources may be a crucial issue. Thus, plaintiffs are demanding the identity of reporters' sources in more and more libel cases. Alarmingly, some courts have ruled that journalists must either name their sources or accept the legal presumption that there was no source. If there is no source, of course, a court is free to decide the reporter fabricated the story—a clear sign of actual malice. In some states, journalists must choose between identifying their sources and losing libel suits they would otherwise win. Indeed, some libel insurance policies are invalid if the reporter refuses to name his or her news sources.

Fortunately, the courts in many states are allowing journalists to keep their sources confidential either under a shield law or reporter's privilege even in libel cases, but there is an alarming trend to the contrary in some states. Sometimes libel suits are filed for the sole purpose of forcing a journalist to identify a news source.

REPORTER'S PRIVILEGE AND JUDICIAL ACTIVISM

A closely related issue facing the mass media is the disputed validity of shield laws and reporter's privilege in other contexts. During the 1970s, at least two reporters spent more than a month in jail for their professional principles. It seems certain new confrontations like the *Farr* and *Farber* cases will arise in the coming years.

Although 26 states have shield laws, the courts have repeatedly carved out judicial exceptions to these laws, requiring reporters to disclose confidential information despite the seeming applicability of a shield law. In a number of states, the appellate courts have significantly weakened state shield laws by judicial interpretation. In response to that trend, the voters in California, for example, placed their shield law in the state Constitution. But almost as soon as that happened, the courts began whittling away at this new constitutional shield law just as if it were still merely an act of the state legislature.

However, there is a dramatic countervailing trend in the development of the reporter's privilege: a surprising number of both federal and state courts have now recognized the privilege judicially, even in the absence of a statutory shield law. In no fewer than seven states lacking shield laws, the state's highest court has taken this step.

Moreover, federal courts in appellate circuits from coast to coast have recognized a reporter's privilege as a matter of federal common law if not constitutional law. This judicially created reporter's privilege is by no means absolute: the courts are reserving the right to weigh the privilege against other factors, such as the relevance of the requested information and the court's need for it. Reporters and judges often clash on this issue, with reporters contending that even to submit the confidential information to a judge privately is a breech of their ethical duty. Judges, meanwhile, feel they alone can weigh all of the issues and must make the final decision. That means many more reporters may be cited for contempt of court and sent to jail before this issue is finally resolved, but at least the courts are beginning to recognize that there is such a thing as a reporter's privilege.

FREEDOM OF INFORMATION: OLD AND NEW THREATS

Even if the fight for a reporter's privilege is ultimately won, journalists will face other newsgathering legal problems. For one, governments are showing no great inclination to open their doors and files willingly. At the federal level, there is a strong Freedom of Information Act and a Sunshine Act, but Congress is under heavy pressure from the bureaucracy to weaken these laws. In recent years no fewer than 30 bills have been introduced in Congress to weaken the FoI Act. None has passed—yet. But the FBI and CIA, to name just two agencies that have sometimes abused the rights of American citizens in the past, have been lobbying for blanket exemptions from the FoI Act. If they get what they want, the public will lose its best means of keeping these agencies accountable for their conduct.

On the state level, the freedom of information picture seems a little brighter. Almost all states have both open meeting and public record legislation. However, it takes constant vigilance to force public officials to obey these laws. Given any glimmer of a chance, some government agencies will close their files and lock their meeting-room doors. In the coming years, a major goal in the FoI field will be to reduce the number of exceptions these laws recognize—and to add effective legal remedies for unlawful government secrecy—while warding off bureaucrats' attempts to rid themselves of the onerous task of doing the public's business in public.

Another legal problem of newsgathering concerns the fair trial-free press dilemma. The alarming trend toward closed courtrooms was slowed considerably by the Supreme Court's *Richmond Newspapers v. Virginia*, *Globe Newspaper v. Superior Court* and *Press Enterprise v. Superior Court* decisions. However, courtroom closures remain a problem in many states, particularly during pretrial proceedings. Judges often cite the alleged threat of prejudicial publicity to justify closing the doors during proceedings that have been routinely open to the public for decades—or centuries.

Journalists have been fighting still another access problem in the nation's courtrooms, but with more success. For years, cameras, tape recorders, and particularly television equipment were unwelcome in most courts. However, that began to change dramatically in the late 1970s. At least 40 states were allowing cameras and broadcast equipment in court under at least some circumstances by 1984. That trend was encouraged by the Supreme Court's *Chandler v. Florida* decision, which said broadcast coverage of court proceedings is not inherently prejudicial to defendants. The court said the states were free to allow television coverage, with the burden on defendants to prove that the coverage violated their rights in specific cases.

The *Chandler* case didn't give the media any special right to take their equipment into the nation's courtrooms, but at least the high court didn't order all cameras out of court with a single stroke of the judicial pen. The question now is how many states will eventually open their courtrooms to cameras, and under what conditions. And when, journalists wonder, will the federal courts finally be opened to photographic and broadcast coverage?

Like the problem of courtroom access for broadcasters and photographers, another major fair trial-free press problem of the late 1960s and early 1970s has largely disappeared. Thanks to the *Nebraska Press Assn. v. Stuart* Supreme Court decision, "gag" orders have rarely been imposed on the media in recent years. News sources in many celebrated cases are still subjected to gag orders, but most trial judges now recognize that directly gagging the press is an unconstitutional prior restraint.

PRIVACY AND PRESS FREEDOM

In other areas of law, the mass media will also face uncertainties in the coming years. Privacy law is still a growing field with many unresolved questions. The *Cox Broadcasting v. Cohn* decision said journalists may truthfully report the contents of public records without civil liability. However, not all states are taking the *Cox* decision literally.

Also, there are other contexts in which the rules on privacy remain unclear. When, for example, may a journalist report embarrassing but truthful private facts? It will take more court decisions to fully outline the scope of the newsworthiness defense. Also unsettled is the extent to which the *New York Times v. Sullivan* doctrine applies in false light privacy cases. Must only public figures prove actual malice to win such privacy lawsuits? Or do the rules in privacy cases differ from those in libel suits? The Supreme Court's *Cantrell v. Forest City Publishing* decision failed to squarely address this issue, leaving it uncertain whether private plaintiffs may now show mere negligence in privacy cases, as they may in libel cases in many states.

One more unsettled question in privacy law surrounds the scope of the right of publicity. Does that right survive a person's death, making it unlawful to commercially exploit a deceased celebrity's name and likeness? Various courts have differed in attempting to answer this question.

Another question involves the extent to which a celebrity can own words or phrases other than his name. The *Carson v. Here's Johnny* case held that entertainer Johnny Carson could prevent others from using "Here's Johnny" as a product name. If so, what other commonly used phrases might become someone's private property? Perhaps at some point the Supreme Court will hear a case on some of these issues.

COPYRIGHT: TECHNOLOGICAL CHALLENGES

The 1976 Copyright Act clarified the law in many respects, but a number of important questions remain unresolved. The 1976 act recognized the judicially created Fair Use Doctrine for the first time, but it left many issues about copyright and technology unsettled.

The Supreme Court's long-anticipated *Sony v. Universal Studios* decision held that the Copyright Act permits consumers to engage in "time-shifting" by video taping television shows for later viewing. Such home taping is a fair use rather than a copyright infringement, the court said.

In the end, the *Sony* decision did nothing more than shift the copyright battlefield from the Supreme Court to Congress: as soon as the case was decided, lobbyists for all sides descended on Congress to seek a legislative solution to the problem.

As a result, Congress faces a difficult dilemma. If Congress changes the law to make home video taping a copyright infringement, it must answer to millions of consumers. If it does not, motion picture and television producers will be denied a new source of revenue which they feel is rightfully theirs. And if Congress solves the problem by simply adding a flat royalty fee to the price of each blank audio and video tape, would that not be an injustice to those who use blank tapes for copying non-copyrighted materials? If people who don't tape anything that is copyrighted must pay the fee, wouldn't it be more correct to call the fee a tax to subsidize the entertainment industry and not a royalty?

Another difficult copyright issue involves cable and the other emerging television technologies. Copyright owners complained for years that cable systems were not paying their fair share. In 1983 the Copyright Royalty Tribunal responded by drastically increasing the fees cable systems must pay for each distant signal they carry. The fee applies even if the distant station is a "superstation" intended for cable retransmission. Even worse, cable operators feel, the fee does not go to the stations (or "superstations") whose signals they retransmit. Instead, it goes into a general fund that is divided among various copyright owners. Congress may have thought it was solving the cable copyright problem when it enacted the 1976 Copyright Act, but it is now apparent that these conflicts will not soon be resolved to everyone's satisfaction.

The dramatic growth of the microcomputer industry has also created new copyright problems. Computer software writers are alarmed and angry about the wholesale copying of their programs by consumers, just as motion picture producers are disturbed about home video taping. And software writers, like movie producers, realize they cannot stop these wholesale copyright infringements by millions of consumers. The fact is that computers, like tape recorders, are capable of copying copyrighted materials accurately and efficiently. Various technical schemes have been devised to make computer floppy disks impossible to copy, but almost as soon as a new copy-prevention scheme is devised, someone finds a way to "crack" it and make copies.

On the other hand, computer manufacturers are taking advantage of the Copyright Act to protect the machine language "code" hidden inside electronic "chips." By doing this, they can often prevent competitors from making computers that will run most if not all of their software. Some say this is a restraint of trade, a misuse of copyright law to force consumers to pay more than they should for hardware—not just software. Others feel it is a legitimate expansion of copyright law into a new field, a way to protect manufacturers from commercial piracy.

In any case, like video cassette recorders and photocopying machines, personal computers have created difficult new copyright problems, problems that it may take Congress years to solve.

In other areas, there are also difficult and controversial unresolved copyright problems. For example, when does the Fair Use Doctrine permit journalists and scholars to use information from copyrighted publications in their own writings? Obviously, it will take more court decisions to clarify the scope of the fair use defense in copyright infringement lawsuits.

A REVOLUTION IN ELECTRONIC COMMUNICATIONS

The electronic media face other legal and ethical issues that could over-shadow the ones involving copyright law. We may be in the midst of a communications revolution even more profound than the one that brought us television some 40 years ago. With cable systems rapidly gaining public acceptance everywhere, and with direct satellite broadcasting and home teletext/videotex services getting established, the old rules of broadcast economics—and law—may be obsolete. The day when three major networks could dominate home entertainment in America may someday disappear forever.

Recognizing these trends, the Federal Communications Commission has taken a new approach in its efforts to get broadcasters to act "in the public interest, convenience, and necessity." After years of trying to foster public service by fine-tuning the Fairness Doctrine and other content controls, the FCC is looking to the marketplace for answers. The FCC now believes the goals of diversification and high program quality may be better served by letting free enterprise set the standards. As a result, the commission has acted to deregulate both the broadcasting and cable industries. Many of the rules and policies that were sacred cows for years are being unceremoniously discarded, victims of the age of deregulation.

In place of regulation, the FCC is trying to open the radio and television marketplace to new voices and new ownerships. In this process, the commission has taken a very tough look at its traditional policies on the use of the radio spectrum. The result has been the greatest expansion in broadcast channel availability in three decades. As the FCC grants licenses for the newly created assignments, the key question will be whether these new broadcast voices will really enhance program diversity—or perhaps just give us more of the same. Many consumer groups are troubled by the latter possibility, and they have strenuously objected to the avalanche of deregulation, but to little avail.

Another potential source of program diversity, of course, is cable—and the other new television delivery systems. As a result of deregulation and advances in satellite communications, cable systems now offer programming alternatives undreamed of a few years ago. But the growth of cable also raises new legal questions.

At a time when the nation's giant media corporations are maneuvering for bigger shares of both the broadcasting and cable industries, one of the major issues is cross-ownership and group ownership. The FCC's rules still forbid ownership of cable systems by broadcasters serving the same market. But are those rules really in the public interest? It is not clear whether the FCC's actions to eliminate ownership restrictions in broadcasting will produce more—or less—public service. And it is by no means certain that either the print-broadcast or cable-broadcast cross-ownership rules themselves will survive.

The growth of technology has raised other difficult questions that must be answered. For instance, what kind of protection from cable retransmissions, if any, should broadcasters be afforded to assure the continuing viability of over-the-air broadcasting? Moreover, as home information systems develop, who should control that potentially important new form of mass communications? Will conventional television stations gain control of that market with one-way teletext systems? Or will cable systems, the phone company, or perhaps newspapers prevail with fully interactive (i.e., two-way) videotex-type communications services? Or will most people want their computerized information systems to be something entirely different from either teletext or videotex as we know it now?

There are good reasons to believe the computer age will in fact lead to something other than more efficient delivery of the news to consumers. For more than a century, the mass media have disseminated information to readers, listeners, or viewers who had no choice but to be merely recipients of the information. But the most popular computerized information services today emphasize *two-way* interpersonal communications over the impersonal mass communications aspects of their business. As the sidebar to Chapter 15 points out, many CompuServe users are on line not to read the news or even access the sophisticated data bases available: *they're there to communicate with other people who share similar interests.*

It may be that the one-way mass communications process we have known ever since the "penny press" era of the 1830s will disappear—rendered obsolete by information systems that only deliver the news as a sideline, a supplement to people-to-people communications.

If this happens, then the longtime dream of open public access to the mass media will have been realized, not as a result of new laws or court decisions but because of computer technology.

NEW, OLD, AND HYBRID MEDIA: SCARCITY OR SURPLUS?

The computer age is creating still other legal problems. For example, as it becomes feasible to transmit newspaper pages to the reader's home electronically without ever printing them, will the print and electronic media somehow merge? When a newspaper is delivered to a subscriber's home electronically and then displayed on what amounts to a television screen, will newspapers be required to obey the stringent content controls that now apply only to broadcasters? Will newspapers lose some of their editorial freedom if they go electronic? Or will broadcasters finally win equal treatment under the First Amendment? Can we really continue to have a double standard, with rules saying a four-letter word is okay on the home television screen if a newspaper-sponsored videotex system puts it there, but illegal if it got there via teletext from a TV broadcaster?

Broadcasters and cable operators are already wrestling with this kind of inconsistency in the law. Cable systems frequently carry uncut versions of movies, including material that could not be shown on broadcast television under today's rules. In fact, so do some of the new over-the-air pay-television services.

Where do these new video technologies fit into the regulatory equation? If the thing that triggers government regulation of program content is the use of the radio spectrum, why are some of the new microwave video delivery systems regulated as broadcasters while others are not? Why aren't all users of the radio spectrum who deliver programming to consumers treated alike? The FCC is allowing direct broadcast satellite operators to *choose* whether to be regulated as broadcasters or common carriers. In fact, the differences between the two services are becoming indistinguishable to everyone except communications lawyers. At some point, Congress must face up to the contradictions in the present laws governing broadcasting, common carriers, and cable.

Given the plethora of new video programming alternatives, the traditional scarcity justification for broadcast regulation may no longer be valid. The primary factor limiting the introduction of new video programming services today is the economic saturation of the marketplace, not the physical saturation of the radio spectrum. The fact that the FCC receives more applications for broadcast licenses than it can accommodate may not be the overriding consideration today, given the alternatives to traditional broadcasting that now exist. Over-the-air broadcasting is just one of many delivery systems available to those who wish to disseminate video programming to consumers.

At this point the same economic factors that serve to limit the number of newspapers also set the limits on television-like services. Either industry could add numerous additional media outlets—if the marketplace would support them. True, a broadcaster must have a government license while a newspaper publisher does not, but that hardly seems to matter: new television-like services are appearing all over the landscape while major newspapers are failing. Is it really still true that "anyone can start a newspaper, but not anyone can start a radio station," as advocates of regulation often contend? Or has the scarcity of radio and television channels ceased to be the bottom line consideration in communications law?

ADVERTISING AND TECHNOLOGICAL CHANGE

In all of these technologies, the basic issue is simply economics: who will pay the bills? One fundamental question about American mass communications is whether advertising will continue to pay most of the cost or whether there will be a major shift to subscriber sponsorship. Will for-pay systems eventually outbid advertiser-supported systems for the best programming? And what will advertising be like in the coming years?

The Federal Trade Commission's once-expansive powers have been curtailed somewhat. Will the FTC restrict itself to enforcing the rules against false and misleading advertising, or will it someday resume the activist role it played in the late 1970s? Meanwhile, will the courts continue the dramatic trend, begun in 1975, toward constitutional protection for commercial speech? Or will the courts at some point again say a message is protected only if its creator is in the business of selling ideas as opposed to products and services?

Obviously, there are complex and difficult questions about the future of the mass media in an era of technological change. Most of these questions cannot be quickly or easily answered. About the only thing of which we can be certain is that change is inevitable in mass communications, and that mass media law must change along with the media themselves.

APPENDIX A: SELECTED AMENDMENTS TO THE U.S. CONSTITUTION

THE FIRST AMENDMENT

Congress shall make no law respecting an establishment of religion, or prohibiting the free exercise thereof; or abridging the freedom of speech, or of the press; or the right of the people peaceably to assemble, and to petition the government for a redress of grievances.

THE FOURTH AMENDMENT

The right of people to be secure in their persons, houses, papers, and effects, against unreasonable searches and seizures, shall not be violated, and no Warrants shall issue, but upon probable cause, supported by Oath or affirmation, and particularly describing the place to be searched, and the persons or things to be seized.

THE SIXTH AMENDMENT

In all criminal prosecutions, the accused shall enjoy the right to a speedy and public trial, by an impartial jury of the State and district wherein the crime shall have been committed, which district shall have been previously ascertained by law, and to be informed of the nature and cause of the accusation; to be confronted with the witnesses against him; to have compulsory process for obtaining witnesses in his favor, and to have the Assistance of Counsel for his defence.

THE FOURTEENTH AMENDMENT

§1.   All persons born or naturalized in the United States, and subject to the jurisdiction thereof, are citizens of the United States and of the State wherein they reside. No State shall make or enforce any law which shall abridge the privileges or immunities of citizens of the United States; nor shall any State deprive any person of life, liberty, or property, without due process of law; nor deny to any person within its jurisdiction the equal protection of the laws.

§2.   Representatives shall be apportioned among the several States according to their respective numbers, counting the whole number of persons in each State, excluding Indians not taxed. But when the right to vote at any election for the choice of electors for President and Vice President of the United States, Representatives in Congress, the Executive and Judicial officers of a State, or the members of the Legislature thereof, is denied to any of the male inhabitants of such State, being twenty-one years of age, and citizens of the United States, or in any way abridged, except for participation in rebellion, or other crime, the basis of representation therein shall be reduced in the proportion which the number of such male citizens shall bear to the whole number of male citizens twenty-one years of age in such State.

§3.   No person shall be a Senator or Representative in Congress, or elector of President and Vice President, or hold any office, civil or military, under the United States, or under any State, who, having previously taken an oath, as a member of Congress, or as an officer of the United States, or as a member of any State legislature, or as an executive or judicial officer of any State, to support the Constitution of the United States, shall have engaged in insurrection or rebellion against the same, or given aid or comfort to the enemies thereof. But Congress may by a vote of two-thirds of each House, remove such disability.

§4.   The validity of the public debt of the United States, authorized by law, including debts incurred for payment of pensions and bounties for services in suppressing insurrection or rebellion, shall not be questioned. But neither the United States nor any State shall assume or pay any debt or obligation incurred in aid of insurrection or rebellion against the United States, or any claim for the loss or emancipation of any slave; but all such debts, obligations and claims shall be held illegal and void.

§5.   The Congress shall have power to enforce, by appropriate legislation, the provisions of this article.

APPENDIX B: GLOSSARY OF LEGAL TERMS

When they are first used in the text, most legal terms are defined. For convenience, brief definitions of some important terms are grouped together here.

Amicus curiae (Latin: "friend of the court")   A nonparticipant in a lawsuit who files a written brief urging the court to decide a case in a certain way.

Appellant   The party who appeals an unfavorable lower court decision to a higher court.

Appellate brief   A written document presented to a court, usually presenting legal arguments for a particular ruling.

Appellate court   A court that reviews the decisions of lower courts, deciding issues of law (as opposed to factual issues). Usually more than one judge participates in each decision; juries are not used.

Appellee   The party who opposes the appellant when a decision is appealed, and who typically has prevailed in the lower court.

Certiorari, writ of   An order from a higher court to a lower one to send up the records of a case for appellate review. A party who has no automatic right to appeal an adverse decision to the Supreme Court may petition the court to issue this writ, thus taking up the case even though not required to. *Certiorari denied* (cert.den.) means the court has decided not to review the case.

Change of venue A transfer of a lawsuit from one county or district to another to ensure a fair trial.

Complainant A synonym for the plaintiff—the party who brings a lawsuit.

Complaint An initial filing to begin a lawsuit.

Concurring opinion An opinion written by a judge who agrees with the decision of the court, but perhaps not with the reasoning that led to the decision.

Damages Compensation that a party receives for a wrong or injury. The injury may be intangible (as in general damages) or may result in a specifically provable monetary loss (as in special damages). Punitive damages are a sort of civil fine, a punishment for a wrongful act, and bear little or no relationship to the magnitude of the injury or wrong.

Defendant The party who must answer the plaintiff's complaint; the party who allegedly committed the civil or criminal wrong that led to the lawsuit.

Demurrer A motion to dismiss a lawsuit in which the defendant says that, even if all of the facts the plaintiff alleges are true, there is no legal basis for the action.

Dissenting opinion An opinion written by a judge who disagrees with the decision of the court.

Disparagement A statement about a business' products that tends to influence consumers not to buy them; also called "trade libel."

Diversity jurisdiction A lawsuit heard in federal court because the parties are citizens of different states.

Equity An alternative to the application of the hard-and-fast rules of the common law, a system based on concepts of fairness that judges may apply when there is no adequate remedy at law.

Ex parte A one-party proceeding or action, taken without the participation of any other parties to the case.

Ex rel. A legal proceeding initiated by a district attorney or attorney general on behalf of the government, but at the behest of a party with an interest in the matter.

Felony A serious criminal offense.

Grand jury A body of people summoned to determine whether there is sufficient evidence to formally charge someone who is suspected of a crime.

Grandfather A term that means a party is being given special consideration based on seniority: a new law sometimes exempts persons who were already doing something the law prohibits before it was adopted (i.e., they are "grandfathered").

Habeas corpus, writ of (Latin: "you have the body")   An order requiring a jailer to bring a prisoner before the court so it may be determined if there is just cause to continue holding him. It allows a second review of a criminal conviction.

In camera (Latin: "in chambers")   A proceeding or action in the judge's chambers (that is, in private).

Indictment   A formal, written document in which a grand jury accuses someone of a crime.

Information   An alternative to a grand jury indictment; a way a prosecutor can bring charges against a person by merely having a magistrate agree that there is probable cause to prosecute.

Injunction   A court order directing a party to do something or refrain from doing something; an example of an action in equity rather than at law.

JNOV (judgment non obstante veredicto; Latin: judgment notwithstanding the verdict)   An order by a judge setting aside a jury verdict and deciding the case differently, sometimes issued when the judge feels the facts will not support the jury's conclusion.

Mandamus, writ of   An order requiring an official to do something he or she is legally required to do, but has failed to do.

Misdemeanor   A minor criminal offense.

Mistrial   A trial that is declared void because of some serious error or flaw in the proceedings.

Per curiam   An unsigned opinion of the court.

Petitioner   The party asking a court to hear or review a case.

Plaintiff   The party that initiates a lawsuit; the person suing.

Precedent   A previously decided case that provides guidance for future decisions.

Preliminary hearing   A hearing held to determine if there is sufficient evidence to bind a person over for trial. A preliminary hearing is a required step in prosecuting a person on an information rather than a grand jury indictment.

Privilege   A legal immunity from prosecution or other sanctions for doing (or failing to do) something that would otherwise be forbidden (or required).

Remand   A decision to send a case back to the court that made the original decision to reconsider it in light of a new interpretation of the law.

Respondent   The party answering the petitioner's statement or request.

Restatement of Torts   The American Law Institute's authoritative summary of the common law of torts, an important source of law in fields such as libel and invasion of privacy.

Reverse To set aside a judgment; an action taken by a higher court when a lower court has erred.

Scienter Sufficient knowledge of the facts to support a conviction where knowledge is an element of the crime, as it often is in prosecutions for selling obscene matter.

Sequestration The process of isolating jurors so they cannot be prejudiced by outside influences such as the mass media and friends.

Stare decisis (Latin: to hold a decision) The concept that future cases will be decided in accordance with precedents established in earlier decisions.

Summary judgment A judgment rendered by a court without awaiting a jury verdict (and often without a trial), an appropriate action when there are no facts in dispute between the two sides in a lawsuit.

Tort A civil wrong not involving breach of contract; an injury to a party's person, property, or reputation by another party who is called the "tortfeasor."

Voir dire An examination of potential jurors to determine if they are competent and impartial.

INDEX